tions had been adopted, without any emendation, in the laſt printed edition in folio, not merely in the orthography and other trivial reſpects, but very frequently in the references to authorities, which are in many inſtances very erroneouſly printed.

It had been propoſed to accompany each Chapter with notice of various judicial determinations and obſervations of later writers, which appear to contradict ſome of the authorities, poſitions and doctrines contained more particularly in the Third and Fourth Inſtitute, as alſo with Notes explanatory of ſuch alterations as have ſucceſſively taken place in the law, relating to the ſubjects of theſe Inſtitutes, ſince the time of Lord *Coke*; and ſome collections and progreſs have accordingly been made towards that undertaking: But it has ſince been found adviſeable to preſerve the original order and connection of Lord *Coke*'s Work, and to preſent, at a future period, thoſe Notes in a ſeparate form, correſpondent to the ſeveral diviſions and chapters of theſe Inſtitutes, in conformity with the arrangement of the text and notes in the laſt improved edition of the Firſt Inſtitute.

Jan. 23,
1797.

A TABLE

Of the ſeveral Courts in this Fourth Part of the INSTITUTES, treated of.

or

out commiſſion; ſome derivative, or delegate by commiſſion. Of all theſe, ſome be of record, and ſome not of record; ſome to enquire, hear, and determine, ſome to enquire only; ſome guided by one law, ſome by another; the bounds of all and every ſeverall courts being moſt neceſſary to be known. For as the body of man is beſt ordered, when every particular member exerciſeth his proper duty: ſo the body of the commonwealth is beſt governed when every ſeverall court of juſtice executeth his proper juriſdiction. But if the eie, whoſe duty it is to ſee, the hand, to work, the feet, to go, ſhall uſurp, and incroach one upon anothers work: as for example, the hands or feet, the office of the eie to ſee, and the like; theſe ſhould aſſuredly produce diſorder and darkneſſe, and bring the whole body out of order, and in the end to deſtruction. So in the common wealth (juſtice being the main preſerver thereof) if one court ſhould uſurp, or incroach upon another, it would introduce incertainty, ſubvert juſtice, and bring all things in the end to confuſion.

Now when I conſidered how much it would tend to the honour of the kings majeſty, and of his laws, to the advancement of juſtice, the quiet of the ſubject, and generally to the good of the whole common wealth (no king in the Chriſtian world having ſuch tribunals, and ſeats of juſtice, as his majeſty hath, which, God willing, in this treatiſe we ſhall make to appear) that all the high, honourable, venerable, and neceſſary tribunals, and courts of juſtice within his majeſties realms and dominions, as well civill as eccleſiaſticall, might be drawn together, as it were, in one map, or table, (which hitherto was never yet done) that the admirable benefit, beauty, and delectable variety thereof might be, as it were, *uno intuitu* beholden, and that the manifold juriſdictions of the ſame might be diſtinctly underſtood and obſerved. We having (as elſe where we have ſaid) collected ſome materials towards the raiſing of this great and honourable building, and fearing that they ſhould be of little uſe after my deceaſe, being

In the preface to the firſt part of the Inſtitutes.

very

very ſhort, and not eaſily of others to be underſtood, if I ſhould have left them as they were.

Out of the duty that I owe to his moſt excellent Majeſty, and my zeal, and affection to the whole common wealth, I have adventured to break the ice herein, and to publiſh more at large thoſe things which in our reading we had obſerved concerning juriſdiction of courts. I confeſſe it is a labour of as great pains, as difficulty: for as in an high and large building, he that beholds the ſame after it is finiſhed, and furniſhed, ſeeth not the carriages, ſcaffolding, and other inviſible works of labour, induſtry, and ſkill in architecture: ſo he that looketh on a book full of variety of important matter, eſpecially concerning ſacred laws, after it is printed and fairly bound and poliſhed, cannot ſee therein the carriage of the materials, the ſearching, finding out, peruſing, and digeſting of authorities in law, rols of parliament, judiciall records, warrants in law, and other inviſible works, *tam laboris, quam* * *ingenii*: yet I was the rather encouraged thereunto, both becauſe I have publiſhed nothing herein, but that which is grounded upon the authorities and reaſon of our books, rols of parliament, and other judiciall records, and eſpecially upon the reſolution of the judges of latter times upon mature deliberation in many caſes never publiſhed before; wherewith I was well acquainted, and which I obſerved and ſet down in writing, while it was freſh in memory.

* *Minerva quaſi nervos minuens.*

There be amongſt the kings records divers and many rols, whereof you ſhall find little or no mention (that we remember) in our books, viz. *Rot. Parliament. Rot. Placitorum Coronæ, Rot. Placitorum Parliament. Rot. Clauſ. Rot. Brevium, Finium, Inquiſitionum, Liberationum, Rot. Cartarum, Eſchaetriæ, Pat. Rot. Ordinationum, Rot. Franciæ, Scotiæ, Vaſconiæ, et Almaniæ, Rot. Romana, Rot. Judæorum, Rot. Ragman, Brangwin, Rot. Contrarienſium* (and the reaſon of the naming of this roll thus, was for that Thomas earl of Lancaſter (a man ſingularly beloved) taking part with

gether under the head in confultation for the common good of the whole realm, there is *ultimum fapientiæ*.

What Properties a Parliament Man fhould have.

Rot. parl. anno 3 H. 6. nu. 3.

It appeareth in a parliament roll, that the parliament being, as hath been faid, called *commune concilium*, every member of the houfe being a counfeller, fhould have three properties of the elephant; firft, that he hath no gall: fecondly, that he is inflexible, and cannot bow: thirdly, that he is of a moft ripe and perfect memory: which properties, as there it is faid, ought to be in every member of the great councell of parliament. Firft, to be without gall, that is, without malice, rancor, heat, and envy, *in elephante melancholia tranfit in nutrimentum corporis*. Every gallifh inclination (if any were) fhould tend to the good of the whole body, the common wealth. Secondly, that he be conftant, inflexible, and not to be bowed, or turned from the right, either for fear, reward, or favour, nor in judgement refpect any perfon. Thirdly, of a ripe memory, that they remembring perils paft, might prevent dangers to come, as in that roll of parliament it appeareth. Whereunto we will adde two other properties of the elephant, the one, that though they be *maximæ virtutis, et maximi intellectus*, of greateft ftrength, and underftanding, *tamen gregatim femper incedunt*, yet they are fociable, and goe in companies; for *animalia gregalia non funt nociva, fed animalia folivaga funt nociva*. Sociable creatures that goe in flocks or heards are not hurtfull, as deer, fheep, &c. but beafts that walk folely, or fingularly, as bears, foxes, &c. are dangerous and hurtfull. The other, that the elephant is *philanthropos, homini erranti viam oftendit*, and thefe properties ought every parliament man to have.

Virg. Georg. Illum non populi fafces, non purpura regum Flexit.——

Ariftotle. Bartholomæus.

*[4]

Of Records of Parliament.

[a] Mich. 5 E. 1. in communi banco. Rot. 100. Linc. Pafch. 19 E. 1. Rot. 145. Abbot de Selby. Pafch. 28 E. 1. coram rege rot. between the King and Venables in Quare Impedit. Mich. 3 E. 2. coram rege rot. 6. and many others where the caufes and reafons, pro et contra have been fet down, &c. 6 E. 3. fo. 5. per Herle. 3 E. 4. 2. b. 7. a. 19 H. 6. 63. a. per Fray. 22 E. 4. 18. per Huffey. rot. par. 19 E. 1. rot. 12. Margery Weylands cafe. Nota quia optime, &c.

The reafon wherefore the records of parliament have been fo highly extolled, is, for that therein is fet down in cafes of difficulty, not only the judgment, or refolution, but the reafons, and caufes of the fame by fo great advice. [a] It is true * that of ancient time in judgements at the common law, in cafes of difficulties either criminall, or civill, the reafons and caufes of the judgement were fet down in the record, and fo it continued in the reigns of E. 1. and moft part of E. 2. and then there was no need of reports: but in the reign of E. 3. (when the law was in his height) the caufes and reafons of judgements, in refpect of the multitude of them are not fet down in the record, but then the great cafuifts and reporters of cafes (certain grave and fad men) publifhed the cafes, and the reafons and caufes of the judgements or refolutions, which from the beginning of the reign of E. 3. and fince we have in print. But thefe alfo, though of great credit, and excellent ufe in their kind, yet far underneath the authority of the parliament rols, reporting the acts, judgements, and refolutions of that higheft court.

The Summons of Parliament.

The king *de advisamento concilii* (for so be the words of the writ of parliament) resolving to have a parliament, doth out of the court of chancery send out writs of summons at the least forty days before the parliament begin: every lord of parliament, either spirituall, as archbishops, and bishops, or temporall, as dukes, marquisses, earls, viscounts and barons; peers of the realm, and lords of parliament ought to have severall writs of summons.

Prov. 13. 16. Sapiens omnia agit cum consilio. Vide infra. These writs of summons you shall find in former times in the close rol, for they are not in the Register, and in that rol are the writs De expensis militum, civium et burgensium, et procuratorum cleri, and these are in the Register also.

Temporall Assistants.

And all the judges of the realm, barons of the exchequer of the coif, the kings learned councell, * and the civilians masters of the chancery are called to give their assistance and attendance in the upper house of parliament, but they have no voices in parliament; and their writs differ from the writs to the barons: for their writs be, *Quòd intersitis nobiscum et cum cæteris de consilio nostro* (and sometimes *nobiscum* only) *super præmissis tractaturi, vestrumque consilium impensuri*; but the writ to the barons is, *Quòd intersitis cum prælatis, magnatibus et proceribus super dictis negotiis tractaturi, vestrumque consilium impensuri.*

* Regist. 261. F. N. B. 229. a. ib. called attendants.

Spirituall Assistants. Procuratores Cleri.

And in every writ of summons to the bishops, there is a clause requiring them to summon these persons to appear personally at the parliament, which is in these words, *Præmonientes decanum et capitulum ecclesiæ vestræ Norwicensis, ac archidiaconos totumque clerum vestræ diocess. quòd iidem decani et archdiaconi in propriis personis suis, ac dictum capitulum per unum, idemque clerus per duos procuratores idoneos plenam et sufficientem potestatem ab ipsis capitulo et clero divisim habentes prædict' die et loco personaliter intersint ad consentiendum hiis quæ tunc ibidem de communi consilio dicti regni nostri divina favente clementia contigerit ordinari:* and the bishop under his seal make certificate accordingly. And these are called *procuratores cleri*, and many times have appeared in parliament as spirituall assistants, to consider, consult, and consent, *ut supra*, but had never voices there, because they were no lords of parliament. Some have thought, that because the clergy were not party to the election of the knights, citizens, and burgesses, that these *procuratores cleri* were appointed to give their consent for them, but then they should have had voices, which questionlesse they never had. And by the words of the writ it was to consent to those things which by the common councell of the realm should happen to be ordained, so as their consent was only to such things as were ordained *de communi concilio regni*, and that there might be an act of parliament without them: and in many cases multitudes are bound by acts of parliament which are not parties to the elections of knights, citizens, and burgesses, as

Mod. tenend. parl. ca. 2. Rot. Clauf. 8 E. 2. m. 15. Dorf. Ib. 5. E. 2. m. 15. Ib. 11 E. 3. part 1. m. 1. Ib. 22 E. 3. part 2. m. 3. Ib. 36 E. 3. m. 16. Rot. par. 18 E. 3. nu. 1. 3 R. 2. 11 R. 2. 21 R. 2. Procuratores Cleri. reg. 261. a. F. N. B. 229. a. Procuratores de Clero. In fascicul. litterarum procurat. &c. 13 H. 4. & 5 H. 5. See hereafter tit. Proxies.

the end, he did in the kings name require the commons to make choice of a learned and discreet man to be their speaker: and when a bishop was lord chancellor, he took a text of scripture which he repeated in Latin, and discoursed upon the same. But when a judge was lord chancellor, he took no text, but in manner of an oration shewed summarily the causes of the parliament.

The Election of the Speaker.

It is true the commons are to chuse their speaker: but seeing that after their choise the king may refuse him, for avoiding of expence of time and contestation, the use is (as in the *conge de eslier* of a bishop) that the king doth name a discreet and learned man whom the commons elect: but without their election no speaker can be appointed for them, because he is their mouth, and trusted by them, and so necessary, as the house of commons cannot sit without him: and therefore a grievous sicknesse is a good cause to remove him, as in 1 H. 4. John Chenye speaker chosen and allowed, was for sicknesse, so as he could not serve, discharged, and Sir John Doreward chosen in his place: and so was William Sturton, after he was chosen and allowed speaker, removed for grievous sicknesse, and Sir John Doreward chosen in his place. At the parliament holden in 15 H. 6. Sir John Tirrell knight was chosen and allowed speaker, and for grievous sicknesse removed, and William Beerly esq; chosen in his place, &c.

Sicknesse cause to remove the speaker. 1 H. 4. nu. 62, 63. Rot. parl. 1 H. 5. nu. 9, 10, 11. Rot. parl. 15 H. 6. nu. 10. & 27.

But sicknesse is no cause to remove any knight, citizen or burgesse of the house of commons: so note a diversity between the speaker, and any other of the house of commons, and this diversity being not observed begat an error by some opinion in 38 H. 8. tit. Parliament, Brook 7. for continuall experience is to the contrary.

Sicknefs no cause to remove a member of the house of commons. 38 H. 8. parl. Br. 7.

The Presentment of the Speaker.

What the speaker shall do when he is chosen.

The king may allow of his excuse, and disallow him, as Sir John Popham was. 28 H. 6. nu. 6.

The protestation of the speaker.

When the commons have chosen their speaker, the person elected standing in his place disabling himselfe to undergoe so weighty a charge, as in his discretion he thinks fit, desires them to proceed to a new choise: which being denied, and he set in the chaire, then he prayeth them to give him leave, that he may disable himselfe to the king: after this they present him to the king in the lords house; where after he hath disabled himselfe to speak before the king, and for the whole body of the realme, and made humble suit to the king, lest by his insufficiency the businesse of the realme may be hindred, to be discharged, and a more sufficient man to be chosen: if he be allowed by his majestie, then he maketh a protestation consisting on three parts: first, that the commons in this parliament may have free speech, as of right and by custome they have used, and all their ancient and just priviledges and liberties allowed to them. Secondly, that in any thing he shall deliver in the name of the commons (if he shall commit any error) no fault may be arrected to the commons, and that he may resort again to the commons for declaration of their true intent, and that his error may be pardoned. The third is, that as often as necessity

necessity for his majesties service, and the good of the common wealth shall require, he may by the direction of the house of commons have accesse to his royall person.

* This is in the parliament rols called a protestation in respect of the first part, the nature whereof is to be an exclusion of a conclusion, and herein that the house of commons be not concluded to speak only of those things which the king or lord chancelor, &c. hath delivered to them to be the causes of the calling of this court of parliament, but in a parliamentary course of all other arduous and urgent businesse, which principally consist in these five branches, as it appeareth in the writs of summons to the lords spirituall and temporall, viz.

Rot. par. 1. R. 2. nu. 15. &c. Rot. Parl. 2 H. 4. nu. 8. Sir Arnold Savage speaker. 5 H. 4. nu. 8. 7 H. 4. nu. 11. Sir Jo. Tibetoft speaker. and ibid. nu. 30. 1 H. 5. nu. 7. 2 H. 5. nu. 10. And so in succeeding times called a protestation.

The Matters of Parliament.

1. Touching the king. 2. The state of the kingdome of England. 3. The defence of the kingdome. 4. * The state of the church of England; and 5. The defence of the same church. And this appeareth by expresse words in the parliament writ in these words: *Pro quibusdam arduis urgentibus negotiis, nos, statum, et defensionem regni nostri Angliæ, et ecclesiæ Anglicanæ concernentibus quoddam parliamentum nostrum, &c. teneri ordinavimus, &c.* And these words [the state and defence of the kingdome] are large words, and include the rest. And though the state and defence of the church of England be last named in the writ, yet is it first in intention, as it appeareth by the title of every parliament: as for example, [a] To the honour of God and of holy church, and quietnesse of the people, &c.

Rot. parl. 9 H. 4. An act intituled. *Indemnitie des seigniors et commons,* not printed.

* See W. 1. anno 3 E. 1. in the preamble, the state of the realme, and of holy church. And the 2 part of the Institutes, W. 1. cap. 1. and in the preamble.

[a] 36 E. 3. 50 E. 3. &c.

Now for as much as divers lawes and statutes have been enacted and provided for these ends aforesaid, and that divers mischiefs in particular, and divers grievances in generall concerning the honour and safety of the king, the state and defence of the kingdome and of the church of England might be prevented, an excellent law was made *anno* 36 E. 3. which being applyed to the said writs of parliament doth in few and effectuall words set downe the true subject of a parliament in these words. For the maintenance of the said articles and statutes, and redresse of divers mischiefs and grievances which daily happen, a parliament shall be holden every year, as another time was ordained by a * statute.

36 E. 3. cap. 10. Parliaments ought to be holden once in a year.

* 4 E. 3. cap. 14. Inter leg. Edgar cap. 5.

Before the conquest parliaments were to be holden twice every year, *Celeberrimus autem ex omni satrapia bis quotannis conventus agitur.* King E. 1. kept a parliament once every two year for the most part, and now it is enacted, that a parliament shall be holden once every year.

The Romans vanquished our ancestors the ancient Britains, for that they assembled not, they consulted not in common with them, nor common councels, as Tacitus in vita Agricolæ saith. *Nec aliud adversus validissimas gentes pro nobis utilius, quam quod in * commune non consulunt. Rarus ad propulsandum commune periculum conventus: ita dum singuli pugnant, universi vincuntur.* But to return to the matters of parliament.

Tacitus in vita Agricolæ, pag. 306.

* Nota, Commune concilium. Conventus.

And

4 H. 8. c. 8.

And it is enacted and declared by authority of parliament in *anno* 4 H. 8. That all suits, accusements, condemnations, executions, fines, amerciaments, punishments, corrections, charges, and impositions at any time from thenceforth to be put, or had upon any member, either of that present parliament, or at any parliament at any time after that act to be holden, for any bill, * speaking, reasoning, or declaring of any matter or matters concerning the parliament, to be communed, or treated of, be utterly void and of none effect. Which latter branch is generall. Now what matter or matters concern the parliament appear before. And this clause of the act of 4 H. 8. is declaratory of the ancient law and custome of the parliament.

* Neq; timida probitas, neque improba fortitudo rei publicæ est utilis.

And this doth not only appear by the writs directed to the lords of parliament, but by the writs for election of the commons. For example. The writ to the sheriffe of Norfolk for election of the knights, citizens, and burgesses within that county is, *Rex vicecomiti Norff. salutem. Quia nos de avisamento et assensu concilii nostri pro quibusdam arduis et urgentibus negotiis, nos, statum, et defensionem regni nostri Angliæ, et ecclesiæ Anglicanæ concernentibus quoddam parliamentum nostrum apud, &c. teneri ordinaverimus, et ibidem cum prælatis, magnatibus, et proceribus dicti regni nostri colloquium habere et tractatum: ipsi vicecom. Norff. præcipimus firmiter injungend', quòd facta proclamatione in proximo comitatu tuo post receptionem ejusdem brevis, duos milites gladiis cinctos, &c. elegi faceret, &c.* [a] *ad faciendum et consentiendum hiis quæ tunc ibidem de communi concilio nostro Angliæ (favente Deo) contingerent ordinari* [b] *super negotiis antedictis, ita quòd pro defectu potestatis hujusmodi, seu propter improvidam electionem militum, civium et burgensium prædict' dicta negotia nostra infecta non remanerent quovismodo.* And this power extendeth equally to all knights, citizens and burgesses of parliament.

The like writ to all the other counties, saving in Wales they have but one knight and one burgesse.

[10]

[a] *Nota, ad faciendum et consentiendum.* And every city two citizens, and out of every burgh two burgesses.

[b] *Nota, super negotiis antedictis.*

What the Speaker shall doe after his Allowance.

After the commons with their speaker are come from the lords house, and that the speaker is set in the chair, then he desireth the commons, that seeing they have chosen him for their mouth, that they would favourably assist him in their arduous and important affairs, and that he will do them the best service he can with all diligence and faithfull readinesse, or to the like effect.

The Writs of Summons of Parliament, which are to be found in the close Roll from time to time.

Seeing the summons of parliament (as hath been said) is by the kings writs, which tend to the beginning of the parliament, it shall be necessary to speak somewhat of those writs. And it is to be observed, that the substance of those writs ought to continue in their originall essence without any alteration, or addition, unlesse it be by act of parliament. For * if originall writs at the common law can receive no alteration, or addition, but by act of parliament, *à multo fortiori*, the writs for the summons of the highest court of parliament can receive no alteration or addition, but by act of parliament.

* Bract. l. 5. f. 413. Britton, 122. 227. Fleta, li. 2. ca. 12. W. 2. ca. 25. 1. pt. of the Inst. sect. 101. Epist. ad lib. um.

liament. Where [c] the writs of summons issued out of the chancery, and were returnable in the court of parliament, the return thereof could not be altered, and returnable into the chancery, but by act of parliament. And because the words of the writ for election of knights, &c. were, [d] *duos milites gladiis cinctos, &c.* it required an act of parliament, that notable esquires might be eligible.

Walsingham saith, that in *anno Domini* 1404. which was *anno* 6 H. 4. in the writs of the summons of parliament, there was added by the king a commandment in the writ, that no lawyer should be returned knight or burgesse, (but the historian is deceived, for there is no such clause in those writs, but it was wrought by the kings letters by pretext of an ordinance in the lords house, in 46 E. 3.) But at the next parliament in 7 H. 4. at the grievous complaint of the commons, being interrupted of their free election by those letters (which were letters of justice and right) it is, amongst other things, enacted, that elections * should be freely, and indifferently made notwithstanding any prayer, or commandment to the contrary, i. *sine prece*, by any prayer or gift, *et sine precepto*, without commandment of the king by writ, or otherwise, or of any other which was a close, and prudent salve, not only for that sore, but for all other in like case, and is but an act declaratory of the ancient law and custome of parliament.

[c] 7 H. 4. ca. 15. Rot. par. 5 R. 2. nu. 1. 2, &c. they be now returned into the chancery, and kept in the office of the clerk of the crown there.
[d] 23 H. 6. ca. 15.
Parl. 6 H. 4. This was called *indoctum parliamentum*, lack-learning parliament. Rot. parl. 46 E. 3. nu. 13. 5 R. 2. c. 4. 7 H. 4. ca. 15. See hereafter more of this matter, in this chapt. pa. and who be eligible, &c.
* Nota. W. 1. ca. 5. 3 E. 1.

Petitions in Parliament.

On the first day of the parliament, after the commons be departed to choose their speaker, then are certain justices assistants, and civilians masters of the chancery attendants, viz. four justices, and two attendants appointed to be receivers of the petitions of England, Ireland, Wales, and Scotland, and that those that will deliver their petitions, are to deliver them within six days following. At that time there are other justices and civilians attendants, viz. three justices and two attendants appointed to be receivers of petitions for Gascoign and other * places beyond the seas, and of the isles, and that they deliver their petitions within six days, &c.

Then are appointed of the nobility lords of parliament and bishops, viz. six of the nobility, and two bishops to be triers of the said petitions for England, Ireland, Wales, and Scotland, they together, or four of the prelates and lords aforesaid, calling to them the kings learned councell, attendants in parliament when need should be, and to sit in the chamber of the treasury. The like appointment of the nobility and bishops to be triers of the petitions for Gascoign, and other places beyond the seas, and of the isles, and a place appointed for their sitting, calling to them the kings learned councell when need should be. For petitions to be preferred into the lords house in parliament for the countries and places aforesaid, this was the ancient constant law, and custome of the parliament continued untill this day. Wherein these three things are to be observed. First, the extent of the jurisdiction of the parliament of England. Secondly, that for expediting of causes, there should be receivers of all petitions, both of judges of the realm for their knowledge in the laws of the realm, and of civilians attendants, who might prepare and in-

[11]
Receivers of petitions of England, Ireland, Wales, Scotland.
* Gascoin, Guyan, Poiters, Normandy, Anjou, &c.
Triers of petitions.

demanded of one that stood by, *Quis vituperavit? ad quod non fuit responsum.* But now let us return to proxies.

At the parliament holden an. 1 Eliz.

A lord of parliament by licence obtained of the queen to be absent, made a proxy to three lords of parliament. *Conjunctim et divisim dans eis potestatem tractandi, tractatibusque auxilium et consilium impendendi, atque statutis et ordinationibus, quæ inaditat' contigerint, consentiendi, ita quod non sit melior conditio occupantis.* And one of the procurators gave consent to a bill, and the two others said, not content. And first it was by order of the lords debated amongst the judges and civilians attendants, and conceived by them that this was no voice, and the opinion was affirmed by all the lords of parliament *seriatim.* Another question was moved at that time, that if a lord of parliament make a proxy, and after come into the lords house of parliament, and sit there without arguing, consenting or speaking any thing: and it was conceived by the judges and civilians, that this sitting there without saying any thing was a revocation in law of his proxy; *à fortiori*, if he moved, or spake to any matter there propounded, and their opinion was resolved by the lords *seriatim.* And these were the proxies of the bishop of Bathe, the lord Howard chamberlain, and of the lord Windesor.

[13]

Lib. Sap. 17. 12. Mat. Par. pa. 233.

King John in the 13 year of his reign being in extream fear of both the pope and the French king, and especially of his own subjects (and what is fear, saith Solomon, but a betraying of the succours that reason offereth?) sent ambassadours to Admiralius Murmelinus great emperour of Turky Sir Thomas Hertington and Sir Ralph Nicholson knights, and Sir Robert of London clerk, *nuntios suos secretissimos,* to offer to be of his religion, and to make his kingdome tributary to him, and he and his subjects to be his vassals, and to hold his kingdome of him. But that infidell great prince, as a thing unworthy of a king, to deny his religion, and betray his kingdome, utterly refused to accept. King John in the 14 year (the next year) of his reign by his charter 15 May, by the threats and perswasion of the popes commissary Pandulphus surrendered his kingdomes of England and Ireland to pope Innocent the third, *cum communi consilio baronum* (as he inserted therein) and that thence forward he would hold his crown as feodary to the pope, paying for both the said kingdomes 1000. marks. Whereupon doing homage and fealty to the pope by the hand of Pandulphus, and taking off the crown from his head surrendred it to the pope by Pandulphus, at whose feet he laid also the royall ensignes, his scepter, sword and ring: all which was afterward accepted, approved, and ratified by the pope, by his bull which was called *Bulla aurea.*

Rot. Cl. an. 3 E. 1. m. 9. in Schedula.

Gregorius papa petiit à rege E. 1. per literas annuum censum 1000 merc. Rex respondet se sine prælatis et proceribus regni non posse respondere, et quod jurejurando in coronatione sua fuit astrictus, quod jura regni sui servaret illibata, nec aliquid quod diadema tangat regni ejusdem absque ipsorum requisit' consilio faceret.

Rot. par. 40 E. 3. nu. 8. an act never yet printed.

In *anno* 40 E. 3. the pope by his ambassador demanded of the king homage for the kingdome of England and land of Ireland, and the arerages of 1000 marks by the year, granted by king John to pope Innocent the third and his successors, and threatened that if it were not paid, the pope was resolved to proceed against the king. Whereupon the king in the same year called his court of parliament

ment, and in the beginning of that parliament (saith the record) *Fuit monstre a les prelates, dukes, countes, barons, les chivaliers des counties, citizens et burgesses en le presence le roy per le chancellor, coment' ils avoient entendue les causes del summons del parliament en generall, mes la volunte le roy fuist que les causes feussent monstres a eux en especiall, lour disoit coment le roy avoit entendue que le pape per force dun fait quel il dit que le roy Johan fesoit au pape de luy faire homage pur le realme d'Engleterre et la terre d'Irland et que per cause du dit homage qil luy deveroit paier chescun an perpetuelment mille marcs, est en volunte de faire proces devers le roy et son roialm pur le dit service et cens recoverir; de qoi le roi pria as dits prelats, dukes, countes et barons lour avys et bon conseil, et ce qil enferroit, en case que le pape vorroit proceder devers luy, ou son dit roialme per celle cause: et les prelats requeroient au roy quils se purroient per eux soul aviser et respondre lendemain, queux prelatz le dit lendemain adeprimes per eux mesmes, et puis les autres dukes, countes, barons et gentz respondirent et disoient, que le dit roy Johan ne nul autre purra mettre lui, ne son roialme, ne son people en tiele subjection sanz assent et accorde deux: et les communes sur ce demandez et avisez respondirent en mesme le manere; sur qui feust ordeine, et assentu per commune assent en manere quensuyt. En se present parlement tenuz a Westm' Lundy proschein apres la invention de la seinte croice lan du reign le roy Edward quarantisme, tant sur lestat de seinte eglise, come des droits de son roialm et de sa corone maintenir, entre autres choses estoient monstrez coment ad este parlee, et dit que le pape per force dun fait quele il dit que le roi Johan, iadis roy d'Engleterre fesoit au pape au perpetuite de luy faire homage pur le roialme Dengleterre et la terre de Irland, et per cause du dite homage de luy rendre un annuel cens: ad este en volunte de faire processe devers le roi pur les ditz services et cens recoverir; la quele chose monstree as prelats, ducs, countes, barons, et la commun' pur ent avoir lour avys et bon conseil, et demandee de eux ce qe le roi enferra en case que le pape vorroit proceder ou rien attempter devers lui ou son roialme per celle cause? Queux prelats, ducs, countes, barons et communes en sur ce plein deliberacion responderont et disoient dune accorde, que le dit roy Johan ne nul autre purra mettre luy ne son roialme ne son people en tiel subjection sanz assent de eux, et come piert per pluseurs evidences, que si ce feust fait, ce feust fait sanz leur assent, et encontre son serement en sa coronacion, et outre ce le ducs, countes, barons, gents et communes accorderent et granterent que en case que le pape se afforceroit ou rien attempteroit per proces, ou en auter manere de fait de constreindre le roi ou ses subjects de per fait ce quest dit q'il voet clamer telle partie qils resistront et contreesterront ove toute leur puissance.*

I have thought good to transcribe it in proprio idiomate.

[14]

No king can put himself nor his realm, nor his people, in such subjection without assent of the lords and commens in parliament, and therefore if k. John had done it by the common councell of his barons as his charter purported, yet it bound not, for that it was not done in parliament by the king, the lords and commons: and albeit it might (as here it appeareth, it cannot be done without authority of parliament) yet it is *contra legem et consuetudinem parliamenti*, to doe such a thing, as by the next record in 42 E. 3. appeareth.

This noble and prudent king took the fairest and surest way to give satisfaction, whereof the pope being certified, the matter ever since hath rested in quiet.

* It is declared by the lords and commons in full parliament, upon demand made of them on the behalf of the king, that they could not assent to any thing in parliament, that tended to the disherison of the king and his crown, whereunto they were sworn. See hereafter in the case of Ireland.

* Ro. pat. 42 E 3. nu. 7. *Lex et consuetudo parliamenti.*

Lex et Consuetudo Parliamenti.

By the ancient law, and custome of the parliament a proclamation ought to be made in Westminster in the beginning of the parliament, that no man upon pain to lose all that he hath, should

7 E. 2. *Stat. de defensione portand. arma.*

2 E. 3. ca. 3. Rot. par. 6 E. 3. nu. 1. 13 E. 3. nu. 2. 14 E. 3. nu. 2. 15 E. 3. nu. 2. 17 E. 3. nu. 3. 18 E. 3. nu. 2. 20 E. 3. nu. 1. 25 E. 3. stat. 1. nu. 58. 25 E. 3. stat. 2. nu. 5. &c. Privy coat or armour. Games or plays. Rot. par. anno 13 E. 3. nu. 5. & 8. * See hereafter pa.

during the parliament in London, Westminster, or the suburbs, &c. wear any privy coat of plate, or goe armed, or that games or other playes of men, women, or children, or any other pastimes or strange shews should be there used during the parliament: and the reason hereof was, that the high court of parliament should not thereby be disturbed, nor the members thereof (which are to attend the arduous and urgent businesse of the church and commonwealth) should not be withdrawn.

* It is also the law, and custome of the parliament, that when any new device is moved on the kings behalf, in parliament for his aid, or the like, the commons may answer, that they tendred the kings estate, and are ready to aid the same, only in this new device they dare not agree without conference with their countries; whereby it appeareth, that such conference is warrantable by the law and custome of parliament.

And it is to be observed, though one be chosen for one particular county, or borough, yet when he is returned, and sits in parliament, he serveth for the whole realm, for the end of his comming thither, as in the writ of his election appeareth, is generall, *ad faciendum et consentiendum hiis quæ tunc et ibidem de communi consilio dicti regni nostri (favente deo) contigerint ordinari super negotiis prædictis.* i. *pro quibusdam arduis et urgentibus negotiis nos, statum, et defensionem regni nostri Angliæ et ecclesiæ Anglicanæ concernentibus*, which are rehearsed before in the writ.

† [15]

Lex et consuetudo parliamenti. Ista lex ab omnibus est quærenda, a multis ignorata, a paucis cognita. Fleta, lib. 2. cap. 2. * Rot. par. 11 R. 2. nu. 7. See the first part of the Institutes, sect. 3. verb. *En la ley.* Rot. par. 2 H. 4. nu. 11.

And as every court of justice hath laws and customes for its direction, some by † the common law, some by the civill and canon law, some by peculiar lawes and customes, &c. So the high court of parliament *suis propiis legibus et consuetudinibus subsistit.* It is * *lex et consuetudo parliamenti*, that all weighty matters in any parliament moved concerning the peers of the realm, or commons in parliament assembled, ought to be determined, adjudged, and discussed by the course of the parliament, and not by the civill law, nor yet by the common laws of this realm used in more inferiour courts; which was so declared to be *secundum legem et consuetudinem parliamenti*, concerning the peers of the realm, by the king and all the lords spirituall and temporall; and the like *pari ratione* is for the commons for any thing moved or done in the house of commons: and the rather, for that by another law and custome of parliament, the king cannot take notice of any thing said or done in the house of commons, but by the report of the house of commons: and every member of the parliament hath a judiciall place, and can be no witnesse. And this is the reason that judges ought not to give any opinion of a matter of parliament, because it is not to be decided by the common laws, but *secundum legem et consuetudinem parliamenti:* and so the judges in divers parliaments have confessed. And some hold, that every offence committed in any court punishable by that court, must be punished (proceeding criminally) in the same court, or in some higher, and not in any inferiour court, and the court of parliament hath no higher.

Rot. parl. 3 H. 6. In le countee de Marshalls case.

Rot. par. 27 H. 6. nu. 18. the earle of Arundels case.

Rot. parl. 31 H. 6. nu. 26. 27, 28. baron Thorps case.

5 H. 4. nu. 22. The earl of Northumberlands case.

Vide rot. parl. 9 H. 4. *Indemnity des seigniors et commons.*

Upon his petition exhibited to the king, wherein the question was, whether the power which he had raised was high treason, &c. which petition (saith the king) let be delivered to the justices by them to be considered. Whereupon the lords made protestation, that the order thereof belonged to them, which was to them allowed, and they resolved it to be no treason.

And

And becauſe we have a caſe in 3 E. 3. 19. concerning the law and cuſtome of parliament, we have thought good to ſet down the record of that caſe *de verbo in verbum*, and then to examine the report of the ſaid caſe, and the opinion there delivered, wherein we ſhall deſire the learned to conſider well the ſtatute of 5 R. 2. ſtat. 2. cap. 4. and thereupon to conſider what (as that ſtatute ſpeaketh) hath been done of old times, &c. And how that act ſaith done, and not ſaid.

Johannes epiſcopus Winton in miſericordia pro pluribus defaltis. Idem Johannes epiſcopus attachiat' fuit ad reſpond' domino regi, de eo quare cum in parliamento regis apud novam Sarum nuper tent' per ipſum dominum regem inhibitum fuiſſet, ne quis ad dictum parliamentum ſummonitus ab eodem recederet ſine licenc' regis: idem epiſcopus durante parliamento prædict. ab eodem ſine licentia regis receſſit in regis contemptum manifeſtum, et contra inhibitionem regis ſupradictum. Et unde idem dominus rex per Adam de Fincham, qui ſequitur pro eo, dicit, quod prædictus Johannes epiſcopus fecit ei tranſgreſſ. et contemptum prædict. &c. in contempt. regis mille librarum. Et hoc offert verificare pro domino rege, &c.

Paſch. 3 E. 3. coram rege rot. 9. in Dorſ. Southt. Nota, that this was by writ originall.

The declaration.

*Et prædictus epiſcopus in propria perſona ſua venit, et defendit omnem contemptum et tranſgreſſ. et quicquid, &c. et dicit, quod ipſe eſt unus de paribus regni, et prælatus ſacroſ. eccleſiæ, et eis in eſt venire ad parliamentum domini regis per ſummonitionem et pro voluntate ipſius domini regis cum ſibi placuerit, * et dicit, quòd ſi quis eorum deliquerit erga dominum regem in parliamento aliquo, in parliamento debet corrigi et emendari, et non alibi in minor' cur' quàm in parliamento: per quod non intendit, quod dominus rex velit in cur' hic de hujuſmodi tranſgr. et contempt. factis in parliamento reſponderi, &c. Et ſuper hoc datus eſt eis dies coram rege à die ſanctæ Trin. in quindecem dies ubicunq; &c. ſalvis rationibus. Ad quem diem præd. epiſcopus venit in propria perſona ſua, et datus eſt ei dies coram domino rege a die ſancti Mich. in 15 dies ubicunq; &c. in eodem ſtatu quo nunc, &c. ſalvis rationibus ſuis, &c. Ad quem diem venit prædict. Adam qui ſequitur, &c. Et ſimiliter prædictus epiſcopus in propria perſona ſua. Et prædictus Adam pro prædicto domino rege dicit, quòd cum placeat ei parliamentum ſuum tenere pro utilitate regni ſui de regali poteſtate ſua facit illud ſommoneri ubi et quando, &c. pro voluntate ſua, et etiam facit prohiberi exiſtentibus tunc ad parliamentum, ne quis eorum abinde recedat contra prohibitionem ſuam, &c. abſq. licentia, &c. Et ſi quis eorum abinde recedat contra prohibitionem, &c. in contempt. regis, &c. bene liceat ipſi domino regi ſumere ſectam erga hujuſmodi delinquentes in qua curia placeat ſibi, &c. Et ex quo dominus rex pro voluntate ſua parliamenta ſua tenet, &c. petit judicium pro ipſo domino regi, ſi idem dominus rex duci debeat, ſeu compelli ad proſequend' in hac parte alibi contra voluntatem ſuam, &c.*

The plea of the biſhop to the juriſdiction of the court.

[16]

* Nota hoc.

This is the allegation of the kings attorney.

Et prædictus epiſcopus dicit ut prius, quòd cum aliquis deliquerit in parliamento, ibidem debet corrigi et emendari, &c. et licet aliquis ſummonitus eſſet veniendi ad parliamentum, et non veniſſet ibidem, debet puniri, per quod non intendit, quòd dominus rex velit alibi reſponderi quam in parliamento, &c. Et ſuper hoc datus eſt eis dies uſq; in cra'. animarum ubicunque, &c. in eodem ſtatu quo nunc, &c. Ad quem diem venit tam prædict. Adam, qui ſequitur pro domino rege, quam prædict. epiſcopus in propria perſona ſua. Et datus eſt eis dies coram domino rege in octab. Sancti Hilarii ubicunq. &c. ſalvis rationibus ſuis, &c. Ad quem diem prædict. epiſcopus venit, et datus eſt ei dies ulterius coram domino

The B. maintains his former plea to the juriſdiction.

rege in octab. Pur. beatæ Mariæ ubicunq', &c. Ad quem diem venit tam prædictus episcopus, quam Johannes de Lincoln' qui sequitur pro domino rege, et datus est eis dies ulterius coram domino rege a die Paschæ in quinque septimanas ubicunq', &c. Salvis rationibus, &c. Ad quem diem venit tam præd. episcopus in propria persona sua, quàm prædict. Johannes de Lincoln, qui sequitur pro dicto domino rege, &c. Et datus est eis dies ulterius a die Sancti Michaelis in 15 dies ubicunq; &c. salvis sibi rationibus suis hinc in dicend' &c.

[17] And this is all that is in the record, whereby it appeareth that the plea of the bishop to the jurisdiction of the court after divers dayes given did stand, and was never over-ruled agreeably to the said resolutions in former times, that judges were not to determine matters concerning the parliament, as is aforesaid. Touching the report of the said case, thus far forth it agreeth, that this contempt cannot be punished in any other court than in the kings bench: so as the question is only for that court. It appeareth that the reporter never saw the said record, only took it by the care of that which was spoken in court (a dangerous kind of reporting, and subject to many mistakings, for seldome or never the right case is but) as in this case it fell out. For first, where the record saith, that the parliament was holden at Sarum, the report is of a parliament holden at Salop. 2. The report saith, that John B. of Winchester was arraigned, which implieth that he was indicted, &c. where he was sued by originall writ. 3. The inhibition made by the king alledged in the record, is not in the report. 4. Concerning the sudden opinion of Scrope in this report: by his opinion the parliament it selfe could not have punished this contempt: for he saith, *Ceux q. sont judges de parliament, sont judges de lour piers, mes le roy nad my pier in son terre demesn, pur q. il ne poet p. eux estre judge, donques ailors que cy ne poet estre judge*, whereas without question the parliament might have punished this contempt: and concludeth with a rule at the common law, that the king may sue in what court it pleaseth him. But matters of parliament (as hath been often said) are not to be ruled by the common law: and it seemeth that the rest of the judges were against Scrope, for the plea was never over-ruled, as by the record it appeareth.

Vide per indictamenta termino Paschæ 1 & 2 Ph. et Mar. coram rege rot. 48. Informations preferred by the attorney generall against 39 of the house of commons for departing without license contrary to the kings inhibition in the beginning of the parliament; whereof 6 being timorous burgesses *ad redimendam vexationem* submitted themselves to their fines, but whether they paid any, or very small, we have not yet found. And * Edmond Plowden the learned lawyer pleaded, that he remained continually from the beginning to the end of the parliament, and took a travers full of pregnancy: and after his plea was *sine die per demise le roign.*

Mich. 3 & 4 Ph. & Mar. rot. 36. inter plac. regis et reginæ.

If offences done in parliament might have been punished elsewhere, it shall be intended that at some time it would have been put in ure. Vid. the first part of the Institutes, sect. 108.

Now the said informations *anno* 1 & 2 Ph. and Mar. against 39 of the house of commons follow in these words. *Pasch* 1 & 2 *Ph. and Mar. regis et reginæ.* Midd. *ss. memorand' quod Edwardus Griffyn ar' attornat' domin. regis et reginæ generalis, qui pro eisdem domino rege et domina regina sequitur, venit hic in cur' dictorum dominorum regis*

Edw. Griffin.

gis et reginæ coram ipsis rege et regina apud Westm' die Sabbathi proxim' post quind' Pasch. isto eodem termino, et dat cur' hic intelligi et informari. Quòd cum ad parliamentum dominorum regis et reginæ nunc tent' apud West' annis regnorum suorum primo et secundo inhibitum fuit per ipsos dominum regem et dominam reginam in eodem parliamento, quod nullus ad idem parliament' summonitus, et ibidem interessens, ab eodem parliamento absque speciali licentia dictorum dominorum regis et reginæ, et cur' parliament' prædict' recederet, seu seipsum aliquo modo absentaret. Quidam tamen Thomas Denton de in com' Oxon' ar' Henricus Cary de in com' gent' Richardus Warde de in com' ar' Edmund. Plowden de Tybmershe in com. Berks armiger, Henricus Chiverton de in com. ar. Robertus Browne de in com. Johannes Courke de in com. Johannes Pethebrige de in com. Johannes Melhewes de in com. Johan. Courtney de in com. Radulphus Michel de in com. Thomas Mathew de in com. Richardus Brasey de in com. Thomas Massye de in com. armig'. Petrus Frechwell de in com. miles. Henricus Vernon de Sydbery in com. Derby armig. Willielmus Moore de villa Derb. in com. Derb. gen. Willielmus Banibrigge de in com. Johannes Eveleigh de in com. gen. Nich. Adamps de Dartmouth, alias Clifton Harnys in com. Devon gen. Richardus Phelipps de in com. ar. Anthonius Dylvington de in com. Andreas Hoorde de in com. Christopherus Hoell de in com. Dors. gen. Johannes Mannocke de in com. gen. Thomas Phelipps de in com. Johannes Hamond de in com. Johannes Phelipps de in com. Willielmus Randall junior, de in com Johannes Moyne de in com. Hugo Smyth de in com. gen. Rogerus Gerrard de in com. gen. Radulphus Scroope de in com. gen. Thomas Moore de Hambled. in com Buck. gen. Willielmus Reade de in com. ar. Henricus Mannock de in com. ar. Joh. Maynarde de villa Sancti Albani in com. Hertf. ar. Nich. Debden de in com. gen. et Philippus Tirwhyt de in com. ar' qui summoniti fuerunt ad dictum parliamentum. et in eodem parliamento comparuerunt, ac ibidem interfuerunt mandat' et inhibitionem dominorum regis et reginæ supradict' parvi pendentes, ac statum reipublicæ hujus regni Angliæ minime curantes aut ponderantes postea scil. 12 die Januarii annis regnorum dictorum dominorum regis et reginæ nunc primo et secundo supradictis, et durante parliamento prædicto ab eodem parliamento sine licentia dictorum dominorum regis et reginæ et cur' suæ prædict. contemptuose recesserunt in ipsorum dominorum regis et reginæ ac mandat' et inhibitionis suorum prædict' curiæq; prædict contempt' manifestum, ac in magnum reipublicæ statum hujus regni Angliæ detriment', nec non in perniciosum exemplum omnium aliorum, &c. Unde idem attornatus dominorum regis et reginæ petit advisamentum cur' in præmis. et debit' legis process. vers. eosdem Thomam Denton, Henricum Cary, Richardum Warde, Edm. Plowden, Henricum Chiverton, Robertum Browne, Joh. Courk, Joh. Pethybridge, Joh. Melhewes, Joh. Courtney, Radulph. Michell, Thomam Mathewe, Richardum Brasey, Thomam Massye, Petrum Frechwell, Henricum Vernon, Will. Moore, Will. Banibrigge, Joh. Eveleigh, Nich. Adamps, Richardum Phelipps, Anthonium Dilvington, Andream Hoorde, Christopherum Hoell, Johannem Mannock, Thomam Phelipps, Johan. Hamond, Joh. Phelipps, Willielmum

Inhibitum fuit.

[18]

Mandatum et inhibitionem.

[19]

mum Randall, Joh. Moyne, Hugonem Smith, Rogerum Gerrard, Radulphum Scroope, Tho. Moore, Will. Read, Henricum Mannock, Johan. Maynard, Nicholaum Debden, et Phil. Tyrwhyt fieri ad respondend. domino regi, et dominæ reginæ de contempt' prædict. &c.

Mich. 3 & 4 Ph. & Mar. ro. 36. inter plac. regis et reginæ.

Et modo scil. die Veneris prox' post crast' animarum isto eodem termino coram domin. rege et domina regina apud West' ven' prædict Edm. Plowden per Andream Tusser attornatum suum; et habit' audit' informationis prædictæ dic', quod ipse non intendit quod dominus rex et domina regina nunc ipsum Edmun' pro præmissis vel aliquo præmissorum impetere seu occasionare velint aut debent: Quia dicit quod ipse ad dict' parliament' in informatione prædict' specificat' interfuit et præsens fuit, ac in eodem parliamento continue remansit, viz. *à principio ipsius parliamenti usq; ad finem ejusdem. Absq; hoc quod ipse idem Edmund. Plowden dicto* 12 *die Januarii, an. primo et secundo supradict' durant' parliament' prædict' ab eodem parliament' sine licentia dictorum dominorum regis et reginæ, et cur' suæ prædict' contemptuose recessit in ipsorum dominorum regis et reginæ ac mandat' et inhibitionis suorum prædict' curiæq; præd' contemp' manifest', ac in magnum reipublicæ stat' hujus regni Angliæ detriment', nec non in perniciosum exemplum omnium aliorum modo et forma prout per informac' prædict' vers. eum supponitur. Et hoc paratus est verificare prout cur. &c. unde pet' judicium: et quod ipse de præmiss. per cur' hic dimittatur, &c.*

Nota, the pregnancy of this travers. Sine die per demise le royne.

Per de annis 1 & 2 Ph. & Mar. Rot. 48.

Midd. *Ve. fac' Thomam Constable de Grimsbye in com. Lincoln. ar. Hen. Leigh, de in com. Francis. Farnham de Querne in com. Leic. ar.* Li. lo. Mic. 2 & 3 Ph. regis et Mar. reginæ. *Joh. Holcroft. sen. de in com. milit. Will. Bromley de in com. ar. Tho. Somerset de in com. ar. Georg. Ferrers de Markyat' in com. Hertf. gen. Nich. Powtrell de Exincton in com. Nott' ar.* F. Hill. 3 & 4 Ph. & Mar. *Tho. Moyle de in com' Kanc' milit. Tho. Waters de in com. ar. Will. Tylcock de civit' Oxon' gen.* Li. lo Hil. 2 & 3 Ph. & Mar. *Tho. Balkden de Weclyngleigh in com. Sur. milit.* Li. lo. Mic. 2 & 3 Ph. & Mar. *Math. Cradock de villa Staff. gen.* Li. lo. Hil. 2 & 3 Ph. & Mar. *Georgium Lye de villa Salop. gen.* Ceff. proceff. per mandat' attornat' dominorum regis & reginæ, quia ulterius prosequi non vult vers. ipsum Geo. Lye. *Joh. Hoord de Bridgenorth in com. Salop. gen.* F. Mic. 5 & 6 Ph. & Mar. *Joh. Alsop de villa de Ludlowe in com. Salop. gen. Wil. Laurence de civ. Winton. gen.* Li. lo. Mich. 2 & 3 Ph. & Mar. *Robert Hudson de civ. Winton gen.* Li. lo. ut antea. *Edm. Rowse de Donwich in com. Suff. mil. Rob. Coppinge de Donwich in com' Suff. ar. Joh. Harman de hospicio dom. regis et dom. reginæ gen. Will. Crowch de Wellowe in com' Somers. ar. Tho. Lewes de villa de Wels in com' Somers. gen.* Li. lo. Hil. 2 & 3 Ph. & Mar. *Wil. Godwyn de Wels præd' in com' Somers gen.* F. Mich. 3 & 4 Ph. & Mar. *Joh. Ashburnham de Ashburnham in com' Suss. ar.* Li. lo. Mic. 2 & 3 Ph. & Mar. *Walt. Reyncum de civ' Cicest' in com' Suss. gen.* Li. lo. Tr. 2 & 3 Ph. & Mar. *Wil. Moodyere de Slindon in com' Suss. gen.* F. Tr. 4 & 5 Ph. & Mar. *Joh. Roberts de in com' Suss. gen. utlegat. &c. Wil. Pellet de Steininge in com' Suss. gen.* F. Pasch. 2 & 3 Ph. & Mar. *Rich. Bowyer de Arundell in com' Suss. gen.* Li. lo. Mic. 3 & 4 Ph. & Mar. *Will. Danby de in com. Westmerl. gen. Rob. Griffyth de civ' Novæ Sarum in com' Wilts, draper.* Li. lo. ut supra. *Joh. Hooper de civ. Novæ Sarum in com' Wilts, gen.* Li. lo. Mic. 2 & 3 Ph. & Mar. *Wil. Clark de in com. Grif. Curtys de*

[20]

de Bradstock in com' Wilts gen. Li. lo. ut supra, &c. *Tho. Hil. de Denyses in com. Wilts gen.* F. Hil. 2 & 3 Ph. & Mar. *Edw. Umpton de London gen.* Li. lo. Mic. 2 & 3 Ph. & Mar. *Tho. Parker de in com' Joh. Reade de London gen.* F. Hil. 2 & 3 Ph. & Mar. *Arth. Allen de civ' Bristol merch. Egid. Payne de civ. Bristol. gen. Wil. Hampshire de London gen.* Li. lo. Mic. 3 & 4 Ph. & Mar. *et Pet. Tayler de Marlborow in com' Wilts, taylor.* Li. lo. Mic. 3 & 4 Ph. & Mar. *resp. regi de quibusdam transgress. et contempt. unde impetit' sunt.*

Cess. processſ. verſ. Georgium Lye.

Sine die per demise le Royne.

Mid. *Ve. fac' cr' Trin Edw. Braxden de civ' Wigorn. gen. Georg. Newport de Droitwich in com' Wigorn. gen. Wil. Wigstone de Wolstone in com' War. mil.* Li. lo. Mic. 2 & 3 Ph. & Mar. *Radulph. Browne de Woodlowes in com. War. gen.* Li. lo. Mich. 3 & 4 Ph. & Mar. *Joh. Harforde de civ' Covent. gen.* Cess. processſ. &c. *Nich. Fryshe de in com' Rich Rayleton de in com. Marc. Wyrley de civ. Lichfield, gen. Walt. Jobson de villa de Kingston super Hull. Jac. Brenne de in com. gen. Joh. Payton de in com. Kanc. ar. Joh. Cheney de in com. Kanc. armigerum Willielmum Oxenden de in com. Kanc. armigerum. Tho. Keys de in com. Kanc. gen. Wil. Hannington de in com. Kanc. Joh. Tyssars de in com. Nich. Crypse de in com. Kanc. ar. Edw. Herbert de Stawley in com. Salop ar.* F. Hil. 4 & 5 præd. Ph. & Mar. &c. *Rich. Lloyde de in com. Kanc. gen. Joh. de Knylle de in com. ar. Hen. Jones de in com. mil. Meredith Gaines de in com. gen. et Rich. Bulkeley de in com. mil. Resp. regi de quibusdam transgr. et contempt. unde impetit' sunt. Et postea, scil. termino sanct. Trin. annis* 4 *&* 5 *Ph. & Mar. pro eo quod sufficienter hic in cur' testatum est quod prædict. Joh. Harford habuit licentiam recedere à parliamento. &c. Ideo Edw. Griffyn ar. attornat. dominorum regis et reginæ generalis qui pro ipsis rege et regina in hac parte sequitur, dicit quod ipse ulterius in hac parte vers. præfatum Joh. Harford prosequi non vult. Ideo cess. hic. process. vers. eum omnino, &c.*

Per cont' rott' de annis 1 & 2 Ph. and Mar. rot. 48.

Non prof. verſ. Harford tantum.

Sine die per demise le Royne.

[21]

And to deal clearly, this is all that we can find concerning this matter. Thus you may observe, that the poor commons, members of the parliament, *in diebus illis*, had no great joy to continue in parliament, but departed. But now to proceed.

Of Writs of Error in Parliament.

If a judgement be given in the kings bench either upon a writ of error, or otherwise, the party grieved may upon a petition of right made to the king in English, or in French (which is not *ex debito justitiæ*, but for decency, for that the former judgement was given *coram rege*) and his answer thereunto, *fiat justitia*, have a writ of error directed to the chief justice of the kings bench for removing of the record *in præsens parliamentum*, and thereupon the roll it self, and a transcript in parchment is to be brought by the chief justice of the kings bench into the lords house in parliament: and after the transcript is examined by the court with the record, the chief justice carrieth back the record it self into the kings bench, and then the plaintife is to assign the errors, and thereupon to have a *scire fac'* against the adverse party, returnable either in that parliament, or the next, and the proceeding thereupon shall be *super tenorem re-*

The house of the lords is a distinct court for many purposes. 22 E. 3. fo. 3. Regist. 17. lib. Intr. Rast. 284.

cordi, et non super recordum. All this, and many more excellent matters of learning are contained in the records following; whereof a light touch is hereafter given, the records at large being too long here to be rehearsed. And the proceeding upon the writ of error is only before the lords in the upper house, *Secundum legem et consuetudinem parliamenti.*

Rot. par. post festum Sancti Hil. anno 18 E. 1. rot. 8.

Queritur Guilielmus de Valencia contra concilium regis, i. Justic' coram rege, pro injusto judicio tangen' allocationem Dionisiæ filiæ Guilielmi de monte Caniso ut hæred': sed dominus rex ratum habet eorum factum, et judicium redditum est contra Guilielmum de Valencia.

Rot. par. 4 E. 3. nu. 13. Rich. earl of Arundels case. Ib. 28 E. 3. nu. 11, 12. Mortimer earl of Marches case. See Pasch. 28 E. 3. coram rege rot. 37 Wigorn. the same case. 33 H. 8. ca. 20. 29 Eliz. ca. 2. rot. par. 7 R. 2. nu. 20. 8 R. 2. nu. 14.

If a nobleman had been erroneously attainted of treason, &c. he might have had his writ of error in parliament, notwithstanding the statute of 33 H. 8. ca. 20. for that must be intended of lawfull records of attainder: but if the attainder be established by authority of parliament, then he must exhibite his petition in parliament to be restored of grace. But now by the statute of 29 El. ca. 2. it is ordained, that no record of attainder of high treason that then was, for the which the party attainted had been executed for the same treason should be reversed for error: but this extendeth only to attainders of high treason, and not to any attainder of high treason after that act, nor to any high treason before, for the which the party was not executed.

The prior and covent of Montague by their petition declare, that Richard Seimour had obtained an erroneous judgement against the said prior in the kings bench, upon a judgement given in the common place upon a fine for the mannor of Titenhull in the county of Somerset, &c. And the principall error was for denying of aid of the king where it was grantable, and that hanging a writ of right, the said Richard sued a *scire fac.* And commandment was given to the chancelor of England, that he should make a writ of possession and seison to be had, and other processe upon that judgment to be made: in this record you shall observe excellent pleading.

Rot. par. 13 R. 2. nu. 15. Sir Thomas Methams case.

Error in parliament upon a judgment in an appeal of death upon an acquitall of the defendant, and inquiry of the abettors, &c.

And (that we may observe it once for all) when one sueth in parliament to reverse a judgement in the kings bench, he sheweth in his bill which he exhibiteth to the parliament some error or errors, whereupon he prayeth a *scire facias.*

Rot. par. 50 E. 3. nu. 48.

The bishop of Norwich sheweth that an erroneous judgment was given against him in the common place for the archdeaconry of Norwich belonging to his presentation, and prayed that those errors might be heard, and redressed there: whereunto answer was made, that errors, by the law, in the common place are to be corrected in the kings bench, and of the kings bench in the parliament and not otherwise.

[22]

1 R. 2. nu. 28, 29. 2 R. 2. nu. 31. A writ of error in parliament between William Mountacute earl of Sarum, and Roger of Mortimer earl of March of a judgment in the kings bench.

[a] The dean and chapter of Litchfield recovered in the common place against the prior of Newport Pannel: the prior by writ of error reverseth the judgment in the kings bench: the dean and chapter by writ of error in parliament reverseth the judgment in the kings bench, and affirmeth the judgment in the common place, and

[a] Rot. par. 15 R. 2. nu. 23. & 18 R. 2. nu. 11, 12, 13, 14, 15. This parliam. of 18 R. 2. is not mentioned in the printed book, because no act passed at this parliament. See 2 H. 4. nu. 40.

and a commandment given to the chancelor, that the judgement in the common place be executed by processe by him to be made.

[b] John Sheppy complains of a judgement in the kings bench in a writ of error.

[b] Rot. par. 15 R. 2. nu. 22.

[c] Error in parliament between William Mountacute earl of Salisbury, and Roger de Mortimer earl of March, for the castle, town, and honour of Denbeigh, &c. upon a judgment given in the kings bench, and had a *scire fac'* returnable the next parliament.

[c] 21 R. 2. nu. 25. 2 H. 4. nu. 13.

[d] William Seward alias Cheddre complaineth, that where he by that name was presented and inducted to the parsonage of Wotton Under Egge in the county of Glouc', and thereof continued the possession by the space of four years, untill the king by untrue suggestion presented Sir John Dawtry to the parsonage of Underhegge in that county, where there was no such parsonage called Underhegge, as the said William pleaded in a *quare impedit* brought by the king in the kings bench; upon which writ the king recovered by the default the parsonage of Underhegge, and not Under Egge, whereby upon a writ sent to the bishop of Worcester, the said William was put from his parsonage of Under Egge: for which mistaking and error, the judgment for the said John in full parliament was reversed, and a writ awarded to the said bishop for the restitution of the said William.

[d] Rot. par. 1 H. 4. nu. 91.

The record and judgment given in the kings bench for the king, against Edmond Basset for certain lands, &c. was for divers errors reversed in parliament, and restitution of the premisses with the mean profits restored to the said Edmond. Rot. par. 15 R. 2. nu. 24. & 2 H. 4. nu. 38.

In error in parliament between Roger Deyncourt, and Ralph de Adderlye for a judgement given in the kings bench for the mannor of Anslye in com' Warr'. Sir William Gascoign chief justice delivered a copy of the record and processe, word for word, under his hand, &c. to the clerk of the parliament, &c. 5 H. 4. nu. 40.

In error in parliament between Richard Quatermayns and Willam Hore, &c. upon an erroneous judgement given in the kings bench in an action of trespasse, and the plaintif entred his atturny of record to proceed therein. Rot. par. 3 H. 5. nu. 19.

John Beauchamp lord Abergaveny complained in parliament upon an erroneous judgment given upon a verdict in the kings bench in a *scire fac'* upon a recognisance in the chancery for keeping the peace. In the record whereof are excellent points of learning, as well touching the recognisance, as the processe, and issue. Rot. par. 10 H. 6. nu. 51. & 11 H. 6. nu. 40.

Error in parliament, Pasch. 31 H. 6. upon a judgment given in an assize in the kings bench, *et intratur super marginem, rot. mittitur in parliamentum per Johannen Fortescue termino Paschæ anno* 31 H. 6. Rot. par. 31 H. 6.

And to omit many others, to descend to some of latter times, Richard Whalley recovered in assise by verdict against divers tenants, who brought a writ of error in the kings bench, where the judgment in the assise was affirmed, the tenant complained in parliament for error in the kings bench. Rot. par. 23 El. Dier 23 El. f. 373.

Error in parliament upon complaint of Sir Christopher Heydon knight of a judgment in a writ of error in the kings bench, between the said Sir Christopher plaintif, and Roger Godsalve and others defendants, Rot. par. 12 Jac.

fendants, upon a judgment given for the ſaid Roger, &c. againſt the ſaid Sir Chriſtopher in an aſſiſe before juſtices of aſſiſe, wherein the judgement in the aſſiſe was affirmed in the kings bench, whereof the complaint was made, *ſed non prævaluit.*

In caſe of treaſon, &c. the lords ſpirituall make their proctors. The peers are judges of treaſon, &c. during the parliament, &c. Rot. par. 5 H. 4. nu. 11, 12. Rot. par. 21 R. 2. ſub tit. Plac. Coronæ, &c. Rot. par. 31 H. 6. nu. 49.

A peer of the realm being indicted of treaſon, or felony, or miſpriſion of treaſon, may be arraigned thereof in parliament, a lord ſteward being appointed, and then the lords ſprituall ſhall make a procurator for them; and the lords, as peers of the realm, during the parliament are judges, whether the offence be treaſon, &c. that is ſuppoſed to be committed by any peer of the realm, and not the juſtices, as it appeareth in the earl of Northumberlands caſe, rot. parl. 5 H. 4. nu. 11, 12. See in the parliament holden 21 R. 2. *ſub titulo Pl. Coronæ,* in a roll annexed, &c. before the ſteward of England and other lords temporall, Richard earl of Arundels caſe. Rot. parl. 31 H. 6. nu. 49. Thomas earl of Devon was arraigned of high treaſon before Humphry duke of Buck' ſteward of England *hac vice,* and was acquited by his peers, 10 E. 4. fo. 6. b. Stanf. Pl. Coron. 153. b.

Of Judicature.

Now order doth require to treat of other matters of judicature in the lords houſe, and of matters of judicature in the houſe of commons. And it is to be known, that the lords in their houſe have power of judicature, and the commons in their houſe have power of judicature, and * both houſes together have power of judicature: but the handling hereof according to the worth and weight of the matter would require a whole treatiſe of it ſelf; and to ſay the truth, it is beſt underſtood by reading the judgements and records of parliament at large, and the journals of the houſe of the lords, and the book of the clerk of the houſe of commons, which is a record, as it is affirmed by act of parliament in *anno* 6 H. 8. ca. 16.

* Vide placita in parliam. anno 33 E. 1. rot. 33. Nicholaus Segrave adjudge per prælatos, comites, barones et alios de concilio. At the parliament at York anno 12 E. 2. *Conſideratum eſt per prælatos, comites, barones, et communitatem Angliæ.* The lord Awdeleys caſe. At the parl. at Weſtm' 15 E. 2. Hugh le pier adjudge per les ſeignours et commons. Rot. parl. 42 E. 3. nu. 20. Sir John at Lee adjudged by the lords and commons. Rot. pat. 50 E. 3. 2. parte, A pardon to the lord Latimer of a judgement in parliament. Rot. parl. 50 E. 3. nu. 34. Lo. Nevils caſe.

See Rot. clauſ. 1 R. 2. m. 5. 8. 38, 39. *A treſage councell le roy, les ſeigniors et commons, &c.* Rot. parl. 1 H. 4. nu. 79. it is no act of parliament but an ordinance, and therefore bindeth not in ſucceſſion. Rot. par. 2 H. 5. nu. 13. error aſſigned that the lords gave judgement without petition or aſſent of the commons. Rot. par. 28 H. 6. nu. 19. and many others in the reign of king H. 6. king E. 4.

And of latter times, ſee divers notable judgements, at the proſecution of the commons, by the lords at the parliaments holden 18 and 21 Jac. *regis,* againſt Sir Giles Mompeſſon, Sir John Michel, viſcount S. Albone lord chancellor of England, the earl of M. lord treaſurer of England, whereby the due proceeding of judicature in ſuch caſes doth appear.

Thomas Long gave the maior of Weſtbury four pound to be elected burgeſſe, who thereupon was elected. This matter was examined and adjudged in the houſe of commons, *ſecundum legem et conſuetudinem parliamenti*, and the maior fined and impriſoned, and Long removed: for this corrupt dealing was to poyſon the very fountain it ſelf. In the book of the houſe of commons at the parliament holden 8 Eliz. Ownſloe ſpeaker. fo. 19.

Arthur Hall a member of the houſe of commons for publiſhing and diſcovering the conferences of the houſe, and writing a book to the diſhonor of the houſe, was upon due examination, *ſecundum legem et conſuetudinem parliamenti*, adjudged by the houſe of commons to be committed to the Tower for ſix months, fined at five hundred marks, and expelled the houſe. 23 El. lib. fo. 14. Popham atturny generall ſpeaker.

Munĉton ſtroke William Johnſon a burgeſſe of B. returned into the chancery of record, for which upon due examination in the houſe of commons, it was reſolved that *ſecundum legem et conſuetudinem parliamenti*, every man muſt take notice of all the members of the houſe returned of record at his perill: but otherwiſe it is of the ſervant of any of the members of the houſe; for there he that ſtriketh, &c. muſt have notice. And the houſe adjudged Munĉton to the Tower, &c. Ib. 2. Aprilis. 1 Mariæ. Vid. 11 H. 6. c. 11. 5 H. 4. ca. 6. [24] See Rot. parl. 8 H. 6. nu. 57.

If any lord of parliament, ſpirituall, or temporall, have committed any oppreſſion, bribery, extortion, or the like, the houſe of commons, being the generall inquiſitors of the realm (comming out of all the parts thereof) may examine the ſame, and if they find by the vote of the houſe, the charge to be true, then they tranſmit the ſame to the lords with the witneſſes and proofs.

Priviledge of Parliament.

And now after judicature, let us ſpeak ſomewhat of priviledge of parliament: experience hath made the priviledges of parliaments well known to parliament men, yet will we ſpeak ſomewhat thereof. Vide inter leges Edw. Confeſſ. c. 3.

Magiſter militiæ Templi petit quòd diſtringat (catalla unius de concilio) tempore parliamenti pro redditu unius domus in London: rex reſpondet, non videtur honeſtum, quod illi de concilio ſuo diſtringantur tempore parliamenti, ſed alio tempore, &c. Whereby it appeareth that a member of the parliament ſhal have priviledge of parliament, not only for his ſervants, as is aforeſaid, but for his horſes, &c. or other goods diſtreinable. Petitiones coram domino rege ad parliament' poſt feſtum Sancti Mich. anno 18 E. 1. fo. 7.

Querela Comitis cornubiæ, verſus Bogonem de Clare et priorem ſanctæ Trinitatis London, quòd ipſi tempore parliamenti ipſum comitem in medio aulæ Weſtm' ad procurationem ipſius Bogonis citaverunt, quòd compareret coram archiepiſcopo Cantuar', &c. Ipſe prior venit et Bogo ſimiliter, et ponunt ſe in gratiam, miſericordiam, et voluntatem regis de alto et baſſo, ob quod mandantur turri London: poſtea venit dictus Bogo et finem fecit domino regi pro prædicta tranſgreſſione per duas mille marcas, &c. et quoad prædict' comitem reſpondeat comiti 1000. li. pro tranſgreſſione ſibi fact', &c. et prædictus prior mittitur ibidem ad faciend' ſecundum quod theſaurarius ei dicet ex parte dni. regis. Plac. coram rege et ejus concilio ad parliam. ſuum poſt feſtum Sancti Hil. anno 18 E. 1. fol. 1. Vide inf. 10 E. 3. more hereof concerning ſerving of a citation.

And yet the ſerving of the ſaid citation did not arreſt, or reſtrain his body, and the ſame priviledge holdeth in caſe of *ſub pœna*, or other proceſſe out of any court of equity.

Rex

Rot. parliam. anno 8 E. 2. in Dorf. cl. 8 E. 2.

Rex mandavit justiciariis suis ad assisas, jurat', &c. capiend. assignat' quòd supersedeant captioni eorundem ubi comites, barones et alii summoniti ad parliamentum regis sunt partes, quamdiu dictum parliam. duraverit.

Ibid. m. 33 & 22.

De non procedendo ad capiend' assisas versus illos, qui ad parliamentum regis apud Eborum venerunt.

In Scacc' ex Originali de anno 10 E. 3. ro. 27. No.

* That is, in court of parliament.

Citationes. This John de Thoresby was then clerk of the parliament.

*Rex omnibus balivis et fidelibus suis ad quos, &c. salutem. Sciatis, quòd cum curiæ nostræ in quibus * negotia regni nostri dedecantur ubiq; adeo liberæ sint et exemptæ, et à tempore quo non extat memoria liberæ et exemptæ fuerunt, quod nec aliqua forum ecclesiasticum concernentia in eisdem curiis nostris fieri seu exequi, nec aliqui easdem curias nostras ad aliqua forum ecclesiasticum contingentia faciendum vel exequendum ingredi debeant, vel consueverunt aliquibus temporibus retroactis, ac magister Henricus de Harewedon clericus, Edmundus de Lukenore et Johannus de Wedlingburgh de eo quòd ipsi nuper in cancellaria nostra in præsentia venerabilis patris I. Cantuariensis archiepiscopi cancellarii nostri quasdam citationes sive monitiones dilecto clerico nostro Johanni de Thoresby, ne non provocationes, appellationes et instrumenta publica super citationibus seu monitionibus prædictis in nostri contemptum et coronæ nostræ ac regiæ dignitatis nostræ præjudicium, et contra libertatem et exemptionem prædict' fecerunt per inquisitionem in quam se inde in curia nostra coram dilecto cancellario nostro et aliis de concilio nostro posuerunt convicti fuissent et ea occasione prisonæ nostræ mancipati in eadem ad voluntatem nostram moraturi. Nos de gratia nostra speciali ad requisitionem Philippæ reginæ Angliæ consortis nostræ charissimæ perdonavimus eidem Henrico, Edmundo et Johanni imprisonamentum prædictum; ita tamen quod nobis satisfaciant de redemptione sua occasione præmissorum, et*

[25]

quod super citationibus, monitionibus, provocationibus, appellationibus seu instrumentis prædictis in dicta cancellaria nostra sic factis processum aliquem non faciant, nec quicquam quod in nostri vel juris coronæ nostræ præjudicium cedere possit attemptent vel attemptare faciant de cætero quovis modo. In cujus, &c. Teste rege apud turrim London 15 die Aprilis, ex originali de anno 10 E. 3. Rot. 27. Not.

* Rot. parl. anno 17 E. 4. nu. 36. Vid. 21 E. 4. fol. 38, 39. Rot. parl. anno 8 H. 6. nu. 57. Vide infra. pa.

* Priviledge of parliament in informations for the king, generally the priviledge of parliament do hold, unlesse it be in three cases, viz. treason, felony, and the peace.

Of Statutes, or Acts of Parliament.

a Vid. 14 R. 2. nu. 15. & 13 H. 4. nu. 25. b 4 H. 7. 18. b. p. touts les justices. 7 H. 7. 14 & 16. 11 H. 7. 27. a. Brook prerogative 134. Fortescue fo. 20. cap. 18. Dier 1 Mar. 92.

There is no act of parliament but must have the consent of the lords, the commons, and the royall assent of the king, and as it appeareth by [a] records and our [b] books whatsoever passeth in parliament by this threefold consent, hath the force of an act of parliament.

The difference between an act of parliament, and an ordinance in parliament, is, for that the [c] ordinance wanteth the threefold consent, and is ordained by one or two of them.

[c] Rot. parl. 25 E. 3. nu. 16. &c. 39 E. 3. 12. 22 E. 3. 3. 8 H. 6. cap. 29. Dier 4 Mar. 144. 39 E. 3. 7. Thorp male erravit. Rot. parl. 37 E. 3. nu. 39. 1 R. 2. nu. 56. diversity between acts of parliament and ordinances. 2 R. 2. stat. 2. nu. 28.

I have

[d] I have read of a reſtitution in blood, and of lands of one William de Laſenby by the king, by the aſſent of the lords ſpirituall, and commons, (omitting the lords temporall) this we hold is an ordinance, and no act of parliament. And when the clergy is omitted and the act made by the king, the lords temporall, and commons. See the rols of parliament and authorities following, viz. Rot. parl. Paſch. [e] 15 E. 2. the caſe of the Spencers. 3 R. 2. cap. 3. in print: Our ſoveraigne lord by the common conſent of all the lords temporall, and at the petition of the commons, &c. 7 R. 2. cap. 12 accord. 11 R. 2. nu. 9, 10, 11. See 1 H. 5. c. 7. [f] 21 R. 2. nu. 9. & 10. 6 H. 6. nu. 27. 7 H. 8. Kelw. 184. the opinion of the juſtices agreeable with the ſaid acts of parliament. And note the mutability in this particular caſe of the Spencers, of this high court of parliament. The judgement by parliament in 15 E. 2. againſt the Spencers, was in the ſame year by act of parliament repealed: that repeale was repealed by authority of parliament in 1 E. 3. that repeal of 1 E. 3. was repealed by act of parliament in 21 R. 2. and that of 21 R. 2. was repealed by authority of parliament in 1 H. 4. And ſo the judgement againſt the Spencers ſtandeth in force.

[d] 13 H. 4. nu. 20.

[e] Repeal 1 E. 3. cap. 2. ſtat. 1. 15 E. 3. tit. Petition. F. 2. See Rot. par. an. 1 H. 4. part 5. m. 36. the Iſle of Man given to the king by the lords temporall and commons.

[f] Repeal. 1 H. 4. cap. 3.

The Diviſion of Acts of Parliament.

Of acts of parliament ſome be introductory of a new law, and ſome be declaratory of the ancient law, and ſome be of both kinds by addition of greater penalties or the like. Againe, of acts of parliament, ſome be generall, and ſome be private and particular. All acts of parliament relate to the firſt day of parliament, if it be not otherwiſe provided by the act.

33 H. 6. fol. 17.

The ſeverall Formes of Acts of Parliament.

In ancient time all acts of parliament were in form of petitions. And for the ſeverall forms of acts of parliament, ſee the princes caſe in the 8 book of Reports. Now for the reading, committing, amending, ingroſſing, voting, and paſſing of bils in either houſe, and touching conferences with the lords, and for the priviledge of any member of either houſes, and of their ſervants more then hath been ſaid, they be ſo ordinary and well known, and in ſuch continuall practice, as it were but expence of time to treat any more of them. And for that many times the rols of the parliament have not been truly ingroſſed, at the requeſt of the commons certain of them are to be appointed, who ſhould be at the ingroſſing of the rols of parliament.

Dier 3. Mar. 131. lib. 8. fo. 1. the princes caſe. Concerning the ingroſſing in rols of acts of parliament. Rot. parl. 7 H. 4. nu. 65.

[26]

In former Times Acts of Parliament were proclaimed by the Sheriffes.

When I read the caſe of premunire in 39 E. 3. upon the ſtatute of 27 E. 3. of proviſors againſt the biſhop of Chicheſter, and obſerving that ſerjeant Cavendiſh of councell with the biſhop objected two things: firſt, that the act whereupon the writ was grounded,

grounded, was no ſtatute. Secondly, that if it were a ſtatute, it was never publiſhed in the county: whom Sir Robert Thorpe chiefe juſtice anſwered. Although proclamation be not made in the county, every one is bound to take notice of that which is done in parliament: for as ſoon as the parliament hath concluded any thing, the law intends, that every perſon hath notice thereof, for the parliament repreſents the body of the whole realm: and therefore it is not requiſite that any proclamation be made, ſeeing the ſtatute took effect before. This gave me to underſtand, that albeit it was not required by law that ſtatutes ſhould be publiſhed in the county; yet ſeeing in thoſe days and long after, the uſe of printing came not into this realm; the uſe was (as it appeareth by Cavendiſhes ſpeech) that they ſhould be publiſhed in the county, to the end that the ſubjects might have expreſſe notice thereof, and not to be overtaken by an intendment in law, which gave me occaſion to ſearch and inquire how this uſage was, and how long it continued. And in the end I found, that at every parliament the acts that paſſed were tranſcribed into parchment, and by the kings writ directed to the ſheriffe of every county of England, and commandement given to him, that all the ſaid ſtatutes in all places through his whole bayliwick, as well within franchiſe as without, where he ſhould finde moſt fit, that he not only ſhould proclaime them, but to ſee that they ſhould be firmly obſerved and kept. And the uſage was to proclaim them at his county court, &c. and there to keep the tranſcript of the acts, that who ſo would, might reade or take copies thereof. And this writ was ſometime in Latine and ſometime in French, as in thoſe dayes the ſtatutes were enacted in Latin or in French. But an example of the one, and of the other will more illuſtrate this matter.

John Moore. Printing was invented in Meath in Germany, anno domini 1441. and came to us in the raign of H. 6. See Bodin De Methodo hiſtoriæ. li. 7. *Una typographia cum omnibus omnium veterum inventis certare facile poteſt.* *Polydor Virgil de invent. rerum lib.* 2. *cap.* 7. *Cardan. de varietate rerum lib.* 3. *cap.* 64.

At the parliament in anno 10 E. 3.

* Nota that the ſheriffe that hath *cuſtodiam comitatus*, ſhould ſee the ſtatutes within his county to be kept.

Edwardus Dei grat' rex Angliæ et Franciæ, et dominus Hiberniæ vic' Norff. ſalut. Quædam ſtatuta p. nos, prælatos, comites, barones, et alios magnates ad parliamentum noſtrum tentum apud Eborum in cro. Aſcenſionis ultim' præterit' ordinavimus et ſtabilivimus, prout ſequitur, and recite the ſeverall ſtatutes *verbatim*. And then the writ concludeth. *Et ideo tibi præcipimus, quod ſtatuta illa et omnes articulos in eiſdem contentos in ſingulis locis in baliva tua, tam infra libertates, quam extra, ubi expedire videris, publice proclamari et * firmiter teneri et obſervari facias. Teſte, &c.*

At the parliament an. 1. R. 2.

Richard p. la grace de Dieu roy Dengliterre et de France, et ſeigniour d'Ireland a noſtre viſcount de Norff. ſalut. Saches que al honeur de Dieu, et reverence de ſaint eſgliſe et pur nurrer peace, unitie, et concord in touts parts deins noſtre realme, le quel nous deſirons mult entirement, del aſſent des prelats, dukes, counts et barons de meſme noſtre realme, al inſtance et ſpeciall requeſt des commons de noſtre realme aſſembles a noſtre parliament tenus a Weſtm. a la quinzim de S. Michael lan de noſtre reigne primier avons fait ordeiner et ſtablier certaine ſtatuts en amendment et relievement de meſme noſtre realme, et en la forme que ſenſuiſt. Primerment eſt aſſentus et eſtablie, que ſaint egliſe eit et enjoy ſe touts les droitures, &c. rehearſing all the ſtatutes that paſſed at that parliament. And the writ concludeth thus. *Et pur ceo vous mandons que touts les ſtatuts faces crier et publier, et firmament tener p. my voſtre baillie ſolonq; la forme et tenor de icel, et ceo ne leſſes en aſcun manner. Done p. teſtmoignants de noſtre grand ſeale al Weſtm. le primier jour de Feverer lan de noſtre reigne primer.* And the like writs continued

untill

untill the beginning of the reign of H. 7. long time after printing within the reign of H. 6. (as hath bin said) came unto us.

[27]

Prorogation, Adjournment, Continuance, and what maketh a Session of Parliament.

The passing of any bill or bils by giving the royal assent thereunto, or the giving any judgement in parliament doth not make a session, but the session doth continue untill that session be prorogued or dissolved: and this is evident by many presidents in parliament ancient and late.

The parliament of 14 E. 3. began at Westminster the Wednesday after Mid Lent: the first Monday of the parliament, the ninth part of their grain, wooll, and lambe, &c. was granted to the king, on condition that the king would grant their petitions in a schedule beginning. These be the petitions which by the commons and lords was drawne into a forme of a statute, and passed both houses, and the royall assent thereunto, and the same exemplified under the great seal. After this the parliament continued, and divers acts made, and petitions granted, and in the end that parliament was dissolved.

Rot. parl. 14 E. 3. stat. primo. nu. 7, 8, 9. &c.

In the parliament holden *anno* 3 R. 2. it is declared by act of parliament that the killing of John Imperiall ambassadour of Jenoa, was high treason, *crimen læsæ majestatis*, and yet the parliament continued long after, and divers acts of parliament afterwards made, and petitions granted: and in the end the parliament dissolved.

Rot. parl. 3 R. 2. nu. 18. &c.

In the parliament begun the first day of March, *anno* 7 H. 4. on Saturday the 8 day of May it was enacted by the king, the lords spirituall and temporall, and the commons, that certain strangers by name, who seemed to be officers to the queen, should by a day depart the realm, and proclamation thereof in kinde made by writ, by authority of parliament, which parliament continued, and divers other acts of parliament made, and petitions answered: and on the 22 day of December 8 H. 4. dissolved.

Rot. parl. 7 H. 4. nu. 29. &c.

The parliament begun 7 November, and on the first day of the parliament it was resolved by all the judges, that those that were attainted of treason, and returned knights, citizens, or burgesses of parliament, that the attainders were to be reversed by authority of parliament before they could sit in the house of commons: and that after the attainders reversed, both the lords, and those of the house of commons might take their places, for such as were attainted could not be lawfull judges, so long as their attainders stood in force: and thereupon the attainders were reversed by act of parliament, and then they took their places in parliament, and the parliament continued, and divers acts made.

Rot. parl. 1 H. 7. nu.
1 H. 7. fo. 4. b.

* The bill of queen Katharine Howards attainder passed both houses about the beginning of the parliament, whereunto the king sitting the parliament by his letters patents gave his royall assent, and yet the parliament continued untill the first day of Aprill, and divers acts of parliament passed after the said royall assent given. Divers more might be produced, but these shall suffice, So as albeit bils passe both houses, and the royall assent given

* Rot. par. 33 H. 8. begun the 16 day of January, and continued till the first of April following.
On the 12 of February the queen was beheaded in the Tower, sitting the parliament.

given thereunto, there is no session untill a prorogation or a dissolution.

The diversity between a prorogation and an adjournment, or continuance of the parliament, is, that by the prorogation in open court there is a session, and then such bils as passed in either house, or by both houses, and had no royall assent to them, must at the next assembly begin again, &c. for every severall session of parliament is in law a severall parliament: but if it be but adjourned or continued, then is there no session: and consequently, all things continue still in the same state they were in before the adjournment or continuance.

And the title of divers acts of parliament be, At the session holden by prorogation, or by adjournment and prorogation, but never by continuance or adjournment *tantum*. And the usuall form of pleading is, *ad sessionem tentam, &c. per prorogationem.*

Prorogo à porro & rogo, unde prorogatio. Adjourner, unde adjournare, et adjournamentum, est ad diem dicere, or diem dare. Rot. parl. 23 H. 8. 24 H. 8. nu. 1. 25 H. 8. nu. 1. 26 H. 8. nu. 1. 27 H. 8. nu. 1. &c. 2 & 3 E. 6. nu. 1. 3 & 4 E. 6. nu. 1. &c. 1 Mariæ sess. 2. 28 Eliz. nu. 1. &c. And in every of them it is said [and there continued untill such a day;] and yet in them divers adjournments were. See the Journall Book in the lords house. *Ultimo Junii* 14 *Eliz. Custos magni sigilli ex mandato dominæ reginæ adjournavit præsens parliament' usq; in festum omnium sanctorum.* And in the parliament in anno 39 Eliz. *Custos magni sigilli ex mandato dominæ reginæ* (the queen being absent.)

[28]

We have been the longer and more curious for the clearing of this point for two reasons, 1. For that the adjournment or continuance (as before it appeareth) is much more beneficiall for the common-wealth for expediting of causes, then a prorogation. 2. In respect of a clause in the act of subsidie in the parliament holden in *anno* 18 Jac. *regis*, which is but declaratory of the former law, as by that which hath been said appeareth.

When a parliament is called and doth sit, and is dissolved without any act of parliament passed, or judgement given, it is no session of parliament, but a convention.

Rot. parl. 18 R. 2. which began 15 Hilarii.

In the 18 year of R. 2. at a parliament holden before the duke of York (the king being in his passage to Ireland) the petitions of the commons were answered: and a judgement given in the kings bench for the prior of Newport-pannell, against the dean and chapter of Lichfield was reversed, but no act of parliament passed, and therefore this parliament is omitted in the print,; but it is no question but it was a session of parliament, for otherwise the judgement should not be of force: and many times judgements given in parliament have been executed, the parliament continuing before any bill passed.

The House of Commons is a distinct Court.

Nota, the house of commons is to many purposes a distinct court, and therefore is not prorogued, or adjourned by the prorogation or adjournment of the lords house: but the speaker upon signification of the kings pleasure by the assent of the house of commons, doth say: this court doth prorogue or adjourn itself; and then it is prorogued or adjourned, and not before. But when it is dissolved, the house of commons are sent for up to the higher house, and there the lord keeper by the kings commandement dissolveth the parliament; and then it is dissolved, and not before.

And the king at the time of the diſſolution ought to be there in perſon, or by repreſentation: for as it cannot begin without the preſence of the king either in perſon or by repreſentation (as before it hath been ſaid) ſo it cannot end or be diſſolved without his preſence either in perſon or by repreſentation. *Nihil enim tam conveniens eſt naturali æquitati, unumquodq; diſſolvi eo ligamine quo ligatum eſt.*

Bracton.

It is declared by act of parliament, that the kings letters patents under his great ſeale, and ſigned with his hand, and declared and notified in his abſence to the lords ſpirituall and temporall, and commons aſſembled in the higher houſe of parliament, is, and ever was of as good ſtrength and force, as if the kings perſon had been there perſonally preſent, and had aſſented openly and publickly to the ſame.

33 H. 8. cap. 21. royall aſſent by letters patents. Dier. 1 Mar. 93. *Commiſſion au 4 Seigniors, &c. a doner royall aſſent, & indorcement fait.* Soit fait come eſt deſire.

Of Subſidies and Aides granted by Parliament.

Subſidie is derived of the verb *ſubſidiari*, which ſignifieth to be ready to help at need, *unde ſubſidium*, which ſignifieth aide and help at need, ſo properly called, when ſouldiers were ready to help the foreward of the battell: and aptly was the word ſo derived, aſwell becauſe that which we call now *ſubſidia*, ſubſidies, were anciently called *auxilia*, aides, granted by act of parliament upon need and neceſſity: as alſo, for that originally and principally they were granted for the defence of the realm, and the ſafe keeping of the ſeas, &c. *Communia pericula requirunt communia auxilia.*

This word [*ſubſidia*] is common, as well to the Engliſh, as to the French. Concerning ſubſidies hear what a ſtranger truly writeth. *Reges Angliæ nihil tale, niſi convocatis primis ordinibus, et aſſentiente populo, ſuſcipiunt. Quæ conſuetudo valde mihi laudanda videtur; interveniente enim populi voluntate et aſſenſu creſcit robur, et potentia regum, et major eſt ipſorum authoritas, et feliciores progreſſus.*

Ph. Cominæus, Lib. 5. fo. 233.

Subſidies taken in their generall ſenſe for parliamentary aides are divided into perpetuall and temporary: perpetuall into three parts, viz. into *cuſtuma antiqua, ſive magna, cuſtuma nova ſive parva*, and in- [29]
to cuſtome of broad cloth. Temporary, whereof there are three kindes, viz. 1. Of tonnage and poundage of ancient time granted for a year or yeares incertainly, and of latter times for life. 2. A ſubſidie after the rate of 4 s. in the pound for lands, and 2 s. 8 d. for goods. And 3 for an aide called a fifteenth. And of theſe in order.

Cuſtuma antiqua ſive magna.

Cuſtuma antiqua ſive magna was by act of parliament granted to king E. 1. his heirs and ſucceſſors for tranſportation of three things, viz. wools, woolfels, and leather, viz. for every ſack of wool containing thirty ſix ſtone, and every ſtone fourteen pound, half a mark; and for three hundred woolfels half a mark, and for a laſt of leather thirteen ſhillings four pence, to be paid as well by ſtrangers as by Engliſh. *Prælati, magnates, et tota communitas conceſſerunt quandam novam conſuetudinem nobis de lanis, pellibus et coriis dimid'*

See hereafter, ca. 11. Verb. de nous Cuſtomes, &c. Rot. finium an. 3 E. 1. Rot. par. 3 E. 1. m. 1. dat. 10 Novemb. which which was in the end of the year, for he began his reign 17 Nov. Confirmat. cartarum Vet. Mag.Cart. 2 part fo. 36. a. * Int. brevia de term Mich. 26 E. 1. In offi. remem. regis. [a] 12 H. 4. nu 45. 6 H. 6. nu. 11. 12 E. 4. ca. 3. 7 E. 4. nu. 30. 1 E. 6. ca. 13. 1 Mar. cap. 18. 1 Eliz. ca. 19. & 3 Jac. regis accord.

dimid' marc', de 300. pellibus dimid' marc', et de lasta coriorum unam marcam. In the statute called *Confirmationes cartarum anno* 25 *E.* 1. there is a saving in these words, *Save a nous, et nous heires la custome des leynes, pealx et quires grant' per le comminalty du realm.* See also the like in the preamble: * *Salva tamen nobis et hæredibus nostris custuma lanarum, pellium et coriorum per communitatem dicti regni nobis prim' concess.*

[a] Note it is said in divers records, *per communitatem Angliæ nobis concess'*, because all grants of subsidies or aides by parliament doe begin in the house of commons, and first granted by them: also because in effect the whole profit which the king reapeth doth come from the commons.

Custuma parva et nova.

Custuma is derived of the French word *coustum*, i. tributum seu vectigal. Rot. cart 31 E. 1. nu. 44. called Carta mercatoria. This was questioned rot. ordinat. anno 5 E. 2. but allowed of in parliament, anno 1 E. 3. 9 E. 3. ca. 1. 27 E. 3. stat. Stapl. ca. 26. F. N. B. 227. d. 259. a.

In the 31 year of E. 1. the merchant strangers in consideration of certain liberties and priviledges granted to them, and a release to them of all prises and takings, gave to the king and his heirs, three shillings four pence, *ultra antiquam custumam ut prius concess.* So as where the subject paid a noble, the stranger paid ten shillings, &c. See the statutes of 1 H. 7. ca. 2. 11 H. 7. cap. 14. 22 H. 8. cap. 8.

Custome of what Things, ex antiquo.

1 El. Dier 165.

And it is to observed, that of ancient time no custome was by English or stranger, but for wools, woolfels, and leather. Hereby it appeareth how necessary the knowledge of ancient records, and of the true originall of every thing is.

Of wools draped into cloth no custome was due.

In the reign of E. 3. a great part of the wools for the which such custome was granted, and paid, as is aforesaid, was draped into broad cloth: whereupon question grew, whether upon the transportation of the cloth, into which the wool was draped, custome should be proportionably paid, having regard to the quantity of the wool so converted into cloth: and it was resolved, that no custome should in that case be paid, because the wool by the labour and industry of man was changed into another kind of merchandize: wherewith the king held himself satisfied, and so it appeareth in the kings own writs and records enrolled in the exchequer.

[30]

The first act of parliament that gave any subsidy of cloth, was in *anno* 21 E. 3. (not printed) viz. fourteen pence of lieges, and one and twenty pence of strangers, for every cloth of assise, and two shillings four pence of lieges, and three shillings six pence of strangers for every cloth of scarlet, &c. *Vide inter original' de scaccario,* 24 E. 3. rot. 13. And the reason of granting the said subsidies of broad cloth was, *Quia jam magna pars lanæ regni nostri in eodem regno pannificitur, de qua custuma aliqua non est soluta, per*

Int. Orig. de Scaccario. 24 E. 3. rot. 13.

per quod proficuum quod de custumis et subsidiis lanarum, si extra dictum regnum ducerentur, percipere debemus, in multo diminuuntur, &c. And yet if in any case the king might by his prerogative have set any imposition, he might have set one in that case, for that, as it appeareth by that record, by making of cloth the king lost his customes of wool: and therefore for further satisfaction of the king for the custome of wool; at the parliament holden in *anno* 27 E. 3. a subsidy was granted to the king his heirs and successors, (* over the customes thereof due) viz. of every whole cloth of assise not ingrained, four pence, and for the half of such a cloth, two pence, and of every cloth ingrained five pence, and of the halfe two pence half penny, and of every cloth of scarlet six pence, and of the half three pence; and the alnegers fee is granted to him by act of parliament, viz. for the measuring of every cloth of assise of the seller a half penny, and of half a cloth a farthing for his office, and no more, nor shall they take any thing for a cloth that is lesse; and that he take nothing of the alnage of any cloth but only of such cloth as is to be sold. And both in this act, and in some acts in the reign of H. 3. *consuetudines et custumæ*, which are englished, customes, are taken for the subsidies that were granted by parliament, for verily those were ancient and right customes or subsidies. And in the statute of 11 H. 4. customes and subsidies are used as *synonymaes*.

Ib. 27 E. 3. rot. 4. See the second part of the Institutes, Mag. Cart. cap. 30. p. 60.

By 27 E. 3. stat. 1. & ca. 4. Custome of cloth.

* Viz. the subsidies granted in anno 21 E. 3.

The alnagers fee of the subject granted by parliament.

Mag. Cart. ca. 30. Consuetudines. stat. de Scaccario. 51 H. 3. Custum. des Leynes.

11 H. 4. ca. 7.

Butlerage.

Butlerage is a custome due to the king of two shillings of every tun of wine brought into this realm by strangers: but Englishmen payeth it not.

In libro rubeo in scaccaria in custodia rememoratoris regis, fol. 265. the grant of king John to the merchants of Aquitain trading for wines thence into England of divers liberties, viz. *De libertatibus concessis mercatoribus vinetariis de ducatu Aquitaniæ, reddendo regi et hæredibus suis* 2. *s. de quolibet dolio vini ducti per eosdem infra regnum Angliæ vel potestate regis.*

Lib. rubeus in Scacc. fo. 265. Vid. 6 E. 3. fo. 5 & 6. the archb. of Yorks case.

All merchant strangers in consideration of the grant to them by the king of divers liberties and freedoms, *Concesserunt quòd de quolibet dolio vini quod adducent vel adduci facerent infra regnum, &c. solvent nobis et hæredibus nostris nomine custumæ duos solidos, &c.*

Rot cartarum anno 31 E. 1. nu. 44. called Carta mercatoria.

Prisage.

Prisage is a custome due to the king of the wines brought in by the merchants of England of every ship having twenty tuns or more, two tuns, viz. one before the mast, and the other behind, paying twenty shillings for each tun; and this is called *certa prisa*, and *recta prisa*, and *regia prisa*, as in the record ensuing appeareth, and hereof merchant strangers are discharged, *per cartam mercatoriam*, 31 *E.* 1. *ubi supra.*

Fleta li. 2. ca. 21. Rot. pat. 40 H. 3. Rot. par. 28 E. 1. pro Math. de Columbar'.

Memorandum quòd rex habet ex antiqua consuetudine de qualibet nave mercatoris vini 6. *carcat' applican' infra aliquem portum Angliæ de viginti doliis duo dolia, et de decem doliis unum de prisa regia pro quodam certo ab antiquo constitut' solvend'.*

P. Rec. 20 R. 2. Vid. Tr. 33 E. 1. rot. 12. Prisæ vinorum in Hibernia.

Hereby it appeareth that priſage is due by preſcription, and that it was a certainty of ancient time ordained to be paid.

43 E. 3. ca. 3. & 1 H. 8. ca. 5.

It is called butlerage becauſe the kings chief butler doth receive it, and priſage, becauſe it is a certain taking or purveyance for wine to the kings uſe.

Concerning the alnaging of new draperies.

[31]

In Hilary tearm, *anno*, 2 *Jac. regis*, upon a ſuit made to the king by the duke of Lenox, queſtion was moved concerning new draperies, as frizadoes, bayes, northern cottons, northern dozens, clothraſh, durances, perpetuanoes, fuſtians, canvas, ſackcloth, worſteads, and ſtuffs made of worſtead yarn, whether the king might grant the alnaging of them with a reaſonable fee, or whether they were within the ſaid ſtatute of 27 E. 3. And theſe queſtions were by the kings commandment in this Hilary Term referred to all the judges of England to certifie their opinions concerning the ſuit to the lords of his privy councell; who upon often hearing of the cauſe, and mature deliberation, and conference amongſt themſelves, in the end in Trinity term following with one unanimous conſent, certified in writing in theſe words following, viz. To the lords and others of his majeſties moſt honourable privy councell. Our duties to your lordſhips remembred. May it pleaſe the ſame to be advertiſed, that according to your letters in that behalf, we have heard the matter touching the fearm of the alnage, and meaſurage, that is ſought to be granted by his majeſty of ſundry kindes, as well of new made drapery, as of other ſtuffs made within this realm. And upon hearing as well of ſome of the part of the maſter of Orkney, as of others, both of the behalf of the duke of Lenox and maſter Shaw, have informed our ſelves touching the ſame. And for our opinions we are reſolved, that all new made drapery made wholly of wool, as frizadoes, bayes, northern dozens, northern cottons, cloth raſh, and other like drapery, of what new name ſoever, for the uſe of mans body, are to yeeld ſubſidy and alnage according to the ſtatute of 27 E. 3. and within the office of the ancient alnage, as may appear by ſeverall decrees in that behalf made in the exchequer in the time of the late queen. But as touching fuſtians, canvas, ſackcloth and ſuch like made meerly of other ſtuff then wool, or being but mixed with wool, we are of opinion, that no charge can be impoſed for the ſearch or meaſurage thereof, but that all ſuch patents ſo made are void, as may appear by a record of the 11. year of H. 4. wherein the reaſon of the judgment is particularly mentioned, which we held not amiſſe to ſet down to your lordſhips, which is thus, The ſame king H. 4. granted the meaſurage of all woollen cloth and canvas that ſhould be brought to London to be ſold by any ſtranger or denizen (except he were free of London) taking one half penny for every piece of cloth ſo meaſured of the ſeller, and one other half penny of the buyer, and ſo after the rate for a greater or leſſer quantity, and one penny for the meaſuring of 100. els of canvas of the ſeller, and ſo much more of the buyer. And although it were averred that two other had enjoyed the ſame office before with the like fees, viz. one Shering by the ſame kings grant, and one Clytheroe before by the grant of king R. 2. yet, amongſt other reaſons of the judgment, it was ſet down and adjudged, that the former poſſeſſion was by extortion, and coertion, and without right, and that thoſe patents were *in onerationem, oppreſſionem et depauperationem*

See Rot. parl. 50 E. 3. nu. 142. Cogware Kerſeys. See hereafter, cap. 67. See Rot. parl. 9 H. 4. nu. 34. Kendall clothes, &c. 17 H. 4. c. 2. enact. 11 H. 4. nu. 26. for remnants of cloth, &c. 11. H. 4. c. 7. ſtat. 2.

pauperationem populi domini regis, et non in emendationem ejusdem populi, &c. and no benefit to the king, and therefore the patents void. And as touching the narrow new stuffe made in Norwich and other places with worstead yarn, we are of opinion that it is not grantable, nor fit to be granted, for we cannot find, that there was ever any alnage upon Norwich worsteads. And for these stuffs, if after they be made and tacked up for sale by the makers thereof, they should be again opened to be viewed and measured, they will not well fall into their old plaits to be tacked up as before, which will be (as is affirmed) a great hinderance to the sales thereof in grosse, for that they will not then appear to be so merchandizable, as they were upon the first making of them up: and even so we humbly take our leaves. Serjeants Inn, the 24. of June. 1605. Which certificate being read by the lords of the privy councell (I being then atturny generall and present) was well approved by them all, and commandment given, that it should be kept in the councell chest to be a direction for them to give answer to all suits of that kind.

And it is to be observed, * that acts of parliament that are made against the freedome of trade, merchandizing, handycrafts, and mysteries, never live long.

37 E. 3. ca. 5, 6. 38 E. 3. ca. 2. lib. 11. fo. 54. de Taylers de Ipswich.

Good Bills or Motions in Parliament seldome die.

[32]

Bils, motions.

It is an observation proved by a great number of presidents, that never any good bill was preferred, or good motion made in parliament, whereof any memoriall was made in the Journall Book, or otherwise, though sometime it succeeded not at the first, yet hath it never died, but at one time or other hath taken effect; which may be a great encouragement to worthy and industrious attempts, as taking some few examples for many, which I have quoted in the margent.

8 E. 2. nu. 17 E. 3. nu. 49. 1 R. 2. nu. 82. 4 R. 2. nu. 36. 9 R. 2. nu. 44. 1 H. 4. nu. 121. 2 H. 4. nu. 83. 2 H. 4. nu. 70. 11 H. 4. nu. 47. 1 H. 5. nu. 23. 7 H. 5. nu. 18.

1 H. 6. nu. 41. 7 E. 4. nu. 20. *Acts of Parliament.* 2 E. 3. cap. 2. 25 E. 3. ca. 5. 4 H. 4. ca. 22. 1 H. 5. cap. 1. 15 H. 6. ca. 14. 1 R. 3. ca. 3. 21 H. 8. cap. 5. 23 H. 8. cap. 4. 26 H. 8. cap. 3. 31 H. 8. ca. 1. 32 H. 8. cap. 32. 2 E. 6. cap. 8. & 13. 1 & 2 Ph. & Mar. cap. 13. Vide Infra, cap. 8, pa.

The Subsidy of Tunnage and Poundage.

By the subsequent records you shall observe 13. things. 1. The grant of poundage only. 2. Of tunnage and poundage, 3. Severall rates, sometimes 6. d. 8. d. 12. d. for poundage. 4. Sometimes 2. s. 18. d. 3. s. 5. *Hac vice*, 1, 2, 3, 4. years, for life. 6. To merchants, &c. 7. To have intermission and to vary, lest the king should claim it as a duty. 8. Expressed upon free gift. 9. Upon condition to keep the seas, and for commerce. 10. That is ever the consideration and cause of the grant. 11. Granted without retrospect. 12. Sometimes double of strangers. 13. Cloth excepted, that it be not subject to tunnage and poundage. 31 H. 6.

The Records.

[a] Of poundage only, and 6. d. in the pound, for two years upon condition, &c.

[a] 47 E. 3. nu. 12.

b 6 R. 2. nu. 13.
c 7 R. 2. stat. 1.
d 5 R. 2. nu. 40.
9 R. 2. nu. 11.
10 R. 2. nu. 18.
11 R. 2. nu. 12.
e 13 R. 2. nu. 20.
f 14 R. 2. nu. 12.
g 17 R. 2. nu. 12.
h 2 H. 4. nu. 9.
i 4 H. 4. nu. 28.
k 6 H. 4. nu. 9.
8 H. 4. nu. 9.
9 H. 4. nu. 27.
l 11 H. 4. nu. 45.
m 13 H. 4. nu. 10.
n 1 H. 5. nu. 17.
o 3 H. 5. nu. 50.
p 2 H. 6. nu. 14.
q 3 H. 6. nu. 17.
9 H. 6. nu. 14.
r 23 H. 6. nu. 16.
s 31 H. 6. nu. 8. & cap. 8.
* Nota.
t 4 E. 4. & 12 E. 4. ca. 3. in print.
u Rot. par. 1 H. 7. not printed, for he had many subsidies, but printed none.
x Rot. parl. 1 H. 8. not printed. Vid. 6 H. 8. ca. 14. in print.

[b] 6. d. for poundage, and 2. s. for tunnage of wine, *hac vice*.

[c] 6. d. of every pound of merchandize, and 2. s. of every tun of wine, upon condition, &c. *hac vice*.

[d] Sometime to have intermission, and to vary, lest the king should claim as duties.

[e] for tunnage of wine 3. s. and 6. d. for poundage for one year.

[f] 3. s. for tunnage of wine, 12 d. for poundage, *hac vice*.

[g] 6. d. for poundage, and 18 d. for tunnage of wine for three years.

[h] 8. d. for poundage and 2. s. for tunnage of wine.

[i] 12. d. for poundage, and 3. s. for tunnage of wine for three years.

[k] 12. d. for poundage, and 3. s. for tunnage of wine for severall times upon condition, sometime for one year. In these and most of the former granted upon condition for due employment [l] of their own good will, and so entred, and the king to have a certain sum [m] more expresly.

[n] 12. d. for poundage, and 3. s. for tunnage of wine for four years.

[o] The like subsidy is granted to the king for his life upon conditions, &c. which was the first grant of tunnage and poundage for life, which was a leading grant, as hereafter appeareth.

[p] The subsidy of poundage only for two years.

[q] Tunnage of wine and poundage granted for severall years.

[r] Tunnage and poundage, *ut prius* of denizens, double of strangers.

[s] Tunnage of wine and poundage granted to H. 6. for life with an exception of all woollen * cloth: and here cloth was first excepted, and was a leading exception in all subsequent acts.

[t] Tunnage of wine and poundage granted to E. 4. for life with no retrospect, but for the time to come.

[u] At the parliament holden *anno* 1 H. 7. a like act was made for the grant of the subsidies of tunnage and poundage to him for his life.

[x] And the like subsidy was granted to king H. 8. at the parliament holden *anno* 1. of his reign for his life.

[33]
1 E. 6. ca. 13.
1 Mar. cap. 18.
1 Eliz. cap. 19.
1 Jac. ca. 33.

The like grant was made to E. 6 queen Mary, queen Eliz. and king James for their severall lives, and in all these it is affirmed, that the like grants were made by act of parliament to king H. 7. and king H. 8.

* Rot. par. 11 H. 4. nu. 45. 13 H. 4. nu. 10.

The consideration of the grant of the subsidies of tunnage and poundage is ever, as is aforesaid, expressed in the grant, for the keeping and safeguard of the seas, and for intercourse of merchandize safely to come into this realm, and safely to passe out of the same. And this pertaineth properly to the office of the lord admirall to see the consideration of the act to be performed. * They are granted of the free good will of the subjects, and so expresly set down in the parliament roll.

A book of rates or values.

In king James his reign, when I was a commissioner of the treasury, these subsidies granted for life amounted to one hundred and threescore thousand pounds *per annum*, and so letten to farm. The values of the merchandize for the which the subsidy of poundage is paid, do appear in a book of rates in print, whereby the mer-

chant

chant knows what he is to pay. The ſubſidy of tunnage of wine is certain in theſe acts by the contents of the veſſels: and none of theſe acts doe extend to any other liquid merchandize imported or exported, but unto wines only: and ſeeing nothing is more incertain then the continuance of the values of merchandizes wherefore the ſubſidy of poundage is paid, it were good at every grant of them to ſet down the rates in a ſchedule annexed to the bill.

Subſidies temporary and uſuall at his Day.

Subſidies temporary and uſuall at this day. And this is when the commons in parliament freely grant to the king an aid to be levied of every ſubject of his lands or goods after the rate of 4.s. in the pound for lands, and 2.s. 8.d. for goods, and for aliens for goods double, to ſuch ends and for ſuch conſiderations, and to be paid at ſuch times, as by the acts thereof (which are uſuall and frequent) doe appear. And in former times in this kind of ſubſidy, this order was obſerved, that over and above the ſubſidy of tunnage and poundage, the commons never gave above one ſubſidy of this kind, and two fifteens, (and ſometime leſſe) one ſubſidy amounting to ſeventy thouſand pounds, and each fifteen at twenty nine thouſand pounds, or near thereabouts; nor above one ſubſidy, which did riſe to twenty thouſand pounds, the clergy gave not.

At the parliament holden in 31 Eliz. the commons gave two ſubſidies, and four fifteens, which firſt brake the circle.

In 35 Eliz. three ſubſidies and ſix fifteens.

In 39 Eliz. three ſubſidies and ſix fifteens.

In 43 Eliz. four ſubſidies and eight fifteens, &c.

In 21 Jac. *regis*, three ſubſidies and ſixe fifteens in ſhorter times then had been before.

In 3 Car. *regis*, five ſubſidies in ſhorteſt time of all.

And it is worthy of obſervation how quietly ſubſidies granted in forms uſuall and accuſtomable (though heavy) are borne; ſuch a power hath uſe and cuſtome: on the other ſide, what diſcontents and diſturbances ſubſidies framed in new molds doe raiſe, (ſuch an inbred hatred novelty doth hatch) is evident by examples of former times:

As that of 4 R. 2. a new invention of ſubſidies of the kings ſubjects of either ſex by the poll, &c. for the furniſhing of the earl of Buckingham for his going into France, whereupon a ſtrong and a ſtrange rebellion enſued, wherein three great and worthy officers were by the raſcall rebels barbarouſly and wickedly murdered, viz Simon Sudbury archbiſhop of Canterbury, chancelour of England, the prior of S. Johns of Jeruſalem, treaſurer of England, and Sir John Cavendiſh chief juſtice of England. Rot. Par. 4 R. 2. nu. 15. 5 R. 2. nu. 32.

In 4 H. 7. another like new found ſubſidy was granted, which raiſed a rebellion in the north, in which the noble earl of Northumberland a commiſſioner in that ſubſidy, was by the rebels cruelly and cauſeleſly ſlain. Hollenſh Chron. 769.

In *anno* 16 H. 8. to furniſh the king for his going in his royall perſon into France, a new device for getting of mony was ſet on foot, which made the headleſſe and heedleſſe multitude to riſe in rebellion, [34] Hollenſh. Chron. 891.

rebellion, untill Charles Brandon the noble duke of Suff quieted, and dispersed them.

Rot. par. 9 E. 3. nu. 5.

At the parliament holden in 9 E. 3. when a motion was made for a subsidy to be granted of a new kind, the commons answered, that they would have conference with those of their severall countries and places, who had put them in trust, before they treated of any such matter.

9 H. 6. nu. 15. 10 H. 6. nu. 50.

Vide 9 H. 6. nu. 15. Every knights fee to pay 20 s. and so according to the value under or over, and so of the clergy for lands purchased since 20 E. 1. And all other having 20 l. lands not holden as is aforesaid, 20 s. &c. This whole subsidy for certain doubts the king utterly released, so as there is no mention made of the same: but hereof thus much shall suffice.

Sæpe viatorem nova, non vetus orbita fallit.

Of Fifteens, Quinzims, &c.

Fifteens, Quinzim or Task, or Quinta decima.

A fifteen is a temporary aid granted to the king by parliament, which without further inquiry is certain, and therein differeth from the subsidy, which is ever uncertain, untill it be assessed.

The fifteen of ancient time was the fifteenth part of goods moveable, but in 8 E. 3. all the cities, boroughs, and towns in England were rated certainly at the fifteenth part of the value at that time generally upon the whole town, whereof you shall read more at large in the second part of the Institutes, in the last chapter of Magna Carta, verb. *Quintam decimam partem bonorum mobilium.*

Second part Inst. Mag. Carta cap. ultimo.

Of Tenths.

There is *decima pars* of the laity, and for the most part of cities and boroughs by their goods (*Vid.* 1 R. 2. nu. 26.) which proportionably is, *secundum decimam quintam partem.* That which we call tax, tallage, tenth, and fifteen, the Saxons called *geldinn**, we use the word changing *g* to *y*, for *gelding*, *yee'ding*, *&c.*

* Doomsday. Norff. in Wanelunt, i. Wayland, & ibid. in Frebringe in Massingham, &c.

No * subsidy before the end of the parliament, because it is to accompany the pardon.

* Rot. par. 11 R. 2. nu. 11. This is contained in the act of subsidy, and so an act of parliament: and accordingly subsidies, &c. have been granted, as in the book of statutes appeareth.

Of Acts of Parliament of Confirmation of Letters Patents.

Rot. par. 2 H. 5. nu. 20. 1 H. 6. nu. 46. 3 H. 7. to the queen. 6 H. 8. to the duke of Suff.

We have read of particular acts of confirmation of letters patents; but the first of lands, &c. that was the more generall, was the statute of 31 H. 8. ca. 13. of monasteries (to make those lands the more passable) but after that, generall acts of confirmation of letters patents have been very frequent.

How the Lords give their Voices.

In the lords houſe, the lords give their voices from the puiſne lord *ſeriatim* by the word of [content,] or [not content.]

A bill was preferred at the parliament holden in *anno* 6 H. 6. that no man ſhould contract or marry himſelf to any queen dowager of England without ſpeciall licence and aſſent of the king, on pain to loſe all his goods and lands. The biſhops and clergy aſſented to this bill, by the word of [content,] as far forth as the ſame ſwarved not from the law of God and of the church, and ſo as the ſame imported no deadly ſin. At this time there were beſides the archbiſhops and biſhops, 27 abbots and 2 priors, (albeit in troth the number was many times uncertain, as in the cloſe roll it appeareth) which ſeverally held *per baroniam*, and were lords of parliament, and ſo continued untill they were diſſolved in the reign of H. 8. The entry of the ſaid act of 6 H. 6. in the roll is: It is enacted by the king, lords temporall, and commons, that no man ſhould contract or marry himſelf to any queen of England, without the ſpeciall licenſe and aſſent of the king, on pain to loſe all his goods and lands. The biſhops and clergy aſſented to this bill, as far forth as the ſame ſwerved not from the law of God, and of the church, and ſo as the ſame imported no deadly ſinne.

Rot. par. 6 H. 6. nu. 27.

[35]

How many lords ſpirituall in former times.

This is holden to be an act of parliament: firſt, for that the aſſent of the clergie could not be conditionall. Secondly, it was not againſt the law of God nor of the church, nor imported any deadly ſinne to make this law by authority of parliament, as it appeareth by Magna Carta, cap. 7. which had by 32 acts of parliament been confirmed, and many others.

This law was made after the marriage of queen Katherine dowager of H. 5. with Owen ap Meredith ap Grono (deſcended of the princes of Wales) by whom ſhe had iſſue Edmond of Hadham aforeſaid, earle of Richmond, and Jaſper of Hatfeild, after earl of Pembroke, and duke of Bedford.

How the Commons give their Voices.

The commons give their voices upon the queſtion, by yea or no, and if it be doubtfull, and neither party yield, two are appointed to number them; one for the yea, another for the no: the yea going out, and the no ſitting: and thereof report is made to the houſe. At a committee, though it be of the whole houſe, the yeas go of one ſide of the houſe, and the noes on the other, whereby it will eaſily appear which is the greateſt number.

Pl. com. 126. miſtaketh it, and that the clerk number them.

How Parliaments ſucceed not well in five Caſes.

It is obſerved by ancient parliament men out of record, that parliaments have not ſucceeded well in five caſes. Firſt, when the king hath been in diſpleaſure with his lords, or with his commons. 2. When any of the great lords were at variance between themſelves. 3. When there was no good correſpondence between the lords

lords and the commons. 4. When there was no unity between the commons themselves. 5. When there was no preparation for the parliament before it began.

[a] Rot. parl. 37 E. 3. nu. 2. and the writ to the clergie, *De orando pro rege & regno*, which was usuall in those dayes.

[b] Rot. parl. 43 E. 3. nu. 1. 25 E. 3. nu. 15. 50 E. 3. nu. 2.

[a] For the 1: so essentiall is the kings good will towards his commons, that it was one of the petitions of the commons to the king, that he would require the archbish. and all others of the clergy to pray for his estate, for the peace and good government of the land, and for the continuance of the kings good will towards his commons: whereunto the thrice noble king assented with these effectual words, The same prayeth the king: and many times the like petitions for the lords. [b] How the king in all his weighty affairs had used the advice of his lords and commons, (so great a trust and confidence he had in them.) Alwaies provided, that both lords and commons keep them within the circle of the law and custome of the parliament.

[c] Rot par. 4 H. 6. nu. 12. See the acts of that parliament.

[c] For the second: at the parliament holden in 4 H. 6. what variance was there between the duke of Gloc. and the b. of Winchester, and their friends on either side: the successe was, that little was done in any parliamentary course at that parliament, and that little was of no moment.

[d] Rot. par. 3 H. 6. nu. 1. & 10.

[d] At the parliament holden in the third year of H. 6. the great controversie was between John earl marshall, and Richard earl of Warwick with like successe.

[e] Rot. parl. 27 H. 6. nu. 18.

[f] Rot. par. 2 H. 4. nu. 14. 5 H. 4. nu. 18. 20.

* Rot. Parl. 21 R. 2. by the court of Arundell to the duke of Lancast. 4 H. 6. nu. 12.

[e] The like controversie between William earle of Arundell and Thomas earl of Devon, for superiority of place, with like event. And many more might be cited. [f] And alwayes in the beginning amity was made between the grandees of the realm by shaking of hands and kissing, and sometime by * submission.

For the third, when it was demanded by the lords and commons what might be a principall motive for them to have good successe in parliament, it was answered, *Eritis insuperabiles, si fueritis inseparabiles. Explosum est illud diverbium; divide, et impera, cum radix et vertex imperii in obedientium consensu rata sunt.*

[36]

Rot. parl. anno 11 H. 4. nu. 10. the king desired this unity. 20 Judicum.

For the fourth, unity between the commons themselves. It is most necessary in both these, and agreeable to the parliament in the book of Judges. *Quasi homo unus, eadem mente, uno consilio.*

1 Chron. cap. 28.

For the fifth, the summons of parliament is by forty dayes or above before the sitting, to the end that preparations might be had for the arduous and urgent affairs of the realme: and that both the king, according to the example of king David, and likewise the nobles and commons should prepare; for *præparatæ meditationes sunt semper saniores et meliores quam properatæ*, wherein both houses may greatly expedite the businesse of the common-wealth in parliament, if they will pursue the ancient custome of parliament, viz. in the beginning thereof to appoint a select committee to consider of the bils in the two last parliaments that passed both houses, or either of them, and such as had been preferred, read, or committed, and to take out of them such as be most profitable for the common-wealth.

The

The Honour and Antiquity of the Parliament.

For the honour and antiquity of the parliament, ſee the firſt part of the Inſtitutes, ſect. 164. verb. *Vcigne les burgeſſes*, and in the preface to the ninth book of my Reports, fo. 1, 2, 3, 4, &c. whereunto you may adde, *Int' leges Edwardi regis*, ca. 8. *de decimis eccleſiæ reddendis*, *ſect. de apibus vero*, &c. *Hæc enim prædicavit beatus Auguſtinus, et conceſſa ſunt à rege baronibus et populo.* A grant by expreſſe act of parliament. *Vide infra*, cap. 79. pag.

7 H. 6. 28. lib. 11. fo. 14
Inter leges Edwardi regis, ca. 8.

The Power and Juriſdiction of the Parliament.

[a] Of the power and juriſdiction of the parliament, for making of laws in proceeding by bill, it is ſo tranſcendent and abſolute, as it cannot be confined either for cauſes or perſons within any bounds. Of this court it is truly ſaid: [b] *Si antiquitatem ſpectes, eſt vetuſtiſſima, ſi dignitatem, eſt honoratiſſima, ſi juriſdictionem, eſt capaciſſima.*

[c] *Huic ego nec metas rerum, nec tempora pono.*

Yet ſome examples are deſired. [d] Daughters and heirs apparant of a man or woman, may by act of parliament inherit during the life of the anceſtor.

[e] It may adjuge an infant, or minor of full age.

[f] To attaint a man of treaſon after his death.

[g] To naturalize a meere alien, and make him a ſubject borne.

[h] It may baſtard a childe that by law is legitimate, viz. begotten by an adulterer, the huſband being within the foure ſeas.

To legitimate one that is illegitimate, and born before marriage abſolutely. And to legitimate *ſecundum quid*, but not *ſimpliciter*. As to take one example for many.

[i] John of Gaunt duke of Lancaſter had by Katherine Swinford before marriage four illegitimate children, viz. Henry, John, Thomas, and Joane. And becauſe they were borne at [k] Beaufort in France, they were vulgarly called Henry de Beaufort, &c. John before the 20 year of R. 2. was knighted, and Henry became prieſt. [l] At the parliament holden 20 R. 2. the king by act of parliament in forme of a charter doth legitimate theſe three ſonnes, and Joane the daughter: and the charter beginneth thus. *Rex*, &c. *chariſſimis conſanguineis noſtris nobilibus viris* [m] *Johanni militi:* [n] *Henrico clerico:* [o] *Thomæ* [p] *domicello, ac dilectæ nobis nobili mulieri* [q] *Johannæ Beaufort domicellæ germanis præchariſſimi avunculi noſtri, Johannis ducis Lancaſtriæ natis ligeis noſtris ſalutem*, &c. *Nos dicti*

[a] See 13 Eliz. cap. 1. 39 H. 6. 15. Vide infra. ca. 79.

[b] Forteſc. ca. 18.

[c] Virgil.

[d] Rot. par. 12 E. 4. nu. 20, 21, 22. the caſe of the wives of the duke of Clarence and Gloceſter.

[e] 12 E. 4. nu. 34. duke of Buckingham.

[f] 21 R. 2. nu. 27. Sir Ro. Pleſington. 31 H. 6. cap. 1.

[g] This is uſuall in many parliaments.

[h] Rot. par. 5 & 6. E. 6. the lo. marquiſſe of Wincheſters caſe.

[i] Rot. pat. anno 20 R. 2. m. 6.

[k] Beaufort came to the houſe of Lanc. by marriage between Blanch of Artois, and Edmond firſt earle of Lancaſt. [l] Rot. pat. 20 R. 2. membr. 9. [m] This John in anno 21 R. 2. was created earle of Somerſet, and marquiſſe Dorſet. But in 1 H. 4. the marquiſhip was taken away by parliament. [n] This Henry was after biſhop of Wincheſter, cardinall of S. Ewſeby, and chancellor of England. [o] This Thomas was in 21 R. 2. created earle of Dorſet. [p] For *domicellus*, &c. See *Lambe inter. leges Edw. fo.* 139. b. *Nos indiſcrete domicellus de pluribus dicimus, quia baronum filios vocamus domicellos, Angli vero nullos, niſi natos regum.* [q] Joane was firſt married to Ralph the firſt earle of Weſtmerland, and after to Robert Ferrers lord of Owſeley.

avunculi

avunculi nostri genitoris vestri precibus inclinati, vobiscum qui (ut asseritur) defectum natalium patimini, ut hujusmodi defectu (quem ejusq; qualitatis quascunq; praesentibus habere volumus pro sufficientur expressis) non obstante ad quaecunque honoris dignitates, (excepta dignitate regali) praeheminencias, status, gradus, et officia publica et privata tam perpetua quam temporalia, atq; feudal' ac nobil' quibuscunque nominibus nuncupantur, etiamsi ducatus, principat', comitat', baronia, vel alia feuda fuerint, etiamsi mediate, vel immediate vel à nobis dependeant seu teneantur, praefici, promoveri, eligi, assumi et admitti, illaq; recipere, retinere, perinde libere et licite valeatis, ac si de legitimo thoro nati existeretis, quibuscunque statutis seu consuetudinibus regni nostri Angliae in contrarium editis seu observatis (quae hic habemus pro totaliter expressis) nequaquam obstantibus; de plenitudine nostrae regalis potestatis, ac de assensu parliamenti nostri tenore praesentium dispensamus, vosque et vestrum quemlibet natalibus restituimus, et legitimamus. In cujus rei testimonium. Teste rege apud Westm. 9 die Febr. Per ipsum regem in parliamento.*

* Nota.

In this act are divers things worthy of observation. 1. The names whereby they were legitimated. 2. That this legitimation was not *simpliciter*, but *secundum quid*: for they were legitimated and made capable of all dignities, except the royall dignity: so as this legitimation extended not to make them or their posterities inheritable to the crown, but to all other dignities. 3. That before their legitimation, they were not created to any of their dignities. 4. The briefe and artificiall penning of this legitimation, with generall words, as if the particularity were expressed, and with a brief *non obstante*, and with as little blemish as may be. 5. And hereby it appeareth, that [a] H. 7. being son of Edmond of Hadham earle of Richmond, and Margaret his wife, daughter and heir of John de Beaufort duke of Somerset: which Margaret lineally descended from the said John de Beaufort, legitimated and made capable of all dignities, as is aforesaid, *excepta regali dignitate*, that the best title of H. 7. to the crown, was by Elizabeth his wife, eldest daughter of E. 4. yet before this marriage the crown was by act of parliament intayled to H. 7. and to the heirs of his body, the right of the crowne then being in the said Elizabeth, eldest daughter of E. 4. 6. In this act the said Thomas before his legitimation could not be called esquire, and therefore he hath this addition of * *domicello*, either derived of the French word *domoicell*, which signifieth a young souldier not yet knighted, or signifieth nobly born. And note, Johan. the daughter, had the addition of de Beaufort and *domicella* in that sense also.

[a] Nota, pro corona. Rot. parl. anno 1 H. 7. not in print. 7 H. 4. cap. 2. the like to H. 4. the right of the crowne being then in the descent from Philip daughter and heir of Lionel duke of Clarence. Vid. 1 H. 7. 12, 13. 25 H. 8. cap. 22. repeal by 28 H. 8. cap. 7. & 1 Mar. parl. 1. cap. 1. See 13 Eliz. ca. 1. in principio.

* See Hovenden, pag. 608. for this word *domicel*.

[b] And albeit I finde an attainder by parliament of a subject of high treason being committed to the tower, and forth-coming to be heard, and yet never called to answer in any of the houses of parliament, although I question not the power of the parliament, for without question the attainder standeth of force in law: yet this I say of the manner of the proceeding, *Auferat oblivio, si potest; si non, utcunque silentium tegat*: for the more high and absolute the jurisdiction of the court is, the more just and honourable it ought to be in the proceeding, and to give example of justice to inferiour courts. But it is demanded, since he was attainted by parliament, what should be the reason that our historians do all agree in this, that he suffered death by a law which he himself had made. For answer hereof, I had it of Sir Thomas Gawdye knight,

[b] Rot. parl. 32 H. 8. The attainder of Tho. Cromwell earle of Essex.

knight, a grave and reverend judge of the kings bench, who lived at that time, that king H. 8. commanded him to attend the chiefe juſtices, and to know whether a man that was forth-coming might be attainted of high treaſon by parliament, and never called to his anſwer. The judges anſwered, that it was a dangerous queſtion, and that the high court of parliament ought to give examples to inferiour courts for proceeding according to juſtice, and no inferior court could do the like; and they thought that the high court of parliament would never do it. But being by the expreſſe commandement of the king, and preſſed by the ſaid earle to give a direct anſwer: they ſaid, that if he be attainted by parliament, it could not come in queſtion afterwards, whether he were called or not called to anſwer. And albeit their opinion was [38] according to law, yet might they have made a better anſwer, for by the ſtatutes of Mag. Cart. ca. 29. 5 E. 3. cap. 9. & 28 E. 3. cap. 5. No man ought to be condemned without anſwer, &c. which they might have certified, but *facta tenent multa, quæ fieri prohibentur;* the act of attainder being paſſed by parliament, did bind, as they reſolved. The party againſt whom this was intended, was never called in queſtion, but the firſt man after the ſaid reſolution, that was ſo attainted, and never called to anſwer, was the ſaid earl of Eſſex; whereupon that erroneous and vulgar opinion amongſt our hiſtorians grew, that he died by the ſame law which he himſelf had made. The rehearſall of the ſaid attainder can work no prejudice, for that I am confidently perſwaded, that ſuch honourable and worthy members ſhall be from time to time of both houſes of parliament, as never any ſuch attainder, where the party is forth comming, ſhall be had hereafter without hearing of him.

[a] *Nunquid lex noſtra judicat hominem, niſi prius audierit ab ipſo, et cognoverit quid faciat?* Doth our law judge any man, before it hear him and know what he doth? [b] It is not the manner of the Romans to deliver any man to die, before that he which is accuſed have the accuſers face to face, and have licence to anſwer for himſelf concerning the crime laid againſt him.

[c] *Ait Joſua ad Acab, fili mi, da gloriam Domino Deo Iſrael, et confitere mihi quid feceris, ne abſcondas.*

[d] *Interrogatus Levita maritus mulieris interfectæ quomodo tantum ſcelus perpetratum eſſet, &c.* And the concluſion is after hearing and diſcerning the cauſe, conſider, conſult, and then give ſentence.

[e] And as evil was the proceeding in parliament againſt Sir John Mortimer, third ſon of Edmond the ſecond earl of March (deſcended from Lionell duke of Clarence) who was indicted of high treaſon for certain words, in effect, that Edmond earl of March ſhould be king by right of inheritance, and that he himſelf was next rightfull heir to the crown after the ſaid earl of March; wherefore if the ſaid earl would not take it upon him, he would: and that he would goe into Wales, and raiſe an army of 20000. men, &c. which indictment (without any arraignment or pleading) being meerly faigned to blemiſh the title of the Mortimers, and withal being inſufficient in law, as by the ſame appeareth, was confirmed by authority of parliament: and the ſaid Sir John being brought into the parliament without arraignment or anſwer, judgement

[a] Lex. divina. John 7. v. 15. Deut. c. 17. v. 10. & ca. 19. v. 15. Mat. Par. 18 Johannis 273. *Incivile videtur et contra canones eſſe in hominem abſentem non vocatum, non convictum nec confeſſum ferre ſententiam.* Hereof ſee *paulo poſtea*

[b] Acts 25. 16. Gen. 3. 9.. Dixit dominus, Adam, ubi es? Vide Gen. 18. 21. Eccleſiaſticus 11. 7, 8.

[c] Praxis ſanctorum Joſua 7. 19, 22, 23. &c.

[d] Jud. 20. 3.

[e] Rot. par. 2 H. 6. nu. 18.

judgement in parliament was given againſt him upon the ſaid indictment; that he ſhould be carried to the tower of London, and drawn through the city to Tiborn, and there hanged, drawn and quartered, his head to be ſet on London bridge, and his four quarters on the four gates of London, as by the record of parliament appeareth.

The Proceeding in Parliament againſt Abſents.

The ancient law and cuſtome of the parliament was, that when any man was to be charged in parliament with any crime or offence, or miſdemeanour, the kings writ was directed to the ſherif to ſummon and injoin the party to appear before the king in the next parliament. For example.

Placita in parliamento domini regis, anno E. I. 33. Northampt.

Dominus rex mandavit vic' quod aſſumptis ſecum quatuor de diſcretioribus et leg' militibus com' ſui in propria perſona ſua accederet ad Nicholaum de Segrave, et ipſum in præſentia prædictorum militum ſummon' et ex parte domini regis firmiter ei injungeret quod eſſet coram domino rege in proximo parliament' ſuo apud Weſtm' in primo adventu domini regis ibidem ad audiendam voluntatem ipſius domini regis ſuper hiis, quæ tunc ibidem proponere intenderet verſ. eum, et ad faciendum et recipiendum ulterius quod curia domini regis conſideraret in præmiſſis. Et vic' modo mandavit quod aſſumptis ſecum Thoma Wale, Waltero filio Roberti [39] *de Daventry. Roberto de Gray de Wollaſton, et Radulpho de Normavill quatuor milit', &c. in propria perſona ſua acceſſit apud Stowe ad manerium prædicti Nicholai, et in præſentia eorundem militum ſummon' prædictum Nicholaum, et ei firmiter injunxit quod eſſet coram domino rege in iſto parliamento nunc juxta formam et tenorem mandati præd', &c.*

Placita coram domino rege, Paſ. 33 E. I. Rot. 19. Oxon.

Almaricus de Sancto Amando, magiſter Johannes de Sancto Amando Willielmus de Monte Acuto, Richardus Attchaw conſtabularius caſtri Oxon, Rich. de Hurle, Thomas de Carleton capellanus, Johannes de Ros, Johannes de Trenbrigg, Willielmus Attewarde frater ejus, et Philippus de Wigenton attachiat' fuerunt per vic' in caſtro Oxon' per præcept' domini regis reſponſur' eidem domino regi in parliamento ſuo in craſtino ſancti Mathæi apoſtoli anno regni ſui xxxiii. *ſuper quibuſdam criminibus et tranſgreſſionibus infra ſcriptis, et inde per manucaptionem ſufficient' adjornat' coram ipſo domino regi hic ad hunc diem, ſcilicet a die Paſchæ in* xv. *dies, &c.*

Or a writ might be directed to the party himſelf, when any complaint was made againſt him, *De injuriis, gravaminibus, aut moleſtationibus*, to appear in his proper perſon before the king and his councell, &c. As for example:

Placita coram rege apud Cantuar' de termino Paſc. anno regni regis E. I. 30. Conſimile breve ubi ſupra eidem Roberto de Burgherſh ad ſectam majoris et baronum quinque portuum.

Dominus rex mandavit breve ſuum Roberto de Burgherſh in hæc verba. Edwardus Dei gratia, &c. Dilecto et fideli ſuo Roberto de Burgherſh conſtabular' caſtri ſui Dover et cuſtod' ſuo quinque portuum, ſalutem. Quia dilectus nobis in Chriſto abbas de Faverſham et Robertus de Gurne balivus ſuus ejuſdem villæ coram concilio noſtro apud Eborum exiſtente de diverſis injuriis, gravaminibus et moleſtationibus eis per vos voluntar' et abſq; cauſa rationabili multipliciter illatis graves querimonias depoſuerunt, petentes inſtanter ut eis ſuper hoc fieri faceremus remedium opportunum; propter quod dedimus eis diem coram nobis et concilio noſtro à die Paſch. in xv. *dies, &c. ad querelas ſuas prædictas tunc oſtendend', et ad faciend'*

ciend' super hoc ulterius et recipiend' quod justitia suaderet; vobis mandamus, quod in propria persona vestra sitis coram nobis et concilio nostro ad diem prædict' præfatis abbati et balivis suis super præmissis respons' factur' et receptur' quod curia nostra consideraverit in hac parte, et ab injuriis, gravaminibus, molestationibus et districtionibus indebitis præfatis abbati et balivis suis interim inferendis penitus desistendo. Et habeatis ibi hoc breve. Teste me ipso apud Linliscum XXX. *die Januarii, anno regni nostri* XXX. *Virtute cujus brevis prædictus Robertus venit, et breve illud protulit ad diem in eodem contentum. Et prædictus abbas venit et querelas suas protulit in quodam rotulo scriptas, et quas in curia hic querelando ostendit et legere fecit, de quibus prima est hæc, &c.*

Now they which absent themselves shall be proceeded withall, vide 50 E. 3. nu. 37. Adam Buries case, 2. parte patent. 21 R. 2. nu. 15, 16. Rot. Par. 17 R. 2. nu. 28. 11 H. 4. nu. 37, 38. 15 H. 6. nu. 4. 33 H. 6. fo. 17. Sir John Pilkingtons case.

And where by order of law a man cannot be attainted of high treason, unlesse the offence be in law high treason, he ought not to be attainted by generall words of high treason by authority of parliament (as sometime hath been used) but the high treason ought to be specially expressed, seeing that the court of parliament is the highest and most honourable court of justice, and ought (as hath been said) give example to inferiour courts.

25 H. 8. ca. 12. Eliz. Barton, and others. And see the act of the attainder of the lord Cromwell, anno 32 H. 8. ubi supra.

There was an act of parliament made in the 11 year of king H. 7. which had a fair flattering preamble, pretending to avoid divers mischiefs, which were, 1. To the high displeasure of almighty God. 2. The great let of the common law, and, 3. The great let of the wealth of this land: and the purvien of that act tended in the execution contrary, *ex diametro*, viz. to the high displeasure of almighty God, the great let, nay the utter subversion of the common law, and the great let of the wealth of this land, as hereafter shall manifestly appear. Which act followeth in these words:

A mischievous act with a flattering preamble in 11 H. 7.

[40]

The king our sovereign lord calling to his remembrance that many good statutes and ordinances be made for the punishment of riots, unlawfull assemblies, reteinders in giving and receiving of liveries, signs and tokens unlawfully, extortions, maintenances, imbracery, excessive taking of wages contrary to the statutes of labourers and artificers, the use of unlawfull games, inordinate apparell, and many other great enormities and offences, which been committed and done daily contrary to the good statutes, for many and divers behoofull considerations severally made and ordained, to the displeasure of almighty God, and the great let of the common law, and wealth of this land, notwithstanding that generally by the justices of the peace in every shire within this realm in the open sessions is given in charge to enquire of many offences committed contrary to divers of the said statutes, and divers enquests thereupon there straitly sworn, and charged before the said justices to enquire of the premisses, and therein to present the troth which any letted to be found by imbracery, main-

11 H. 7. ca. 3.

maintenance, corruption and favour; by occaſion whereof the ſaid ſtatutes be not, nor cannot be put in due execution: for reformation whereof, for ſo much that before this time the ſaid offences, extortions, contempts, and other the premiſſes might not, nor as yet may be conveniently puniſhed by the due order of the law, except it were firſt found and preſented by the verdict of twelve men thereto duly ſworn, which for the cauſes afore rehearſed will not find nor yet preſent the truth: wherefore be it by the advice and aſſent of the lords ſpirituall and temporall, and the commons in this preſent parliament aſſembled, and by authority of the ſame enacted, ordained and eſtabliſhed, that from henceforth as well the juſtices of aſſiſe in the open ſeſſions to be holden afore them, as the juſtices of peace in every county of the ſaid realm, [a] upon information for the king before them to be made, have full power and authority [b] by their diſcretion to hear and determine all offences and contempts committed and done by any perſon or perſons againſt the form, ordinance, and effect of [c] any ſtatute made and not repealed, and that the ſaid juſtices upon the ſaid information have full power and authority to award and make like proceſſe againſt the ſaid offenders and every of them, as they ſhould or might make againſt ſuch perſon or perſons as been preſent and indicted before them of treſpaſſe done contrary to the kings peace, and the ſaid offender, or offenders duly to puniſh according to the purport, form, and effect of the ſtatutes. Alſo be it enacted by the ſaid authority, that the perſon which ſhal give the ſaid information for the king ſhall by the diſcretion of the ſaid juſtices content and pay to the ſaid perſon or perſons againſt whom the ſaid information ſhall be ſo given his reaſonable coſts and dammages in that behalf ſuſtained, if that it be tried or found againſt him, that ſo giveth or maketh any ſuch information. Provided always, that any ſuch information extend not to treaſon, murder, or felony, nor to any other offence, wherefore any perſon ſhall loſe life, or member, nor to loſe by nor upon the ſame information any lands, tenements, goods or chattels to the party making the ſame information. Provided alſo that the ſaid informations ſhall not extend to any perſon dwelling in any other ſhire, then there, as the ſaid information ſhall be given or made, ſaving to every perſon or perſons, cities, and towns, all their liberties and franchiſes to them and every of them of right belonging and appertaining.

[a] Upon information without any indictment.

[b] By their diſcretion, and not *ſecundum legem & conſuetudinem Angl.* as all proceedings ought to be.

[c] Obſolete ſtatutes and all, and ſpecially ſuch as time had ſo altered from the originall cauſe of the making thereof, as either they could not at all, or very hardly be obſerved and kept.

[41]

But it extended to a premunire, miſpriſion of treaſon, &c.

By pretext of this law Empſon and Dudley did commit upon the ſubject unſufferable preſſures and oppreſſions, and therefore this ſtatute was juſtly ſoon after the deceaſe of H. 7. repealed at the next parliament after his deceaſe, by the ſtatute of 1 H. 8. ca. 6.

1 H. 8. ca. 6.

A good caveat to parliaments to leave all cauſes to be meaſured by the

the golden and ſtreight metwand of the law, and not to the incertain and crooked cord of diſcretion.

It is not almoſt credible to foreſee, when any maxime, or fundamentall law of this realm is altered (as elſewhere hath been obſerved) what dangerous inconveniences doe follow, which moſt expreſly appeareth by this moſt unjuſt and ſtrange act of 11 H. 7. for hereby not only Empſon and Dudley themſelves, but ſuch juſtices of peace (corrupt men) as they cauſed to be authorized, committed moſt grievous and heavy oppreſſions and exactions, grinding of the face of the poor ſubjects by penall laws (be they never ſo obſolete or unfit for the time) by information only without any preſentment or triall by jury being the ancient birthright of the ſubject, but to hear and determine the ſame by their diſcretion, inflicting ſuch penalty, as the ſtatutes not repealed impoſed: theſe and other like oppreſſions and exactions by or by the means of Empſon and Dudley and their inſtruments, brought infinite treaſures to the kings coffers, whereof the king himſelf in the end with great grief and compunction repented, as in * another place we have obſerved.

See the 2. part of the Inſtitutes, W. 1. ca. 26. See the preface to the 4. part of the Reports. The danger enſuing by alteration of any of the maximes of the law.

* In the chapter of the Court of Wards and Liveries.

This ſtatute of 11 H. 7. we have recited, and ſhewed the juſt inconveniences thereof, to the end, that the like ſhould never hereafter be attempted in any court of parliament. And that others might avoid the fearfull end of thoſe two time-ſervers, Empſon and Dudley. *Qui eorum veſtigia inſiſtunt, eorum exitus perhorreſcant.*

See the ſtatute of 8 E. 4. ca. 2. the ſtatute of liveries, an information, &c. by the diſcretion of the judges to ſtand as an originall, &c. This act is deſervedly repealed.

Vide 12 R. 2. cap. 13. Puniſhment by diſcretion, &c. Vide 5 H. 4. ca. 6. 8. See the * Commiſſion of ſewers. Diſcretion ought to be thus deſcribed. *Diſcretio eſt diſcernere per legem quid ſit juſtum.* And this deſcription is proved by the common law of the land, for when a jury doe doubt of the law, and deſire to doe that which is juſt, they find the ſpeciall matter, and the entry is, *Et ſuper tota materia, &c. petunt diſcretionem juſticiariorum*, and ſometime, *adviſamentum et diſcretionem juſticiariorum in præmiſſis, &c.* that is, they deſire that the judges would diſcern by law what is juſt, and give judgement accordingly.

* Lib. 5. fo. 100. Rooks caſe. Lib. 10. fo. 128. &c.

Pl. com. 348. Barnards caſe.

Acts againſt the Power of the Parliament ſubſequent bind not. [42]

An article of the ſtatute made in 11 R. 2. cap. 5. is, that no perſon ſhould attempt to revoke any ordinance then made, is repealed, for that ſuch reſtraint is againſt the juriſdiction and power of the parliament, the liberty of the ſubject, and unreaſonable. And likewiſe the laſt will and teſtament of king R. 2. under the great ſeal, privy ſeal, and privy ſignet, whereby he deviſed certain mony, treaſure, &c. to his ſucceſſors upon condition to obſerve all the acts and orders at the parliament holden in *anno* 21 of his reign, was holden unjuſt and unlawfull, for that it reſtrained the ſoveraign liberty of the kings his ſucceſſors.

1 H. 4. nu. 144. 21 R. 2. nu. 20. repealed by 1 H. 4. ca. 3. 1 H. 4. nu. 48. Vid. 7 H. 4. nu. 37.

Sundry lords of parliament (but no biſhops) or ſix of them, and certain knights of ſhires of the commons or three of them are authoriſed by authority of parliament to examine, anſwer, and plainly

21 R. 2. ca. 16. 21 R. 2. nu. 44.

determine all the petitions exhibited in that parliament, and the matters contained in the same by their good advice and discretion, &c. The high power of a parliament to be committed to a few is holden to be against the dignity of a parliament, and that no such commission ought to be granted.

1 H. 4. nu. 70.

2 H. 4. ca. 22. Vide 21 R. 2. nu. 44.

An act in 11 R. 2. ca. 3. that no man against whom any judgment, or forfeiture was given should sue for pardon or grace, &c. was holden to be unreasonable without example, and against the law and custome of parliament, and therefore that branch by authority of parliament was adnichaled, and made void.

26 H. 8. ca. 1. Acts of parliament ought to be plainly, and clearly, and not cunningly and darkly penned, specially in criminall causes.

Also I find that in times past the houses of parliament have not been clearly dealt withall, but by cunning artifice of words utterly deceived, and that in cases of greatest moment, even in case of high treason, as taking one example for a warning in like cases hereafter.

King H. 8. after the clergy of England had in their convocations acknowledged him supream head of the church of England, thought it no difficult matter to have the same corroborated and confirmed by authority of parliament, but withall secretly and earnestly desired that the impugners and deniers thereof, though it were but by word, might incur the offence of high treason, and finding the one, that is, the acknowledgement of his supremacy likely to have good passage, and having little hope upon that which he found to effect the other concerning high treason, sought to have it passe in some other act by words closely cowched, though the former act of supremacy had been the proper place. * And therefore in the act of recognition of his supremacy it is enacted, that he should have annexed and united to the crown of this realm the title and stile thereof: † and afterwards towards the end of the parliament, a bill was preferred whereby many offences be high treason, and thereby it is enacted, That if any person or persons by [a] word or writing, 1 practise or attempt any bodily harm to the king, the [b] queen or their heirs apparent, 2 or to [c] deprive them or any of them, of their dignity, [d] title, or name of their royall estates, 3 or that the king should be an [e] heretique, schismatique, tyrant, infidell, or usurper of the crown, &c. that every such person so offending should be adjudged traytors, &c. So as now by this latter act, he that by word or writing attempts to deprive the king of the title of his royall estate is a traytor, but the former act had annexed to the crown the title of the stile of supremacy, and therefore he that should by word or writing attempt to deprive the king thereof should be a traytor. And [f] upon this law of 26 H. 8. ca. 13. for denying of the kings supremacy divers suffered death as in case of high treason, whereas all laws, especially penall, and principally those that are penall in the highest degree [g] ought to be so plainly and perspicuously penned, as every member of both houses may understand the same, and according to his knowledge and conscience give his voice. [h] *Erit autem lex honesta, justa, possibiiis, secundum naturam et secundum consuetudinem patriae, temporique conveniens, necessaria et utilis, manifesta quoque, ne aliquid per obscuritatem incautum captione* * *contrudat, nullo privato commodo, sed pro communi civium utilitate conscripta, ideo in ipsa constitutione ista consideranda sunt, quia cum leges institutae fuerint non erit liberum arbitrium judicare de ipsis, sed oportebit judicare secundum ipsas*, which be excellent

* 26 H. 8. ca. 1.

†26 H. 8. ca. 13.

[a] By word, &c. this by construction referres to the 2. clause.

[b] Shadowed with the queen or prince.

[c] Deprive, an obscure word.

[d] Note this word [title] in the former act.

[e] Parker B. of Cant. *Lib. de Antiquitate Brit. Ecclesiae. Clerus animo toto obstupuit, nondum enim quid sibi hic novus vellet titulus, aut quorsum tenderet, prospexit, &c.*

[f] But this act lived not long, for twice it was repealed, viz. by 1 E. 6. c. 12. & 1 Mar. c. 1.

[g] What qualities laws ought to have.

[h] Isidor. 2. Etymol.

*[43]

cellent rules for all parliaments to follow. But the statute of 5 Eliz. ca. 1. hath concerning the * supremacy dealt plainly and perspicuously as by the same appeareth.

5 Eliz. ca. 1. * Exod. 4. 16. *Tu, i. Moses erit ei, i. Aaron, in his quæ ad deum pertinent, &c.* Exod. 32. 15, 16. *Moses custos utriusque tabulæ.* Numb. 10. 1, 2. *Moses custos utriusque tubæ.* Joshua 24. 1. *Congregavit Josua, &c.* 28. *dimisit.* 1 Chron. 15. 4. 1 Chron. 16 43. *Rex David.* 2 Chron. 5. 2. *Rex Solomon.* 2 Chron. 29. 15. &c. *Ezekias.* Nota. 1 Sam. 15. 17. *Et ait Samuel ad Saul, nonne cum parvulus esses caput in tribubus factus es?* and the tribe of Levi was one. 1 Maccab. 14. 44. See hereafter ca. 74.

And albeit it appeareth by these examples, and many other that might be brought, what transcendent power and authority this court of parliament hath, yet though divers parliaments have attempted to barre, restrain, suspend, qualifie, or make void subsequent parliaments, yet could they never effect it, for the latter parliament hath ever power to abrogate, suspend, qualifie, explain, or make void the former in the whole or in any part thereof, notwithstanding any words of restraint, prohibition, or penalty in the former: for it is a maxime in the law of the parliament, *quod leges posteriores priores contrarias abrogant.*

Subsequent parliaments cannot be restrained by the former. 43 E. 3. ca. 1. 11 H. 7. ca. 1. 28 H. 8. ca. 17. 1 E. 6. ca. 11. lib. 4. to 46. the B. of Cant. case.

Acts of Parliament enrolled in other Courts.

For the better observation of any act of parliament enacted for the commonwealth, or of a petition of right, or judgment in parliament, or the like, and to incourage the judges that the same may be duly executed, the same may be inrolled in the courts of justice in this manner. The tenor of the record must be removed into the chancery by writ of *certiorari*, and delivered into the kings bench by the hands of the chancelor or lord keeper, and sent by mittimus to the court of common pleas, and by like mittimus into the exchequer, and the king by his writ may command any court to observe and firmly to keep such an act of parliament, as it appeareth by these two precedents. *Ex Rotulo Clauf. anno* 28 *E.* 1. *m.* 2. *Dorf. Rex thesaurat' et baronibus suis de scaccar' salutem. Quia volumus quod Magna Carta domini Henrici quondam regis Angliæ patris nostri de libertatibus Angliæ quam confirmavimus et etiam innovavimus in omnibus et singulis articulis suis firmiter et inviolabiliter observetur. Vobis mandamus quod cartam prædictam in omnibus et singulis suis articulis quantum in vobis est coram vobis in dicto scaccario observari faciatis firmiter et teneri. T. R. apud Dunfres* 23. *die Octobris.*

Int. placita parl. 18 E. 1. rot. 18. Ibid. 20 E. 1. Magnum placitum int. com. Gloc' & com. Heref. & Essex irr. rot. claus. an. 28 E. 1. in Dors. irr. le Magna Carta. Pasch. 33 E. 1. rot. par. Nich. Segraves case, rot. 22. Tr. 12 E. 2. ro. 60. de irr. Petition in parliament, *al banke le rey.*

Rex justic' suis de banco salutem: Cum in alleviationem gravaminum quæ populus regni nostri occasione guerrarum hactenus toleravit, ac in emendationem status ejusdem populi, nec non ut ex hoc se exhibeat ad nostra servicia promptiorem, nobisque in agendis nostris libentius subsidium faciat in futurum, quosdam articulos eidem populo plurimum (annuente domino) profuturos de gratia nostra speciali duxerimus concedendos. Vobis mandamus quod dictos articulos quos vobis mittimus sigillo nostro consignatos coram vobis in banco prædicto quantum in vobis est juxta vim, formam et effectum eorundem observari faciatis firmiter et teneri. T. R. apud Dunfres 30. *die Octobris.*

Every Member of the Parliament ought to come.

5 R. 2. ſtat. 2. c. 4. rot. par. 31 H. 6. nu. 46. fines were ſet, &c. If any of the lords or commons come not, &c. they ſhall be fined.

Every lord ſpirituall and temporall, and every knight, citizen, and burgeſſe ſhall upon ſummons come to the parliament, except he can reaſonably, and honeſtly excuſe himſelf, or elſe he ſhall be amerced, &c. that is, reſpectively, a lord by the lords, and one of the commons by the commons.

By the ſtatute of 6 H. 8. ca. 16. no knight, citizen or burgeſſe of the houſe of common's ſhall depart from the parliament without licence of the ſpeaker and commons, the ſame to be entred of record in the book of the clerk of the parlirment, upon pain to loſe their wages.

[44]

Vi. 3 E. 3. 18. ſup. If any of the lords or commons depart, &c. they ſhall be fined. 1 & 2 Ph. and M. rot. 48. ut ſup.

* 5 R. 2. ſtat. 2. ca. 4.

If a lord depart from parliament without licence, it is an offence done out of the parliament, and is finable by the lords: and ſo it is of a member of the houſe of commons, he may be fined by the houſe of commons. Vide 1 & 2 Ph. and Mar. coram rege. Rot. 48. divers informations by the attorney generall for departing without licenſe, *ut ſupra*.

* The puniſhment of ſheriffes for their negligence in retorning of writs, or for leaving out of their retorns any city or borough which ought to ſend citizens and burgeſſes.

Advice concerning new and plauſible projects and offers in Parliament.

See before pa. 14. Rot. par. 13 E. 3.

When any plauſible project is made in parliament to draw the lords and commons to aſſent to any act (eſpecially in matters of weight and importance) if both houſes do give upon the matter projected and promiſed their conſent, it ſhall be moſt neceſſary, they being truſted for the common-wealth, to have the matter projected and promiſed (which moved the houſes to conſent) to be eſtabliſhed in the ſame act, leſt the benefit of the act be taken, and the matter projected and promiſed never performed, and ſo the houſes of parliament performe not the truſt repoſed in them. As it fell out (taking one example for many) in the reigne of H. 8. On the kings behalfe the members of both houſes were informed in parliament, that no king or kingdome was ſafe, but where the king had three abilities. Firſt, to live of his own, and able to defend his kingdome upon any ſudden invaſion or inſurrection. 2. To aide his confederates, otherwiſe they would never aſſiſt him. 3. To reward his well deſerving ſervants. Now the project was, that if the parliament would give unto him all the abbies, priories, friories, nunneries, and other monaſteries, that for ever in time then to come, he would take order that the ſame ſhould not be converted to private uſe: but firſt, that his exchequer for the purpoſes aforeſaid ſhould be enriched. Secondly, the kingdome ſtrengthened by a continuall maintenance of 40 thouſand well trained ſouldiers with ſkilfull captains and commanders. Thirdly, for the benefit and eaſe of the ſubject, who never afterwards (as was projected) in any time to come ſhould be charged with ſubſidies, fifteenths, loanes, or other common aides. Fourthly, leſt the honour of the realme ſhould receive any diminution of honour by the diſſolution of the ſaid monaſteries,

nasteries, there being 29 lords of parliament of the abbots and priors (that held of the king *per baroniam*, whereof more in the next leafe) that the king would create a number of nobles, which we omit. The said monasteries were given to the king by authority of divers acts of parliament, but no provision was therein made for the said project, or any part thereof; * only *ad faciend' populum* these possessions were given to the king his heirs and successors to do and use therewith his and their own wils, to the pleasure of almighty God, and the honour and profit of the realme.

27 H. 8. de monasteries, & 31 H. 8. cap. 13. 32 H. 8. cap. 14. * 27 H. 8. ca. 28.

Now observe the catastrophe; in the same parliament of 32 H. 8. when the great and opulent priory of Saint Johns of Jerusalem was given to the king, he demanded and had a subsidie both of the clergie and laity. And the like he had in 34 H. 8. and in 37 H. 8. he had another subsidie. And since the dissolution of the said monasteries he exacted divers loanes, and against law received the same.

32 H. 8. ca. 23. 50. 34 H. 8. cap. 16. & 27. 37 H. 8. cap. 24.

Whom the King may call to the Lords House of Parliament.

If the king by his writ calleth any knight or esquire to be a lord of the parliament, he cannot refuse to serve the king there in *communi illo concilio*, for the good of his country. But if the king had called an * abbot, prior, or other regular prelate by writ to the parliament to the common councell of the realme, if he held not of the king *per baroniam*, he might refuse to serve in parliament, † because *quoad secularia*, he was *mortuus in lege*, and therefore not capable to have place and voice in parliament, unlesse he did hold *per baroniam*, and were to that common councell called by writ, which made him capable: and though such a prelat regular had been often called by writ, and had *de facto* had place and voice in parliament, yet if *in rei veritate* he held not *per baroniam*, he ought to be discharged of that service, and to sit in parliament no more.

Rot. Claus. in dors. 10 H. 7. 20 Septemb. Writs to divers *ad ordinem militiæ de balneo suscipiend. juxta antiquam consuetudinem in creatione usitatam.*

* Of regular prelats that hold *per baroniam.*

† [45] And so was it adjudged in the parliament at York, an. 12 E. 2. in the case of the abbot of S. James extra Northamp. Stanf. pl. cor. 153. a.

[a] For that the abby of Leicester was founded by Robert Fitz-Robert earle of Leicester (albeit the patronage came to the crowne by the forfeiture of Simon de Mountford earle of Leic.) yet being of a subjects foundation, it could not be holden *per baroniam*, and therefore the abbot had no capacity to be called to the parliament, and thereupon the king did grant, *quod idem abbas et successores sui de veniendo ad parliamenta et concilia nostra vel hæredum nostrorum quieti sint et exonerati imperpetuum.*

[a] Rot. pat. an. 26 E. 3. part. 1. m. 22. See Rot. claus. in dors. 11 E. 3. part 2. m. 11 *Religious que teignont per barony sont tenus de venier au parliament.* Vid. ibid. 13 E. 3. part. 2. m. 28 & 1.

[b] *De jure et consuetudine Angliæ ad archidiaconatum Cantuariensem, &c. abbates, priores, aliosq; prælatos quoscunque per baroniam de domino rege tenentes pertinet in parliamentis regiis quibuscunque ut pares regni prædicti personaliter interesse, ibiq; de regni negotiis ac aliis tractari consuetis cum cæteris dicti regni paribus ac aliis ibidem jus interessendi habentibus consulere et tractare, ordinare, statuere, et diffinire, ac cætera facere quæ parliamenti tempore ibid. immunient faciend'.*

[b] Rot. pat. 11 R. 2. part. 1. m. 2. artic. 34.

No man ought to sit in that high court of parliament, but he that hath right to sit there: for it is not only a personall offence in him that sitteth there without authority, but a publick offence to the court of parliament, and consequently to the whole realme. But all the cases abovesaid, and others that might be remembered touching this point, as little rivers, do flow from the fountain of *modus tenendi parliamentum*, where it is said. *Ad parliamentum summoneri*

Modus tenendi parl. ca. 2.

This is *infra* explained by the assise of Clarendon.

moneri et venire debent ratione tenuræ suæ omnes et singuli archiepisc', episcopi, abbates, priores et alii majores cleri qui tenent per comitatum vel baroniam ratione hujusmodi tenuræ, et nulli minores, nisi eorum præsentia necessaria vel utilis reputetur, &c.

One rare and strange creation of a lord regular of parliament we cannot passe over, which was, that king H. 8. in the fifth year of his reign, by his letters patents under the great seale, did grant unto Richard Banham abbot of Tavestock in the county of Devon, being of his patronage, and to the successors of the said abbot, *ut eorum quilibet, qui pro tempore ibidem fuerit abbas, sit et erit unus de spiritualibus et religiosis dominis parliamenti nostri, hæredum et successorum nostrorum, gaudend' honore, privilegio et libertatibus ejusdem.*

By that which hath been said, it appeareth that this creation of a regular lord of parliament was voide, for that the abbot was neither *baro*, nor had *baroniam*, &c. And if the king might create abbots or priors lords of parliament in this manner, by the same reason he might create deans and archdeacons lords of parliament, which without question he cannot.

10 H. 2. cap. 11. Mat. Par. 97. Assisa de Clarendon.

By the act of parliament of 10 H. 2. called the assise of Clarendon, it is declared, *Ut pars consuetudinum et libertatum antecessorum regis*, viz. *Henrici primi et aliorum, quæ observari debent in regno et ab omnibus teneri*, viz. *archiepiscopi, episcopi, et universæ personæ regni, qui de rege tenent in capite habeant possessiones suas de rege sicut baroniam, et inde respondeant justiciariis et ministris regis, et sequantur et faciant omnes consuetudines regias, et sicut cæteri barones debent interesse judiciis curiæ regis cum baronibus, quousq; perveniatur * ad diminutionem membrorum vel ad mortem.* So as by this act a tenure of the king in chiefe was in equipage with a barony.

Rot. parl. 11 & 21 R. 2.

Cart. libertat. a rege Johanne anno 17 regni sui concess. Mat. Par. 343.

And king John by his great charter of liberties made *anno* 17 of his reigne, granteth, *Quod faciemus summoneri archiepiscopos, episcopos, abbates, comites, et majores barones regni singulatim per literas nostras.* Out of this clause we are to observe these things: First, that these barons called here *majores*, were lords of parliament, and called thereunto by the kings writs. Secondly, that they were called *majores* comparatively, and that was in respect of others which were called *barones minores*, or *nobiles minores*, and were freeholders that * hold by knights service and escuage. i. *Servitium scuti*, of three sorts, viz. *milites, armigeri, et generosi*, knights, esquires, and gentlehomes, or gentlemen. These *barones minores* were lords of mannors, and had not the dignity of lords, but had courts of their freeholders, which to this day are called court barons, *curiæ baroniar'*. Of this baron it is said in that law made by king Edward before the conquest: *Barones qui suam habent * curiam de suis hominibus, videant ut sic de eis agant, quatenus erga deum reatum non incurrant, et regem non offendant.*

[46]

* Nota, a knights fee is the service of a knight, that is of a man at arms, or of war. Hereof see the second part of the Instit. cap. de Militibus.

1 E. 2. Inter leges Edw. cap. 21 Ib. ca. 9.

* 1. Curiam baronis. Glanv. li. 8. cap. 11. acc'. Bract. li. 3. 154. b. Camd. Brit. 121.

Baro à bar, Germanica lingua liberum et sui juris significat. 1. which agreeth well with that which hath been said. 2. That *baro major* was called *baro major regni.* 3. That every greater baron was severally summoned by the kings writ, which continueth to this day.

The

The Fees of the Knights, Citizens, and Burgesses of Parliament.

First, for the knight of any county it is 4 s. *per diem*, and so it hath been time out of mind, which is particularly expressed in many records, but let us take one in *hæc verba. Johannes Shordich unus militum comitatus Middlesex venientium ad parliamentum tent' apud Westm' in cro. animarum ultim' præterit' habet allocationem* 4 *li. et* 4 *s. pro* 21 *diebus pro expensis suis veniendo ad parliament' prædict' ibid. morando, et exinde ad propria redeundo, capiendo per diem* 4 *s. Teste rege apud Westm'* 24 *die Novemb. anno* 46. Every citizen and burgesse is to have 2 s. *per diem, ut supra, mutatis mutandis.*

[a] Nota the writ *de expensis militum, &c.* doth comprehend the summe according to the abovesaid computation, and a commandement to the sheriffe to levie the same [b] *de communitate comitatus prædict' tam infra libertates, quam extra. (Civitatibus et burgis de quibus cives et burgenses ad parliamentum nostrum, &c. venerunt duntaxat exceptis.)* The like writs to the sheriffes *de expensis civium et burgensium*, to levie the same in cities and boroughs.

[c] An. 1 R. 2. nu. 11. the commons petitioned in parliament, that all persons having lay fee might contribute to the charge of the knights, and to all tallages. The king answered, [The lords of the realm wil not lose their old liberties,] note the writ is *de communitate.*

[d] Also there is a writ in the Register *de expensis militis non levandis ab hominib' de antiquo d'nico, nec ab nativis.* [e] Other discharges *de expensis militum.*

[f] For the wages of the knights of the shire of Cambridge see the statute of 34 H. 8. cap. 24. *Consimile pro insula de Ely, &c.*

[g] H. 4. an. 14. of his reigne summoned a parliament *cro. Purificationis*, and he deceased 20 *Martii* following, so as the parliament was dissolved by his decease. Thereupon it was a question, whether the knights and burgesses should have their wages seeing nothing passed in that parliament. And it was resolved, that if upon view of the kings [h] records any like presidents may be found, allowances of their fees shal be made. [i] Also the clergy were contributory by reason of their benefices to the expences of the procurators of the clergy.

[k] But chaplains which are masters of the chancery and attendants at the parliament, shal not be contributory by reason of their benefices to the expences of the clergy, as by the Register *ubi supra* appears: and this was by an act of parliament made in * 4 E. 3. which in generall words is recited in the writ directed to the arch-deacon for their discharge.

Indors. claus. an. 46 E. 3. nu. 4. Rot. claus. 7 R. 2. nu. 1. de expensis milit. Regist. fo. 192. a. acc' *Diota. Veniendo, morando, redeundo, per diem* 4 *s.* Par. 51 E. 3. nu. 45. 35 H. 8. cap. 11. See the ancient treatise, *De modo tenendi parl.*

[a] Regist. f. 192. a. See the stat. of 12 R. 2. ca. 12. and see 23 H. 6. ca. 11. how the sheriffe shall levie the same. See 8 R. 2. tit. Avowrie 260. what the common law was.

[b] Nota, de communitate. Vid. sup. pa. 1. For the legall understanding of this word commons.

[c] Rot. par 1 R 2. nu. 11.

[d] Regist. 261. 7 H. 6. 35. b. F. N. B. 14 E.

[e] Regist. 191, 192. 12 R. 2. ca. 12.

[f] 34 H. 8. ca. 24. 9 H. 6. nu. 46.

[g] Rot. par. 1 H. 5. nu. 26.

[h] Nota, for presidents.

[i] Regist. 261. F. N. B. 229. a. [k] Vid. sup. pa. 4, 5. * Parl. an. 4 E. 3. apud Winton, whereof there is no roll now remaining.

Who be eligible to be a Knight, Citizen, or Burgeſſe of Parliament.

See the ſtat, of 5 R. 2. cap. 4. Vid. ſup. pa. 4, 5. Rot. brev. 7 R. 2. [47] Dorſ. clauſ. 7 R. 2. m. 10. & 37.

A knight baneret being no lord of parliament is eligible to be knight, citizen, or burgeſſe of the houſe of commons being under the degree of a baron, who is of the loweſt degree of the lords houſe. But Thomas Camois was not only a knight baneret, but a baron and lord of parliament in *anno* 7 R. 2. and ſerved in that parliament as a baron of the realme, and therefore as of a thing notorious he was diſcharged. One under the age of 21 years is not eligible, neither can any lord of parliament ſit there untill he be of the full age of 21 years.

Vi. ſtat. de 1 Mar. cap.

An alien cannot be elected of the parliament, becauſe he is not the kings liege ſubject, and ſo it is albeit he be made denizen by letters patents, &c. for thereby he is made *quaſi, ſeu tanquam ligeus:* but that will not ſerve, for he muſt be *ligeus revera*, and not *quaſi, &c.* And we have had ſuch an one choſen and diſallowed by the houſe of commons, becauſe ſuch a perſon can hold no place of judicature; but if an alien be naturalized by parliament, then he is eligible to this or any other place of judicature.

39 E. 3. 35, 36.

But it is objected that Gilbert de Umphrevill earle of Andgos in Scotland, was called by the kings writ to the parliament in 39 E. 3. by the name of Gilbert earle of Andgos: and in a writ of raviſhment of ward brought againſt him, by the name of Gilbert Umphrevill chivaler, he pleaded to the writ, that he was earle of Andgos not named in the writ: and for that he was ſummoned to every parliament by the name of the earle of Andgos, and the king ſent to him a writ of parliament under the great ſeale, as to a peer of the land, by judgement of the court the writ did abate. We have ſearched for the truth of this caſe, and do finde it in the plea rolls in this manner.

Richard de Umphrevill baron of Prodhowe and Redeſdale in the county of Northumberland, had iſſue Gilbert, who after the death of his father was a baron of this realm, and in the reign of H. 3. married with Mawde daughter and heir of the earl of Andgos in Scotland, who by her had iſſue Gilbert, who was earle of Andgos as heir to his mother, and baron of Prodhow and Redeſdale as heir to his father: he ſat in parliament upon ſummons by writ in 27 E. 1. 28 E. 1. 30 E. 1. 35 E. 1. 1 E. 2. and 2 E. 2. by the name of Gilbert earle of Andgos. Robert his ſonne ſat in parliament, *anno* 12 E. 2. by the ſame name of dignity, and ſo forth, all E. the ſeconds reign. And Gilbert his ſonne ſat in parliament in 6 E. 3. and in every parliament following untill. and in 4 R. 2. by the ſame name. And in Gilbert his ſonne (who deceaſed in *anno* 15 H. 6.) that ſirname of Umphrevil ceaſed. Hereby it appeareth that the ſaid Richard Umphrevil and his poſterity, from whence ſoever they originally deſcended, were liege Engliſhmen: for if they had been aliens, they could not have enjoyed the lordſhips of Prodhowe, Otterborne, Harbottle, and Redeſdale in England, nor the barony of Kime in Lancaſhire, which the two laſt Gilberts enjoyed. And note, the book in 39 E. 3. concludeth, that Gilbert

All this doth appear in the rols of parliament in all the ſeveral times.

These two were commonly called the earls of Kime.

Gilbert Umphrevil was summoned to the parliament under the great seale, *come un pier del realme*.

A bishop elect may sit in parliament as a lord thereof. Hil. 18 E. 1. fo. 4. nu. 105.

Of Knights, Citizens and Burgesses of Parliament.

None of the judges of the kings bench, or common pleas, or barons of the exchequer that have judiciall places can be chosen knight, citizen, or burgesse of parliament, as it is now holden, because they be assistants in the lords house; and yet you may reade in the * parliament roll, an. 31 H. 6. that Thorp baron of the exchequer was speaker of the parliament. But any that have judiciall places in the court of wards, court of duchie, or other courts ecclesiasticall, or civill, being no lord of parliament, are eligible.

* Rot. par. 31 H. 6. nu. 26, 27, 28. Note, he could not be speaker unless he were knight of the shire, &c. in the book of burgesses of the house of commons.

[a] None of the clergy, though he be of the lowest order, are eligible to be knight, citizen, or burgesse of parliament, because they are of another body, viz. of the convocation.

a Alex. Nowels case, who after was deane of Pauls being a prebend. 1 Mar.

A man attainted of treason or felony, &c. is not eligible: for concerning the election of two knights, the words of the writ be, *Duos milites gladiis cinctos magis idoneos, et discretos eligi fac.* And for the election of citizens and burgesses, the words of the writ be, *Duos, &c. de discretioribus et magis sufficientibus*, which they cannot be said to be, when they are attainted of treason or felony, &c.

[48]

Maiors and bailiffes of townes corporate are elegible against the opinion in Brook, *anno* 38 H. 8. tit. Parliament.

Any of the profession of the common law, and which is in practice of the same, is eligible. For he which is eligible of common right cannot be disabled by the said ordinance in parliament in the lords house in 46 E. 3. unlesse it had been by act of parliament: and if it had been by authority of parliament, yet had the same been abrogated by the said statutes of 5 R. 2. stat. 2. cap. 2. and 7 H. 4. cap. 15. which are generall lawes without any exception, as hath been said.

Rot. par. 46 E. 3. nu. 10.

5 R. 2. stat. 2. ca. 4. 7 H. 4. ca. 15.

At a parliament holden at Coventry *anno* 6 H. 4. the parliament was summoned by writ (and by colour of the said ordinance) it was forbidden, that no lawyer should be chosen knight, citizen, or burgesse, by reason whereof this parliament was fruitlesse, and never a good law made thereat, and therefore called *indoctum parliamentum*, or lack-learning parliament. And seeing these writs were against law, lawyers ever since (for the great and good service of the common-wealth) have been eligible: for as it hath been said, the writs of parliament cannot be altered without an act of parliament: and albeit the prohibitory clause had been inserted in the writ, yet being against law, lawyers were of right eligible, and might have been elected knight, citizen, or burgesse in that parliament of 6 H. 4.

Rot. Claus. anno 6 H. 4. See before pa. 10. 4 Petty acts passed at this parliament of little or no effect, as by the same appears.

Rot. parl. 50 E. 3. nu. 83. an ordinance that no sheriffe should be justice of peace, &c. bound not the subject until a statute made 1 Mar. c. 8.

By speciall order of the house of commons the attorny generall is not eligible to be a member of the house of commons.

At the parliament holden 1 *Caroli regis*, the sheriffe for the county of Buckingham was chosen knight for the county of Norff. and returned into the chancery: and having a *subpena* out of the chancery served upon him, at the suit of the lady C. *pendente parliamento*, upon motion, he had the priviledge of parliament allowed

allowed unto him by the judgement of the whole house of commons.

Who shall be Electors of Knights, Citizens, and Burgesses, how and when: and of Elections.

Who shall be electors, and who shall be chosen, and the time, place, and manner of election, and therein the duty of the sheriffe, you may reade in the positive lawes of 7 H. 4. cap 15. 11 H. 4. cap. 1. 1 H. 5. cap. 1. 8 H. 6. cap. 7. 10 H. 6. ca. 2. 23 H 6. cap. 15. 6 H. 6. cap. 4. &c. which need not here be particularly rehearsed.

5 Eliz. cap. 1. No knight, citizen or burgesse can sit in parliament before he hath taken the oath of supremacy.

Vide Rot. claus. 7 R. 2. 7 *Octobris in dors.* Sir Thomas Moreville elected one of the knights for the county of Hertford, *ibid.* James Berners chosen to serve in parliament, and both of them discharged. See the record.

No election can be made of any knight of the shire but between 8 and 11 of the clock in the forenoone: but if the election be begun within that time, and cannot be determined within those hours the election may be made after.

For the election of the knights, if the party of the freeholders demand the poll, the sheriffe cannot deny the scrutiny, for he cannot discerne who be freeholders by the view: and though the party would wave the poll, yet the sheriffe must proceed in the scrutiny.

If the king doth newly incorporate an ancient borough (which sent burgesses to the parliament) and granteth that certain selected burgesses shall make election of the burgesses of parliament, where all the burgesses elected before, this charter taketh not away the election of the other burgesses. And so, if a city, &c. hath power to make ordinances, they cannot make an ordinance that a lesse number shall elect burgesses, for the parliament then made the election

[49] before: for free elections of members of the high court of parliament are *pro bono publico,* and not to be compared to other cases of election of maiors, bailiffes, &c. of corporations, &c.

Ro. par. 5 H. 4. nu. 38. If one be duly elected knight, citizen, or burgesse, and the sheriffe returne another, the returne must be reformed, and amended by the sheriffe: and he that is duly elected must be inserted: for the election in these cases is the foundation, and not the return.

By originall grant or by custome, a selected number of burgesses may elect and binde the residue.

Concerning Charters of Exemption.

The king cannot grant a charter of exemption to any man to be freed from election of knight, citizen, or burgesse of the parliament (as he may do of some inferiour office or places) because the elections of them ought to be free, and his attendance is for the service of the whole realme, and for the benefit of the king and his people, and the whole common-wealth hath an interest therein:

Pasch. 3 E. 3. fo. 19. tit. Coron. F. 161.

and

and therefore a charter of exemption that king H. 6. had made to the citizens of York of exemption in that case, was by act of parliament enacted and declared to be voide. And though we finde some presidents that lords of parliament have sued out charters of exemption from their service in parliament, yet those charters are holden to be void: for though they be not eligible, as is aforesaid, yet their service in parliament is for the whole realme, and for the benefit of the king and his people, of which service he cannot be exempted by any letters patents. And if he hath *læsam phantasiam*, or be extremely sick, or the like, these be good causes of his excuse in not comming, but no cause of exemption, for he may recover his memory and health. &c. So as the said presidents were grants *de facto*, not *de jure*: for if the king cannot grant a charter of exemption from being of the grand assise in a writ of right, or of a jury in an attaint for the mischiefe that may follow in those private actions, *à fortiori*, he cannot grant any exemption to a lord of parliament: for his service in parliament is publick for the whole realme. But if any lord of parliament be so aged, impotent, or sick, as he cannot conveniently without great danger travell to the high court of parliament, he may have license of the king under the great seale to be absent from the same during the continuance or prorogation thereof: but if the rehearsall be not true, or if he recover his health, so as he become able to travell, he must attend in parliament. Or without any such license obtained, if he be so aged, impotent, or sick, as is aforesaid, and yet is amerced for his absence, he may reasonably and honestly excuse himselfe by the statute of 5 R. 2.

29 H. 6. cap. 3. Rot. par. 1 part. 11 E. 3. Rot. pat. 4 part. 1 E. 4. m. 15. pro. Do. Beauchamp. Rot. pat. 2 E. 4. part 2. m. 2. pro Dom. Vesey.

39 E. 3. 15. 34 H. 6. 25. 35 H, 6. 42.

5 R. 2. c. 4. stat. 2.

After the precept of the sheriffe directed to the city or borough for making of election, there ought *secundum legem et consuetudinem parliam.* to be given a convenient time for the day of the election; and sufficient warning given to the citizens or burgesses that have voices, that they may be present: otherwise the election is not good, unlesse such as have voyces doe take notice of themselves and be present at the election.

Any election or voyces given before the precept be read and published, are void and of no force: for the same electors after the precept read and published may make a new election and alter their voyces, *secundum legem et consuetudinem parliamenti.*

Thus much have we thought good to set down concerning knights, citizens, and burgesses, because much time is spent in parliament concerning the right of elections, &c. which might more profitably be imployed *pro bono publico*.

Now to treat more in particular (as it hath been much desired) of the lawes, customes, liberties and priviledges of this court of parliament (which are the very heartstrings of the common-wealth, whereof we have remembred some: and you may see some * few other examples in the margent too long here to be rehearsed) † would take up a whole volume of it selfe: certain it is, as hath been said, that *curia parliamenti suis propriis legibus subsistit.*

See before pag. 24, 25.

* 16 R. 2. rot. clauf. in dorf. rot. parl. 11 R. 2. nu. 7. 1 H. 4. nu. 143. 2 H. 4. nu. 11. 2 H. 4. ca. 1. Rot. parl. 9 H. 4. *Indemnity des Seigniours & commons.* 1 H. 5. nu. 9. cap. 1. 4 H. 8. ca. 8. verf. finem. a generall law. 6 H. 8. c. 6. in the preamb.

All the justices of England and barons of the exchequer are assistants to the lords to informe them of the common law, and there-

† [50]

unto

[a] Rot. parl. 5 H. 4. nu. 12. 23 H. 6. nu. 45. 27 H. 6. nu. 18. 31 H. 6. nu. 26, 27. Lamb. *inter leges Edw. Confessoris, ca. 3. Ad synodos, ad capitula venientibus, sive summoniti sunt, sive per se quid agendum habuerint, sit summa pax.*

unto are called severally by writ. [a] Neither doth it belong to them (as hath been said) to judge of any law, custome, or priviledge of parliament. And to say the truth, the lawes, customes, liberties, and priviledges of parliament are better to be learned out of the rols of parliament, and other records, and by presidents and continuall experience, then can be expressed by any one mans pen.

Per varios actus legem experientia fecit.

Multa multo exercitamentis facilius, quam regulis percipies.

Consultations in Parliament for Maintenance of the Navie.

Rot. par. 45 E. 3. nu. 32. The decay of the navy.

In many parliaments consultations have been had for the maintenance of the navie of England, and remedies provided against decay of the same: as taking one example for many. In the parliament holden in *anno* 45 E. 3. the commons amongst their petitions do affirme, that the decay of the navy doth arise by three causes. First, for that sundry mens ships are seised for the king, long before they serve, whereby the owners are driven at their charges to find their mariners, to their undoing. Secondly, for that merchants, the nourishers of the navy, are oft restrained in their shipping, whereby mariners are driven to seek other trades and livings. Thirdly, for that the maisters of the kings ships do take up masters of other ships as good as their selves are, whereby the most of those ships do lye still, and the mariners enforced to seek new livings: whereof they prayed remedy. To this petition of right the kings royall answer was, That he would provide remedy.

The kings navy exceeds all others.

The kings navy exceeds all others in the world for three things, viz. beauty, strength, and safety. For beauty, they are so many royall palaces: for strength (no part of the world having such iron and timber as England hath) so many moving castles and barbicans: and for safety, they are the most defensive wals of the realm. Amongst the ships of other nations, they are like lions amongst silly beasts, or falcons amongst fearfull fowle.

In the reign of queen Elizabeth (I being then acquainted with this businesse) there were 33 besides pinnaces; which so garded and regarded the navigation of the merchants, as they had safe vent for their commodities, and trade and traffick flourished. A worthy subject for parliaments to take into consideration, and to provide remedy as often as need shall require. For navigation, see Gen. 6. 14. Sapient 14. 6. * *Remp. quasi navem existimare debemus, quæ omnium manibus officioq; indiget, &c.* A leak in a ship is timely to be repaired: for as it is in the naturall body of man, so it is in the politick body of the common-wealth. *Non morbus in plerisq; sed morbi neglecta curatio corpus interficit.* And thus much for consultations in parliament concerning the navy of England.

* Patricius, lib. 5. De institutione reipublicæ.

Of the burgesses of parliament. About 300 sessions of parliament since the conquest.

See the first part of the Institutes. Sect. 164. verb. [*Veigne les burgesses al parliament.*] And there have been since the conquest about 300 sessions of parliament, whereof divers are not printed.

In perusing over the rols of parliament we find first divers acts of parlia-

parliament in print that are not of record in the roll of parliament. Secondly, many acts of parliament that be in the rols of parliament, and never yet printed. Thirdly, divers clauses omitted in the print which are in the parliament roll. Fourthly, more in the print than in the record. Fifthly, many variances between the print and the roll. Sixthly, statutes repealed or disaffirmed, and yet printed, &c. Seventhly, whole parliaments omitted out of the print. Eightly, whole parliaments repealed, or a great part.

And of every of these taking some examples; for to handle all at large would require a whole treatise, which (we having broken the ice) some good man and lover of his countrey (we hope) will undertake to wade thorow. [51]

To the first.

As to the first, these are in print, and not of record, * 20 E. 3. the oath of the judges. 27 E. 3. cap. 4, 5, 6, 7, 8. concerning the Alneger and Gascoigne wines. 37 E. 3. cap. 7. touching silver vessell. 37 E. 3. cap. 19. of hawkes. 2 R. 2. cap. 5. of newes. Vid. 11 R. 2. 11. 2 R. 2. cap. 3. of fained guifts. 7 R. 2. cap. 15. against maintenance. 9 R. 2. cap. 3. of error and attaint. 11 R. 2. cap. 4, 5, & 6. not of record. 13 R. 2. cap. 11. touching clothes. 13 R. 2. cap. 19. concerning salmons. 13 R. 2. cap. 2. touching pilgrims. 13 R. 2. cap. 15. concerning the kings castles and gaoles. 14 R. 2. ca. 7. concerning tinne. 17 R. 2. cap. 8. of unlawfull assemblies. 17 R. 2. cap. 9. concerning salmons. 27 H. 6. cap. 3. touching imployments, &c.

* See the third part of the Institutes, *De corrupto judice.*

To the second. See the Princes case, lib. 8. fo. 1.

As to the second: these acts of parliament are of record, and not in print. an. 11 E. 3. the creation of the duke of Cornwall, &c. by authority of parliament. 3 R. 2. nu. 39. concerning justices of peace, a profitable law for them. 8 R. 2. nu. 31. concerning the jurisdiction of the constable and marshall. 20 R. 2. concerning the legitimation of the children of John of Gaunt duke of Lanc. by Kath. Swinford. 5 H. 4. nu. 24. a commission or act of parliament for arraying and mustering of men. 8 H. 4. nu. 12. clergy exempted from arraying and mustering of men. 11 H. 4. nu. 28. against bribery and brocage in great officers, judges, &c. 11 H. 4. nu. 63. concerning attornies, &c. 6 H. 6. nu. 27. that a queen of England dowager, shall not contract her selfe or marry without the kings license. 9 H. 6. nu. 25. concerning fees of privy counsellors, and other head officers. And very many others.

To the third.

As to the third: in these acts of parliament divers clauses are omitted out of the print, which are in the parliament roll. 36 E. 3. cap. 3. in the act of purveyors, &c. in the clause of the penalty, the steward, treasurer, and controller are expresly named, but omitted in the print. 2 R. 2. stat. 2. cap. 4. in confirmation of liberties, &c. saving the kings regality, is omitted. 13 R. 2. cap. 1. concerning presentations of the king, the last clause, concerning ratifications of the king, is omitted. 13 R. 2. cap. 2. touching provisions. 14 R. 2. cap. 4. nu. 9. concerning regrators of wools, high prices omitted in the print. 17 R. 2. cap. 4. of malt, leaveth out Hertfordshire. 2 H. 5. cap. 3. nu. 38. concerning enquests. 2 H. 5. ca. 1. nu. 30. concerning justices of peace. 9 H. 4. cap 8. nu. 43. concerning provisions. 8 H. 6. nu. 50. cap. 10. concerning proces during the kings will, omitted in the print.

To the fourth.

As to the fourth: in these there is more in the print then in the record.

record. 9 H. 4. cap. 8. nu. 43. touching provisions. 2 H. 5. stat. 2. cap. 3. nu. 38. touching jurors, &c.

To the fifth.

The fifth: In these the print vary from the record in some materiall thing. Generally in all the statutes made concerning provisions, or other the usurpations of the pope, the biting and bitter words are left out in the print. As to take an example or two. Vi. 38 E. 3. in print. cap. 1, 2, 3, 4. and in the roll, nu. 9. &c. 3 R. 2. cap. 3. in print. Rol, nu. 37. &c. the bishops being lord chancellors. 9 R. 2 nu. 1. the print mistake the beginning of the parliament, viz. Monday after S. Luke, for Friday. 9 H. 4. cap. 2. nu. 26. concerning attornies, &c. A roll of parliament intituled 14 E. 4. where it should be 13 E. 4. 9 H. 5. cap. 2 & 3. printed as perpetuall in some books, where they were to endure but untill the next parliament.

To the sixth.

The sixth: statutes pretended to be enacted, and after disaffirmed, and yet printed. 5 R. 2. cap. 5. stat. 2. touching inquiries of heresies. *Anno* 6 R. 2. nu. 52. disaffirmed by the commons, for that they protested it was never their meaning to be justified, and to binde themselves and their successors to the prelats no more then their ancestors had done before them. Robert Braibroke bishop of London was then lord chancellor. By this and that which followes, it appeareth how necessary it was in those dayes to have some of the commons to be (as hath been said) at the ingrossing of the parliament rols, as appeareth rot. parl. *anno* 6 H. 4. nu. 56. 7 H. 4. nu. 65. &c. *et modo tenend'* parl. cap. 8. 2 H. 4. cap. 15. disavowed by the commons, and yet the pretended act printed. 2 H. 5. cap. 6. against preachers, disavowed the next parliament by the commons, for that they never assented, and yet the supposed act printed.

[52]

Rot. par. 11 H. 4. nu. 12. vide 7 H. 4. nu. 11.

To the seventh.

The seventh: whole parliaments omitted out of the print, wherein there be many notable things to be observed. an. 3 E. 2. a parliament holden at Westm. 3 Sept. Dors. claus. 2 E. 2. m. 14. & 22. *annis* 4 E. 2. *apud London.* 5 E. 2. *apud Westm.* 6 E. 2. ib. *bis.* 7 E. 2. ib. 8 E. 2. *apud Eborum.* 11 E. 2. *apud Westm.* 16 E. 2. *apud Rippon, et postea apud Eborum.* an. 6 E. 3. a parliament holden at Westminster the Monday after the feast of S. Gregory. *anno* 8 E. 3. a parliament holden at York the day before the feast of S. Peter *in cathedra. anno* 11 E. 3. at Westm. whereat the prince was created duke of Cornwall, &c. an. 13 E. 3. holden at Westm. in 15 Mich. 22 E. 3. at Westm. the Monday next after the week in the middest of Lent. 29 E. 3. a parliament holden at Westm. the day after S. Martin. 40 E. 3. at Westm. the Monday after the invention of the crosse. 7 R. 2. at Westm. the Friday after the feast of S. Mark, &c.

To the eighth.

The eighth: whole parliaments repealed and made void by subsequent parliaments. 1 H. 4. cap. 3. repealed. 21 R. 2. which had repealed the parliament of 11 R. 2. and reviveth the same. By 39 H. 6. cap. 1. a parliament holden at Coventry *anno* 38 H. 6. is wholly repealed. Rot. par. 12 E. 4. nu. A whole parliament holden *anno* 49 H. 6. *et readeptionis regni sui primo*, is repealed and reversed. [a] *Vide* the parliament of 15 E. 3. repealed. rot. parl. *anno* 17 E. 3. nu. 23. For there it is agreed that the statute of 15 E. 3. shall be utterly repealed, and lose the name of a statute, as contrarie to the laws and prerogative: and for that some articles there made are rea-

[a] Where the printed book suppose that there was another parliament in anno 15 E. 3. whereby the former statute was repealed, the truth is, the parliament was holden at Westm. 15 Pasch. anno 17 E. 3.

reaſonable, it is agreed, that ſuch articles and others agreed in this parliament ſhall be made into a ſtatute by the advice of the juſtices.

[b] Many records of parliament can hardly be underſtood, unleſſe you joyne thereunto the hiſtory of that time. For example: [c] the cardinall of Wincheſter, uncle of the king, declareth in open parliament, that he being in Flanders, in his journey to Rome, returned back of his own will to purge himſelfe of a bruit, that he ſhould be a traytor to the realm, whereof (no accuſation being againſt him) he was eaſily purged by the duke of Gloc. protector, by the kings commandement. But adde the hiſtory thereunto, that the cardinall having certain of the kings jewels in gage, meant to have them brought after him: but theſe jewels being arreſted and ſtay'd at Sandwich by the kings commandement, and the bruit hereof comming to the cardinals eare (he being therewith exceedingly troubled) for the recovery of them, returned in poſt to the parliament. Now after he was purged of the bruit of ſuppoſed treaſon; touching the ſaid jewels ſtayed at Sandwich to the great hindrance of the cardinall, as he complained. It was on a motion on his behalfe, ordered that the cardinall ſhould pay to the king ſix thouſand pound more for them, and lend to the king thirteen thouſand pound, which was done.

[b] Hiſtories ſometime explaine records of parliament.

[c] Rot. parl. 10 H. 6. nu. 14.

This appeareth in the ſame parliament nu. 15.

And for a concluſion hereof, and of this chapter of the high court of parliament, it is to be remembred, that by the ſtatute of 42 E. 3. cap. 1. all ſtatutes are repealed that are againſt Magna Carta, or Carta de Foreſta.

See hereafter cap. 75. how and in what manner parliaments be holden in Scotland. And cap. 77. how and what manner parliaments be holden in Ireland, and how bils ſhall paſſe there, never before this time publiſhed, as we know.

Parliaments in Scotland.
In Ireland.

CAP. II.

Of the Councell Board, or Table.

THIS is a moſt noble, honourable, and reverend aſſembly of the king and his privy councell in the kings court or palace: [a] with this councell the king himſelf doth ſit at his pleaſure. Theſe councellors, like good centinels and watchmen, conſult of, and for the [b] publique good, and the honour, defence ſafety, and profit of the realm. *A conſulendo, ſecundum excellentiam*, it is called the councell table. [c] private cauſes, leſt they ſhould hinder the publique, they leave to the juſtices of the kings courts of juſtice, and meddle not with them: they are called *concilium regis privatum, concilium ſecretum, et continuum concilium regis.* [d] The num-

[a] Rot. clauſ. 12 E. 3. parte 2. m. 19. 39 E. 3. fo. 14. rot. pat. 1 R. 2. parte m. 16. 8 H. 4. nu. 76. &c. Rot. par. 2 H. 6. nu. 15.

[b] Pro bono publico.

[c] 20 E. 3. ca. 1. 25 E. 3. ca. 1. ſtat. 4. 42 E. 3. ca. 3.

Rot. par. 1 R. 2. nu. 87. 112. Rot. par. 7 H. 4. nu. 41. 11 H. 4. nu. 14. 23. 47. [d] Rot. par. 50 E. 3. nu. 10. 12. 1 R. 2. nu. 4. Rot. pat. 1 parte, m. 10. Rot. parl. 7 H. 4. 31. 41, 66, 67. 1. parte of the Inſtitutes, ſect. 164. rot. clauſ. 16 E. 2. m. 5. in Dorſ. *Hen. de bello mente baro de magno et de ſecreto concilio regis jurat'.*

ber

ber of them is at the kings will, but of ancient time there were twelve, or thereabouts. Of the diversity of the kings severall councels, you may read in the first part of the Institutes, sect. 164.

See Rot. pat. 42 E. 3. parte 1. m. 13. *de concilio regis.*

King E. 3. would have his councellors to have four properties. 1, That he be *parcus sui*, knowing that he would never be provident for him, that would not be a good husband for himself. 2. That he should not be *cupidus rei alienæ*, no covetous, nor greedy man, for *ei nihil turpe, cui nihil satis.* 3. That he should be *avarus reipublicæ*, covetous for the kings treasure and commonwealth: and 4. That he *super omnia sit expertus;* in what place the king shall employ him, that he be expert; for great offices are never well managed by deputy, where the officer himself is but a cipher.

Stanf. 72. F. *Senatores sunt partes corporis regis.* Rot. par. 3 H. 6. nu. 3. [e] Inas ca. 46.

To these councellors all due honour and reverence is to be given, for they are incorporated to the king himself, and bear part of his cares, they are his true treasurers, and the profitable instruments of the state. Such honour was given to counsellors of state in ancient time, [e] that if one did strike in a senators or councellors house, or elsewhere in his presence, he was fined.

[f] Alvredus c. 15. Hugh Spencer the father, and Hugh the son evill counsellors.

[f] See Vet. Mag. Cart. fo. 51. 2. parte. Hugh Spencer the father, lord Spencer earl of Winchester, and the kings chamberlain, and Hugh his son earl of Gloc' were adjudged in parliament to be exiled, &c. amongst other articles, six were. First, for that they by their evill covin would not suffer the grandees of the realm, nor the kings good councellors to speak with or come neer the king, or to give him good councell, or that the king might speak with them, but only in the presence or hearing of the said Hugh the father, and Hugh the son or of one of them, and at their wil, and according to such things as pleased them. Secondly, for giving evill councill to the king, not to answer the petitions of the great men and others, but at their pleasure. Thirdly, that they, to attain by their malice and covetousnesse to the disheritance of the great men of the realm, and destruction of the people, put out good and covenable ministers, which had their places by assent, and put in others false and evil of their covin, that they should not cause right to be done. And sherifs, escheators, constables of castles, and others in the offices of the king, not covenable for the king, nor for the people they did make, and caused justices to be made not conusants in the laws of the land, to hear and determine things touching the great men and people of the realm, &c. And so, that which ought to be for the maintenance of the

[54] peace, and of good men, and punishment of evill, was turned to the disheritance of the great men, and destruction of the people. Fourthly, that they falsely and maliciously did counsell the king to raise horse and arms, &c. in destruction of the good people, against

Magna Carta. the form of Magna Carta, and so by their evill counsell would have moved war within the realm, to the destruction of holy church, and of the people, for their proper quarrell. Fifthly, for defeating by their evill counsell that which the king had granted in his parliament by his good counsell, by the assent of the peers of the land, to the dishonour of the king, and against right and reason.

ſon. Sixthly, they would not ſuffer the king to take reaſonable fines, &c. upon alienations, &c. Read the whole.

Hereby it appeareth that one or two ought not to be ſole counſellors, and to make a monopoly thereof: for true it is that Homer ſaith.

Haud quaquam poteris tu fortiter omnia ſolus,
Namque aliis divi bello pollere dederunt,
Huic ſaltandi artem, voce huic, citharaque canendi.
Inſeruitque ſagax alii ſub pectore magnus
*Jupiter ingenium, at multis eſt * utilis ille.*

Homer. See the articles againſt cardinal Woolſey, hereafter cap. Chancery, pa. Art. 9, 10. 15.

* Utilis ſed non ſolus.

[a] The duty of a privy counſellor appeareth by his oath, which conſiſteth on theſe articles or parts.

[a] Ro. par. 11 H. 4. nu. 14. Nota. Vid. Vet. Mag. Cart. parte 1. fo. 165. *juramentum conſiliariorum.* Vide Fleta lib. 1. ca. 17. Nota, vide inf. 5.

1. That he ſhall as far forth as cunning and diſcretion ſuffereth, truly, juſtly and evenly counſell and adviſe the king in all matters to be commoned, treated, and demeaned in the kings councell, or by him as the kings counſellor.

2. Generally in all things that may be to the kings honour and behoof, and to the good of his realms, lordſhips and ſubjects, without partiality, or exception of perſons, not leaving, or eſchewing ſo to do for affection, love, meed, doubt, or dread of any perſon or perſons.

3. That he ſhall keep ſecret the kings counſell, and all that ſhall be commoned by way of councell in the ſame, without that he ſhall common it, publiſh it, or diſcover it by word, writing, or in any otherwiſe to any perſon out of the ſame councell, or to any of the ſame councell, if it touch him, or if he be party thereof.

4. That he ſhall not for gift, meed, nor good, ne promiſe of good by him, nor by mean of any other perſon receive or admit for any promotion, favouring, nor for declaring, letting, or hindring of any matter or thing to be treated or done in the ſaid councell. Rot. par. 11 H. 4. nu. 28.

5. That he ſhall with all his might and power help and ſtrengthen the kings ſaid councell in all that ſhall be thought to the ſame councell for the univerſal good of the king and his land, and for the peace, reſt, and tranquillity of the ſame. Nota, ſupra 2.

6. That he ſhall withſtand any perſon or perſons of what condition, eſtate or degree they be of, that would by way of feat, attempt, or intend the contrary.

7. And generally that he ſhall obſerve, keep and doe all that a good and true counſellor ought to doe unto his ſoveraign lord.

By force of this oath and the cuſtome of the realm he is a privy counſellor without any patent or grant during the life of the king that maketh choice of him.

It is enacted that all the kings counſellors and other head officers there named ſhall have yearly out of the exchequer ſuch fees by way of reward as are there expreſſed. Rot. par. 9 H. 6. nu. 25.

Every privy counſellor hath a voice and place in the court of ſtar-chamber, as in the chapter of the court of ſtar-chamber appeareth.

For the better performance of which oath, king H. 8. would wiſh that his counſellors would commit ſimulation, diſſimulation and partiality to the porters lodge when they came to sit in councell.

[55]

Of the President of the Councell.

Principalis consiliarius.
Capitalis consiliarius.
You shall have what we have observed by our own reading, of others learn that which is here wanting.

There is, and of ancient time hath been a president of the councell, who was sometime called *principalis consiliarius,* and sometime *capitalis consiliarius,* Rot. par. 9 E. 2. *comes Lancast'.* 50 E. 3. 1 R. 2. 1. pars. pat. nu. 22. 1 H. 6. nu. 26, 27. *dux Bedf.* Rot. pat. 1 H. 6. parte 3. *dux Gloc'.* Rot. parl. 10 H. 6. nu. 9. *dux Gloc'.* See rot. parl. 11 H. 6. nu. 19. rot. parl. 22 H. 6. *dux Eborum.* Rot. pat. 13 E. 4. part 1. *Johannes Russel episcopus Roffen' et postea Lincoln' presidens consilii. Int' record curiæ stellat' Johannes Fisher episcopus Roff' præsidens consilii* 12 H. 7. A. 25 H. 8. usq; 37 H. 8. *Carolus Brandon dux Suff' in libro pacis,* rot. parl. 1 E. 6. Pawlet. In the Journall book of parliament. 5 E. 6. & 7 E. 6. *dux Northumb.* 1 & 2 Ph. and Mar. *comes Arundel,* &c.

Acts of parliament naming the presidents of the councell, 21 H. 8. cap. 20. 31 H. 8. ca. 10. 34 H. 8. ca. 1.

This office was never granted but by letters patents under the great seal *durante beneplacito,* and is very ancient: for John bishop of Norwich was president of the councell *in anno 7 regis Johannis,* Holl. fo. 169. Math. Paris 205. and Math. Westm': *dormivit tamen hoc officium regnante magna Elizabetha.*

21 H. 8. ca. 20.
Vid. rot. parl. 50 E. 3. nu. 12.

The lord president is said in the statute of 21 H. 8. ca. 20. to be attending upon the kings most royall person, and the reason of his attendance is, for that of latter times he hath used to report to the king the passages, and the state of the businesse at the councell table. See 50 E. 3. *ubi supra.*

Lord Privy Seal.
See rot. parl. 50 E. 3. nu. 10. & nota bene.

Next to the president of the councell, (as more fully appeareth in the chapter of presidency) sitteth in councell, &c. the lord privy seal, who besides his oath of a privy counsellor taketh a particular oath of the privy seal, which consisteth on four parts: 1. That he, as far forth as his cunning and discretion suffereth, truly, justly, and evenly execute, and exercise the office of the keeper of the kings privy seal to him by his highnesse committed. 2. Not leaving or eschewing so to do for affection, love, meed, doubt, or dread of any person or persons. 3. That he shall take special regard, that the said privy seal in all places where he shall divert unto, may be in such substantiall wise used and safe kept, that no person without the kings speciall commandment or his assent, or knowledge, shall move, seal, or imprint any thing with the same. 4. Generally, he shall observe, fulfill, and doe all and every thing, which to the office of the keeper of the kings privy seal duly belongeth, and appertaineth.

The oath of the Lo. Privy Seal.

This is an office of great trust and skill, that he put this seal to no grant without good warrant, nor with warrant, if it be against law, undue, or inconvenient, but that first he acquaint the king therewith.

27 H. 8. ca. 11.

Upon the lord privy seal are attendant four clerks of the privy seal: now how, and in what wise, the kings grants, writings, and leases, shall passe the three seals, viz. the privy signet, the privy seal,

seal, and the great seal, and the duties of the clerks of the privy signet, and privy seal, and what fees shall be paid, and where none at all, &c. and many articles concerning the passing of the kings grants, &c. you may read in the statute of 27 H. 8. a law worthy of observation. And of this act you may read Lib. 8. fo. 18. b. in the Princes case. This officer is named in the statutes of 2 R. 2. ca. 5. and 12 R. 2. ca. 11. * clerk of the privy seal. In rot. parl. 11 H. 4. nu. 28. *Garden del privy seal:* and in the statute of 34 H. 8. ca. 4. lord privy seal. This seal is called by severall names. By the statute of 11 R. 2. cap. 10. it is provided that letters of the signet, nor of the kings secret seal shall be from henceforth sent in dammage or prejudice of the realm, nor in disturbance of the law. Vide Mir. ca. 3. §. *Exception al power de judge.*

27 H. 8. ca. 11.

* An humble name of a great officer, and in those acts ranked amongst the grandees of the kingdome.

In the statute of *Articuli super Cartas*, cap. 6. 28 E. 1. it is called the little seal, and likewise in the statute of 2 E. 3. cap. 8. it is so called. Regist. fo. 186. *parvum sigillum.* 50 E. 3. nu. 185. F. N. B. 180. Fleta, lib. 2. cap. 12. §. *Est int.' &c. Custos privati sigilli*, clerks of the signet, *clerici signetti* are named in the said act of 27 H. 8. &c. and are four in number attendant upon the kings principall secretary who always hath the keeping of this seal or signet, for sealing of the kings privy letters: these four clerks sit at the secretaries board. He that desireth to read more of the duty of privy counsellors, and how, and for what causes they are to be punished, if they offend; let him read the parliament roll of the 50 year of E. 3. nu. 15, 16, 17, 18, 19, 20, 21, 22, 23, 24, 25, 26, 27, 28, 29, &c. 34, 35, &c.

See the 2 part of the Instit. Artic. super Cart. ca. 6.

[56]

F. N. B. 85. a. See artic. super Cartas, ubi supra, lib. 8. ubi supra.

Acts of parliament concerning the kings privy councell, 25 E. 3. ca. 4. stat. 4. 28 E. 3. cap. 31. 42 E. 3. cap. 3. in print. 9 R. 2. nu. 12. 11 H. 4. nu. 28. 13 H. 4. cap. 7. 3 H. 7. cap. 14. 3 E. 6. cap. 5. 21 Jac. ca. 3. concerning warrants of assistance, &c. 3 Caroli. ca. 1. in the petition of right, concerning loans, &c. imprisonment, &c. martiall law, soldiers, &c.

9 R. 2. nu. 12. and 11 H. 4. nu. 28. not in print. 3 E. 6. ca. 5. repealed.

See hereafter pa.   in the chapter of the Chancery in the articles against cardinall Woolsey, artic. 9, 10, 15, &c. concerning privy councellors.

It appeareth by the writs and records of parliament, that the high court of parliament is resolved to be holden by the king *per advisamentum consilii sui*, that is, by advice of his privy councell.

Orders of parliament for the privy councell, and other things concerning them in the rols of parliament. 50 E. 3. nu. 10. 12. 15. 21. 34. 42 E. 3. nu. 27. Sir John Lees case. 1 R. 2. nu. 87. 1,12. Rot. pat. 1 R. 2. parte 1. m. 16. 2 R. 2. stat. 1. nu. 49. Rot. parl. 1 H. 4. nu. 2. 7 H. 4. nu. 31, 32, 33. 41. 66, 67, 68, &c. 11 H. 4. nu. 14. 13 H. 4. nu. 3. 1 H. 6. nu. 30, 31, 32. 2 H. 6. nu. 15, 16, 17. 8 H. 6. nu. 27, 28. certain articles to the number of eighteen touching the order of the kings councell (amongst which the eleventh is, that all offices and benefices of the kings gift, such as had served him or his father, should be preferred thereunto) are established by the king, the bishops and lords. 9 H. 6. nu. 25. 11 H. 6. nu. 19. Six articles, whereof the last was, that a roll should be made of such as at any time had served in the wars, or otherwise, to the end they should be preferred to offices and benefits. 12 H. 6. nu. 4. *De intendentiis consiliariorum.* 31 H. 6. nu. 30. Vide Rot. pat. 32 H. 6. parte 1. m. 22.

Acts of councell concerning the same. Rot. *finium.* 20 E. 3. m. 8. rot. clauf. 4 H. 4. in dorf. m. 13. clauf 25 E. 3. m. 10. pat. 19 R. 2. parte 2. m. 8. clauf. 20 E. 3. parte 1. m. 26. The clerks of the councell are attendants upon the lords and others of the privy councell. Concerning the clerks of the councell and their duty, see rot. parl. *anno* 1 H. 6. nu. 32. 2 H. 6. nu. 17. &c.

Of these acts of parliament, orders in parliament, and acts of councell we have referred you (for avoiding of tediousnesse) to the originals. *Qui ambulat fradulenter revelat arcana, qui autem fidelis est celat, &c.* (Prov. 11. 13.)

Bonum est abscondere sacramentum regis, opera autem dei revelare honorificum. (Tobie 12. 7.)

Nihil magis optandum, quam ut rerum gerendarum consilia, quoad ejus fieri poterit, quam maxime occulta sint. (Valerius lib. 4. Regulæ.)

(Ovid.)

Eximia est virtus præstare silentia rebus,
Ac contra gravior culpa tacenda loqui.

Nulla sunt meliora consilia, quam quæ ignoraverit adversarius antequam facias, &c. Quid fieri debeat, tractato cum multis; quod facturus sis, cum paucissimis ac fidelissimis, &c. Consilia nisi sint abscondita, exitum raro prospiciunt. (Vegetius lib. 3. de re militari.)

Consilia callida et audacia prima fronte læta, tractatu dura, eventu tristia. (Erasmus in Epist.)

In consiliario imprimis requiritur temperantia, quia * *novandis, quam gerendis rebus aptiora ingenia illa ignea.* And it is certain that men of fiery and furious spirits easily become factious. (* Curtius.)

In consiliario principis tria maxime requiruntur, libertas, fides, et veritas: libertas consilii est ejus vita et essentia, qua erepta, consilium evanescit. (Plinie.)

Privatæ res semper officere, officientque publicis consiliis, pessimum veri affectus et judicii venenum sua cuique utilitas. (Tacitus.)

[57]

Tu civem patremque geris, tu consule cunctis;
Non tibi, nec tua te moveant, sed publica vota.

All which, and much more are comprehended within the orth abovesaid.

Some rules of counsell, which in councell we have observed, we will adde. First, that it is safest to give a king counsell, when he demandeth it. Secondly, the truest and best counsell is ever given to a king, when the question is so evenly propounded, as the counsellor knoweth not which way the king himself inclineth. Thirdly, that * *præpropera concilia sunt raro prospera:* for resolution should never goe before deliberation, nor execution before resolution. Fourthly, when upon debate and deliberation it is by the councell table well resolved, the [a] change thereof upon some private information is neither safe nor honourable, [b] nor that after resolution timely execution be delayed. Fifthly, it is a mean of prosperous successe when the question is debated with a few, not that he should rely upon them, but that thereby the state of the question may be wel understood, to the end the same may be plenarily and fully propounded to the whole board. Sixthly, [c] good counsel is the soul of the state. Seventhly, when counsellors doe hide or disguise

* Book of Judg. 19. ver. ultimo. Consider, consult, and then give sentence.

[a] Seneca. Non semper in uno gradu, sed in una via, non semitat, sed aptat.

[b] Saluft. Priusquam incipias, consulto, & ubi consulueris mature facto opus est.

[c] 11 H. 4. nu. 14.

disguise the truth, it is full of danger both to the king and to [d] themselves. Eighthly, violent courses are like to hot waters that may do good in an extremity, but the use of them doth spoil the stomach, and it will require them stronger and stronger, and by little and little they will lessen their own operation. Lastly, such fear as doth not fal *in constantem virum*, is an enemy to good counsel: for what is fear, [e] but a betraying of such succours, as reason (and counsell) should afford.

d Malum consilium consultori pessimum. Rot. claus. 18 H. 3. nu. 19. Segraves case. Rot. par. 50 E. 3. nu. 24. Segnior Latimers case.

No lord of parliament takes any place of precedency in respect he is a privy counsellour. But under that degree such place a privy councellor shall take, as is set down *in serie ordinum tempore* H. 7. hereafter remembred in the chapter of Precedency.

e Sap. 12.

CAP. III.

[58]

Of the Power and Authority of the Protector and Defender of the Realm and Church of England during the Kings tender Age.

SEE Rot. parl. *anno* 1 H. 6. nu. 26. & 27. 2 H. 6. nu. 16. 6 H. 6. nu. 22, 23, 24. 8 H. 6. nu. 13. 11 H. 6. nu. 19. 32 H. 6. nu. 71. where you shall finde his authority, place, and precedency well expressed and described.

The surest way is to have him made by authority of the great councell in parliament.

See Hollingsheds Chronicle, pa. 1069. which may give you occasion to search for the records of such protectors as are there rehearsed.

CAP. IV.

The Court of the High Steward of England, intituled, *Placita Coronæ coram Thom. Duce N. Seneschallo Angliæ.*

HIS stile is *seneschallus Angliæ*. This office is very ancient, and was before the conquest. For I reade in an ancient and authenticall manuscript, intituled *authoritas seneschalli Angliæ*: where putting an example of his authority, saith: *Sicut accidit Godwino comiti Kanciæ tempore regis Edwardi antecessoris Willielmi ducis Normandiæ pro hujusmodi male gestis et consiliis suis (per seneschallum Angliæ) adjudicatus et forisfecit comitivam suam.*

His stile.
The antiquity of his office.
Nota, then a judge of the peers of the realm.
1 H. 4. 1.
13 H. 8. 13.
Cust. de Norm. cap. 10.

In the time of the Conqueror William Fitz-Eustace was steward of England. And in the reign of William Rufus and H. 1. Hugh

Hugh Grantſemenel baron of Hinkley held that barony by the ſaid office.

Of ancient time this office was of inheritance, and appertained to the earldome of Leiceſter, as it alſo appeareth by the ſaid record: *Seneſchalcia Angliæ pertinet ad comitivam de Leiceſter, et pertinuit ab antiquo.* That is, that the earldome of Leiceſter was holden by doing of the office of ſteward of England. Other records teſtifie that it ſhould belong to the barony of Hinkley. The truth is, that Hinkley was parcell of the poſſeſſions of the earle of Leiceſter, for Robert Bellomont earle of Leiceſter in the reigne of H. 2. married with Petronil daughter and heir of the ſaid Hugh Grantſemenel baron of Hinkley and lord ſteward of England, and in her right was ſteward of England. And ſo it continued, untill by the forfeiture of Simon Mountfort it came to king H. 3. who in the 50 year of his reign, created Edmond his ſecond ſon earle of Leiceſter, baron of Hinkley, and high ſteward of England, which continued in his line untill Henry of Bullinbroke * ſon and heir of John of Gaunt duke of Lancaſter and earl of Leiceſter, who was the laſt that had any eſtate of inheritance in the office of the ſteward of England. Since which time it was never granted to any ſubject, but only *hac vice.* And the reaſon was, for that the power † of the ſteward of England was ſo tranſcendent, that it was not holden fit to be in any ſubjects hands: for the ſaid record ſaith, [b] *Et ſciendum eſt quod ejus officium eſt ſupervidere, et regulare ſub rege, et immediate poſt regem totum regnum Angliæ, et omnes miniſtros legum infra idem regnum temporibus pacis et guerrarum,* &c. and proceedeth particularly with divers exceeding high powers and authorities, which may well be omitted, becauſe they ſerve for no preſent uſe.

[c] And albeit their power and authority have been ſince the reign of H. 4. but *hac vice,* yet is that *hac vice* limited and appointed. As when a lord of parliament is [d] indicted of treaſon or felony, then the grant of this office under the great ſeal is to a lord of parliament, reciting the indictment, [e] *Nos conſiderantes quod juſtitia eſt virtus excellens et altiſſimo complacens, eaq; præ omnibus uti volentes, ac pro eo quod officium ſeneſchalli Angliæ, cujus præſentia pro adminiſtratione juſtitiæ et executione ejuſdem in hac parte facien' requiritur, ut accepimus, jam vacat: de fidelitate, ſtrenuitate, provida circumſpectione, et induſtria veſtris plurimum confidentes ordinavimus et conſtituimus vos ex hac cauſa et cauſis ſeneſchallum noſtrum Angliæ ad officium illud cum omnibus eidem officio in hac parte debitis et pertinentibus hac vice gerend', accipiend', et exercend',* [f] *dantes et concedentes vobis tenore preſentium plenam et ſufficientem poteſtatem et authoritatem, ac mandatum ſpeciale indictamentum prædict.* &c. So as it appeareth, that this great officer is wholly reſtrained to proceed only upon the recited indictment. And he to whom this office is granted, muſt be a lord of parliament, and his proceeding is to be [g] *ſecundum leges et conſuetudines Angliæ,* for ſo is his commiſſion. And hereof you may reade more at large in the third part of the Inſtitutes, cap. High Treaſon. [h] Alſo at every coronation he hath a commiſſion under the great ſeale *hac vice,* to hear and determine the claimes for grand ſerjeanties and other honourable ſervices to be done at the coronation for the ſolemnization thereof: for which purpoſe the high ſteward doth hold his court ſome convenient time before the coronation.

* Rot. par. 21 R. 2. nu. 4. Int. placita coronæ *John of Gaunt* duke of Lanc. and earl of Leiceſter, ſteward of England.

His authority *hac vice:* and therefore he is not mentioned in the ſtatute of 31 H. 8. ca. 10. concerning the placing of great officers.

† [59]

[b] Herewith agreeth the cuſtom. of Norm. cap. 10. fo. 17. Hollenſh. Chron. pa. 866.

[c] His authority (*hac vice*) limited.

[d] See the ſecond part of the Inſtitutes, Mag. Cart. cap. 29. 1 H. 4. cap. 1.

[e] He is ſole judge by the common law, and can make no deputy.

[f] Stanf. pl. cor. 152. 1 H. 4. fo. 1. 13 H. 8. fo. 11. b.

[g] His rule.

[h] His further authority.

nation. See a prefident hereof before the coronation of king R. 2. John duke of Lancafter then fteward of England, (who in claymes before him was ftiled *trefhonorable feignior le roy de Caftle et Leon, et fenefchal D'anglitere)* and held his court in *Alba Aula apud Weftm. die Jovis proxime ante coronationem. Quæ quidem coronatio habita et folemnizata fuit die Jovis fequente,* viz. 16 *Julii anno* 1 R. 2.

The firft that was created *hac vice* for the folemnization of the coronation of H. 4. was Thomas his fecond fon. [i] And upon the arraignment of John Holland earl of Huntingdon, the firft that was created fteward of England *hac vice*, was Edward earl of Devon.

Rot. parl. 37 H. 6. nu. 49. Thomas Courtney earl of Devon was arraigned of high treafon before Humphrey duke of Gloc. *hac vice* fteward of England, and acquited. And fo was [k] the lord Dacres of the north arraigned of high treafon before Thomas duke of Norff. *hac vice* fteward of England and acquited by 20 peers.

[i] V. 1 H. 4. fo. 1. Therefore Tho. Walfingham, p. 363. and others who affirme that he was beheaded at Pleffy in Effex by the commons, do erre.

[k] Term. Pafch. 26 H. 8. of juftice Spilmans report.

When he fitteth by force of his office he fitteth under a cloth of eftate, and fuch as direct their fpeech unto him, fay, Pleafe your grace my lord high fteward of England. The ftile of the faid John of Gaunt was, *Johannes filius regis Angliæ, rex Legionis et Caftellæ, dux Aquitaniæ et Lancaftriæ, comes Derbiæ, Lincolniæ, et Leiceftræ, fenefchallus Angliæ.* And in refpect his power before it was limited was fo tranfcendent, I finde no mention made of this great officer in any of our ancient authors, the Mirror, Bracton, Britton, or Fleta. It feemeth they liked not to treat of his authority. Neither do I finde him in any act of parliament, nor in any book cafe before 1 H. 4. and very few fince: which hath caufed me to be the longer in another place to fet forth his authority and due proceeding upon the arraignment of a peer of the parliament, by judiciall record and refolution of the judges, agreeable with conftant experience.

See the third part of the Inftitutes, cap. Treafon.

For the etymologie and fignification of *(fenefchallus)* fee the firft part of the Inftitutes: and though it hath feverall derivations, yet as being applied to England, it is properly derived from *fen*, that is juftice, and *fchale*, that is, governour or officer, that is, *præfectus feu officiarius juftitiæ*. And this agreeth well with his authority and duty to proceed (as hath been faid) *fecundum leges et confuetudines Angliæ*.

[60]

First part of the Inftit. fect. 78.

It is to be obferved, that as the peers of the realm that be triors or peers, are not fworne, fo the lord fteward being judge, &c. is not fworn: yet ought he according to his letters patents to proceed *fecundum legem et confuetudinem Angliæ*.

CAP. V.

The Honourable Court of Star-Chamber, *coram Rege et Concilio suo:* Of ancient Time, *coram Rege in Camera*, &c.

That it is an eminent court proved by records and acts of parliament.

IN [a] the 28 year of the reign of E. 3. it appeareth, that the retorns *coram nobis*, are in three manners, *coram nobis in camera* (which, it is said, was afterwards called *camera stellata.*) 2. *Coram nobis ubicunque fuerimus in Anglia*, which is the kings bench; and *coram nobis in cancellaria.* And of all the high and honourable courts of justice, this ought to be kept within his proper bounds and jurisdiction.

[a] 22 Lib. ass. pl. 52.

[b] In 38 E. 3. *coram rege et concilio,* John Redland complained of Robert Spinke for delivery of prisoners upon false suggestion made to the king: upon hearing the cause, the defendant was acquitted, the plaintife imprisoned.

[b] Rot. pat. 1 part. m. 13. *Fraud and falsehood.*

[c] In 39 E. 3. Ralph Brantingham one of the chamberlains of the exchequer complained before the king and his councell of Richard Cesterfield clerk deputy of the kings treasurer, in the receipt for divers allowances, payments, &c. unduly made, and for rasing of records, &c. Upon the hearing of the cause by the whole councell, the defendant was acquitted, and the plaintife removed from his office, and committed to prison.

[c] Rot. pat. 1 part. m. 13. *Falshood in an officer and rasing of a record.*

[d] The abbot de Bruera, and Ragge his monk sentenced *coram rege et concilio*, for rasing of letters patents, and inserting other words: and the letters patents by sentence cancelled.

[d] Rot. claus. 42 E. 3. m. 8. in dorf. Vid. rot. pat. 2 R. 2. 1 part. m. *camera stellata.* for rasing. 12 R. 2. cap. 11. dev. le councel.

[e] In *anno* 41 E. 3. in a bill of complaint exhibited to the king by Elizabeth the widow of Nicholas Awdeley plaintife, against Jane Awdeley defendant, who appeared before the kings councell, viz. the chancellour, treasurer, justices, and others assembled *en la chamber des estoiels pres de la receits.*

[e] Rot. claus. 41 E. 3. Cambd. Brit. 130.

[f] A suit depending before the king and councell between the abbot of Saint Austen of Canterbury and others concerning wrecks, &c. The abbot brought his action at the common law against the parties, who being thereupon arrested and imprisoned, the sheriffe was commanded by the kings writ to deliver them, and to forbear to serve any other proces against them: and the reason there yeilded is notable, *Quia non est juri consonum, aut honestum, quod aliquis de hiis quæ coram nobis et concilio nostro in discussione pendent, alibi inde interim placitari debeat, aut apparere.*

[f] Rot. claus. 16 R. 2. in dorf. m. 11.

[g] A suit depending before the king and his councell, beween W. G. of the one part, and H. S. of the other part: a sequestration is ordered for the preservation of the things in question.

[g] Pat. 6 H. 5. & consimile anno 7 H. 5. pro manerio de Fishherwicke in Com' Norff.

In

h In 17 H. 6. an inrolment of a confession of John Ford of Lon. mercer before the lord treasurer and others of the kings councell in the star chamber for the * fraudulent packing and transporting of wooll, with a writ to the sheriffe of London to set him on the pillory. h Rot. claus. 17 H. 6.

The abbot of Westminster exhibited his bill to the king against the sheriffes of London for arresting and drawing out with force a priviledged person out of the sanctuary of S. Martins le grand belonging to the said abbey: which matter after due proceedings being heard in the court of star-chamber before the lords and others of the kings councell, and Hodey and Newton chief justices, which justices determining, that by law the party ought to enjoy the priviledge of sanctuary, the sheriffes were grievously fined in the star-chamber by particular name: which sentence the lord Dier, as he hath reported under his own hand, saw upon a reference to him and justice Southcote out of the star-chamber, Trin. 11 *reginæ Eliz.* concerning the sanctuary of Westm. for Hampton and Whitacres being in for debt. And the lord Dier made this note with his own hand. *Nota, pur le star-chamber.* And this is a notable proof of the jurisdiction of the court for fining, &c. That the bill was exhibited to the king, and that the two chief justices then did sit, and were judges (amongst others) in that court. Anno 29 H. 6. Trin. 1. Eliz. Dier. manuscript not imprinted.

For divers riots, extortions, oppressions, and grievous offences by divers persons done against the kings peace and lawes, to divers of his liege people, commandement hath been given by the kings writs under the great seale (which continue untill this day) to appear before the king in the chancery, or before him and his councell at certain dayes to answer to the premisses, which commandement hath been many times disobeyed. Provision is made by that act for the punishment of such disobedience, as by that act appeareth. True it is, that this act was but temporary, yet it affirmeth so much as before hath been said, Stat. de 31 H. 6. cap. 2. Vide Rot. parl. 1 H. 6. nu. 41.

Anno 35 H. 6. A writ of *certiorari* was directed: *Thomæ Kent clerico concilii: volentes certis de causis certiorari super tenorem cujusdam actus Pasch. ultime præterito apud Westm. in camera stellata concernen' Johannem ducem Norff.* And see there proces of rebellion against the said duke. Ex bundello brevium regis. 35 H. 6.

Robert Davers a counsellor at law by bill exhibited to the king, &c. for defamation of rasing a record. And the said Robert by the kings councell in *camera stellata* was acquited, and John Broket that made the rasure sentenced. Rot. claus. 11 H. 6.

The kings councell assembled in the star-chamber. The lord Cromwels case. Rot. claus. 28 H. 6.

An order in the star-chamber for the duke of Yorks councell to have accesse to him, because called into the chamber by privy seale, &c. Rot. pat. 32 H. 6. m. 20.

An exemplification of a complaint by Richard Heron against John Prout, *coram rege et consiliariis suis in camera stellata*, for a great misdemeanour concerning wools. Pat. 3 E. 4. part. 1.

Anno 8 E. 4. proceeding by English bill, answer, replication, &c. *coram rege et concilio.* Rot. petit. 8 E. 4.

Anno 20 E. 4. a sentence in the star-chamber for turbulent and undue elections between the abbot of Bury and the inhabitants. Rot. pat. 20 E. 4. part. 2.

We

We have omitted many other records, but because they be of like nature we have contented our self with these. And now we will consult with our book cases, and reports of law: wherein either *coram rege et concilio*, or *coram rege et concilio in camera stellata*, is named.

Book cases and reports of law. 39 E 3. fo 14. 19 ass. pl. 1. 40 ass. 38. 13 E. 4. 9. *in camera stellata.* Vid. 27 E. 3. cap. 13. 21 E. 4. 71. *in camera stellata.* 2 R. 3. fo. 2. & 11. *in camera stellata.* 1 H. 7. 3. *in camera stellata.* This court in ancient times sat but rarely, for three causes. First, for that enormious and exorbitant causes which this court dealt withall only in those days rarely fell out. Secondly, this court dealt not with such causes, as other courts of ordinary justice might condignely punish, *ne dignitas hujus curiæ vilesceret.* Thirdly, it very rarely did sit, lest it should draw the kings privie council from matters of state, *pro bono publico*, to hear private causes, and the principall judges from their ordinary courts of justice.

[62]

3 H. 7. ca. 1. That which now is next to be considered in *serie temporis* is the statute of 3 H. 7. the letter whereof followeth:

21 H. 8. ca. 20. The president of the kings councell added.

It is ordained that the chancelour and treasurer of England, and the keeper of the kings privy seal, or two of them, calling to them a bishop and a temporal lord of the kings most honourable privy councell, and the two chief justices of the kings bench and common place for the time being, or other two justices in their absence, upon bill or information put to the said lord chancelour or any other against any person for unlawfull maintenance, giving of liveries, signs and tokens, and reteyners by indentures, promises, oaths, writings or otherwise, imbraceries of his subjects, untrue demeaning of sherifs in making of pannels, and other untrue returns, by taking of mony, by injuries, by great riots, and unlawfull assemblies, have authority to call before them by writ or privy seale the said misdoers, and they and other by their discretion, by whom the truth may be known to examine, and such as they find therein defective, to punish them after their demerits, after the form and effect of statutes thereof made in like manner and form as they should, and ought to be punished, if they were thereof convict after the due order of law.

Camden Brit. *Cameræ stellatæ authoritatem prudentissimus princeps Henricus septimus ita parliamentaria adauxit et constabilivit, nonnulli primum instituisse falso opinantur.*

Upon this statute and that which formerly hath been said, these six conclusions do follow. The first conclusion is, that this act of 3 H. 7. did not raise a new court: for there was a court of starchamber, and all the kings privy councel judges of the same. For if the said act did establish a new court, then should those four or any two of them be only judges, and the rest that they should call to them should be but assistants, and aidants, and no judges: for the statute of 31 E. 3. cap. 12. which raiseth a new court, and before

fore new judges, is introductory of a new law, by having conusance of error in the exchequer, which shall be reversed in the exchequer chamber before the chancelour and treasurer, or calling to them two judges, there the chancelour and treasurer are only judges in the writ of error, and so in the like. But it is clear that the two justices in the star-chamber are judges, and have voices, as it hath been often resolved, and daily experience teacheth. And further to clear this point, if the justices should be but assistants and no judges in the star-chamber, for that they are to be called, &c. then, and for the same reason should neither lord spirituall nor temporall, nor other of the privy councell be judges, nor have voices in the court of star-chamber. And therefore the sudden opinion in 8 H. 7. and of others not observing the said distinction between acts declaratory of proceedings in an ancient court, and acts introductory of a new law in raising of a new court, is both contrary to law, and continuall experience. 8 H. 7. 13. Plow. Com. 393.

The second conclusion is, that the act of 3 H. 7. being in the affirmative is not in some things pursued. For where that act directeth that the bill or information should be put to the lord chancelour, &c. all bils and informations in that court are constantly and continually directed to the kings majesty, as they were before the said act; and it is a good rule, that where the act of 3 H. 7. is not pursued, there (if there be many judiciall presidents in another sort) they must have warrant from the ancient court; and yet it is good (as much as may be) to pursue this act, there being no greater assurance of jurisdiction then an act of parliament. And where there be no such presidents, then the statute as to the judges must be pursued: and that was the reason that in default of others, Sir Christopher Wray chief justice of England for a time was made lord privy seal to sit in the star-chamber, *ne curia deficeret in justitia exhibenda*. [63]

Thirdly, that this act being (as hath been said) in the affirmative, and enumerating divers particular offences, albeit (injuries) is a large word, yet that court hath jurisdiction of many other, as is manifest by authority, and daily experience, and this must of necessity be in respect of the former jurisdiction.

Fourthly, this act in one point is introductory of a new law, which the former court had not, viz. to examine the defendant, which being understood after his answer made, to be upon oath upon interrogatories, which this ancient court proceeding in criminall causes had not, nor could have but by act of parliament, or prescription, the want whereof especially in matters of frauds and deceits (being like birds closely hatched in hollow trees) was a mean that truth could not be found out, but before the statute the answer was upon oath.

Fifthly, where it is said in this act, And to punish them after their demerits after the form and effect of statutes made, &c. The plaintife may choose whether he will inform upon such statutes as this act directeth, or for the offence at the common law, as he might have done before this act, which proveth that this act taketh not away the former jurisdiction.

6. Lastly, that the jurisdiction of this court dealeth not with any offence, that is not *malum in se*, against the common law, or *malum prohibitum*, against some statute.

It

It is to be obſerved that neither the ſtatutes of 37 E. 3. ca. 18. 38 E. 3. cap. 9. 42 E. 3. ca. 3. 17 R. 2. ca. 6. nor any other ſtatute taketh away the juriſdiction of any ſetled court of juſtice, neither is the court of ſtar-chamber named in any of them, and yet was it a court then and before that time.

Divers ſpeciall acts of parliament have been alſo juriſdiction to this court, viz. 12 R. 2. ca. 11. 2 R. 2. cap. 5. 13 H. 4. cap. 7. 33 H. 8. cap. 1. 4 & 5 Ph. and M. cap. 8. 5 Eliz. ca. 9, 10. & cap. 14. 27 Eliz. cap. 4.

The juriſdiction of this court

And ſeeing the proceeding according to the laws and cuſtomes of this realm cannot by one rule of law ſuffice to puniſh in every caſe the exorbitancy and enormity of ſome great horrible crimes and offences, and eſpecially of great men, this court dealeth with them, to the end that the medicine may be according to the diſeaſe, and the puniſhment according to the offence, *Ut pœna ad paucos, metus ad omnes perveniat*, without reſpect of perſons, be they publique or private, great or ſmall.

Camden Brit. 130. *In camera ſtellata tractantur criminalia, perjuria, impoſturæ, dolus malus, exceſſus, &c.*

As for oppreſſion, and other exorbitant offences of great men, (whom inferiour judges and jurors (though they ſhould not) would in reſpect of their greatneſſe be affraid to offend) bribery, extortion, maintenance, champerty, imbracery, forgery, perjury, diſperſers of falſe and dangerous rumours, news, and ſcandalous libelling, falſe and partiall miſdemeanours of ſherifs and bailifs of liberties, frauds, deceits, great and horrible riots, routs, and unlawfull aſſemblies, ſingle combats, challenges, duels, and other hainous and extraordinary offences and miſdemeanours; but ordinary, and ſuch offences as may be ſufficiently and condignly puniſhed by the proceeding of the common laws, this court leaveth to the ordinary courts of juſtice and dealeth not with them, *ne dignitas hujus curiæ vileſceret*, as before is ſaid.

For proceeding, *ore tenus*, ſee before ro. clauſ. 19 H. 6. John Fords caſe. Rot. clauſ. 42 E. 3. the abbot of Brueries caſe, &c. *In notoriis ordo eſt ordinem juris non ſervare.*

The proceeding in this court is by bill or information, by examination of the defendant upon interrogatories, and by examination of witneſſes, and rarely *ore tenus*, upon the confeſſion of the party in writing under his hand, which he again muſt freely confeſſe in open court, upon which confeſſion in open court, the court doth proceed. But if his confeſſion be ſet down too ſhort, or otherwiſe then he meant, he may deny it, and then they cannot proceed againſt him but by bill or information, which is the faireſt way.

[64]

The informations, bils, anſwers, replications, &c. and interrogatories are in Engliſh, and ingroſſed in parchment, and filed up. All the writs and proceſſe of the court are under the great ſeal: the ſentences, decrees and acts of this court are ingroſſed in a fair book with the names of the lords and others of the kings councell and juſtices that were preſent and gave their voices.

Paſc. 12 Ja. Reg.

In an information in this court by the atturny generall againſt Sir Stephen Procter, Birkenhead and others for conſpiracy againſt, and ſcandall of the earl of Northampton, and Edward lord Wootton two of his majeſties privy counſell: at the hearing of which cauſe there ſat eight in court, and four of them condemned the defendant: and the lord chancelour, the two biſhops, and the chancelour of the exchequer acquitted him. And the queſtion was, whether the defendant ſhould be condemned or no: and herein it was moved by the kings learned councell, that when the voices be

equall,

equall, that in that caſe, of which part the lord chancellor was, on that ſide it ſhould be decreed, without regard, whether it was for the plaintif or defendant: and it was reſolved, that regularly *et de communi jure*, in reſpect of the equality of the voices no ſentence could be given in that caſe, as it holdeth in the high court of parliament, and all other courts, according to the old rule, *paribus ſententiis reus abſolvitur*. And therefore the preſidents of this court were to be ſearched; for except preſidents could make a difference between this court and others, the defendant could not be ſentenced. Whereupon the court referred this queſtion to the two chief juſtices, that they calling unto them the kings learned councell to view preſidents, whether by the cuſtome of this court the common rule in other courts is altered. Before whom in the preſence of the kings learned councell two preſidents were produced for proof of the ſaid cuſtome, viz. one Termino Hil. *anno* 39 Eliz. between Gibſon plaintif, and Griffith and others defendants: wherein the complaint was for a riot. And upon hearing of the cauſe eight ſat in court, and four gave their ſentence that the defendants were guilty, and the other four, whereof the lord chancelour was one, did acquit the defendants, and no ſentence of condemnation was ever entred. But the juſtices took it, that that preſident tended not to prove any ſuch cuſtome, for it agreed with the rule in other courts. Another preſident was ſhewed, Termino Hil. 45 Eliz. in an information by the queens atturny generall againſt Bathern and others for forging of a will, &c. Upon the hearing of the cauſe, the preſence conſiſting of eight, whereof four gave ſentence againſt the defendant for forgery, and to be puniſhed according to the ſtatute of 5 Eliz. the other four, whereof the lord chancelour was one, found him guilty of a miſdemeanour, and not of the forgery, and impoſed a fine of five hundred pound only, and impriſonment, and that was entred according to the lord chancelours voice. But no rule of court was ſhewed for entring thereof in that manner: ſo as it appeared not that it was ever moved, or debated in court, and in that caſe all concluded againſt the defendant, and it is but one preſident. Now whether this one, being ſuch a one as it is, and ſo late, be ſufficient to alter the generall law and courſe of all other courts, I leave to the judgment of this honourable court: and ſentence was never given againſt Sir Stephen Procter agreeable to the generall rule in other courts. See Rot. parl. 8 H. 6. nu. 28.

Erodius fo. 112.

Hil. 39 Eliz. in camera ſtellata, Gibſons caſe.

Hil. 45 El. in camera ſtellata, Batherns caſe.

Lawrence Hide and Henry Hide eſquires, exhibited a bill of complaint againſt George Coriet and others upon the ſtatute of 32 H. 8. cap. 9. for unlawfull maintenance; and complained for three ſeverall leaſes for certain years of the parſonage of Dynton in the county of Wiltſ. whereof the leſſor nor any of his anceſtors were in poſſeſſion within a year before, &c. and purſued the ſtatute: upon which part of the bill (for the bill concerned riots and other things) the defendant demurred in law, and the cauſes of the demurrer were. Firſt, that by the ſaid act this court had no juriſdiction of this cauſe upon this ſtatute, becauſe that the act which is introductory of a new law did not give juriſdiction to this court, but the ſuit muſt be in the courts of the common law upon this act, which (ſaid they) alſo appeared, in that in the remedy given by the act in this clauſe, *In which action, bill, plaint,* or

Mic. 36 & 37 El.

or information no essoign, protection, wager of law, or injunction shall be allowed, and that no essoign, &c. did lie in this court. The second objection was, this court had no power to give the plaintif remedy to have execution in this court of the penalty given by this act. Whereunto upon great advisement it was answered and resolved. As to the first: that the statute did give jurisdiction to this court, for it is one of the kings courts, &c. intended in the act: and the statute of 3 H. 7. declareth that this court hath jurisdiction of maintenance, and this act of 32 H. 8. doth adde but a greater penalty: and as to the clause of essoin, &c. it must be construed *reddendo singula singulis, &c.* for as no essoin, &c. lieth in this court, so no injunction is awarded in the court of common pleas, &c. As to the second: it was resolved that this court had power in this case to grant execution of the penalty inflicted by this act, as in a like case had been done, in the case of James Taverner. And both these points had formerly been resolved in this court, 14 Maii. 27 Eliz. between Robert Bradshaw esquire plaintif, and Robert Charnock esquire defendant, upon this statute, and the case decreed accordingly, and a commission awarded out of this court, to enquire of the value, &c. And for these causes by the rule of the whole court, the demurrer was over-ruled, and the defendant ordered to answer.

Dier Mich. 6 & 7 Eliz. fo. 236.

Dier 15 El. 323. in camera stellat'. Taverners case. Pasc. 27 El. in camera stellata. Charnocks case.

This court sitteth twice in the week in the term time, viz. on Wednesdays, and Fridays, except either of those dayes fall out to be the first or last day of the terme, and then the court sitteth not, but it constantly holdeth the next day after the terme ended: but if any cause be begun to be heard in the terme time, and for length or difficulty cannot be sentenced within the term, it may be continued and sentenced after the term.

The dignity of this court.

It is the most honourable court, (our parliament excepted) that is in the Christian world, both in respect of the judges of the court, and of their honourable proceeding according to their just jurisdiction, and the ancient and just orders of the court. For the judges of the same are (as you have heard) the grandees of the realm, the lord chancelor, the lord treasurer, the lord president of the kings councell, the lord privy seal, all the lords spirituall, temporall, and others of the kings most honourable privy councell, and the principall judges of the realm, and such other lords of parliament as the king shall name. And they judge upon confession, or deposition of witnesses: and the court cannot sit for hearing of causes under the number of eight at the least. And it is truly said, *Curia cameræ stellatæ, si vetustatem spectemus, est antiquissima, si dignitatem, honoratissima.* This court, the right institution and ancient orders thereof being observed, doth keep all England in quiet.

The judges of this court.

Camb. ubi supra.

Albeit the stile of the court be *coram rege et concilio*, yet the kings councell of that court hear and determine causes there, and the king in judgment of law is always in court. As in the kings bench the stile of the court is *coram rege*, and yet his justices who are his councell of that court doe hear and determine, and so *coram rege in cancellaria*, and the like.

So this court being holden *coram rege et concilio*, it is or may be compounded of [a] three severall councels. That is to say, of the lords and others of his majesties privy councell, always judges without

[a] See the 1. part of the Institutes. sect. 164. *Verb. veigne les Burgesses al parliament.* 4 E. 3. 2. 3 ass. pl. 15.

§ out

out appointment, as before it appeareth. 2. [b] The judges of either bench and barons of the exchequer are of the kings councel for matter of law, &c. and the two chief juſtices, or in their abſence other two juſtices, are ſtanding judges of this court. 3. The lords of parliament are properly *de* [c] *magno concilio regis*, but neither theſe, being not of the kings privy councell, nor any of the reſt of the judges or barons of the exchequer are ſtanding judges of this court.

[b] 39 E. 3. 5. 19 E. 3. Judgment. 174. W. 1. ca. 1. 17 E. 2. *Stat. de Templariis.* 16 R. 2. *Stat. de Premunire.* 43 Aſſ. pl. 15. Regiſt. 124, 12: 191. 27 H. 6. 5. 2 R. 3. 10.

[c] 27 Aug. 5 H. 4. in the exchange between the king and the earl of Northumberland, *in turre.* 37 E. 3. ca. 18. &c. Note the parliament is called *commune concilium.*

The name of this court.

[66]

It is now, and of ancient time hath been called the chamber of the [d] ſtars, the [e] ſtar-chamber, the [f] ſtarred chamber, in reſpect the roof of the court is garniſhed with golden ſtars. Some have imagined that it ſhould be called the ſtar-chamber, becauſe *crimina ſtellionat'* are there handled: others of this Saxon word *ſteeran*, to ſteer or rule as doth the pilot, becauſe this court doth ſteer and govern the ſhip of the common-wealth. Others, becauſe it is full of windows: but the true cauſe of the name is, becauſe, as is aforeſaid, the roof is ſtarred. In all records in Latin, it is called *camera ſtellata.*

[d] 41 E. 3. ubi ſup.
[e] In many of the records before cited.
[f] 25 H. 8. ca. 1. Lambard. Sir Tho. Smith. lib. 2. ca. 4.

The proceſſe.

The proceſſe in this court is *ſuppœna*, attachment, proceſſe of rebellion, &c. all under the great ſeal.

Officers of the court ſworn.

In this court there is the clerk of the councell, which is an office of great account, and truſt, for he is to receive, endorſe, enter, keep, and certifie the bils, pleadings, records, orders, rules, ſentences and decrees of the court: and I find that in former times men of great account have had that office in this court: as to give you a little taſte thereof: king H. 6. by his letters patents, 15 July *anno regni ſui* 22. granted the ſame to Thomas Kent doctor of the law for his life, calling him *clericum concilii noſtri*, and ſoon after ſwore him of his privy councell. King H. 7. *anno* 1. of his reign, granted the ſame office to John Bladeſwell doctor of laws for tearm of his life: but hereof this little taſte ſhall ſuffice.

Laſtly, it remaineth to be ſeen what juriſdiction this court hath in puniſhment, and where, and in what caſes this court may inflict puniſhment by pillory, papers, whipping, loſſe of ears, tacking of ears, *ſtigmata* in the face, &c. (For it extendeth not to any offence that concerns the life of man or obtruncation of any member, the ears only excepted, and thoſe rarely and in moſt hainous and deteſtable offences.) But herein the ſureſt rule is, that ſeeing it is an ancient court, the preſidents of the court are to be followed, and the rather for that the court conſiſteth of ſuch learned and honourable judges. And novelties without warrant of preſidents are not to be allowed: generally ſome certain rules are to be followed, eſpecially where no preſidents are extant in the caſe. * *Quod arbitrio judicis relinquitur, non facile trahit ad effuſionem ſanguinis:* for generall acts of parliament which inflict puniſhment, viz. *ſur forfeiture de corps et de avoir, &c.* theſe are expounded not to extend to life, or member, but to impriſonment, &c.

Eccleſiaſticus 20. 8. *Qui poteſtatem ſibi ſumit injuſte, odietur.*

* *See ſtatut. de moneta temps* E. 1. 35 E. 1. *de Carliſle.* 20 E. 3. ca. 4. Vid. 23 El. ca. 2. And note where he ſhall loſe his ears for defamation of the queen.

See the firſt part of the Inſtitutes, ſect. 745. verb. Felony. *Majore*

jore pœna affectus, quam legibus statut' est, non est infamis. Pœna gravior ultra legem posita æstimationem conservat. Confessus in jure pro judicato habetur, cum quodammodo sua sententia damnatur. Cum confitente sponte mitius est agendum.

In hac curia non agitur de delictis ordinariis, ne dignitas hujus curiæ vilesceret.

Quicquid judicis authoritati subjicitur, novitati non subjicitur.

[67]

CAP. VI.

A Court for Redresse of Delayes of Judgements in the Kings great Courts.

14 E. 3. cap. 5. stat. 1. Rot. parl. 2 R 2. nu. 63. confirmed by parliament.

THIS court is raised by the statute of 14 E. 3. which followeth in these words.

Judgements delayed.

Item, Because divers mischieves have happened of that, that in divers places, as well in the chancery, as in the kings bench, the common bench, and in the exchequer, before the justices assigned, and other justices to hear and determine deputed, the judgements have been delayed, sometimes by difficulty, sometimes by divers opinions of the judges, and sometime for some other cause: it is assented, established, and accorded, that from henceforth at every parliament shall be chosen a prelate, two earls, and two barons, which shall have commission and power of the king to heare by petition delivered unto them the complaints of those that will complaine them of such delayes and grievances made, and they shall have power to do come before them at Westminster, or elsewhere, where the places or any of them shall be, the tenor of records and processes of such judgements so delayed, and to cause the same justices to come before them, which shall be then present to hear their cause and reasons of such delayes: which cause and reason so heard by * good advice of themselves, the chancelor, treasurer, the justices of the one bench, and of the other, and other of the kings councell, as many and such as shall seem convenient, shall proceed to take a good accord, and make a good judgement: and according to the same accord so taken, the tenor of the same record, together with the judgement which shall be accorded, shall be remaunded before the justices, before whom the plea did depend; and that they shall give judgement according to the same record: and in case it seemeth to them that the difficulty be so great, that it may not well be determined without assent of the parliament, that the said tenor or tenors shall be brought by the said prelate, earles, and barons in the next parliament

* Nota, by good advice of the chancellour, treasurer, and justices.

Good accord.

Vide Regist. fo. 124. b. Rex Johanni de B. Militi, &c.

parliament, and there shall be a final accord taken what judgement ought to be given in this case, and according to this accord it shall be commanded to the judges before whom the plea did depend, that they shall proceed to give judgement without delay.

Before the making of this statute delay of judgements was forbidden both by the common law, and by acts of parliament. By the common law. 1. It is required, that *plena et celeris justitia fiat partibus*, &c. not *plena* alone, nor *celeris* alone, but both *plena et celeris*. All writs of *præcipe quòd reddat*, are, *Quòd juste et sine dilatione reddat*, &c. All judicial writs are *sine dilatione*, &c. 2. There did and yet doth lye a writ *de procedendo ad judicium*, when the justices or judges of any court of record, or not of record, delayed the party plaintife or defendant, demandant or tenant, and would not give judgement: and thereupon an *alias plur'*, and an attachment, &c. doth lye. And the words of the writ be, *Quia redditio judicii loquelæ quæ est coram vobis*, &c. *de quadam transgressione eidem A. per præfat' B. illata, ut dicitur, diuturnam cepit dilationem ad grave damnum ipsius A. sicut ex querela sua accepimus, vobis præcipimus quod ad judicium inde reddendum cum ea celeritate quæ secundum legem et consuetudinem regni nostri procedas*, &c.

Regist. 131. a, F. N. B. 23. c. And so upon conusans granted.

Regist. fo. 22. F. N. B. 153. b. &c. Cust. de Norm. cap. 27.

[68]

Diuturna dilatio.

3. Likewise when justices or judges of any court of record, or not of record gave judgement, and delayed the party of his execution, the party grieved may have a writ *de executione judicii*; by which writ the justices or judges are commanded, *Quod executionem judicii nuper redditi*, &c. *de loquela quæ fuit*, &c. *per breve nostrum*, &c. *sine dilatione fieri fac'*. And thereupon an *alias*, *plur'* and attachment, &c. do lye.

Regist. fo. 18. F.N.B. fo. 20. a. &c.

4. By the meeting together upon adjournment of the cause out of the court, where the cause dependeth, &c. All the judges, &c. which now we call an exchequer chamber cause, warranted by the common law and ancient presidents before this statute: and the frequent use of this court of exchequer chamber hath been the cause that this court upon the act of 14 E. 3. hath been rarely put in ure.

See hereafter, ca. Exchequer and Exchequer Chamber.

5. By the kings writ comprehending *quod si difficultas aliqua interfit*, that the record should be certified into the parliament, and to adjourne the parties to be there at a certain day. *Si obscurum et difficile sit judicium, ponantur judicia in respect' usque magnam curiam.* An excellent record, whereof you may read in the parliament holden at Westminster the Tuesday after the translation of Becket, *anno* 14 E. 3.

2 E. 3. fo. 7. Ellys Callers case. Bract. lib. 1. ca. 2. rot. parl. 14 E. 3. nu. ult. Sir Geff. Stantons case.

Secondly, by acts of parliament. *Nulli vendemus, nulli negabimus, aut differemus justitiam vel rectum.*

Mag. Cart. ca. 29.

That it shall not be commanded neither by the great-seale, nor by the little-seale, nor by letters, nor any other cause to delay right: and albeit such commandement come, &c. that by them the justices surcease not to do right in no manner. *Vide* 2 E. 3. cap. 8. 14 E. 3. cap. 14. 18 E. 3. stat. 3. 2 R. 2. a statute not in print, Rot. parl. nu. 51. whereby it is enacted, that no justice shall stay justice for any writ, letter of the great-seal or privy-seal, or other commandement whatsoever against the laws and statutes before that

2 E. 3. fo. 3. per Aldham. 14 E. 3. jour. 24. 18 E. 3. 47. 57. 31 E. 3. an. 161. 39 E. 3. 37. 11 H. 4. 5. 76. 9 H. 6. 58. b. 5 E. 4. 132. Fortesc. cap. 5. F. N. B. 240. d.

that time made, Rot. par. 2 H. 4. nu. 64. *anno* 5 H. 4. nu. 33. all which are declaratory of the common law. * And upon the said act of 2 E. 3. a writ is framed, directed to the justices, by which they are commanded, *Quod ad justitiam partibus, &c. faciend' virtute alicujus mandati de magno sigillo, et parvo sigillo vobis direct' seu dirigend' nullatenus supersedeatis, &c.* And thus much for the common law and acts of parliament.

* Regist. fo. F.N.B. 240. d.

This statute of 14 E. 3. cap. 5. consisteth of two generall parts, viz. the preamble and the body of the act. In the preamble three things are to be observed. 1. That (notwithstanding the provision of the common law) mischiefs do happen by delay of judgements. 2. It enumerateth in what courts these delayes do happen, viz. in the chancery, in the kings bench, the common bench, and the exchequer, the justices assigned, and other justices to hear and determine deputed. 3. It declareth how these delayes have grown, viz. sometime for difficulty of the matter in law, sometime in diversity of opinion of the judges, and sometimes for some other cause, that is, by commandements, letters, or messages of the king or great men, &c. In the body of the act we have collected many observations. 1. That at every parliament there shall be chosen a prelate, two earls, and two barons, (or one bishop, two earles, and two barons.) viz. At this parliament were chosen, 1. John Stratford archbishop of Canterbury, (a man famous for learning, loyalty, and vertuous living.) 2. Rich. Fitzalan earle of Arundel, a man of great wisdome, prowes, and integrity. 3. William Clynton earle of Huntingdon, and admirall of England, a man lately before advanced for his singular valour, wisdome, and vertue. 4. The lord Wake of Lidel. and 5. Ralph lord Basset of Drayton, two of the most renowned barons of England. *Quos omnes honoris causa nomino.*

[69]

2. This act doth appoint that the prelate, two earls, and two barons are to have a commission and power of the king under the great seal (and none of them can be absent) which commission is to endure untill the next parliament.

3. This commission and power consisteth on ten parts. 1. *Ad audiendum*, to hear the petition delivered to them, the complaints of those that will complain to them of such delayes or grievances made. 2. *Ad venire faciend'* to do come before them at Westminster, or elsewhere, the tenor of the records and processes of such judgements so delayed; and this is to be done by the kings writ of *certiorari.* 3. *Ad venire faciend'*, to cause the same justices to come before them. 4. *Ad audiend' suas rationes et causas talium dilationum*, to hear their reasons and causes of such delayes which ought to be entred of record. 5. Which causes and reasons so heard, *ad procedendum*, to proceed to make a good accord. 6. But this must be done not only by themselves, but by the good advice of certain assistants appointed by the act, viz. the chancelour, treasurer, the justices of the one bench and the other, and other of the kings councell, as many, and such as they shall think convenient. 7. *Ad capiendum*, to take a good accord of the assistants. 8. *Ad faciendum*, to make a good judgement. 9. *Ad remandandum*, to remaund before the justices, before whom the plea did depend, the tenor of the said record, together with the judgement that so shall be accorded.

corded. Lastly, that those justices shall presently give judgement according to the said record.

A commission granted in 18 E. 3. grounded upon this statute, and referring to the same being enacted, as there it appeareth, at a parliament holden *die Mercurii proxim' post medium quadragesimæ anno* 14 *E.* 3. *regni Angliæ et Franciæ primo*, there being two parliaments in that year, which you may reade, being worthy of observation, for it is a good exposition of this act.

Rot. pat. 18 E. 3. 2 part.

4. It is further provided by the said act of 14 E. 3. that in case it seemeth to them, that the difficulty is so great, that it cannot well be determined without assent of parliament, that the tenor or tenors shall be brought by the said prelate, earls, and barons unto the next parliament, and there shall finall accord be taken what judgement shall be given in this case.

Rules concerning delayes.

[a] It is better that the demandant be delayed, then the tenant disherited, or that the law be altered. Shard. We cannot nor will delay any man in respect of our oath.

[b] The justices ought to delay no man in the name of the king where the king hath no right. The demandant shall not be legally delayed twice for one cause.

[c] Delay in a *quare impedit*, though it be by essoign, is a disturbance. [d] *Semper fur est in mora.* [e] *In circuitu impii ambulant.*

[f] In divers cases the party grieved shall have an action for unjust delay.

[g] *Tolle moram, semper nocuit differre paratis*

But seeing neither the common law, nor any of the acts of parliament do extend to ecclesiasticall courts, it is then demanded, what if an inferiour ordinary will refuse, or delay to admit and institute a clerk presented by the right patron, to a church within his dioces, or the like: or delay, or refuse to give sentence in a cause depending before him. It is answered, that the archbishop of the province may grant his [h] letters under his seale to all and singular clerks of his province, to admonish the ordinary, within nine dayes to performe that which by justice is desired, or otherwise to cite him to appeare before him or his officiall at a day in those letters prefixed, and to cite the party that hath suffered such delay, then and there likewise to appeare, and further to intimate to the said ordinary, that if he neither perform that which is enjoyned, nor appear, he himselfe without further delay will performe the justice required. Or in the former of the said cases, the party delayed may have his *quare imp.* but that is thought not to be so speedy a remedy.

[a] 18 E. 3. 54. a. 13 H. 4. 4. 24 E. 3. 64. a.

[b] 4 E. 3. 2. a. 22 H. 6. 39. per Newton. 10 E. 3. 57. 40 E. 3. 22. &c.

[c] 4 E 3. 14. 6 E. 3. 4.

[d] Bracton.

[e] Psal. 12. 9.

[f] 44 E. 3. 4. 18 E. 3 12, 13. 20 H. 6. 10. 21 E. 4. 22. 23. F. N. B. 96. f. 97. b.

[g] *Ovidius.*

[h] This is called *duplex querela*, necessary to be known for finding of institutions, &c.

CAP. VII.

The Court of Kings Bench, *coram Rege.*

Lib. 3. cap. 7. fo. 105. b.

BRACTON doth make in few words a notable expression of this court. *Habet rex plures curias in quibus diversæ actiones terminantur, et illarum curiarum habet unam propriam, sicut aulam regiam, et justiciarios capitales qui proprias causas regias terminant, et aliorum omnium, per querelam, vel per privilegium, sive libertatem.*

Fo. 108. a.

And soon after speaking of the justices of this court saith: *Item justiciariorum quidam sunt capitales, generales, perpetui, et majores à latere regis residentes, qui omnium aliorum corrigere tenentur injurias, et errores.*

* Nota.

* A granter prohibitions.

And Britton saith: *In droit des justices que sont assignes de nous suer et tener nostre lieu ou q. nous seons en Angliterre. * Voilons que eux eiant conusans de amender faux judgements et de terminer appeales et auters trespasses faitz enconter nostre peace, et * enconter nostre jurisdiction, et lour record se esteant solonq; ceo que nous manderons per nostre bre.*

Fleta in describing this court saith: *Habet et rex curiam suam et justiciarios suos tam milites quam clericos locum suum tenentes in Anglia, coram quibus, et non alibi nisi coram semetipso et concilio suo vel auditoribus specialibus falsa judicia et errores justiciariorum revertuntur et corriguntur: ibidem etiam terminantur brevia de appellis, et alia brevia super actionibus criminalibus et injuriarum contra pacem regis illatarum impetrata, et omnia, in quibus continetur ubi tunc fuerimus in Anglia.*

Liber niger in scaccario, cap. 4.

In the Black Book of the exchequer, it is thus said of the chief justice of this court: *capitalis justitia præsidet primus in regno.* Out of these three ancient authors we observe these six conclusions.

* Note this word

a See Britton, f. 1. speaking of the king, *Et pur ceo que nous ne suffisons in nostre proper person a oier & terminer touts querels del people. Avomus partie nostre charge en plusors parts come est ordeine, &c.* 20 E. 3. cap. 1.

b Stat. de Marlb. 52 H. 3. ca. 1. Vi.. 4 H. 4. ca. 22.

c 24 H. 8. cap. 2. in effect.

d Bract. lib. 1. ca. 5. fol. 3. b.

e 20 E. 3. cap. 1. speaking in the kings person.

First, where Bracton saith, *Habet rex plures curias in quibus diversæ actiones * terminantur;* hereby, and in effect by [a] Britton, and this conclusion followeth, that the king hath committed and distributed all his whole power of judicature to severall courts of justice, and therefore the judgement must be *ideo consideratum est per curiam.* And herewith do agree divers acts of parliament and book cases, some whereof, for illustration, we will briefly remember; and leave the judicious reader to the rest.

[b] *Provisum, concordatum et concessum est, quod tam majores, quam minores justitiam habeant et recipiant in curia domini regis.* [c] That the lawes ecclesiasticall and temporall were and yet are administred, adjudged, and executed by sundry judges, &c. [d] *Expedit etiam magistratus reipublicæ constitui, quia per eos qui juredicendo præsunt effectus rei accipitur; parum est enim jus in civitate esse, nisi sint qui possunt jura gerere.*

[e] For the pleasure of God and quietnesse of our subjects as to save our conscience, and to keep our oath, by the assent of our great men and other of our councell, we have commanded our justices, that they shall from henceforth do even law and execution of right to all our subjects, rich and poor, without having regard to any person, without letting to do right for any letters or commandement

mandement which may come to them from us, or from any other, or by any other cause.

W. 1. an. 3 E. 1. cap. 1. Fleta lib. 1. ca. 29.

Agreeable to that great canon of the law *anno* 3 E. 1. which we have translated into Latin: *Rex præcipit quòd pax sacrosanctæ ecclesiæ et regni solidè custodiatur et conservetur in omnibus, quodq; justitia singulis tam pauperibus quam divitibus administratur, nulla habita personarum ratione.* See the second part of the Institutes, W. 1. cap. 1.

[71]

8 H. 4. fo. 19.

8 H. 4. the king hath committed all his power judiciall, some in one court, and some in another, so as if any would render himselfe to the judgement of the king in such case where the king hath committed all his power judiciall to others, such a render should be to no effect. And 8 H. 6. the king doth judge by his judges (the king having distributed his power judiciall to severall courts) and the king hath wholly left matters of judicature according to his lawes to his judges.

8 H. 6. 20 & tit. Grant. F. 5.

2 R. 3. fol. 11.

And albeit it be enacted that the delinquent shall be fined at the will of the king, *Non dominus rex in camera sua, nec aliter nisi per justiciarios suos (finem imponit) et hæc est voluntas regis,* viz. *per justiciarios et legem suam, unum est dicere.*

The second conclusion is, that in those dayes this court of kings bench did follow the court: and therefore Bracton calleth it *aulam regiam,* because they sat in the kings hall. Britton calleth the justices of this court, *justices assignes de nous suer:* and Fleta, *ubi tunc fuerimus in Anglia.*

The third is, that it is called the kings bench, and the pleas thereof *coram rege:* because in this court (as Bracton saith) those *capitales justiciarii proprias regis causas terminant,* and therefore the king himselfe cannot be judge *in propria causa.*

Of these you may read in Glanvil. lib. 1. cap. 2. &c. & lib. 10. cap. 18. and in the third part of the Institutes *per totum,* & Stanf. *per totum.*

* And in Ireland of errors in the kings bench there. lib. 7. fo. 18. F. N. B. 22. 34 Ass. 7. 39 E. 3. Error 88.

a Lib. 11. fo. 98. Jam. Bagges case Vid. 10 E. 3. ca. 3. Marshalsea.

The fourth is, that under these words [*proprias causas*) are included three things. First, all pleas of the crowne; as all manner of treasons, felonies, and other pleas of the crown which *ex congruo,* are aptly called *propriæ causæ regis,* because they are *placita coronæ regis.* Secondly, regularly to examine and correct all and all manner of errors *in fait,* and in law, of all the judges and justices of the * realm in their judgements, processe, and proceeding in courts of record, and not only in pleas of the crown, but in all pleas, reall, personall, and mixt, (the court of the exchequer excepted, as hereafter shall appear.) And this is *proprium quarto modo* to the king in this court: for regularly no other court hath the like jurisdiction, and therefore may be well called *propria causa regis.* and these two be of high and soveraign jurisdiction. [a] Thirdly, this court hath not only jurisdiction to correct errors in judiciall proceeding, but other errors and misdemeanours extrajudiciall tending to the breach of the peace, or oppression of the subjects, or raising of faction, controversy, debate, or any other manner of misgovernment; so that no wrong or injury, either publick or private, can be done, but that this shall be reformed or punished in one court or other by due course of law. As if any person be committed to prison, this court upon motion ought to grant an *habeas corpus,* and upon returne of the cause do justice and relieve the party wronged. And this may be done though the party grieved hath no priviledge in this court. It granteth prohibitions to courts temporall and ecclesiasticall, to keep them within their proper jurisdiction. Also this court may baile any person for any offence whatsoever. And if a freeman in city, burgh, or town corporate be disfranchised unjustly, albeit he hath no priviledge in this court, yet this court may relieve the party, as it appeareth in James Bagges case, *ubi supra, et sic in similibus.*

F. N. B. 89. 92. * Tr. 19 E. 3. coram rege rot. 56. Linc.

Fourthly, this court may hold plea by writ out of the chancery of all trespasses done *vi et armis*, of replevins, of * *quare impedit*, &c.

b 2 part of the Institutes, Magna Carta, cap. 11.

b See the second part of the Institutes, the 11 chapter of Mag. Carta, *Communia placita non sequantur curiam nostram.*

Fifthly, this court hath power to hold plea by bill for debt, detinue, covenant, promise, and all other personall actions, *ejectione firme*, and the like, against any that is *in custodia mareschalli*, or any officer, minister, or clerk of the court: and the reason hereof is, for that if they should be sued in any other court they should have the priviledge of this court: and lest there should be a fayler of justice (which is so much abhorred in law) they shall be impleaded here by bill though these actions be common pleas, and are not restrained by the said act of Magna Carta, *ubi supra*. Likewise the officers, ministers, and clerks of this court privileged by law in respect of their necessary attendance in court, may impleade others by bill in the actions foresaid. And all this appeareth by Bracton, who lived when Magna Carta was made, *ubi supra*: where he saith, *Et aliorum omnium per querelam vel per privilegium sive libertatem.* And continuall experience concurreth with antiquity herein.

[72]

See the second part of the Institutes, ubi supra. 27 H. 3. coram rege. rot. 9. *Hus & Haut.*

H. P. captus per querimoniam mercatorum Flandriæ et imprisonatus offert domino regi hus *et* haut *in plegio ad standum recto, et ad respondendum prædictis mercatoribus, et omnibus aliis qui versus eum loqui voluerint*, &c. This plea was after the statute of Magna Carta, *anno* 9 H. 3. Of these words *hus* and *haut*, two French words. *Hus* signifying an elder-tree, and *haut* the staffe of a halbert, &c. I leave the conjecture that some have made thereof to themselves: we think it was then common bail changed now to *Do* and *Ro*, and the rather for this word [*offert.*] And it is observable, that then putting in baile at one mans suit, he was in *custodia mareschalli* to answer all others which would sue him by bill, and this continueth to this day. If any person be in *custodia mareschalli*, &c. be it by commitment, or by latitat', bill of Mid' or other proces of law, it is sufficient to give the court jurisdiction: and the rather, for that the court of common pleas is not able to dispatch all the subjects causes, if the said actions should be confined only to that court. And seeing none but serjeants at law can practise in the court of common pleas, it is necessary that in this court of kings bench apprentices and other counsellors of law might by experience inable themselves to be called serjeants afterwards; otherwise serjeants must want experience, which is the life of their profession. And the proceedings in that court for so long time, and under so many honourable judges and reverend sages of the law, hath gotten such a foundation, as cannot now without an act of parliament be shaken. And the errors in the kings bench cannot be reversed (but in certain particular actions by the statute of 27 Eliz. cap. 8. wherein the jurisdiction of the court is saved) but in the high court of parliament, as before in the chapter of the court of parliament appeareth.

31 H. 6. 10. b. adjudge.

Sixthly,

Sixthly, if a writ in reall action be abated by judgement in the court of common pleas, and in a writ of error the judgement is reversed in this court, and the writ is adjudged good, this court shall proceed upon this writ, and is not restrained by Magna Carta, *ubi supra, ne curia domini regis deficeret in justitia exhibenda.*

1 H. 7. 12. 14 H. 7. 14. 21 E. 3. 46. 11 H. 4. 49. in nativo habendo.

This court may hold plea in assise of *novel disseisin* without any patent, for it is *querela* and not *placitum*, and so not within these words *communia placita*, as it hath been expounded and warranted by continuall experience.

F. N. B. 177. 30 Ass. 35. Ass. de mord.

A *scire fac'* to repeal a patent of the king may be brought in this court. And where Fleta saith, *Nisi coram semetipso et concilio suo, vel auditoribus specialib' falsa judicia ac errores justiciariorum revertuntur:* It is to be known that all the common law errors in the court of exchequer (being the proper court of the king for his revenue and profit) were examinable before commissioners appointed by the kings writ under his great seal, which Fleta here calleth *auditores speciales.* But now by the statute of 31 E. 3. the chancelour and treasurer taking to them the justices and other sage persons, such as to them seemeth to be taken, shall examine the errors in the exchequer, &c.

3 H. 4. 7.

See more hereof in the chapter of the Exchequer. 31 E. 3. cap. 12.

[a] In ancient time, when pleas were holden in parliament, when the parties descended to issue, the record was adjourned into the kings bench to be tried there.

[b] See the statute of W. 1. against preposterous hearings in this court, and the exposition of the same in the second part of the Institutes.

[c] By the statute of *Artic' super Cart.* the chancelour and the justices of the kings bench were to follow the court: but notwithstanding both the chancery and the kings bench were at this time setled courts during the severall terms * of the year, as by infinite records both before and after this statute doth appear. So as at this time they did not attend in the kings court, but when they were called yet were accounted as parcell of the kings houshold as long as they followed the court: but this cumbersome attendance wholly ceased in the reign of E. 3. and yet the lord chancelour would have had his purveyance, as if he had continued still as one of the houshold, untill he and all others, but those of the kings, queens, or princes houshold only, were restrained by act of parliament. 34 E. 3. cap. 2.

[a] Rot. par. 18 E. 1. nu. 97. Placit. int. Jo. de novo Burgo & Regman, &c.

[b] W. 1. cap. 14. Against preposterous hearings.

[c] Art. sup. cart. 28 E. 1. cap. 5. Glan. temps. H. 2. lib. 2. ca. 6. & lib. 11. ca. 1. *Coram justiciis domini regis in banco sedentibus. Vid adjudicat' coram rege* in every terme, from 1 E. 1. during all his reign in every severall term in the yeare. And in all those times and termes the court of chancery did sit. 34 E. 3. ca. 2.

*[73]

Also upon perusall of the records in the reign of H. 3. from the beginning of his reign untill the ending of it, this court sat in the term time where the other courts of justice did sit. And the pleas were stiled to be holden *coram rege* as to this day they are: and this appeareth by Fitzh. Abridgement, in the titles of Corone, of Brief, of Wast, &c. and by Bracton who in many places voucheth judgments in the reign of H. 3. in terms *coram rege.* And this appeareth also in elder times: but hereof thus much shall suffice to prove, that at the making of the said act of 28 E. 1. and long before, this court in term times sat with the kings other courts, and specially for pleas of the crown, &c. and that the said act

And so did the chancery both of them being to some purposes but one court as it appeareth in the chapter of the court of chancery.

is to be intended, that the chancelour and the judges of this court should attend the king and follow the court when they were required.

3 El. Dier 187. 27 Ass. p. 1.

It is truly said that the justices *de banco regis* have supream authority, the king himself sitting there as the law intends. They be more then justices in eire.

7 E. 4. 18. 4 H. 7. 18. 14 H. 7. 21. li. 9. fo. 118. a & b. Segnior Sanchers case.

The justices in this court are the soveraign justices of oier and terminer, gaol-delivery, conservators of the peace, &c. in the realm. See the books in the margent, you shall find excellent matter of learning concerning the supream jurisdiction of this court.

In this court the kings of this realm have sit in the high bench, and the judges of that court on the lower bench at his feet; but judicature only belongeth to the judges of that court, and in his presence they answer all motions, &c.

17 E. 3. 13. a. lib. 4. fo. 57. in the Sadlers case. Pl. Com. 262.

The justices of this court are the soveraign coroners of the land, and therefore where the sherif and coroners may receive appeals by bill, *à fortiori* the justices of this court may do it.

a 21 Ass. 12. 27 ass. 1. 28 ass. 52. 21 H. 7. 29. b Pasch. 12 E. 3. coram rege, Ro. 99. Chichest. W. 1. cap. 3. lib. 9. fo. 118, ubi supra.

[a] So high is the authority of this court, that when it comes and sits in any county, the justices of eire, of oier and terminer, gaol-delivery, [b] they which have conusance, &c. doe cease without any writing to them. But if any indictment of treason or felony in a foraign county be removed before certain commissioners of oier and terminer in the county where this court sits, yet they may proceed, because this court (for that this indictment was not removed before them) cannot proceed for that offence. But if an indictment be taken in Midd. in the vacation, and after this court sit in the next term in the same county (if this court be adjourned) then may speciall commissioners of oier and terminer, &c. in the interim proceed upon that indictment, but the more usuall way is by speciall commission. And all this was resolved by all the judges of England at Winchester term, *anno* 1 *Jacobi regis*, in the case of Sir Everard Digby and others; and so had it been resolved, Mich. 25 & 26 Eliz. in the case of Arden and Somervile, for this kind of special commission of oier and terminer: and herewith agreeth Pl. Com. in the earl of Leic' case, *anno* 1 *Mar. reginæ*.

Hil. 1 Jac. Sir Walter Raleighs case, &c. Pl. Com. fo 388. count de Leic' case acc'.

22 E. 3. 6. b. 24 E. 3. 73. 29 ass. 52. Stanf. pl. cor. 15.

And so supream is the jurisdiction of this court, that if any record be removed into this court, it cannot (being as it were in his centre) be remaunded back, unlesse it be by act of parliament. And this appeareth by the judgment of the parliament in *anno* 6 H. 8. but by the authority of that act indictments of felonies and murders removed into the kings bench may by the justices of that court be remaunded, and this court may send down as well the bodies of all felons and murderers, as their indictments into the counties where the same murders or felonies were committed or done, &c. in such manner, &c. as if the indictments had not been brought into the kings bench.

6 H. 8. cap. 6. It extendeth only to felonies and murders.

[74]

See before cap. Parliam. pag. 21. when a writ of error is sued of a judgment, *coram rege*, they proceed *super tenorem recordi*, and the record it self remaineth in this court.

But the justices of the kings bench of their own authority may grant a *nisi prius* in case of treason, felony, and other pleas: for there they send but the transcript of the record, and not the record itself, as shall be said in the chapter of Justices of *nisi prius*. But if the justices of the kings bench doe perceive that any indictment is to be removed into that court by practise or for delay, the court may refuse to receive the same, before it be entred of record, and remand the same back again for justice to be done.

2 H. 4. cap. 10.

By the statute of 2 H. 4. the clerk of the crown of this court, if fourscore

fourſcore or an hundred men be indicted of felony or treſpaſſe, of one felony, or one treſpaſſe, and they plead to an iſſue, as not guilty, the ſaid clerk ought not to take for the *venire fac'*, nor for the entring of the plea but two ſhillings only, and not two ſhillings for every one, which act is made in affirmance of the common law. So if one man be indicted of two ſeverall felonies or treſpaſſes, and is acquited, he ſhall pay but for one deliverance. 26 Aſſ. p. 47.

Out of this court are other courts derived, as from one fountain ſeveral ſprings and rivers, in reſpect of the multiplicity of cauſes, which have increaſed. *Juriſdictio iſtius curiæ eſt originalis ſeu ordinaria, & non delegata.* The juſtices of this court have no commiſſion, letters patents or other means to hold pleas, &c. but their power is originall and ordinary. They were called anciently * *juſticiæ, juſticiarii, locum tenentes domini regis, &c.* The chief juſtice, [a] *juſtitia Angliæ, juſtitia prima, juſticiarius Angliæ, juſticiarius Angliæ capitalis,* and *juſticiarius noſter capitalis ad placita coram nobis terminand'.* To obſerve the changes of theſe names, and the reaſon and change thereof, is worthy of obſervation.

Deſignatio juſticiariorum eſt à rege, juriſdictio vero ordinaria à lege.

* Glanvil lib. 1. ca. 6, 13. &c. ſæpenumero.

a Lib. nigro in ſcaccario. par. 1. ca. 4.

Never in any legall record (which we have ſeen) they were called *ſummi juſticiarii.*

Before the reign of E. 1. the chief juſtice of this court was created by letters patents, and the form thereof (taking one example for all) was in theſe words.

Rot. cart. 45 H3. 13 Aug.

Rex, &c. archiepiſcopis, epiſcopis, abbatibus, prioribus, comitibus, baronibus, vicecomitibus, foreſtariis, et omnibus aliis fidelibus regni Angliæ, ſalutem. Cum pro conſervatione noſtra, et tranquillitatis regni noſtri, et ad juſtitiam univerſis et ſingulis de regno noſtro exhibendam conſtituerimus dilectum et fidelem noſtrum Philippum Baſſet juſticiarium Angliæ quamdiu nobis placuerit capitalem. Vobis mandamus in fide qua nobis tenemini firmiter injungentes, quatenus in omnibus quæ ad officium juſticiarii prædicti, nec non ad conſervationem pacis noſtræ et regni noſtri eidem dum in officio prædicto ſteterit, plenius ſitis intendentes. Teſte rege, &c.

Capitalis juſticiarius Angliæ.

Herein 6 things are to be obſerved. 1. That the creation of his office was by letters patents. 2. That this officer was originally inſtituted for three things. 1. *Pro conſervatione noſtra.* 2. *Tranquillitatis regni noſtri.* 3. * *Ad juſtitiam univerſis et ſingulis de regno noſtro exhibendam.* The third thing to be obſerved is, that he was ſtiled *juſticiarius Angliæ capitalis.* 4. That Philip Baſſet was conſtituted chief juſtice of England, and after made knight, for he was not knight at the making of the letters patents. This Philip was of Welledby in the county of Northampton, and was excellently learned in the laws of the realm; he was younger brother of baron Baſſet of Draiton Baſſet in the county of Staff. 5. That he was conſtituted *quamdiu nobis placuerit.* Laſtly, the clauſe of attendance, and the perſons that are to give attendance, &c. to him, are very remarkable. This Philip Baſſet was the laſt of this kind of creation by any like letters patents, and he died chief juſtice neer to the end of the reign of H. 3. king E. 1. being a wiſe and prudent prince knowing that *cui plus licet quam par eſt, plus vult quam licet,* (as moſt of theſe *ſummi juſticiarii* did) made three alterations, 1. By limitation of his authority. 2. By changing *ſummus juſticiarius,* to *capitalis juſtic'* 3. By a new kind of creation, viz. by writ, leſt, if he had continued his former manner of creation, he might

* This was the original juriſdiction of this court.

might have had a desire of his former authority, which three doe expresly appear by the writ yet in use, viz.

Rex, &c. E. C. militi salutem. Sciatis quod constituimus vos justiciarium nostrum capitalem ad placita coram nobis tenenda, durante beneplacito nostro. Teste, &c.

Which writ being called breve doth in few words comprehend the substance of the former letters patents: for *capitalis justiciarius noster* and *ad placita coram nobis tenenda* includes all that which was truly intended to be granted to him in the former letters patents, which alterations were made by authority of parliament, though not now extant. For it is a rule in law, that ancient offices must be granted in such forms and in such manner, as they have used to be, unlesse the alteration were by authority of parliament. And continuall experience approveth, that for many successions of ages without intermission, they have been, and yet are called by the said writ, *et optimus legum interpres consuetudo.* But after the said alteration, viz. in *anno* 25 E. 1. Reginaldus de Grey (was stiled) *justiciarius Angliæ*, and he was in legall proceedings called *capitalis justiciarius noster*, when his patent was, *capitalis justiciarius Angliæ.*

See in the chapter of the Constable and Marshall for this point.

Rot. par. 25 E. 1. so named in the writ of parliament to him directed.

We have seen a fine in these words: *Hæc est finalis concordia facta in curia domini regis apud West' à die sancti Michaelis in tres septimanas, anno regni regis Henrici filii regis Johannis 3. coram domino Huberto de Burgo capitali justiciario Angliæ et aliis domini regis fidelibus tunc ibi præsentibus.*

Nota, this fine was levied, *Inter Martinum Abbatem de Missenden querentem, et Thurstanum Basset deforcientem de 3 carucat' terræ in lega.* before him in the kings bench, in 3 H. 3. before Mag. Car. and stiled *capit. justiciar' Angliæ*, Lib. *de Missenden* fo. 109. divers other fines with the same stile.

[a] In the writ *de homine replegiand'*, he (which was formerly called *capitalis justiciarius Angliæ*) is called *capitalis justic' noster*, and sometime *cap. justic' regis.* The stile of this court of kings bench is *Anglia* in the margent: and in divers acts of parliament he is called chief justice of England. 34 H. 8. cap 26. 37 H. 8. cap. 12. 2 E. 6. cap. 13. 5 E. 6. cap. 11.

The chief justice in Ireland is called *capitalis justiciar' Hiberniæ* at this day.

Pasch. 13 E. 1. (the pleas in this court are *coram rege*) then were stiled thus, *Placita coram locum domini regis tenentibus, &c. ideo venit inde jurata coram rege vel ejus locum tenentibus.* 15 *Paschæ*, &c. within which words all the judges of the kings bench were included.

[a] Regist. fo. 77. 24 E. 1. *stat' de consultat'* 3 E. 3. coron. 361. Lib. Int. Co. tit. *action sur le case*, sect. 5.

[b] *Anno domini* 969. in the abby of Ramsey this epitaph was engraven, &c. *De Ailivinus inclyti regis Edgari cognatus totius Angliæ* * *aldermannus, &c.* who was without question chief justice of all England. *Inter leges Aluredi* cap. 34. he is called *cyninger ealdorman*, i. *regis aldermannus sive senator, sive judex.* Vide cap. 3. 15. & 38. *et inter leges Edovardi* ca. 35.

[b] Aldermanni judices dicti sunt in diebus illis.

The rest of the judges of the kings bench have their offices by letters patents in these words. *Rex omnibus ad quos præsentes literæ pervenerint, salutem. Sciatis quod constituimus dilectum et fidelem Johannem Doderidge militem unum justiciariorum ad placita coram nobis tenenda durante beneplacito nostro, teste, &c.* [c] These justices of the kings bench are stiled 1. *Capitalis.* 2. *Generales.* 3. *Perpetui.* 4. *Majores à latere regis residentes:* but the chief justice is only called by the king *capitalis justiciarius noster.* They are called 1. *Capitales*, in respect of their supream jurisdiction. 2. *Generales*, in respect of their generall jurisdiction throughout all England, &c. 3. *Perpetui*, for that they ought not to be removed without just cause,

[c] Bract. li. 3. f. 108.

cause. 4. *Majores à latere regis residentes*, for their honor and safety, that they should be protected by the king in administratton of justice, for that they be *à latere regis*.

And where in 5 E. 4. it is holden by all the justices in the exchequer chamber that a man cannot be justice by writ but by patent or commission, it is to be understood of all the judges, saving the chief justice of this court. But both the chief justice, and the rest of the judges may be discharged by writ under the great seal. L. 5 E 4. 137.

None can be a judge of this court unlesse he be a serjeant of the degree of the coif, and yet in the writ of patent to them made, they are not named serjeants.

If a writ be returnable *coram justiciariis nostris apud Westm'*, it shall be returned in the common place: but if it be returnable in this court, it must be *coram nobis ubicunque fuerimus in Anglia*. See the second part of the Institutes, Mag. Cart. cap. 11. and the exposition upon the same. [76]

In former times some ill disposed clerks of this court, because they could have no originall out of the chancery for debt returnable into this court, they would sue out an originall action of trespasse (a meer feigned action) returnable into this court, and so proceed to exigent, (where in truth the cause of action is for debt) and when the defendant appeared, &c. all the former proceedings were waved, and a bill filed for the defendant for debt. This is an unjust practice in derogation of the dignity and honour of this court, and worthy of severe punishment according to the statute of W. 1. c. 29. when it is found out: Vide in the chapter of the court of common pleas in the end thereof.

W. 1. ca. 29. Vid. 30 H. 6. 37. a. 30 E. 3. 32. It is fraud where one thing is pretended and another done.

Now that we may here say somewhat to a vulgar objection of the multiplication of suits in law both in this court, and other of his majesties courts at Westm' more then hath been in the reigns of E. 3. R. 2. H. 4. H. 5. H. 6. E. 4. and R. 3. It is to be observed, that there be six causes of the increase of them, whereof two be general, and the other four particular. The generall be peace, and plenty: the particular, 1. The dissolution of so many monasteries, chanteries, &c. and the dispersing of them into so many severall hands. 2. The swarm of informers. 3. The number of concealors. 4. The multitude of atturnies.

Multiplication of suits. Peace. Plenty. Dissolution of monasteries, &c. Informers. Concealors. Atturnies.

For the first generall: in the reigns of E. 3. R. 2. H. 4. H. 5. and part of the reign of H. 6. in respect of the wars in France, &c. and in the residue of the reign of H. 6. and in the reign of E. 4. in respect of the bloody and intestine wars, and in almost continuall alarums within the bowels of this kingdome, between the houses of Lancaster and York, there could not be so many suits in law, as since this kingdome hath enjoyed peace, which is the first generall cause, peace is the mother of plenty, (which is the second general cause) and plenty the nurse of suits. In particular, by the dissolution of monasteries, chanteries, &c. and dispersing of them, &c. Upon the statutes made concerning the same (there being such a confluence of ecclesiastical possessions) there arose many questions and doubts, whereupon suits were greatly increased, 2. Informers and relators raised many suits, by informations, writs, &c. in the kings courts at Westm' upon penall statutes, many whereof were obsolete, inconvenient, and not fit for those days,

Silent leges inter arma.

Concordia parvæ res crescunt ex pulentialites.

and yet remained as snares upon the subject, so as the subject might justly say with Tacitus, *Prius vitiis laboravimus, nunc legibus.* 3. Concealors, *helluones*, that endeavoured to swallow up cathedrall churches and the ecclesiasticall possessions of church-men, and the livings of many others of the kings subjects. Lastly, the multitude of * atturnies, more then is limited by law, is a great cause of increase of suits.

* See the preambles of the stat. of 4 H. 4. ca. 18. 33 H. 6. ca. 7.

a Diminution of suits.

[a] But now on the other side, to shew what great hope there is, that suits in law shall decrease, for that in effect all the particular causes of the increase of them are taken away, which we have thought good to remember.

b Possessions of monast. and chanteries, &c. 35 El. ca. 3. 21 Ja. cap. 2. Concealors.

[b] For the first, the statute of 35 Eliz. cap. 3. hath remedied part, but the statute of 21 Jac. ca. 2. hath given a plenary salve for the whole mischief, whereof you may read at large in the third part of the Institutes, cap. 87. against concealors, *turbidum hominum genus.*

c 21 Jac. ca. 4. Informers. See the third part of the Inst. cap. against vexatious relators informers &c.

[c] For the second, by the statute of 21 Jac. cap. 4. Informations, &c. upon penall statutes are to be heard and determined in their proper counties, and not in the courts at Westminster, whereby the vexatious swarm of informers, who are best trusted where they are least known, are vanished and turned again to their former occupations.

d Atturnies. Rot. par. 20 E. 1. rot. 4. *De apprenticiis et atturnatis.* 15 R. 2. nu. 28. 4 H. 4. ca. 18. 33 H. 6. ca. 7. See Rot. parl. 13 H. 4. nu. 63. not in print.

e 21 Jac. ca. 16.

[d] Concerning atturnies, the number are set down, and that they ought to be learned and vertuous, and as I understand, the judges at this time have this matter in consideration. But besides these, there are some other statutes made for avoiding and decreasing of vexatious suits. As an [e] act in 21 Jac. regis, cap. 16. for limitation of actions and avoiding suits in law, a good and beneficiall law. Another act at the same parliament, cap. 13. for the further reformation of jeofails, * a good law for ending of suits. Another at the same parliament, cap. 8. to prevent and punish abuses in procuring of processe of *supersedeas* of the peace and good behaviour, out of his majesties courts at Westminster, &c. whereby infinite vexations, troubles and charges of the subjects are prevented. Another at the same parliament, ca. 23. for avoiding of vexatious delays in causes by removing of actions and suits out of inferiour courts, wherein the former abuse was vexatious, grievous, and chargeable to the subject. A branch of an act at the same parliament, cap. 16. for pleading of tender of amends in an action of trespasse, *quare claus. fregit*, for a trespasse by negligence, or involuntary, wherein the defendant maketh no title, &c. an excellent and necessary law for avoiding of trifling and vexatious suits, especially in champion countries. An act at the same parliament, cap. 2. against monopolies and new projects, &c. a great quiet for the time to come. *Anno 3 Caroli Regis, nunc*, cap. 1. The petition of right concerning the rights and liberties of all the subjects of this realm for their repose and quiet. Lastly, the repeal of so many obsolete penall statutes is a great mean of diminution of suits.

*[77]

See the 3 part of the Inst. cap. against Monopolists and Projectors.

3 Car. regis c. 1. 21 Jac. ca. 28. 3 Car. ca. 4.

For the abovesaid generall causes, viz. peace and plenty, long may they happily by the goodnesse of God continue without abuse within this realm.

The kings bench hath authority for great misprisions and offences, to adjudge and inflict corporall punishment, as pillory, papers, and the like: whereof you may read many presidents in the third part of the Institutes, pag. 219, 220.

CAP.

CAP. VIII.

The Court of Chancery.

CERTAIN it is, that both the Brittish and Saxon kings had their chancelors and court of chancery, the only court out of which originall writs doe issue: as taking some few examples before the conquest.

The antiquity of this court. 26 E. 3. ass. p. 24. and the preface to the third book of Reports. History of Ely, Hugo Petroburgensis, Leland. Fortesc. cap. 17.

Edward the Confessor had Reinbald his chancelor. This Edward granted many mannors, lands, &c. and franchises to the abbot of Westminster, and endeth his charter thus. *Ad ultimum, cartam istam sigillari jussi, et ipse manu mea propria signum crucis impressi, et idoneos testes annotari praecepi:* and amongst those witnesses this you shall finde *Swardus notarius ad vicem Reinbaldi regiae dignitatis cancellarii hanc cartam scripsi et subscripsi.* He had also Lefrick to his chancelor.

King Etheldred also had a worthy name, and a worthy man to his chancelor. *Rex Etheldredus statuit atque concessit quatenus ecclesiam de Elye ex tunc et semper in regis * curia cancellariae ageret dignitatem, &c.* This king began his reign, *anno domini* 978, which albeit it was void in law to grant the chancelorship of England in succession, yet it proveth that then there was a court of chancery.

In the second book of the History of Ely, written in the reign of king Stephen soon after the conquest.
* Curia Canc'.

King Edgar had Adulph: king Edred had Thurkettle: king Edmond the same: king Athelstane Wolsine their chancelors, &c.

Nota.

For further proof that there was a court of chancery before all these kings time, out of which writs remediall issued, as they doe to this day: hear what the Mirror saith, *Le primer constitutions ordenus per les viels roys, &c. ordein fuit que chescun eyt del chancery le roy brief remedial a son pleint sans difficultie.* Hereby it appeareth that in the reign of king Alfred there was a court of chancery out of which writs remediall issued, which was not then instituted, but affirmed to be a court then *in esse*, and enacted that out of that court writs remediall should be granted without difficulty, which law continueth to this day. And thus much touching the court of chancery before the conquest: and therefore * Polydor Virgill, who affirmeth this court to come in with the Conqueror, *perperam erravit.*

Mirror ca. 1. §. 3. & vide ca. 5. §. *pur le enrolments de pardon le roy in le chancery en temps le roy Alfred.* King Alfred began to reign anno dom. 872, and was father to king Edward senior, father of the said Athelstane.
* Error Polydori.

In a charter to the abbot of Westminster by William the Conqueror, and amongst the witnesses it is written thus, *Ego Mauritius regis cancellarius favendo legi, et sigillavi.* Arfastus bishop of North-elmham in Norff, who translated his see to Thetford, was also chancellor to the Conqueror.

Cancellarii Angliae dignitas est, ut secundus à rege in regno habeatur, ut altera parte sigilli regii, quod et ad ejus pertinet custodiam, propria signet mandata, &c.

Fitz. Stephen. tempore H. 2. in the end of Stows survey of Lond.

Omnia brevia de pace, &c. irrotulari debent in rotulo cancellariae.

Bracton fo.

Fleta saith, *Est inter caetera quoddam officium quod dicitur cancellaria, quod uno provido et discreto, ut episcopo vel clerico, magnae dignitatis debet committi simul cum cura magni sigilli regni, cujus substituti sunt*

See Glanv. li. 12. ca. 1. & 5. &c. Fleta li. 2. ca. 12.

cancellar'

cancellar' omnes in Anglia, Hibernia, Wallia, et Scot' omnesque sigilla regis custodientes ubique praeter custodem sigilli privati. Cui associentur clerici honesti, circumspecti domino regi jurati, qui in legibus et consuetudinibus Anglicanis notitiam habeant pleniorem, quorum officium sit supplicationes et querelas conquerentium audire et examinare, et eis super qualitatibus injuriarum ostensarum debitum remedium exhibere per brevia regis.

W. 2. 13 E. 1. c. 1. 13 E. 1. ca. 23, 24.

Breve de forma donationis in reverter e satis est in usu in cancellaria. In cancellaria et in registro cancellariae.

[79]

1 part Instit. sect. 101. Epist. lib. 9.

For the antiquity and authority of this book of the register of the chancery, see the first part of the Institutes, *verb. per le Register*, and in the epistle to the ninth book of my Commentaries.

Vid. postea ca. 10. of the court of common pleas.

But to proceed (omitting many others) Robert Parning took the state and degree of a serjeant at law in 3 E. 3. and became the kings serjeant, and for his profound and excellent knowledge of the laws, in Trin. term 14 E. 3. was 24 Julii by writ created chief justice of England: in which office he remained untill the 15 of December following, on which day he was made lord treasurer of England. In that office he remained untill the 15 year of the reign of the same king, and then was constituted lord chancelour. This man knowing that he that knew not the common law, could never well judge in equity (which is a just correction of law in some cases) did usually sit in the court of common pleas, (which court is the lock and key of the common law) and heard matters in law there debated, and many times would argue himself, as in the report of 17 E. 3. it appears.

Ubi non est scientia, non est conscientia. 17 E. 3. fo. 11. 14. 23. 37.

In the 30 year of E. 3. Sir Robert Thorpe chiefe justice of the common pleas (not Sir William Thorpe chiefe justice of England, convicted of sordid bribery) a man of singular judgement in the laws of this realm, was constituted lord chancelour of England. And in the parliament *anno* 45 E. 3. a grievous complaint was made by the lords and commons, that the realme had bin of long time governed by men of the church in disherison of the crown, and desired that lay men only might be principall officers, &c.

Rot. parl. 45 E. 3. Rot. 22. nu. 15.

After the decease of Sir Robert Thorpe 5 Julii *anno* 46 E. 3. Sir John Knivet knight, chief justice of England, a man famous in his profession, was made lord chancellor of England, who deceased in *anno* 50 E. 3. &c.

Rot. par. 5 R. 2. nu. 20.

In perusing the rolls of parliament in the times of these lord chancelours, we finde no complaint at all of any proceeding before them. But soone after, when a chancelour was no professor of the law, we finde a grievous complaint by the whole body of the realm, and a petition that the most wise and able men within the realm might be chosen chancelours, and that he seek to redresse the enormities of the chancery. But leaving many other records to their proper places hereafter, we will conclude this point concerning the antiquity and jurisdiction of this court with the opinion of all the judges of the realm in 9 E. 4. in a suit in the court of exchequer against the clerk of the hamper in the chancery upon his account in the exchequer, where it was holden by all the justices in the exchequer chamber, that all the courts of the king have been time out of memory, so as a man cannot know which of them is the ancientest court. And justice Young the plaintife demanded of the justices, what if the chancelour command me upon a payne, that

that I ſhall not ſue him? To whom Billing the chief juſtice anſwered, you are not bound to obey it, becauſe that commandment is againſt law; but ſeing that toucheth upon the juriſdiction of the court, let us in the next place handle that point.

The Juriſdiction of the Court.

In the chancery are two courts, one ordinary, *coram domino rege in cancellaria*, [a] wherein the lord chancelour or lord keeper of the great ſeale proceeds according to the right line of the laws and ſtatutes of the realm, *ſecundum legem et conſuetudinem Angliæ*. [b] Another extraordinary according to the rule of equity, *ſecundem æquum et bonum*. And firſt of the former court.

[a] 8 E. 4. 5. 9 E. 4. 15. 14 E. 4. 7.
[b] Stan. prær. c. 20. fo. 65. b. Pl. com. fo. 72.

[c] He hath power to hold plea of *ſcire fac'* for repeal of the kings letters patents, of petitions, *monſtrans de droits*, traverſes of offices, partitions in chancery, of *ſcire fac'* upon recogniſances in this court, writs of *audita querela* and *ſcire fac'* in the nature of an *audita querela* to avoid executions in this court; [d] dowments in chancery, the writ *de dote aſſignanda* upon offices found, execution upon the ſtatute ſtaple, or recogniſance in nature of a ſtatute ſtaple upon the act of 23 H. 8. but the execution upon a ſtatute merchant is retornable either into the kings bench, or into the common place, and all perſonall actions by or againſt any officer or miniſter of this court in reſpect of their ſervice or attendance there. [a] In theſe if the parties deſcend to iſſue, this court cannot try it by jury, but the lord chancelour or lord keeper delivereth the record by his proper hands into the kings bench to be tried there; becauſe for that purpoſe both courts are accounted [b] but one, and after triall had to be remanded into the chancery, and there judgement to be given. But if there be a demurrer in law, it ſhall be argued and adjudged in this court. Nota, the legall proceedings of this court be not inrolled in rolls, but remaine *in filaciis* being filed up in the office of the pety-bag. [c] Upon a judgement given in this court a writ of error doth lie retornable into the king's bench: [d] the ſtile of the court of the kings bench is *coram rege* (as hath been ſaid) and the ſtile of this court of chancery is *coram domino rege in cancellaria, et additio probat minoritatem*. And in this court the lord chancelour or the lord keeper is the ſole judge: and in the kings bench there are four judges at the leaſt.

[c] Rot. par. 8 H. 4. nu. 122. 2 R. 3. 1.
[d] Regiſt. 297. F. N. B. 263. Stanf. prær. ca. Rot. par. 18 E. 3. nu. 41, 42.
[80]
[a] 13 E. 2. coram rege, rot. 51. London.
[b] 10 E. 3. 61. 24 E. 3. 65. 73.
[c] 18 E. 3. 25. 17. aſſ. 24. 14 Eliz. Dier 315. Pl. com. 393. a.
[d] In par. Tr. 9. H. 6. rot. 5. int. placita regis.

This court is *officina juſtitiæ*, out of which all originall writs and all commiſſions which paſſe under the great ſeal go forth, which great ſeal is *clavis regni*, and for thoſe ends this court is ever open.

Officina juſtitiæ.

Of this court Fleta *ubi ſupra*, ſaith, *Dicuntur brevia cum ſint formata ad ſimilitudinem regulæ juris, quæ breviter, et paucis verbis intentionem proferentis exponunt, ſicut regula juris, rem quæ eſt breviter enarrat: non tamen ita debet eſſe bre. quin rationem et vim intentionis contineat. Et ſunt quædam brevia formata ſub ſuis caſibus, et quædam de curſu quæ conſilio totius regni ſunt approbata, quæ quidem mutari non poterunt abſque eorundem contraria voluntate. Sunt et brevia ex eis ſequentia quæ dicuntur judicialia, et ſæpius variantur ſecundum varietatem placitorum proponent' et reſpondent', petentis et excipientis et ſecundum varietatem reſponſionum. Sunt et quædam quæ dicuntur magiſtralia et ſæpius variantur ſecundum diverſitatem caſuum, factorum et querelarum, et quorum*

Fleta lib. 2. ca. 12. Bract. li. 5. fo. 413. Britton ca. 84. Fleta lib. 6. ca. 35. & 36.

quædam

quædam sunt personalia, et quædam realia, et quædam mixta, secundum quod sunt actiones diversæ vel variæ, quia tot erunt formulæ brevium, quod sunt genera actionum, quia non potest quis sine brevi agere, præcipue de libero tenemento suo, quia non tenetur quis respondere sine brevi, nisi gratis voluerit, et cum hoc fecerit quis, ex hoc ei non injuriabitur: volenti enim et scienti non fit injuria. De eadem autem re, plures alicui competere poterunt actiones, ordine autem, ut convenit, observato. Breve quidem regis in se nullam debet continere falsitatem, nec aliquem errorem: apparere debet vel in prima sui figura non vitiosum, maxime si fuerit patens sive apertum, quia originalia quædam sunt clausa, et quædam aperta. Et sive aperta, sive clausa, apparere non debent abrasa, nec abolita: et si inveniatur abrasio, tunc refert quo loco, à quo, et quando. Quo loco? videlicet utrum in narratione facti vel juris. Si autem in narratione facti, cadet coram justic' quasi suspectum. Facta enim et nomina mutari non debent, sed jura ubique scribi possunt. A quo? utrum videlicet per clericum cancellar' cui autoritas data fuerit, vel ausu temerario per alium, sicut clericum justic,' vel vic' ad procurationem alicujus partis: quo casu omnes agentes et consentientes tanquam falsarii puniantur. Item quando? videlicet utrum hoc fiat antequam bre. in curia resuscitatum et publicatum, vel post. Si autem post, erit breve suspectum et cadet, si à tenente fuerit hoc calumpniatum. Fiunt autem brevia judicialia in cancellaria ex recognitionibus et contractibus habitis et in rotulis cancellariæ irrotulatis et ex recordo cancellario et clericis sibi associatis per hac constitutionem concesso. Quia de hiis quæ recordata sunt coram cancellar' domini regis, et ejus justic' qui recordum habent et in rotulis eorum irrotulantur, non debet fieri processus placiti per summonitionem, vel attachiament', essonia, visus tre. et alias solempnitates cur' sicut fieri consuevit ex contractibus, et conventionibus factis extra curiam. Observandum est de cætero quod ea quæ inveniuntur irrotulata coram hiis qui recordum habent vel in finibus contenta, cum sint contractus sive conventiones vel obligationes sive servicia aut consuetudines recognitæ sive alia quæcunq; irrotulata quib' cur' regis sine juris et constitutionis offensa authoritatem præstare potest' [81] talem de cetero habeat vigorem, quod non sit necesse de hiis placitare in posterum, sed cum venerit querens ad curiam domini regis, si recens sit cognitio, vel finis, viz infra annum per bre. levatus, statim habeat bre. de executione illius recognitionis factæ: et si forte à majore tempore transacto facta fuerit illa recognitio, vel finis levatus: præcipiatur vic' quod scire fac' parti de qua fit queremonia, quod sit ad certum diem, ostens. si quid sciat dicere quare hujus irrotulata vel in fine contenta executionem habere non debeant. Et si ad diem venerit, et nihil sciat dicere quare executio fieri non debeat, præcipiatur vic' quod rem irrotulatam vel in fine contentam exequi fac'. Eodem modo mandetur ordinario in suo casu, observato nihilominus quod inferius dicetur in statuto de medio qui per judicium aut recognitionem est obligatus. Ex hac quidem constitutione oriuntur bria. judicialia in cancellaria sicut coram ipsis justic. Ipsi autem collaterales et socii cancellarii esse dicuntur præceptores, eo quod bria. causis examinatis remedialia fieri præcipiunt, et hoc quoque cum fine denar' ad opus domini regis, et quoque sine fine, eo quod omnia bria. non sunt omni tempore æquipollentia. De brevibus autem coram justic' ad primas assisas cum in partes illas venerint, fines capere non consueverunt, eo quod ad tempus itineris justic' ligat constitutio Magnæ Cartæ quæ talis est; Nulli justitiam negabimus, vendemus, vel differemus: sed non inhibetur quin fines capiantur pro brevibus possessionum, et actionum personalium, pro celeriore justitia habenda; qui quidem pro qualitatibus et quantitatibus

portionem

portionem concessi in eisdem brevibus imbreviabuntur, et in rotulis cancellariæ irrotulantur. Qui quidem rotuli singulis annis ad scaccar' liberabuntur, et fines hujus extrahuntur et per summon' scaccarii leventur. Clausula vero finis talis est, Et cape securitatem à præfato tali de 40 solid. ad opus nostrum pro hoc brevi. *Verba autem extract' de scaccario sunt hæc.* De A. de B. pro brevi habend' dim marc' *vel amplius prout finis factus fuerit. Conceduntur aliquando conquerentib' ob favorem paupertatis quod ubi præsumi potest sic quod plegios invenire non possunt de prosequend' clamorem suum quod securitatem præstent vic' per fidei interpositionem suam, non tamen in actionibus personalibus hoc concedendum est. Habet et rex clericos in officio illo expertos et legales qui formulas brevium cognoscunt, qui approbanda admittunt et defectiva omnino repellunt, quib' omnia bria. priusquam ad sigillum proveniunt cum deliberatione distincte et aperte in ratione, dictione, litera et syllaba examinare injunctum est. Et sciendum quod nullum bre. nisi per manus eorundem ad sigillum debet admitti. Habet etiam sex clericos suos prænotarios in officio illo, qui cum clericis memoratis familiares, &c. esse consueverunt et præcipue ad victum et vestitum qui ad bria. scribenda secundum diversitates querelarum sunt intitulati. Et qui omnes pro victu et vestitu de proficuo sigilli in cujuscunque usus pervenerit debent honeste inveniri. Sunt etiam nihilominus clerici juvenes et pedites quibus de gratia cancellar' concessum est pro expeditione populi bria. facere cursoria, dum tamen sub advocatione clericorum superiorum fuerint qui eorum facta in eorum receperint pericula. Et in quolibet bri. debet scribentis nomen inbreviari qui warrantizare poterint in peccatores si necesse fuerit. Et ne præfati clerici superflua petant stipendia pro scriptura sua, constitutum est quod tam clerici justic' quam cancellar' de solo denario pro scriptura unius brevis se teneant contentos.*

And this court is the rather alwayes open, for that if a man be wrongfully imprisoned in the vacation, the lord chancelour may grant a *habeas corpus* and do him justice according to law, where neither the kings bench nor common pleas can grant that writ but in the term time; but this court may grant it either in term time or vacation. So likewise this court may grant prohibitions at any time either in terme or vacation; which writs of prohibition are not retornable: but if they be not obeyed, then may this court grant an attachment upon the prohibition retornable either in the kings bench or common place.

* The author of that book speaking of the court of chancery, and of the jurisdiction it then had, saith, *Curia cancellariæ regiæ est curia ordinaria pro brevibus originalibus emanandis, sed non placitis communibus tenendis.*

* New Tales, or *Novæ Narrationes*, written about the beginning of E. 3.

Divers acts of parliament give authority to the lord chancelour to heare and * determine divers offences and causes in the court of chancery, which is ever intended in this court proceeding in Latin, *secundum legem et consuetudinem Angliæ*, and the defendant shall not be sworn to his answer, nor examined upon interrogatories, and upon issue joyned it shall be tried in the king's bench, *ut in similibus casibus solet.* But our purpose is not to enumerate all these statutes, for our aim is principally at the generall jurisdiction of this court.

27 E. 3. cap. 13. 2 R. 3. fo. 3. 13 E. 4. Dier 12 El. 288. a resolve.

*[82]

The officers and ministers of this court of common law doe principally attend and doe their service to the great seal, as the * twelve masters of the chancery, whereof the master of the rols is

Officers and ministers of this court.

See the 2 part of the Inst. W. 2. ca. 24. *verb. Clerici de Cancellaria.*

* In the parliament rol of 5 R. 2. nu. 23. they are called chief clerks.

the chief, who by their originall inſtitution, as it is proved before, ſhould be expert in the common law, to ſee the forming and framing of originall writs according to law, which are not of courſe; whereupon ſuch are called in our ancient authors *brevia magiſtralia.* The clerk of the crown, the clerk of the hamper, the ſealer, the chafe wax, the controller of the chancery, twenty four curſitors for making writs of courſe or formed writs according to the regiſter of the chancery, the clerk of the preſentations, the clerk of the faculties, the clerk examiner of letters patents, the clerks of the pettibag, and the ſix atturnies. The proceſſe in this court is under the great ſeal according to the courſe of the common law.

Having ſpoken of the court of ordinary juriſdiction, it followeth according to our former diviſion, that we ſpeak of the extraordinary proceeding according to the rule of equity, *ſecundum æquum et bonum*, wherein we will purſue our former order.

Of the antiquity of this court of equity. Henry Beaufort ſon of John of Gaunt biſhop of Winch. cardinal of St. Euſebius, lord chancelor in the beginning of the reign of H. 6. and in that kings reign John Kemp cardinall of S. Rufeline archbiſhop of York, lord chancelor. See Rot. parl. 28 H. 6. nu. 10. & 35 H. 6. fo. 3. [a] 36 E. 3. cap. 9.

Albeit our ancient authors, the Mirror, Glanvill, Bracton, Britton and Fleta doe treat of the former court in chancery, and of originall writs and commiſſions iſſuing out of the ſame, yet none of them do once mention this court of equity. We have alſo conſidered what caſes in this court of equity have been reported in our books, and we find none before the reign of H. 6. and in that kings time, and afterwards plentifully, we then turned our eies to acts of parliaments and parliament rols.

[a] Some have thought that the ſtatute of 36 E. 3. gave the chancelor his firſt authority for his proceeding in courſe of equity, by which it is enacted, That if any man think himſelf grieved contrary to any of the articles above written, or others contained in divers ſtatutes, will come to the chancery or any for him, and thereof make his complaint, he ſhall preſently have there remedy by force of the ſaid articles and ſtatutes, without elſewhere purſuing to have remedy. But certainly this act giveth the chancelor no power to proceed in courſe of equity, but that he grant to the party grieved originall writs which are called remediall grounded upon any ſtatute for his relief, and there is no ſtatute that gives the party grieved remedy in equity. Laſtly, the laſt words of the act, without elſewhere purſuing to have remedy, doe manifeſt that the meaning of the makers of the act is to direct the party to be relieved by the common law, by actions upon theſe ſtatutes, and not elſewhere.

Rot. par. 13 R. 2. nu. 30.

In the parliament holden 13 R. 2. the commons petitioned to the king, That neither the chancellor nor other counſellor doe make any order againſt the common law, nor that any judgment be given without due proceſſe of law. Whereunto the kings anſwer was, The uſages heretofore ſhall ſtand, ſo as the kings royalty be ſaved. In the ſame parliament another petition was, That no perſon ſhould appear upon a writ *De quibuſdam certis de cauſis*, before the chancelor or any other of the councell, where recovery is therefore given by the common law: whereunto the kings anſwer is, The king willeth as his progenitors have done, ſaving his regalty.

17 R. 2. ca. 6.

In the parliament holden in 17 R. 2. it is enacted at petition of the commons, That foraſmuch as people was compelled to come before the kings councell, or in chancery, by writs grounded upon untrue ſuggeſtions, that the chancelor for the time being preſently after

after that ſuch ſuggeſtions be duly found and proved untrue, ſhall have power to ordain and award dammages according to his diſcretion * to him which is ſo travelled unduly as is aforeſaid. This act extendeth to the chancelor proceeding in courſe of equity, and extendeth not to a demurrer in law upon a bill, but upon hearing of the cauſe upon theſe words in the act [duly found and proved] and this is the firſt parliament that I find touching this matter. And in the roll of the ſame parliament, I finde the firſt decree in chancery that ever I obſerved, the effect whereof was: John de Windſor complaineth and requireth to be reſtored to the mannors of Rampton, Cottenham and Weſtwick with their appurtenances in the county of Cambridge, the which were adjudged to him by the kings award, then in the poſſeſſion of Sir John Liſley, and now withholden by Sir Richard le Scrope, who by champerty bought the ſame: the cauſe was this. Upon a petition of Windſor againſt Liſley they both compromitted the matter to the kings order, the king committed the ſame to the councell, they after digeſting of the ſame made a decree for Windſor under the privy ſeal, they ſend warrant to the chancelor to confirm the ſame, which was done under the great ſeal by a ſpecial injunction to Liſley, and to write to the ſherif to execute the ſame. After this, Liſley by petition to the king requireth that the ſame may be determined at the common law, notwithſtanding any former matter: the king accordingly by privy ſeal giveth warrant to the chancelor to make a *ſuperſedeas*, the which was done by privy ſeal, after which Sir Richard Leſcrope bought the ſame. Upon the ripping of the whole matter, this ſale was thought no champerty, whereupon it was adjudged, that the ſaid Windſor ſhould take nothing by his ſaid ſuit, but to ſtand to the common law, and that the ſaid Sir Richard ſhould goe without day.

7 E. 4. fo. 14.

Rot. par. 17 R. 2. nu. 10. William Courtney ſon of Hugh earl of Devon, was then biſhop of Cant. and lo. chancelor when this decree was made.

Champerty.

The commons petitioned that no writs or privy ſeals be ſued out of the chancery, exchequer or other places to any man to appear at a day upon a pain, either before the king and his councell, or in any other place, contrary to the ordinary courſe of the common law: whereunto the king anſwered: that ſuch writs ſhould not be granted without neceſſity.

Rot. par. 2 H. 4. nu. 69.

Amongſt the petitions of the commons you ſhall find this, that all writs of *ſubpœna* and *certis de cauſis*, going out of the chancery and the exchequer may be enrolled, and not granted of matters determinable at the common law, on pain that the plaintif doe pay by way of debt to the defendant forty pound: whereunto is anſwered, the king will be adviſed.

Rot. par. 3 H. 5. nu. 46. Edmund Stafford archb. of York, was lord chancellor at this time.

It is enacted, to endure untill the next parliament, that the exception (how that the party hath ſufficient remedy at the common law) ſhall diſcharge any matter in chancery. At the next parliament you ſhall find a petition in theſe words. No man to be called by privy ſeal or *ſubpœna* to anſwer any matters but ſuch as have no remedy by the common law, and that to appear ſo by the teſtimony of two juſtices of either bench, and by indenture between them and the plaintif, which plaintif ſhall always appear in proper perſon, and find ſurety by recognizance to proſecute with effect the matters of the bill only, and to anſwer dammages if the ſame fall out againſt the plaintif.

Rot. Par. 9 H. 5. nu. 25.

Rot. Par. 1 H. 6. nu. 41.

Never good petition in parliament dieth, but firſt or laſt will take effect. Vid. ſup. pa. 32. 15 H. 6. ca. 4.

H 2 But

But in *anno* 15 H. 6. for a perpetuall law, and for the true jurisdiction of this court it is enacted in these words.

30 H. 6. fo. 26. 4 E. 4. 8. 14 E. 4. 1. 16 E. 4. 9. b. 18 E. 4. 13. 6 E. 4. 10. b. 7 H. 7. 12. Fortesc. ca. 34. Rot. par. 14 E. 4. nu. 5. William. Shetfords case Doct. & Stud. cap. 18. 24. 50. 31 H. 6. ca. 2.

Item, forasmuch as divers persons have before this time been greatly grieved by writs of *subpœna*, purchased for matters determinable by the common law of his land, to the great dammage of such persons so vexed, in subversion, and impediment of the common law aforesaid; our soveraign lord the king will, that the statutes thereof made shall be kept after the form and effect of the same. And that no writ of *subpœna* be granted from henceforth till surety be found to satisfie the party so grieved and vexed for his dammages and expences, if so be that the matter may not be made good, which is contained in the bill. In *anno* 31 H. 6. cap. 2. there is a proviso in these words. Provided that no matter determinable by the law of this realm shall be by the said act determined in other form then after the course of the same law in the kings courts having determination of the same law.

[84]

Trin. 2 Jac.

Tr. 2 Jac. *regis*, upon suit made to the king for erecting of a new office for taking of surety according to the said act of 15 H. 6. cap. 4. the king referred the cause to Popham chief justice, who upon conference with the judges in Fleetstreet, resolved that the surety was by force of that act to be by obligation, and to be made by the party grieved himself, because it concerneth his dammages and costs, and the court was to set down the form and sum of the obligation, and in the end the suit prevailed not.

* Pasch. 29 El. in Scaccario Woods case. Vide 7 El. Dier 238. Seignior Shandois case.

* Pasch. 29 Eliz. *in scaccario*, in Woods case adjudged upon the statute of 2 E. 6. cap. 13. for the like reason that the forfeiture for non-payment of tithes shall goe to the party grieved.

Reasons, 1. à majori ad minus. Rot. par. 2 R. 2. nu. 18. Rot. par. 13 R. 2. nu. 10.

1. Rot. par. 2 R. 2. nu. 18. the high court of parliament relieveth but such as cannot have remedy but in parliament.

The parliament for matters determinable at the common law doth remit the parties thereunto.

2 *Regula.*

2. *Nunquam decurritur ad extraordinarium, sed ubi deficit ordinarium.*

3.

3. Whereas matters of fact by the common law are triable by a jury of twelve men, this court should draw the matter *ad aliud examen*, that is, to judge upon deposition of witnesses, which should be but evidence to a jury in actions real, personall, or mixt.

37 H. 6. 14. 27 H. 8. 18.

This court of equity proceeding by English bill is no court of record, and therefore it can bind but the person only, and neither the state of the defendants lands, nor property of his goods or chattels.

Trin. 3 Jac. reg. in scaccario. Sir Thomas Themilthorps case.

Egerton lord chancelour imposed a fine upon Sir Tho. Themilthorp knight, for not performing his decree in chancery concerning lands of inheritance, and estreated the same into the exchequer: and upon processe the party appearing pleaded that the fine was imposed by the lord chancelour for not performance of his decree, and that he had no power to assesse the same. The atturny generall confessed the plea to be true, *et petit advisamentum curiæ*, concerning the power of the chancelor in this case,

case, and upon debate of the queſtion in court, and good adviſement taken, it was adjudged that the lord chancelor had no power to aſſeſſe any ſuch fine, for then by a mean he might bind the intereſt of the land where he had no power, but of the perſon only, and thereupon the ſaid Sir Thomas Themilthorp was diſcharged of the ſaid fine.

Afterward the ſaid lord chancelor decreed againſt Waller certain lands, and for not performance of the decree impoſed a fine upon him, and upon proceſſe out of the court of chancery extended the lands that Waller had in Midd. &c. whereupon Waller brought his aſſiſe in the court of common pleas, where the opinion of the whole court agreed *in omnibus*, with the court of exchequer. **Wallers caſe.**

The lord chancelor or the lord keeper is ſole judge both in this court of equity, and in the court concerning the common law; but in caſes of weight or difficulty he doth aſſiſt himſelf with ſome of the judges of the realm, and no greater exception can be taken hereunto then in caſe of the lord ſteward of England being ſole judge in triall of the nobility, who alſo is aſſiſted with ſome of the judges. *The Judge of this court of equity, &c.*

For this court of equity the ancient rule is good. Three things are to be judged in court of conſcience: covin, accident, and breach of confidence.

All covins, frauds, and deceits, for the which is no remedy by the ordinary courſe of law.

Accident, as when a ſervant of an obligor, morgageor, &c. is ſent to pay the mony on the day, and he is robbed, &c. remedy is to be had in this court againſt the forfeiture, and ſo in the like.

The third is breach of truſt and confidence, whereof you have plentifull authorities in our books.

[85] Mich. 42 & 43 El. in Cancellar'. SirMoyl Finches caſe.

The caſe in the chancery between the earl of Worceſter and other laintifs, and Sir Moyl Finch and Eliz. his wife defendants was this. The queen being ſeiſed of the mannor of Raveſton and of certain lands in Stokegoldington, (which the plaintif pretended to be a mannor either in right or reputation) granted by her letters patents the mannors of Raveſton and Stokegoldington to the ſaid Sir Moyl, and John Awdelye, and their heirs: but this was upon confidence, that they ſhould grant the mannor of Raveſton to Sir Thomas Heneage and Anne his wife, and to the heirs of Anne: and the mannor of Stokegoldington to Sir Thomas and Anne, and the heirs of Sir Thomas. Sir Moyle and Awdelye by deed indented and inrolled *termino Trin.* 1588. 30 Eliz. in this court for a thouſand pound bargained and ſold to Sir Thomas Henage and his wife the mannors of Raveſton and Stokegoldington, and the ſcite of the priory of Raveſton in the county of Buck. and all other their lands, tenements and hereditaments in Ravenſton, Weſton, Pidington, and Stokegoldington, in the county of Buck. To have and to hold the mannor of Raveſton and the ſcite of the ſaid priory, and all the premiſſes in Ravenſton, Weſton, Pidington, and Stokegoldington (other then the ſaid mannor of Stokegoldington) to the ſaid Sir Thomas and dame Anne, and the heirs of the ſaid dame Anne: and to have and to hold the ſaid mannor of Stokeg. to the ſaid Sir Thomas and dame Anne, and to the heirs of Sir Thomas. Sir Thomas had iſſue by the ſaid dame Anne the ſaid Elizabeth one of the defendants his only child, and afterwards the ſaid dame Anne died: the defendant alleadged that Sir Thomas was diſſeiſed of Stokegoldington, and the plaintif denied it. And after Sir Thomas by deed indented and inrolled, bargained and ſold the mannor of Stokegoldington to the plaintif for payment of his debts and died: and for payment of his debts, they exhibited their bill againſt Sir Moyl, and the ſaid Eliz. his wife, for the ſaid mannor of Stokegoldington, and the lord chancelor decreed it for the plaintif. And upon a petition preferred by the defendants to queen Elizabeth, ſhe referred the conſideration of the whole caſe to all the judges of England: and after hearing of the counſell of both parts on ſeverall days, and conference between themſelves, theſe points for rules in equity were reſolved. Firſt, that if there were any diſſeiſon, that nothing paſſed to the plaintif either in right or equity, for the diſſeiſor was ſubject to no truſt, nor any *ſubpœna* was maintainable againſt him, not only becauſe he was in the *poſt*, but becauſe the right of inheritance or freehold was determinable at the common law and not in the chancery, neither had *ceſti que uſe* (while he had his being) any remedy in that caſe. Secondly, it was reſolved by all the juſtices, that admitting that Sir Thomas Heneage had a truſt, yet could not he aſſign the ſame over to the plaintif, becauſe it was a matter in privity between them, and was in nature of a *choſe* in action, for he had no power of the land, but only to ſeek remedy by *ſubpœna*, and not like to *ceſti que uſe*, for thereof there ſhould be *poſſeſſio fratris*, and he ſhould be ſworn on juries in reſpect of the uſe, and he had power over the land by the ſtatute of 1 R. 3. cap. and if a bare truſt and confidence might be aſſigned over great inconvenience might thereof follow by granting of the ſame to great men, &c. Thirdly, when the land deſcended to Elizabeth one of the defendants, as heir to her mother, and the truſt deſcended to her from her father, the truſt was drowned and extinguiſhed. Fourthly, when any title of freehold or other matter determinable by the common law come incidently in queſtion in this court, the ſame cannot be decided in chancery, but ought to be referred to the triall of the common law where the party grieved may be relieved by error, attaint, or by action of higher nature. And when the ſuit is for evidences, the certainty whereof the plaintif ſurmiſeth he knoweth not, and without them he ſuppoſeth that he cannot ſue at the common law: It was reſolved that if the defendant make no title to the land, then the court hath juſt juriſdiction to proceed for the evidence; but if he make title to the land by his anſwer, then the plaintif ought not to proceed, for otherwiſe by ſuch a ſurmiſe, inheritances, freeholds, and matters determinable by the common law ſhall be decided in chancery in this court of equity. And thus were theſe points reſolved by Sir John Popham, Sir Edmond Anderſon, Sir William Periam, and Walmeſlye, Gawdye, Fenner, and Kingeſmill juſtices, and Clark and Savill barons of the exchequer, and all this amongſt other things they certified under their hands into the chancery, and thereupon the former decree was reverſed. And in debating of this caſe it was reſolved by the two chief juſtices, chief baron, and divers other juſtices, that if a man make a conveyance, and expreſſe an uſe, the party himſelf or his heirs ſhall not be received to averre a ſecret truſt, other then the expreſſe limitation of the uſe, unleſſe ſuch truſt

A diſſeiſor ſubject to no truſt.

A truſt cannot be aſſigned over. 22 El. Dier fo. 369. pl. 50.

Matters determinable by the common law cannot be decided in chancery.

Suit for evidence.

[86]

truſt or confidence doe appear in writing, or otherwiſe declared by ſome apparent matter. And Popham ſaid, that covin, accident, and breach of confidence were within the proper juriſdiction of this court.

Thomas Throckmorton eſquire exhibited a bill in this court againſt Sir Moyl Finch knight, claiming a leaſe of the mannors of R. and S. for many years to come, and ſhew clear matter in equity to be relieved againſt a forfeiture pretended by Sir Moyle for breach of a condition where there was no default in the plaintif, &c. Unto which bill the defendant pleaded this plea, that for the triall of the forfeiture of which leaſe, he made a leaſe for years to one priviledged in the exchequer, who brought an *ejectione firme* againſt the plaintif, and upon pleading a demurrer in law, the leſſee had judgment to recover againſt Thomas Throckmorton (now plaintif in chancery:) whereupon Thomas Throckmorton brought a writ of error in the exchequer chamber, where upon due proceeding the judgement was affirmed, and demanded judgment, if after theſe judgements given at the common law he ought to be drawn to make any further anſwer in this court of equity. And Egerton lord chancelor delivered his opinion in court, that the defendant ſhould anſwer to the bill: and foraſmuch as the caſe was of great conſequence, the conſideration of the demurrer was by the queen referred to all the judges of England: before whom the councell of Throckmorton ſaid, that the intent of the lord chancelor was not to impeach the ſaid judgments, but confeſſing the ſaid judgments, to be relieved upon matter in equity: as if a man hath (as he is adviſed) two matters to aid him, matter at the common law, and matter in equity, and being impleaded at the common law, doth by advice of his councell aſſay the common law, where his adverſary prevaileth againſt him, and hath judgment accordingly, yet in this caſe the party may, confeſſing the judgment, ſue to be relieved upon a collaterall matter in equity: and thereupon they ſhewed ſome preſidents in time of H. 8. E. 6. &c. and one in the point between Ward and Fulwood. But upon great deliberation it was reſolved by all the judges of England, that the plea of Sir Moyl Finch was good, and that the lord chancelor ought not to examine the matter in equity after the judgement at the common law: for though the lord chancelor (as hath been ſaid) would not examine the judgment, yet he would by his decree take away the effect of the judgment: and for the preſidents, they were grounded upon the ſole opinion of the lord chancelor, and paſſed *ſub ſilentio.* But that ſuch a courſe ſhould be permitted, it ſhould be not only full of inconvenience, but directly againſt the laws and ſtatutes of the realm, againſt which no preſident or preſcription can prevail; * which you may read at large in the third part of the Inſtitutes, cap. Premunire. Which reſolution of the judges was ſignified by Popham chief juſtice to the lord chancelor, and thereupon no further proceeding was againſt Sir Moyle Finch, but his plea ſtood.

Mich. 39 & 40 El. in Cancellar'.

* 27 E. 3. cap. 1. 4 H. 4. cap. 22. &c. in the preamble. Doct. & Stud. 30. W. 2. ca. 5.

Vid. Paſch. 5 E. 4. coram rege rot. 35. Sir Simon Norres caſe.

Nota.

In a caſe depending in chancery by Engliſh bill between Mears plaintif and Saint-John and his wife adminiſtratrix of John Alnion defendant, the caſe was this: that the inteſtate took the profits of the lands of the plaintif being within age by force of a truſt repoſed in him by the father of the plaintif by his laſt will, the

Mich. 37 & 38 El. in Cancellar.

yearly value of which lands was fourscore pounds *per annum*, and the intestate took the profits from the 23 year of queen El. untill the 33 year of her reign, and with parcell of the profits purchased lands in fee which descended to his heir, and left assets to his ad-

[87] ministratrix one of the defendants to satisfie the plaintif, all debts paid. The question was, whether in this case the administratrix might not be charged in equity for the said mean profits: and Sir Thomas Egerton master of the rols said, that he had seen a case in chancery in *anno* 34 H. 6. resolved by all the judges of England remaining in the Tower, that where the feoffees to use took the profits of the land, and received the rents, and made their executors, and died leaving assets to satisfie all debts over and above the said rents and profits, that the executors should be charged to satisfie *cesti que use* for the said rents and profits, and accordingly it was decreed in Mears case against the defendant: but whether the heir should be contributory or no, it was doubted.

Pasch. 32 El. in Cancellaria. Withams case. Eborum. Vide 7 E. 4. 14. & 18 E. 4. 11. & 12.

Withams case in the chancery was, that a tearm for years was granted to the use of a feme sole, she took husband and died, whether the husband should have the use, or the administrators of the feme, was referred to the judges; and by them it was resolved, that the administrators should have it, and not the husband, because that this trust of a feme was a thing in privity, and in nature of an action, for which no remedy was but by writ of *subpœna*. And so it was resolved by the justices in Waterhouses case, Hil. 8 Eliz. *Eborum*, for the trust runneth in privity in this case, and a husband should not be tenant by the curtesie of an use, nor the lord of the villain should have it at the common law.

Trin. 28 El. adjudge in the kings bench, in Peacocks case.

A man possessed of a tearm for years in lands, by his last will devised the same to one and the heirs of his body begotten, made his executors and died, the devisee entreth by the assent of the executors, hath issue and aliens the tearm and dieth: this alienation barreth the issue, for a tearm for years cannot be entayled. And afterwards *anno* 31 Eliz. in a case depending in chancery between Higgins and Milles it was certified by the lord Anderson and justice Walmsley (to whom it was referred) that no estate taile could be of a tearm, and that the alienation of the devisee did bar the issue.

31 Eliz. between Higgins and Mils in Cancellaria.

Mic. 26. & 27 El. coram rege. Perrots case. 10 H. 6. 15. in London by prescription. Nota this resolution is against the court of requests. See hereafter, cap. 9.

In a premunire between John Perrot plaintif, and T. M. H. W. and others defendants, it was resolved by Sir Christopher Wray chief justice, and the court of kings bench, that the queen could not raise a court of equity by her letters patents, and that there could be no court of equity but by act of parliament, or by prescription time out of mind of man. But the queen might grant power *tenere placita*, or *conusans de plea*, for all must judge according to one ordinary rule of the common law, but otherwise it is of proceedings extraordinary without any certain rule.

These cases which upon so great and mature deliberation have been resolved by the judges of the realm, and whereunto we were privy and well acquainted with, we have thought good to report, and publish for the better direction in like cases hereafter.

How he is created. Camden, p. 131.

He is made lord chancelor of England, or lord keeper of the great seal, *per traditionem magni sigilli sibi per dominum regem*, and by taking his oath, *forma cancellarium constituendi regnante Henrico secundo fuit appendendo magnum Angliæ sigillum ad collum cancellarii electi.*

Some have gotten it by letters patents, [a] at will, and [b] one for tearm of his life; but it was holden void, becaufe an ancient office muft be granted, as it hath been accuftomed.

[a] 35 H. 6. 3. B. of Winch. 1 H. 6. nu. 16.

[b] Cardinal Woolfey.

[c] It is enacted and declared, that the common law of this realm is and always was, and ought to be taken, that the keeper of the great feal of England for the time being hath always had, ufed, and executed, and from thenceforth may have, take, ufe, and execute the fame and the like place, authority, preheminence, jurifdiction, execution of laws, &c. as the lord chancelor of England for the time being lawfully ufed, &c.

[c] 5 El. ca. 18.

And fo it appeareth in 18 E. 3. nu 41. that the lord chancelor, or lord keeper for the time being ought to have conufance.

Rot. par. 18 E. 3. nu. 41.

[88]

[a] I finde that king H. 5. had two great feals, one of gold, which he delivered to the bifhop of Durefme, and made him lord chancelour of England, and another of filver, which king Henry the 5 delivered to the bifhop of London to keep.

[a] Rot. par. 1 H. 6. nu. 13, 14. 13 R. 2. nu. 7. Vide Camden ubi fupra.

[b] *William de Ayremin garden des rolles del chancelar' et fes compagnions gardens del grand feale.* At this time was Robert Burnel bifhop of Bath and Wels chancelour of England.

[b] Stat. de forma mittendi extract. in fcaccarium, anno 16 E. 1. vet. Mag. Carta, 2 part. fo. 47. b.

[c] It is to be obferved, that where divers ancient ftatutes fpeak of the chancelour and of his lieutenant, it muft of neceffity be intended of fuch a lieutenant, as the law doth allow of, and that cannot be of a deputy, for the chancelour cannot make a deputy, but *locum tenens* is to be taken for one that holdeth the place, or hath equall authoritie of the chancelour, and that is *cuftos magni figilli*: and this agreeth with the judgement of the faid parliament in 5 Eliz. But all queftions are now taken away by the faid act of 5 Eliz. and at this day there being but one great feale, there cannot be both a lord chancelour and a lord keeper of the great feale at one time, becaufe both thefe are but one office, as it is declared by the faid act.

[c] An. 27 E. 1. de libertatibus perquirendis. Vet. Mag. Carta, part 1. fo. 126, & 2 part fo. 57, &c.

Cancellarius unde.

It is faid before, that the chancelour by his ordinary power may hold plea of *fcire fac'* to repeale the kings letters patents under the great feal being always inrolled in this court, which we (to make a true derivation of his name) fhall now particularly touch. This writ of *fcire fac'* to repeal letters patents doth lye in this ordinary courfe of juftice in three cafes. The firft, when the king by his letters patents doth grant by feverall letters patents one and the felf fame thing to feveral perfons, the former patentee fhall have a *fcire fac'* to repeal the fecond patent. Secondly, when the king granteth any thing that is grantable upon a falfe fuggeftion, the king by his prerogative *jure regio* may have a *fcire fac'* to repeal his own grant. Thirdly, when the king doth grant any thing, which by law he cannot grant, he *jure regio* (for advancement of juftice and right) may have a *fcire fac'* to repeal his own letters patents. Now the judgement in all thefe three cafes is, *Quòd prædictæ litteræ patentes dicti domini regis revocentur, cancellentur, evacuentur, adnullentur, et vacuæ, et invalidæ, pro nullo penitus habeantur, et teneantur; ac etiam quod irrotulamentum eorundem cancelletur, caffetur, et adnihiletur, &c.* Hereof our lord chancelour of England (for forein chancelours, it may be, have not like authority) is

6 E. 4. 9. Dier 3 Eliz. 137. 2 E. 3. 7. 17 E. 3. 59. 21 E. 3. 47.

Lib. 2. fo. 14. &c.

is called *cancellarius, à cancellando, i. à digniori parte*, being the higheſt point of his juriſdiction to cancell the kings letters patents under the great ſeale, and damming the inrolment thereof, by drawing ſtrikes through it like a lettice.

The Lord chancellors oath.

[a] Rot. Par. 10 R. 2. rot. 8. The oath recited. Vid. rot. parl. 11 H. 4. 1. nu. 28.

[b] Becauſe he hath power of judicature, as is aforeſaid.

[c] 10 R. 2. rot. par. nu. 8. 2 H. 4. nu. 10. 15 E. 3. nu. 10. 15. 37. 41, 42.

[d] Laine is an ancient French word, and ſignifieth to hide.

[e] Rot. par. 10 R. 2. nu. 6, 7, 8. &c. the caſe of *Mich. de la Pole* Chancelour of England.

And all this which hath been ſaid concerning the office of the lord chancelour, or lord keeper is included within his [a] oath, which followeth in theſe words, and conſiſteth upon ſix parts. He ſhall ſweare,

1. That well and truly he ſhall ſerve our ſoveraigne lord the king and his [b] people in the office of chancelour (or lord keeper.)

2. That he ſhall doe right to all manner of people, poore and rich, after the [c] lawes and uſages of the realm.

3. That he ſhall truly counſel the king, and his counſell he ſhall [d] layne and keep.

4. That he ſhall not know nor ſuffer the hurt or diſheriting of the king, or [e] that the rights of the crowne be decreaſed by any meanes as far as he may let it.

5. And if he may not let it, he ſhall make it clearly and expreſly to be known to the king, with his true advice and counſell.

6. And that he ſhall do and purchaſe the kings profit in all that he reaſonably may, as God him help, and by the contents of this book.

[89]

Articles againſt Cardinall Woolſey.

Vid. artic. 20, 21, 26, 38. 41. 42. 44. 46.

Now for as much as the articles exhibited to king H. 8. 1 *die Decembris anno* 21 of his reign, by the lords and others of his privy councell (whereof Sir Thomas More lord chancelour was one) and by two of the principall judges of the realm againſt cardinall Woolſey, do in divers of the articles concern the juriſdiction of the chancery, (viz. the 20 and 26 articles, &c.) and other titles of this fourth part of the Inſtitutes, we have thought good juſtly and truly to tranſcribe from the very originall, under the proper hands of the lords and others of the privy councell, and of the ſaid judges, (which we have ſeen and had in our cuſtody) and have compared this tranſcript with the originall it ſelfe, and have (becauſe they are of great weight and uſe to many purpoſes) tranſcribed it *de verbo in verbum*, without omiſſion of any thing, as matters of that nature ought to be: and the rather, for that in our Chronicles they are very untruly rehearſed: and before this time (that we finde) the true articles were never printed.

Conſtrained by neceſſity of our fidelity and conſcience, complaine and ſhew to your moſt royall majeſty, we your graces humble, true, faithfull, and obedient ſubjects: that the lord cardinall of York, lately your graces chancelour, preſuming to take upon him the authority of the popes legat *de latere*, hath by divers and many ſundry wayes and faſhions committed high and notable grievous offences, miſuſing, altering, and ſubverting the order of your graces lawes: and otherwiſe contrary to your high honour, prerogative, crown, eſtate, and dignity regall, to the ineſtimable great hinderance, diminution, and decay of the univerſall wealth of this your graces realm. And it is touched ſummarily and particularly in certain articles here following, which be but a few in compari-

ſon;

ſon of all his enormities, exceſſes, and tranſgreſſions committed againſt your graces lawes. That is to ſay:

1. Firſt, where your grace and noble progenitors within this your realm of England, being kings of England, have been ſo free, that they have had in all the world none other ſoveraigne, but immediate ſubject to Almighty God in all things touching the regality of your crown of England, and the ſame preeminence, prerogative, juriſdiction, lawfull and peaceable poſſeſſion your grace and your noble progenitors have had, uſed, and enjoyed, without interruption or buſineſſe therefore by the ſpace of 200 years and more: whereby your grace may preſcribe againſt the popes holineſſe, that he ſhould not, nor ought to ſend or make any legat, to execute any authority legatine contrary to your graces prerogative within this your realme. Now the lord cardinall of York being your ſubject and naturall liege borne, hath of his high, orgallous, and inſatiable minde, for his own ſingular advancement and profit, in derogation, and to the great imbleniſhment and hurt of your ſaid regall juriſdiction and prerogative, and the long continuance of the poſſeſſion of the ſame, hath obtained authority legatine: by reaſon whereof he hath not only hurt your ſaid preſcription, but alſo by the ſaid authority legatine, hath ſpoyled and taken away from many houſes of religion within this your realm much ſubſtance of their goods. And alſo hath uſurped upon all your ordinaries within this your realme much part of their juriſdiction, in derogation of your prerogative, and to the great hurt of your ſaid ordinaries, prelates, and religious.

The ſoveraignty, prerogative, regall juriſdiction, and freedome of the crowne of England.

Preſcribe.

Cardinall of York.

Authority legatine.

Spoyled many houſes of religion.

Uſurped upon ordinaries.

2. Alſo the ſaid lord cardinall being your ambaſſadour in France, made a treaty with the French king for the pope, your majeſty not knowing any part thereof, nor named in the ſame; and binding the ſaid French king to abide his order and award of any controverſie or doubt ſhould ariſe upon the ſame, betwixt the ſaid pope and the French king.

Ambaſſadour.

3. Alſo the ſaid lord cardinall being your ambaſſadour in France, ſent a commiſſion to Sir Gregory de Caſſalis under your great ſeale in your graces name, to conclude a treaty of amity with the duke of Ferrare, without any commandment or warrant of your highneſſe, nor your ſaid highneſſe advertiſed or made privy to the ſame.

Ambaſſadour.

[90]

4. Alſo the ſaid lord cardinall, of his preſumptuous minde, in divers and many of his letters and inſtructions ſent out of this realm to outward parts, had joyned himſelf with your grace, as in ſaying and writing, The king and I would ye ſhould do thus. The king and I do give unto you our hearty thankes. Whereby it is apparent that he uſed himſelf more like a fellow to your highnes, then like a ſubject.

The king and I.

5. Alſo where it hath ever been accuſtomed within this realm, that when noble men do ſware their houſhold ſervants, the firſt part of their oath hath been, that they ſhould be true liege men to the king and his heirs kings of England: the ſame lord cardinall cauſed his ſervants to be only ſworne to him, as if there had been no ſoveraign above him.

Oath.

6. And alſo whereas your grace is our ſoveraign lord and head, in whom ſtandeth all the ſurety and wealth of this realm; the ſame lord cardinall knowing himſelfe to have the foul and contagious

Great pocks.

gious disease of the great pocks broken out upon him in divers places of his body, came daily to your grace, rowning in your eare and blowing upon your most noble grace with his perilous and infective breath, to the marvellous danger of your highnesse, if God of his infinite goodnesse had not better provided for your highnesse. And when he was once healed of them, he made your grace to beleeve, that his disease was an imposthume in his head, and of none other thing.

Provision. Premunire.

7. Also the said lord cardinall by his authority legatine, hath given by prevention the benefices of divers persons, as well spirituall as temporall, contrary to your crown and dignity, and your lawes and statutes therefore provided: by reason whereof he is in danger to your grace of forfeiture of his lands and goods, and his body at your pleasure.

Counselour. Forein ambassadors.

8. Also the said lord cardinall taking upon him otherwise then a true counsellour ought to do, hath used to have all ambassadours to come first to him alone, and so hearing their charges and intents, it is to be thought he hath instructed them after his pleasure and purpose before that they came to your presence, contrary to your high commandment by your graces mouth to him given: and also to other persons sent to him by your grace.

Letters sent from beyond sea. First to him.

9. Also the said lord cardinall hath practised so, that all manner letters sent from beyond the sea to your highnesse, have comen first to his hands, contrary to your high commandment by your own mouth, and also by others sent to him by your grace: by reason whereof, your highnesse nor any of your councell had knowledge of moe matters but of such as it pleased him to shew them: whereby your highnesse and your councell have been compelled of very force to follow his devices, which oftentimes were set forth by him under such crafty and covert meanings, that your highnesse and your councell have often times been abused: insomuch that when your councell have found and put divers doubts and things which afterwards have ensued, he to abuse them used these words, [I will lay my head that no such thing shall happen.]

Councell.

Foreign intelligence to him, &c.

10. Also the said lord cardinall hath practised, that no manner person having charge to make espiall of things done beyond the sea, should at their returne come first to your grace, nor to any other of your councell, but only to himself: and in case they did the contrary, he punished them for their so doing.

Licenses to transport grain and victuall.

11. Also the said lord cardinall hath granted licences under your great seal, for carrying out of grain and other victuals after the restraint hath been made thereof, for his own lucre and singular advantage of him and his servants for to send thither as he bare secret favour, without your graces warrant or knowledge thereof.

Ambassadours resident with other princes.

[91]

12. Also the said lord cardinall used many years together, not only to write unto all your ambassadours resident with other princes in his own name, all advertisements concerning your graces affairs being in their charge, and in the same his letters wrote many things of his own mind without your graces pleasure known, concealing divers things which had been necessary for them to know: but also caused them to write their advertisements unto him. And of the same letters he used to conceal for the compassing of his pur-

pose

poſe many things both from all your other counſelours, and from your ſelf alſo.

13. Alſo where good hoſpitality hath been uſed to be kept in houſes and places of religion of this realm, and many poore people thereby relieved, the ſaid hoſpitality and relief is now decayed and not uſed: and it is commonly reported that the occaſion thereof is, becauſe the ſaid lord cardinall hath taken ſuch impoſitions of the rulers of the ſaid houſes, as well for his favour in making of abbots and priors, as for his viſitation by his authority legatine. And yet neverthelеſſe taketh yearly of ſuch religious houſes, ſuch yearlie and continuall charges, as they be not able to keep hoſpitalitie as they were uſed to do: which is a great cauſe that there be ſo many vagabonds, beggers, and thieves.

Hoſpitality in houſes of religion decayed.

Impoſitions.

Yearly charges.

14. Alſo where the ſame l. cardinal ſaid before the ſuppreſſion of ſuch houſes as he hath ſuppreſſed, that the poſſeſſions of them ſhould be ſet to ferme among your lay ſubjects after ſuch reaſonable yearly rent as they ſhould well thereupon live, and keep good hoſpitality: and now the demeſne poſſeſſion of the ſame houſes ſince the ſuppreſſion of them hath been ſurveyed, met, and meaſured by the acre, and be now ſet above the value of the old rent. And alſo ſuch as were fermors by covent ſeal, and copieholders be put out and amoved of their fermes, or elſe compelled to pay new fine contrary to all equitie and conſcience.

Suppreſſion of houſes.

Reaſonable rents.

Above the value.

New fine.

15. Alſo the ſaid lord cardinall ſitting among the lords and other of your moſt honourable privie councell, uſed himſelf, that if any man would ſhew his minde, according to his duty, contrary to the opinion of the ſaid cardinall, he would ſo take him up with his accuſtomable words, that they were better to hold their peace then to ſpeak, ſo that he would heare no man ſpeak but one or two great perſonages, ſo that he would have all the words himſelfe, and conſumed much time with a fair tale.

Abuſed the privy councell.

All the words himſelfe.

16. Alſo the ſaid lord cardinall by his ambition and pride hath hindred and undone many of your poore ſubjects for want of diſpatchment of matters, for he would no man ſhould meddle but himſelf, inſomuch that it hath been affirmed by many wiſe men, that ten of the moſt wiſeſt and moſt expert men in England were not ſufficient in convenient time to order the matters that he would retain to himſelfe. And many times he deferred the ending of matters, becauſe that ſuiters ſhould attend and wait upon him, whereof he had no ſmall pleaſure, that his houſe might be repleniſhed with ſuiters.

Ambition and pride.

Want of diſpatch.

No man to meddle but himſelfe.

Suters to attend.

17. Alſo the ſaid lord cardinall by his authority legatine hath uſed, if any ſpirituall man having any riches or ſubſtance, deceaſed, he hath taken their goods as his own, by reaſon whereof their wills be not performed: and one mean he had to put them in fear, that were made executors, to refuſe to meddle.

Taken the goods of ſpirituall men deceaſed.

18. Alſo the ſaid lord cardinall conſtrained all ordinaries in England yeerly to compound with him, or elſe he will uſurp halfe, or the whole of their juriſdiction by prevention, not for good order of the dioceſſes, but to extort treaſure: for there is never a poore archdeacon in England, but that he paid yearly to him a portion of his living.

All ordinaries, &c. to compound with him.

19. Alſo the ſaid lord cardinall hath not only by his untrue ſuggeſtion to the pope ſhamefully ſlandered many good religious houſes,

Slandered religious houſes to the pope.

By authority of his bull ſuppreſſed 30 houſes of religion.

houſes, and good vertuous men dwelling in them, but alſo ſuppreſſed by reaſon thereof above thirty houſes of religion. And where by authority of his bull he ſhould not ſuppreſſe any houſe, that had mo men of religion in number above the number of 6 or 7, he hath ſuppreſſed divers houſes that had above the number. And thereupon hath cauſed divers offices to be found by verdict untruly, that the religious perſons ſo ſuppreſſed had voluntarily forſaken their ſaid houſes, which was untrue, and ſo hath cauſed open perjury to be committed, to the high diſpleaſure of Almighty God.

Cauſed divers offices to be found untruly. Perjury.

Examined matters in chancery after judgements

[92]

20. Alſo the ſaid lord cardinall hath examined divers and many matters in the chancery after judgement thereof given at the common law, in ſubverſion of your lawes, and made ſome perſons reſtore againe to the other party condemned that, that they had in execution by vertue of the judgement at the common law.

Injunctions.

21. Alſo the ſaid lord cardinall hath granted many injunctions by writ, and the parties never called thereunto, nor bill put in againſt them: and by reaſon thereof, divers of your ſubjects have been put from their lawfull poſſeſſion of their lands and tenements. And by ſuch means he hath brought the more party of the ſuiters of this your realm before himſelf, whereby he and divers of his ſervants have gotten much riches, and your ſubjects ſuffered great wrongs.

His ſervants rich.

The popes pardons.

22. Alſo the ſaid lord cardinall to augment his great riches hath cauſed divers pardons granted by the pope to be ſuſpended, which could not be revived, till that the ſaid lord cardinall were rewarded, and alſo have a yearly penſion of the ſaid pardon.

Oppreſſion.

23. Alſo the ſaid lord cardinall not regarding your lawes nor juſtice, of his extort power hath put out divers and many fermors of his lands, and alſo patentees of the arch-biſhoprick of York and the biſhoprick of Wincheſter, and of the abbey of St. Albons, which had good and ſufficient grant thereof by your lawes.

Elections of abbots, priors, &c.

24. Alſo the ſame lord cardinall, at many times when any houſes of religion have been void, he hath ſent his officers thither, and with crafty perſwaſions hath induced them to compromit their election in him. And that before he named or confirmed any of them, he and his ſervants received ſo much great goods of them, that in manner it hath been to the undoing of the houſe.

Viſited. Extortion.

25. Alſo by his authority legatine, the ſame lord cardinall hath viſited the moſt part of the religious houſes and colledges of this your realm, and hath taken from them the twenty fifth part of their lively-hood, to the great extortion of your ſubjects and derogation of your lawes and prerogative, and no law to bear him ſo to do.

26. Alſo when matters have been near at judgement by proces at your common law, the ſame lord cardinall hath not only given and ſent injunctions to the parties, but alſo ſent for your judges, and expreſly by threats commanding them to defer the judgement, to the evident ſubverſion of your lawes, if the judges would ſo have ceaſed.

Injunctions. Threatned judges.

27. Alſo whereas neither the biſhop of York nor Wincheſter, nor the abbey of S. Albons, nor the profit of his legation, nor the benefit of the chancery, nor his great penſion out of France, nor his wards, and other inordinate taking could not ſuffice him, he hath

Penſion out of France.

hath made his ſonne *Winter* to ſpend ſeven and twenty hundred pounds by the year, which he taketh to his own uſe, and giveth him not paſt two hundred pounds yearly to live upon.

His ſon Winter.

28. Alſo where the ſaid lord cardinall did firſt ſue unto your grace to have your aſſent to be legat *de latere*, he promiſed and ſolemnly proteſted before your majeſtie, and before the lords both ſpirituall and temporall, that he would nothing do nor attempt by the vertue of his legacie, that ſhould be contrary to your gracious prerogative or regalitie, or to the damage or prejudice of the juriſdiction of any ordinary, and that by his legacie no man ſhould be hurted nor offended: and upon that condition, and no other, he was admitted by your grace to be legate within this your realm: which condition he hath broken, as is well known to all your ſubjects. And when that he made this promiſe, he was buſie in his ſuit at Rome to viſit all the clergy of England both exempt and not exempt.

Legat *De latere.* His promiſe. Nothing againſt prerogative or regality. Or to the prejudice of ordinary juriſdiction.

Breach of promiſe.

29. Alſo upon the ſuit of the ſaid lord cardinall at Rome to have his authority legatine, he made untrue ſurmiſe to the popes holineſſe againſt the clergie of your realm: which was, that the regular perſons of the ſaid clergie had given themſelves *in reprobum ſenſum;* which words S. Paul writing to the Romans applyed to abominable ſinne: which ſlander to your church of England ſhall for ever remain in the regiſter at Rome, againſt the clergy of this your realm.

Untrue ſurmiſe to the pope of the clergy.

[93]

30. Alſo the ſaid lord cardinall had the more part of the goods of doctor Smith late biſhop of Lincoln, biſhop Savage of York, maſter Dalbye archdeacon of Richmont, maſter Tonyers, doctor Rothall late biſhop of Durham, and of doctor Foxe late biſhop of Wincheſter, contrary to their wils, and your laws and juſtice.

Oppreſſion and extortion.

31. Alſo at the oier and terminer at York, proclamation was made that every man ſhould put in their bils for extortion of ordinaries, and when divers bils were put in againſt the officers of the ſaid lord cardinall of extortion, for taking twelve pence of the pound for probation of teſtaments, whereof divers bils were found before juſtice Fitzherbert and other commiſſioners, the ſaid lord cardinall removed the ſaid indictments into the chancery by *certiorari*, and rebuked the ſaid Fitzherbert for the ſame cauſe.

Extortion of ordinaries. Indictments of extortion of ord. removed into the chancery.

32. Alſo the ſaid lord cardinall hath buſied and endeavored himſelf by crafty and untrue tales to make diſſention and debate amongſt your nobles of your realm, which is ready to be proved.

Made debate between the nobles of the realm.

33. Alſo the ſaid lord cardinals officers have divers times compelled your ſubjects to ſerve him with carts for carriage, and alſo his ſervants have taken both corn and cattle, fiſh, and all other victuall, at your graces price, or under, as though it had been for your grace, which is contrary to your laws.

Purveyance for him. Purveyance at the kings price, Vid. inf. 35, 36.

34. Alſo the ſaid lord cardinall hath miſuſed himſelf in your moſt honourable court, in keeping of as great eſtate there in your abſence, as your grace would have done if you had been there preſent in your own perſon.

Keeping great eſtate in court.

35. Alſo his ſervants by vertue of your commiſſion under your broad ſeal by him to them given, have taken cattel and all other victuall at as low a price as your purveyors have done for your grace by your prerogative, againſt the laws of your realm.

Purveyance. Prerogative in purveyance.

36. Alſo where it hath been accuſtomed that your purveyors for your

Purveyance.

your honourable houſhold, have had yearly out of your town and liberty of S. Albons three or four hundred quarters of wheat, truth it is, that ſince the lord cardinall had the room of the abbot, that your ſaid purveyors could not be ſuffered by him and his officers to take any wheat within the ſaid town or liberty.

Injunction not to ſue for pardon for cauſes in the ſtar-chamber.

37. Alſo he hath divers times given injunctions to your ſervants that have been for cauſes before him in the ſtar-chamber, that they, nor other for them ſhould make, labour by any manner way, directly or indirectly, to your grace to obtain your graces favour or pardon; which was a preſumptuous intent for any ſubject.

A great preſumption.

Oppreſſion.

38. Alſo the ſaid lord cardinall did call before him Sir John Stanly knight, which had taken a farm by covent ſeal of the abbot and covent of Cheſter, and afterward by his power and might contrary to right committed the ſaid Sir John Stanly to the priſon of Fleet by the ſpace of a year unto ſuch time as he compelled the ſaid Sir John to releaſe his covent ſeal to one Leghe of Adlington, which married one Larks daughter, which woman the ſaid lord cardinall kept, and had with her two children. Whereupon the ſaid Sir John Stanly upon diſpleaſure taken in his heart made himſelf monke in Weſtminſter, and there died.

Legh of Adlington.

The card. kept Larkes daughter and had by her two children.

Clerk of the market.

Prices of victuals.

39. Alſo on a time your grace being at S. Albons according to the ancient cuſtome uſed within your verge, your clerk of the market doing his office, did preſent unto your officers of your moſt honourable houſhold the prices of all manner of victuals within the precinct of the verge. And it was commanded by your ſaid officers to ſet up the ſaid prices both on the gates of your honorable houſhould, and alſo within the market place within the town of S. Albons as of ancient cuſtome hath been uſed. And the lord cardinall hearing the ſame, preſumptuouſly, not like a ſubject cauſed the aforeſaid prices which were ſealed with your graces ſeal, accuſtomably uſed for the ſame, to be taken off and pulled down in the ſaid market place, where they were ſet up: and in the ſame places ſet up his owne prices ſealed with his ſeale, and would if it had not been letted in ſemblable manner, uſed your ſeal ſtanding upon your gates. And alſo would of his preſumptuous mind have openly ſet in the ſtocks within your ſaid town your clerk of your market. By which preſumption and uſurpation your grace may perceive that in his heart he hath reputed himſelf to be equall with your reall majeſty.

Pulled down the prices, &c.

[94]

The cardinals hat in the kings coin of groats, &c.

40. Alſo the ſaid lord cardinall of his further pompous and preſumptuous mind hath enterpriſed to join and imprint the cardinals hat under your arms in your coin of groats made at your city of York, which like deed hath not been ſeen to be done by any ſubject within your realm before this time.

41. Alſo where one Sir Edward Jones clerk parſon of Crowly in the county of Buck' in the eighteenth yeer of your moſt noble reign let his ſaid parſonage with all tithes and other profits of the ſame to one William Johnſon by indenture for certain years, within which years, the dean of the ſaid cardinals colledge in Oxenford pretended title to a certain portion of tithes within the ſaid parſonage, ſuppoſing the ſaid portion to belong to the parſonage of Chichelly, which was appointed to the priory of Tykeford lately ſuppreſſed, where (of truth) the parſons of Crowly have been peaceably

peaceably poſſeſſed of the ſaid portion out of the time of mind. Whereupon a *ſubpœna* was directed to the ſaid Johnſon to appear afore the lord cardinall at Hampton-court, out of any tearm, with an injunction to ſuffer the ſaid dean to occupy the ſaid portion. Whereupon the ſaid Johnſon appeared before the ſaid lord cardinall at Hampton-court, where without any bill, the ſaid lord cardinall committed him to the Fleet, where he remained by the ſpace of twelve weeks, becauſe he would not depart with the ſaid portion. And at the laſt upon a recogniſance made that he ſhould appear before the ſaid lord cardinall whenſoever he was commanded, he was delivered out of the Fleet; howbeit as yet the ſaid portion is ſo kept from him that he dare not deal with it. Subpœna.

42. Alſo where one Martin Decowra had a leaſe of the mannor of Balſall in the county of Warwick for tearm of certain years, an injunction came to him out of the chancery by writ upon pain of a thouſand pounds, that he ſhould avoide the poſſeſſion of the ſame mannor, and ſuffer Sir George Throckmorton knight to take the profits of the ſame mannor to the time the matter depending in the chancery between the lord of S. Johns and the ſaid Decowra were diſcuſſed. And yet the ſaid Decowra never made anſwer in the chancery, ne ever was called into the chancery for that matter, and now of late he hath received a like injunction upon pain of two thouſand pounds contrary to the courſe of the common law. Injunction.

43. Alſo whereas in the parliament chamber, and in open parliament communication and deviſes were had and moved, wherein mention was an incident made of matters touching hereſies, and erroneous ſects, it was ſpoken and reported by one biſhop there being preſent, and confirmed by a good number of the ſame biſhops, in preſence of all the lords ſpirituall and temporall then aſſembled, that two of the ſaid biſhops were minded and deſired to repair unto the univerſity of Cambridge for examination, reformation, and correction of ſuch errors as then ſeemed and were reported to reign amongſt the ſtudents and ſcholars of the ſame, as well touching the Lutherane ſect and opinions, as otherwiſe. The lord cardinall informed of the good minds and intents of the ſaid two biſhops in that behalf, expreſly inhibited and commanded them in no wiſe ſo to doe. By means whereof, the ſame errors, as they affirmed, crept more abroad and took greater place; ſaying furthermore that it was not in their defaults, that the ſaid hereſies were not puniſhed, but in the ſaid lord cardinall, and that it was no reaſon any blame or lack ſhould be arrected to them for his offence: whereby it evidently appeareth that the ſaid lord cardinall beſides all other his hainous offences, hath been the impeacher and diſturber of due and direct correction of hereſies, being highly to the danger and perill of the whole body, and good chriſtian people of this your realm. Hereſies and erroneous ſects.

44. Finally, foraſmuch as by the aforeſaid articles is evidently declared to your moſt royall majeſty, that the lord cardinall by his outrageous pride hath greatly ſhadowed a long ſeaſon your graces honor, which is moſt highly to be regarded, and by his inſatiable avarice and ravinous appetite to have riches and treaſure without meaſure, hath ſo grievouſly oppreſſed your poor ſubjects with ſo manifold crafts of bribery and extortion, that the common-wealth of this your graces realm is thereby greatly decayed and impove- [95]

 riſhed.

rished. And also by his cruelty, iniquity, affection, and partiality, hath subverted the due course and order of your graces laws to the undoing of a great number of your loving people.

Please it your most royall majesty therefore of your excellent goodnesse towards the weal of this your realm and subjects of the same, to set such order and direction upon the said lord cardinall, as may be to the terrible example of other to beware so to offend your grace, and your laws hereafter. And that he be so provided for that he never have any power, jurisdiction or authority hereafter to trouble, vex, and impoverish the common-wealth of this your realm, as he hath done heretofore, to the great hurt and dammage of every man almost high and low, which for your grace so doing, will daily pray, as their duty is, to almighty God for the prosperous estate of your most royall majesty, long to endure in honor and good health, to the pleasure of God, and your hearts most desire. Subscribed the first day of December the 21 year of the reign of our soveraign lord king Henry the 8.

T. More. T. Norffolk. Charl. Suff. Tho. Dorset. H. Exon. John Oxinford. H. Northumberland. G. Shrewsbury. R. Fitzwater. T. Rocheford. T. Darcy. W. Mountjoy. William Sandys.

William Fitzwilliam. Henry Guldeford. * John Fitz James. * Anthony Fitz Herbert.

So these articles began to be subscribed by Sir Thomas More lord chancelor, and ended with the two judges of the law.

There be in this court many officers, ministers, and clerks of the court, the principall whereof is the [a] master of the rols, anciently called *garden des rolles*, *clericus rotulorum*, *custos rotulorum*. And this is an ancient office, and grantable either for life, or at will, at the pleasure of the king. [b] The house annexed to his office, is called *domus conversorum*, so called because * king H. 3. founded this house to be a house of Jews as should be converted to the true religion of Jesus Christ, and there should have maintenance and allowance, which continueth to this day. King E. 3. *anno* 15 of his reign, by letters patents annexed this house to the office of *custos rotulorum*, and this office is grantable by letters patents: for the more assurance whereof, and of divers things worthy of observation, we have thought good to set down an act of parliament concerning this matter in these words.

[c] King E. 3. by his charter *anno* 51 of his reign did grant after the death of William Burstall then keeper of the rols and of the same house of converts of the kings grant to the keeper of the rols for the time being, and annexed it to the said office *imperpetuum*, and further granted that after the decease of the said William, the chancelor or keeper of the great seal after the voidance of the said office of keeping of the rols to institute successively the keepers of the rols, *in dicta domo conversorum, et custodes illos ponend' in possessione ejusdem, &c.* This charter was confirmed by act of parliament, as by that which followeth appeareth.

[d] *A nostre tresdoute H. le roy et son honourable counseil en cest parliament supplie son petit clerke William de Burstall gardeiner des rolles de la cancellarie, et gardeiner de la meason des converses de Londres quele est de vostre honorable patronage que come le dit William a ses tresgraundes custages et reparille la chappelle de les edifices du dit meason, et nostre seignior le roy dareine (que dieu assoil) pur maintenance de la dit chappelle* et

* Chief justice of England.
* Sir Anth. Fitzh. a justice of the court of common pleas.
[a] He was not called master of the rols, untill 11 H. 7. ca. 20. but never so called in any letters patents of this office.
[b] Fortesc. ca. 24.
* See the charter of erection by king H. 3. Holling. 1281. Vid. Rot. parl. 18 E. 1. nu. There were above fourscore converts in 18 E. 1. and petitioned in parliament for more relief.
[c] Rot. pat. 11 Ap. 51 E. 3. which you may read at large in Hollingsh. pa. 1281. 1282.
[d] Ex bundello petic. parl. anno 1 R. 2.
Garden des rolles de la chancery et de la meason des converses de Londres.
Nota the master of the rols or keeper is garden of the house of converts of the patronage or gift of the king.

et meason a la prier du dit William granta pur luy et ses heires per ses letters patents que le dit meason de converse apres le decease du dit William demerera a tous jours as gardein' de dits rolles pur le temps esteants tanque come ils seront en le dit office sans certain forme comprise en letters sursdites, please a nostre dit seignior le roy et seigniors deu parliament confirmer la dit grant et les letters patents issint ent faitz, et les choses comprises en ycels en ouier de charitie. Whereunto full assent was given by authority of parliament.

After which act of parliament John de Waltham gardein or keeper of the rols obtained of R. 2. in the sixth year of his reign letters patents, whereby the king granted to him *et successoribus suis custodibus rotulorum* the said house of converts; and the reason hereof seemeth to be, for that in the said charter of 51 E. 3. *sibi et successoribus suis* wanted. This John of Waltham was in 12 R. 2. bishop of Salisbury, and after treasurer of England. Hereby it appeareth what estate the master of the rols hath *in domo conversorum.* And this house is the place where the rols of the chancery are kept, and are so called because they are written in parchment, and made up in bundels of rols, that is to say, of charters, letters patents, commissions, deeds enrolled, recognisances, &c. Rot. pat. 6 R. 2.

These records since the beginning of H. 7. remain in the rols, and all before were transmitted into the Tower, and there remain.

Also for further manifestation hereof, we have thought good to set down a letters patents of this office in the 25 year of H. 6. and the rather for that it was granted *authoritate parliamenti*, in these words, *Henricus Dei gratia rex Angliæ, et Franciæ, et dominus Hiberniæ, omnibus ad quos præsentes lræ. pervenerint. Sciatis quod cum nos tertio decimo die Novembris, anno regni nostri decimo septimo constituimus dilectum clericum nostrum Johannen Stependen custodem rotulorum et librorum cancellariæ nostræ cum omnibus ad officium illud spectantibus, percipiend' in eodem officio feoda, commoditates, et proficua consueta, quamdiu nobis placuerit. Et ulterius dederimus, et concesserimus eidem Johanni custodiam domus nostræ conversorum præfato officio pro inhabitatione dicti custodis per progenitores nostros quondam reges Angliæ ab antiquo deposita, et annexæ: habendum et tenendum custodiam illam cum omnibus juribus et pertinentiis spectantibus ad eandem, prout in lris. nostris patentibus inde confectis plenius continetur. Nos bonum et gratuitum servicium quod dilectus clericus noster Thomas Kirkby nobis ante hæc tempora multipliciter impendit, indiesque impendere non desistit merite contemplantes, ac de fidelitate, circumspectione et industria ipsius Thomæ plenius confidentes, constituimus ipsum Thomam custodem rotulorum et librorum cancellariæ nostræ cum omnibus ad officium illud spectantibus, percipiendo in eodem officio feoda, commoditates, et proficua consueta à tempore quo officium illud per cessionem seu alio modo quocunque proximo vacare contigerit, quamdiu nobis placuerit. Et ulterius dedimus et concessimus, ac p. præsentes damus et concedimus eidem Thomæ custodiam dictæ domus nræ. conversorum præfato officio pro inhabitatione ejusdem custodis per dictos progenitores nros. ab antiquo (ut præmititur) disposita et annexæ. Habend' et tenend' eidem Thomæ custodiam illam cum omnibus juribus et pertinentiis spectantibus ad eandem quamdiu ipsum Thomam dictum officium custodis rotulorum et librorum prædictorum habere et tenere sive occupare contigerit. Eo quod expressa mentio de vero valore annuo officii prædicti et cæterorum præmissorum seu alicujus eorum, aut de aliis donis seu concessionibus per nos præfato Thomæ ante hæc tempora factis in præsentibus facta non*

Clericus noster custos rotulorum et librorum cancellar' nostræ cum omnibus ad officium illud spect'. Custodia domus nostræ conversorum.

Custos rotulorum, &c.

 existit,

existit, aut aliquibus actibus sive ordinationibus in contrarium editis sive ordinatis, aut aliqua alia causa, re, seu materia in aliquo non obstantibus. In cujus rei testimonium has lras. nras. fieri fecimus patentes. Teste meipso apud Maidston vicesimo nono die Martii, anno regni nri. vicesimo quinto. Authoritate parliamenti.

[97] Of latter times in the grant of this office he is stiled *clericus* * *parvæ bagæ, custos rotulorum, et domus conversorum.*

* Belonging anciently to his office.

See the statute of 14 H. 8. cap. 8.

The master of the rols hath *in jure officii*, the gift of the offices of six clerks in the chancery.

In the absence of the lord chancellor he heareth causes and giveth orders.

See in the third part of the Institutes, cap. Præmunire.

CAP. IX.

The Court of Requests.

See hereafter the Courts of Audience and Faculties. pa.

HAVING spoken of the court of chancery, swayed and governed by the lord chancelour, or keeper of the great seale; it shall be fit in this place to treat of the jurisdiction of the court of requests, wherein the lord privie seale at his pleasure, and the masters of requests doe assemble and sit. And the originall institution hereof was, that such petitions as were exhibited to the king, and delivered to the masters of the requests, should be perused by them, and the party directed by them to take his remedy according to their case, either at the common law, or in the court of chancery. And thereupon they were called *magistri à libellis supplicum:* and in this respect this meeting and consultation was called the court of requests, as the court of audience and faculties are called courts, albeit they hold no plea of controversie.

Cassaneus 7 part. fo. 136. b.

Those which in former times would have this court to be a court of judicature, took their aime from a court in France, which is called *curia eorum quos requestarum*, i. *supplicationum palatii magistros vocant, apud quos causa eorum tantum agitur, qui regis obsequiis deputati, vel privilegio donati sunt: hujus curiæ judices octo sunt.* But others taking this jurisdiction to be too narrow, contend to have it extend to all causes in equitie equall with the chancery, and their decrees to be absolute and uncontrollable. But neither of these are warranted by law, as shall evidently appear.

See before cap. Chancery. Perots case, pag. 87. See the articles against cardinall Woolsy, p. 89. See Hals Chronicle ubi supra. and Guines learned preface to his reading in the Inner Temple, about 16 El.

In the reign of H. 8. the masters of requests thought (as they intended) to strengthen their jurisdiction by commission, to hear and determine causes in equity. But those commissions being not warranted by law (for no court of equity can be raised by commission) soon vanished, for that it had neither act of parliament, nor prescription time out of minde of man to establish it.

* Mich. 40 & 41 Eliz. In the court of common pleas, upon a bill

* Tr. 40 El. in communi banco inter Stepney et Lloyd. Rot. 1157. See Hals Chron. 8 H. 8. fo. 5 . agreeth with the law.

a bill exhibited in the court of requeſts againſt Flood, for default of anſwer an attachment was awarded againſt Flood under the privie ſeale, to Stepney then ſheriffe of Carnarven, who by force of the ſaid writ attached Flood, and would not let him go, untill he had entred into an obligation to the ſheriffe to appear before his majeſties councell, in the court of requeſts: upon which obligation the ſheriffe brought an action of debt for default of appearance, and all this matter appeared in pleading. And it was adjudged upon ſolemne argument, that this which was called a court of requeſts, or the white hall, was no court that had power of judicature, but all the proceedings thereupon were *coram non judice*, and the arreſt of Flood was falſe impriſonment, ſo as he might avoid the bond by dures at the common law, without aide of the ſtatute of 23 H. 6. ca. 10.

The puniſhment of perjury in the court of Whitehall by the ſtatutes of 33 H. 8. cap. 9. and 5 Eliz. cap. 9. doth not give it any juriſdiction of judicature, no more than the ſtatutes that give againſt a gaoler an action for an eſcape, or puniſheth a gaoler of his owne wrong for extortion, an officer of his own wrong ſhall be puniſhed by the ſtatutes in that caſe provided, and yet the ſtatutes thereby make them no lawfull officers: for it is one thing to puniſh, and another to give authority. So it was juſtice in the parliaments to puniſh perjury in the Whitehall, although the court were holden by uſurpation, and ſo before it appeareth to be by the judgement in Stepneys caſe. See Beverlyes caſe, lib. 4. 123, 124. and the caſe of the orphans of London, lib. 5. fo. 73. where it is called the court of requeſts, taking the ſame to be according to the originall inſtitution. And as gold or ſilver may as currant money paſſe even with the proper artificer, though it hath too much allay, untill he hath tried it with the touchſtone: even ſo this nominative court may paſſe with the learned as juſtifiable in reſpect of the outſide by vulgar allowance, untill he adviſedly looketh into the roots of it, and try it by the rule of law: as (to ſay the truth) I my ſelf did: but *errores ad ſua principia referre, eſt refellere*, to bring errors to their firſt, is to ſee their laſt. [98]

The author of the book of diverſity of courts written in 21 H. 8. doth not ſo much as mention any ſuch court: nor the Doctor and Student who wrote in 23 H. 8. treating of matters of equity never mentioneth any ſuch court: nor in any of the reports of H. 8. or of any other before him, we finde any mention made of any ſuch court. Herein, as in all other things, we have dealt clearly and plainly, upon what authorities and reaſons we have grounded our opinion: and when we undertook to write, we reſolved to publiſh nothing *reluctante conſcientia*, which we (by Gods ſpeciall grace) have performed, without any ſpark of contradiction, or reſpect of any private whatſoever: that charge ever ſounding in mine eare, that is given to all that take upon them to write, *Ne quid falſum audeant, ne quid verum non audeant.* And although the law be ſuch as we have ſet down; yet in reſpect of the continuance that it hath had by permiſſion, and of the number of decrees therein had, it were worthy of the wiſdome of a parliament, both for the eſtabliſhment of things for the time paſt, and for ſome certaine proviſion with reaſonable limitations (if ſo it ſhall be thought conve-

Error, qui non reſiſtitur, approbatur.

Regula.

nient to that high court) for the time to come: *et sic liberavi animam meam.*

[99]

CAP. X.

The Court of Common Pleas.

Mag. Cart. ca. 11.

Bracton lib. 3. fo. 105. b.

* Ut sup. fo. 108. a.

BY the statute of Magna Carta, cap. 11. it is provided, *Quòd communia placita non sequantur curiam nostram, sed teneantur loco certo. Habet rex etiam curiam, et justiciarios in banco residentes, qui cognoscunt de omnibus placitis, de quibus authoritatem habent cognoscendi, et sine warranto jurisdictionem non habent nec coercionem. Et paulo post. Sunt etiam alii justiciarii * perpetui, certo loco residentes, sicut in banco, loquelas omnes de quibus habent warrantum terminantes, qui omnes jurisdictionem habere incipiunt prestito sacramento.*

Britton fo. 2. Vide Fleta lib. 2. cap. 2. & lib. 1. cap. 54.

Oustre ceo voilons q. justices demorgent continualment a Westm. ou ailors la, ou nous voudrons ordeiner, a pleader comunes pleas solonq; ceo que nous les manderons per nous breifes; issint que des parols deduces devant eux per nous breifes eyent record.

Out of these, three things are to be observed: first what shall be said *communia placita.* They are not called *communia placita* in respect of the persons, but in respect of the quality of the pleas. Regularly pleas are divided into pleas of the crown, and into common or civill pleas. Pleas of the crowne are treason and felony, and misprision of treason and felony, &c. This court is the lock and the key of the common law in common pleas, for herein are reall actions, whereupon fines and recoveries (the common assurances of the realm) do passe, and all other reall actions by originall writs are to be determined, and also of all common pleas mixt or personall: in divers of which, as it appeareth before in the chapter of the Kings Bench, this court and the kings bench have a concurrent authority.

See the second part of the Institutes Mag. Cart. cap. 11. Vid. 17 E. 3. 50. *Quare incumbravit,* and in the chapter of the kings bench here before.

* Vid. sup. pa 79.

* Robert Parning the kings serjeant at law 24 July 14 E. 3. was created chief justice of England, in which office he remained untill the 15 of December following, and then he was made lord treasurer of England; in which office he continued untill the 15 year of E. 3. when he was made lord chancelour of England: and while he was lord chancelour, he would come and sit in this court being the lock and key of the common law, as is aforesaid: and there debate matters in law of greatest difficulty, as it appeareth in the report of the year of 17 E. 3. fo. 11. 14. 23. 37. &c. knowing assuredly, that he that knowes not the common law, can never rightly judge of matters in equity: whereof at that time very few matters were depending before him in chancery.

2. These words of Bracton, [*sine warranto jurisdictionem non habent,*] are well expounded by Britton, that that warrant is by the kings writs, *solonq; ceo que nous les manderons per nous breifes.* So as regularly this court cannot hold any common plea in any action, reall, personall, or mixt, but by writ out of the chancery, and retornable into this court.

3. That

3. That in certain cases this court may hold plea by bill without any writ in the chancery, as for or against any officer, minister, or priviledged person of this court.

Also this court without any writ may upon a suggestion grant prohibitions to keep, as well temporall as ecclesiasticall courts, within their bounds and jurisdiction, without any originall or plea depending: for the common law which in those cases is a prohibition of it self stands in stead of an originall, whereof there be infinite presidents in this court. And Sir Thomas Egerton lord chancelour Mich. 7 Jac. regis called Fleming chief justice and all the judges of the kings bench, and Tanfeild chief baron, and the rest of the barons of the exchequer, of whom the chancelour demanded whether the court of common pleas had authority to grant any prohibition without writ of attachment or plea depending: who upon mature deliberation unanimously resolved, that this court might grant prohibitions upon suggestions without any writ of attachment or plea depending for the reason aforesaid, and according to a multitude of presidents. The justices of the common pleas were not called, because they had often resolved the point before. So as now this point concerning the jurisdiction of this court for granting of prohibitions upon suggestions, where there is neither writ of attachment, nor plea depending, is in peace, being resolved by the justices of the bench and of the common pleas, and by the barons of the exchequer.

8 R. 2. Attachment sur prohib. pl. ultimo. 9 H. 6. 61. 10 E. 2. action sur lestat. 34.

[100]

4. This court upon an adjournment upon a forein voucher may hold plea likewise upon other foreign pleas, and upon generall bastardy, *Ne unques accouple in loiall matrimony, &c.* for none but the kings courts, and no inferiour court shall write to the bishop. So likewise upon ancient demesne pleaded, &c.

See the second part of the Institutes all these points.

The chiefe justice of the common pleas is created by letters patents. *Rex, &c. Sciatis quod constituimus dilectum et fidelem E. C. militem, capitalem justiciarium * de communi banco. Habendum quamdiu nobis placuerit, cum vadiis et feodis ab antiquo debitis et consuetis. In cujus rei testimonium has literas nostras fieri fecimus patentes. Teste, &c.*

* So called the common bench in respect of the common pleas there holden.

And each of the justices of this court hath letters patents. *Sciatis quod constituimus dilectum et fidelem P. W. militem unum justiciariorum nostrorum de communi banco, &c.* But none can be constituted judge of this court unlesse he be serjeant at law of the degree of the coife, and yet in the letters patents to them made, they are not named serjeants.

The jurisdiction of this court is generall, and extendeth throughout all England.

For the antiquity of this court see before in the chapter of the kings bench adjoining thereunto, 6 E. 3. where a fine was levied in this court 6 R. 1. and in 39 E. 3. a plea in this court in 1 H. 3. And that I may speak once for all the justices of the kings bench, or of this court of the common bench, that they observe the ancient rule of law, *Nemo duobus utatur officiis*, for none of them can take any other office, or any fee, or reward but of the king only. And it were behoovefull to the common-wealth and advancement of justice and right, and preferment of well deserving men, if the like course were holden concerning all offices, as well ecclesiasticall as temporall and civill: and that no man following the example of the

See the second part of the Institutes, Mag. Cart. cap. 11. 6 E. 3. 52. 39 E. 3. 24. 18 E. 3. stat. 3.

reverend judges should enjoy two offices. For severall offices were never instituted to be used by one man.

Term. Trin. anno 19 E. 1. in communi banco, rot. 146. Rotel. in Thesaur.

The jurisdiction of this court for punishment of their officers and ministers. *Petrus de Luffenham indictatus quod ipse in curia hic à die Sancti Hillarii in 15 dies anno regni regis nunc 19, falso et maliciose delevit adjornationem ejusdem essoin' ad diem illum intrati de com' Rotel. pro Roberto Attehale de South-Luffenham petente et Radulph. de Kirkeby tenent' de placito terre, &c. Et quesitus qualiter se velit inde acquietare, dicit quod in nullo est inde culpabilis, et de hoc ponit se super juram' de sociis in cur' hic. Et qui jurati dicunt super sacramentum suum, quod prædictus Radulphus prædictis die et anno fuit in cur' hic, et dixit prædicto Petro quod prædictum essoinum fuit adjornat' et prædictus Petrus intravit infra bancum et rotulos de essoin', et cum perpendisset quod le aff. fuit appositum molivit ipse policem suum et inde frotavit super le aff. quousq; illud fere omnino delevit ut sic faceret prædictum Robertum amisisse breve suum, &c. Ideo consideratⁱ est quod prædictus Petrus committitur gaolæ de Fleete custodiend' per unum annum et unum diem pro falsitate et deceptione prædictis, et tunc redimendus pro voluntate domini regis, &c. Et sciend' quod liberatus fuit gaolæ die Mercurii prox' ante festum Sanctæ Margaretæ virginis hoc anno, &c. Postea die Veneris prox' ante festum Sanctæ Margaretæ virginis anno 20 deliberatus est prædictus Petrus, et inhibitum est ei, quod nihil habet nisi vestes pendentes in dorso, admittitur ad dimid' marc. per 20 li. Wil. de Okeham, ita tamen quod si ad plus sufficiat, &c. Justic' reservant eis potestatem, &c.*

[101]

Mich. 19 E. 1. in banco rot. 191. Northampton.

*Et quia prædictus Johannes de Vpton in cur' hic' recognovit quod hoc anno in æstate concessit quod prædictam defaltam remitteret, et pro illa concessione recepit 20 s. in autumpno, et postea ad prædictam tertiam septimanam Sancti Michaelis idem Johannes remisit prædictam defaltam, per quam prædictus Willielmus recuperasse potuit prædictum ten' in fraudem et deceptionem prædicti Willielmi; ideo ipse pro falsitate prædicta committitur gaolæ de Fleet commoraturus per annum et diem, &c. per formam * statuti, &c. Postea post annum et diem, &c. prædictus Johannes venit et deliberatus est secundum statutum, &c. et inhibitum est ei, &c. et finivit pro una marca.*

* W. 1. cap. 29.

Eodem rot. nu. 210. London.

Bene examinatur fraus de brevi in jur' per vic' retorn' termin' Trin' et per quendam alium panellum ejusdem mutatum et contrefectum, unde contrefactor per jur' est culpabilis, et adjudicatur gaolæ de Fleete per annum et diem. Et quia scriptor ejusdem brevis licet de falsitate et malitia non fuit particeps, nec aliquid mali fecisse putavit, &c. Custodiatur, &c. et finem fecit per unam marcam.

Hil. 20 E. 1. in banco rot. 109. Northampton.

Et quia Rogerus de Langeport attornatus est malæ famæ, et defatigavit cur' : ideo committitur gaolæ, &c. Et quæsitis rotulis de indictamentis attornatorum, &c. compertum est quod idem Rogerus indictatus fuit, quod ipse fuit conversans in cancell' et socius Adæ de Pontefracto, qui falsavit sigillum domini regis, et falsa brevia composuit, &c. Et quæsitus qualiter se velit acquietare, dicit quod clericus est, et non potest in curia hic domino regi inde respondere. Et quia nullus ordinarius ipsum petit, &c. nec ipse Rogerus aliter se velit inde acquietare, ideo ipse committitur gaolæ quousque, &c. Et mittitur ad turrim London, &c.

The officers of this court are many, viz. *Custos brevium, tres prothonotarii,* three prothonotaries: *clericus warrantorum,* clerk of the warrants: *clericus argenti regis,* clerke of the kings silver: *quatuor exigendarii,* exigenters: *quatuordecem falazarii,* filazers: *clericus juratorum,*

ratorum, clerk of the juries: *clericus essoniorum*, clerk of the essoignes: *clericus utlagariorum*, clerke of the outlawries: this belongs to the office of the attorny generall, who exerciseth it by deputy.

In former times great abuses have been by attornies of this court, by suing out a judiciall proces without any originall: which when it hath been found out, it hath beene severely punished; for many inconveniences thereupon doe follow. For example, in 20 H. 6. an attorny of the common place had made a *capias* directed to the sheriffe of York, whereof there was no originall; at which day of the retorne an attachment was awarded by the court against the attorny to answer the deceipt, whereupon he was taken and examined, and confessed it, and thereupon by the court he was committed to the Fleet, imprisoned for a moneth, and that his name should be drawn out of the roll of attornies, and never should be attorny either in this court or any other, and thereunto he was sworne. Note the severity of this judgement doth shew the heynousnesse of the offence.

20 H. 6. 37. a. W. 1. cap. 29.

[102]

An attorny sued out an *habere facias seisinam* against one, by force whereof the true tenant was put out of his freehold, where in truth there was no record of any recovery: the party grieved brought an action of deceit against the attorny, and recovered damages, and the attorny imprisoned.

17 E. 3. 51, 52. Nota, he may be punished for the crime, and the party grieved may have his action.

Memorandum quod magister Johannes Lovell qui fuit custos rotulorum et brevium domini regis de banco per manus suas proprias liberavit Johanni Bacon clerico de mandato domini regis in hæc verba. Edwardus, &c. Dilecto clerico suo Johanni Lovell salutem. Cum commiserimus dilecto clerico nostro Johanni Bacon custod' rotulorum et brevium nostrorum de banco; habendum quam diu nobis placuerit: vobis mandamus quod eidem Johanni rotulos et brevia prædicta quæ sunt in custodia vestra ex commissione nostra per chirographum inde inter vos et ipsum conficiend' sine dilatione liberetis custod' in forma prædicta. T. me ipso apud Stebenheth 17 Aprilis anno regni nostri 20.

Pasch. 20 E. 1. in banco, rot. post. 135.

Super quo prædictus Johannes liberavit dicto Johanni Bacon rotulos et brevia de termino Sancti Michaelis anno 17, usque hunc terminum, et similiter rotulos de esson'. Et scripta dedicta et suspecta cum talleis dedict', una cum compotis dedict', ac etiam 160 not' finium, duas ligulas de recordis sine die, et 14 certificat' episcoporum.

[103]

CAP. XI.

The Court of Exchequer.

THE authority of this court is of originall jurisdiction without any commission. Of this court Britton speaking in the kings person saith. [a] *Volons nous que a nous eschekers a Westm' et ailors eyent nous* [b] *treasorers, et nous* [c] *barons illonques jurisdiction et record de choses que touchent lour office a oier et determiner touts les causes que touchent nous debts, et auxi a nous fees, et les incident choses, sans les queux tiels choses ne purront estre tries, et que ilz eyent power a co-nuster*

[a] Britton fo. 2. b.
[b] Nota treasurers in the plurall number.
[c] Of ancient time they were barons and peers of the realm, lib. nigro. scaccar' parte 1. ca. 4. See the 14 chap. of Mag. Cart. and the exposition of the same.

nuster de dettes que lon doit a nous dettors per ou nous puissons pluis tost aprocher a nre. dett.

d Et fo. 29. b.

[d] *En droit des purprestures voilons nous que le noisances soient oustes aux costages des purprestours, et les sufferables soient prise in nostre maine a la value per an soit inrolle, et solonque le discretions des treasors et des barons de nous eschequers soient arenes a fee farm a eux que pluis voilent doner.*

e Et fo. 38. b.

[e] *Et soit auxi enquis de nos customes de quirs et de leynes qui les ount coilles, et combien les coillours ount bien suffert de passer de sackes de leyne sauns payer custome, et combien eit valu la custome chescun au en chescun mannere de custome a nous apurtenant et ceux articles soient termines a nostre escheker selonc la discretion de nos barons.*

See the Custumer of Normandy, cap. 5. & 6. touching the exchequer there, both of another jurisdiction, and of other judges, and officers, then our court of exchequer is.

Mirror ca. 1. §. 14 *De la place del Eschequer.*

Lescheker est un place quarre que solement est ordeine pur le prou le roy ou deux chivaliers. 2 Clerks, ou 2 homes, lres. sont assignes pur oier et terminer les torts faits al roy et a sa corone en droit de ces fies et ces franchises, et les accounts des bayliffs, et des receivors de deniers le roy et des administrators de ces biens per la viewe de une soveraign que est treasorer de Angliterre. Les deux chivaliers soloient estre appeles deux barons pur afferer les amerciaments de counties, et des barons et des tenants counties et baronies cy que nul ne fuit affere forsque per ces piers.

A celle place estoit assigne un seale ove garden pur faire ent acquittance de chescun payment que avoir le voloit, et de sealer les bres. et les estrets south cere verte issant de celle place pur le prou le roy. En celle place sont auxi chamberleines et plusors auters ministers que ne touch my molt a la ley.

Et ca. 1. § 3.

* This was in respect of the tenure, for all earldomes and baronies were holden in capite.

20 E. 3. ass. 120. 26 ass. 37.

f Artic. sup. Cart. cap. 4. 28 E. 1. Stat. de Roteland. 10 E. 1. reg. 187.

g Fleta li. 2. ca. 2.

h Ockam.

*Ordeine fuit leschequer in manner come ensuist, et les paines pecuniels de countees et barons en certein, et auxi de tenants, counties et * baronies dismemlies et que ceux amerciaments fuissent affered per les barons del eschequer, et que lein envoast les estreets de lour amerciaments al eschequer ou que ilz fuissent amercies en la court le roy.*

[f] *Ouster ceo nul common plea ne soit deformes tenus en leschequer encounter la forme de la grand charter.*

[g] Fleta (for Bracton treateth not of this court) saith. *Habet et rex curiam suam et justiciarios suos residentes ad scaccarium.* And this is all I finde in him.

This court is divided into two parts, viz. judiciall accounts, called *scaccarium computorum*, and into the receipt of the exchequer. [h] *Una origo utriusque scaccarii, superioris scilicet, et inferioris, sed quicquid in superiori computatur, in inferiori solvitur.*

[104]

Before we observe any thing out of these ancient authors and acts of parliament, it shall be necessary to set down the great officers, the judges, and other officers and ministers of this court, as they be at this day.

Fiscus in one sense is taken for the exchequer, properly it is *sporta* a hamper, wherein the confiscations, sessements, and other moneys of the king were carried into the treasury.

The officers of this court.

Rot. par. 13 R. 2. nu. 6. & 7.

1. *Dominus thesaurarius Angliæ:* which office he hath at this day by the delivery of a white staffe, at the kings will and pleasure. In former times he had this great office by delivery of the keys (golden keys) of the treasury: when treasure failed, the white staffe

ſtaffe ſerved to reſt him upon it, or to drive away importunate ſuiters.

2. *Theſaurarius ſcaccarii*, anciently called *arcarius ab arca*, and this office he hath by letters patents. For both theſe offices he hath 365. l. fees, robes out of the wardrop 15. l. 7. s. 8. d. in toto 380. l. 7. s. 8. d. * Hugo Pateſhull was firſt treaſurer of the exchequer, and after *ſummus theſaurarius*.

Vide rot. pa. 13 E. 3. part 1. for this office.

* Math. Paris 18 H. 3. pa. 391. & 19 H. 3. anno dom. 1234. And ſo was Tho. Wimondham, anno dom. 1258. 50 H. 3.

Cancellarius ſcaccarii, that keepeth the ſeal. See Pl. com. 321. *Leſchequer ad chancelor et ſeale; et les bres. uſuall in le chancery in leſchequer, &c. ſont pluis ancient que le regiſter.* See of the chancelor of the exchequer hereafter in the court of the exchequer chamber.

Capitalis baro et barones alii.

Subtheſaurarius ſcaccarii, anciently called *locum tenens theſaurarii. Petrus de Willebye locum tenens theſaurarii, anno* 30 E. 1. *et plures alii:* he nameth the two praiſers of all the goods ſeiſed or not cuſtomed, and ordereth whether the party ſhall have been at the price or not, he appointed the ſteward, cook and butler for the proviſion of the ſtar-chamber: he in the vacancy of the treaſurer doth all things in the receipt, that the treaſurer doth. In the ſtatute of 39 El. ca. 7. and 43 El. in the ſubſidy of the clergy he is called under-treaſurer of England. Concerning this matter I finde of record this writ following.

Edwardus rex Angliæ et dominus Hiberniæ baronibus et camerariis ſuis de ſcaccario ſuo, ſalutem. Quum pro eo quod [a] *venerabilis pater W. archiepiſcopus Eborum nuper theſaurarius ſcaccarii prædicti, circa diverſa negotia in partibus borealibus eſt occupatus, quo minus intendere poſſit ad ea quæ ad officium illud in* [b] *dicto ſcaccario pertinent exercenda, conſtituerimus venerabilem patrem Johannem Wintonienſem epiſcopum* [c] *tenentem locum theſaurarii ſcaccarii prædicti, quouſque de officio illo aliter duximus ordinandum, percipiendo in eodem officio (dum illud ſic tenuerit) feodum conſuetum,* [d] *prout in literis noſtris patentibus præfato epiſcopo inde confectis plenius continetur. Vobis mandamus quod ipſum epiſcopum ad officium admittatis et ei in his quæ ad officium prædictum pertineant intendatis in forma prædicta. Teſte Edwardo filio noſtro primogenito cuſtode regni noſtri, apud Hereford ſexto die Novembris, anno regni noſtri viceſimo.*

Rot. brevium. 20 E. 2.

[a] Archbiſhop treaſurer of the exchequer.

[b] Nota in dicto ſcaccario.

[c] Under-treaſurer.

[d] Treaſurerſhip of the exchequer granted by letters patents.

Cuſtos regni.

The office and duty of the lord treaſurer of England doth appear by his oath, which ſtandeth upon eight articles.

Vid. the lord chancelors oath in the chapter of the Chancery.

1. That well and truly he ſhall ſerve the king and his people in the office of treaſurer.
2. That he ſhall doe right to all manner of people, poor and rich, of ſuch things as concern his office.
3. The kings treaſure he ſhall truly keep and diſpend.
4. He ſhall truly counſell the king.
5. The kings councell he ſhall * layn and keep.
6. That he ſhall neither know nor ſuffer the kings hurt, nor his diſheriting, nor that the rights of the crown be decreaſed by any mean, as far forth as he may let it.
7. And if he may not let it, he ſhall make knowledge thereof clearly and expreſly to the king with his true device and counſell.
8. And he ſhall doe and purchaſe the kings profit in all that he may reaſonably doe: which in effect agreeth with the oath of the lord chancelor, as you may read *ubi ſupra*.

* Lain is an old French word, to hide.

Imprimis

Forma constitutionis thesaurarii Angliæ.

Imprimis post sigillationem patentium de illo officio vocetur in cur' cancellariæ, coram domino cancellario genibus flexis facit sacramentum, ut superius scribitur, et deinde sigillatum erit breve regis directum baronibus et camerariis de scaccario de attendenc' recitans effectum dictarum literarum patentium. Et inde recesserit dictus dominus cancellarius ad curiam scaccarii et ibidem (dicto thesaurario stante) ad barram legantur literæ patentes prædict' et similiter prædictum bre. et vocatus est idem thesaurarius ad locum suum per dictum dominum cancellarium accipiens cessum, et liberatæ erunt tunc et ibidem claves officii thesaurarii, et omnes officiarii sub se recedent cum ipso thesaurario in thesaurum et dantes ei attendenc'. This we have transcribed *de verbo in verbum in eisdem verbis.*

Vid. Rot. Cartarum anno 17 H. 3.

The lord treasurer of England hath also granted to him by letters patents under the great seal, *thesaurariam scaccarii regis Angliæ*, which of ancient time was a distinct office by itself. The office of the treasurer of the exchequer did principally take care of the green wax, fees, and tenures, as it is said; he hath also with the barons the custody of records as by the insuing record appears.

Hil. 25 El. coram baronibus.

Note the statute speaketh of the chancelor and treasurer generally which is intended of the treasurer of England, *in digniori sensu.* See lib. 1. fo. 11. Sir William Pelhams case.

* Note hereby it clearly appeareth that the treasurer and barons of the exchequer are keepers of the records judiciall of the exchequer. Vide 9 E. 3.

In an information of intrusion in the exchequer against Brace, judgment was given for the queen against Brace, who brought a writ of error directed to the lord chancelor and lord treasurer, and they made a warrant under their seals to the barons to bring the record before them. And Manwood chief baron objected against both the writ and the warrant, for that the statute of 31 E. 3. c. 12. that giveth this writ of error is generall, that the lord chancelor and lord treasurer shall cause to come before them the record and processe of the exchequer, and in as much as no speciall writ was given by the statute, therefore the writ ought to be directed to them that have the keeping of the record according to the course of the common law. * And for that the treasurer of the exchequer and barons have the keeping of the records of the exchequer, the writ of error ought to have been directed to them, and that the lord chancelor and lord treasurer of England are judges in this case, and not the treasurer of the exchequer. And upon search of presidents all the writs of error from the making of the statute untill 7 Eliz. were directed to the treasurer of the exchequer, and barons to bring the record before the lord chancelor and lord treasurer: but in 7 El. and since divers writs have been directed as this writ was, &c. But it was resolved by the lord chancelor, lord treasurer, and the two chief justices assistants, that the writ ought to be directed to the treasurer of the exchequer and barons that have the record in their custody according to the ancient course and presidents, and thereupon this writ abated.

Here four things are to be observed. 1. That albeit the barons, as hath been said, are the sole judges, yet the treasurer of the exchequer is joyned with them in keeping of the records, whereof the barons are judges, for they are parcell of the kings treasure. 2. That writs of error are to be directed to them that have the custody of the record wherein any judgment is given; as a writ of error to reverse a judgment in the court of common pleas, shall be directed to the chief justice only who hath the custody of the body of the record wherein the judgment is given, but the originall writ and warrant of atturny are not in his custody. 3. That albeit the lord treasurer is also treasurer of the exchequer, yet the writ of error

ror is directed to him as treasurer of the exchequer, and the barons, to have the record before himself as treasurer of England and the chancelor. 4. That at the making of the statute of 31 E. 3. that giveth the writ of error, the offices of treasurer of England and the treasurer of the exchequer were in severall hands, as by the writs of error brought soon after appeareth. Before the said statute of 31 E. 3. the errors in the exchequer were sometimes examined in parliament, and sometimes before commissioners by force of the kings writ under the great seal.

Par. 18 E. 3. nu. 40 &c. Vid. 1 R. 2. nu. Sir William de la Pools case. Mich. 33 & 34 E. 1. coram Rogero de Hegham & al is justiciariis, &c.

It was petitioned in parliament in 22 E. 3. nu. 25. that erroneous judgments in the exchequer might be reversed in the kings bench, but it succeeded not.

[106]

Vide term. Pasch 14 E. 3. a writ directed to the treasurer and barons calling to them such justices as they should think fit, to examine the record, &c. of the judgement in the exchequer, &c. for the countesse of Kent against the abbot of Ramsey, upon which judgement the abbot brought his writ of error. Fitzherbert for another purpose abridgeth the case, tit. *scire fac.* 122.

Hil. 11 E. 3. *in libro rubeo in scaccario* fo. 322. the case of John de Lecestre chamberlaine of the exchequer, a notable president to the like effect. *Lege, quia optime.*

Nota in the act of 31 E. 3. that is called the councell chamber, which now is called the exchequer chamber, because there was the assembly of all the judges being the kings councell for deciding of matters in law.

The chamberlaines of the exchequer. For these officers see in the first part of the Inst. lib. 2. cap. Grand' Serjeanty, sect. 153. the office mentioned in the letters patents is, *officium unius camerariorum de recept' scaccarii, sive officium unius camerariorum de scaccario*, and is granted for term of life to be exercised by him or his deputy. To this office belong the office of one of the dorekeepers of the receipt.

1 part of the Institutes, cap. Grand serjanty, sect. 153.

Contrarotulator. Of so great regard is the right use of the pipe, as there is a controller thereof, which no other office in this court hath. And the chancelour of the exchequer is the controller of the pipe.

Rememeratores. 3. viz. *regis, thesaurarii, et primorum fructuum.*

Clericus pipe. Of this officer somewhat is necessary to be said. The originall institution of this court was taken from a conduit or conveyance of water into a cisterne: for as water is conveyed from many fountains and springs by a pipe into a cisterne of a house, and from thence into the severall offices of the same: so this golden and silver stream is drawne from severall courts as fountains of justice, and other springs of revenue reduced and collected into one pipe, and by that conveyed into the cistern of his majesties receipt, &c. Therefore all accounts and debts to the king are delivered and collected out of the offices of the kings remembrancer, and treasurers remembrancer, &c. and drawn down and put in charge in the pipe. So as whatsoever is in charge in this roll or pipe, is said in law to be duly in charge. The clerk of the pipe in the patent of his office, is called *ingrossator magni rot. in scaccario.*

See the stat. of 5 R. 2. c. 14. stat. 1. 26 Ass. p. 60.

Duly in charge.

Also the treasurers remembrancer is by his office to charge and enter from the originall into the annuall, otherwise called the great roll,

The annuel or great roll.

roll, all fee-farme rents and other rents whatſoever upon leaſes of lands within the ſurvey of this court: and whatſoever is in charge in this roll is ſaid to be duly in charge. Alſo he ought to keep another roll, commonly called a roll of reverſions, as of grants of lands and offices in taile, for life or years *abſque compoto, aut aliquid inde reddendo*, to the end, as often as need ſhall require, writs may be granted to enquire whether the iſſue be ſpent, the leſſee dead, &c.

Duly in charge. The roll of revenues.

5 Auditors. 1 H. 7. 4. a. 7 El. Dier 238. b. Sir Rich. Lees caſe.

There be five auditors of the kings revenues within the ſurvey of this court, and their office is to take the accounts of the kings receivers, ſheriffs, eſcheators, collectors, and cuſtomers, and to audite and perfect them. But an auditor cannot allow any licenſe or grant, for the auditor knoweth not whether the licenſe or grant be good or no: but upon petition it ought to be allowed by the barons who know the law, *et ſic de ſimilibus*. Neither can the auditor put any thing in charge, for his office is (as hath been ſaid) but to take and audite accounts: for the words of his patent be, *Conceſſimus B. officium unius auditorum ſcaccarii noſtri quod I. S. nuper habuit et occupavit: habendum et tenendum prædictum officium præfato B. quam diu ſe bene geſſerit in eodem per ſe vel ſufficient' deput' ſuum.* Nay, though the barons do order upon ſight of any record or evidence, that any thing ſhall be put in charge, this is uſed to be done to bring it in queſtion, but it is not in law accounted to be duly in charge (untill it be recovered, received, and accounted for of record: for it is not judicially done, becauſe it may be done in the abſence of the party. Neither can any auditor make a *ſuper*, but of that that hath been received and accounted for before.

Quamdiu ſe bene geſſerit.

[107]

Auditor of the preſts take and audite the accounts of Ireland, Barwick, the mint, and of any money impreſted to any man.

Auditor of the receipts. Firſt, he is a kinde of filacer, for he fileth the tellers bils and entreth them. Secondly, he is a remembrancer, for he giveth to the lord treaſurer a certificate of the money received the week before. Thirdly, he is an auditor, for he maketh debentures to every teller before they pay any money, and taketh and auditeth their accounts. Beſides all theſe he keepeth the black book of receipts, and the lord treaſurers key of the treaſury, and ſeeth every tellers money locked up in the new treaſury.

Green wax.

Forinſec' oppoſitor, the forein oppoſer, he doth oppoſe all ſheriffes and bailiffs of liberties of their green wax: under theſe words [green wax] are included fines, iſſues, and amerciaments, recognizances for the peace, recognizances for appearance in any other court, and good behaviour, and ſuch like incertainties certified in ſeveral ſtreats into the office of the lord treaſurers remembrancer, who delivereth the ſame to the clerk of the extreats to be put into proces. And becauſe the extreats annexed to the writ are under a ſeale in green wax, they are vulgarly called greenwax. But felons goods, waifes, ſtrayes, outlawes goods, deodands, and ſuch like, are within the ſheriffes accounts, with which the eſcheator was wont to deale.

42 E. 3. cap. 9. 7 H. 4. cap. 3.

Clericus extractorum, clerk of the extreats, his office is partly touched before.

Here it may be demanded what the meaning of theſe words (of eſtreats that ſowne not) is. The act of 4 H. 5. cap. 2. being ori-

4 H. 5. cap. 2.

ginall in French, is *in proprio idiomate*, *Des estreats nient sovvenn*, which by turning the two single *v v* into a *w* was first made *sowenn*, and afterwards *sowne*. Now *sovvenn* properly signifieth to be remembred, and such casualties, as are not to be remembred run not in demand, that is, are not leviable.

Clericus nihilorum maketh a roll of all such summes as the sheriffe upon proces for the greenwax retorn *nihil*, and delivereth that roll into the office of the lord treasurers remembrancer to have execution done of it for the king. See the statute of 5 R. 2. cap. 13. stat. 1. concerning those retorns of *nihil* and the discharge thereof. See the stat. of Rotel. vers. finem.

Clericus placitorum, clerk of the pleas. In this mans office all the officers and priviledged persons in this court are to sue and be sued. Of this matter more hereafter.

Mareschallus, marshall. To this officer the court committeth the keeping of the kings debtors during the sitting of the term, to the end they may provide to pay the kings debts, or else to be further imprisoned. Such offices as are found *virtute officii*, and brought into the exchequer, are delivered to him, to be delivered over to the lord treasurers remembrancer. He also appointeth auditors to sheriffs, escheators, customers, and collectors for taking their accounts. Stat. de 51 H. 3. statut. 5.

Clericus summonitionum, clerk of the summons.

Deputati camerarii duo, called under-chamberlains of the exchequer: they cleave the tallies written by the clerk of the tallies, and read the same, that the clerk of the pell and the controllers thereof may see their entries be true: they also search for all records in the treasury.

Secundarii rememoratoris regis duo.

Secundarii rememoratoris thesaurarii duo.

Secundarii pipæ duo.

In the other part of the exchequer which is called the receipt. Concerning the course of the receipt of the exchequer, see Rot. Claus. 39 E. 3. m. 26. Rot. claus. 39 E. 3. memb. 26.

The two chamberlaines. Of the duty of these officers see in the first part of the Institutes. Vide 51 H. 3. stat. 5. 14 E. 3. cap. 14. First part of the Instit. Sect. 153.

[108]

Clericus talliarum. There be two kind of tailes or tallies, the one is called a talley of [a] debt, and the other is called a tally of [b] reward; of both which you may read in divers acts of parliament.

[a] 1 R. 2. cap. 5.

[b] 27 H. 8. ca. 11. 31 H. 8. cap. 16. 2 E. 6. cap. 4.

Clericus pellis, clerk of the pele. His duty is to enter every tellers bill into a roll, called *pellis receptorum*. His duty also is to enter in another roll payments called *pellis exitus*; and by what warrant the payment was made.

Numeratores, 4 tellers. The office of a teller consisteth in four duties. 1. To receive monies due to the king. 2. To give to the clerk *pellis receptorum* a bill thereof, whereby he may be charged. 3. To pay to all persons monies by warrant of the auditor of the receipt. 4. They make yearly and weekly books of their receipts and payments, which they deliver to the lord treasurer.

Junctores talliorum duo.

Deputati camerarii duo.

Custos thesauriæ.

Tabellarii

Tabellarii ordinarii 4.
Scribæ duo.
Officiarii decimarum et primitiarum.

Parl. 5 R. 2. ca. 16. ſtat. 1.

By the ſtatute of 5 R. 2. for making a commiſſion in the exchequer the clerk ſhall not take for his fee above 2 s. only; nor for a record of *niſi prius* with the writ but 2 s. only, as afore this time was wont to be done and uſed.

Vid. in the office of the kings remembrancer. Mich. 26 H. 6. rot. 46.

See in the end of a book containing many little books, as Fitzherberts juſtice of peace, *Carta feod'*, *&c.* the fees of the officers of the exchequer.

But it ſhall be neceſſary to ſet down the duties of the kings remembrancer, and of the lord treaſurers remembrancer.

The duties of the kings remembrancer.

The office of the kings remembrancer conſiſteth principally in eight duties. His firſt is to write proces againſt collectors of cuſtomes, ſubſidies, and fifteens. 2. He entreth in his office all recognizances before the barons, and taketh bonds for any of the kings debts, for obſerving of orders, or for appearances, and his duty is to make out proces upon every of them. 3. He maketh proces upon informations upon penall ſtatutes, all which informations are entred in his office. 4. He maketh bills of compoſition upon informations upon penall ſtatutes, 5. He taketh the ſtalment of debts and entreth them. 6. The clerk of the ſtar-chamber certifieth into his office the fines ſet in the ſtar-chamber; this officer maketh a record thereof, and draweth them down into the pipe. 7. Into this office ought to be delivered to be ſafely kept, all aſſurances, conveyances, and evidences, whereby any lands, tenements, hereditaments, or other things are granted to the king. 8. Alſo there is a court of equity holden in the exchequer chamber by Engliſh bill: all the bils and proceedings thereupon are entred in the office of this officer. See the ſtatute of 5 R. 2. cap. 14. ſtat. 1.

The duties of the lord treaſurers remembrancer.

The office of the lord treaſurers remembrancer principally conſiſteth in eight duties. 1. His duty is to preſerve the broadſpreading and fruitfull tree of tenures ſo many wayes beneficiall to the crown, and the juriſdiction of the court of wards, which ſometimes were within the ſurvey of this court, but ſince taken from it. He maketh out proces for the kings revenue by reaſon of the tenures of the king (wards excepted.) 2. He maketh proces of *fieri fac'* and extent for debts due to the king either in the pipe, or with the auditors. If a clerk of this court make any writ of proces for a debt which hath been paid and the tallies thereof joyned and allowed, he ſhall loſe his office, and be impriſoned untill he hath ſatisfied the party ſo much as by the diſcretion of the treaſurer and barons he is endamaged. 3. He maketh proces againſt all ſheriffs, eſcheators, receivers, and bayliffs, to bring them to account. 4. To make an entry of record, whereby it appeareth whether ſheriffs and other accountants pay their proffers due at Eaſter and Michaelmas. 5. He maketh another entry of record, to the end it may be known whether ſheriffs and other accountants keep their dayes of prefixion. 6. The green-wax is certified into his office, and are by him delivered to the clerk of the eſtreats, as hath been ſaid. [109] 7. There ought to be brought into this office all the accounts of cuſtomers, controllers, and all other accounts to make thereof in this office an entry of record, to avoid all

See hereafter in the chapter of the court of Wards.

1 R. 2. cap. 5.

all delay and concealment in the kings busines. 8. See the statute of 5 R. 2. cap. 14. stat. 1.

Concerning these officers there is an excellent law made in 5 R. 2. whereby it is enacted. [that from henceforth no baron of the exchequer, clerk of the pipe, remembrancer, opposer, controller, clerk of the pleas, and clerk of the foreign summons, auditor, or other chief officer of the exchequer be made, unlesse he be well learned in the law, or otherwise very skilfull in the courses and usages of the exchequer.] Here is the heartstring of this court, for albeit the lawes and orders thereof be most excellent, yet the benefit thereof consist in good and skilfull officers and ministers. Rot. Parl. 5 R. 2. nu. 105. and worthy to be printed.

These things being understood, let us now peruse our ancient authors, for out of the old fields must come the new corne.

Eyent nous treasorers. Hereby it appeareth being in the plurall number, that there be two treasurers, whereof we have spoken before. There is also a treasurer of the kings chamber, *thesaurarius cameræ regis*, which is not accountable in the exchequer, but to the king himself. If the king appoint some whom he trusts to take his account, this is esteemed to be done by the king himself, *Qui per alium facit, per ipsum facere videtur.* Rot. parl. 3 H. 6. nu. 47.

Et nous barons illonques jurisdiction. * All judiciall proceedings according to law in the exchequer, are *coram baronibus*, and not *coram thesaurario et baronibus*: but the court of equity holden in the exchequer chamber, is holden before the lord treasurer, chancelor, and barons. Of this court we have given a touch before, and shall treat more hereafter. Note the judiciall proceedings before the barons are in rols, but they are not numbred as in other courts. 28 H. 6. 11, 12. 5 R. 2. ca. 9. stat. 1. 20 E. 3. cap. 2. *The court of equity in the exchequer, Chamber.* See hereafter cap. 13. pa. 118. Rols not numbred.

The oath of the barons of the exchequer expressing their duties consisteth upon ten articles. 1. That well and truly he shall serve in the office of baron of the kings exchequer. 2. That truly he shall charge and discharge all manner of people, as well poor as rich. 3. That for highnesse nor for riches, nor for hatred, nor estate of no manner of person or persons, nor for any deed, gift, nor promise of any person the which is made to him, nor by craft, nor by ingen he shall let the kings right. 4. Nor none other persons right he shall disturbe, let or respite contrary to the lawes of the land. 5. Nor the kings debts he shall put in respite, where that they may goodly be levied. 6. That the kings need he shall speed before all others. 7. That neither for gift, wages, nor good deed, he shall * layne, disturbe, nor let the profit or reasonable advantage of the king in the advantage of any other person, nor of himself. 8. That nothing he shall take of any person for to do wrong or right, to delay or to deliver, or to delay the people that have to doe before him; but as hastily as he may them goodly to deliver without hurt of the king, and having no regard to any profit that might thereof to him be therein, he shall make to be delivered. 9. Where he may know any wrong or prejudice to be done to the king, he shall put and do all his power and diligence that to redresse, and if he may not do it, that he tell it to the king: or to them of his councell, which may make relation to the king, if he may not come to him. 10. The kings councell he shall keep and layne in all things. *The oath of the barons.* See the statute of 20 E. 3. cap. 2.

* Layne, *i.* to conceale or hide.

Triall by record.

In the exchequer at the suit of the king in an information of intrusion of lands, wherein issue is joyned, which may be tried by the country; yet where the king hath a direct record or records for the manifestation of his title, the kings attorny may pray that the triall may be by records, whereof you may reade a notable case, Mich. 27 & 28 Eliz. in the exchequer where the case was, that in an information of intrusion into certain lands, &c. against Savil, the issue was whether certain lands belonged to a house or no, and upon a tryall by record judgement was given against Savil. Afterwards Savil the defendant died, and his sonne and heir brought a writ of error in the exchequer chamber, where it was holden, that this kinde of tryall by records was before the statute of 33 H. 8, cap. 39. the words whereof be, That all and every triall and trials of all manner of suits, bils, plaints, informations, &c. and issues in the court of exchequer, shall be made and tried by due examination of witnesse, writings, proofes, or by such other wayes or means, as by the court of exchequer shall be thought expedient; and that every such judgement, decree or decrees, shall be good, perfect, and in full strength, force, and effect in law, to all intents, constructions and purposes. And yet, notwithstanding the generality of these words, if a judgement be given upon a triall by record, a writ of error doth lie thereupon; because, as to that point, this act is but in affirmance of the common law.

Mic. 27 & 28 El. in scaccar. inter Leroigne et Savil.

33 H. 6. 19. 51, 52.

[110]

For triall by records, vid. Mich. 32 & 33 E. 1. coram Rege. Robertus archiep. Cant. &c. Hil. 8 E. 2. coram rege, Cornwall. Walterus episc. Exon, &c.

22 E. 3. nu. 17.

It was petitioned in parliament, that remedy might be found, that no accountant in the exchequer do run in issues before he be warned. The kings answer was, the proces therein shall be first a *venire fac'*, then a *distringas*, and after a writ out of the chancery to the treasurer and barons.

51 E. 3. nu. 27.

It was also petitioned in parliament, that such as owe to the king may upon their account be allowed of all such lones, as be due unto them, or to any of his ancestors: whereunto the king answered, the treasurer and barons shall make allowance of due debts.

So great care was taken by the court of exchequer (which is the centre of the kings revenue and profit) that no man might sue or plead for their discharge of any debts, account, or other demand, without having expresse commandement by writ or letter of the great seal. But by the statute of 5 R. 2. it appeared, that the parties ought to have been received thereunto, according to the law, without any such writ or letter: and that the obtaining of such writs or letters was to the great disquietnesse, mischiefe, and delay of the parties impeached, and no advantage to the king. And where before that time no plea could be allowed in the exchequer by attorny, but in proper person: by the said act it is ordained that the barons of the exchequer shall have full power to hear every answer of every demand made in the same: so that every person that is impeached or impeachable of any cause by himself or by * any person, shall be received in the exchequer, to plead, sue, and have his reasonable discharge without carrying or suing any writ or other commandement whatsoever. So as by this act both these mischiefs are provided for. And out of this act this generall conclusion may be justly collected, that such course of the exchequer as tendeth to the disquietnesse, mischiefe, and delay of the subject, and no advantage to the king, is against law, and ought not to be allowed. And

5 R. 2. cap. 9. Course of the exchequer against law, &c.

* That is, by his attorny: and therefore the admittance of an attorny in these cases, is not *ex gratia curiæ* (as is said in the common pleading) but *ex debito justitiæ*.

And it is to be observed, that Britton doth joyn in this clause, the treasurers and barons.

[a] And into the exchequer chamber or the like, all cases of greatest difficulty in the kings bench or common pleas, &c. are, and of ancient time have been adjourned and there debated, argued, and resolved by all the judges of England and barons of the exchequer. See more of this court *infra*, cap. 13. pagin. 121.

[a] *Tempore regis Johannis*, the abbot of Crowlands case. *Justiciarii hæc audientes surgentes de banco, cum baronibus scaccarii et domini regis fidelibus illic residentibus colloquium, &c. Rot. in scaccario de Crowland. Pl. Coronæ coram justic' itinerantibus apud Turrim London. an.* 4 E. 1. *Rot. Claus.* 13 E. 1. *infra. p.* 121. *Hil.* 32 E. 1. *coram rege Wigorn.* Mic. 6 E. 2. *in communi banco* Despencers case. Mic. 11. E. 6. *coram rege*, case of the burgesses of Great Yarmouth.

A oier et terminer touts les causes que touchont nous debts. Here debts are taken for all manner of duties due to the king. 4 H. 6. 12. b. 5 E. 4. 7. 7 E. 4. 14. b. 16. b.

Et auxi a nous fees. Here the tenures of the king (whereof we have spoken before) are expressed. And albeit there be many tenures of the king both in *capite*, and by knights service of some honor or mannor, &c. yet there be many more by the error or negligence of sollicitors, by suing out of licences or pardons of alienation, where in troth the mannors or lands were not holden of the king *in capite*.

But Mich. 39 & 40 Eliz. it was resolved by all the judges of England, when I was attorny generall: that if a man purchase a license or pardon, and after being called into the exchequer do plead the license or pardon, that neither the purchase nor pleading is any conclusion, but the tenure may afterwards upon another alienation be traversed or denied. For the words of the license or pardon be, *Quæ de nobis tenentur in capite (ut dicitur;)* for neither the charge in this case is direct being grounded upon a license or pardon, nor the plea; for the license or pardon is pleaded, as it is, *ut dicitur:* and therefore neither the one nor the other doth conclude. But if he in his plea doth by expresse words (with a *bene et verum est, &c.)* confesse a tenure, *in capite*, and in discharge thereof plead the pardon or license in discharge thereof, there is a conclusion wrought: and so are the books to be intended: which resolution I heard and observed, and have reported it for advancement of truth and right. Mich. 39 & 40 El. *per touts les justices.* [111] 46 E. 3. 33. 29 Ass. 38. 7 E. 6. Estoppel. Br. 222. pl. com. 398.

Concerning licenses of alienation, and the short pleading of licenses and pardons, there is a profitable statute made *anno* 18 Jac. *regis*, and another *anno* 1 Jac. cap. 26. concerning orders of the exchequer. 18 Jac. cap. 1 Jac. reg. ca. 26.

Et les incident choses sauns les queux, &c. Quando lex aliquid alicui concedit, concedere videtur et id sine quo res ipsa esse non potest.

Et que ils eyent power a conuster des detts que lendoit a nous dettors per ou nous puissons pluis tost approcher a nostre dett. This is the ancient prerogative of the king as it appeareth in our books. 20 E. 3. ley 52. 8 H. 5. 4.

The king brought an action of debt in this court against a prior alien. The prior had proces against A who deteined goods from him, without which he could not answer the king. A came and claimed the goods as his tithes as parson of D, the prior claimed the tithes as parson of S; and thereupon issue taken for the king triable in the exchequer. 38 Ass. p. 20.

If he that is in execution will in this court confesse himself debtor to the king, where he is no debtor of record, he shall be 1 R. 2. cap. 12.

remanded to the first prison, and after the creditor be satisfied, then to be committed to the Fleet untill he hath paid the summe confessed.

Solonq; le discretion des treasorers et barons, &c. soients arents a fearme a eux que pluis voilent doner. To the end that no lands in the kings hands, which ought to be to the kings profit, should be without a farmor that should yeild a rent to the king, the treasurer in certain cases, and with certain cautions ought to make a warrant to the great seal for demising thereof, that is to say, not only of lands extended, of lands during the vacation of any abbey, and of lands seised for an alienation without license, and before 23 H. 8. of land in ward, or the like upon uncertainties, but also of the demeans of the crown out of lease, &c.

In original. Anno 16 E. 4. rot. 13. Nota herein five things. 1. *Per manucaptionem.* 2. *Commisimus.* 3. *Custodiam.* 4. Yielding a rent. 5. *Proviso, quod si quis alius plus dare voluerit.* Nota Britton sup. *A eux que pluis voilent doner.* See 27 H. 8. cap. 11.

The lease will be best expressed by an example, first of lands extended. *Rex omnibus ad quos, &c. salutem. Sciatis quod per manucaptionem Walteri Mathew de Westm' in com' Mid. yeoman, et Nich. Whitfeild de eadem, yeoman. Commisimus Rico. Foster, custodiam unius shopæ, 30 acr' terræ, 3 acr' prati, et 4 acr' pasturæ cum pertin' in Stanford in com' Lincoln, quæ fuerunt Silvani Southorpe, quæ in manus regis Edwardi nuper regis Angliæ tertii pro 138 li. 6 s. 8 d. in quibus idem Silvanus prefato nuper regi tenebat', seisiti fuerunt, et in manibus nostris ea de causa adhuc existunt. Habendum à festo Sancti Michaelis anno regni nostri 13 usque finem 10 annorum ex tunc proxime sequen' et plenarie complendorum. Reddendo inde nobis per annum in custodia prædicta 25 s, prout nobis responsum est, ad festa Paschæ, et Sancti Michael' per æquales portiones. Proviso semper quod si aliquis alius dare voluerit de incremento per annum pro custodia prædicta sine fraude vel malo ingenio, quod tunc dictus Richardus tantum pro eadem solvere teneatur, si custodiam prædictam habere voluerit. In cujus rei, &c. Teste R. apud Westm. 7 die Novemb. anno regni nostri decimo sexto.*

Note by many presidents the lord treasurer may make a warrant to grant the lands extended, either for years, or *quam diu in manibus nostris fore contigerit.*

Rot. pat. 5 H. 6.

[112]

11 H. 6. 28. b. 8 H. 6. 34. Br. Lease 71. Register 295. See for this word Commisimus. Vide 27 H. 8. ca. 1. a speciall proviso for the lo. treasurer. * 32 H. 6. ca. 5. 17 R. 2. ca. 5. 4 H. 4. cap. 18. Dier fo. 303.

The lord treasurer made a warrant to the lord chancelour to demise to John Pempons land parcell of the dutchy of Cornwall for the tearm of fifteen years in the like form of words as the before recited lease was. This lease was pleaded in 11 H. 6. and though the lease was by the words of *commisimus*, and *commisimus custodiam terræ, &c.* yet in pleading the lessee pleaded a demise of the land it self, and there allowed to be good, which is worthy of observation.

Vide in original' in scaccario de anno 21 & 22 H. 7. rot. 4. *et ibid.* 23 H. 7. rot. 12. many such leases. But of ancient time, as it appeareth by Britton, both the treasurer and barons did demise, &c. * Letters patents of the alnage shall passe only by the lord treasurers warrant. And the gift of the office of the escheator belong to his office. Vide in the chapter of the Court of Escheator.

See in the chapter of the Court of Wards. * Vid. pl. co'. 491.

By the statutes of 8 H. 6. cap. 16. and 18 H. 6. cap. 6. it appeareth that the chancelor or treasurer had power to make leases in certain cases of wards lands: but that is altered by the statute of 32 of H. 8. of erection of the court of wards. * Note the statute of 18 H. 6. ca. 1. extends only to the kings warrant, and not to the warrant of the lord treasurer.

* It is to be obſerved, that when in any act of parliament or other record the treaſurer is named for demiſing, or other intermedling with any of the kings revenue, it is to be intended of the treaſurer of the exchequer.

De nous cuſtomes de quirs et leynes, &c. What theſe cuſtomes were appeareth in the ſecond part of the Inſtitutes, by the ſtatute of confirmation *cartarum*, the laſt branch, and the expoſition upon the ſame, whereby it appeareth that the king had no cuſtome but ſuch as was granted to him by act of parliament.

Leſchequer eſt un place quarre. It is fourſquare and the carpet that ſometime lay upon it had wrought in it the form of a cheſſe board, and thereupon it was called the exchequer: and about the end of the reign of E. 1. this court was new built, and therefore in 2 E. 3. it was called the novel eſchequer, and it was new built upon this occaſion. Both the parts of the eſchequer were of an ancient building, and weak; fourſcore and one perſons (whereof the abbot of Weſtm' and forty eight of his monkes were part) brake into the receipt, and feloniouſly robbed the king of a hundred thouſand pounds, *ad damnum inæſtimabile*, ſaith the record. All theſe fourſcore and one were indicted of this felony, and committed to the tower of London, &c. and this was the occaſion of the new building of both theſe parts of the eſchequer.

Qui ſolement eſt ordein pur le prowe le roy. Here is a ſhort, but an effectuall deſcription of the juriſdiction of this court, that is, for the profit of the king. This profit is either immediate, or mediate: [a] immediate, as of lands, rents, franchiſes, hereditaments, debts, duties, accounts, goods, chattels, and other profits, and benefits whatſoever due to the king. [b] Mediate, as firſt, the priviledge of the officers, and * miniſters of the court: for two things doe principally ſupport the juriſdiction of a court, viz. the juſt preſervation of the dignity of it, and the due attendance of the officers and miniſters of the ſame to ſue and be ſued in this court. 2. [c] By *quo minus*. 3. It extendeth (as hath been ſaid) to the debtor of the kings debtor. 4. To priſoners in this court to be ſued here. 5. To accountants that have entred into their account, except [d] collectors of diſmes, they ſhall not be ſued by bils, neither if he be ſued in any other court, ſhall he have the priviledge of this court.

Ou deux chivaliers, et 2 clerks, ou 2 homes lettres. 2. *Chivaliers* be hereafter explained. 2 *Clerks, ou 2 homes lettres*, the one is intended to be the baron of courſe, the other the clerk of the pipe.

† *De ſes fees et franchiſes.* Of fees, that is tenures, whereof we have ſpoken before. Franchiſes, being flowers of the crown, are notorious and known.

Et les accounts, &c. All accounts to the king ought to be made upon oath, and it is beſt for the king to have the accounts to be taken in this court, for accounts taken by commiſſion are little for

* Hil. 18 E. 1. f. 9. nu. 128.

Second part of the Inſt. Confir. Cart. Vid. ſupra cap. Parl. p. 29.

Mirror. Ockham.

2 E. 3. 25. rot. par. 31 E. 1. m. 12. Dorſ.

Nota, the robbery of the king of his treaſure is *damnum inæſtimabile.*

[a] 2 E. 3. 25. Jeffery Sharlags caſe. 14 E. 3. tit. Scire fac' 122. 44 E. 3. 27. Regiſt. 187. b. Prohibit. 38. aff. p. 20. rot. par. 1 R. 2. nu. 64. 2 H. 4. 11. rot. par. 2 H. 4. 101. *Dat' eſt nobis intelligi.* Rot. par. 11. H. 4. 54. 56. 64. ibid. 13 H. 4. 32. 8 H. 5. Ley 66. 20 E. 3. Ley 52. 32 H. 6. 24. 5 E. 4. 4. b. 7 E. 4. 30. 21 E. 4. 44, 45. &c. 8 H. 6. 34. 36 H. 6. 26. li. 5. f. 62. action ſur le caſe. 11 H. 7. 26.

[b] Stat. de Rutland. 10 E. 1. * Regiſter 187. F. N. B. 90. f. Information de intruſion ou trans. & 217. c. terræ taile. Vid. 32 H. 8. cap. 39. 16 Eliz. Dier 328. [c] 14 E. 3. brev. 789. 20 E. 3. Ley 52. 2 H. 4. 9. 8 H. 5. 6. 10. 8 H. 5. Ley 66. 11 H. 7. 26. Pl. Com. 322. Lib. 6. fol. 18. [d] 1 R. 3. cap. 14. 5 R. 2. cap. 10. ſtat. 1. the barons ſhall hear, &c. without any writ, letter or commandment. 4 H. 4. cap. 9. 7 H. 4. cap. 11. concerning commiſſions. 13 Eliz. cap. 9. Sewers. 14 E. 3. cap. 12. Weights. 13 R. 2. cap. 2. No recognizanc or bond in double.

[113]

e Stat. de Rutland. 10 E. 1.
f Ro. par. 21 E. 1. rot. 3.
g 5 R. 2. ca. 11.
h Rot. par. 3 H. 6. nu. 47.

the kings benefit. [e] The keeper of the wardrobe is to make his account once in the year in the exchequer. [f] Once in the year the treasurer of Ireland shall account in the exchequer of England. [g] The accounts of the exchequer to be more shortly heard, made, and ingrossed, &c.

[h] The treasurers of the kings chamber are only accountable to the king, and not in this court of exchequer, but yet the king, by the advice of some whom he may trust in secret doth take account thereof, as before is said.

18 H. 3. nu. 110.

Vide recordum et processum contra Petrum de Rivalles alias Petrum de Oriall, thesaurarium et camerarium regis totius Angliæ et Hiberniæ, et custodem omnium forestarum, et omnium portuum maris de compoto reddit' de officiis prædictis, et de judicio contra ipsum reddito per defaltam, quia venire recusavit, nisi salvo regis conductu, quod rex denegavit, quasi insolitum et indebitum.

Per le view de un soveraign que est treasurer Dengliterre. Of this great officer we have spoken before.

Bracton lib. 3. fo. 116. b.
See the 2 part of the Inst. Mag. Cart. ca. 14.

Le 2. chivaliers soloient ee. 2 barons, &c. And herewith agreeth Bracton, *Comites vero vel barones non sunt americiandi, nisi per pares suos secundum modum delicti, et hoc per barones de scaccario vel coram rege.*

En cel place sont auxi chamberleins, et plusors auters ministers, que ne touch my molt a la ley. Hereof we have spoken before.

Artic sup. Cart. ubi supra. Stat. de Rotland. 10 E. 1. acc.
* Pl. com. 209.

Nul common plea ne soit disormes tenus in leschequer encounter le form del grand charter. Upon this act four severall opinions have been conceived. * 1. That this court might originally have holden plea of all common pleas; and this they think to prove by the title of Glanvils book, which taking it altogether is this, *Tractatus de legibus, &c. tempore Henrici 2. compositus, justitiæ gubernacula tenente illustri viro Ranulpho de Glanvilla, juris regni et antiquarum consuetudinum eo tempore peritissimo, et illas solum leges continet et consuetudines, secundum quas placitatur in curia regis ad scaccarium coram justiciariis ubicunque fuerint.* 2. Others think that at the making of Magna Carta, the court of the exchequer was parcel of the kings bench, which they infer upon the words of this act, No common plea shall be holden in the eschequer against the great charter, in which charter *curia nostra* is only intended of the kings bench. 3. That in Magna Carta, to which this statute refers, there is no restraint, and therefore this statute of *artic' super cartas* restraineth not. 4. That the ordinance of Rutland is no statute, but made by the king for the order of this court. In the second part of the Institutes, in the exposition of Magna Carta, cap 11. we have spoken nothing of this matter, but thought good to referre it to this act being his proper place.

As to the first: it appeareth by the said ancient authors, and by the authority of our books, that the institution and jurisdiction of this court have been only for the kings businesse and profit, &c. as hath been said. For the title of Glanvils book: first, it was never of his own making, for he would never have given himselfe such high and superlative titles, as *Illustri viro juris regni, &c. eo tempore peritissimo.* 2. He that added the title speaketh of three courts, viz. 1. *In curia regis.* 2. *Ad scaccarium.* 3. *Coram justiciariis ubicunque fuerint.* For the first, viz. *in curia regis*, he intendeth justice in *eire, &c.* for example, *Inquirentur purpresturæ vel in capitali curia, vel coram justiciis regis ad tales inquisitiones faciend' in di-*

Glanv. lib. 9. cap. 11. &c.

versas

versas regni partes transmissas per juratam patriæ sive vicenet'. 2. *Ad scaccarium,* this court he doth mention but once (that I remember) in all his book in these words. *Si vero dominus rex aliquam custodiam alicui commiserit, tunc distinguitur utrum ei custodiam pleno jure commiserit ita quod nullum eum inde reddere compotum oporteat ad scaccarium,* which agreeth with the originall institution and jurisdiction of the court concerning the profit of the king. 3. *Coram justiciariis ubicunque fuerint* is the kings bench, whereof Glanvil was chief justice, and of the pleas in that court is in effect the sum of his treatise.

Lib. 7. cap. 10.

[114]

As to the second: 1. Glanvile who wrote in the reign of H. 2. doth (as hath been said) name the exchequer as a distinct court for the accounts to be made to the king. 2. In the * black book of the exchequer dedicated to H. 2. of the observations of the exchequer, it is said, *Nulli licet statuta scaccarii infringere, vel eis quavis temeritate resistere, habet in hoc commune cum ipsa domini regis curia, in qua ipse in propria persona jura discernit, nec recordationi nec sententiæ in eo latæ liceat alicui contradicere.* Whereby it appears that the kings bench and exchequer were distinct courts in the reign of H. 2.

* The author of this book is Gervasius Tilburiensis a learned man and an officer of the exchequer cap. 1.

To the third, our statute is intituled *articuli super cart'* that is, articles upon *Magna Carta et Carta de Foresta:* so as the sense of this act is, that the exchequer should hold no common plea no more then the kings bench: for the form of the great charter is, *Quod communia placita non sequantur curiam nostram.* Secondly, our statute is but an affirmance of the common law concerning the jurisdiction of this court, and this doth expresly and notably appear in the Register in these words. *Rex thesaurar' et baronibus de scaccario salutem. Cum secundum legem et consuetudinem regni nostri communia placita coram vobis ad scaccarium predict' placitari non debeant, nisi placita illa nos vel aliquem ministrorum nostrorum ejusdem scaccarii specialiter tangant, &c.* Here it is to be observed that this writ of prohibition is not grounded upon the statute of *artic' super cart'* or any other statute, but upon the common law and custome of the kingdome, which concerning the jurisdiction of this court doth *in omnibus* agree with our ancient authors and year-books, wherein you shall observe an admirable harmony and consent in so many successions of ages.

Regist. 187. b.

This is a statute proved by the title thereof, and for that it is entred in the parliament roll, and in the Register 187. b. it is called *statutum de Rotland.*

Stat. de Rotland. 10 E. 1. Vid. Pl. Com. 221. per 2 barons. Regist. 187. b.

Now it is good to know, how the law commonly called *respondeat superior,* holdeth in this court and in other courts, and first by the records of this court, and then by acts of parliament.

Respondeat superior.

Memorand' quod allocuto præfato Willielmo morantur nuper vic' super levatione 40. s. extract' in magno rotulo de anno 12 in kanc' sub nomine William Herlizan unius coronatorum com' Kanc' pro falso returno. Idem Willielmus vic' dic' super sacramentum suum quod præfatus Willielmus Herlizan non habet terr' vel ten'ta, bona, seu catalla in balliva sua, nec habuit unde dict' denar' levari possint. Et quia ipse coronator electus erat per comitatum juxta formam statuti, &c. ita quod in defectu ejusdem coronator' totus comitatus ut elector et superior, &c. habeant regi respondere, præcip' nunc vic' quod de terris et tenementis hujusmodi totius comitatus in balliva sua fieri fac' prædict' xl. s. et eos habeat hic in cro. clausi Paschæ super proffrum suum regi solvend'. Ad quem diem vic' non re-

Int' præcept' de termino Sancti Hil. anno 14 E. 3. exparte remem. regis rot. 9. in scac'. *Coronator.*

torn' breve. Ideo ſicut alias in cro' Sancti Johan' Baptiſtæ. For more preſidents in the exchequer of this kind, ſee Mic. 17 R. 2. rot. Mic. 19 H. 8. rot. 4. *Eborum.* Paſch. 30 H. 8. rot. 30. Wilteſ. Mich. 5 E. 6. rot. 130, &c. Stat. de 52 H. 3. *de ſcaccario.*

How it holdeth in other courts. Vid. 11 E. 2. tit. Det. 172, where the ſherifs be removable as in London for their inſufficiency, *reſpondeat ſuperior*, that is, the maior and comminalty of London.

45 E. 3. 9, 10. *Prior datiſe et removeable ſuffer eſchape, reſpondeat ſuperior.* 14. E. 4. *Pur inſufficiency del bailie dun libertie reſpondeat dominus libertatis.* Vid. 44 E. 3. 13. 50 E. 3. 5. 14 H. 4. 22. 11 H. 6. 52. 30 H. 6. 32. W. 2. cap. 2. *Si non habeat balivus unde reddat, reddat ſuperior.*

2 H. 6. cap. 10. There is a generall ſtatute concerning all the courts of the king, worthy of obſervation in theſe words.

Item, To the intent that better and more ſure government [115] be had within the courts of our lord the king for his profit, and eaſe of his people, which have to purſue, and doe in the ſame. It is ordained and eſtabliſhed that all the officers made by the kings letters patents royall within the ſaid courts, which have power and authority by vertue of their offices of old times accuſtomed, to appoint clerks and miniſters within the ſame courts, ſhall be charged and ſworn to appoint ſuch clerks and miniſters, for whom they will anſwer at their perill, which be ſufficient, faithfull, and attending to that which pertaineth to them in performance of the buſineſſe, as well of the king as of his people.

20 E. 3. ca. 2. Hereby it appeareth that to them belongeth doing of right and reaſon in legall proceedings.

In the ſame manner we have ordained in the right of the barons of the exchequer, and we have expreſly charged them in our preſence, that they ſhall doe right and reaſon to all our ſubjects, great and ſmall, and that they ſhall deliver the people reaſonably and without delay of the buſineſſe which they have to doe before them, without undue tarrying as hath been done in times paſt.

Mich. 13. Ja. *In Banke le roy in probibition.* 8 H. 5. 4. 45 E. 3. *Decies tantum.* 12.

It was reſolved in the caſe of auditor Povie, that if A be indebted to B, and B is indebted to the king, that the king by his prerogative may levie his debt upon A: but this levying ought to be of an immediate, and not of a mediate debtor to the debtor of the king. As if A be indebted to B, and B to C, and C to the king, the king cannot levy his debt of A, for then it might be levied *in infinitum, quod reprobatur in jure*, and this appeareth in our books.

Li. 5. fo. 89, 90. For aſſignment of debts made to the king, ſee in my Reports.

7 Jac. cap. 15. By the ſtatute of 7 Jac. no debt ſhall be aſſigned to the king his heirs or ſucceſſors by or from any debtor or accountant to his majeſty, his heirs or ſucceſſors, other then ſuch debts as did before grow due originally to the kings debtor.

No obligation, recognizance or ſtatute made for ſaving harmleſſe or performance of covenants, &c. though it be forfeited, or for any cauſe, other then a due debt, can be aſſigned to the king by any of his debtors. Theſe aſſignments of debts to the king are not favoured

voured in law when the kings immediate debtor is able to pay his debt; for by the aſſignment at the kings ſuit the body, lands and goods of the debtor to the kings debtor are liable to the king, whereas at the ſubjects ſuit, he could have had but his body only by *capias ad ſatisfaciend'*, or his goods only by *fieri fac'*, or half his lands and goods by *elegit*. By the ſtatute of 1 R. 2. a penalty is provided for him who confeſſeth a debt to the king (that is not debtor to the king of record) to delay the execution of others. 1 R. 2. ca. 12.

The barons of the exchequer are the ſoveraign auditors of England, for if a man aſſign auditors to a bailif or receiver to account, and the auditors will not allow juſt and reaſonable allowances but commit the bailif or receiver to priſon, ſuch priſoner may have an originall writ of *ex parte talis* returnable before the treaſurer and barons of the exchequer, &c. for his relief in that behalf. Fleta li. 6. ca. 64. 2 E. 3. 12. 14 E. 3. account 74. 8 E. 4. 16. F. N. B. 129. f. Regiſt. 137.

Upon the accountant in the exchequer of B. Fulham the kings butler, he demanded allowance of certain parcels of wines given by the king to certain perſons by word of mouth without writing, and it was diſallowed by the rule of the court. Rot. clauſ. anno 4 E. 3. m. 2.

Upon the account in the exchequer of Richard Bury keeper of the wardrobe, he demanded allowance for certain veſſels of gold and ſilver and certain jewels given by the king *ore tenus* to Iſabell queen of England, and others to Philip queen of England conſort of the king, *et non allocatur*, by the like rule of the court: for the gifts by word in both theſe caſes are void, which with Petilians caſe that followeth are good rules to eſtabliſh the law in a caſe wherein there hath been variety of opinions in our books. Rot. clauſ. anno 4 E. 3. m. 19. 35 H. 8. Prærog. B. 61. 14 E. 4. 2. a.

Hil. 6 E. 4. rot. 14. *in ſcaccario inter brevia in dorſ.* Petilians caſe. A warrant under the ſignet is not ſufficient to iſſue any treaſure of the king out of the receipt, but it muſt be under the great or privy ſeal. [116]

If the barons doe not allow unto an accountant before them ſuch juſt demands as he maketh, he may have a writ *De allocatione facienda*, directed to the treaſurer and barons commanding them to allow the ſame. Regiſt. 192. a. b. & 193.

Of a Liberate *for payment of a penſion or debt, &c.*

A *liberate* is an originall writ iſſuing out of the chancery, and is directed to ſome officers that have of the kings mony in his hands to pay over a penſion, debt, or duty. And it is not called a *liberate* by reaſon of any ſuch word contained in the writ, (as for the moſt part writs are) for the words be *quod ſolvas* or *ſolvatis*, but it is ſo named *ab effectu*. But ſuch a writ cannot be directed to the kings fermor to pay a penſion, &c. becauſe, though the ferm or rent be behind, yet it is not the kings untill it be paid, and all the writs in the Regiſter are directed as is aforeſaid to officers, as to the treaſurer and chamberlain, to a cuſtomer, &c. The form of the writ appeareth in the Regiſter 192, 193. And there it appeareth that there be two kinds of writs of *liberate*, one dormant or currant and continuall, and another *hac vice* and particular. And it is ſometimes accompanied with a writ of allowance, as there you may read.

If the officer have sufficient in his hands to pay, &c. at the time of the *liberate* delivered to him, he is become debtor (by act of law) to the party, for which he may have an action of debt: but after the *liberate* sued out, and before the delivery, the king may discharge the officer of the kings money in his hands. And if the king decease before the delivery of the *liberate*, the officer hath no warrant to pay it.

If the officer at the time of the delivery of the *liberate* have of the kings money to pay but part, and not the whole, the writ is no warrant to him to pay part. See 21 H. 6. tit. det. 43. 27 H. 6. 9. 37 H. 6. 24, 25. 9 E. 4. 12. 14. 1 H. 7. 8. 2 H. 7. 9. F. N. B. 121. f. *br. tit. Taile deschequer.*

Vid. Mag. Cart. cap. 22. *Liberationem antiquitus statut', id est, precium antiquitus statutum.*

The course of the eschequer is, that as soon as a sherif or escheator enter into his account for issues, amerciaments and mean profits, to mark upon his head O. *Ni.* which is as much as to say, *oneratur, nisi habeat sufficientem exonerationem,* and presently he is become the kings debtor, and a *debet* set upon his head, and thereupon the parties *peravaile* are become debtors to the sherif or escheator, and discharged against the king.

Dier 7 El. 238. The ancient course of the eschequer hath been, that if in an information of intrusion into lands or tenements the defendant plead not guilty, he shal lose the possession; and it is said that the reason of this course is, first for that regularly the kings title appeareth of the record, and therefore the defendant may take knowledge thereof, and the rather for that in every information of intrusion it is specified of whose possessions the lands, &c. were: but if the defendant plead not guilty, the kings learned councell cannot know the defendants title, to provide to answer the same, as the defendant may doe to the kings title.

[117]

CAP. XII.

A Court to enquire of, and certifie unlawfull and untrue Accounts in the Exchequer.

6 H. 4. cap. 3. See rot. parl. 6 H. 4. nu. 59. for the print swarveth from the record.

THIS court sitteth by commission under the great seal by force of the statute of 6 H. 4. directed and sent, together with the tenour of the account, to the most lawfull and discreet persons in the counties, where the accountants be officers, to enquire and certifie the profits which the sheriffs, escheators, alnagers, controllers, and other the kings officers have received, &c. by them upon their said accounts deceitfully concealed, &c. and being attainted of the said frauds and deceipts, they shall forfeit treble the value, and their bodies to prison, untill they have made fine and ransome to the king, after the discretion of the judges.

But (as hath been said before) it is certain, that it is ever most for the kings benefit that accounts be yearly taken in the exchequer, and

and not by commission: and to that end an ordinance was made in the parliament holden *anno* 21 E. 1. in these words: *Dominus rex vult et præcipit, quòd de cætero singulis annis semel in anno compotus Vasconiæ et Hiberniæ per constabularium Burdegaliæ, et thesaurarium Hiberniæ reddantur ad scaccarium Angliæ, et ibid. audiantur per thesaurar' et barones suos. A fortiori* of accounts within the realm.

Rot. parl. anno 21 E. 1. Rot. 3. Vide rot. parl. 28 E. 1. Nich. de Clere thesaurarius Hiberniæ.

And of the court of the exchequer we will end with an old verse ingraved in stone in the exchequer wall,

Ingrediens Jani, rediturus es æmulus Argi.

The chief baron is created by letters patents, and the office is granted to him *quamdiu se bene gesserit,* wherein he hath a more fixed estate (it being an estate for life) then the justices of either bench, who have their offices but at will: and *quamdiu se bene gesserit* must be intended in matters concerning his office, and is no more then the law would have implyed, if the office had been granted for life.. And in like manner are the rest of the barons of the exchequer constituted, and the patents of the attorney generall, and solicitor are also *quam diu se bene gesserit.*

See Lit. 1 part of the Instit. sect.

CAP. XIII.

[118]

The Court of Equity in the Exchequer Chamber.

THE judges of this court are the lord treasurer, the chancelour, and barons of the exchequer. Generally, their jurisdiction is as large for matter of equity, as the barons in the court of the exchequer have for the benefit of the king by the common law: for all the proceedings both in this court of equity, and of that by the common law ought to be, as hath been said, for the profit or benefit of the king, or touching the king: and if in either court they hold any plea, which is not for the profit or benefit of the king, or which toucheth not the king, there lyeth a prohibition, which, as is aforesaid, appeareth in the Register: for all are said *communia placita* which are not *placita coronæ.*

Art cler. cap. 4. Regist. fol. 187. b. stat. de Rotland. cap. ultimo.

By the statute of 33 H. 8. cap. 39. they have full power and authority to discharge, cancell and make void, all and singular recognizances and bonds made to the king for payment of any debt or summe of money, or for performance of conditions, &c. upon shewing the acquitance, &c. or any proof made of payment and performance. Also to cancell and make void by their discretion all recognizances made for any appearance or other contempt. And that if any person of whom any such debt or duty is demanded, alledge, plead, declare, or shew in the said court sufficient cause and matter in law, reason and good conscience in barre or discharge of the said debt or duty, and the same matter sufficiently prove in the said court: then the said court shall have power and authority to judge and allow the said proof, and clearly acquit and discharge

Cancell.

Cancell.

Matter in law, reason and good conscience.

§ such

Lib. 7. fo. 18. Sir Thomas Cecils case, and resolved by English bill in the exchequer chamber. See there divers presidents. * Lib. 7. fo. 20. ubi supra. Et lib. 3. fo. 12. Sir Wil. Herberts case. Inheritance. Freehold.

such person and persons. Also lands chargeable to the kings debts in the seisin and possession of divers and sundry persons, the same shall be wholly and * intirely, and in no wise severally liable to the payment of the said debt and duty: but in the said act of 33 H. 8. all manner of estates, rights, titles, and interests, as well of inheritance as freehold, other then joyntures for term of life, are excepted.

By the said act of 33 H. 8. speciall jurisdiction is given to the court of augmentation, when title is pretended to any mannors, lands, tenements, or hereditaments, bargained, sold, or exchanged by the king, upon which letters patents there is or shall be reserved any annuall rents or farms, paiable in the court of augmentations, and divers other clauses which gave to the court of augmentation jurisdiction. But the court of augmentation is but in shew annexed to the court of the exchequer, and not *de jure*, as hereafter it appeareth in the chapter of the Court of Augmentations. And therefore this court of exchequer chamber cannot claime any jurisdiction given and appropriated to that court, for that the court of augmentations is dissolved.

I. S. holdeth lands of the king by fealty and a yearly rent, and maketh a lease thereof for years to A. B pretends that I. S. leased the same to him by a former lease; albeit there is a rent issuing out of these lands to the king, yet neither A nor B can sue in this court by any priviledge in respect of the rent, for that the king can have no prejudice or benefit thereby, for whether A or B doth prevaile, yet must the rent be paid: and if this were a good cause of priviledge, all the lands in England holden of the king by rent, &c. might be brought into this court.

32 E 3. tit. Aid. *Le roy*. 1. 35 H. 6. 56.

But if Black acre be extended to the king for the debt of A as the land of A, and the king leaseth the same to B for years, reserving a rent: C pretends that A had nothing in the land, but that he was seised thereof, &c. this case is within the priviledge of this court, for if C prevaile the king loseth his rent.

[119]

The king maketh a lease to A of Black acre for years reserving a rent and A is possessed of a tearm for years in White acre, the king may distrain in White acre for his rent, yet A hath no priviledge for White acre, to bring it within the jurisdiction of this court.

44 E. 3. 45. 13 E. 4. 6. 8 H. 5. 4. Pl. com. 323. a. This prerogative holdeth not only in case of rent, service, but in case of a rent charge, and rent secke.

Note reader, where our books say, that the king may distrain for his rent in all the other lands of his tenant, of whomsoever the same be holden, it is thus to be understood, that the other lands must be in the actuall possession of the kings tenant, for he cannot distrain in those lands in the possession of his tenant for life, tenant for years, or at will.

Some are of opinion that a court of equity was holden in the exchequer chamber before the statute of 33 H. 8. And then it must be a court of equity by prescription: for we find no former act of parliament that doth create and establish any such court: and if it be by prescription, then judiciall presidents in course of equity must guide the same: as to the jurisdiction, certain it is that there hath been of ancient time an officer of the exchequer called *cancellarius scaccarii*, of whom amongst other officers of the exchequer Fleta saith thus: *Officium vero cancellarii est sigillum regis custodire simul cum controrotulis de proficuo regni.* And the Mirror saith, *Perjure est per la ou il fuit chancelor del eschequer vea a tiel a faire*

Cancellarius scaccarii. Mirror. cap. 2. § 13. & cap. 5. § 2.

luy

luy acquittance de tant que avoit pay al eschequer de la dett le roy south le seale del eschequer ou delay a faire acquittance de tiel jour tanq. a tiel jour, &c. His ancient fee is 40 marks. Livery out of the wardrobe 12 li. 17 s. 4 d. *in toto* 39 li. 10 s. 8 d. See 25 H. 8. cap. 16.

* The exchequer hath a chancelour and seal, and the writs usuall in the chancery in the exchequer to sease land, are more ancient then *prerog. regis*. * Pl. com. 321.

Hereupon it is collected, that seeing there hath been time out of minde of man a chancelour of the exchequer, that there should also be in the exchequer a court of equity.

Where some doe vouch 22 E. 4. tit. Petition 9. for the naming of the chancelour of the exchequer in granting of writs of search to the treasurer and chancelour, the book is false printed, for it should be the chamberlaines and treasurer of the exchequer: for no writ of search is directed to the chancelour, &c. but to the treasurer and chamberlain of the exchequer, who have the custody of the records, &c.

[a] We find a petition of the commons in 2 H. 4. that no writs or privie seals be sued out of the chancery, exchequer, or other place, to any man to appear upon a pain, &c. to answer, &c. contrary to the ordinary course of the common law: whereunto the king answered, that such writs should not be granted without necessity. [a] Rot. par. 2 H. 4. nu. 69.

[b] *Anno* 3 H. 5. the commons petitioned that all writs of *subpœna* and *certis de causis* going out of the chancery and the exchequer might be inrolled, and not granted of matters determinable at the common law on pain of 40 li. The kings answer was, That he would be advised. [b] Rot. parl. anno 3 H. 5. nu 46. [c] 7 H. 6. 44. 6 H. 7. 15. 8 H. 7. 13. lib. 1. fo. 11. Vet. N. B.

[c] So as in the exchequer there are these seven courts. 1. The court of pleas, 2. The court of accounts, 3. The court of receipt, 4. The court of the exchequer chamber being the * assembly of all the judges of England for matters in law, 5. The court of exchequer chamber for errors in the court of exchequer. 31 E. 3. cap. 8. and 31 Eliz. cap. 1. 6. A court in the exchequer chamber for errors in the kings bench. 27 Eliz. ca. 8. 31 Eliz. ca. 1. Co. pl. Intr. fo. 2. 24. 37. and 7. This court of equity in the exchequer chamber. * Rot. claus. in. Dors. an. 13 E. 1. In schedula pend. *Et si contingat quod, &c.* Vide supra, pag. 110. 31 E. 3. cap. 8. 31 Eliz. cap. 1. 27 Eliz cap. 8. 31 Eliz. cap. 1. Co. pl. Intr. fo. 2. 24. 37.

CAP. XIV. [120]

Of First-fruits and Tenths Ecclesiasticall.

A Court of the first-fruits and tenths was raised, officers constituted, of chancelour, treasurer, kings attorny, two auditors, and two clerks: authority given them to compound for first-fruits, bonds taken therefore should be of like force as a statute staple: but this court was dissolved by queen Mary parl. 1. sess. 2. cap. 10. Stat. de 32 H. 8. cap. 45. Rot. par. 47 E. 3. nu. 30. 7 H. 4. nu. 43. acc.

These were granted to the crown by the statute of 26 H. 8. cap. 3. But all the clergy were exonerated and discharged thereof afterwards, *anno* 2 & 3 Ph. and Mar. cap. 4. 26 H. 8. cap. 3. 2 & 3 Ph. and M. cap 4.

The

1 Eliz. cap. 4. obſerve the alteration and alternation.

The ſtatute of 26 H. 8. revived, and firſt-fruits and tenths of the clergy reunited to the crown by *anno* 1 Eliz. cap. 4. But no court is revived, but firſt-fruits and tenths to be within the rule, ſurvey, and government of the exchequer, and created a new office, and officer, viz. a remembrancer of the firſt-fruits and tenths of the clergy, who taketh all compoſitions for the ſaid firſt-fruits and tenths, and maketh proces againſt ſuch as pay not the ſame.

25 H. 8. cap. 5. 1 Eliz. cap. 4.

Firſt-fruits, or annates, *primitiæ*, are the firſt-fruits after avoidance of every ſpirituall living for one whole year (except vicarages not exceeding 10 li. and perſonages not exceeding 10 marks) but all are to pay tenths.

Eccleſiaſticall livings were ſometimes valued by a book of taxation made in 20 E. 1. which remaineth in the exchequer, and by another taxation in 26 H. 8. which alſo remaineth in that court. And according to this latter taxation are the values of eccleſiaſticall livings computed for the firſt-fruits and tenths. What pope firſt impoſed firſt-fruits, untill [a] hiſtorians do agree, I will not trouble my ſelf.

[a] Walſ. an. Dom. 1316. Trivet. Ranulphus Ciſtrenſis, li. 7. c. 42. Polyd. Virg. lib. 8. cap. 2. Platina. Fox, &c.

What we finde of record concerning firſt-fruits, we will ſummarily relate.

[b] The king forbiddeth H. P. the popes nuntio to collect firſt-fruits, &c.

[b] 2 E. 3. Rot. clauſ. m. 4.

[c] That the popes collector be willed no longer to gather the firſt-fruits of benefices within this realm being a very novelty, and that no perſon do any longer pay them.

[c] Parl. 1 R. 2. nu. 66.

[d] The commons do petition that proviſion may be made againſt the popes collectors for levying of the firſt-fruits of eccleſiaſticall dignities within the realm. The anſwer of the king in parliament is, There ſhall be granted a prohibition in all ſuch caſes where the popes collectors ſhall attempt any ſuch [e] novelties.

[d] Rot. par. 4 R. 2. nu. 44.

[e] Note they were not ſo ancient with us, as is pretended.

[f] Upon complaint made by the commons in parliament, the king willeth that prohibitions be granted to the popes collectors for receiving of firſt-fruits.

[f] Rot. par. 6 H. 4. nu. 50.

[g] Againſt firſt-fruits by arch-biſhops and biſhops to the pope of Rome, terming it a horrible miſchief and damnable cuſtome.

[g] 6 H. 4. cap. 1.

[h] It is enacted, that the popes collectors ſhould not from thenceforth levy any money within the realm for firſt-fruits of any eccleſiaſticall dignity by any proviſion from Rome upon pain of the ſtatute of proviſors: but this is omitted out of the print of 9 H. 4. cap. 8.

[h] Rot. par. 9 H. 4. nu. 43.

[i] The biſhop of Norwich had in 19 E. 3. by preſcription time out of minde of man firſt-fruits within his dioces of all churches after every avoidance. But theſe alſo were given to the crowne [k] by the ſtatute of 26 Hen. 8. cap. 3.

[i] 19 E. 3. tit. Juriſdiction. 22.

[k] 26 H. 8. cap. 3.

[121]

Tenths eccleſiaſticall, *decimæ*, theſe are the tenth part of the value of all eccleſiaſticall livings yearly payable to the king, his heirs and ſucceſſors by the ſaid ſtatute of 26 H. 8. and 1 Eliz. to be valued as is aboveſaid.

Num. 18. 26. &c. Vi. Jerom. in Eze. ca. 44. v. 28. &c.

Theſe the pope (as the canoniſts hold) pretended to have *de jure divino*, as due to the high prieſt by pretext of theſe words, *Præcipe Levitis atq; denuncia, cum acceperitis à filiis Iſrael decimas quas dedi vobis, primitias earum offerte Domino, id eſt decimam partem decimæ, ut reputetur vobis in oblationem primitiarum tam de areis, quam de torcularibus et univerſis quorum accipietis primitias offerte Domino, et*

date

date ea Aaron ſacerdoti. But the parliaments in 25 H. 8. and 26 H. 8. were not of opinion that theſe tenths did belong to the biſhop of Rome; as by the ſeverall preambles thereof appeareth, which we have added; for that we have endeavoured to ſhew through all this work the ſeverall claims or pretences of every thing whereof we have treated. And king Philip and queen Mary yeilded not theſe tenths to the pope, but (as hath been ſaid) by authority of parliament diſcharged the clergy thereof: which they would never have done, if they had taken them to be due to the pope *de jure divino.* And the biſhop of Norwich could not have preſcribed to have firſt-fruits within his dioces, if they had been due to the pope *de jure divino:* and the rather, for that Anthony de Becke, for whom the preſcription was made, was a reteiner to the court of Rome, and made biſhop of Norwich by the pope. 19 E. 3. tit. Juriſdiction, ubi ſup.

CAP. XV.

The Court of Augmentations of the Revenues of the Crowne of England.

THIS court was erected by authority of parliament in *anno* 27 H. 8. conſiſting of a chancelour, treaſurer, attorny, ſolicitor. And all lands, &c. belonging to monaſteries, and purchaſed lands were within the ſurvey and governance of this court. This court could not be erected but by parliament, becauſe a chancelour and a court of equity were conſtituted. More hereof in the next chapter. 27 H. 8. cap. 27.

CAP. XVI. [122]

The Court of Generall Surveyours of divers of the Kings Lands with Power to make Leaſes for Twenty-one Years erected by Act of Parliament in 33 H. 8. 33 H. 8. cap. 39.

BOTH theſe courts king H. 8. by his letters patents *anno regni ſui* 38 diſſolved, and erected a new court of augmentations by his letters patents. The diſſolution was holden void, becauſe they were created by authority of parliament. Vid. the rehearſall of the ſtatute of 7 E. 6. cap. 2. and the erection was alſo void for the cauſe aforeſaid. And thereupon the ſaid letters patents, as well for the diſſolution of the former, and for the erection of the new court of augmentations were confirmed and eſtabliſhed by the ſaid act of 7 E. 6.

Bract. Nihil tam conveniens eſt naturali æquitati, unumquodque diſſolvi eo ligamine quo ligatum eſt. 7 E. 6. cap. 2. 1 Mar. cap. 10.

Queen Mary according to the power given to her for diſſolution of of the ſaid court by act of parliament holden the fifth of October in the firſt yeare of her reigne, did afterwards by her letters patents, bearing date 23 *Januarii* in the ſame yeare diſſolve the ſaid court of augmentations; and the next day following by other letters patents united the ſame to the exchequer, which was utterly void, becauſe ſhe had diſſolved the ſame before: ſo as ſhe purſued not her authority.

Dier 4 Eliz. 16. So reſolved by all the judges.

[123]

CAP. XVII.

The Honourable Court of Chivalry before the Conſtable and Marſhall.

The ſtile of the court.

ROT. Pat. 12 H. 4. m. This court is called *curia militaris* and rot. parl. 2 H. 6. nu. 9. the marſhall court.

The judges. 43 E. 3. fo. 3. See the firſt part of the Inſtitutes. ſect. 745. many other authorities cited.

The judges of this court are the lord conſtable of England and the earl marſhall of England, and this court is the fountain of the marſhall law. And the earl marſhall is both one of the judges, and to ſee execution be done.

The name. 1. part of the Inſtitutes, ſect. 102 & 153.

Conſtable or *cunſtable* is compounded of two Saxon words, *cuninge per contractionem kinge*, and *ſtable*, *id eſt*, *columen*, *quaſi columen regis*, anciently written *cuningſtable*. *Marſhall* anciently written *marſcalc*, likewiſe of two Saxon words, viz. *marc* for *equus*, and *ſtalc curator*, *quaſi curator equorum:* for the marſhall *mariſchallus*, and the derivation thereof, ſee the firſt part of the Inſtitutes, ſect. 102. fol. 74. ſect. 154. fo. 106. ſection 745. fo. 391.

The place.

This court of chivalry was anciently holden in the kings hall.

The juriſdiction.

The juriſdiction is declared by the ſtatute of 13 R. 2. ſtat. 1.

Rot. par. 8 R. 2. nu. 31. not in print. 13 R. 2. ſtat. 1. ca. 2. Rot. parl. 8 H. 6. nu. 38.
* The judges, vide infra.
1 H. 4. cap. 14.

* Nota declared.

Becauſe the commons doe make a grievous complaint, that the court of the * conſtable and marſhall have incroached to them, and daily doe encroach contracts, covenants, treſpaſſes, debts and detinues, and many other actions pleadable at the common law, in great prejudice of the king and of his courts, and to the great grievance and oppreſſion of his people, the king willing to ordain a remedy againſt the prejudices and grievances aforeſaid, hath * declared in this parliament by the advice and aſſent of the lords ſpirituall and temporall the power and juriſdiction of the ſaid conſtable in the form that followeth.

The power and juriſdiction.

To the conſtable it appertaineth to have conuſance of contracts and deeds of arms, and of war out of the realm, (1) and alſo of things that touch war within the realm, which cannot be determined or diſcuſſed by the common law, with other uſages and cuſtomes to the ſame matters pertaining, which other conſtables have heretofore duly and reaſonably uſed in their time, joyning to the ſame that every plaintif ſhall declare plainly his matter in his petition afore that any man be ſent for to to anſwer thereunto. And if any will complain that any plea be commenced before the conſtable and marſhall, that might be tried by the law of the land, the ſame complainant ſhall have a privy ſeal of the king without difficulty directed to the ſaid conſtable and marſhall to ſurceaſe in that plea, till it be diſcuſſed by the kings councell, if that matter ought and of right pertaineth to that court, or otherwiſe to be tried by the common law of the realm of England, and alſo that they ſurceaſe in the mean time.

See the third part of the Inſtitutes, cap. High Treaſon, pag. 26. Rot. pat. 25 E. 3. parte 1. m. 16. 1 H. 4. between the lord Morly and the earl of Sarum, the record whereof we have ſeen. Rot. pat. 2 H. 4. parte 1. m. 7. between Kighly and Scroop. Rot. pat. 3 H. 4. Balleſhuls caſe. Rot. Vaſcon. 9 H. 5. nu. 14. Bullemers caſe. Rot. parl. 21 R. 2. nu. 19. &c. Rot. parl. 2 H. 6. nu. 9. Holl. Chron. 424. 3 H. 4. Sir John Anneſleys caſe. See this caſe Walſing. pa. 237. *Duellum percuſſum. Ibidem* 8 R. 2. 446. John Walſhes caſe. For this caſe of Walſh, ſee Walſing. pa. 311. and Stowes Annals 477. Howes Chron. 8 H. 6. 371. between John Upton and John Down. Vide Stowes Survey of London 385. See this caſe, rot. pat. 8 H. 6. parte 2. m. 7. Annals 609. Stow. *ibid. anno* 25 H. 6. *anno domini* 1446. between John Davye and William Catur his maſter, Annals 655. *ibid.* 386. battell joyned between Thomas Fitz-Thomas prior of Kilman and James Butler earl of Ormond; but when it came to the point the king forbad it. Vide Rot. parl. 2 H. 6. nu. 9. John lord Talbot lievetenant of Ireland accuſed the earl of Ormond of high treaſon before the earl of Bedford conſtable of England in his marſhals court, the king did aboliſh the accuſation. [124]

What judgment ſhall be given when either party is vanquiſhed, ſee the articles of the duke of Glouc' conſtable of England about the beginning of the reign of R. 2. The law of arms is, that the appellant being overcome ſhall incurre the ſame puniſhment, that the defendant ought to have done if he had vanquiſhed.

See an ancient manuſcript in French entituled *Modus faciend' duellum coram rege. Bone foy et droit et ley de arms voet que lappellant encourge meſme peyne que le defendant deveroit, ſil ſoit convict et diſcomfit.* * And this ſeemeth to be conſonant to the law of God.

This manuſcript treateth both of the juriſdiction and manner of the proceeding before the conſtable and marſhall, and for that it is long, and I doubt not but copies thereof are in many hands, I have not inſerted it here.

There are many in forain parts that have written of combats, &c. in Latine, French, and Italian. As Alciat, Lancelottus, Conradus, Johannes de Lignano, Mutio Juſtino Politano, Berandler, Beutheus, Deſdiguieres, &c. to whom we refer the reader, for that it is ſafe to follow the acts of parliament concerning the juriſdiction of this court, and ſuch preſidents as have been before the conſtable and marſhall in the marſhals court within this realm.

(1) *Out of the realm.*] This is to be underſtood in any forain part beyond the ſeas, *in partibus exteris et tranſmarinis.* For upon the ſea the admirall hath juriſdiction, which admirall (our Engliſh Neptune)

* Deut. 19. 18. And the judges ſhall make diligent inquiſition, and if the accuſer be found falſe, and that he hath given falſe witneſſe againſt his brother, then ſhall you doe to him, as he had thought to doe to his brother, and thou ſhalt put evill away from the middeſt of thee.

Neptune) cannot meddle with any thing beyond the seas upon the land, and the constable and marshall have no conusance of any thing done upon the sea.

26 H. 8. ca. 13. 35 H. 8. cap. 2. 5 E. 6. cap. 11.

Where by these acts it is provided, that all treasons, misprision of treasons, or concealment of treasons committed out of this realm of England, should be inquired of, heard and determined in the kings bench by good and lawful men of the same shire where the said bench shall sit, or else before such commissioners and in such shire, as should be assigned by the kings commission by good and lawful men of the same shire, in like manner and form to all intents and purposes as if such treasons, &c. had been done within the same, &c. None of these acts doth take away the jurisdiction of the constable and marshall, where one accuseth another of high treason done out of the realm: for of such an accusation of one against another of any high treason done out of the realm the constable and marshall should have conusance thereof: because high treason is not triable by jury according to the course of the common laws of the realm in that case for want of proof, as by all the presidents aforesaid it appeareth. Neither doth the said act of 35 H. 8. or 5 E. 6. take away the statute of 28 H. 8. cap. 15. for tryall of treasons done upon the sea, albeit they be done out of the realm. See hereafter cap. 23. and the third part of the Institutes, cap. of Piracy, pa. 111, & 112. and there was no doubt conceived of the triall of them. See the preamble of the statute of 35 H. 8. and of 5 E. 6.

See 1 E. 6. ca. 12. & 5 E. 6. ca. 11. in the 3 part of the Inst. p. 24.

See 5 El. ca. 5.

* If any merchant English be spoiled, or his goods taken from him beyond sea by any merchants strangers, and the English merchant cannot upon suit attain † to justice there, he shall have upon testimony thereof a writ out of the chancery to arrest the merchants strangers if they come into England or their goods, &c. untill they be satisfied. See hereafter the chapter of Admiralty.

*Vid. Regi. 129. F. N. B. 114. b. Note remedy by the common law for wrong done beyond the sea.

†[125]

Before this act at a parliament holden in the 8 year of R. 2. it was enacted, that no plea which should concern the common law should be tried before the constable and the marshall.

Rot. par. 8 R. 2. nu. 31. not printed.

No addition either of persons or of jurisdiction can be added to this court, unlesse it be by act of parliament; * for ancient courts ought to be exercised according to the ancient and right institution.

Rot. par. 5 R. 2. nu. 39. Bennet Wilmots case. 6 H. 7. 5. Simile. * Regul. 6 H. 7. 4, 5.

In the appeal aforesaid between Upton and Down in 8 H. 6. after battell joyned, the kings writ out of the court of chancery issued to the sherifs of London, as we find it entred and recorded in the great book of the abby of Bury fo. 87. as followeth.

Breve Vic' London pro listis & barris, &c. pro duello fac'. Lex armorum. Pro duello, &c. See the articles set down by Tho. of Woodstock duke of Glouc' constable of England, about the beginning of the reign of R. 2.

Rex vic' London salutem: precipimus vobis firmit' injungentes quod quasdam listas et barras de meremio fortes et satis sufficientes pro quodam duello inter Johannem Upton appellantem et Johannem Down defendentem, secundem legem armorum die Lunæ prox' futur' apud Westsmithfield in suburb' civitatis prædictæ Deo dante perficiend' contra diem prædictum nostris sumptibus et expensis erigi, construi, et fieri fac' in omnibus prout in ultimo duello ibidem facto fact' fuerunt, et quod terra infra listas prædict' cum sabulo sufficiente et equalit' cooperatur, ita quod aliqui lapides grandes aut arena infra easdem listas minime inveniantur quovismodo: et de omnibus et singulis pecuniarum summis quas circa premissa applicaveritis, nos vobis in compoto vestro ad scaccarium nostrum

per

per presens mandatum nostrum, debitam allocationem habere faciemus, &c.

By this writ we observe 4. things. 1. That sherifs ought to make the lists, &c. 2. The manner how they are to make them. 3. That they ought to make them by the kings writ. 4. That they are to be made at the kings charges. See mod' fac' duellum coram rege.

By the statute of 1 H. 4. all appeals of things done within the realm shall be tried and determined by the good laws of the realm, &c. And that all appeals made of things done out of the realm shall be tried and determined before the constable and marshall of England for the time being, and that no appeal be pursued in parliament. 1 H. 4. cap. 14. Rot. par. 11 H. 4. nu. 24.

They proceed according [a] to the customes and usages of that court, and in cases omitted, according * to the civil law, *secundum legem armorum*. And therefore upon attainders before the constable and marshall of England for the time being no land is forfeited, or corruption of bloud wrought. [a] 13 H. 4. fo. 4, 5. *By the civil law, &c.* * 37 H. 6. fo. 3. Fortesc' cap. 32. fo. 38.

For records, book-cases, and other authorities in law as well for the exposition of the said statutes, as for the jurisdiction and proceedings of this court, [b] see the first part of the Institutes, sect. 102. and 745. and peruse the authorities there cited. See also the petition of right, 3 Car. cap. 1. [b] 11 H. 4. nu. 24. All statutes made touching the courts of the constable and marshall and admiral of England shal be observed. Vide rot. parl. 5 H. 4. nu. 24. An act not in print touching a commission for araying and mustering of men, which at this day is of force, and no other. Vide 8 H. 4. nu. 12. Clergy exempt out of that. See also 14 E. 3. stat. 2. nu. 53. a commission of lieutenancy. See hereafter amongst the ecclesiasticall courts, tit. Appeals.

It is to be observed that after sentence pronounced in this court of chivalry in case of arms the party grieved may appeal to the king, whereof you may read a notable record, Rot. pat. 13 R. 2. parte 3. Note also a speciall rol, an. 14 R. 2. intituled *rot. process' in curia militari in causa armorum, int' Ric'um le Scroop chivalier, et Robertum Grovener chivalier.*

And for this cause (amongst others) [c] the heralds are attendants upon this court. Of these heralds there be *tres reges*, viz. *Garter rex armorum, Clarenceux * rex armorum ex parte australi. Norroy rex armorum ex parte boreali, et sex alii heraldi.* These English heralds are messengers of war and peace, skilfull in descents, pedegrees, and armories; they marshall the solemnities at coronations, they manage combats before the constable and marshall, and upon request they solemnize the funerals of noble, honourable, reverend, and worshipfull parsonages. [a] They were first incorporated by king R. 3. and afterwards newly incorporated by king Philip and queen Mary. Their learning and faithfull dealing in descents and pedegrees upon just proof may be a mean to quiet many controversies about the titles of honors, dignities, and inheritances.

[b] In the Prophet Ezechiel it is thus written: *Dicit dominus deus, et erit manus mea super prophetas, qui vident vana, et divinant mendacium: in concilio populi mei non erunt, et in scriptura domus Israel non scribentur.*

Upon these latter words divines doe hold, *Quod mos erat in Israel, quod unaquæque familia genealogiam ejus scriberet, in qua dinoscebatur* Vid. Glover 82, 83.

[c] Saxonicè Ejnhold *i.* honorem tenens, Latine fæciales. 5 E. 4. 6. b. Pl. Com. 12. b. [a] Rot. pat. 1 R. 3. rot. pat. 2 & 3 Ph. and Mar. 18 July: their colledge is in the parish of S. Bennet in Castle Bainard awrd granted to the corporation of the heralds by letters patents bearing date 18 July 1555. anno 2 & 3 Ph. and Mar. [b] Ezech. 13. 8, 9. Psalm. 69. *Deleantur de libro viventium, et cum justis non scribantur.* 1 Esdr. ca. 2. 62. *Hi quæsierunt scripturam genealogiæ suæ et non invenerunt, et ejecti sunt.*

* [126]

quilibet de qua tribu erat, et de qua familia, et quæ hæreditas ejus esse deberet, et ille qui penitus destrueretur non scriberetur.

c Discharged of subsidies.

c These heralds are discharged of subsidies, tols and other charges of the common-wealth, by letters patents of E. 6. *anno* 3. of his reign.

See the first part of the Institutes for degrees, and creations of nobility, and triall thereof, Sect. 9. fo. 16. and Sect. 95. fo. 69. whereunto you may adde a notable writ in d the Register, when a baron or any higher degree of nobility is sued in the * court of common pleas, and processe awarded against him by *capias* or *exigent*, then may he sue out this writ.

d Regist. 287. b. F. N B. 247. c.

* Or in the kings bench or other court.

Nota, *pro barone*. Vid. 8 H. 6. 9, 10. 14 H. 6. 2. lib. 6. fo. 53. b. e Countes de Rutlands case.

Rex justiciariis suis de banco salutem. Mandamus vobis, quod si G. T. miles coram vobis ad sectam alicujus per actionem personalem implacitatus existit, talem processum et non alium versus ipsum in actione prædicta fieri faciatis, qual' versus dominos, magnates, comites sive barones regni nostri Angliæ qui ad parliamentum nostrum de sommonitione nostra venire debent aut eorum aliquem secundum legem et consuetudinem regni nostri Angliæ fuerit faciend', quia prædict' G. T. *unum baronum regni nostri prædict' ad parliamenta nostra de sommonitione regia venientium recordari, &c.*

The barony of Edmond de Eincourt commonly Deincourt of Langley in Lincolnshire originally created by writ, had long continued in his firname, and having no issue male, desirous that his firname, arms, and barony, all which he held in fee simple might continue, by humble suit importuned king E. 2. for that he conceived, *Quod cognomen suum et arma post mortem suum delerentur, et corditer affectabat ut post mortem ejus in memoria haberentur, ut de maneriis et armis suis feoffaret quemcunque voluerit*: and in the end he obtained his suit by the kings letters patents under the great seal, and afterwards about 19 E. 2. he assigned according to the kings grant his firname, arms, and possessions. For we find in the close rols that the said Edmond baron of Eincourt sat in parliament untill and in 18 E. 2. and that after his decease his assignee sat in parliament in 1 E. 3. by the name of William de Eincourt, and in his heirs males the dignity, firname, and possessions continued * untill 21 H. 6. and then his heir male together with the name and dignity ceased.

10 E. 2. Camden Brit. rot. cart. 23 H. 3. nu. 32. 34. Almarick earl of Leic' Math. Par. pag. 647.

* Inquisit' 21 H. 6. post mortem Willielmi domini de Eincourt.

And I did hear the baron of Burghley lord treasurer deputy to the earl of Shrewsbury then earl marshall of England, in hearing of the cause by the queens commandement between Edward Nevil and lady Mary Vane daughter and heir of Henry lord of Aburgaveny for the right of the barony of Aburgaveny, vouch a record in the reign of E. 4. That the lord Hoe, who bare for his ensigns of honor quarterly silver and sable, having no issue male, by his deed, under his seal granted his name, arms and dignity over, but having not the kings licence and warrant, the same was in parliament adjudged to be void.

Hil. anno 31 El.

[127]

Our heralds are constituted by letters patents, and have many ceremonies done unto them at their creation, but those ceremonies are not of the essence of their office, but the letters patents only: and so was it adjudged in the kings bench in the reign of Queen Eliz. in the case of Dethick king of arms. But thus much of heralds upon this occasion shall suffice; and now let us return to our constable and marshall.

In

In ancient laws before the conquest, you shall read *de heretochiis* or *heretogiis*, i. *ductoribus exercitus, ab here exercitus et toech, ducere.* Int' leges Edwardi regis. Lamb. 136. Hovenden annal. cap. 35. De Heretochiis.

Heretochius agreeth with either of these great officers, *constabularius* or *marischallus: isti vero eligebantur per commune concilium pro communi utilitate regni per provincias et patricos in pleno folkmote.*

This office of the constable of England was afterwards of inheritance by the tenure of the mannors of Harlefield, Newman, and Whitenhurst by grand serjeanty, in the line of the Bohuns earls of Hereford, and Essex, and afterwards of right in the line of the Staffords and dukes of Buckingham as heirs generall to them; at the last by the opinion of * all the judges it was lawfully descended to Edward duke of Buckingham, who was attainted of treason, in anno 13 H. 8. whereby this office became forfeited to the crown, and since that time both in respect of the amplitude of the authority both in war and peace, and of the charge, it was never granted to any subject, but now of late *hac vice.* Of ancient time eligible. Lambard ubi sup. Hovend. ubi sup.

* See 11 El. Dier 285. so resolved in 6 H. 8.

For the office of the earl marshall, see the first part of the Institutes, sect. 102. & 135.

The effect of the grant of this office of constable of England is in very few words, viz. *officium constabularii Angliæ una cum omnibus feodis, proficuis, commoditatibus, et emolumentis quibuscunque officio prædicto qualitercunque pertinentibus, et ab antiquo debitis et consuetis.* And by no means we are to follow the irregular president of the grant thereof by king E. 4. in the 7 year of his reign to Richard Widevile earl Rivers and lord of Grafton and De la mote for his life: which patent you shall find rot. pat. anno 7 E. 4. part 1. and is directly against the common law and the statutes concerning the jurisdiction of this office: and therein to over-reach all the good and wholesome laws made for the declaration of the jurisdiction of this great office, power was given to the earl Rivers to have conusance in case of high treason, and other causes and affairs, *quæ in curia constabularii Angliæ ab antiquo, viz. domini Guilielmi Conquestoris progenitoris regis, seu aliquo tempore citra, tractari, audiri, examinari et decidi consueverunt, seu de jure debuerunt sive debent, et diversa alia perperam.* And therefore by no means the same or the like is to be drawn into example.

For grants of this great office of constable of England, see the presidents, and by that which hath been said choose the best. Rot. pat. 1 H. 4. parte 1. *Henrico comiti North pro vita.* Rot. pat. 4 H. 4. parte 2. *Johanni filio regis, ad placitum.* Rot. parl. 1 H. 6. nu 23. *Duci Glouc' ad placitum.* Rot. pat. 1 H. 6. parte 2. *Johanni duci Bedford pro vita.* Rot. pat. 8 H. 6. parte 1. *Richardo duci Eborum in absentia Johannis ducis Bedford.* Rot. pat. 25 H. 6. parte 1. *Johanni vicecom' de bello monte.* Rot. pat. 28 H. 6. parte 2. m. 22. *Henrico com. Northumbr. ad placitum.* Rot. pat. 29 H. 6. parte 1. *Edmundo duci Somerset ad placitum.* Rot. pat. 1 E. 4. parte 3. m. 188. *Johanni com. Wigorn'.* Rot. pat. 7 E. 4. parte 1. *Johanni domino Tiptoft.* Rot. pat. 7 E. 4. *Ubi supra Richardo com' Rivers.* Pat. 8 E. 4. parte 1. Pat. 9 E. 4. *Georgio duci Clarenc'.* Pat. 9 E. 4. parte 2. *Richardo duci Gloc'.* Pat. 10 E. 4. parte. * *Johanni Tiptoft comiti Wigorn. pro vita.* Pat. 16 E. 4. parte 1. *Ricardo duci Eborum. Henricus Stafford dux Buckingham jure hæreditario.* Pat. 1 R. 3. *Thomas dominus Stanley. Edwardus dux Buck' jure hæreditario.*

Hic omnium immanissimus: but the debts of cruelty are never unpaid, *respice finem.*

This great office hath been usually granted, as by the presidents aforesaid

[128]

aforesaid appeareth, *exercendum per se vel per sufficientes deputatos suos, seu per sufficien' deputatum suum.*

There is also an office of *subconstabularius* granted to Thomas Kent doctor of laws. Pat. 23 H. 6. parte 2. Simile pat. 22 E. 4. m. 2.

There is also *clericus constabulariæ Angliæ, et promotor causarum et negotiorum regiam majestatem tangen'.* This office was granted to Thomas Appulton with a fee of five marks. Pat. 8 E. 4. parte 1.

Concerning the grants of the office of earl marshall of England: for this office ever passed by the grants of the king, and never belonged to any subject by reason of tenure, as the stewardship, and constableship of England sometime did.

Ro. Cart. 20 R. 2. m. 1. n. 3.

*Rex, &c. sciatis quòd cum nos nuper de gratia nostra speciali concesserimus dilecto consanguineo nostro Thomæ comiti Notingham officium mareschalli Angliæ: habendum ad totam vitam suam. Nos jam de ulteriori gratia nostra concessimus præfato consanguineo nostro officium prædictum * una cum nomine et honore comitis mareschalli. Habendum sibi et hæredibus suis masculis de corpore suo exeuntibus cum omnibus feodis, proficuis et pertinentiis quibuscunque dicto officio qualitercunque spectantibus imperpetuum. Hiis testibus, &c. Dat' 12 Junii anno regni sui 20.*

* This is the first stile that ever came in any patent.

Ro. Cart. 9 R. 2. nu. 17.

This charter of creation is confirmed by act of parliament. The former grant before recited, yet shorter then this, was made anno 9 R. 2.

For other grants of this office in Rot. Cartarum, pat. & parl. See Rot. Cart. 1 Johannis parte 2. nu. 85. Rot. Cart. 9 E. 2. nu. 32.

Vide Rot. Pat.
- 1 H. 3. m. 14. 16.
- 22 R. 2. parte 1. m. 12.
- 1 H. 4. parte 1. & 5. m. 6.
- 1 R. 3. parte 1. m. 12.
- 1 H. 7. parte 3.
- 2 H. 8. parte 2.
- 25 H. 8. parte 2.
- 1 E. 6. parte 2. m. 19. & 22.
- 19 Ja. parte 13. nu. 5.

Vide Rot. Parl.
- 3 H. 6. m. 181.
- 1 Mariæ, nu. 34.
- 1 R. 2. m. 4. & 3.
- 20 R. 2. nu. 33.
- Parl. 21 E. 1. rot. 1. *Quæ pertinent ad officium comitis mareschalli, &c.*

Pat. 22 E. 4. m. 2.

There was also *vicemareschallus*, which office was granted to Tho. Grey *hac vice.*

Vide *lib. nigr. de scaccario*, concerning the offices of the constable and marshall, *et lib. rubro fo.* 36.

See also the marshall of England, Fleta lib. 2. cap. 4, 5. and Britton *in principio libri.*

See Mich. 13 E. 2. *in scaccario pro feodis constabularii Angliæ.*

Hil. 5 E. 3. *in scaccario certificatio facti' regi pro officio mareschalli.* 1 E. 3. fo. 16. 2 E. 3. fo. 12. 48 E. 3. 3. Rot. parl. 2 R. 2. nu. 47. 5 R. 2. tit. Triall. 54. Rot. par. 5 H. 4. nu. 39. Keylwey 172. Stanf. Pl. Cor. 65. Fortescue ca. 32. fo. 38. 5 Mar. Br. tit. Battell 15.

Herestita

Hereſlita ſignifieth a ſoldier hired and departing without licence, derived of *here*, *exercitus*, and *ſliten*, to depart.

If any ſoldier have covenanted to ſerve the king in his war, and appear not at the time and place appointed, there lyeth by the common law an original writ of *capias conductos ad proficiſcendum*, directed to two of the kings ſerjeants at arms to arreſt and take him wheresoever he may be found, and to bring him *coram concilio noſtro* with a clauſe of aſſiſtance: but of this matter ſee the third part of the Inſtitutes, cap. [Soldiers that depart, &c.] See 3 Car. the petition of right concerning martiall law, and the commiſſion to lieutenants, &c. Regiſt. fo. 191. a, & Par. 5 E. 3. nu. 18. [129]

To conclude with ſome ſhort touch concerning right of war. *Si quando acceſſeris ad expugnandam civitatem, offeres ei primum pacem:* and ſee there many things concerning right of war. *Quis rex iturus committere bellum adverſus alium regem, non ſedens prius cogitat ſi poſſit cum decem millibus occurrere ei qui cum viginti millibus venit ad ſe, alioquin illo adhuc longe agente legationem mittens rogat ea quæ pacis ſunt.* Deut. 20. 10. &c. Luc. 14. 31.

Haud facile vincitur qui de ſuis et adverſarii copiis vere poterit judicare. *Qui colloquium offert, ſemper paveſcit,* he that offereth parly is ever afraid. *Nulla ſunt meliora conſilia quam quæ ignoraverit adverſarius antequam facias.* *Tacitus.* *Vegetius de re militari.*

Nullum bellum eſt juſtum niſi aut pro rebus petitis geratur, aut ante denunciatum ſit, et indictum. *Cicero offic'.*

Jure gentium non licet indictas inimicitias exercere et bellum gerere, priuſquam ille à quo injuria ſit orſa moneatur illicitam injuriam reſarcire, et ab injuria abſiſtere. *Camden.*

Juſtum autem bellum eſt quod tria hæc habet, authorem, cauſam, finem. *Lipſius.*

Semper in prælio hiis maximum periculum, qui maxime timent. *Saluſt.*

Longa belli præparatio celerem dat victoriam. *Veget. et Seneca.*

Ideo ſuſcipienda ſunt bella, ut ſine injuria in pace vivatur. *Cicero ubi ſup.*

In republica maxime conſervanda ſunt jura belli. *Ariſt.* 10.

* *Olim veteri lege armorum cives et burgenſes militiam tractare prohibiti fuerunt.* * Vid. 24 E. 3. tit. coron.

We vouch *Vegetius* for his own honor and worthineſſe, and for that Forteſcue, fo. 70. b. citeth him.

CAP. XVIII.

The Court of the Marſhalſea.

The name. 1 part of the Inſtitutes, §. 102. & 135. *The antiquity and honor.* 4 H. 6. 8. L. 5 E. 4. 229. *Wherefore it is called the court of the marſhalſea.*

FOR the derivation of *mareſchallus et mareſchalcia*, ſee before in the next preceding chapter of the court of the conſtable and marſhall, that they be derived from two Saxon words which we conceive tendeth much for the proof of the antiquity and honor of our nation, ſeeing other nations have the ſame officers and offices; and in reſpect their name is derived from the language of our anceſtors, it is like they took the ſame from us.

Albeit in this court the ſteward and marſhall of the houſhold are judges, and the ſteward hath the precedency, yet the court is called the court of marſhalſea for three cauſes. Firſt, he is not only a judge, but ſeeth that execution (which is the life of the law) be done. Secondly, his office is in force both in time of peace, and in time of war. Thirdly, though the conſtable hath the precedency of the marſhall of England, yet the court holden before them is called the marſhall court for the cauſes aforeſaid. See before in the chapter of the conſtable and marſhall, ſee alſo rot. par. *anno* 8 H. 4. nu. 82. that the court of the marſhall can hold no plea but ſuch as were holden in the reign of E. 1.

The juriſdiction of this court is original and ordinary. 4 H. 6. 1.

For the juriſdiction of this court, and within what precinct, ſee in my Reports, lib. 10. fo. 68, 69, &c. *Le caſe del marſhalſea.* Lib. 6. fo. 20, 21. Michelbornes caſe. 7 H. 4. 15. in Calvins caſe Lib. 4. fo. 46, 47. Swifts caſe. See parl. 30 E. 1. rot. 2. All inquiſitions concerning any citizen of London ſhall be taken in London.

Hil. 20 R. 2. coram rege rot. 58. Midd.

Pertinet ad mareſcallum cur' hic venire fac' juratores ſuper felones captos cum manuopere in aula regis.

This court hath his foundation from the common law of England.

W. 1. ca. 26. fees.

This marſhall by the ſtatute of W. 1. can take no fee for doing of his office but only of the king, but ſuch fees as latter acts of parliament have given him, he may take. See the third part of the Inſtitutes, cap. Extortion.

For the fees of the marſhall of the kings houſe, and of ſtaffe bearers, and ſervitors of bils, ſee the ſtatute of 2 H. 4. cap. 23.

Rot. par. 17 E. 3. nu. 31.

To conclude this chapter with an act of parliament not in print. It is enacted that every perſon arreſted into the marſhalſea, may tell his own tale, and that the officers doe not paſſe the verge. See par. 50 E. 3. nu. 91. 162.

CAP.

CAP. XIX.

The Counting-house of the Kings Household.

Domus Compotus Hospitii Regis.

IT is commonly called the green cloth, in respect of the green-cloth upon the table, whereat the honourable officers hereafter mentioned do sit, viz. the lord steward, the treasurer of the kings house, the controller of the kings house, the master of the houshold, the cofferer, and two clerks controllers continually sitting in this counting-house for these purposes. First, for daily taking the accounts for all expences of the said houshold. Secondly, for making of provisions for the said houshold, according to the laws and statutes of the realm. Thirdly, for making of payment for the same accordingly. Fourthly, for the good government of the kings servants of houshold. Fifthly, the cofferer is to pay the wages to the kings servants beneath the staires, and the lord chamberlaine above the stairs of the kings houshold. Vide 39 Eliz. cap. 7. and he is to account in the exchequer for about 40000 li. 33 H. 8. cap. 12.

See Fleta *de officio thesaurarii hospitii regis, &c. Habet enim rex alios clericos in hospitio suo, et thesaurar' garderobæ suæ quæ est locus clericis tantum assignatus, quæ in Francia camera clericorum appellatur. Huic enim thesaurario cur' expens' regis et familiæ suæ committit', q. cum clerico provido sibi associato pro controt'latore recordum habet ut in hiis q. officium suum contingunt.* Fleta lib. 2. ca. 13. Thesaurarius. Garderobæ.

Officium thes. garderobæ est pecuniam, jocalia exemna. regi facta recipere et recepta regisque secreta custodire, et de receptis expens' facere rationabiles, expensarumque particulas inbreviare, et de particulis comp' reddere ad scaccarium singulis annis in festo Sanctæ Margaretæ absque sacr'o præstando, eo quod de consilio regis est juratus, et unde primo debet distincte et aperte comp' reddere de omnibus recept' separatim per se in uno rotulo. In alio autem rotulo de expensis cotidianis de quibus sen' audiverit comp', simul cum thes. et consocio suo. Item de necessariis expens. in quibus emptiones equorum, cariagia et plura alia continent'. Item de donis. Item de oblationibus et eleemosynis. Item de vadiis militum. Item de vadiis balistar'. Item de feod' forinsecis. Item de præstit' et accommodat'. Compotum reddere. De consilio regis juratus. Modus compoti.

Item de expens. garderobæ in quib' emptiones pannorum, pelure, cere sperū tele, et hujusmodi comprehenduntur. Item de jocalibus. Item de expens. forinsecis, in quibus diversi onerant' in compot' reddend. Item de nunciis. Item de falconar'.

Thes. autem memoratus convenire debet singulis noctibus sen. hospitii, camerar' controt'latorem et clericum ejus, coffrarium, mar' aulæ et hostiar' milites, mar' servientem et duos hostiar' aulæ et hostiar' cameræ servientes, assessorem ferculorum, pincernam, panetr' pistorem et clericum eorundum officiorum, q. de expens. dictæ, viz. panis, vini, et cervis. pichiorum, ciphorum, salis, fructus, casei et hujusmodi respondebit. Convenire singulis noctibus. Coffrarius.

Magistri Cocorum clericus Coquinæ.

Item duos magistros cocorum, lardenar', poletar', scutellar', salsar' et clericum coquinæ qui de eisdem officiis pro omnibus in eorum præsentia de expens. illius dietæ reddit rationem, quorum omnium præsentia necessaria est. Item eleemosinar', janitor' servientem ad custodiam summar' et carectarum deputatum et clericum de marescalcia cum marescall' fractore equorum, qui quidem clericus de expens. feni et aven' litere fracture equorum et harnesie pro equis et carectis ac de vadiis servient' scutiferarum clericorum et garc' respondebit, cuj' interest scire tam de hiis qui de novo erunt admissi ad vad' regis, quam de vagantibus et in hiis vadia minuere et augere. Vadia autem absentibus sine speciali præcepto regis nisi obsequio reg' fuerint minime concedunt', præsentia autem coronatoris regis necessaria erit [132] *in pleno compoto, compoti auditores super foro frumenti et aven. instruet et edocēt qualit' proclamat' in eisdem partibus per quod melius scire possint quot panes obolati fiere debent de quart' frument. quibus omnibus congregatis audire debent expens. et rationabilem compot' illius dietæ.*

Mareschalli autem de supervenientibus debent inferiori mar' testimonium perhibere. Hostiarius miles hostiariis aliis de numero ferculorum lardenar', coco, camerar', hostiario camer' regis, et sic quibus alii et sic audiat compotus de tota dieta.

And then followeth a description of the duties of the severall officers abovesaid, worthy the reading.

Artic. sup. Cart. cap. 2.

The cofferer is in Fleta called *coffrarius* of the coffer: because he should have money in his cofer to pay wages, &c. as is aforesaid. It is enacted by the statute of 28 E. 1. cap. 2. That all purveyours shall account in the * household, or in the wardrobe. Rot. par. 28 E. 3. nu. 34. no purveyour arrested shall be brought before the councell, &c. but take his remedy by the common law. See the third part of the Institutes, cap. Purveyours.

* Counting house having the greencloth. Rot. par. 28 E. 3. nu. 34. * 36 E. 3. ca. 2, 3, 4. &c.

* See the statutes concerning purveyours, *anno* 36 E. 3. cap. 2, 3, 4, 5, 6, &c. But observe that there is left out of the print the pain on the steward, treasurer, controller, and other officers of the household at the kings will, for not executing the statute: which omission hath made those of the greencloth the bolder.

Rot. par. 36 E. 3. nu. 18.

At that parliament it was also enacted, that the kings cariages should be made in as easie manner as might be, and that in the summer, and other times convenient, as in August (which is also left out of the print.) For the kings cariages see Mag. Cart. cap 21. and the exposition upon the same in the second part of the Institutes.

For the Wardrobe, vide 15 E. 2. rot. *per se.* 1 E. 4. ca. 1. clerk of the wardrobe, Rot. parl. 7 H. 7. the expences of the kings household and wardrobe. 1 H. 8. an act concerning the great wardrobe. 3 H. 8. the assignment for the kings wardrobe. 39 Eliz. cap. 7. master of the wardrobe, whose office is accountable in the exchequer. See W. 1. cap. 44. what issues the kings justices are to estreat into the wardrobe: more of the wardrobe, Rot. claus. 33 E. 1. m. 3. rot. *liberationum,* 11 E. 2. m. 4. To conclude, see Rot. claus. 18 E. 4. m. 13. where it appeareth that letters and writings concerning matters of state, which were not fit to be made vulgar, were inrolled in the wardrobe, and not in the chancery, as leagues were and ought to be, as it appeareth in 19 E. 4. 6. And thus much of the wardrobe being mentioned in Fleta.

Vid. infra cap. 26.

The officers of the counting-house never held plea of any thing.

CAP.

CAP. XX.

The Court of the Lord Steward, Treasurer, and Controller of the Kings Household, concerning Felony by compassing or Conspiracy to kill the King, or any Lord or other of the Kings Councell, &c.

THEY have jurisdiction by act of parliament, to enquire, heare, and determine the said offence, as particularly and at large appeareth in the third part of the Institutes, cap. Felony, by compassing, or conspiracy to kill the king, &c.

3 H. 7. cap. 14. 3 part of the Institutes cap. Felony by compassing or conspiracy to kill the king, fo. 67.

CAP. XXI.

The Court of the Lord Steward of the Kings House, or in his Absence of the Treasurer, and Controller of the Kings House, and Steward of the Marshalsea.

THEY have jurisdiction by act of parliament to enquire of, hear, and determine all treasons, misprision of treasons, murders, manslaughters, bloodshed, and other malitious strikings, whereby blood shall be shed in any of the palaces and houses of the king, or in any other house where the king in his royall person shall be abiding. And by that act the * limits and bounds of the kings palaces or house, or the house where the royall person is abiding, are particularly and expresly set forth and described. In this and like cases we refer you to the statute it selfe, for *compendia sunt dispendia.*

33 H. 8. cap. 12. See the statute for the triall and manner of proceeding. Rastall pl. 124. See the third part of the Institutes, cap. Misprision. fol. 229.
* Vide 28. ca. 12.

CAP.

CAP. XXII.

The Court of the Admiralty proceeding according to the Civill Law.

Articuli Admiralitatis.

Articuli Admiralitatis. The articles of the admiralty. The proces and proceedings in this court are in the name of the lord admirall.

The complaint of the lord admirall of England to the kings most excellent majesty against the judges of the realme, concerning prohibitions granted to the court of the admiralty 11 *die Febr. penultimo die termini Hilarii, anno* 8 *Jac. regis:* the effect of which complaint was after by his majesties commandement set downe in articles by doctor Dun judge of the admiralty; which are as followeth, with answers to the same by the judges of the realme: which they afterwards confirmed by three kinds of authorities in law. 1. By acts of parliament. 2. By judgements and judiciall proceedings: and lastly, by Book cases.

The title of the complaint.

Certain grievances whereof the lord admirall and his officers of the admiralty do especially complain, and desire redresse.

1 Objection.

THAT whereas the conusance of all contracts and other things done upon the sea belongeth to the admirall jurisdiction, the same are made triable at the common law, by supposing the same to have been done in Cheapside, and such places.

The answer.

By the lawes of this realm the court of the admirall hath no conusance, power, or jurisdiction of any manner of contract, plea, or querele within any county of the realm, either upon the land or the water: but every such contract, plea, or querele, and all other things rising within any county of the realm, either upon the land or the water, and also wreck of the sea ought to be tried, determined, discussed, and remedied by the lawes of the land, and not before, or by the admirall nor his lieutenant in any manner. So as it is not materiall whether the place be upon the water *infra fluxum et refluxum aquæ*: but whether it be upon any water within any county. Wherefore we acknowledge that of contracts, pleas, and querels made upon the sea, or any part thereof which is not within any county (from whence no triall can be had by twelve men) the admirall hath, and ought to have jurisdiction. And no president can be shewed that any prohibition hath been granted for any contract, plea, or querele concerning any marine cause made or done upon the sea, taking that only to be the sea wherein the admirall hath jurisdiction, which is before by law described to be out of any county. See more of this matter in the answer to the sixth article.

The description and limitation of the (sea) wherein the lord admirall hath jurisdiction.

When

When actions are brought in the admiralty upon bargains and contracts made beyond the seas, wherein the common law cannot administer justice, yet in these cases prohibitions are awarded against the admirall court. 2 *Objection.*

Bargains or contracts made beyond the seas wherein the common law cannot administer justice (which is the effect of this article) do belong to the constable and marshall; for the jurisdiction of the admirall is wholly confined to the sea, which is out of any county. But if any indenture, bond, or other specialty, or any contract be made beyond sea for doing of any act or payment of any money within this realm, or otherwise, wherein the common law can administer justice, and give ordinary remedy; in these case neither the constable and marshall, nor the court of the admiralty hath any jurisdiction. And therefore when this court of the admiralty hath dealt therewith in derogation of the common law, we finde that prohibitions have been granted, as by law they ought. *The answer.* See hereafter in the proofs by judgements and judiciall presidents. [135]

Whereas time out of minde the admirall court hath used to take stipulations for appearance and performance of the acts and judgements of the same court: it is now affirmed by the judges of the common law, that the admirall court is no court of record, and therefore not able to take such stipulations: and hereupon prohibitions are granted to the utter overthrow of that jurisdiction. 3 *Objection.*

The court of the admiralty proceeding by the civill law is no court of record, and therefore cannot take any such recognisance as a court of record may do. And for taking recognisances against the lawes of the realme, we finde that prohibitions have been granted, as by law they ought. And if an erroneous sentence be given in that court, no writ of error, but an appeale before certain delegates do lye, as it appeareth by the statute of 8 Eliz. *reginæ*, cap. 5. which proveth that it is no court of record. *The Answer.* 8 Eliz. cap. 5.

That charter-parties made only to be performed upon the seas are daily withdrawn from that court by prohibitions. 4 *Objection.*

If the charter-party be made within any city, port town, or county of this realm, although it be to be performed either upon the seas, or beyond the seas, yet is the same to be tried and determined by the ordinary course of the common law, and not in the court of the admiralty. And therefore when that court hath incroched upon the common law in that case, the judge of the admiralty and party suing there have been prohibited, and oftentimes the party condemned in great and grievous damages by the laws of the realm. *The Answer.*

That the clause of *non obstante statuto*, which hath foundation in his majesties prerogative, and is currant in all other grants, yet in the lord admirals patent is said to be of no force to warrant the determination of the causes committed to him in his lordships patent, and so rejected by the judges of the common law. 5 *Objection.*

Without all question the statutse of 13 R. 2. cap. 3. 15 R. 2. cap. 5. and 2 H. 4. cap. 11. being statutes declaring the jurisdiction of the court of the admirall, and wherein all the subjects of the realm have interest, cannot be dispensed with by any *non obstante*, and therefore not worthy of any answer: but by colour thereof, the court of the admiralty hath contrary to those acts of parliament incroched upon the jurisdiction of the common law, *The Answer.* 13 R. 2. cap. 3. 15 R. 2. cap. 5. 2 H. 4. cap. 11.

to

to the intolerahle grievance of the subjects, which hath oftentimes urged them to complain in your majesties courts of ordinary justice at Westm. for their relief in that behalf.

6 Objection. To the end that the admirall jurisdiction may receive all manner of impeachment and interruption, the rivers beneath the first bridges, where it ebbeth and floweth, and the ports and creeks are by the judges of the common law affirmed to be no part of the seas, nor within the admirall jurisdiction: and thereupon prohibitions are usually awarded upon actions depending in that court, for contracts and other things done in those places; notwithstanding that by use and practise time out of mind, the admirall court have had jurisdiction within such ports, creeks, and rivers.

The Answer. The like answer as to the first. And it is further added, that for the death of a man, and of mayhem (in those two cases only) done in great ships, being and hovering in the maine streame only beneath the points of the same rivers nigh to the sea, and no other place of the same rivers, nor in other causes, but in those two only, the admirall hath cognisance. But for all contracts, pleas, and querels made or done upon a river, haven, or creek, within any county of this realm, the admirall without question hath not any jurisdiction, for then he should hold plea of things done within the body of the county, which are triable by verdict of twelve men,
[136] and meerly determinable by the common law, and not within the court of the admiralty according to the civil law. For that were to change and alter the laws of the realm in those cases, and make those contracts, pleas, and querels triable by the common laws of the realm to be drawn *ad aliud examen*, and to be sentenced by the judge of the admiralty according to the civil laws. And how dangerous and penall it is for them to deal in these cases, it appeareth by judiciall presidents of former ages. See the answer to the first aricle.

The 7 Object. That the agreement made in *anno domini* 1575, between the judges of the kings bench and the court of the admiralty for the more quiet and certain execution of admirall jurisdiction is not observed as it ought to be.

The Answer. The supposed agreement mentioned in this article hath not as yet been delivered unto us, but having heard the same read over before his majesty (out of a paper not subscribed with the hand of any judge) we answer, that for so much thereof as differeth from these answers, it is against the laws and statutes of this realm: and therefore the judges of the kings bench never assented thereunto, as is pretended, neither doth the phrase thereof agree with the tearms of the laws of the realm.

The 8 Object. Many other grievances there are, which in discussing of these former will easily appear worthy also of reformation.

The Answer. This article is so generall, as no particular answer can be made thereunto, only that it appeareth by that which hath been said, that the lord admirall his officers and ministers principally by colour of the said void *non obstante*, and for want of learned advice have unjustly incroached upon the common laws of this realm, whereof the marvail is the lesse, for that the lord admirall, his lieutenants, officers, and ministers have without all colour incroached and intruded upon a right and prerogative due to the crown, in that they have

have seised, and converted to their own uses goods and chattels of infinite value taken by pirates at sea, and other goods and chattels which in no sort appertain unto his lordship by his letters patents, wherein the said *non obstante* is contained, and for the which he and his officers remain accountable to his majesty. And they now wanting in this blessed time of peace causes appertaining to their naturall jurisdiction, they now incroach upon the jurisdiction of the common-law, lest they should sit idle and reap no profit. And if a greater number of prohibitions (as they affirm) hath been granted since the great benefit of this happy peace, then before in time of hostility, it moveth from their own incroachments upon the jurisdiction of the common law. So as they do not only unjustly incroach, but complain also of the judges of the realm for doing of justice in these cases.

Touching our proceedings in granting of prohibitions concerning any of the said articles, two things are to be considered of. First, the matter; and secondly, the manner. For the matter nothing hath been done therein by your majesties courts at Westminster, but by good warrant of law and former judiciall president. And for the manner, we have granted none in the time of vacation, nor in the term time in any of our chambers, nor in the court in the terme time *ex officio*, but upon motion made in open court by learned councell, and after a day prefixed, and warning given to the adverse party, and upon reading of the libell in open court, and hearing of the councell learned of such of the parties as were warned and did attend.

The said answers are proved and confirmed (as is aforesaid) by three kind of authorities in law. First, by authority of the high courts of parliament. Secondly, by judgments and judiciall presidents. Thirdly, by book-cases, and the authority of our books.

1 By acts of parliament.

13 R. 2. cap. 5.

Concerning the acts of parliament: it is enacted by the statute made in 13 R. 2. ca. 5. That the admirals and their deputies shall not meddle from henceforth with any thing done within the realm of England, but only with things done upon the sea, according to that which hath been duly used in the time of the noble king Edward grandfather of king R. 2. By the which it is manifest, that the jurisdiction of the court of admiralty is only confined to things done upon the sea, which the adverse party yeelded, but claimeth by a colour of a *non obstante*, &c. which is utterly void, as hath been said. [137]

15 R. 2. ca. 3.

By the statute of 15 R. 2. cap. 3. it is enacted and declared, That the court of the admirall hath no manner of conusance, power nor jurisdiction of any manner of contract, plea or querell, or of any other thing done or rising within the bodies of the counties, either by land or by water, and also of wreck of the sea, but all such manner of contracts, pleas, and querels, and all other things rising within the bodies of the counties as well by land as by water, as is aforesaid, and also wreck of the sea shall be tried, termined, discussed, and remedied by the laws of the land, and not before, nor by the admirall nor his lieutenant in no manner. Nevertheless of the death of a man, and of a mayhem done in great ships, being and hovering in the main stream of the great rivers only beneath the points of the same rivers, and in no other place of

Nota, the lord admirall hath greater jurisdiction in case of the death of a man, and mayhem, then in other cases.

of the ſame rivers, the admiral ſhall have conuſance. This latter clauſe giveth the admirall further juriſdiction in caſe of death and mayhem, (with neither of which we ever medled) but in all other happening within the Thames, or in any other river, port, or water, which are within any county of the realm, (as all rivers and havens be, as hereafter ſhall manifeſtly appear) by expreſſe words of this act of parliament, the admirall or his deputy hath no juriſdiction at all. Wherein it is to be obſerved, how curious the makers of this ſtatute were to exclude the admirall of all manner of juriſdiction within any water which lyeth within any county of the realm.

2 H. 4. cap. 11.

The ſtatute of 2 H. 4. cap. 11. enacteth, That the ſaid act of 13 R. 2. cap. 5. be firmly holden and kept, and put in due execution, and further at the prayer of the commons that as touching a pain to be ſet upon the admirall or his lieutenant, that the ſtatute and common law ſhall be holden againſt them, and the party grieved ſhall recover his double dammages. By which act it appeareth, that the ſtatute of 13 R. 2. is but an affirmance of the common law, as ſhall alſo manifeſtly appear hereafter.

Which three acts cannot be diſpenſed withall by a *non obſtante*, as hath been ſaid before, but remain in full force, and hath been put in due execution in all ages.

27 El. cap. 11.

5 El. cap. 5.

The ſtatute of 27 Eliz. cap. 11. deſcribeth particularly the limits of the lord admirals juriſdiction in theſe words. All and every ſuch of the ſaid offences before mentioned, as hereafter ſhall be done on the main ſea, or coaſt of the ſea, being no part of the body of any county of this realm, and without the precinct, juriſdiction and liberty of the cinque ports, and out of any haven or pier, ſhall be tried and determined before the lord admirall, &c. So as by the judgment of the whole parliament the juriſdiction of the lord admirall is wholly confined to the main ſea, or coaſts of the ſea being no parcell of the body of any county of this realm.

And by theſe four acts of parliament all the ſaid objections that have been made, or can be made againſt the proceedings of the kings courts at Weſtminſter (being grounded on the ſame) are fully anſwered. And we will conclude this firſt part with the ſaying of God himſelfe. Almighty God (as he himſelf out of a whirlwind ſpake) hath ſhut up the ſea within certain dores and bounds, *Quis concluſit oſtiis mare, quando erumpebat, quaſi de vulva procedens: circumdedi illud terminis meis, et poſui vectem et oſtia, et dixi, Uſque huc venies, et non procedes amplius, et hic confringes tumentes fluctus ejus.*

Job 38. 8. 10. 11.

2 By judgements and judicial preſidents.

Concerning the ſecond kind of proof, viz. by judgments and judicial preſidents, every of them in all ſucceſſions of ages *in ſerie temporis*, taking ſome in every age for many that might be cited.

Regiſt. Origin. fo. 129. F. N. B. 114.

Regiſter Origin. fo. 129. F. N. B. 114. If goods be taken from an Engliſh man in Spain beyond the ſea, and the party cannot obtain juſtice there, he ſhal have a writ to the ſherif to arreſt the body of the offenders, and to ſeiſe of their goods to the value: which proveth that the admirall cannot hold plea thereof, for that the party hath remedy by the common law, and the admirals power is only *ſuper altum mare*.

[138]

Hil. 6 H. 6. Rot. 303. in Banc.

Hil. 6 H. 6. rot. 303. in the court of common pleas between John Burton plaintif, and Bartholomew Put defendant, the caſe was this upon the ſaid ſtatutes. The ſaid Bartholomew ſued the ſaid

ſaid John Burton in the admirall court before Thomas duke of Exeter then admirall of England, for that the ſaid John Burton with force and arms the ſecond day of September, *anno* 1 H. 6. three ſhips of the ſaid Bartholomew with his priſoners and merchandizes to the value of 960 marks, 5 s. 5 d. *ob.* in the ſame ſhips being did take and carry away, ſuppoſing by his libell the ſame to be taken away, *ſuper altum mare*, upon the high ſea. Although the taking aforeſaid was *infra corpus comitatus in Briſtow* (the ſaid ſhips lying in the haven of Briſtow) and not upon the high ſea, contrary to the form and effect of the ſaid ſtatutes; the parties deſcended to an iſſue, which was found for the plaintif and dammages aſſeſſed for the plaintif, to 700. l. And it appeareth by the record, that this being the firſt caſe that we can yet find that received judgment in the court of common pleas upon the ſaid ſtatutes, the ſame depended in adviſement and deliberation eight terms: and then the record ſaith, *Et ſuper hoc audito tam recordo quam veredicto prædicto, et per curiam plenius intellect': conſideratum eſt quod præd' Johannes Burton recuperet verſ' præfat' Bartholomæum damna ſua præd'cta occaſione attachiamenti, proſecutionis, et vexationis, quam miſarum et cuſtagiorum ad ſeptingentas libras per juratores præd' ſuperius aſſeſſ' in duplum per ſtatutum, &c. quæ damna in duplo ſe extendunt ad mille et* 400. *l. et idem Barth. pœnam decem librarum erga dominum regem nunc per idem ſtatut' incurrat, et capiatur, et querens remittit* 400. *l.* Upon which judgment four things are to be obſerved. Firſt, that it is *contemporanea expoſitio*, being made within twenty years of the making of one of the ſaid ſtatutes, and *contemporanea expoſitio eſt optima.* Secondly, that albeit the ſaid three ſhips with the priſoners and merchandizes in them lay in the haven, *inter fluxum et refluxum aquæ*, and *infra primos pontes*, yet that the haven is *infra corpus comitatus*, and that for taking of the ſhips and the priſoners, and merchandizes in the ſame no ſuit ought to be in the admirall court, but at the common law. Thirdly, that the court of admiralty hath no juriſdiction but *ſuper altum mare*, which is not within any county, for the record ſaith, that the ſaid three ſhips with the priſoners and merchandize in the ſame, did lye *infra comitat' Briſtoliæ, et non ſuper altum mare*, as the plaintif in the admirall court ſuppoſed the ſame to be. Laſtly, that judgment ſo ſolemnly, and with ſuch adviſement given, if it were alone, were ſufficient to give full ſatisfaction in this point: for *judicium eſt tanquam juris dictum*, and *judicium pro veritate accipitur.* But to proceed.

In Portu.

Paſch. 12 H. 6. rot. 124. a like action brought by Robert Cupper upon the ſaid ſtatutes in the court of common pleas (reciting the ſaid three ſtatutes) againſt John Rayner of Norwich, for that the ſaid Rayner did ſue the ſaid Cupper in the court of admiralty before John countee of Huntingdon and Ivery lieutenant to John duke of Bedford admirall of England, for that Rayner having a ſhip *in portu aquæ Jernemuthæ infra corpus com' Norff.* ready for a voyage to Zealand the ſaid Cupper entered the ſaid ſhip lying in the ſaid haven, and took away divers goods in the ſame being, *aſſerendo per prædictum placitum res illas ſuper altum mare emerſiſſe, ac ſi res illæ ſuper altum mare emerſiſſent, cum non ibi, ſed apud Jernemutham contra formam ſtatutorum præd'*, which alſo proveth that the haven is within the body of the county.

Paſch. 12 H. 6. rot. 124. in banc.

In Portu.

In the same terme in the same court a like action between John Widewell and the said John Rayner, rot. 123. which with many others being to one effect we omit.

a Mich. 31 H. 6. rot. 315. in banc. Hil. 2. Ph. & Mar. rot. 130. Cr. a prohibition upon a charter-party. Hil. 17 Eliz. rot. 410. Cr. Spencers case, and infinite others upon charter-parties.

*[139]

[a] Mich. 31 H. 6. rot. 315. between William Hore, and Jeffery Unton for a suit in the court of admiralty before Henry duke of Exeter, admirall of England, concerning a contract of fourscore pounds upon a charter-party of affrait of a ship of the said Jeffery called the Trinity of Harflew to goe from the port of Pole * towards the parts of Iseland, *cum contractus ille apud novam Sarum infra corpus comitatus, et non super altum mare factus et junctus fuit, contra formam statutorum præd.'* The defendant pleaded to issue, which was found against him, and dammages assessed to a hundred marks, and costs to forty pound: and thereupon judgment is given by the court, that he should recover his dammages *in duplo*, according to the statute, &c. Which judgment directly proveth, that if a charter-party or any other contract be made within city, town, or county of the realm, though the performance thereof be to be done and performed upon the high sea, yet the admirall hath no jurisdiction, because it may be tried by the common law, as by the said record it appeareth. But where the whole is to be done *super altum mare*, and no part of it *infra corpus comitatus*, the admirall hath jurisdiction.

32 H. 8. ca. 14.

The statute of 32 H. 8. c. 14. concerning fraights of ships giveth to the lord admirall or his deputy power to make certificate concerning the ships of aliens in ports, &c. And if the lord admirall or his deputy be not resiant, then it giveth power to the customer and controller, or their deputy to make certificate: but without question this giveth no power to the lord admirall to hold plea of fraights of ships more then he had before, no more then it doth to the customer and controller, to whom equall power is given by the act to make certificate concerning the ships of aliens, &c. in the absence of the lord admirall or his deputy, as to the lord admirall or his deputy being present: and yet no man will affirm, that the customer and controller can hold plea of fraights.

Mich. 38 H. 6. rot. 36. cr.

Mich. 38 H. 6. rot. 36. cr. A premunire brought by John Cassy esquire, *Qui tam, &c.* against Richard Beuchamp, Thomas Paunce esquires, and others upon the statute of 16 R. 2. for suing *in curia Romana vel alibi*, of matters belonging to the common law. For that the defendant did sue the plaintif in the admirall court before Henry duke of Exeter, that the said John Cassye did take and carry away certain jewels *super altum mare, ubi idem Johannes Cassye bona illa apud Stratford at Bowe infra corpus comitatus Midd' et non super altum mare cepit*, which is so evident, and of so dangerous consequent, as no application shall be made thereof.

Book of entries. fo. 23.

In the book of entries fo. 23. tit. Admiralty, it appeareth that the taking of a ship called the Trinity of London lying upon the river at E. in the county of Kent is not *super altum mare*, but *infra corpus comitatus Kantiæ*. And therefore a suit for the taking of that ship lying there in the admirall court before John earl of Huntingdon admirall of England appeareth to be against the said statutes, and yet no question that taking was *infra fluxum et refluxum maris, et infra primos pontes*.

Book of entries. ubi supra.

9 H. 7. A premunire brought for a suit in the admiral court before John earl of Oxford for taking and carrying away *quandam*

naviculam apud Horton Key at Southlyn, &c. supposing the same to be *super altum mare*, where it was *infra corpus comitatus*.

Mich 16 H. 8. rot. 140. The river of Thames at Belingsgate is not within the jurisdiction of the admirall, but *infra corpus comitatus*. Mich. 16 H. 8. rot. 140.

35 H. 8. A prohibition to John Dudley knight, viscount Lisle for holding plea in the court of admiralty for a contract made in *rivo Thamesiæ*, supposing the same to be *super altum mare*, where in truth it was in *rivo Thamesiæ apud B. in com' Essex*, which notwithstanding was *infra fluxum et refluxum aquæ, et infra primos pontes*. Book of entries, ubi supra.

Hil. 36 H. 8 rot. 38. cr. The like prohibition *inter Wheler et Warner, eodem termino rot. Inter Tooly et Lewes*, a prohibition for a contract made at Danske, *in partibus transmarinis*. And in 2 Jac. *regis*, the whole court of common pleas, because the libell supposed the act to be done *in partibus exteris et transmarinis*, granted a prohibition. Hil. 36 H. 8. rot. 38. cr. Hil. 2 Jac. regis. *In communi Banc. int' Theodor Tomlinsun Quer' et Philips Def.* Tr.

Trin. 38 H. 8. rot. 126. between Crane and Bell a promise made at Dartmouth, that a ship called the Mary Fortune should passe safely without taking and surprising, &c. which ship was after taken by the Spanyards *super altum mare* is not determinable in the court of the admiralty, for that albeit the taking was upon the high sea, yet the promise was made upon the land, whereupon an action doth lye at the common law. 38 H. 8. rot. 126.

[140]

Tr. 3 & 4 Ph. and Mar. rot. 709. between Lawrence Mashe-rode, and Richard Wyn, a prohibition out of the court of common pleas to the court of the admiralty, William lord Howard then lord admirall being. Tr. 3 & 4 Ph. & Mar. rot. 709. in banco.

Tr. 3 & 4 Ph. and Mar. rot. 811. the like prohibition granted out of the same court to the court of admiralty between Robert Inne plaintif, and Roger Garland defendant. Eodem termino rot. 181. in banc.

Hil. 4 & 5 Ph. and Mar. rot. 831. the like prohibition. Hil. 4 & 5 P. & M. rot. 831.

Many are the presidents in the reign of the late queen Eliz. in the court of common pleas, the kings bench and exchequer, which we purposely omit, and insist rather upon the more ancient, yet one or two we will remember concerning things happening beyond sea, whereupon an action did lye at the common law agreeable with the president in the reign of H. 8.

Mich. 39 & 40 Eliz. rot. 3158. A prohibition out of the court of common pleas for a suit in the admirall court upon a bill under the parties hand and seal for French crowns, for that the bill was made beyond sea. Mich. 39 & 40 El. rot. 3158.

And Mich. 3 Jac. a prohibition was granted in the like case to the admirall court by the court of eschequer, for Sir John Swinarton having the priviledge of that court for a matter rising beyond the sea. And divers prohibitions granted also in the like case in the kings bench. Mic. 3 Jac. in scaccar'.

For causes of actions which are transitory done out of the realm, an action may lye at the common law, but if the cause be criminall or locall done beyond sea, then before the constable and marshall only. See in the chapt. of the Court of the Constable, and Marshall.

Concerning the last manner of proof, viz. by book-cases and authorities of our books. 3. *By book cases and authorities in law.*

In the Regiſter the moſt ancient book of the law, fo. F. N. B. fo. 87. I. & 88. F.

Temps E. 1. Avowry 192. in communi banc.

In temps E. 1. tit. Avowry 192. a replevyn was brought for the taking of a ſhip in the coaſt of Scarborow in the ſea, and for carrying the ſame from thence into the county of N. Mutford the plaintif counteth of a taking in the coaſt of Scarborow, which is neither town nor place, out of which a jury may be taken, for that the coaſt is four miles long, and alſo of a thing done in the ſea, this court hath no conuſance, for certain judgement is given thereof to mariners. Berry chief juſtice of the common place; the king willeth, that the peace be as well kept on the ſea, as on the land, and we find that you are come hither by due proceſſe, and therefore ruled him to anſwer. Out of which four things are to be obſerved. Firſt, that it is called the ſea which is not within any county from whence a jury may come. Secondly, that the ſea (being not within any county) is not within the juriſdiction of the court of common pleas, but belongs to the admirall juriſdiction. Thirdly, that when the ſhip came within the river, then it is confeſſed to be within the county of Northumberland. Laſtly, that when a taking is partly on the ſea, and partly in a river, the common law ſhall have juriſdiction.

8 E. 2. tit. Coron 399.

8 E. 2. tit. coron. 399. It is no part of the ſea, where one may ſee what is done of the one part of the water, and of the other, as to ſee from one land to the other, that the coroner ſhall exerciſe his office in this caſe, and of this the country may have knowledge; whereby it appeareth that things done there are triable by the country (that is, by jury) and conſequently not in the admirall court.

43 E. 3. Vid. 5 E. 3. 3. tit. Replevin. 41.

43 E. 3. Norff. as the ſaid lord Dier voucheth the record in Mich. 15 & 16 El. ſaying *(quod vidi)* the caſe was, that the abbot of Ramſey was ſeiſed of the mannor of Brancaſter in Norf. bordering upon the ſea, upon ſixty acres of marſh of which mannor the ſea did flow and reflow; and yet it was adjudged parcell of the abbots mannor, and by conſequence within the body of the county unto the low water mark.

Paſch. 17 El. in ſcaccario.

[141]

And it was adjudged Paſch 17 El. in the exchequer, Diggs being plaintif, that the land between the flowing and reflowing of the ſea belonged to the lord of the mannor adjoyning, as the lord Dier doth there report.

48 E. 3. 3.

48 E. 3. 3. If a mariner makes a covenant with me to ſerve me in a ſhip upon the ſea, yet *ſi lower ne ſoit pay*, it ſhall be demanded in this court by the common law, *et ne per la ley de mariner.*

46 E. 3. tit. Conuſans 36.

46 E. 3. tit. Conuſans 36. An action of treſpaſſe was brought for taking of a ſhip in the haven of Hull againſt certain perſons; the maior and bailiffes of Hull demanded conuſance by the charter of the king granted unto them, that the citizens and burgeſſes of Hull ſhould not be impleaded *alibi de aliquibus tranſgreſſionibus, conventionibus et contractibus infra burgum, &c. quam infra burgum.* And the conuſans was granted; which proveth that the haven of Hull where the ſhip did ride was *infra burgum de Hull*, and by conſequence *infra corpus comitatus*, and determinable by the common law, and not in the admirall court.

7 R. 2. Treſpaſſe in Stathom pl. 54.

7 R. 2. tit. *treſpaſſe in Stathom*, pl. 54. In treſpaſſe for a ſhip and certain merchandize taken away (which treſpaſſe muſt of neceſſity

cessity be alledged in some town and county in some river or haven) the defendant pleaded, that he did take them *in le haut mere ove les Normans queux sont enemies le roy.* And it is ruled a good plea, which concurreth with the other books.

7 H. 6. 22. 35. An action lieth at the common law for forestalling, &c. in a port or haven, for that it is *infra corpus comitatus*, and triable by the common law, and by consequence the admirall hath no jurisdiction there. 7 H. 6. 22. 35.

19 H. 6. 7. The statute doth restraine that the admirall shall not hold plea of any thing rising within any of the counties of the realm, but executions he may make upon the land. And therefore where it is said in 22 Ass. pl. 93. that every water, which flows and reflows, is an arme of the sea, yet it followeth not that the admirall shall have jurisdiction there, unlesse it be out of every county, or else such a place whereof the countrey cannot take knowledge, as it appeareth in the book of 8 E. 2. before cited. But of this more hereafter. 19 H. 6. 7. 22 Ass. p 93.

Fortescue, cap. 32. fo. 38. *Nam si quæ super altum mare extra corpus cujuslibet comitatus regni illius fiant quæ postmodum in placito coram admirallo Angliæ deducantur per testes, illa juxta legum Angliæ sanctiones terminari debent*, which proveth by expresse words that the jurisdiction of the admirall is confined to the high sea, which is not within any county of the realm. Fortesc. cap. 32. fo. 38.

2 R. 3. fo. 12. *Hibernici sunt sub admirallo Angliæ de re facta super altum mare*, which agreeth with the former, viz. that the jurisdiction of the admirall is *super altum mare*. 2 R. 3. 12.

Stanford, lib. 1. pl. cor. fo. 51. b. If one be slaine upon any arme of the sea, where a man may see the land of the one part and of the other, the coroner shall inquire of this, and not the admirall, because the country may take conusance of it, and doth vouch the said authority of 8 E. 2. whereupon he concludeth in these words. So this proveth, that by the common law before the statute of 2 H. 4. &c. the admirall had no jurisdiction but upon the high sea, which only authority were sufficient to overrule all the said questions. For hereby appeareth, that the jurisdiction of the admirall is only confined by the common law to the high sea, and agreeth with all the former book cases and acts of parliament. Stanf. pl. cor. fo. 51. b.

4 & 5 Ph. and Mar. Dier 159. b. By the libell in the admirall court the cause is supposed to commence *sur le haut mere et infra jurisdictionem del admiralty ubi revera facta fuit in tali loco infra corpus comitatus et non super altum mare.* Whereby it also appeareth, that the lord admirals power is confined to the high sea. 4 & 5 Ph. and Mar. Dier 159. b.

Pasch. 28 Eliz. in the kings bench the case was, that a charter-party by deed indented, was made at Thetford in the county of Norfolk, between Evangelist Constantine of the one party, and Hugh Gynne of the other part, by the which Constantine did covenant with Gynne that a certain ship should saile with merchandizes and goods of Hugh Gynne to Muttrell in Spaine, and there should remain by certain dayes, &c. Upon the breach of which covenant Gynne brought an action of debt of 500 l. upon a clause in the same charter, and alledged the breach of the covenant, for that the ship did not remain at Mutterel in Spaine by so many dayes as were limited by the covenant. Whereupon issue was Pasch. 28 Eliz. [142]

taken and tried before Sir Christopher Wray chief justice of England, and found for the plaintife: and in arrest of judgement it was shewed, that this issue did rise out of a place totally and meerly in a forein kingdome out of the realme, from whence no jury of twelve men could come, and therefore the triall was insufficient. But it was adjudged by Sir Christopher Wray, Sir Thomas Gawdy, and the whole court of kings bench after great deliberation that the plaintife should recover 500 li. besides his damages and costs, for that the charter party whereupon the action is brought was made at Thetford within this realme, and that the triall being in the same place where the action was brought was sufficient.

Mich. 30 & 31 Eliz. coram rege.

And the like case was after adjudged in the same court, Mich. 30 & 31 Eliz. in an action upon the case upon an assumpsit grounded upon an instrument called a policy, commonly made between merchants for assurance of their goods, whereby the undertaker did assume that such a ship should saile from Melcome Regis in the county of Dorset unto Abvile in France safely without violence, &c. and declared that the said ship in failing towards Abvile, that is to say, in the river of Somne in the realme of France was arrested by the French king, &c. whereupon issue was taken and tried, where the action upon the assumpsit was brought, and againe the validity of the triall newly questioned, and in the end resolved and adjudged as before; which judgement proves, that where part of the contract or other thing is made in any place within any of the counties of the realm, though the performance thereof be upon the high sea, the triall and determination of the whole act belongeth to the common law, and consequently the court of the admiralty ought not to deale therewith.

These answers being delivered to king James, *magna est veritas et prævaluit.*

The kings prerogative of the sea, &c.
The antiquity of the court of admiralty long before the reign of E. 3. in whose days some have dreamed it began.

Now for the great prerogative and interest that the king of England hath in the seas of England, and for the antiquity of the court of the admiralty of England, and of the name of the admirall, we have seen an ancient and a notable record, intituled, *De superioritate maris Angliæ et jure officii admiralitatis in eodem.* * So much whereof as we finde in *archivis regis*, we will transcribe *de verbo in verbum*, as it is in the record it self.

* In archivis in Turri London.

This cause was handled in or about the 22 year of E. 1. as by divers parts of the record it appeareth.
Admirall of the sea of England.
Time out of minde.
Lawes, statutes, and ordinances.

A vus seignieurs auditors deputes per le rois de Engliterre et de France a redresser les damages faits as gents de lour roialmes et des auters terres subgits a lour seignuries per mer et per terre en temps de pees et de trewes. Monstrent les procurours de prelats et nobles, et del admirall de la mier d'Engliterre et de cominalties des cities et des villes, et des merchants, mariners, messagiers, et pelerins et des touts aultres du dit royalme d'Engliterre et des aultres terres subgits a la seignurie du dit roy d'Engliterre et daillours sicome de la marine de Genue, Cateloigne, Espaigne, Alemaigne, Seland, Hoyland, Frise, Dennemarch, et Norway et de piusours aultres lieux del empier, que come les roys d'Engliterre per raison du dit royalme du temps dont il ny ad memoire du contrarie eussent est en paiceable possession de la soveraigne seignurie de la mier d'Engliterre et des isles esteants en ycele per ordinance et establicement des leis, estatuts, et defenses et des vesseaux autrement garnies

garnies que vesseaux de merchandise et de seurte prendre et sauue gardes doner en tous cas que mestier serra et par ordinance entre tout manere des gents taunt dautre signurie come de lour propre de tous aultres faitz necessaries a la garde de pees, droiture et equitie par elenques passants et per souveraigne garde et toute manere de conisance et justice haulte et basse sur les dites lois, estatuts, ordenances et defences, et pur touts autres faits queux a le government de souveraigne seignurie appertenir purrent es lieux avandits. Et A de B admirall de la dit mier deputey per le roy d'Englitere, et tous les aultres admirals par mesme celui roy d'Englitere et ces ancesters iades royes d'Englitere eussent est en paiseble possession de la dit souveraigne garde ove la conisance et justice et touts les aultres appurtenances avantditz forprise en case dappele et de querele fait de eux a lour souveraignes reys d'Englitere de defalte de droit ou de malvais judgement, et especialment pur empechement metre et justice faire seurte prendre de la pees de tout manere de gents usants armes en la dit mier ou menans niefs aultrement apparreilles ou garnies que nappertient au nief de marchants et en teuts aultres points en queux homme poit avoir reasonable cause de suspition vers eux de robbery, ou des aultres mesfaitz. Et come le maistre de niefs du dit roialme d'Englitere en absence des dits admirals eussent este en paisible possession de conustre et juger des touts faits en la dite mier entre touts manere de gents selone les lois estatuts et les defenses, franchises et custumes.*

De Botertort, admirall of the sea. Note for the antiquity of the admirall of England. The said De Botertort was admirall of the sea coasting upon Yarmouth in Norfolk (right over against France) and of that station in anno 22 E. 1.

Et come en le primer article de lailliance nadgaires fait entre les dites rois en les traites sur le darreine pees de Paris soient comprises les paroles que sensuient en une sedule annexe a yceste.

The league between E. 1. and the French king.

Primerment il est traite et accorde entre nous et les messagers et les procurours de surdiz en nom des dits roys que yceux roys serrent lun a lautre desores en avant bons verrois et loyaux amyes et eydans countre tout homme sauue lesglise de Rome en tiels manere que si ascun ou plusours quicunques ilz fuissent voloient deponticer, empescher, ou troubler les dits roys en franchises et liberties, priviledges es droits, es droitures, ou es custumes de eux et de lour roialmes quils serront bons et loyaux amys et aydans countre toute homme que puisse venire et morir a defendre, gardir et maintenir les franchises, les liberties, les privileges, les droitz, les droitures, et les custumes de susdites, except le dit roy d'Englitere monsieur John duc de Brebon en Brabant et ses heires descendus de lui et de la fille le roy Denglitere, et except pur le dit nostre seignior le roy de France excellent prince Dubert roy d'Alemaigne ses heires roy d'Alemaigne, et mounsieur Johan counte de Henan en Henan, et que lun ne serra en consaile ne en aide ou lautre perde vie, membre, estate ne honour temporel. Monsieur Reymer Grimbald maistre de la navie du dit roy de France que se dit estre admirall de la dit mier deputey per son seignior avantdit pur sa guerre contre les Flemings apres le dite alliance faite et affirmee contre le forme et la force de mesme lalliance et lintention de ceux qui la firent loffice del admirall en la dite mier Denglitere par commission du dit roy de France torseousement emprist et usa un an et plus en pernant le gents et marchants du roialme d'Englitere et daillours per la dite mier passaints ovesque lour biens et les gents ainsi prises livera a la prison de son dit seigniour le roy de France lour biens et marchandizes a les resceivors per mesme celuy roy de France a ceo deputey en les ports de son dit royalme come a luy forfait et acquis fist amener per son juggement et agard, et la prise et detenue des dites gents ove lour dites biens et marchandises et son dit juggement, et agard sur la forfaiture de eaux et acquest ait justifie devant vous seigneurs auditors en escripts per my lautoritie de sa dite commission

Margaret the third daughter of E. 1. was married to John the duke of Brabant an. dom. 1290, & 18 E. 1. Monsier Raymer Grimbald master of the French navie.

[144]

mission sur l'admiralte avantdite per lui ainsi usurpe et per une defense comunement fait per le roy d'Englitere per my son poer lelonc la forme de le tiers article de lalliance avantdite qui contient les paroles desuscripts en requerant que de ceo il en fusse quitz et absoluts en grand damage et prejudice du dite roy d'Englitere et des prelats et nobles et aultres desusnomes. Purquoy les dits precurours et les noms de lours ditz seigniours a vous seigniours auditors avantditz pryent que deliverance dewe et hastine des dites gents ovesq; lour biens et marchandises ainsi prises et detenues faicets estre fait al admirall du dit roy d'Englitere a qui la conisance de ceo apertient de droit sicome dessus est dit ainsi quils sauns disturbance de vous et d'aultre puisse de ceo conoistre et faire ceo que apertient a son office avantdit. Et que le dit monsieur Reymer soit condempne et distreint a faire due satisfaction a touts les dits damages seavant come il purra suffire et en sa defalte son dit seignior le roy de France per que il estoit deputey al dit office, et que apres dewe satisfaction faitz as dits damages le dit monsier Raymer soit si duement punis pur le blemissement de la dite alliance, que la punission de luy soit as aultres example pur temps a venir.

The admirall of England to whom the conusance appertain, &c.

Item in alio rotulo annexo.

Item, a la fin que venes et consideres les formes des proces et les letters ordenees per les consaillers le aiel nostre seignior le roy, &c. especialment a retenir et maintenir le souveraign que ses dits auncesters roys d'Englitere soloyent avoir en la dite mier d'Englitere quant al amendment declaration et interpretation des loix per eux faites a governer touts maneres des gents passants per la dite mier. Et primerement a son admirall et as maisters et mariners des niefs de Cync ports d'Englitere, et des autres terres annexes a la corone d'Englitere emendant a sa armee en la dite mier pur retenir et maintenir la garde des lois avantditz, et la punission de touts faitz al encountre en la mier susdite.

Admirall of England.

Item in alio rotulo de articulis super quibus justitiarii domini regis sunt consulendi de anno regni regis E. 3. 12.

*Item ad finem quod resumatur et continuatur ad subditorum prosecutionem forma procedendi quondam ordinata et inchoata per * avum domini nostri regis et ejus consilium ad retinendum et conservandum antiquam superioritatem maris Angliæ, et nos officii admiralitatis in eodem quoad corrigendum, interpretandum, declarandum et conservandum leges et statuta per ejus antecessores Angliæ reges dudum ordinata ad conservandum pacem et justitiam inter omnes gentes nationis cujuscunque per mare Angliæ transeuntes, et ad cognoscendum super omnibus in contrarium attemptatis in eodem, et ad puniendum delinquentes et damna passis satisfaciendum. Quæ quidem leges et statuta per dominum Richardum quondam regem Angliæ in reditu suo à terra sancta correcta fuerunt, interpretata et in insula Oleron publicata et nominata in Gallica lingua.* La ley Olyronn.

* E. 1. avus E. 3.

R. 1. Insula de Olyron in Gallia.

[145]

And long before this king Edgar in his charter saith thus: *Mihi concessit propitia divinitas cum Anglorum imperio omnia regna insularum oceani cum suis ferocissimis regibus usque Norwegiam ac maximum partem Hiberniæ*

See this charter in the epistle to the 4 book of Reports.

Hiberniæ cum sua nobilissima civitate de Dublina Anglorum regno subjugare, &c.

We have also found a record in 10 E. 3. in these words. Rot. Scotiæ 10 E. 3. m. 16.

Rex dilecto et fideli suo Galfrido de Say admirallo flotæ suæ navium ab ore aquæ Thamesiæ verss. partes occidentales, salutem. Cum nuper vobis per literas nostras mandaverimus quod vos una cum quibusdam navibus de quinque portubus nostris quas de guerra pro obsequio nostro muniri et parari mandavimus supra mare proficisceremini ad obviand' et resistend' quibusdam galeis in diversis partibus exteris provisis et hominibus armatis munitis quæ ad partes dominii nostri ad gravand' nos et gentes nostras, vel ad partes Scotiæ in inimicorum nostrorum ibidem succursum divertere ut accepimus proponebant. Et quia jam nobis ab aliquibus est relatum quod galeæ hujusmodi usque ad numerum viginti et sex ad partes Britan' et Norman' noviter accesserunt et ibidem adhuc se tenent ad mala, ut creditur, contra nos et nostros quæ poterunt perpetrand', vel ad succurrend' dictis nostris, ut prædicitur, inimicis. Nos advertentes quod progenitores nostri reges Angliæ domini maris Anglicani circumquaque et etiam defensores contra hostium invasiones ante hæc tempora extiterunt, et plurimum nos tæderet, si honor noster regius in defensione hujusmodi nostris (quod absit) deperiat temporibus, aut in aliquo minuatur, cupientesque hujusmodi periculis auxiliante domino obviare, ac salvationi ac defensioni regni et populi nostrorum providere, malitiamque hostium nostrorum refrenari: vobis in fide et ligeancia quibus nobis astricti estis, et sicut de vobis specialiter confidimus, mandamus firmiter injungendo quod statim visis præsentibus et absque ulteriori dilatione naves portuum prædictorum, ac alias naves quæ jam paratæ existunt supra mare teneatis, &c.

And because the reader by this record shall discern, that of ancient time there were several admirals (for the wisdom of those dayes would not trust one man with so great a charge, nor any man to have a certain estate in an office of so great trust). I will briefly give the reader such light thereof as I have found of record.

Rex commisit Galfrido de Lucy maritimam Angliæ custodiend' quamdiu domino regi placuerit, &c. Rot. pat. anno 8 H. 3.

Rex commisit Richardo Aguillum marinam regis Norf. et Suff. &c. quamdiu nobis placuerit. Rot. pat. anno 9 H. 3.

Petrus de Rival capitaneus Pictanie habet ad totam vitam suam custodiam omnium portuum et totius costeræ marinæ Angliæ, excepto portu de Dovor, qui est in custodia Huberti de Burgo. Rot. Car. 15 H. 3.

Willielmus de Leybourne constituitur capitaneus nautarum et marinariorum de regno et potestatis regis, quamdiu regi placuerit. Rot. Vascon. 22 E. 1. m. 8.

Willielmus de Leybourne admirallus Angliæ. Rot. par. 23 E. 1.

Willielmus de Leybourne capitaneus marinariorum, &c. 2 parte pat. anno 25 E. 1. m. 14.

To let you know what we have observed in those times: there were also two other, the one had the government of all the fleet from the mouth of the Thames westward, and the other from the mouth of the Thames northward. Claus. in Dors. m. 18.

Johannes Botetort custos regis portuum maritimorum versus partes boreales. 25 Martii. 1 parte pat. 25 E. 1. m. 9.

Nicholaus Kyriell constituitur admirallus flote omnium navium ab ore aquæ Thamesis tam quinque portuum, quam aliorum portuum et locorum per costeram maris versus partes occidentales, quamdiu regi placuerit. Teste rege apud Turrim London 8 Decembris. 1 parte pat. 10 E. 2.

Clauf. 15 E. 2. pat. 15 E. 2. Tefte rege apud Ebor. 19 Maii.

Robertus de Leyborn admirallus quarundam navium regis ſup' mare occidentali.
Robertus Battayli admirallus flotæ navium ab ore aquæ Thameſis de ſingulis portubus verſus auſtrum.

1 parte pat. anno 1 E. 3. m. 21.

Johannes Perbrome conſtituitur capitaneus, et admirallus flotæ navium magnæ Geremuthe et omnium aliorum locorum ab ore aquæ Thameſis per coſteram maris verſus partes boreales, quamdiu, &c. Teſte rege apud Stamf. 21 Aprilis.
Warroſius de Valloignes conſtituitur capitaneus et admirallus flotæ navium ab ore aquæ Thameſis tam quinque portuum quam aliorum portuum et locorum per coſteram maris verſus partes occidentales, quamdiu, &c. ut ſupra.

2 parte clauf. 12 E. 3. in Dorf.

Petrus Bard admirallus navium ab ore aquæ Thameſis verſus partes occidentales. 18 Auguſti.
Thomas de Drayton admirallus ab ore aquæ Thameſis verſus partes boreales. 18 Auguſti.

And ſo in the reigns of R. 2. H. 4. H. 5. H. 6. But in theſe and in former times there was a great admirall of England, vid. ſupra pa. 142, 143, 144.

Rot. pat. anno 14 H. 6. 25 Oct. 18 E. 4.

The king did by charter conſtitute John Holland duke of Exeter and Henry his ſon to be *admirallos Angliæ, Hiberniæ, et Aquitaniæ, pro termino vitæ.*

This charter being of a judiciall office and granted to two, we hold to be void: for ſuch ancient offices muſt be granted as they formerly have been. This duke is he that is mentioned in the former records, who being a great peer of the realm endeavoured to incroach upon the common law, but the ſubjects by courſe of law were defended and recompenſed.

Rot. parl. 7 H. 4. nu. 19, 20. &c. 26. & 142. 9 H. 4. nu. 19.

The merchants, mariners, and owners of ſhips undertook the ſafeguard of the ſeas for the ſubſidies of tunnage and poundage, &c. and that merchants ſhould name two perſons, the one for the ſouth part, the other for the north part, who by commiſſion ſhould have the like power as other admirals have had touching the ſame.

Addition of ſome Records of Parliament.

11 H. 4. nu. 24. Rot. par. 17 R. 2. 48. 4 H. 4. nu. 47. 11 H. 4. nu. 61.

All ſtatutes made concerning the court of the admirall ſhall be obſerved.

Sundry towns of the weſt part prayen remedy againſt the officers of the admiralty for holding plea of matters determinable by the common law, the which they pray may be revoked: the kings anſwer was, The chancelor by the advice of the juſtices upon hearing of the matter ſhall remit the matter to the common law, and grant a prohibition.

7 R. 2. nu. 14.

The earl of Northumberland admirall of the north, and the earl of Devon' admirall of the weſt, to receive the ſubſidy of tunnage and poundage, and to keep the ſeas.

Addition of Books.

1 part Inſtit. § 459. & 677. 11 H. 4. fo. 11.

See the firſt part of the Inſtitutes, ſect. 459. and ſect. 677. where Littleton ſpeaketh of a man out of the realm, or beyond ſea;

ſea, and adde thereunto the notable caſe in Mich. 11 H. 4. fo. 11. pl. 85. Sovingles caſe, the defendant in an appeal of death being outlawed, brought his writ of error, and aſſigned for error, that at the time of the outlawry, and before, he was in the kings ſervice upon the ſea in the company of the lord Berkley then admirall, and had a writ unto him to certifie. Lord Berkeley admirall.

6 R. 2. tit. Protection 46. 7 R. 2. tit. Treſpaſſe Statham. 10 H. 7. fol. 7. a. Vide 18 H. 6. nu. 53. where the owner of a ſhip ſhall anſwer for hurt done by his ſhip, though he be not party thereunto.

Vid. Lacies caſe, Cr. 25 El. li. 2. fo. 93. Vid. li. 5. fo. 106, 107. and 108. Sir Henry Conſtables caſe. Lib. 6. fo. 47. Dowdales caſe, Brook, tit. Error 177.

See certain ſtatutes, viz. 27 E. 3. cap. 13. Stat. Staple. 31 H. 6. cap. 4. 2 R. 3. cap. 6. 28 H. 8. cap. 16.

It appeareth by the former records, that the admiralty is ſometime called *admiralitas*, ſometime *admirallatus*, and ſometime by other names, as *admirallus*, *capitaneus* or *cuſtos maris*, or *marinæ*, or *maritaniæ*, *or flotæ navium*, that is, of the navy floating on the ſea. *Ley marine*, *ley des mariners*. *The name.* [147]

The officer is called admirall indifferently both in Engliſh and in French. We name him in Latin *admirallus*, and the court *curia admiralitatis*, derived of *amir*, *id eſt*, *præfectus*, *et* ἁλιός i. *marinus*, *præfectus marinus*, *admiralius*, *admirallus*, *admiralli curia res maritimas tractat: in hac numerantur admirallus Angliæ*, *locum tenens et judex*, *ſcribæ duo*, *ſerviens curiæ viceadmirallii Angliæ*. Camden.

Hæda or *hitha*, i. *portus* a haven, as Queen-hithe, Lamb-hithe, &c. *Hafne courts*, now haven or port courts, *hable*, i. *portus*.

To conclude, the king of Englands navy doth excell the ſhipping of all other forain kings and princes: for if you reſpect beautifull ſtatelineſſe, or ſtately beauty, they are ſo many large and ſpacious kingly and princely palaces. If you regard ſtrength and defence, they are ſo many moving impregnable caſtles, and barbicans, and were tearmed of old the wals of the realm. When our Engliſh navy is among the ſhips of other nations, it is like lions *inter pecora campi*, and like a falkon *inter phaſianos*, *perdices*, *et alia volatilia timida cœli*.

Beſides, no part of the world have ſuch timber for building and reparing of ſhips as our king hath.

CAP.

CAP. XXIII.

The Court of the Commiſſion under the Great Seal by Force of the Statute of 28 H. 8. cap. 15.

28 H. 8. cap. 15.

The commiſſioners. THIS court muſt be holden *coram admirallo Angliæ, ſeu ejus locum tenente*, and 3 or 4 ſuch other ſubſtantiall perſons, as ſhall be named by the lord chancellor for the time being.

The juriſdiction. Their juriſdiction is to hear and determine all treaſons, felonies, robberies, murders, and confederacies committed or done upon the ſea, &c.

To be heard and determined by the common law. Theſe offences ſhall be heard and determined according to the courſe of the common law, and therefore ſome of the judges of the realm are ever in this commiſſion.

See the 3 part of the Inſtit. cap. Piracy. pa. 111, 112. &c.

Concerning the miſchief that was before the making of this ſtatute, and how the ſaid act hath been formerly expounded, you may read plentifull matter in the third part of the Inſtitutes, cap. Piracy.

The proceſſe and proceedings herein are in the name of the king: ſee before cap. Chivalry, p. 124. that the ſtatute of 35 H. 8. cap. 2. nor that of 5 E. 6. c. 11. taketh not away this act of 28 H. 8. concerning treaſons; Note, that in all the commiſſions granted for the execution of this act of 28 H. 8. ſince the ſaid acts of 35 H. 8. 5 E. 6. power and authority is given to hear and determine all treaſons, &c. done upon the ſea.

[148]

CAP. XXIV.

Of Port-mootes, *alias* Port Courts, *alias* Portmote Courtes.

A Portmote is a court kept in haven towns, or ports, and thereof taketh his name *curia portus, &c.*

Portus eſt locus in quo exportantur et importantur merces, a portando. And they are *portæ regni* the * gates of the realm, [a] *Hitha* and *heda* often in Domeſday is taken for a haven or port, anciently written *hafne* and now haven, by changing the *f* into *v* as is uſuall.

Every haven is within the body of the county, &c. whereof ſee before plentifull matter in the chapter of the court of the admiralty proceeding according to the civil law. See 43 Eliz. cap. 15.

* See in the chapt. of the Courts of the Foreſt.

[a] Hereof commeth in London Queenhithe, and in Lambith Lambhithe, &c.

CAP.

CAP. XXV.

The Power and Authority of Commissioners and others for the maintaining and erecting of Beacons, Signes of the Sea, or Light-houses, and Sea-marks, and concerning Watches.

See the 3. part of the Inst. cap. Buildings, p. 204.

BEACON, this word is derived of the Saxon word *beacon*, i. *speculum, unde speculantur adventus hostium*, and is often called *signum speculatum*, and *bechan* in the Saxon language is *signum dare*, and we use the word to becken to at this day.

Before the reign of E. 3. there were but stacks of wood set upon high places, which were fired when the comming of enemies were descried, but in his reign pitch boxes, as now they be, were in stead of those stacks of wood set up, and this properly is a beacon.

Light-houses.

Light-houses, *ignes speculatorii, seu monitorii, seu lumen maritimum, seu* * *pharus, unde versus,*

Lumina noctivagæ tollit pharus æmula lunæ.

* ἀπὸ τοῦ φανοῦ, *id est, lucidum.*

These light-houses are properly to direct seafaring men in the night when they cannot see marks, and these are also *signa speculatoria.*

Sea-marks.

Sea-marks, as steeples, churches, castles, trees, and such like for direction of seafaring men in the day time, and these are called *signa marina*, or *speculatoria*, or *signa nautis*, whereof Virgill 5 Eneids.

Hic viridem Æneas frondenti ex ilice metam
Constituit * *signum nautis pater, unde reverti*
Sciverit, et longos ubi circumflectere cursus, &c.

* Id est insignium.

So as you may divide *specula* or *signa speculatoria*, or *signa nautis* into three branches, viz. into beacons, light-houses, and sea-marks.

At the common law none but the king only could erect any of these three, which ever was done by the kings commission under the great seal, as taking some few examples for many.

[149]

De signis super montes per ignem faciend'. Rot. Scotiæ. 10 E. 3.

De signis super montes faciend'. Rot. Clauf. Vasc' 10 E. 3.

Rex assignavit [a] *Henricum Epu. Norwic' et* [b] *Willielmum comitem Suff. et alios, &c. (inter alia) ad signa speculatoria super montes in com' Norf. ponend'. Et similes commissiones in aliis comitatibus.* Rot. Franc' 47 E. 3. m. 20.

Vide Rot. clauf. 1 *R.* 2. *m.* 41. *in dors' pro vigiliis et ignibus speculatoriis, et monitoriis.*

He that is desirous to see more of beacons, &c. and watching of the same, let him read the [c] act of 5 H. 4. which is an act of parliament, and Dors' pat. *anno* 28 H. 6. parte 2. m. 21. *in com' Kanc' et memb.* 13. *pro com' Norf. pro signis, anglice* beacons, *et vigiliis. Et* Dors' pat. *anno* 1 E. 4. parte 3. &c.

But of latter times by the letters patents granted to the lord admirall

[a] Henricum Spencer, he of a soldier became a bishop.

[b] William Ufford comes Suff.

[c] Rot. par. 5 H. 4. nu. 24. not in print worthy to be read.

mirall he hath power to erect beacons, ſeamarks, and ſigns for the ſea. &c.

8 Eliz. cap. 13.

By the act of 8 Eliz. it is provided and enacted, That the maſter, wardens and aſſiſtants of the Trinity houſe of Debtford ſtrond (a company of the chiefeſt and moſt expert maſters and governors of ſhips) ſhall and may lawfully from time to time at their will and pleaſure, and at their coſts, make, erect, and ſet up ſuch and ſo many beacons, marks, and ſigns for the ſea in the ſea-ſhoars, and uplands neer the ſea coaſts, or forelands of the ſea only for ſeamarks, as to them ſhall ſeem moſt meet, whereby the dangers may be avoided, and ſhips the better come to their ports. And all ſuch beacons, marks and ſigns ſo by them to be erected ſhall be continued, renewed and maintained from time to time at the coſts and charges of the ſaid maſter, wardens and aſſiſtants. An excellent law, that this power and authority was given to them which had greateſt ſkill, ſeeing they were works for the ſafety of the realm, and ſafeguard of the lives of ſeafaring men, and that theſe works ſhould be erected, and made, and continued by them at their own coſts and charges, becauſe they knew to goe the neareſt way.

Paſch. 1 Jac. It was reſolved by the two chief juſtices, atturny, and ſolicitor, that this act extended as well to light-houſes in the night, as to beacons, &c. by the day.

Beconagium ſignifieth money due or payable for the maintenance of beacons, or the watching of the ſame. What puniſhment they incur which take down, fell, or otherwiſe cut down any ſeamarks, ſee the ſaid act of 8 El. *ubi ſupra*, wherein it is to be obſerved, that if the perſon offending be not able to pay the penalty therein inflicted, he ſhall be deemed convict of outlawry, *ipſo facto*, to all conſtructions and purpoſes: the like whereof we have not obſerved in any other ſtatute.

Convict of outlawry.

Wardwite, *aliàs warwite*, or *ward penny*, to be free from contribution of money to watches and wards.

We have out of an ancient manuſcript tranſcribed this ordination that followeth, which in the county of Norf. hath been ever obſerved, and it is very probable, that the like hath been done by like authority in other maritime counties.

Norf.

Ordinatio pro vigill' obſervand' in com' prædict' à Lynne uſque Yermouth.

Robertus de Monte alto and Tho. de Bardolfe ſat in parliament, 14 E. 2. as barons of the realm, as appeareth in the parliament rols.

*Hæc igitur authoritate mandati nos Robert de Monte alto et Thomas de Bardolfe mandamus vic' Norf. quod venire faciat coram nobis apud Norwic' die Mercurii in feſt' decollationis Sancti Johannis Baptiſt' prox' futur' omnes milites, omnes capit' conſtabul' hundred', et conſtabul' vill' et duos homines de diſcretior' cujuſlibet villæ ubi portus vel applicat' navium in balliva ſua tam infra libertat' quam extra in com' prædict' ad conſulend', formand', auxiliand' qualiter et quomodo dict' cuſtod' ſecurius pro ſalvatione partium illarum fieri poſſit, et ad faciend' quod ex parte dom. regis ſuper præmiſſis injungitur. Ad quem diem nos dict' Robert' et Thomas perſonaliter acceſſimus ibidem, ac milit', capit' conſtabul' hundred', conſtabul' vill' cum omnibus hominibus vill' ubi applicat' navium exiſt' de portu Lynne et de portu Yarmouth coram nobis ibidem compar', et aſſeruerunt, quod valde neceſſe eſſet pro ſalvat' totius patriæ quod vigill' fiant in † locis periculoſis ſicut * antiquo more fieri ſolebant juxta mare. Et quod omnes homines corpor' valid' de com' Norf. contribuend' ad ill' faciend', per quod,*

* 5 H 4. cap. 3. Watches to be made upon the ſea coſt by the number of the people, in the places, and in manner and form as they were wont to be.

† [150]

ordinat'

ordinat' et consens' eorum concordat' est quod duæ vigill' per sex homines de corpore potenti tam per dies quam per noctes fieri in hundred' de Freebrigge, viz. *apud Wolverton, et apud Clencherne, eo quod dict' hundred jung' se mari à Wisbiche usque Dersingham per* 14 *leucas. Et quod quilibet vigilans capiet per diem et per noctem pro vadiis suis* 3 *d. Et quod hundred de Clackclose adjung' eidem hundred' de Freebrigge ad contribuend' ad vigill' illa faciend'* viz. *pro qualibet septiman'* 4 *s.* 6 *d. et idem hundred. de Freebrigge* 6 *s. pro septiman'. Et sciend' est* 77. *vill. continentur in dict' hundredo quæ assignantur ad dict' vigill' faciend.* Freebrigge. Clackclose.

Fiat etiam una vigill' apud Southlynne in Clynchern, &c.

Item quod una vigill' fiet in hundred' de Smithdon apud Thornham per sex homines, eo quod dictum hundred' jungit se mari de Dersingham usq; Deepedal fenn per 12 *leucas. Et quod hundred de Southgrenhoe et Laundiche adjung' eidem hundred' de Smythdon ad contribuend' ad vigill' ill' faciend',* viz. *hundredo de Southgrenhoe* 3 *s.* 6 *d. per septimam' et hundred. de Landiche* 4 *s. per septimam', et hundred. de Smythden* 3 *s. Et continent' in dict' hundred'* 79. *vill' ad vigill' illa faciend.* Smythdon. Southgrenhoe. Laundiche.

Et fiat una vigill' in hundred' de Gallowe apud Burnham per 4. *homines, eo quod dict' hundred. jungit se mari de Deepedale usque Holkham per* 3. *leucas. Et hundred. de Brothercrosse adjungit' eidem hund' ad contribuend. ad vigill' ill' faciend',* viz. *hundred' de Brothercrosse* 3 *s. per septim' et idem hundred. de Gallowe* 4 *s. per septim.' Et sciend' est* 45. *vill' sunt in dict' hundred' ad vigill' illa faciend.* Gallow. Brothercrosse.

Item fiet un' vigill' in hundred' de Northgrenhoe apud Holkham per 6. *homines, eo quod dict' hundred' jungit se mari, a Holkham usque Marston per* 6. *leucas. Et hundred' de Weyland, Giltcrosse, Grimshoe, et Ersham adjung' eidem hundred' ad contribuend' ad vigill' illa faciend',* viz. *Weylond* 2 *s. per septim', Grimshoe* 2 *s. per septim', Giltcrosse* 2 *s. per septim', et Ersham* 2 *s. per septim', et idem hundred' de Northgrenhoe* 2 *s. per septim'. Et sciend' est quod* 76 *vill' sunt in dict' hundred' ad vigill' ill' faciend.* Northgrenhoe. Weyland. Giltcrosse. Grimshoe. Ersham.

Item fiet unum vigill' in hundred' de Holt apud Wabornn per sex homines, eo quod dict' hundred' jungit se mari à Marston usque Sheringham per 7 *leucas. Et hundred. de Eynsford et Hempsteed adjung' eidem hundred de Holt ad contribuend' ad vigill' faciend',* viz. *Eynsford* 4 *s. per septim', Hemsteed* 3 *s.* 6 *d. per septim' et idem hundred' de Holt* 3 *s. per sept. et sciend. est quod* 70 *vill. sunt in dict' hundred' ad vigill' ill' faciend.* Holt. Eynsford. Hemsteed.

Item fiet unum vigill' in hundred. de Northerpingham in duobus locis, viz. *apud Runton et Trimmingham per* 5 *homines, eo quod dict. hundred. jung se mari à Sheringham usque Munslye becke per decem leucas, et hundred. de Sutherpingham et Mitford cum vill. infra libert' adjung. eidem hundred. ad vigill' illa facienda,* viz. *Southerpingham* 6 *s.* 8 *d. per sept. Mitford* 3 *s.* 6 *d. per sept. et Northerpingham* 12 *s.* 6 *d. per sept. Et sciend' est quod* 77. *vill' sunt in hundred. præd. ad vigill. ill. faciend.* Northerpingham. Southerpingham. Mitford.

Item fiet unum vigill. in hundred. de Tunsted apud Bastwick per sex homines, eo quod dict. hundred' jungit se mari à Munsley usque Walcote per 4 *leucas. Et hundred. de Humbleyard et Fowrehoe adjung. eidem hundred. ad contribuend. ad vigil. ill. faciend',* viz. *Humbleyard* 3 *s. per sept. Fowrehoe* 3 *s. per sept. et Tunstead* 4 *s.* 6 *d. per sept. et sciend. est quod* 76 *vill. sunt in dict. hund. ad vigil. ill. faciend.* Tunstead. Humbleyard. Fowrehoe. [151]

Item fiet unum vigil. in hundred. de Happing in duobus locis, viz. *apud Happisborow per* 4 *homines et apud Wastuesham per* 4 *homines, eo quod dict.* Happing.

dict. hund. jungit se mari à Walcote usque Wimbesdele in loco periculoso per 6. leucas. Et hundred. de Taverham, Depwade, Shropham et Disse adjung. eidem hund. de Happing ad contribuend. ad vigil. ill. faciend. viz. *hund. de Taverham 2 s. per sept. Depewade 3 s. per sept. Shropham 5 s. per septim. et Disse 2 s. per sept. et dict. hund. de Happing 2 s. per sept. Et sciend. est quod* 60. *vill. sunt in hund. prædict. ad vigil. ill. faciend.*

Eastflegge. Westflegge.

Item fiet unum vigil. in hund. de Eastflegge et Westflegge in tribus locis, viz. *apud Winterton per 6 homines, apud Saltivos haven per sex homines, et apud Fordham per sex homines, eo quod dict. hund. jungit se mari à Wykeldock usque Bunton in Mitford in loco periculoso per 7 leucas. Et hund. de Walsham, Blowfeild, Loddon, et Clavering adjung. eidem hund. ad contribuend. ad vigill. illa faciend.* viz. *Walsham 4 s. 6d. per sept. Blowfield 4 s. 6 d. per sept. Loddon 5 s. 6 d. per sept. Clavering 5 s 6 d. per sept. Westflegg 2 s. per sept. Eastflegg 2 s. per sept. Et sciendum est quod* 102 *vill. sunt. in dict. hund. ad vigil. ill. faciend.*

Walsham. Blowfeild. Loddon. Clavering.

Præcept. est omnibus capital. constabul. de hund. adjung. mari in locis prædict. in forma prædicta hac instant. die dominica prox. futur. et similiter præcept' est eisdem capital. constabul. et omnibus aliis subconstabul. hundred. totius com. quod sine dilatione levari et reparari fac. signa et fierbares super mont. altior. in quolibet hund. ita quod tota patria per illa signa quotiescunque necesse fuit premuniri posset, et quod ipse constabul. capital. per avizam. constabul. villarum et aliorum proborum hominum agist. fac. fideliter denar. pro vad. vigil. in hundred. prædict. instant. quod. ordinat. solvend. de septimana in septim. ita quod defect. in vigil. prædict. nullo modo inveniatur per eorum defect. et similiter quod omnes qui agist. sunt ad arma et potent. ad portanda arma, et omnes illi qui loco potent. ad arma sua portanda assignat. sint providi et parati sint indies nocte ad veniend. solemniter distinct. et aperte in præsent. domini Walteri de Norwic. episcopi juxta nos assiden. ibidem cur. * *cācar. totius com. Norf. coram nobis vn. fecimus proclamar. Et similiter præcept. est vic. quod levar. fac. denar. agist. in hundred. prædict. pro costis et vad. præd. solvend.*

Signa. Fierbares.

* Vigiliarium.

For watches, and against night-walkers, see the statute of Winch. 13 E. 1. cap. 4. 5 E. 3. cap. 14. Vid. 5 H. 7. 5.

Vide Lamb. inter leges Edovardi regis, fo. 136. *b. et inter leges Willielmi regis, fo.* 125. *a.*

Dorf. Claus. 8 H. 4. m. 8. & 10.

Quod homines de Larkefield, Filbarow street, Newchurch, et Worth in com' Kanc' tenentur facere vigilias in Romney Marsh.

CAP.

CAP. XXVI.

De Conſervatore ſeu Cuſtode Treugarum, i. Induciarum et ſalvorum Regis Conductuum,

And incidently of the Office, Authority, and Priviledge of Ambaſſadours; and of Leagues, Treaties, and Truces.

BY the ſtatute of 2 H. 5. robbery, ſpoyling, breaking of truces, and ſafe conducts by any of the kings liege people and ſubjects within England, Ireland, and Wales, or upon the main ſea, was adjudged and determined to be high treaſon: but this branch concerning high treaſon is repealed by the ſtatute of 20 H. 6. But by the ſaid act of 2 H. 5. for the better obſervation of truces and ſafe conducts, *conſervator induciarum et ſalvorum regis conductuum* was raiſed, and appointed in every port of the ſea by letters patents: his office was to enquire of all offences done againſt the kings truces and ſafe conducts upon the main ſea (out of the counties, and out of the liberties of the cinque-ports) as admirals, of cuſtome, were wont. 2 H. 5. ca. 6. ſtat. 1. 20H. 6. cap. 11.

It concerneth the juriſdiction of divers courts, and eſpecially of the ſaid court before mentioned upon the ſaid ſtatute of 28 H. 8. and of the court of the admiralty, to know the rights of leagues and ambaſſadours, as far as the lawes of England extend unto, for of them we will only treat.

All leagues or ſafe conducts are, or ought to be of record, that is, they ought to be inrolled in the chancery to the end the ſubject may know, who be in amity with the king, and who be not: who be enemies, and can have no action here; and who in league, and may have actions perſonall here. * In all treaties, the power of the one party and the other ought to be equall. 19 E. 4. 6. b. 18 H. 6. cap. 4. 20 H. 6. cap. 1. Vide ſupra. p. 132. * Regula.

A league may be broken by leavying of war, or by ambaſſadour or herald.

Bryan held opinion in 19 E. 4. *ubi ſupra*, that if all the ſubjects of England would make war with a king in league with the king of England without the aſſent of the king of England that ſuch a war was no breach of the league. See the ſtatute of 2 H. 5. cap. 6. in the preamble. 19 E. 4. ubi ſupra. See the third part of the Inſtit. cap. Treaſon. verb. League. 2 H. 5. cap. 6.

In the duke of Norf. caſe Hil. 14 Eliz. the queſtion was, whether the lord Heriſe and other ſubjects of the king of Scots, that without his aſſent had waſted and burnt divers towns in England, and proclaimed enemies, were enemies in law within the ſtatute of 25 E. 3. the league being between the king and the Scot: and reſolved that they were enemies. Hil. 14 Eliz.

And in the biſhop of Roſſes caſe, *ann.* 13 Eliz. the queſtion being, *An legatus, qui rebellionem contra principem ad quem legatus concitat,* Hil. 13. Eliz.

legati privilegiis gaudeat, et non ut hoſtis pœnis ſubjaceat. And it was reſolved that he had loſt the priviledge of an ambaſſadour, and was ſubject to puniſhment.

Hil. 12 Jac.

Samuel Palache affirming himſelfe to be the ſubject and ambaſſadour of Mula Sedan king of Morocco to the ſtates of the United Provinces, to treat and negociate with them of divers matters between them; and they of the United Provinces having accepted him for an agent or legat. And the laſt of June 1611, there being enmity between the king of Morocco and the king of Spaine, the king of Morocco made a commiſſion to the ſaid Samuel to take Spaniards and their goods. The 25 of October 1613, the king of England gave him letters of ſafe conduct as a publick miniſter ſent to the ſtates of the United Provinces. 3 Martii 1613, the ſtates licenſed him to leavie men to furniſh his ſhips, &c. In June

[153]

Carvel, or caravel, is a ſwift bark.

1614 he took a carvell of the Spaniards at the Canaries laden with ſugar, and another ſhip there alſo laden with hides, of the goods of Spaniards; and after, with diſtreſſe of wind, he with the ſaid priſes was driven to Plimouth, there being at that time league both between England and Spain, and between England and the United Provinces, and wars between Spain and the United Provinces. And againſt this Samuel the Spaniſh ambaſſadour here in England complained at the councell table, and charged him with piracy. The ſaid Samuel and his company being arreſted, and the goods ſeiſed, the Spaniſh ambaſſadour prayed that he might proceed againſt him as a pirat upon the ſaid ſtatute of 28 H. 8. cap. 15. The lords of the councell referred the conſideration of this requeſt to the chiefe juſtice of England being preſent at the table, and to the maſter of the rols, and Sir Daniel Dun judge of the admiralty, to conſider of the caſe, and to direct a courſe of juſtice therein indifferently. And the ſaid referrees heard the councell learned both in the common and civill lawes on both ſides on two ſeverall dayes in this terme: and after conference between themſelves, and with others, theſe points were reſolved. Firſt, that at this day there could be no ambaſſadour without letters of credence of his * ſoveraigne, to another that had ſoveraigne authority. *Legatus per literas de ſua legatione fidem facere debet, ſi exigantur, et commonitorium,* ſ. *inſtructiones privat'*, for the ambaſſadour himſelf for his direction.

* Nulli niſi abſoluti principes et qui majeſtatis jura habent, legatos conſtituere poſſunt.

Secondly, that of ancient time ambaſſadours were called *oratores.*

Virgil. Idem, 11 Æneid, *Legati reſponſa ferunt.* Idem, 12 Æneid. *Nuntius hæc Idmon Phrygio mea dicta tyranno Haud placitura refer.*

> *Jamq; oratores aderant ex urbe Latina*
> *Velati ramis olei—*

And afterwards they were called *legati à legando, nuntii à nuntiando*, and afterwards *ambaſſiatores* or *embaſſiotores*, and ſometimes agents: for *omnis legatus eſt agens*, but *omnis agens* is not *legatus:* for if he be ſent from a king or abſolute potentate or ſtate to a king or abſolute potentate or ſtate to treat between them, although he in his letters of credence be termed an agent or *nuntius*, yet he is an ambaſſadour or legate.

Thirdly, it was reſolved, that ambaſſadours ought to be kept from all injuries and wrongs, and by the law of all countries, and of all nations they ought to be ſafe and ſure in every place, in ſo much that it is not lawfull to hurt the ambaſſadours of our enemies: and herewith

herewith agreeth the civill law. And if a baniſhed man be ſent as ambaſſadour to the place from whence he is baniſhed, he may not be detained or offended there, and this alſo agreeth with the civill law. L. fi. F. de Lega. In aut'de ſanctiſſ. § Rerum Col. 9.

The caſe (which we have ſeen reported) in the reign of H. 8. was this: there being amity between king H. 8. and the French king, and enmity between H. 8. and the pope, * R. Pole a rebell and traitor to the king of England flyeth to Rome, whom the pope being in amity with the French king ſendeth as ambaſſadour to him: the king of England demandeth his rebell of the French king, notwithſtanding he was ſent as ambaſſadour, *ſed non prevaluit*. And it is truly ſaid, whoſoever ſaid it, *Quia veritas à quocunque dicitur à Deo eſt, fuit ſemper etiam apud Gentiles (qui nul'am tenebant veræ fidei rationem) inviolabile nomen nuncii et legati, etiamſi ab hoſtibus mitterentur ſemper ſalvi, et hodie apud Saracenos et Turcos, à quibuſcunque tutæ deſtinantur legationes et literæ, etiamſi illis ad quos deferantur moleſtæ ſint et injurioſæ*. But if a forein ambaſſadour being *prorex* committeth here any crime, which is *contra jus gentium*, as treaſon, felony, adultery, or any other crime which is againſt the law of nations, he loſeth the priviledge and dignity of an ambaſſadour as unworthy of ſo high a place, and may be puniſhed here as any other private alien, and not to be remanded to his ſoveraigne but of curteſie. And ſo of contracts that be good *jure gentium* he muſt anſwer here. But if any thing be *malum prohibitum* by any act of parliament, private law or cuſtome of this realme, which is not *malum in ſe jure gentium*, nor *contra jus gentium*, an ambaſſadour reſiding here ſhall not be bound by any of them: but otherwiſe it is of the ſubjects of either kingdome, &c.

* See the third part of the Inſtitutes, cap. High Treaſon, verb. *Overt fact.* pa. 14. Tempore H. 6.

Paſch. 36 Eliz. Henry de Vale and other Frenchmen imported divers manufactures, as cloth of tiſſue, cawles, points, &c. Whereupon Tomlinſon and other good merchants of London exhibited divers informations upon the ſtatute of 19 H. 7, which prohibit the ſame; of whom the Frenchmen complained at the councell table, and it was reſolved by the lord treaſurer Burghleigh and the whole councell, that it was no breach of the league between this kingdom and France, for that in the articles of the league the lawes of either kingdome be excepted: and therefore if Tomlinſon the ſubject being a French merchant ſhould trade into France, he muſt obſerve the laws and cuſtomes of France. Paſch. 36. in ſcac. [154] 19 H. 7. cap. 21.

Fourthly, it was reſolved, that admit the ſaid Palache was no ambaſſadour, notwithſtanding becauſe there was enmity between the king of Spain and the king of Morocco, he could not be indicted as a pirat before commiſſioners upon the ſaid ſtatute of 28 H. 8. Becauſe that one enemy cannot be a felon for taking of the goods of another enemy. And the words of the ſaid act be, [that the commiſſioners by force of the ſaid act ſhall proceed, as if the offence had been committed upon the land, and according to the courſe of the common law.]

See 2 R. 3. by all the juſtices, that this is no felony, which caſe is in his parts remembred hereafter. For it is very obſervable what the law of England is in that caſe. It was holden by ſome of the civilians, that albeit the Spaniard could not proceed againſt him *criminaliter*, upon the ſaid act of 28 H. 8. yet the goods being *in ſolo amici*, that is, in the ſoile of the king of England, who was in 2 R. 3. fo.

league with both, that the Spaniard might proceed againſt Palache, *civiliter* in the admirall court: but that was reſolved to the contrary by Popham chiefe juſtice, and the whole court of the kings bench Trin. 2. Jac. to be againſt the law of England in that caſe: where the caſe was this, that where the king of England was in league with the king of Spain, and with thoſe of Holland, &c. and there was enmity between the king of Spain and thoſe of Holland, &c. and one of Holland upon the high ſea *in aperto prælio* took the goods of a ſubject of Spain, and brought them into England, *infra corpus comitatus*, and for that the goods were *in ſolo amici*, the Spaniard whoſe goods were taken libelled for them *civiliter* in the admirall court. It was reſolved by the whole court of the kings bench upon conference and deliberation, that the Spaniard had loſt the property of the goods for ever, and had no remedy for them in England. And relyed principally upon the book in 2 R. 3. *ubi ſupra*, being of ſo great authority: for by that book, he that will ſue to have reſtitution of goods robbed at ſea, ought by law to prove two things. Firſt, that the ſoveraigne of the plaintife was at the time of the taking in amity with the king of England. Secondly, that he that took the goods was at the time of the taking in amity with the ſoveraigne of him whoſe goods were taken: for if he which took them was in enmity with the ſoveraigne of him whoſe goods were taken, then was it no depredation or robbery, but a lawfull taking, as every enemy might take of another: all which appeareth in the ſaid book. See the ſtatutes of 27 E. 3. and 31 H. 6. well expounded in 2 R. 3. *ubi ſupra*. Vide 7 E. 4. 14. 13 E. 4. 9. 22 E. 3. fo. 23. concerning this matter. And for that there was enmity between the king of Spain and thoſe of Holland, therefore it could not be depredation, but a lawfull taking. It was alſo reſolved by the court of the kings bench, that the goods ſo taken being within this realm, viz. *infra corpus comitatus, in ſolo amici*, that if the Spaniard ſue for them *civiliter* in the court of the admiralty, that a prohibition ſhould be granted, and that it ſhould be determined by the laws and ſtatutes of England, and not by the civill law.

Trin. 2. Jac. coram rege.

27 E. 3. ca. 13. & cap. 17. 31 H. 6. cap. 4. 7 E. 4. fo. 14. 13 E. 4 9. 22 E. 3. 16, 17. Regiſt. 129. F. N. B. 114. Prohibition. Nota.

With this reſolution of the kings bench doctor Taylor an Engliſhman, and ſolicitor for the king of Spain, was at the firſt much offended, but when he had taken advice and underſtood the reaſon of the reſolution, he was well ſatisfied.

Lib. 5. fo. 106.

If a ſhipwrack be on the ſea, yet if any of the goods come to land within this realm, the admirall ſhall not have juriſdiction, but it belongeth to the common law.

See the third part of the Inſtitutes, cap. Treaſon: what offence it hath been, and what it is at this day to kill a foreign ambaſſadour: and ſee there 3 R. 2. John Imperials caſe, ambaſſadour of Genoa. It appeareth in the holy hiſtory, viz. in the firſt book of the Chronicles, that injury and diſgraces offered to king Davids ambaſſadours which he ſent to Hanon king of the Moabites, *ad conſoland' ei ſupra mortem patris ſui, grandem etiam contumeliam ſuſtinuerunt, &c.* was a juſt cauſe of warre by David againſt the Moabites, and was ſeverely revenged, as by the holy hiſtory it appeareth.

[155]
1 Chro. 19. 2. &c.

There be four kindes of leagues. 1. *Fœdus pacis*, and that a Chriſtian prince may have with an infidell. *Si fieri poſſit, quod ex vobis eſt, cum omnibus hominibus pacem habeatis.* 2. *Fœdus congratulationis ſive*

Rom. 12. 18. Gen. 14. 13. &c. Abrah. cum rege Sodom.

ſive conſolationis. And this may a Chriſtian prince make with an infidell as David did with Hanon: *ubi ſupra.* 3. *Fœdus commutationis mercium ſive commercii.* And this alſo may be made with an infidell, as king Solomon did with Hiram an infidell, and Joſua did with the Gibionites. 4. *Fœdus mutui auxilii*, and this cannot be done with an infidell or an idolater. Jehoſaphat king of Juda, made *fœdus mutui auxilii* with Achab king of Iſrael, an idolater: for Achab ſaid to Jehoſaphat, *Veni mecum in Ramoth Gilead. Cui ille reſpondet, Ut ego et tu, et ſicut populus tuus, ſic et populus meus tecum erimus in bello:* in which warre Achab was ſlain, and Jehoſaphat was in extreame danger. And after, as the text ſaith, *Reverſus eſt autem Jehoſaphat rex Judæ in domum ſuam pacifice in Jeruſalem, cui occurrit * Jehu filius Hanani, et ait ad illum, impio prebes auxilium, et hiis qui oderunt dominum amicitia jungeris, et idcirco iram quidem domini merebaris.* And the laws of England concerning theſe four leagues are as you perceive grounded upon the law of God.

Joſua cap. 9. 2 Kings 5. 1. &c. & 34. 35. 2 Chron. 18. Jeremy 15. 4. See 1 Mac. 8. 19, 20. & cap. 10. 2 Chron. 19. 2. & cap. 20. 35, &c.

* The prophet of God.

But here ariſeth a queſtion, that ſeeing *fœdus pacis*, or *fœdus commercii* may be ſtricken between a Chriſtian prince and an infidell pagan and idolater, and thoſe leagues are to be eſtabliſhed by oath, whether the infidell or pagan prince may ſwear in that caſe by falſe gods, ſeeing he thereby offendeth the true God by giving divine worſhip to falſe gods. This very doubt was moved by Publicola to S. Auguſtine, who reſolveth the ſame thus: he that taketh the credit of him that ſweareth by falſe gods not to any evill but good, he doth not joyn himſelfe to that ſinne of ſwearing by devils, but is partaker with thoſe lawfull leagues wherein the other keepeth his faith and oath. But if a Chriſtian ſhould any way induce another to ſweare by them, herein he ſhould grievouſly ſin. And ſeeing the leagues in theſe caſes are warranted by the word of God, *et per praxin ſanctorum in ſacra ſcriptura*, all incidents thereunto are permitted: for *per praxin ſanctorum* the practiſe of holy men in ſcripture, may often time be collected how the commandements in it are to be underſtood, and *praxis ſanctorum* appeareth before.

Aug. Epiſt. 154. *ad Publicolam.*

Auguſt. lib. de mendacio cap 2. 15. Praxis ſanctorum interpres præceptorum.

And it is to be obſerved that of ancient time, and untill latter dayes no ambaſſadour came into this realme before he had a ſafe conduct. For as no king, &c. can come into this realm without a licence or ſafe conduct, ſo no *prorex*, *&c.* which repreſenteth a kings perſon can doe it. For ſafe conducts ſee the writs in the Regiſter *de ſalvo conductu*, and the ſtatutes of 15 H. 6. 18 H. 6. and 20 H. 6. with all incidents thereunto. And king H. 7. that wiſe and politique king would not in all his time ſuffer lieger ambaſſadors of any foraine king or prince within his realm, nor he any with them, but upon occaſion uſed ambaſſadors.

Rot. parl. 9 H. 6. nu. 12. and long after. See lib. 7. Calvins caſe, *De rege Manne.* Regiſt. fo. 25, 26. 15 H. 6. cap. 3. 18 H. 6 cap. 8. 20 H. 6. cap. 1. 1 H. 7. fo. 10. Legate of the pope ſworne, &c.

* Every ambaſſador ought to have four qualities, expreſſed in this verſe

Nuncie, ſis verax, tacitus, celer, atque fidelis.

* Foure qualities ought to be in an ambaſſadour.

And of him another ſaith.

Fœderis orator, pacis via, terminus iræ,
Semen amicitiæ, belli fuga, litibus hoſtis.

William de la Pole duke of Suff. by the commons was charged (amongſt other things) with this, that he procured the king, in his preſence only without any other of the councell, to have ſecret conference with the French ambaſſadors, &c. for the which

Rot. pl. 28 H. nu. 28.

(amongſt other things) he was baniſhed, &c. as by the record appeareth.

20 Decemb. 21 H. 8.

* Cardinall Wolſey was charged with theſe notable high and grievous offences (amongſt others) viz. That he being the kings ambaſſador in France made a treaty with the French king for the pope, the king not knowing any part thereof nor named in the ſame, and binding the French king to abide his order and award, if any controverſie or doubt ſhould ariſe between the ſaid pope, and the ſaid French king.

See theſe articles before *in hæc verba*, cap. Chancery, artic. 2, 3. 9, 10. 12.

Alſo that the ſaid lord cardinall being the kings ambaſſador in France ſent a commiſſion to Sir Gregory de Caſſalis under the great ſeal in the kings name to conclude a treaty of amity with the duke of Ferrare without the kings commandement or warrant, nor the king advertiſed nor made privy to the ſame.

Alſo the ſaid lord cardinall taking upon him otherwiſe then a true privy councellor ought to doe, hath uſed to have all ambaſſadors to come firſt to him alone, and to hear their charges and intents, &c.

Alſo the ſaid lord cardinall uſed many years together not only to write to all the kings ambaſſadors in forain parts with other princes in his own name all advertiſements concerning the kings affairs being in their charge, and in the ſame letters wrote many things of his own mind without the kings pleaſure known, concealing divers things which had been neceſſary for them to know, but alſo cauſed them to write their advertiſements to him, and of the ſame letters he uſed to conceal, for the compaſſing of his purpoſe, many things both from the kings councell and the king himſelf.

The difference between a league and a truce is, that a truce is a ceſſation from warre for a certain time: a league is an abſolute ſtriking of peace.

[a] A truce. Rot. Franc' 19 E. 3. m. 10. part 1.
[b] See the truce at large, lib. par. fo. 5.

[a] Of a truce we have read in *anno* 19 E. 3. to this effect. *Rex poſt initas inducias cum Francorum rege per mediationem* [b] *Romani pontificis, copias ſuas bellicas demum reduxit, poſtea deprehendens præfat' regem Franc' hoſtilia contra ipſum moliri, et nuntios præfati pontificis ſimulata pace diſſidium fovere, præmiſſa omnia per literas patentes exponenda duxit, et bellum cum præfato rege reſumpſit.*

[c] A league. rot. par. 4 H. 5. nu. 14.
[d] 9 E. 4. 2. a.
[e] 39 H. 6. 39.
[f] Ro. pat. 35 E. 5. part 2. m. 24. clauſ. 10 H. 4. m. 15. *nuntius papæ*. Rot. clauſ. 14 H. 3. m. 1. rot. clauſ. 12 R. 2. m. dorſ.
[g] Ro. pat. 17 R. 2. part 1. m. 23. Rot. Franc. 12 H. 6. m. 2. Rot. pat. 12 H. 6. 12 part. m. 6.

[c] A league and alliance was made between king H. 5. his heirs and ſucceſſors, and Sigiſmond king of the Romans his heirs and ſucceſſors kings of the Romans, and was confirmed by act of parliament. The inſtrument whereof is very long, but not ſo long as effectuall and worthy of obſervation.

[d] It is ſaid in 9 E. 4. that a league made between two kings (without naming of ſucceſſors) doth not extend to ſucceſſors, although by our law *rex non intermoritur*.

[e] Juſtice Aſhton is of opinion, that no ambaſſador ought to be ſent to the pope, but there may be many preſidents to the contrary, for beſides his ſpirituall juriſdiction he is a temporall prince, whereof ſee a preſident among many others, [f] Rot. pat. 35 E. 3. parte 2. memb. 24. and likewiſe the pope ſent ambaſſadors into England, who were ſworn not to attempt any thing prejudiciall to the king or kingdome.

[g] And that we may give ſome taſte of every kind: in times paſt the king of England ſent ambaſſadors to generall councels, as taking one

one example of that sort for many. *Ad concilium Basiliens' sub Eugenio papa, quorum destinati sunt per regem ambassiatores et oratores episcopi * Robertus London', Philippus Exoniens', Johannes Roffens', Johannes Baiocens' et Bernardus Aquarens' Ed'us comes Moriton, abbates Glaston' et beatæ Mariæ Eborum, prior Norwici, Henricus Bromflet miles, (dominus Vesciæ) Thomas Browne legum doctor decanus Sarum, Johannes Colleville miles, et alii.* Their authority was in these words. *Dantes et damus eis et ipsorum majori parti potestatem et mandatum tam generale quam speciale nomine nostro et pro nobis in eodem concilio interessendi, tractandi, communicandi, et concludendi tam de hiis quæ reformationem ecclesiæ universalis in capite et in membris, quam in hiis quæ fidei orthodoxæ fulcimentum, regumque ac principum pacificationem concernere poterunt, nec non de et super pace perpetua, guerrarumve abstinentia inter nos et Carolum † adversarium nostrum de Francia, ac etiam tractandi, communicandi, et appunctuandi, consentiendi insuper, et si opus fuerit, dissentiendi hiis quæ juxta deliberationem dicti concilii inibi statui, et ordinari contigerit. Promittentes et promittimus bona fide nos ratum, gratum, et firmum perpetuo habiturum totum et quicquid per dictos ambassiatores, oratores, et procuratores nostros, aut majorem partem eorundem actum, factum, seu gestum fuerit in præmissis, et in singulis præmissorum, et hoc idem cum de et super hiis certiorati fuerimus quantum ad nos et Christianum principem attinet, executioni debitæ curabimus demandar'. In cujus rei testimonium has literas nostras fieri fecimus patentes. Dat' sub magni sigilli nostri testimonio in palatio nostro Westm'* 10 *die Julii.*

* Robert Gilbert doctor of divinity. John Langdon doctor of divinity died at this councell. *Nicholaus Abbas Glaston, Willielm. Abbas beatæ Mariæ Eborum.* The letters of the pope whereby generall councels are called, you may read in Mat. Par. anno dom. 1245. pa. 886.

†[157]

We have expressed this ambassage the more particularly, for that, to this councell also I find that Henry Beauford (son of John of Gaunt by Katherin Swinford) bishop of Winchester and cardinall of S. Eusebye addressed himself and had licence to transport and carry with him 20000 l. of gold and silver (mute, but moving ambassadors) notwithstanding the statutes of 9 E. 3. cap. 1. and 5 R. 2. cap. 2. &c. For the form of a safe conduct (which is called *de salvo conductu*) see the Register. And for the effect and validity thereof, see the statutes of 15 H. 6. cap. 3. 18 H. 6. cap. 4. 20 H. 6. cap. 1.

Rot. pat. anno 11 H. 6. parte 1. m. 10 & 12. & anno 12. part. 2. m. 13. 9 E. 3. ca. 1. 5 R. 2. ca. 2. Safe conduct. Reg. fo. 25, 26

Recordum et process' contra Petrum de Rival thesaurarium et camerarium totius Angliæ et Hiberniæ, et custod' omnium forestarum et omnium portuum maris, &c. de compoto regi reddito de officiis prædictis et de judicio contra ipsum reddito per defaltam, quia venire recusavit, nisi salvo regis conductu, quod rex denegavit quasi insolitum et indebitum.

Anno 18 H

What reward legats have had in former times you may read, Rot. liberat. 11 H. 3. m. 13. Rot. claus. 11 H. 3. m. 11. in dors. Rot. liberat 3 E. 1. m. 9. Eodem rot. 1 E. 1. m. 2. Rot. alman. 11 E. 3. *per totum rotulum.*

See Beda in his history of England, Lib. 1. cap. 11. hereafter cap. 75. Of Scotland, *in fine*, the danger of unwise and incertain leagues.

CAP. XXVII.

The Court of the Justices of Assise, and *Nisi Prius.*

Glanvil lib. 13. cap. 32, 33. &c. Bract. lib. 4. fo. 164. b. Britton fo. 106. b. 112. 118. Fleta li. 4. cap. 1. & 5. Mirror ca. 2. § 15. Stat. Walliæ in Vet. Mag. Car. 2 part. fo. 12. 26 ass. p. 24. * F. N. B. 177. Reg. See the 1 part of the Inst. sect. 442. Mag. Car. ca. 30. 39 H. 6. 19. b. mord. When justices of assise by patent first began. † The patent of the justice of assise. a *Justic' nostros ad assisas.* Hereunto belong commissions of associat' writs of admittance, and of *si non omnes, &c.* F. N. B. 177. Register, and a writ to the sherif to bring before them *omnia brevia assis' jurat' et certificat' &c.* b *Jurat'* when the recognitors are turned *in juratum.* 19 E. 2. ass. 418. 29 ass. p. 78. &c. c Certificat. hereof you may read in F. N. B. and the Register. d Nota. e W. 2. ca. 25.

FOR the writ of assise, whereof the justices take their name; in all ancient authors, it is called *assisa novæ disseisinæ*, or *petit brief de novel disseisin.* Of which writ Bracton saith. *Recognitio assisæ novæ disseisinæ multis vigiliis excogitata et inventa fuit recuperandæ possessionis gratia, ut per summariam cognitionem absque magna juris solennitate, quasi per compendium, negotium terminetur.* And the Mirror saith, that for expedition of justice, and ousting of delayes, it was ordained by Ranulph de Glanvill; but I finde the writ more ancient, as it appeareth in 26 Ass. pl. 24.

At the common law assises were not taken but either in * bank, or before justices in eire, and this was a great delay to the plaintif, and a great molestation and vexation of the recognitors of the assise. For remedy whereof, it is enacted by the statute of Magna Carta, *Quod recognitiones de nova disseisina, et de morte antecessoris non capiantur nisi in suis propriis comitatibus, et hoc modo nos si extra regnum fuere capitales justiciarii nostri, mittent justiciarios nostros per unumquemque comitatum semel in anno, qui, &c. capiant comitatibus illis assisas prædictas.* By force of this act, these three conclusions are to be observed. First, that no assise can be returnable in the kings bench, or common bench, unlesse the disseisin be done in the county where the benches sit respectively, or if both benches sit in one county, then the plaintif hath election to make it returnable in which bench he will. Secondly, that the justices of both benches in that case have jurisdiction originally and ordinary without any patent. Thirdly, that upon the said act of Magna Carta letters patents to justices of assise were framed for the taking of assises in the proper counties in these words.

† *Rex, &c. dilectis et fidelibus suis R. M. uni justic' suorum de banco, et I. L. uni justic' suorum ad placita coram nobis tenend' assign' salutem. Sciatis quod constituimus vos justiciarios nostros una cum hiis quos vobis associaverimus, ad omnes* a *assisas,* b *jurat',* c *certificat' coram quibuscunque justic' tam per diversa brevia domini Johannis nuper regis Angliæ patris nostri, quam per diversa brevia nostra in com' nostris Southt' Wiltes. Dors. Somerset' Devon' et Cornub' ac in civitate Exon' arranian' capiend'. Et ideo vobis mandamus, quod ad certos dies et loca quos vos ad hoc provideritis, assis', jurat', et certificationes illas capiatis;* d *facturi inde quod ad justitiam pertinet secundum legem, et consuetudinem regni nostri Angliæ. Salvis nobis amerciamentis inde provenien'. Mandavimus enim vicecomitibus nostris com' et civitat' prædict', quod ad certos dies et loca quos eis scire faciatis assis', jurat' et certificat' illas una cum brevibus origin' et omnibus aliis ea tangen' coram vobis venire fac'. In cujus rei testimonium, &c.*

e By this writ the seisin and possession was recovered, and became most frequent. *Quia non est aliud breve in cancellaria, per quod querentes*

querentes habent tam festinum remedium, quam per assisam. [f] And after the statute of W. 2. was made and thereby it was provided, *quod assignentur duo justiciarii jurati, coram quibus, et non aliis, capiantur assisæ, &c. ad plus ter per annum.*

[f] W. 2. ca. 30. vid. 4 E. 3. cap. 2.

[g] *Dominus rex, &c. præcepit, quod de cætero assignentur octo justiciarii circumspecti et discreti ad assisas, jurat', et certificat' capiend' per totum regnum Angliæ,* viz. and divideth the realm into eight parts, and to every part assigneth two justices.

[g] Ro. par. 21 E. 1. rot. 3. De justiciariis assignatis.

[159]

But divers acts of parliament have given unto justices of assise authority in many cases.

[b] *Per lestatut' de finibus cap. 3. justiciarii ad assisas capiendas assignati deliberent gaolas in com' illis tam infra libertates quam extra de prisonariis quibuscunque.* [c] Appeals of murder, robbery and rape may be commenced before justices of assise. [d] Power given to justices of assise to try the appeals of approvers. [e] *Justiciarii ad assisas capiend' assignati non compellant juratores dicere præcise.*

[b] 27 E. 1. stat. de finibus cap. 3. To deliver gaols. [c] 22 E. 4. 19. [d] Stat. de Appellatis. an. 28 E. 1. [e] W. 2. cap. 30.

[f] Justices of assise shall enquire for non-returning, and false returns of sherifs.

[f] W. 2. cap. 39. 2 E. 3. cap. 5.

[g] Justices of assise may hear and determine of conspirators, false informers, and wicked procurers of dozens, enquests and juries at the complaint of any without writ, and without delay, and of confederacies and champerties and maintainers, bearers, and alliances by bond, &c. [h] Of defaults of sherifs, escheators, bailifs, and other officers.

[g] Artic. sup. Car. 28 E. 1. 4 E. 3. c. 11. 7 R. 2. c. 15. Regist. 186. 188. 4 E. 3. ca. 12. Of maiors and baylifs, *que ne serche wines.* [h] 20 E. 3. ca. 6.

[i] Justices of assise may enquire of defaults, &c. of punishment of victuallers, &c. which sell at unreasonable prices.

[i] 23 E. 3. ca. 6.

[k] They have power to hear and determine riding and going armed, &c. and to punish justices of peace, sherifs, baillies, and others for not doing their office in that case.

[k] 2 E. 3. ca. 3. de Northampton. 1 R. 2. ca. 7. Of unlawful maintenance.

[l] They may hear and determine treason in counterfeiting of money, &c. [m] They shall do execution of the statute of 13 H. 4. of riots done in their presence upon pain of an hundred pound. [n] And by the statute of 2 H. 5. commissions shall be awarded to enquire of the default of justices of assise, and of justices of peace in that behalf.

[l] 3 H. 5. ca. 7. [m] 13 H. 4 cap. 7. [n] 2 H. 5. cap. 8.

[o] They shall enquire of, hear, and determine all offences contrary to the statute of 23 H. 6. concerning sherifs, under-sherifs, and their clerks, coroners, stewards of franchises, bailifs, and keepers of prisons for extortion, and for letting to bail such as were not bailable, or for denying of bail to them that ought to be bailed, &c.

[o] 23 H. 6. ca. 10. 33 H. 8. ca. 9. for shooting.

[p] Justices of assise shall take bail of him that is acquitted of murder within the year to answer to the appeal of the party, 5 Eliz. cap. 5. of Informers. 5 Eliz. cap. 4. of Labourers.

[p] 3 H. 7. cap. 1.

[q] Justices of assise of gaol-delivery, and of the peace, shall enquire of the default of coroners.

[q] 1 H. 8. 8. ca. 7.

[r] Justices of assise, &c. shall enquire of false making of leather. [s] Of amending of high-ways. [t] Of hunters in parks. [u] Of unlawfull taking of fishes. [x] Of forgery of false deed. [y] Against deceipt in linnen-cloth. [z] Against perjury. * Of usury and many other things.

[r] 18 El. cap. 9. [s] 18 El. cap. 10. [t] 5 El. cap. 3. [u] 5 El. cap. 5. [x] 5 El. cap. [y] 1 El. ca. 14. [z] 5 El. ca. 9. * 13 El. cap. 8.

[a] Justices of assise twice in the year ought to proclaim the statute of 32 H. 8. and other statutes against unlawfull maintenance, champerty, imbracery, and unlawfull reteyners. [b] They ought to proclaim

[a] 32 H. 8. ca. [b] 33 H. 8. ca. 9.

proclaim the statute of unlawfull games in their circuit. See the Custumer of Normandy, cap. 19.

c W. 2. c. 30. See the 2 part of the Inst. the exposition of this act. Vid. Fleta l. 4. c. 5. Vid. Hil. 32 E. 3. m. 5. see the authority of justices of nisi prius, in libro meo. fo. 54. b. the pl. begun, *Et auxint en nisi prius grant devant Stonf.*

[c] Now concerning justices of *nisi prius*, they were first instituted by the statute of W. 2. of issues joyned in the common bench, and kings bench: and their authority is annexed to the justices of assise, and is by force of a judiciall writ, and therefore we have joyned them under one title. And this appeareth in the judiciall writ of *nisi prius*, which is:

The writ of nisi prius.

Rex vicecomiti salutem. Præcipimus tibi quod venire fac' coram justiciariis nostris apud Westm' in octab. Sancti Michaelis, vel coram justiciariis nostris ad assisas in com' tuo per formam statuti nostri inde provis' capiend' assignatis, si prius die Lunæ prox' ante festum, &c. apud, &c. venerint 12. tam milites quam alios, &c.

Reg. judic. 48.

75. W. 2. ca. 30. 6 E. 6. Dier 77.

And by the said act the justices of *nisi prius* have power to give judgment in assise of *darrein presentment* and *quare impedit*.

[160]

7 R. 2. ca. 7.

By the statute of 7 R. 2. *nisi prius* shall be granted as well in the exchequer as elsewhere.

18 El. ca. 12.

Of issues joyned in the kings bench, common bench, and eschequer, the chief justices, or chief baron, or in their absences two other justices or barons of the said severall courts, as justices of *nisi prius* for the county of Midd. within the terme, or four days after shall severally try, &c. and that commissions, and writs of *nisi prius* shall be awarded, &c. It is to be observed that there is but a transcript of the record sent to the justices of *nisi prius*.

9 El. Dier 261.

27 E. 1. de finibus. F. N. B. 241. e. Stat. de York. 12 E. 2. c. 3. & 4. 2 E. 3. ca. 16. & 4 E. 3. cap. 2. 14 E. 3. ca. 16.

By the statute of 27 E. 1. *de finibus*, ca. 4. it is provided, *Quod inquisitiones et recognitiones capiantur tempore vacationis coram aliquo justiciario de utroque banco, coram quibus placitum deductum fuerit.* See the statutes of York, 2 E. 3. cap. 16. 4 E 3. ca. 2. and the statute of 14 E. 3. cap. 16. which statute doth provide that *nisi prius* may be taken in every plea real and personall before two, so that one be justice of one of the benches, or the chief baron or serjeant sworn, without any regard where the plea depended, and this standeth yet at this day. Vid. 42 E. 3. cap. 11. 19 H. 6. fol. 47. 33 H. 6. fol. 14. 16 H. 7. fol. 14. 5 Mariæ Dier fol. 163.

Rot. claus. 10 E. 2. m. 10.

Concordatum fuit per totum concilium regis, quod nullus vicecomes aut coronator fiat justiciarius ad assisas capiend', gaolas deliberand', transgress' audiend' et terminand', seu ad aliquod aliud officium justic' faciend', eo quod debent esse intendentes aliis justiciariis. Which act is declaratory of the common law, for that (as by the reason yeelded in the act it appeareth) these offices be incompatible, the one being attendant unto, and within the controlment of the other.

F. N. B. 240. e. Stanf. 156. Nisi prius in case of felony and treason. 4 E. 3. cap. 11.

14 H. 6. cap. 1. Justices of *nisi prius* have power in all cases of felony and treason to give judgment as well where the prisoner is acquitted, as where he is attainted, and to award execution.

a 24 E. 3. f. 23. rot. par. 37 E. 3. nu. 18. F. N. B. 241. e.

[a] Where the king is a party, a *nisi prius* may be granted, if the kings atturny assent unto it.

In appeal of murder, robbery, and rape brought in the kings bench, if the parties be at issue, a *nisi prius* may be granted before justices of assise. 25 E. 3. 30. 14 E. 3. *Nisi prius* 16. 22 E. 4. 19. 21 H. 7. 36. 9 El. Dier 261. 42 E. 3. c. 11. 8 H. 5. 6.

b 10 E. 4. fo. 14. 22 E. 4. 18. 2 Mar. Dier 120, 121. & 171.

[b] But it is to be observed, that if the appellee be acquited before

justices

juſtices of *niſi prius*, they have power to acquit, &c. and give judgement, as is aforeſaid.

[c] They may alſo enquire and judge of the abbettors and dammages by the ſtatute of W. 2. cap. 12. and not by the ſaid act of 14 H. 6. And ſo it is if the appeal be brought before the juſtices of aſſiſe, they have alſo power to enquire and judge, *ut ſupra*.

[c] See the 2 part of the Inſt. upon this act of W. 2. cap. 12.

[d] Theſe juſtices of *niſi prius* were inſtituted for two cauſes, viz. 1. *Propter intolerabilem jacturam juratorum, et in exonerationem juratorum.* 2. *Ad celerem juſtitiam in ea parte exhibendam.*

[d] 27 E. 1. ſtat. de finibus, cap. 4. Regiſt. 186.

Inquiſitiones et jurat' in placito terræ capiend' quæ magnæ non ſunt examinationes, capiantur in patria, &c.

W. 2. cap. 30.

And hereupon a prohibition is grantable to juſtices of aſſiſe, *Quod non caperent in patria inquiſitiones quæ magna indigent examinatione.*

Regiſt. 186.

By the originall inſtitution of juſtices of aſſiſes and of *niſi prius*, the tryall ſhould be before two at the leaſt, and it were much for the advancement of juſtice and right, to have the law put in due execution, for *plus vident oculi quam oculus*, and ſpecially in pleas of the crown concerning the life of man, in regard whereof they ſhall be worthy of greater allowance.

14 E. 3. aſſ. Br. 413. & tit. Aſſ. Fitzh. 110.

Before the juſtices of aſſiſe *in pays* a forain plea, viz. villenage was pleaded, for tryall whereof the record was removed into the common bench, and there a *venire fac'* was awarded, and retorne, *ſervie*, and a *habeas corpus* with a *niſi prius* was prayed. And it was objected that the iſſue was not joyned in bank, nor judgment to be given there, and yet in the end the prayer was granted, as in a * certificate, upon an aſſiſe a *niſi prius* ſhall be granted: [a] and ſo it is upon a forain voucher, receipt ſhall be granted, and a tryall by a *niſi prius* had.

Dier manuſcript. Hil. 11 Eliz. 26 aſſ. p. 3.

[161]

* 7 H. 4. 45. 8 E. 4. 16. F. N. B. 183. h.

[a] 18 E. 3. 1. 49 E. 3. 21. 3 H. 4. 18.

[b] The juſtice of *niſi prius* may grant a *tales de circumſtantibus*, either when but one or more appear of the principall pannell, or where eleven doe appear: and all the jury may be of the *tales de circumſtantibus*, as it was upon a *tales* at the common law.

[b] 35 H. 8. cap. 6. 23 El. Dier 376. 4 & 5 Ph. & Mar. cap. 7. 14 El. c. 9. 18 El. cap. 12. Vid. 8 Eliz. Dier 145.

[c] Where the king is party, a *niſi prius* is grantable for the king, but not for the party without aſſent of the kings atturny, and ſo are the books to be intended.

[c] 25 E. 3. 39. 18 E. 3. 58. 14 E. 3. Niſi prius 16. 24 E. 3. 23. 21 H. 7. 34. F. N. B. 140. Stanf. pl. cor. 156. a. b.

[d] In attaint the plaintif craved a *niſi prius*, and becauſe one of the petit jury was priſoner in Newgate, and came in ward and pleaded, and was remanded, and if a *niſi prius* ſhould be granted he ſhould loſe his challenges, the court denyed to [e] grant any *niſi prius* otherwiſe a *niſi prius* may be granted in an attaint.

[d] 44 E. 3. fo. 2. 44 aſſ. p. 20. 8 H. 4. 23. 21 E. 3. 17. 6 aſſ. p. 7.

[e] 15 E. 3. Niſi prius. 22. ſimile. 21 E. 3. ibidem 21.

[f] In treſpaſſe between the duke of Exeter and the lord Cromwell, the councell of the duke moved for a *niſi prius*, and for that the duke was a prepotent prince in that country, and the *venire fac'* being returned, there was a great rout in the hall, ſo as if a *niſi prius* ſhould be granted great michief might enſue, therefore no *niſi prius* was granted.

[f] 32 H. 6. 9. 22 E. 3. 16. F. N. B. 241. a. Dier 4 El. 215.

More you may read of the writs of aſſiſe and of *niſi prius* in our books, that which hath been ſaid concerning the juriſdiction may ſuffice. It is commonly called a writ of *niſi prius*, but the words of the writ are *Si prius, &c.* And albeit the authority of juſtices of aſſiſe (as it hath appeared) hath by act of parliament been exceedingly enlarged both in dignity and multitude of cauſes, yet they retain their firſt and originall name, albeit aſſiſes are in theſe days very

very rarely taken before them. See in the chapter of Justices of Peace powers and authorities lately granted to justices of assise and justices of *nisi prius*.

[162]

CAP. XXVIII.

Justices of Oier and Terminer.

For generall commissions, see 42 ass. pl. 5. 2 R. 2. cor. 47. pl. com. 390. *Countee de Leic' case.*

THE authority of justices of *oier* and *terminer* is by commission. Of commissions of *oier* and *terminer* there be two sorts, one generall, so called because it is generall, in respect of the persons, the offences, and the places where the offences are committed, the which commission followeth in these words,

Hereupon they are called justices of oier and terminer.

* Nota, these generall words.

* Note.

*Elizabeth Dei gratia Angliæ, Franciæ, et Hiberniæ regina, fidei defensor, &c. Charissimis consanguineis suis Willielmo marchioni Winton, Henrico comiti Southt', &c. ac dilectis et fidelibus suis Rogero Manwood uni justic' suorum de banco, Johanni Jefferay uni justic' ad placita coram nobis tenend' assign', Johanni Arundell militi, &c. Johanni S. John, Humf. Walrond, William Pool, Petro Edgecombe, Thomæ Morton, &c. salutem. Sciatis quod assignavimus vos et tres vestrum, quorum aliquem vestrum vos præfat' Rogerum Manwood et Johannem Jefferay unum esse volumus justiciarios nostros ad inquirendum per sacramentum proborum et legalium hominum de com' nostris Southt' Wiltes. Dorset, Somerset, Devon. et Cornub. et eorum quolibet, ac aliis viis, modis, et mediis quibus melius sciveritis, aut poteritis tam infra libertates quam extra, per quos rei veritas melius sciri poterit de quibuscunque proditionibus misprisionibus proditionum, insurrectionibus, rebellionibus, murdris, feloniis, homicidiis, interfectionibus, burglariis, raptibus mulierum, congregationibus et conventiculis illicitis, verborum prolationibus, coadjutationibus, misprisionibus, confœderationibus, falsis allegantiis, transgressionibus, riotis, routis, retentionibus, escapiis, contemptibus, falsitatibus, negligentiis, concelamentis, manutenentiis, oppressionibus, cambipartiis, deceptionibus, et * aliis malefactis, offensis, et injuriis quibuscunque, nec non accessar' eorundem infra com' prædict' et eorum quemlibet, tam infra libertates, quam extra per quoscunque et qualitercunque habit', fact', perpetrat' sive commiss'. Et per quos vel per quem, cui vel quibus, quando, qualiter, et quomodo, ac de aliis articulis et circumstantiis præmiss. et eorum aliquod vel aliqua qualitercunque concernen. Et ad easdem proditiones et alia præmissa (hac vice) audiend. et terminand. secundum legem et consuetudinem regni nostri Angliæ. Et ideo vobis mandamus quod ad certos dies et loca quos vos, vel tres vestrum, quorum aliquem vestrum ex vobis præfat. Rogerum Manwood et Johannem Jefferay unum esse volumus, ad hoc provideritis diligenter super præmissis faciatis inquisitiones, et premissa omnia et singula audiatis et terminetis, ac ea faciatis et expleatis in forma prædicta * facturi inde quod ad justitiam pertinet secundum legem et consuetud:nem regni nostri Angliæ. Salvis nobis amerciamentis et aliis ad nos inde spectantibus. Mandavimus enim vicecomitibus nostris com' prædict. quod ad certos dies et loca, quos vos vel tres vestrum, quorum aliquem vestrum*

ex

*ex vobis præfat. Rogerum Manwood et Johannem Jefferay unum esse volumus, eis scire feceritis venire fac' coram vobis, vel tribus vestrum, quorum aliquem * vestrum vobis præfat' Rogerum Manwood et Johannem Jefferay unum esse volumus, tot et tales probos et legales homines de ballivis suis tam infra libertates, quam extra per quos rei veritas melius sciri poterit et inquiri. In cujus rei testimonium has literas nostras fieri fecimus patentes, Teste me ipsa apud Westm' 27 die Junii anno regni nostri decimo octavo.*

2 Particular commissions of oier and terminer so called in respect of the persons of the offences, or of the places, whereof you shall finde five presidents in the Register: † 1. Against the bishop of Winchester and his ministers. 2. *De nave fracta*, if the goods ought to be taken for wreck. 3. Of divers oppressions, &c. extortions, &c. by the kings ministers. 4. Of oier and terminer for the prior of Daventry. And 5. for the king in time of vacation, which you may reade there.

[a] Concerning commissions of oier and terminer ten conclusions are to be observed. 1. That oiers and terminers shall not be granted, but before the justices of the one bench or the other, or the justices errant, and that for great or horrible trespasses, of the kings especial grace, according to the statute in the time of his [b] grandfather.

[c] And in the Register there is a *supersedeas, quia non enormis transgressio*, which word [*enormis*] is in the statute of W. 2. *ubi sup.* [d] To commissioners of oier and terminer a writ of *supersedeas* was delivered, *quia enormis transgressio non est, ideo supersedeant*, for it was not but for cutting down of trees. [e] And afterward a writ of *procedendo* under the great seal of later date was delivered to them to proceed *secundum legem et consuetudinem Angliæ non obstante aliquo mandato, &c.* by vertue whereof, notwithstanding the former writ, they did proceed by advice of all the justices. For a writ of *supersedeas* is one thing, and an absolute repeale or countermand of the commission it selfe is another. A *supersedeas* is but to stay, or forbear the proceedings, * that is, *super advisamentum sedere*, and is not *mes un surcesse de advisement*. And such may the cutting down of trees be, as it may be *enormis transgressio*, and therefore notwithstanding a *supersedeas* the cause may proceed by a writ of *procedendo*. But after an absolute repeale or countermand by the king of the commission it self, the commissioners cannot proceed after by force of any *procedendo*, but there must be a new commission.

The second conclusion is, that commissions are like to the kings writs, such are to be allowed which have warrant of law and continuall allowance in courts of justice. For all commissions of new invention are against law untill they have allowance by act of parliament. [f] Commissions of *novell inquiries* are declared to be void: [g] commissions to assay weights and measures (being of new invention) are declared to be void, and that such commissions should not be after granted. So as a commission is a delegation by warrant of an act of parliament, or of the common law, whereby jurisdiction, power, or authority is conferred to others. *Sapientis judicis est cogitare tantum sibi esse permissum, quantum commissum et creditum.* And it is a good rule for all commissioners to hold the like, and ever to keep themselves within their commission.

† Regist. 125, 126, 127. F. N. B. 110, 111. For particular commissions see 42 ass. pl. 12. 34 ass. p. 8. 29 E. 3. 30, 31. Rot. claus. 18 H. 3 m. 15. de Petro de Rivall.

[a] 2 E. 3. cap. 2. 34 E. 3. cap. 1. To be named by the court and not the party. See the statute of 42 E. 3. cap. 4. which extends to Enquiries. 4 H. 4. cap. 9. Vide. rot. parl. 50 E. 3. nu. 51. for commissions of inquiry what persons ought to be named: so note a diversity between commissioners of enquiry, and of oier and terminer.

[b] W. 2. 13 E. 1. cap. 29.

[c] Regist. 124, 125. 2 E. 3. cap. 2.

[d] 12 Ass. p. 21. Vide Br. com. 12. and oier and terminer 4.

[e] Regist. 124, 125.

* Superfed. unde.

[f] 18 E 3. cap 1.

[g] 18 E. 3. cap. 4.

Rot. par. 2 H. 4. nu. 22. The commons do petition, that certaine commissions lately sent to cities for the making of certaine boats and bullingers being done without assent of parliament, might be repealed. The king doth answer, That after conference with the lords, reasonable answer should be made. And that these commissions took no effect, appeareth in this, that no further complaint was thereof made, and no such commission was ever after granted.

Rot. parl. 5 H. 4. nu. 39. At the petition of the commons, the king granted that one Bennet Wilman, who was imprisoned to answer before the constable and marshall of England, should be tried according to the common laws of this realm, notwithstanding any commission to the Vid. 42 ass. p. 5. contrary. And thereupon a writ was accordingly directed to the justices of the kings bench, as there it appeareth. Of these kindes [164] many more authorities might be cited, but let us return to our justices of oier and terminer.

42 Ass. p. 12. Vi. F. N. B. 110. b. Register 125. &c. In the reign of E. 3. the justices were so carefull, that no innovation should creep in concerning commissions of oier and terminer, that certain justices having their authority by writ, where they ought to have had it by commission, though it were of the forme and words that the legall commission ought to be, John Knivett chief justice by the advice of all the judges resolved, that the said writ was *contra legem*. And where divers indictments were before them found against T. S. the same, and all that was done by colour of that writ was damned.

3 Mar. Br. commissions 23. The third conclusion is, that justices of oier and terminer cannot proceed upon any indictment, but upon indictments taken before themselves, for their authority is, *ad inquirend', audiend', et terminand'*.

The fourth conclusion, that justices of oier and terminer may upon an indictment found proceed the same day against the party indicted. But against this there seems to be great authority: for in Vide 29. ass. 33. Kelwey fo. 159. b. it is thus said. *Mem. que en breife de oier et terminer. P. 9 H. 8. sur le insurrection in Londres il fuit determine clerement per touts justices Dengliterre, que justices d'oier et terminer ne puir inquire un jour, et mesme le jour determine, nient pluis que justices de peace; mes justices de gaol delivery et justices in eire poien bien.* It may be that he that set down this case took it upon trust, for it agreeth in effect *totidem verbis* with the Chronicle in 9 H. 8. fo. 843. and it is erroneous in divers main points. 1. That the oier and terminer was by writ, where it was and ought to be by commission, as hath been said. 2. That justices of oier and terminer cannot enquire one day, and determine in the same day, which without question they may do: for proof whereof we will cite some few records in stead of many.

Hil. 2 H. 4 rot. 4. Thomas Marks bishop of Carlisle before commissioners of oier and terminer was indicted, tried, and adjudged all in one day, for high treason.

1 H. 8. Sir Rich. Empsons case. Northampton. *Die Lunæ post festum Sancti Michaelis, anno* 1 H. 8. before Fisher, Brudnell, Palmes, &c. commissioners of oier and terminer, Sir Richard Empson was indicted of high treason and tried all in one day. And we desirous to see the entry, upon not guilty pleaded, it is thus: *Ideo inter dict' dominum regem et dict' Rich. Empson militem in instant' diem ad horam primam post meridiem, &c. apud castrum de Northampton venerunt, &c. qui nec, &c. ad recognosc', &c. Ad*

quos quidem diem horam, et castrum de Northampt' venit coram praefat' justic' praed' Rich. Empson, &c.

2 *Dec' anno* 3 E. 6. at Westm. before Richard Lister, Edward Mountague, Roger Cholmeley, Edmond Merton, William Portman, and Humfrey Browne, and other commissioners of oier and terminer, Robert Bell was indicted of high treason and tried the same day, 10 Dec' *anno* 3 E. 6. before Sir William Portman and other justices of oier and terminer at Reading in the county of Berks Thomas Bonham was indicted of high treason and tried the same day, 4 Augusti 10 Eliz. John Felton was before commissioners of oier and terminer in London indicted of high treason, and tried the same day by the advice of all the judges of England. [a] Nota, the award in the roll by the justices of oier and terminer to the sheriffe to returne a jury, is not sufficient; but there ought to be a precept to the sheriffe, under the seals of the commissioners for the returning of a jury, but otherwise it is in the kings bench.

[a] And with this constant experience agreeth 4 H. 5. tit. Enquest. 55.

[b] The third error in the said case of 9 H. 8. that justices of peace cannot inquire and try the same day, which without question they may, for they are speciall justices of oier and terminer: and wherefore justices of oier and terminer should not try the same day, as well as justices of gaole-delivery, and justices in eire, no sound reason can be given.

[b] 22 E. 4. cor. 44. holden for no law.

[c] The fifth conclusion is, that if any offence be prohibited by any statute, and name not in what court it shall be punished; or if the statute appoint that it shall be punished in any court of record: in both these case it may be heard and determined before justices of oier and terminer. And so it seemeth to me if *the statute appoint the penalty to be recovered in any of the kings courts of record, according to the opinion of Catlyn, Sanders, and Whiddon; for the court of oier and terminer is the kings court of record.

[c] Vide *Lestatut de* 5 E. 6. cap. 14. Of forestallers, ingrossers, and regrators. 33 H. 8. ca. 9. Of unlawfull games. 7 Eliz. Dier 236. See many statutes wherein justices of oier and terminer are expresly named.

*[165]

The sixth conclusion is, that the king may make a commission of association directed to others to joyn with the justices of oier and terminer, and a writ of admittance to the justices of oier and terminer to admit the others into their society, which writ is close. There is also a writ of *Si non omnes* directed to the justices of oier and terminer and to their associates: the formes of all which you may read in the Register *ubi supra*, and in F. N. B. *ubi supra*. And in all these commissions and writs, the justices are directed with this rule, *Facturi quod ad justitiam pertinet secundum legem et consuetudinem Angliae*, which is a true mark of a lawfull commission.

The seventh. If the justices sit by force of the commission, and do not adjourne the commission, it is determined.

Commissions Br. 12.

The eighth. Justices of oier and terminer, or justices of peace, cannot assigne a coroner to an approver; for it is not within the commission of either of them, but justices of gaole-delivery may do it.

9 H. 4. coron. 457. Stanf. pl. co. 143. c.

The ninth. Justices of oier and terminer shall send their records and proces determined, and put in execution to the exchequer at Mich. every year to be delivered there to the treasurer and chamberlains, &c. to keep them in the treasury.

9 E. 3. cap. 5.

The tenth. None of these commissioners, or of assise, or gaole-delivery, or of the peace, or other of the kings commissioners are countermanded by any new commission, unlesse the new commission

34 Ass. p. 8. L. 5 E. 4. fo. 12. 10 E. 4. fo. 7 20 H. 7. 8.

Kelwey 116. Br. commiss. 6. 19 Eliz. Dier 355. Vi. infra pag. 169. The statute of 2 & 3 Ph. and M. cap. 18. for cities or towns corporate being no counties, but it extendeth not to commissioners of oier and terminer.

sion be shewed unto them for so many as it is shewed unto; or that it be proclaimed in the county, or that the new commissioners do sit and keep their sessions by force of the new commission, the former commission is countermanded.

1 E. 6. ca. 7.

* Nota, the generall words.

And a right profitable statute is made concerning this matter, viz. That no proces or suit before any justices of assise, gaole-delivery, oier and terminer, justices of the peace, or * other of the kings commissioners, shall not in any wise be discontinued by the making or publishing of any new commission or association, or by altering of the names of any of the said justices or commissioners, but that the new justices and commissioners may proceed in every behalfe, as if the old justices and commissioners had still remained and continued not altered.

[166]

CAP. XXIX.

The Courts of Speciall Justices of Oier and Terminer, of and concerning, 1. Purveyours. 2. Misdemeanours of Villaines, &c. 3. Sums of Money collected for Houses of Correction, &c. 4. Colledges, Hospitals, and charitable Uses.

And first of Purveyours.

36 E. 3. cap. 4. Of purveyours.

Buyers of victuall, &c. Takers of carriage.

THIS court is raised by the statute of 36 E. 3. whereby it is enacted, That commissions shall be made to two good men and lawfull of every county, and the third to be of the kings house. So that if any of the three come not, the two shall proceed to enquire of the behaviour and acts of the said buyers and takers, and how much the said buyers have taken and bought; and how much carriage: and to heare and determine the contempts, outrages, and trespasses in that behalfe, as well at the kings suit, as of every man that will complaine of them.

These commissions are to be granted *ex merito justitiæ*, and cannot be denied. And it is to be observed, that the action or suit given by the said act is not popular; for either the king only is to have it, or the subject only that will complaine.

And for better information to be made to the said justices of the things aforesaid, the steward, treasurer, and controller of the two houses, (viz. of the king and queen) at every quarter or halfe year shall certifie into the chancery the parcels taken in every towne, and of every person; and the chancelor shall send the said certificate

certificate to the justices which shall be so assigned. And that this act extend and hold place as well against the purveyors of the great horses of the said two houses, as against the buyers or takers before named.

2. *Concerning Misdemeanours, &c. of Villains.*

See the statute of 1 R. 2. cap. 6. 1 R. 2. cap. 6.

3. *Of and for Sums of Money collected for Houses of Correction, or for the Poore, &c.*

This court is raised by the statute of 39 Eliz. cap. 4. as by the same appeareth, wherein this is to be observed, that their proceedings, judgements, and executions shall remain good and aileable in law, without any redresse to be had by suit in any other court.

39 Eliz. cap. 4. 1 Jac. cap. 7.

See the Second part of the Institutes the exposition of these statutes.

4. *Concerning Colledges, Hospitals, or Almes-houses, or for charitable and lawfull Purposes and Uses.*

It is lawfull for the lord chancelour or lord keeper of the great seale, and for the chancelour of the duchy of Lancaster (for lands within the county palatine of Lancaster) to award commissions under the great seale, or seale of the county to the bishop of the dioces and his chancelor, and to other persons of * good and sound behaviour, to enquire by the oathes of twelve lawfull men, &c. as by all other good and lawfull means of all and singular colledges, hospitals, and other places, founded or ordained for the charitable reliefe of poore, aged, and impotent people, maimed souldiers, schooles of learning, orphans, or for such other good, charitable, and lawfull purposes and intents. And also of lands, tenements, and hereditaments, leases, goods and chattels given or appointed for the like lawfull and charitable uses. As also for reparation of highwayes, of bridges, and seabanks, for maintenance of free-schooles and poore scholars, and of orphans and fatherlesse children, and such like good and lawfull charitable uses. And to enquire of the abuses of misdemeanours, mis-imployments, falsities, defrauding the trusts, alienations, and misgovernments, &c. And after such inquiry made upon hearing and examining thereof to set downe such orders, judgements, and decrees as the said good and charitable uses may be truly observed in full, ample, and most liberall sort, &c. Which orders, judgements, and decrees (not being contrary to the orders, statutes, and decrees of the donors or founders) shall stand * firme and good, according to the tenor and purport thereof: which orders, judgements, and decrees are to be certified under the seals of the commissioners respectively, either

39 Eliz. cap. 6.

[167]

* No person interested, &c. to be a commissioner.

Colledges in both universities, of Westm. Eaton, or Winchester, and cathedrall churches, &c. are excepted.

It extends not to lands in cities or towns corporate where there is a speciall governour, &c.

Nor to any colledge, hospitall, or freeschoole, which have speciall visitors, &c. But this exception extends not to leases, goods or chattels..

* The party grieved may complain to the lord chancelour or lord keeper, or to the chancelour of the said duchy, for their redresse therein, &c. and they have power to judge, &c. according to equity.

into the chancery of England, or of the county palatine of Lancaster.

It is to be observed that when any act of parliament doth authorise the lord chancelour or lord keeper to make or grant any commission under the great seale, that he may make or grant the same without any further warrant, because the king is party to the act of parliament, and there cannot be a greater warrant to the lord chancelour, &c. then the act of parliament.

[168]

CAP. XXX.

Justices of Gaole Delivery.

Their Authority is by Commission in these Words.

The commission of gaol-delivery. Note, they are called the kings justices.
* Their commission extends only to them that are in prison.
a Nota.

*ELIZABETH, &c. Dilectis et fidelibus suis AB. CD. &c. Salutem. Sciatis quod constituimus vos, tres, et duos vestrum, quorum aliquem vestrum vos præfat' AB. &c. unum esse volumus, justiciarios nostros ad gaolam nostram castri nostri de C. de * prison' in ea exist' hac vice deliberand. Et ideo vobis mandamus quod ad certum diem quem vos, tres vel duo vestrum (quorum vos præfat' A B. &c. unum esse volumus) ad hoc provideritis, conveniatis apud castrum prædict' ad gaolam illam deliberand'* [a] *facturi inde quod ad justitiam pertinet secundum legem et consuetudinem regni nostri Angliæ. Salvis nobis amerciamentis et aliis ad nos inde spectantibus. Mandavimus enim vic' nostro com' nostri M. quod ad certum diem quem vos, tres, vel duo vestrum (quorum vos præfat' AB. et CD. unum esse volumus) ei scire feceritis, omnes prisones ejusdem gaolæ et eorum attachiamenta coram vobis, tribus, vel duobus vestrum, (quorum aliquem vestrum ex vobis præfat. AB. et CD. unum esse volumus) ibidem venire fac. In cujus rei testimonium has literas nostras fieri fecimus patentes. Teste, &c.*

See the second part of the Instit. stat. de Glouc' cap. 9.
b 4 E. 3. cap. 2.
17 R. 2. cap. 9.
c Thrice in the year, and oftner if need be.
d Nota, few but effectuall words.
e 4 E. 3. cap. 2.
f 4 E. 3. cap. 2.
3 Mar. Br. Commissions. 23.
2 R. 3. coron. 47.

[b] By the law of the land, *ne homines diu detineantur in prisona*, but that they might receive *plenam et celerem justitiam*, this commission was instituted, and by this commission gaols ought to be delivered [c] thrice in the year, and oftner if need be.

Their authority is by this commission, which consisteth in [d] few words. *Constituimus vos justiciarios nostros ad gaolam nostram castri nostri de C de prisonibus in ea existentibus hac vice deliberand.* [e] These justices ought to be, *bone gents et sages auters que des places, &c.*

Upon this authority and by statutes given unto them, thirteen conclusions do follow.

1. [f] Justices of gaole delivery may arraign any man that is in prison in that gaole upon an indictment of felony, trespasse, &c. before justices of peace, though it were not found before themselves, which (as hath been said) justices of oier and terminer cannot do. Justices of peace shall deliver their indictments to the justices of gaole delivery.

4 H. 5. enquest 55.

2. They shall take a panell of a jury retorned by the sheriffe, without making any precept to him, as justices of oier and terminer (as hath been said) ought to make, and the reason of the difference

difference is, because a generall commandment is made to the sheriffe by the justices of gaole delivery to retorn juries against their comming: but if they have a speciall commission, otherwise it is by Hankeford.

3. They may deliver suspects for felony, &c. by proclamation, against whom there is no sufficient evidence produced to the great inquest to indict them, &c. which justices of oier and terminer, or justices of peace cannot do. 2 R. 3. coron. 47.

4. They may inquire and take indictments of felony, &c. of prisoners before them, and proceed upon them. And so was it resolved in an appeal of murder brought by Apharry against Morgan, who pleaded that he was *auterfoitz* indicted and convicted of the same felony, and had his clergy before justices of gaole delivery, and pleaded over to the felony (and the plea allowed.) And so may justices of oier and terminer doe, which is to be observed by the judicious reader, for both of them have authority to enquire, heare, and determine of such as be prisoners in the gaole: and in that case they have a concurrent authority. Pasch. 29 Eliz. coram rege, inter Apharry and Morgan in appeal. 9 H. 7. 9. 2 R. 3. coron. 47. [169]

5. If a man be indicted before justices of peace, and thereupon outlawed, and is taken and committed to prison, the justices of gaole delivery may award execution of this prisoner. 15 H. 7. 5. b.

6. They may assigne a coroner to an approver, and make proces against the appellee in a forein county. Stat. de Appellat. 28 E. 1.

7. * They may punish those that let men to baile or mainprise, which are not bailable by law, or suffer them to escape. Stanf. pl. cor. 143. c. * 27 E. 1. stat. De finibus cap. 3. 4 E. 3. cap. 2. 1 & 2. Ph. and Mar. cap. 13.

By the statute of 1 E. 6. it is provided in these words. 1 E. 6. cap. 7. Treason, &c.

And be it, &c. That in all cases where any person or persons heretofore have been, or hereafter shall be found guilty of any manner of treason, murder, manslaughter, rape, or other felony whatsoever; for the which judgement of death should or may ensue, and shall be repried to prison without judgement at that time given against him, her, or them so found guilty, that those persons, that at any time hereafter shall by the kings letters patents be assigned justices to deliver the gaole where any such person or persons found guilty, shall remain; shall have full power and authority to give judgement of death against such person so found guilty and repried, as the same justices before whom such person or persons was or were found guilty might have done, if their commission of goale delivery had remained and continued in full force and strength.

8. Here by the judgement of the whole parliament this conclusion doth follow, that justices of gaole delivery, according to the generality of the words of their commission, may deliver the gaole of prisoners committed for high treason, which we prefer before any private opinion, especially concluding with a *quere*. 27 E. 1. de finib. cap. 3. See 28 E. 1. De Appellatis, the recitall. V. 2 R. 3. cor. 47. case de Colinborne.

9. [a] Justices of gaole delivery shall send their records and proces determined, and put in execution to the exchequer at Michaelmas every year to be delivered there to the treasurer and chamberlains, &c. to keep them in the treasury. Stanf. pl. cor. 57, 58. & 182. a. [a] 9 E. 3. cap. 5.

10. [b] Justices of gaol delivery may receive appeals of robbery and murder by bill, but the appellees must be in prison before them. 14 H. 7. fo. 15. b. [b] 13 H. 4. fo. 10. Dier fo. 99. 3 H. 7. cap. 1. Stanf. pl. cor.

11. [c] To these justices commissions of association, and writs of admittance, [c] 2 E. 3. cap. 2.

admittance, and *si non omnes* (as hath been said of the justices of oier and terminer) are directed.

d 6 R. 2. cap. 5.

12. [d] Justices of gaole delivery shall keep their sessions in the principall and chief towns of the counties where the shire courts of the same counties be holden.

2 & 3 Ph. and Mar. cap. 18.
* 11 H. 6. cap. 6.

13. By the statute of 2 & 3 Ph. and Mar. it is provided, that all commissions of the * peace or gaole delivery to any city or towne corporate not being a county of it selfe, shall stand and remaine, the granting of any like commission of the peace or gaol delivery in any shire, lathe, rape, riding, or wapentake, being of a latter date, to the contrary notwithstanding.

See in the chapter of oier and terminer *conclusione* 9. more concerning justices of gaole delivery. Vide 44 Ass. pl. 21.

See authorities lately granted to justices of gaole delivery in the chapter next ensuing of justices of peace,

[170]

CAP. XXXI.

Justices of Peace.

SIR Anthony Fitz-Herbert, one of the justices of the court of common pleas, and divers others have written of the jurisdiction and power of justices of the peace, both in the court of the sessions of peace, as without; to whose labours I refer the reader.

And it is such a forme of subordinate government for the tranquillity and quiet of the realm, as no part of the Christian world hath the like, if the same be duly executed.

Before the conquest, *De pace violata.*
4 H. 7. cap. 12.

To the former treatises are necessary to be added certain acts of parliament made in the 21 year of our late soveraigne lord king James, and certain caveats, additions, and observations necessary to be known. *De pace violata*; *vide int' leges Alvredi*, *cap*. 36. *Edwardi cap*. 6.

But as a preface to all that shall be said of the office and duty of justices of peace, we will begin with that which is enacted by the statute of 4 H. 7. as a necessary caveat to all justices of peace, viz. The king considereth that a great part of the wealth and prosperity of the land standeth in that, that his subjects may live in surety under his peace in their bodies and goods: and that the husbandry of this land may increase and be upholden, which must be had by due execution of lawes and ordinances, chargeth and commandeth the justices of the peace to endeavour them to do and execute the tenor of their commission, the said lawes and ordinances ordained for subduing of the premises, as they will stand in love and favour of his grace, and in avoiding the pains that be ordained, if they do the contrary. And over that he chargeth and commandeth, that every man, what degree or condition that he be of, that let them in word or deed to execute their said authority in any manner or forme abovesaid, that they shew it to his grace; and if they do it not,

not, and it come to his knowledge by other then by them, they ſhall not be in his favour, but taken as men out of credence, and be put out of commiſſion for ever. And over this he chargeth and commandeth all manner of men, as well the poore as the rich, which be to him all one in due miniſtration of juſtice, that is hurt or grieved in any thing, that the ſaid juſtice of peace may heare, determine, or execute in any wiſe, that he ſo grieved make his complaint to the juſtice of the peace that next dwelleth unto him, or to any of his fellowes, and deſire a remedy: and if then he have no remedy, if it be nigh ſuch time as his juſtices of aſſiſes come into that ſhire, that then he ſo grieved ſhew his complaint to the ſame juſtices; and if he then have no remedy, or if the complaint be made long afore the comming of the juſtices of aſſiſe, then he ſo grieved come to the kings highneſſe or to his chancelour for the time being, and ſhew his griefe: and his ſaid highneſſe then ſhall ſend for the ſaid juſtice to know the cauſe why his ſaid ſubjects be not eaſed, and his lawes executed. Whereupon if he finde any of them in default of executing of his lawes in theſe premiſes, according to his high commandment, he ſhall doe to [171]
him ſo offending to be put out of the commiſſion, and furthermore to be puniſhed according to his demerits. And over that his ſaid highneſſe ſhall not let for any favour, affection, coſt, charge, nor none other cauſe, but that he ſhall ſee his lawes to have plain and true execution, and his ſubjects to live in ſurety of their lands, bodies and goods according to his ſaid laws, and the ſaid miſchiefs to be avoided, that his ſubjects may increaſe in wealth and proſperity to the pleaſure of God.

And where the words of the ſaid act be: and further to be puniſhed according to his demerits. Theſe words are ſo to be underſtood, that he ſhall be puniſhed in an ordinary courſe of juſtice by way of indictment upon this act, for his contempt, &c. and not by any abſolute power, as hath been often obſerved.

It is to be obſerved, that when juſtice Fitzherbert and ſome others did write of the authority of juſtices of peace, the commiſſion of the peace ſtood overburdened and incumbered with divers ſtatutes, ſome whereof were before, and ſome ſince repealed: and with ſome, whereas there was none ſuch, and ſtuffed with many vain and unneceſſary repetitions, and many other corruptions crept into it by miſtaking of clerks, &c. For amendment and correction whereof (being a matter of ſo great importance) Sir Chriſtopher Wray chief juſtice of England, Mich. 32 & 33 Eliz. aſſembled all the judges of England, and upon peruſall had of the former commiſſion of the peace, and upon due conſideration had thereupon, and often conferences between themſelves, they reſolved upon a reformation of the former, with divers additions and alterations both in matter and method, as it now ſtandeth at this day: and there needeth yet another reformation of that alſo; for ſince that time divers ſtatutes then in force have been repealed, and divers have expired, As for example, all the ſtatutes of liveries inquirable by juſtices of peace are repealed by the ſtatute of 3 Car. cap. 4. ſaving the ſtatute of 1 R. 2. cap. 7. inquirable before juſtices of aſſiſe, *vide ſupra*, pa. 159. Alſo the ſtatute of 27 H. 8. cap. 22. that the owner of any ſcite or precinct, &c. of any diſſolved religious houſe under the value of 200 l. *per annum*, for the keeping of

Compare the old with the new commiſſion, and the reformations, additions, and alterations will appear.

Mich. 32 & 33 El. the commiſſion of the peace reformed by all the judges of England.

12 H. 4. ca. 3.
8 H. 6. ca. 4.
8 E. 4. ca. 2, &c.
27 H. 8. ca. 22.
5 El. ca. 2.

of honest and continuall houshold thereupon, and inquirable by justices of peace is repealed by 21 Jac. *regis* cap. 28. And the statute of 13 R. 2. cap. 8. and 4 H. 4. cap. 25. for taking by any inholders in gain above a half penny in a bushell of oats over the common price in the market, and inquirable by justices of peace be also repealed by the said act of 21 Jac. Likewise the statute of 39 El. cap. 2. concerning husbandry and tillage, which being but a probationer for a time, was discontinued 21 Jac. And the statutes concerning houses of husbandry and tillage in 4 H. 7. 7 H. 8. 27 H. 8. 5 E. 6. and 5 Eliz. are all repealed by 21 Jac. and divers others, &c.

13 R. 2. ca. 8. 4 H. 4. ca. 25. 39 El. ca. 2. 4 H. 7. ca. 19. 7 H. 8. ca. 1. 27 H. 8. cap. 22. 5 E. 6. cap. 5. 5 El. ca. 2.

It is a good rule therefore for all judges and justices whatsoever, that have jurisdiction by any statute which at the first was temporary, or for a time, to consider well before they give judgement, whether that statute have been continued or made perpetuall: and if it were at the first made perpetuall, whether it be not repealed or altered by any latter statute. *Erudimini qui judicatis terram*. See in the second part of the Institutes the exposition upon the statute of 22 H. 8. ca. 5.

42 E. 3. cap. 9. W. 1. cap. 19. 7 H. 4. ca. 3.

Justices of peace may enquire if estreats be not shewed by sherifs, &c. to the party indebted and totted. A necessary law for the ease of the subject.

Rot. par. 28 E. 3. nu. 17. 37 E. 3. nu. 18. 50 E. 3. nu. 64.

Concerning the nomination of justices of peace, see the statutes of 12 R. 2. cap. 2. 2 H. 5. stat. 2. cap. 1. 18 H. 6. ca. 11. whereunto you may add, that before all these another act not in print was made in 28 E. 3. as well for their nomination, as how and by whom they shall be discharged. Certain it is that he, that is named in the commission of peace under the great seal to be a justice of peace is a lawfull justice of peace.

[172] 21 Jac. reg. ca. 4.

At the parliament holden *anno* 21 Jac. *regis*, there was an excellent law made, entituled, An act for the ease of the subject concerning informations upon penall statutes, which act for that it principally concerneth justices of peace, is here inserted *in hæc verba* as followeth.

This was the ancient and prudent policy of parliament (as before it hath appeared) that justice might be administred and tried in their proper counties, and not to be drawn up to the courts at Westminster for the causes in this preamble expressed.

Whereas the offences against divers and sundry pœnall laws and statutes of the realme may better, and with more ease and lesse charge to the subject, be commenced, sued, informed against, prosecuted and tried in the counties where such offences shall be committed. And whereas the poor commons of this realm are grievously charged, troubled, vexed, molested, and disturbed by divers [a] troublesome persons, commonly called relators, informers, and promoters, by prosecuting and enforcing them to appear in his majesties courts at Westminster, and to answer offences supposed by them to be committed against the said pœnall laws and statutes, or else to compound with them for the same.

[a] Of this kind of men, it was formerly truly said, *Hoc genus hominum semper vitabitur, et tamen semper in civitate retinebitur*. But this law consisting of seven parts remedied all the former inconveniences, and the abuses of these troublesome persons.

1. For

1. For remedy whereof be it enacted by the authority of this preſent parliament, that all offences hereafter to be committed againſt any penall ſtatute, for which any common informer or promoter may lawfully ground any popular action, bill, plaint, ſuit or information [b] before juſtices of aſſiſe, juſtices of niſi prius, or gaol-delivery, juſtices of oier and terminer, or juſtices of the peace in their generall, or quarter ſeſſions, ſhall after the end of this preſent ſeſſion of parliament be commenced, ſued, proſecuted, tried, recovered and determined by way of action, plaint, bill, information or indictment before juſtices of aſſiſe, juſtices of niſi prius, juſtices of oier and terminer, and juſtices of gaole-delivery, or before the juſtices of peace of every county, city, borough, or town corporate, and liberty, [c] having power to enquire of, heare and determine the ſame within this realm of England or dominion of Wales, wherein ſuch offences ſhall be committed, in any of the courts, places of judicature, or liberties aforeſaid reſpectively, only at the choice of the parties, which ſhall or will commence ſuit, or proſecute for the ſame, [d] and not elſewhere, ſave only in the ſaid counties, or places uſuall for thoſe counties or any of them

[b] Nota before juſtices of
1. Aſſiſe.
2. Niſi prius.
3. Gaol delivery.
4. Oier & term.
5. Peace.
But the greateſt care for the due execution of this act will belong to the juſtices of peace, whereof there be many learned in the laws.

[c] Note this act giveth juſtices of peace no new power in caſes where former acts gave them none, and ſo of the reſt of the juſtices here named.

[d] So as they cannot be commenced, &c. in any of the kings courts at Weſtminſter.

2. [e] And that like proceſſe upon every popular action, bill, plaint, information or ſuit, to be commenced, or ſued, or proſecuted after the end of this preſent ſeſſion of parliament by force of, or according to the purport of this act, be had and awarded to all intents and purpoſes as in an action of treſpaſſe *vi et armis* at the common law.

3. [f] And that all and all manner of informations, actions, bils, plaints, * and ſuits whatſoever hereafter to be commenced, ſued, proſecuted, or awarded either by the atturny generall of his majeſty, his heirs, or ſucceſſors for the time being, or by any officer or officers whatſoever for the time being, or by any common informer, or other perſon whatſoever in any of his majeſties courts at Weſtminſter, for or concerning any of the offences, penalties, or forfeitures aforeſaid, ſhall be void, and of none effect, any law, cuſtome, or uſage to the contrary thereof notwithſtanding.

4. And be it further enacted by the authority aforeſaid, that in all informations to be exhibited and in all bils, counts, plaints, and declarations in any action or ſuit to be commenced againſt any perſon or perſons, either by, or on the behalf of the [g] king or any other for or concerning any offence committed, or to be committed againſt any penall ſtatute, the offence [h] ſhall be laid and alleadged to have been committed in the

[e] By this branch proceſſe of outlawry doth lye upon every popular action, a neceſſary clauſe for execution of juſtice.

[f] This clauſe was added that the kings majeſty ſhould be bound expreſly by this act, that no information in the courts at Weſtminſter ſhould be exhibited by the kings atturny generall, by any common informer, or other perſon whatſoever. Note the generality of theſe words.

[g] Note, the king expreſly named.

[h] Shall be laid in the proper county. This clauſe is but in affirmance of the true inſtitution of the common law, for *vicini viciniora facta præſumuntur ſcire*, and for theſe informers they were beſt truſted, where they were leaſt known. This is a very beneficiall clauſe for every defendant to take hold of.

*[173]

the said county where such offence in truth was committed and not elsewhere. And if the defendant to any such information, action or suit, pleadeth that he oweth nothing, or that he is not guilty, and the plaintif or informer in such information, action or suit upon evidence to the jury that shall try the issue, shall not both prove the offence laid in the said information, action or suit, and that the same offence was committed in that county, then the defendant and defendants shall be found not guilty.

5. And be it further enacted by the authority aforesaid, that no officer or minister in any [i] court of record shall receive, file, or enter of record any information, bill, or plaint, count, or declaration, grounded upon the said penall statutes or any of them, which before by this act are appointed to be heard and determined in their proper counties, untill the informer, or relator hath first taken a [k] corporall oath before some of the judges of that court, that the offence or offences laid in such information, action, suit, or plaint, was or were not committed in any other county, then where by the said information, bill, plaint, count or declaration the same is, or are supposed to have been committed, and he beleeveth in his conscience the offence was committed [l] within a year before the information or suit within the same county, where the said information or suit was commenced, the same oath to be there entred of record.

i That is in any of the courts before justices of assise, and other justices named in the first part of this act.

k The informer must take an oath before his information, &c. be received. A beneficiall clause also for the defendant.

l Note, within a year before the information.

Vide 7 Jac. ca. 5. 21 Jac. cap. 12.

6. And be it also enacted by the authority aforesaid, that if any information, suit, or action shall be brought, or exhibited against any person or persons for any offence committed, or to be committed against the form of any penall law either by, or on the behalf of the king, or by any other, or on the behalf of the king and any other, it shall be lawfull for such defendants to plead the generall * issue, that they are not guilty, or that they owe nothing, and to give such speciall matter in evidence to the jury that shall try the same, which matter being pleaded had been a good and sufficient matter in law, to have discharged the said defendant or defendants against the said information, suit, or action; and the said matter shall be then as available to him or them to all intents and purposes as if he, or they had sufficiently pleaded, set forth, or alleadged the same matter in bar, or discharge of such information, suit, or action.

Provided alwayes that this act or any clause contained therein shall not extend to any information, suit, or action, grounded upon any law or statute made against popish recusants, or for, or concerning popish recusancy, or against those that shall not frequent the church and heare divine service, nor

The reasons of this clause were, 1. For that in the courts aforesaid, specially before justices of peace, there are not such skilfull prothonotaries and clerks for good pleading as were in the kings courts at Westminster; and therefore the makers of this law provided that the defendant might plead the generall issue. 2. For the ease and benefit of the subject, great charges growing by speciall pleading. 3. For avoiding of demurrers upon strict, and nice points of pleading. 4. For avoiding of writs of error, which often are brought in respect of speciall pleading.

*[174]

to

to any information, suit, or action for maintenance, champetry, or buying of titles, nor to any suit, or information grounded upon the statute made in the first year of the reign of our soveraign lord the king, of a subsidy granted to the king, of tunnage, poundage, wool, &c. nor for or concerning the concealing or defrauding the king, his heirs or successors of any custome, tunnage, poundage, subsidy, impost, or prisage, or for transporting of gold, silver, ordinance, powder, shot, munition of all sorts, wool, woolfels, or leather, but that such offence may be laid or alleadged to be in * any county, at the pleasure of any informer, any thing in this act to the contrary notwithstanding.

* This proviso referreth only to the county, &c. So as no information, &c. grounded upon any of the statutes in this proviso mentioned can be commenced, &c. in any of the kings courts at Westminster but before the justices of assise, justices of nisi prius, or gaol delivery, justices of oier and terminer, or justices of peace.

There was another mischief which lay heavy upon the subject, whereof advantage might be taken by any informer, which was not provided for by this act, viz. divers former statutes, which in respect of the alteration of times lay as snares upon the people, and at this day could not be performed. For example: that a yard of broad-cloth of the finest making scarlet grayned, or other cloth grayned, what colour soever it be, should not be sold above the value of 16 s. a broad yard, &c. Which act and many other acts of parliament of like nature, and other obsolete laws to a very great number were at this parliament utterly repealed, and made void. We advise therefore the justice of peace (for to him we principally direct our speech, though it concern the rest of the justices before named) seriously to read over that act, where all those obsolete laws are particularly mentioned and repealed, and therefore no information, &c. can be commenced, &c. upon any of them.

4 H. 7. cap. 8.

21 Jac. ca. 18.

At the same parliament also *anno* 21 Jac. *regis*, an other good and profitable law was made concerning justices of peace and others, the tenor whereof is as followeth.

The Title. *An Act to enlarge and make perpetuall the Act made for ease in pleading against troublesome and contentious suits prosecuted against Justices of the Peace, Maiors, Constables, and certain others his Majesties Officers for the lawfull execution of their office, made in the 7. year of his Majesties most happy reign.*

21 Jac. ca. 12.

Whereas an act intituled, an act for ease in pleading against troublesome and contentious suits prosecuted against justices of the peace, maiors, constables, and certain others his majesties officers for the lawfull execution of their office made in the seventh year of his majesties most happy reign of England, was made to continue but for seven years, and from thence to the end

[175]

7 Jac. regis ca. 5. That act extended to 1 Justices of peace.

2 Maiors or bailifs of cities or towns corporate. 3 Headborows. 4 Portreves. 5 Constables. 6 Tithingmen. 7 Collectors of subsidies and fifteenths, and not to any officer not named in that act. Made perpetuall.

end of the next parliament, after the said seven years which by experience hath since been found to be a good and profitable law. Be it therefore enacted by the kings most excellent majesty, the lords spirituall and temporall, and the commons in this present parliament assembled, and by the authority of the same, that the said act shall from and after the end of this present session of parliament be perpetuall, and have continuance for ever.

This act of 21 Jacobi extendeth to 1. Churchwardens. 2. All persons called sworn-men executing the office of churchwardens. 3. All overseers of the poor. 4. All others in their aid and assistance, and not to any other officer or person not named in this act.

And be it further enacted by the authority aforesaid, that all churchwardens, and all persons called sworn-men executing the office of the churchwardens, and all overseers of the poor, and all others, which in their aid or assistance, or by their commandement shall doe any thing touching or concerning his or their office, or offices, shall hereafter be enabled to receive and have such benefit and help by vertue of the said act, to all intents, constructions, and purposes, as if they had been specially named therein.

And whereas notwithstanding the said statute, the plaintif is at liberty to lay his action which he shall bring against any justice of peace, or other officer in any forain county, at his choice, which hath proved very inconvenient unto sundry of the officers, and persons aforesaid, that have been impleaded by some contentious and troublesome persons in countries far remote from their places of habitations.

This branch extendeth to 1 Actions upon the case. 2 Trespasse. 3 Battery. 4 False imprisonment.

Be it therefore further enacted by the authority aforesaid, that if any action, bill, plaint, or suit upon the case, trespasse, battery, or false imprisonment shall be brought after the end of this present session of parliament against any justice of peace, maior, or baylif of city, or town corporate, headborow, portreve, constable, tything-man, collector of subsidy or fifteens, churchwardens, and persons called sworn-men executing the office of churchwarden, or overseer of the poor, and their deputies, or any of them, or any other which in their aid, or assistance, or by their commandment, shall do any thing touching or concerning his or their office or offices, for or concerning any matter, cause or thing by them or any of them done by vertue or reason of their or any of their office or offices, that the said action, bil, plaint, or suit shall be laid within the county where the trespasse or fact shall be done and committed, and not elsewhere And that it shall be lawfull to and for all and every person, and persons aforesaid, to plead thereunto the generall issue, that he or they are not guilty, and to give such speciall matter in evidence to the jury which shall try the same, as in or by the said former act is limited or declared. And that if upon the tryal of any such action, bill, plaint, or suit, the plaintif or plaintifs therein shall not prove to the jury which shall try the same, that the trespasse, battery, imprisonment,

The actions aforesaid shall be laid in the proper county.

To plead the generall issue.

[176]

imprisonment, or other fact, or cause of his, her, or their such action, bill, plaint, or suit was, or were had, made, committed, or done within the county where such action, bill, plaint, or suit shall be laid, that then in every such case, the jury which shall try the same, shall find the defendant and defendants in every such action, bill, plaint, or suit, not guilty, without having any regard or respect to any evidence given by the plaintif or plaintifs therein touching the trespasse, battery, imprisonment, or other cause, for which the same action, bill, plaint, or suit is, or shall be brought: and if the verdict shall passe with the defendant or defendants in any such action, bill, plaint, or suit, or the plaintif or plaintifs therein become nonsuit, or suffer any discontinuance thereof, that in every such case the defendant or defendants shall have such double costs, and all other advantages and remedies, as in and by the said former act is limited, directed, or provided.

The plaintif upon the evidence must prove that the cause of action was done or had in the proper county.

See also another act the same parliament, *anno* 21 Jacobi *regis*, intituled,

21 Jac. ca. 15.

An Act to inable Judges and Justices of the peace to give restitution of possession in certain cases.

Be it enacted by the authority of this present parliament, that such judges, justices, or justice of the peace, as by reason of any act or acts of parliament now in force are authorised, and inabled upon inquiry to give restitution of possession unto tenants of any estate of freehold, of their lands, or tenements which shall be entred upon with force, or from them withholden by force, shall by reason of this present act have the like and the same authority and ability from henceforth (upon indictment of such forcible entries, or forcible withholdings before them duly found) to give like restitution of possession unto tenants for tearm of years, tenants by copy of court-rol, guardians by knights service, tenants by elegit, statute merchant and staple of lands, or tenements by them so holden, which shall be entred upon by force, or holden from them by force.

See 8 H. 6. cap. 9. and 31 El. cap. 11.

1. Judges or justices of the kings bench. 4 H. 7. 18 b. 7 E. 4. 18. 2. Justices of the peace. 8 H. 6. cap. 9. lib. 9. f. 118. b. 2 H. 8. Kelw. 159. Not justices of oier and terminer, nor any other justice. In stead of *disseisivit* which was formerly in the indictment, now it shall be said, *ejecit, expulit, et amovit*, or *detinuit*. This act extendeth to

1. Tenant for years. 2. Tenant by copy, &c. 3. *Guardens en chivalry*. 4. Tenant by elegit. 5. By statute merchant. 6. By statute staple, which no former act extended unto.

In termino Pasch. 6 E. 1. *Coram rege prima fuit institutio justiciariorum pro pace conservanda.*

Rot. parl. 18 E. 1. fo. 3. nu. 41. *Homines de Chesershire qui onerati sunt de servientibus pacis sustentandis, petunt exonerari de oneribus statut' Winton, &c. Rex non habet consilium mutandi consuetudines, nec statuta sua revocandi.*

The lord chancelor and others of the privy councell doe remove divers justices of peace for that they were retayning to the archbishop, &c.

Dors. claus. an. 8 R. 2. m. 5.

See

Rot. par. 3 R. 2. nu. 39.

See a profitable and good law for justices of peace in the parliament roll, and not in print.

Regula.

But let us return to the duty of a justice of peace, for *melius est recurrere quam male currere.*

One or more justice or justices of peace cannot make a warrant upon a bare surmise to break any mans house to search for a felon, or for stoln goods, for they being created by act of parliament have no such authority granted unto them by any act of [177] parliament: and it should be full of inconvenience, that it should be in the power of any justice of peace being a judge of record upon a bare suggestion to break the house of any person of what state, quality, or degree soever, and at what time soever, either in the day or night upon such surmises. But if the party suspected be indicted, then the sherif by force of the kings writ may demand the party indicted to be delivered; and that not done, he may break open the house, &c. and apprehend the felon, for that the kings writ is a *Non omittas propter aliquam libertatem:* but if the kings processe be in debt, trespasse, &c. at the suit of a party, there the sherif by force of the kings writ cannot break open the house of the subject. And so is the book in 13 E. 4. fo. 9. which saith; it was holden, that for felony or suspition of felony a man may break the house to take the felon, and two reasons are yeelded in the book. 1. Because it is for the common weale to take them. 2. Because the king hath an interest in the felony, and in such case the writ is a *Non omittas propter aliquam libertatem:* but otherwise it is for debt, or trespasse, the sherif or any other cannot break the house to take him. And yet it is to be understood, that if one be indicted of felony, the sherif may by processe thereupon after denyall made, &c. break the house for his apprehension, or upon hue and cry of one that is slain or wounded, so as he is in danger of death, or robbed, the kings officer that pursueth may (if denyall be made) break a house to apprehend the delinquent: but for justices of peace to make warrants upon surmises, for breaking the houses of any subjects to search for felons, or stoln goods, is against Magna Carta, *Nec super eum ibimus, nec super eum mittemus, nisi per legale judicum parium suorum, vel per legem terræ:* and against the * statute of 42 E. 3. cap. 3. &c. And we hold the resolution of the court, viz. of Brudnell, Pollard, Broke, and Fitzherbert in 14 H. 8. to be law, that a justice of peace could not make a warrant to take a man for felony, unlesse he be indicted thereof, and that must be done in open sessions of the peace. For the justice himself cannot arrest one for felony, unlesse he himself suspect him, (as any other may) and by the same reason he cannot make a warrant to another. And all this appeareth in that book, and is agreeable with our former books, in 42 Ass. p. 5. & 12. & 24 E. 3. tit. Com. Br. 3. and with reason, for this warrant to take a felon should be in nature of a *capias* for felony, which cannot be granted before indictment, nor after indictment, but in open court. And this is the reason wherefore justices of peace before indictment could not have let any charged with felony or suspition to bail, or mainprise, because justices of peace are judges of record, and ought to proceed upon record, and not upon surmises. *Sed distinguenda sunt tempora, et concordabis leges*; for since the statutes of 1 & 2 Ph. & Mar.

13 E. 4. 9. 20 E. 4. 6. b. He may enter into the house the door being open. See lib. 5. f. 91, 92. Semains case.

7 E. 3. 16. 29 E. 3. 9. 2 E. 4. 8. 9 E. 4. 26.

Mag. Cart. c. 29.

* Read the stat.

14 H. 8. f. 16. a.

Vid. 1 R. 3. ca. 3. 3 H. 7. ca. 3. 1 & 2 Ph. and M. ca. 13. & 2 & 3 Ph. and Mar. c. 10.

Mar. cap. 13. and 2 & 3 Ph. & Mar. cap. 10. (the words whereof be, That the said justices, or one of them being of the quorum, when any such prisoner is brought before them for any manslaughter, or felony, shall take examination, &c.) if any person be charged with any manner of felony, and information be given to a justice of peace of the felony or suspition of felony, and feareth that the kings peace may be broken in apprehending of him, the said justice may make a warrant to the constable of the town to see the kings peace kept in the apprehending and bringing of the party charged with or suspected of the felony before him, and the party that giveth the information of his knowledge or suspition to be present and arrest the delinquent; and in this manner it is implied and intended by the said statutes for the prisoner to be brought before them: and this (as we take it) agreeth with the common use and observance ever since those statutes. And this agreeth also with the said book in 14 H. 8. that a justice of peace may make his warrant for the salvation of the peace, meaning to assist the party that knoweth or hath suspition of the felony. But in this case neither the constable, nor any other can break open any house for the apprehension of the party suspected or charged with the felony, for it is in law the arrest of the party that hath the [a] knowledge or suspition, who cannot break open any house: but if the * door of the house be open, he may enter into the same, and arrest the party. Thus much upon reading of some that have written of the office of justices of peace, we have thought good to adde. For though commonly the houses or cottages of poore and base people be by such warrants searched, &c. yet if it be lawfull, the houses of any subject, be he never so great, may be searched, &c. by such warrant upon bare surmises.

[a] 2 H. 7. 3. & 15. 4 H. 7. 2, 3. 5 H. 7. 4. 10 H. 7. 17. 20 H. 7. 12. 7 E. 4. 20. 8 E. 4. 3. b. 10 E. 4. 17. 9 E. 4. 26. 11 E. 4. 4. 13 E. 4. 9. 7 H. 4. 35. 17 E. 4. 5. 27 H. 8. 23. a. Dier 7 Eliz. 236. b.

[178]

* 20 E. 4. fo. 6. 17 E. 4. 5. a. Lamb. fo. 188, 189.

Baile and mainprise.

* Concerning bailement and mainprise, and what offenders were baileable by the common law, you may reade in the second part of the Institutes, W. 1. ca. 15. Now something is necessary to be added in respect of some variety of opinions touching the true diversity and signification of bailment, mainprize, *fideijuss.* surety, pledges, *plevin*, *plevina*, *replevin*, borough, and the like. And first of baile.

See the second part of the Institutes. W. 1. ca. 15. fol. 472, &c. Glanv. li. 14. ca. 1. W. 1. cap. 15. 27 E. 1. stat. de finibus cap. 3.

Of bail and bailment.

Some derive this word from the French word *bailler*, *id est*, *tradere*, to deliver, because the prisoner is delivered out of prison; but it cannot be so derived: for the entry is, *traditur in* or *per ballium*, and then the sense (or non-sense) should be, he is delivered into delivery. But this word *ballium* is truly fetched from the French nown *bail*, that signifieth a gardian, keeper, or gaoler: [a] and herewith agreeth Bracton, who saith, *Non erit ulterius per ballium dimittendus.* And againe, *Per ballium dimittatur usque adventum justitiariorum, alioquin remaneat in prisona:* and in the same page, *tradas in ballium 12 probis hominibus.* We reade not in Britton of this word baile, but of some other words hereafter following, *Que plevissent corps de home ceux ne sont my proprement pledges mes sont manipernors pur ceo que ilz supposent que ceux plevisable sont livers a eux per baile corps pur corps.*

[a] Bracton lib. 3. fol. 123. And herewith agreeth the Regifter. fo. 133. b. Fleta lib. 1. ca. 26. Mirror ca. 2. § 14.

* There bailment is called a living prison.

* Cust. de Norm.

[b] A man arrested or imprisoned (and bailable) for felony shal be bailed before it appeareth whether he be guilty or no. But if a man be convicted by verdict or confession, &c. he is not bailable, because

[b] 24 E. 3. 33. 25 E. 3. 42. b mainprise 1. 3 E. 3. cor. 354. 2 Eliz. Dier. 179. F. N. B. 246. c.

because it appeareth that he is guilty. So, if upon examination a man confesseth a felony, if the mittimus be for felony confessed, he cannot be bailed.

[c] 33 E. 3. mainprise 12.
[d] This agreeth with the former etymologie.

[c] By Shard there is a diversity between bail and mainprise; for the entry of the bail is, that such an one *traditur in ballium*, in which case they be his [d] gardians: and if they suffer him to escape, they shall answer for it.

[e] 36 E. 3. ib. 13 ac' 4 H. 6. 8. 22 H. 6. 59. 32 H. 6. fo. 4. ac' 39 H. 6. 27. 21 H. 7. 33.
* Vid. infra †.

[e] And where it is said there, *Et per quosdam ilz serra pende*, it was spoken but *in * terrorem*, and thereupon a *quere* is made of it. And that it was no felony in ancient time, hear what the Mirror saith. It is abusion to think that such pain should be awarded to the bail, as to the principals which made default, where they were but amerciable in that case.

[f] 36 E. 3. ubi sup. Br. Mainprise 89.

[f] And where any man is delivered *in ballium*, he may safely be kept by his bail for their indempnity, because the court of justice doth deliver him unto them to be safely kept.

The manner of the severall entries of the bail is worthy of observation, because it is only attained unto by observation of presidents, and the course of courts.

21 H. 7. 20. b. per Fineux. F. N. B. 251. d.

And first in case of bailment for felony by the common law, those that do bail him are severally bound to the king by recognisance in a certain summe, that the prisoner shall appear at a certain day, &c. *Et ultra quilibet eorum corpus pro corpore, &c.*

See Lamb. fo. 352, 353. F. N. B. 251. f.

The bail of a felon before two justices of the peace, whereof one to be of the quorum by the statutes of 1 & 2 Ph. & Mar. & 2 & 3 Ph. & Mar. is for the felon in double, and for each of the bail in single. As for example: if the felon be 40 li. the bail is 20 li. a piece. And herein to observe in effect three things. 1. *Ad comparendum* at the next gaole delivery. 2. *Ad standum recto de felonia prædicta.* 3. *Ad respondendum dicto domino regi, &c.* See the second part of the Institutes, the statute of Marlebridge, cap. 27. if the party bailed *propter privilegium clericale respondere noluerit, non amercientur illi quibus traditus fuit in ballium.* There must be also a *liberate* in that case to the gaoler, if the felon be formerly committed to prison, to deliver him out of prison.

Nota, amercientur.
* Vid. supra †.

[179]
25 E. 3. 39. 3 E 3. tit. cor. 40 Ass. 42. 3 E. 1. cap. 15. 27 E. 1. stat. de finibus, cap. 3.

Before the said statutes of 3 E. 1. cap. 15. 27 E. 1. cap. 3. and 1 & 2 Ph. and M. cap. 13. If any person had been let to bail that was not bailable: by law this amounteth to a negligent escape, and shall be punished as a negligent escape of a felon shall be, that is, to be fined at 5 li. But by the statute of 1 & 2 Ph. and Mar. the justices of gaole delivery shall in that case set what fine upon the justices of peace, &c. they shall think fit. Upon a *capias*, and a *cepi corpus* returned, the entry is *traditur in ballium* 8 *die Maii anno* 16 *regis H.* 8. *Jo. Long, &c. usq; diem Mercurii prox' futur', et sic de die in diem, et termino in terminum, quousq; placitum prædictum terminetur*, viz. *quilibet eorum corpus pro corpore.*

Hil. 18 H. 8. Bendl. This bail is determined by the judgment, if the principall be then there.

If A be *in custodia mareschal'* in the kings bench, and a bill of debt be brought against him; and the defendant finde B for his bail, B entreth a recognisance to the plaintife with this condition precedent, *Quod si contigerit præd' defendentem debit' et damna illa præfato querenti minime solvere, aut se prisonæ mareschalli ea occasione non reddere*, that then he would satisfie the same.

21 H. 7. 40. b.

Nota, in these personall actions the baile is only bound, and their

their recognisance is generall, and of no certain summe, as it is in case of felony: and against him that is by bail in the kings bench, any stranger in the same term may sue him by bill in any personall action; otherwise it is if he were by mainprise *de die in diem.* But if A be outlawed in any personall action, and taken by force of a *capias utlegatum*, and plead any plea triable by the country in avoidance of the outlawry, as that he was commorant in another county, &c. In this case A shall be bailed, and the entry is, *Super hoc, T B. et B T. manuceperunt præfat. A habendum corpus ejus hic, &c. et sic de die in diem in quemlibet diem placiti, quousque placitum prædictum terminetur, et judicium inde redditum fuerit,* viz. *quilibet eorum corpus pro corpore: et prædictus A assumpsit pro seipso essendi tunc hic ad quemlibet diem placiti prædicti subpœna* 40 *li. &c. si contingat ipsum A. ad aliquem diem, &c. defaltum facere, aut sectam suam in hac parte non prosequi.* Note, wheresoever the principall is bound, it is in a certain summe.

9 E. 4. 2. a. See before cap. of the kings bench.

Here the bail are bound in no sum but *corpus pro corpore*, the principall in a certain sum.

And where some do hold, that in all cases when any statute enacteth that the body of the delinquent shall be committed to prison at the will of the king, he cannot be let to mainprise before the kings will be known; the rule is good if it be rightly understood; for he cannot in that case by force of any such statute be imprisoned, before he be indicted, convicted, and judgement given, and then he cannot be bailed or letten to mainprise, because his offence appeareth, as hath been said.

Stanf. pl. cor. 77. b.

And the case there cited in 24 E. 3. upon the statute of 2 E. 3. cap. 3. for going armed in Westm. hall, &c. the book saith, that Thomas Figgot *chivaler fuit arraine per Shard, &c.* which proveth that he was indicted, arrained, and legally proceeded with, neither was his armour forfeited before conviction. And note, that the said act in that case giveth the forfeiture of his armour, and imprisonment: and therefore in that case he shall not be fined: but Sir Thomas Figgot might have been bailed before conviction.

24 E. 3. 33. Sir Tho. Figgots case.

In the next place we are to speak of mainprise, *manucaptio,* which deriveth it self, and signifieth a taking into the hand.

Of mainprise.

Every bail is mainprise, (for those that are bail take the person bailed into their hands and custody) but every mainprise is not a bail, because no man is bailed but he that is arrested, or in prison: for he that is not in custody or prison cannot be delivered out, as before it appeareth. But a man may be mainperned which never was in prison, and therefore mainprise is more large then bail. As in an appeal of felony, the defendant wage battell, &c. and a day appointed, &c. the plaintife shall finde mainprise, &c. to appear, &c. And yet he never was in prison or under custody. And * sometime these mainpernors are called pledges. Also if A be in execution for debt, &c. at the suit of T, and sueth a *scire fac'* upon a release or the like, the entry is, *Et super hoc prædictus A. dimittitur per manucapt' E D. E F. qui eum manuceperunt, ad habendum corpus ejus hic ad præfatum terminum, et sic de die in diem, &c. quousque inde judicium redditum fuerit. Et si pro prædict. T. transierit, exequatur,* viz. *quilibet sub pœna* 40 *li. quas quilibet recognovit, &c. ad opus ipsius T. levari, &c. si contigerit ipsum A. ad aliquem diem placita defaltam facere, seu idem placitum cum effectu minime prosequi, vel se ab executione judicii, si pro præd. T. reddatur versus ipsum A. faciend. retrahere, &c.* And this is properly in the entry said, by mainprise, and no baile, because it is for the plaintife in the *scire fac'* who was in execution.

17 E. 3. fo. 2. 17 Ass. p. 1. 5 E. 3. 21. 32 E. 3. Mainprise 23. * 9 H. 4. 3. 1 H. 6. 6. 30 E. 3. 20. 26 E. 3. 12. 11 H. 4. 43. 12 R. 2. conusance 37. 8 H. 6. 30.

[180]

cution. Now for as much as every bail is a mainprise (as hath been said) bail is oftentimes tearmed in our books by the name of mainprise as before it hath partly appeared, and as it appeareth in the * writ *de manucaptione*. 38 E. 3. fo. 14. 11 H. 6. 31. 50 E. 3. 11. 1 H. 7. 1. And in divers acts of parliament, Acton Burnell 11 E. 1. 4 E. 3. cap. 2. 23 H. 6. cap. 10. 1 & 2 Ph. and Mar. cap. 13.

Lastly, [a] there is a manifest diversity between *de die in diem*, and a bail: for he that is by mainprise *de die in diem* no bill can be maintainable against him: otherwise it is against him that is by bail *per cursum curiæ*.

Plegii and *plegiatio* are derived of the French word *pleige*, which signifieth one that undertaketh for another, a surety, *fidei jussor*. Now as every bail is a mainprise, so every bail and mainprise is *ex vi termini plegiatio:* which see in Glanvile for the act of suretiship. But in legall understanding it is taken, first for the pledges which the demandant or plaintife finde in such writs as begin *Si A* (i. *querens) fecerit te securum de clamore suo prosequendo, &c.* And these are called *plegii de prosequendo*, and the reason of these were, for the answering of the king of the amerciament if the demandant or plaintife were barred or nonsuit, &c. so cautious were the founders of our law, that the king should ever be answered of such duties as belonged to him: but the writ of the [b] king, queen, or of an infant, shall not comprehend that clause, *si fecerit te securum, &c.* because they shall not in those cases be amercied. But it is observable, that the tenant or defendant shall finde no pledges: and yet if judgement be given against him he shal be amercied, &c. for * *melior est conditio possidentis et rei, quam actoris.*

[c] Pledges may be found in the chancery, or may be entred at any time hanging writ or bill by the discretion of the justices, upon gaging deliverance by the avowant he shall finde pledges *de liberatione illa facienda.*

[d] There be also *plegii de retorno habendo* by the statute of W. 2. of pledges *come plevin, replevyn, replegiari, &c.* See the statute of Marlebridge, ca. 27. that *traditus in ballium, replegiatus, et per plegios* is all one and *synonyma.*

[e] When the defendant commeth in by cap. or exigent he shall not finde pledges but mainprise.

[f] He that sueth by bill shall finde pledges *de prosequendo in fine billæ*, which have been controverted in books.

We have hitherto spoken of pledges in a judiciall course. [g] There be also voluntary pledges, as you may reade in Fleta, lib. 2. cap. 5. 32 E. 3. *monstrans des faitz*. 179. 42 E. 3. 11. 44 E. 3. 21. 48 E. 3. 20. 22 Eliz. Dier 270. F. N. B. 137. c.

Surety comprehendeth all the former. And note, there is a surety by the common law, and surety by statute. By the common law, [h] as in a writ *de securitate invenienda ne exeat regnum, &c.* There is surety of the peace, and surety of the good behaviour *de bono gestu*. The surety of the peace cannot be broken without some act, as an affray, or battery, or the like. But the surety *de bono gestu* consisteth chiefly, that a man demean himself well in his port and [k] company, doing nothing that may be cause of the breach of the peace, or of putting of the people in fear or trouble; and that it doth not consist in observation of things that concern not the peace,

* Register. F.N.B. 249, 250. Bract. lib. 3. 154.
[a] 33 E. 3. mainprise 12. 36 E. 3. ib. 13. 1 R. 2. tit. bill 9. 9 E. 4. 12. 7 H. 8. 4. 31 H. 6. 10. 32 H. 6. 4. 39 H. 6. 37. 21 H. 7. 33. a. Vid. 4 H. 6. 8. per Cokeine.

Of pledges. Glanvil li. 10. c. 5. Stat. de offic. cor. 4 E. 1. Plegii de prosequendo.

[b] F. N. B. 31. f. & 195. h. 17 E. 3. 75. b. Lib, 8. 61. & lib. 5. 49. a. Bract. li. 4. f. 254. a.
* Regula.
[c] Regist. 288. F. N. B. 19. 18 E. 4. 9.
[d] Vid 2 H. 6. f. 15. 2 part of the Inst. W. 2. cap. 2.
[e] 31 E. 3. mainprise 21. 42 E. 3. 7. acc'
[f] 12 El. Dier 288. 20 E. 3. pledges 11. 9 E. 4. 27. 2 H. 4. 17. 18 E. 4. 9. 2 H. 7. 1, 17.
[g] See Mag. Cart. cap. 8. 2 part of the Institutes.

Surety, Securitas.
[h] Regist. F. N. B. 85. See the third part of the Instit. cap Fugitives.
[i] 2 H. 7. fo. 2. 13 H. 7. 10. b.
[k] 13 H. 7. fo. 10. b 14 H. 7. 8. per Fineux & Trem. These words are well explained. Hil. 30 Eliz. coram rege intra.

peace, as in not well doing his art or occupation. Thus far is the authority of the book in 2 H. 7. by the resolution of all the justices assembled for that purpose. But in mine opinion, the reporter *male se gessit* in the last words of the case.

[1] At a generall sessions holden at Bridgewater in the county of Sommerset, *anno* 28 Eliz. one William King with sureties was bound by recognisance to appear at the next generall sessions of the peace in the same county, *et quod interim se bene gereret erga dictam dominam reginam, et cunctum populum suum.* And after at the next sessions, William King appeared and was indicted for slanderous words spoken since his binding, viz. for saying at one time to Edw. Kyrton, esq; Thou art a pelter, thou art a liar, and hast told my lord lies, and I will make thee a poor . And he was further indicted, that since the said recognisance, *clausum cujusdam Johannis Wich, vi et armis fregit et intravit et averia et catalla ipsius Johannis in clausu prædicto depascent' illicite vexavit et chasiavit.* And afterwards at another time he said to the said Kyrton, Thou art a drunken knave: which indictment was removed into the kings bench. And hereupon two questions were debated divers times both at the barre and the bench. First, admitting that all that is contained in the indictment to be true, whether any therein was in judgement of law a breach of the said recognisance. The second, for how much the said indictment was good in law. As to the first it was resolved, that neither any of the words, nor the trespasse, were any breach of the good behaviour, for that none of them did tend immediately to the breach of the peace, for though the said words (especially thou art a lyar, &c. thou art a drunken knave) are motives and mediate provocations for breach of the peace, yet tend they not immediately to the breach of the peace; as if William King had challenged Kyrton, or sent him a challenge to fight with him, or had threatened Kyrton to beat or wound him, or the like: these tend immediately to the breach of the peace, and therefore are breaches of the recognisance of the good behaviour. And this diversity was justly collected upon the coherence and context of the statute of 34 E. 3. whereby justices of peace are assigned for keeping of the peace, and to restrain the offenders, rioters, and all other barattors, and to chastise them according to their trespasse and offence; and to inquire of pillors and robbers, in the parts beyond the seas, and be now come again, and go wandring and will not labour, &c. (And thus much for punishment of offences against the peace after they be done: now followeth an expresse authority given to the justices, for prevention of such offences before they be done.) viz. * And to take of all them that be not of good fame, (that is, that be defamed and justly suspected that they intend to break the peace,) where they shall be found sufficient surety and mainprise of their good behaviour towards the king and his people (which must concerne the kings peace, as is also provided by the word subsequent) to the intent that the people be not by such rioters troubled or indamaged, nor the peace blemished, nor merchants nor other passing by the highwayes, disturbed, nor put in the perill that may happen of such offenders. For the trespasse, &c. Although every wrongfull trespasse is, *quare vi et armis et contra pacem*, yet these force and arms, or *contra pacem* implyed in law are not taken to be such as shall

[1] Hil. 30 Eliz. coram rege.

[181]

34 E. 3. cap. 2.

* This was the first statute that gave this expresse authority to justices of peace.

make a breach of the good behaviour; because they are trespasse upon the land or touching goods or chattels, and not the person of a man.

21 E. 4. 10.

As to the second point it was holden, that the indictment concerning the words was void and *coram non judice*, and good only for the trespasse, *quare clausum, &c.* But if there be any just cause of breach, he ought to have a *scire fac'* upon the recognisance.

21 H. 6. 26.

In an account, if a *capias ad computand'* be awarded against the defendant, and thereupon he is outlawed, and rendreth himself to the prison of the Fleet, and auditors be assigned to him, before whom they be at issue, and the auditors bring the record into the common place, and the defendant found surety in 200 li. to appeare in proper person every day *pendente placito*; and if the issue passe against him, that he rendreth himselfe to prison.

[a] 45 E. 3. Surety 24. Register 291. b. Nota. F. N. B. 79 g. 2 H. 7. 1. 4. &c. 36 H. 6. 23. 3 H. 4. 9. [b] 6 E. 4. 8. 12 E. 4. 4. a. 5 H. 7. 3. a. 13 H. 7. 17. a. [c] 3 H. 7. 3.

[a] A fine *sur conusance de droit* was levied to an infant, and because the infant ought to pay the fine to the king, he found *securitatem de fine solvendo.*

There is also a writ *de securitate pacis, et de bene gerendo.*

[b] In *homine replegiando* the defendant avow for that the plaintife is his villain regardant. The plaintife said that he is free, and thereupon they were at issue, the plaintife prayed that he might gage deliverance. And it was awarded that he should have deliverance of his goods, and finde no surety that the avowant should have the goods again if it were found for him. But note when the avowant be at issue upon the villenage, [c] then the plaintife shall find surety to sue *cum effectu.*

[182]
See F. N. B. 151. g.

Surety; by statutes: see the statute of W. 1. cap. 20. *De malefactoribus in parcis* in the second part of the Institutes in the exposition of the same: the statute of Gloc, cap. 4. and W. 2. cap. 21. for finding of surety in a *cessavit*. See also the second part of the Institutes in the exposition thereof.

The statute of W. 2. c. 4. *Et statut. de defensione juris, anno* 20 E. 1. of finding of surety by tenant by resceipt. See the second part of the Institutes the exposition of the same. And many other whereof we need not to make mention; only this is observable, that when any statute doth require pledges or surety to be found, they ought to be sufficient, for insufficient pledges are no pledges in judgement of law; and surety cannot be *ex vi termini* unlesse it be sufficient.

W. 2. ca. 29. Mag. Cart. cap. 26. * Reg. 133, 134. 28 E. 3. cap. 9. Stanf. pl. cor. 77. g. See Hil. 32 E. 1. coram rege rot. 71 & 79. Regist. 268. b. F. N. B. 250. a. Bract. li. 3. f. 154. 28 E. 3. cap. 9.

It appeareth by W. 2. cap. 29. that the * writ *de odio et atia* concerning the bailment of prisoners is grounded upon Magna Carta. And it is holden by some, that writ is not now in use, but is taken away by the statute of 28 E. 3. But this writ is revived again by the statute of 42 E. 3. cap. 1. whereby it is enacted that if any statute be made against *Magna Carta*, or *Carta de Foresta*, it is enacted to be void. See more of this matter in the second part of the Institutes, Mag. Cart. cap. 26. which were unnecessary here to be rehearsed. This writ *de odio et atia* is omitted by Fitzh. in his N. B. Concerning the writ *de manucaptione*, one kind thereof directed to the sherif is a writ grounded upon, and rehearsing the statute of W. 1. cap. 15. and how that before him by a certain inquisition of office A B standeth indicted *de quodam latrocinio cujusdam equi, &c.* Now in as much, as by the statute of 28 E. 3. he

cannot

cannot take such inquisitions by force of any writ or commission, therefore that writ *de manucaptione* ceaseth. But the writ of *manucaptione* may be directed to other justices, as to the justices of the forest, justices of peace and to other: for the statute of 28 E. 3. extends only to sherifs, and to sherifs only upon taking of inquisitions. But a writ of *manucaptione* may in other cases be directed to the sherif. Vide the statute of 4 E. 3. cap. 2. for the court of the marshalsea, F. N. B. 25. I.

Regist. 80. a. Regist. 133. b. F.N.B. 250. k. l. & 251. a. b. c.

Regist. 79. F. N. B. 250. d, f. i.

For the writ of *homine replegiand'*, see the Register, fo. 133. F. N. B. 66. E. Hil. 43 E. 3. *coram rege* rot. 110. Sussex. Mich. 5 H. 4. rot. 26. *Devon' per breve regis in duobus com'* William Scuttes case. 11 H. 4. 15. F. N. B. 68. c. cap. in Withernam.

See Bract. ii. 3. 121. 154. Fleta li. 2. ca. 2.

So odious was unjust imprisonment, or unjust deteyning of any freeman in prison, as in ancient time there lay a writ *de pace et imprisonamento, &c. ubi liber homo, &c. uno modo propter injustam captionem, et alio modo propter injustam detentionem, &c.* And there you may read the form of the writ of appeal, *de pace et imprisonamento*, which we have the rather remembred, that it may be observed what severall remedies the law hath allowed for the relief and ease of the poor prisoner. But the readiest way of all is by *habeas corpus* in the term time, or in the vacation out of the chancery, as you may read at large in the second part of the Institutes, Mag. Carta cap. 29. and statut. de Gloc. c. 9. and the exposition upon the same.

Bract. li. 3. fo. 145. Britton fo. 49. Fleta, li. 1, ca. 40. Mirror ca. 2. §. 11. *la appeal de imprisonment.*

The clerk of the crown, clerk of the peace, and clerks of assise shall certifie briefly a transcript of such attainder, outlawry or conviction as is had for any kind of felony before justices of oier and terminer, justices of gaol delivery, and justices of peace before the king in his bench, there to be and remain of record, &c. [a] See the statute, a very necessary law for the plea of *auterfoitz attaint* or convict for ousting of clergy, &c. and for escheats and forfeitures to the king.

34 H. 8. cap 14. This is expounded to be *reddendo singula singulis respective.* Vide 8 E. 4. 18.

[a] Vid. Dier 8 El. 253. 254. upon another branch of this act.

[b] For the better understanding of this act of parliament, it is to be understood, that such attainders of outlawry and convictions of felony before any of the justices named in this act, as are certified, or delivered into the kings bench, are under the custody of the clerk of the crown of that court, and for that cause he is named in this act.

[b] 14 H. 7. 20. *per Keble. Br.* Judg. 8. to be understood of the kings bench.

14 H. 7. 15. b. *per Mordaunt.*

See the statute of 9 E. 3. cap. 5. by which it is ordained and established, that justices of assise, gaol delivery, and of oier and terminer, shall send all their records and processes determined, and put in execution to the exchequer at Mich. every year once to be delivered there, and the treasurer and chamberlains, &c. shall keep them in the treasury as the manner is, so that the justices always doe first take out the estreats of the said records and processes against them to send to the exchequer, as they were wont before.

[183]

By the statute of 11 H. 4. ca. 3. justices assigned (*id est*, justices of assise) shall cause to be delivered into the kings treasury all the records of assises, mordancestor, and of certifications before them determined every second year.

11 H. 4. cap. 3. 13 H. 4. error 91.

All indictments and presentments in the sherifs turn, or law days shall

3 E. 4. cap. 3. Vid. 4 E. 4. f. 31. 8 E. 4. 10. 5.

ſhall be delivered to the juſtices of peace of the ſame county, at their next ſeſſions of peace to award proceſſe, &c.

3 H. 7. ca. 1. lib. Intr. Raſt. 43.

After the murder or manſlaughter found before the coroners they ſhall deliver their inquiſitions afore the juſtices of the next gaol delivery.

3 H. 7. ca. 1.

If any perſon be murdered in the day, and the murderer eſcape untaken, the townſhip ſhall be amercied, and the coroner hath power to enquire thereof upon view of the body, and the juſtices of peace have power to inquire of ſuch eſcapes, and to certifie afore the king in his bench.

And (that we may ſay ſomewhat of every thing) foraſmuch as the charge to be given at the ſeſſions of the peace conſiſteth on two parts, laws eccleſiaſticall for the peace of the church, and laws civill or temporall for the peace of the land, it ſhall be very fit to lay, as a foundation of the charge, that excellent law eſtabliſhed by authority of parliament, which we have tranſlated into Latin. *Imprimis rex vult, et præcipit quod pax ſacroſanctæ eccleſiæ, et terræ ſolide cuſtodiatur et conſervetur in omnibus, quodque juſtitia ſingulis, tam pauperibus, quam divitibus adminiſtretur, nulla habita perſonarum ratione.*

W. 1. an. 3 E. 1. cap. 1.
Pax { Eccleſiæ. Terræ.
Juſtitia pacis mater & nutrix.

Firſt of all, the king willeth and commandeth that the peace of holy church, and of the land be well kept and maintained in all points, and that common right (*i.* juſtice) be done to all, as well poor as rich, without reſpect of perſons.

Hereupon the charge to conſiſt upon two parts. 1. Of laws eccleſiaſticall, and 2. Of laws civill, or temporall, with an exhortation to doe juſtice.

1 Mar. cap. 12.
3 & 4 E. 6. ca. 5.
Though the body of theſe acts be repealed, yet the *axiome* rehearſed in the preamble ſhall continue for ever.

Or an other axiome or principle of the law may be the foundation of the charge. *Imprimis intereſt reipublicæ, ut pax in regno conſervetur, et quæcunque paci adverſentur provide declinentur.*

It is moſt neceſſary in a commonwealth to provide, that tranquillity and peace be continued in the realm, and that all things being contrary thereunto may by foreſight be eſchewed.

* Or that of 32 H. 8. There is nothing within this realm that conſerveth the ſubjects in more quietneſſe, reſt, peace, and good concord, then the due adminiſtration of his laws.

* 32 H. 8. cap. 9.

Or the like, ſee the third part of the Inſtitutes, in Epilogo.

CAP.

CAP. XXXII.

A Court of Inquiry of the Defaults of the Juſtices of Peace, Juſtices of Aſſiſe, Sherifs, and Under-Sherifs, touching the Execution of the Statute of 13 H. 4. cap. 7. concerning Riots, Aſſemblies, and Routs.

THIS court is raiſed by the ſtatute of 2 H. 5. and is a court only of inquiry, and to certifie the inqueſts incontinent into the chancery, as by the ſaid ſtatute more at large appeareth.

2 H. 5. cap. 8. See 19 H. 7. c. 13.

CAP. XXXIII.

Juſtices in Eire.

THEY were originally inſtituted for the good rule of the ſubjects, and for the eaſe of the countries, and that ſuch as had franchiſes might claime them.

See the 2 part of the Inſt. W. 1. cap. 27.

They were called *juſticiarii in itinere*, or *itinerantes*, in reſpect of other juſtices that were *reſidentes*. In the black book in the exchequer, cap. 8. they are called *juſticiarii deambulantes, et perluſtrantes.* See Vet. Mag. Cart. 2 part. fo. 72. *Artic', et ſacramenta in itinere.*

Bracton lib. 3. fo. 116. Britton fo. 1. 2 E. 3. fo. 27. Kelw. fo. 143.

Their authority was by the kings writ in nature of a commiſſion, they had juriſdiction of all pleas of the crown, and of all actions reall, perſonall, and mixt: they road from ſeven years to ſeven years (but now by the ſtatute of 27 H. 8. ca. 24. all juſtices in eire muſt be by letters patents under the great ſeal.) In what county ſoever they came, all other courts during the eire ceaſed, and all thoſe pleas in that county, or riſing there before any other, the juſtices in eire might proceed upon as the others might have done. For example: a writ was directed to the juſtices of the common pleas to adjorn, and ſend all the pleas of that county which were in the court of common pleas before the juſtices in eire to be determined before them, &c. And if judgment had been within that county, the juſtices in eire might award execution without a *ſcire fac'*. See the firſt part of the Inſtitutes, ſect. 514. and read the ancient books and other authorities there quoted for their antiquity and juriſdiction, and the cauſes wherefore they vaniſhed away. But the other juſtices of eire, viz. of the foreſt, continue to this day according to their originall inſtitution. See the chapter of the Court of the Foreſt. See alſo the ſecond part of the Inſtitutes,

Regiſt. F. N. B. 243. 14 H. 7. 29. 15 H. 7. 5.

Institutes, Marlbridge 24, 25. 27. W. 1. cap. 18. & W. 2. cap. 10. and the exposition of every of them.

What franchises and liberties ought to be claimed before justices in eire, see lib. 9. fol. 24. the case of the abbot of Strata Marcella.

The stile of their court was, *Placita de juratis et assisis et coron. de itinere Johannis de Vallibus et sociorum justic' itiner' apud Ockham in com' Rutland in crastino epiphaniæ Domini, anno regni regis Edw.* 14.

[185]

Bract. lib. 3. fo. 115. b. 116. b. Fleta li. 2. cap. 29. *vers. finem.*

Vide postea, ca. 60 of Pipowders.

These justices in eire did hold their courts, as hath been said, from seven years to seven years, and first they began with pleas of the crown, for saith Bracton, *Imprimis incipere debent de placitis coronæ, in quibus terminantur actiones criminales tam majores quam minores.* And one could not be indicted for any thing, concerning the pleas of the crown, done before the last eire: for so it appeareth by Bracton, *Non erit quærendum de placitis illis coronæ quæ emerserunt ante aliud iter justiciariorum, et quæ coram eis proposita non fuerunt.* And by Fleta, *Ex capitulis de veteribus placitis coronæ alias præsentatis et nondum terminatis, solet exceptio quibusdam indictatis oriri, quod de novo indictamento de fact' ante ultimum iter imposito non tenetur respondere; et si non sit allocabilis, sequitur quod juratores hundredi puniendi sunt de concelamento, vel de perjurio convincendi.*

And it were to be wished that in criminall causes at the kings suit, there were a limitation of time, specially in cases concerning the life of man. The common law in appeals at the suit of the party hath in those cases limited a time, viz. that they must be brought within the year and the day after the offence committed: and the reason thereof was, that the cause might be tryed, whiles it was fresh in memory, and that such as could testifie were living.

Vid. Hil. 15 E. 1. *in banco* rot. 56. they could adjorn into another county.

Rot. par. 20 E. 1. rot. 6.

The justices in eire might inquire of the deeds of justices of gaol delivery.

Bracton saith, *Et si post intervallum accusare velit, non erit de jure audiendus, nisi docere potest se fuisse justis rationibus impeditum.* And Bracton also saith, that after the charge given the justices in eire, *debent transferre se in locum secretum, et convocatis ad se quatuor, vel sex, vel pluribus de majoribus de com' qui dicuntur * busones com' ad quorum nutum dependent vota aliorum qualiter à d'no. rege et concilio suo sit provisum, quod omnes tam milites quam alii qui sunt* [c] 15 *annorum et amplius jurare debent,* &c.

* *Busones sive bursones*, of the French word *bourson*; for as it is in the proverb, He that beareth the purse ruleth the roast, which agreeth with Bractons description here, *Ad quorum nutum dependent vota aliorum.* So vulgarly called, which also Bracton insinuateth, when he saith, *Qui dicuntur busones.* [c] It is misprinted, and should be 12 *annorum*, 2 for 5. See the 2 part of the Inst. Mag. Car. ca. 7. & 35.

Br. Jurisd. 116. 27 ass. 1. F. N. B. Fleta li. 1 ca. 10. § *Ex capitulis vers. finem.*

So great was the authority of justices in eire, that if they came into the county where the justices of the court of common pleas sat, the jurisdiction of that court during the eire ceased, but they yeelded to the kings bench.

See cap. Itineris, Vet. Mag. Cart. part. 1. fo. 150. 151, &c.

See Hovenden, *ann' D'ni.* 1176. Vid. Hil. 13 R. 2. pl. 2. Of proceedings before them.

Regist. 19. b. * *Vide* W. 2. c. 10. Nota the Register is a good exposition of this statute. See the 2 part of the Inst. W. 2. cap. 10.

*Rex justiciariis suis prox' itinerantibus in com. N. salutem. Quia per * commune concilium regni nostri Angliæ provisum est, quod qui-*

libet

libet liber homo libere poſſit facere attornatum ad libertates ſuas vendicandas, exigendas, proſequendas, et defendendas; vobis mandamus, quod attornat' quem A per literas ſuas patentes ſui loco attornare voluerit, ad libertates ſuas vendicandas, exigendas, proſequendas, et defendendas coram vobis in itinere veſtro in com' prædicto, loco ipſius A ſine difficultate ad hoc recipiatis, &c.

See alſo another writ in the Regiſter, *ubi ſupra, De clamore admittend' in itinere, &c.*

CAP. XXXIV. [186]

The Court of Juſtices of Trailbaſton.

THESE juſtices ſat by force of the kings commiſſion of oier and terminer grounded, as ſome hold, upon an ordinance made by king E. 1. and the lords at a parliament holden in *anno* 33 E. 1. for the haſty proceeding. And therefore they were called juſtices of trailbaſton, becauſe they proceeded as ſpeedily as one might draw, or trail a ſtaffe. They ſay upon the ſaid ordinance in the ſame year, viz. 33 E. 1. a commiſſion of oier and terminer *vocat' trailebaſton ſecundum ordinationem inde fact' in parliamento de anno* 33 E. 1. By this it appeareth, as ſome have conceived, that this commiſſion was builded upon an ordinance in parliament, and not upon an act of parliament. 33 E. 1. in Dorſ. pat. parte 1.

Others ſay that this commiſſion was grounded upon an act of parliament in *anno* 33 E. 1. intituled, *Statutum quod vocatur Ragman de juſticiariis aſſignatis.* See the ſtatute, and that the ordinance mentioned in the commiſſion of 32 E. 1. is the ſtatute *Ragman*, ſtatutes being often called by the name of ordinances, for every ſtatute is an ordinance, *ſed non è converſo.* Vet. Mag. Cart. 2 parte fo. 28.

But let us now conſider what light our books have given us, the ſtatute being ſomewhat obſcure and dark.

In Trin. 2 E. 3. we read this caſe. William de B. ſued a writ of error returnable in the kings bench upon a judgement given in a plea of land at the ſuit of John Hodey, which was pleaded by bill before juſtices of trailbaſton, where becauſe the juſtices of trailbaſton did ſend only the record of the plea, they were commanded to ſend the tranſcript of their commiſſion, and the bill alſo with the pannell, the which they did, and again the record alſo. In which caſe you may obſerve theſe five concluſions. Firſt, it was aſſigned for error, that John Hodey made his plaint of certain land againſt William de B. being preſent in court before the juſtices of trailbaſton, and he was put to anſwer without making of proceſſe againſt him, and therefore they erred in receiving the plea without proceſſe, &c. *ſed non allocatur.* Secondly, for the juſtices of trailbaſton be in their caſe as juſtices in eire; and in eire when the party puts in his bill againſt another which is preſent in court, the juſtices in eire ought to receive it. Thirdly, another error was aſſigned, that it appeared by the record, that 2 E. 3. fo. 27.

preſently the juſtices of trailbaſton took an inqueſt *de circumſtantibus*, which came not in by proceſſe to give their verdict, and alſo it appeared by the record, that the twelve gave their verdict, *ſuper ſacramentum ſuum*, without ſaying *de conſenſu partium*; *ſed non allocatur*. For in trailbaſton and in eire certain men are made to come by whom thoſe juſtices doe inquire *ex officio*, that is, without proceſſe, whereunto the parties which have pleaded to iſſue agree to be tryed by them, the court erreth not if they take an enqueſt of them, and it is not found of record, that William de B. did diſſent: and as to the other point, the court ſhall intend an aſſent where there appeareth no diſaſſent. Fourthly, the errors aſſigned being no errors, the court did ſearch for errors, and to affirm the judgment or to reverſe it. And the court did find in the firſt record which was ſent, that William de B. *dicit quod in nullo eſt inde culpabilis, et de hoc ponit ſe ſuper patriam*, where John de Hodey
[187] which was plaintif did not joyn with him, *et prædictus querens ſimiliter*, which joyning was in the ſecond record certified; but for that, that record came in without warrant, and the firſt record certified is the record in law, thereupon the former judgement was reverſed. Fifthly, that no error was aſſigned, that the juſtices of trailebaſton had no lawful juriſdiction, but a writ of error brought upon their judgement, whereby, and by all the context of this caſe their juriſdiction was affirmed, the judges of the kings bench
2 E. 3. 28. having, as is aforeſaid, a tranſcript of their commiſſion. Alſo they had juriſdiction in caſe of indictment of death, and ſo allowed, but appeals of felony were excepted in the ſaid ſtatute.

14 E. 3. Vide Dorſ. Pat. *anno* 14 E. 3. part 3. m. 8. & 2. A commiſſion of trailbaſton was granted to Robert Parning treaſurer and others in London, Middleſex and Surrey, and like commiſſions were granted in other counties.

Rot. parl. 1 R. 2. 101. A petition was exhibited by the commons in full parliament, who prayed that no manner of eire or trailbaſton might be holden during the warres, or 20 years, &c. but it was not granted.

But *præcipitatio eſt noverca juſtitiæ*: and both in reſpect of the precipitation and of ſome reference to the next parliament by the ſtatute of Ragman, this commiſſion wholly long ſince vaniſhed, and is left out of the Regiſter as not to be put in execution. But the commiſſion of oier and terminer there remaineth as neceſſary and uſeful for the puniſhment of horrible and enormious offences. See before the chapter of Oier and Terminer.

CAP.

CAP. XXXV.

The Court of Wards and Liveries raised by Authority of Parliament.

FIRST, the king our said soveraigne lord by the authority aforesaid, ordaineth, maketh, establisheth, and erecteth a certaine court commonly to be called for ever The Court of the Kings Wards: which court by authority aforesaid continually and for ever shall be a court of record, and shall have one seale to be graven and made after such form, fashion, and manner, as shall be appointed by the kings highnesse, and shall remaine and be ordered, as hereafter shall be declared.

The statute of 32 H. 8. cap. 46. *The court of the kings wards.* A court of record. by the statute of 33 H. 8. cap. 22. the office of the liveries is annexed to the court of wards. So as now it is in the court of wards and liveries.

Also be it enacted by authority aforesaid, that all wards which the kings highnesse now is, or hereafter shall be intituled to have, with their mannors, lands, tenements, rents, remainders, reversions, services, and all other hereditaments whatsoever they be, as well in possession as reversion, and all revenues, issues, and profits of the same, and every part thereof, for the time the same shall be, or ought to be in the kings possession, shall be in the order, survey, and governance of the said court, and the ministers of the same, in manner and forme, as by this act is declared and limited.

See the first part of the Institutes. sect. 441. All wards, mannors, lands, &c.

In the order, survey, &c.

Also that the said master of the wards for the time being shall have full power and authority to award under the seale to be appointed to the said court in the kings name such proces and precepts with reasonable pains to be therein limited, as be now commonly used in the court of the kings duchy chamber of Lancaster being at Westm. against every person or persons whatsoever they be, for and concerning the interest, right and title of the kings majesty, his heirs and successors, of in or for any wards lands, tenements, rents, account, receit, services, or other cause in any wise touching or concerning any thing appointed by the order of the said court, or any part thereof, for and on the behalfe of our said soveraigne lord the king, or to or for any debt, rising and growing by occasion of the same.

Proces.

Duchy chamber.

In any wise touching or concerning, &c.

Debt.

Also be it enacted by the authority aforesaid, that the said attorny, receiver generall, and auditors shall diligently from time to time attend upon the said maister in the said court for the hearing and ordering of matters and causes in the same court for the time of four terms in the year usually kept for the

Attend.

By the said act of 33 H. 8. the surveyour is added, and to take place before the attorney.

the law at Westm. and procure with all diligence, that all rents, fermes, profits, casualties, improvements, and other emoluments of the wards mariages, ideots, and all mannors, lands, tenements, and hereditaments being in the survey and governance of the said court, shall be truly and justly paid, and answered to the said receiver generall of the said court to the use of the kings highnesse without concealing any part thereof. And shall also cause and procure processe to be made against such as shall be indebted to the kings highnesse and their sureties of and for any part thereof, from time to time, as the time and case shall require without any delay.

[189]
Indebted.

No proces out the exchequer for or concerning any ward, &c.

Also be it enacted by the authority aforesaid, that all manner of proces that shall be made out of the kings exchequer to or against any person or persons for any ferme, rents, issues or profits concerning the premisses or any part thereof, or any other thing limited in this act to be in the survey, order, and governance of the said court, and the ministers thereof, shall be clearly void and of none effect to all intents and purposes.

Widowes.

Also be it enacted by the authority aforesaid, that the said master by the advice of the said attorny, receiver generall, and auditors, or three of them, whereof the said master to be one of them, shall have authority by this act to survey all the kings widows, and to treat, commune, and conclude as well with all and every of the kings widows that now be, or hereafter shall be, and that have married themselves without the kings license, or that hereafter shall happen to marry themselves without the kings license, for their reasonable fines to be made to the kings use, and to tax and assesse the same by their discretion according to the statute of *Prærogativa Regis*: the same fines to be paid to the receiver generall of the wards lands, as the same may appear yearly in his account.

Ideots.
Naturall fools.

Also be it enacted by the authority aforesaid, that the said master by the advice of the said attorny, receiver generall and auditors, or three of them, shall have authority by this act to survey, govern and order all and singular ideots and naturall fools now being in the kings hands, or that hereafter shall come and be in the kings hands. And also to survey and order all the mannors, lands, tenements, and other hereditaments whatsoever, now being in the kings hands, or in the hands of any other person or persons to their uses, or to the use of any of them, that hereafter shall come and be in the kings hands, his heirs and successors in the right of any of them by reason of his graces prerogative royall: and also by the advice of the said attorny, receiver generall, and auditors, or three or two of them, to let and set the mannors, lands, and tenements to the kings use for the time of the kings interest for such rent and fine, as by their discretion shall be thought convenient; the finding and keeping of the said persons their wives and children, and the reparations of their houses and lands alwayes to be considered in the doing thereof; the same rents and fines

To let and set.

reserved

reſerved to the kings grace to be paid alwayes to the hands of the receiver generall of the wards lands for the time being, as the ſame may appeare in his account, and be recorded in the court of wards.

And alſo be it enacted by the authority aforeſaid, that the ſaid maſter for the time being ſhall have power and authority to take recogniſances of all and every perſon and perſons that ſhall be called into the court of wards and liveries to anſwer to any matter alledged againſt them in the ſaid court, to make their daily appearance in the ſaid court, to anſwer to ſuch matters as to them then and there from time to time ſhall be alledged. And that all ſuch recogniſances of what ſumme ſoever they be, ſhall be as good and effectuall in the law to all intents and purpoſes, as recogniſances taken in the kings high court of chancery, or elſewhere before any judge of record within this realm. And that the ſaid maſter for the time being with the advice of the court, or of ſuch member of the ſame as then ſhall be preſent, ſo that they be two beſide the ſaid maſter, ſhall have full power and authority to moderate ſuch recogniſances as be or ſhall be there forfeited, and to ſet fines for the ſame to the kings uſe under the ſummes contained in the ſaid recogniſances; the ſaid fines to be levied by like proces of *ſcire facias*, as by the ſtatute made in the 27 yeare of our ſoveraigne lord the kings reigne is given to the chancelour of the court of augmentations of the revenues of his graces crown. And that the ſaid maſter for the time being with the advice aforeſaid ſhall have power and authority to commit to ward any perſon or perſons for his or their diſobedience, contempt, or other offence made, or to be made triable within the kings court of the wards and liveries, and upon the ſaid matters ordered or decreed there, to deliver them from priſon, and to cancell and make void all recogniſances and obligations taken or hereafter to be taken in the ſame court to the kings uſe when and as often as the ſaid maſter, with the advice of the ſaid court or three of them, ſhall ſee and perceive the matters and cauſes, for the which any ſuch recogniſances or obligations hath or hereafter ſhall happen to be taken, to be finiſhed and ended, and the kings grace his heirs and ſucceſſors, or the party thereupon ſatisfied, without any other warrant for the ſame.

Called by proces.

[190]

To moderate recogniſances.

And alſo ſhall have full power and authority to hear and determine all and all manner of debts, detinues, treſpaſſes, accounts, reckonings, waſts, deceipts, negligences, defaults, contempts, complaints, riots, quarrels, ſuits, ſtrifes, controverſies, forfeitures, offences, and other things whatſoever they ſhall be, which ſhall hereafter grow, be moved, ſtirred, procured, purſued, or ariſe in, for, or upon any matter, cauſe, or other thing * aſſigned, committed, or appointed to the ſeverall directions, orders, and governances of the ſame courts, or any of

The authority of the courts of exchequer, wards and duchy.

A clauſe of the ſtatute of 33 H.8. cap. 39.

*Aſſigned.

of them, or for or upon any manner of thing or things which may or ſhall touch or in any wiſe concern the ſame, wherein the king ſhall be only party. And alſo all manner of ſtates for tearme of years between party and party concerning the premiſes, and to correct and puniſh by their diſcretions all and every perſon and perſons which before them ſhall be convicted of any of the premiſes according to the nature, quality, or quantity of his or their offence or offences, cauſe or cauſes, matter or matters (all and all manner of treaſons, murders, felonies, eſtates, rights, titles, and intereſts as well of inheritance as freehold, other then joynctures for tearm of life, only excepted and alwayes foreprisẽd.)

Before we deſcend to the ſeverall parts and branch of theſe acts, it ſhall be expedient for advancement of truth to handle and clear two queſtions. Firſt, when wards became due to the kings of England, by what title, and upon what reaſon. Secondly, who had the charge of the kings wards; how they were diſpoſed of, and in what court this revenue was anſwered before the reign of H. 8.

[191] The firſt contains three things. Time, title, and cauſe. And in all theſe three Polydor, and ſuch as follow him, do erre. For Polydor ſaith that *Henricus* 3. *anno domini* 1219. *qui avitum regnum civili bello, ac diſſenſionibus vaſtatum, opibus ſpoliatum, atque prope confectum paulo ante adeptus erat, cum rei domeſticæ inopia preſſus, non poſſet ſine auxilio ſuorum, Aſiaticum bellum juvare, vitamque regiam decenter degere, principes ſoluto prius tributo, pro eo bello gerendo poſtea excogitato novo vectigalis genere, ut regem ſuum ea inopia levarent,* [a] *ultro conceſſerunt, ut quoties quiſpiam eorum, qui poſſeſſiones haberent* [b] *quarum rex eſſet dominus, ante moreretur quam liberi quos feciſſet hæredes vigeſimum alterum agerent annum, tum eatenus tam ipſe hæres quam patrimonium in poteſtate atque tutela regis foret, et ille patrimonii hujuſmodi proventus caperet, quoad hæres ad eam ætatem perveniret: quia apud Anglos more majorum pervetuſto conſervandarum facultatum cauſa, filius mas natu grandior fit ſolus hæres, vel filiæ ſi mares liberi nulli ſint. Egit rex gratias omnibus generatim pro munere, ac ut ne id humanitatis in oblivionem iret, deinceps iſtiuſmodi nobilium hæredum tutelas ut rem ſibi valde utilem accuratiſſime ſuſcepit. Sed illud beneficium nequaquam ipſi nobilitati poſtremo bono fuit, quando cæteri reges qui ſecuti ſunt, non habita ratione, quod à principibus olim in Henricum duntaxat collocatum fuiſſet, ut qui pauper eſſet decentius perſonam regiam per illud ſuſtineret ſibi etiam perpetuatum voluerunt. Quid, quod ita res curæ omnibus fuit, ut non modo reges, ſed reliqui locorum domini in hæreditates nobilium defunctorum eodem modo invaſerint, id quod etiam nunc fit, et lege certa obſervatur. Unum iſtud inſtitutum eſt tandem aliquando corrigendum, quippe quod quantum uni vel alteri commodi, tantum aliis incommodi affert: ſane ita uſu venit, ut populorum quibus hæreditates veniunt tutulæ ſæpe à locorum dominis ad tempus ſicut dictum eſt, illorum tutoribus per auctionem vendantur, quo ſic facto lucro, ab ea educandorum puerorum cura vacui ſint, et qui emunt, emunt autem tam nobiles, quam homines novi, ſi modo plus dederint, ea præſertim de cauſa redimant, ut pupillos nobilium ſuis liberis matrimonio conjungent. Idq; ſæpiſſime faciunt, antequam illi pubeſcant, quo ſimul vivendo, cum primum per etatem liceat, urgente voluptatum*

Polydor lib. 16. pag. 288.

Excogitato novo vectigalis genere [a] Ultro conceſſerunt. [b] Quarum rex eſſet dominus.

luptatum titillatione invicem commisceantur, ut ne postea, cum adoleverint, jam mutui polluti nuptias repudiare queant, qui sic sese ab ineunte ætate libidinibus dedecorantes interdum non homines, sed ob virium infirmitatem plane homunciones gignunt à majoribus degenerantes. Atqui nobilitas cum primis eo damnum facit longe ingentissimum quod homines humili loco nati per ejusmodi connubia sanguinem cum ea socient, contaminentque in dies singulos ejus vetustum genus, et pupilli ipsi à sinu matrum per emptionem erepti parum interdum honestis in aliena domo instituantur. Oritur vel hinc res alia indigna de qua nunc tacere libet, istorum enim conjugum gratia admodum modica aliquoties existit cum ante ætatem, et aliquando contra voluntatem nobiles fæminæ, virique plebeis copulati perraro inter se ament. Præterco et illud, quantum patrimonia nobilium, causa hujusce tutelæ lacerentur à novis possessoribus; qui suis avare commoditatibus servientes pecus omne non modo tondent, sed deglubunt egregie. Atque hoc est principum munus, quod regias opes maxime adauxit.

Herein Polydor hath erred in all three. For first, where he affirmeth for the time, that this *novum vectigalis genus* was *excogitatum*, and granted to king Henry the third *anno domini* 1219. which was in the third year of his reigne, Glanvil who wrote in the reign of H. 2. treateth of wardships due to the king and other lords: to the king in these words. *Notandum tamen quod si quis in capite tenere debet, tunc ejus custodia ad dominum regem plene pertinet, sive alios dominos habere debeat sive non, quia dominus rex nullum potest habere parem, multo minus seniorem, &c.* And he treateth *ubi supra* of wardships then due, (which holdeth law till this day) and speaketh nothing of the beginning of them. [192] Lib. 7. cap. 9, 10. And Ockham who wrote *tempore* H. 2. treateth also of wardships and liveries.

King John in the seventeenth year of his reign made a great charter, and granted *concilio baronum, quòd custos t're hæredis qui infra ætatem fuer' non capiat de terra hæredis nisi rationabiles exitus, et rationabiles consuetudines et rationabilia servitia, et hæc sine destructione et vasto hominum vel rerum. Et si nos commiserimus custodiam alicui talis terræ vicecomiti vel alicui alii, qui de exitib' terræ illius nobis debent respondere, et ille destructionem de custodia fecerit vel vastum, nos ab illo capiemus emendam, et terra committatur duobus legalibus et discretis hominibus de feudo illo, qui similiter nobis respondeant, sicut prædictum est. Custos autem quamdiu custodiam t'ræ habuerit, sustentet domos, parcos, vivaria, stagna, molendina, et cætera ad illam terram pertinentia de exitibus terræ ejusdem. Et reddat hæredi, cum ad plenam ætatem pervenerit, terram suam totam instauratam de carucis, et omnibus aliis rebus, ad minus secundum quod illa recepit.* Matth. Paris pag. 246.

2. Where Polydor saith, *Ultro concesserunt ut quoties, &c.* he affirmeth that it came from the grant of the subject to the king. The truth is, that all tenures by knights service, which since the conquest draweth ward and mariage (for reliefe was due before) were either created and reserved by the king, or before of 18 E. 1. *quia emptores terrarum* by the subjects of the realm. If by the king, it is either of the person of the king, *ut de corona*, which we call *in capite*, or of some honour or mannor. If by a subject, either of his person or of an honor or manor. And all these tenures have been created according to this rule, *cujus est dare, ejus est disponere*. And all the lands in England originally moved from the king, and are holden of him mediately or immediately. 1 part of the Institutes. sect. 103. Polydor saith, that this *novum vectigalis genus* was granted to the king. 1 part of the Inst. sect. 1.

3. He utterly mistaketh the end of the creation of these tenures by knights service, which were originally created for the defence of

Britton fo. 162. b. Lib. Rub.

of the realm by his own subjects, which is more safe then to trust to foreigners. But hereof you may reade at large in Littleton, sect. 95, 96. & 103. and Li. Rub. *Mavult enim princeps domesticos, quam stipendiarios bellicis apponere casibus.*

The charter of king Kenulfus, anno dom. 821. The like charter of king Ethelred to a knight called Athelweg, anno dom. 995. The charter of king Ethelred. 1001. Bracton lib. 2. fo. 36, 37. &c. 1 part of the Institutes sect. 103. Verb Chivaler. Castle. Comming of enemies.

This tenure which now is called escuage, or *servicium scuti*, was of ancient time named *expeditio hominum cum scutis*, as you may reade in the charter of king Kenulphus, who *anno domini* 821 *et regni sui* 25 granted to the abbot of Abbandon many mannors and lands, and reserved *quòd expeditionem duodecim virorum cum tantis scutis exerceant, antiquos pontes, et arces renovent, &c.* Of all other services and charges he and his successors were discharged.

In nomine excelsi tonantis, cujus nutu et miseratione à pio patre praeditus, ego Ethelred rex totius insulae cum consensu et licentia optimatum meorum aliorumque meorum fidelium dabo, et libenti ànimo concedo Closic. quandam ruris particulam, hoc est, 20 *mansos in loco quem ruricolae vocitant* at yceantun *in haereditatem perpetuam, et semper liber permaneat notis et ignotis, magnis et modicis, ad habend' et tradend' qualicunq. voluerit relinquat ob omni tributo et * servicio regali, nisi constructione pontis, et arcis aedificatione, et hostium expeditione. Actum est autem hoc mea concessionis donum anno dominicae incarnationis* 1001. *&c.*

Ditone. Regist fo. 2. Domesday tit. Cestresc.

In the book of Domesday you shall finde it thus recorded.

Sudrie. Episcopus Baioc'

Ille qui tenet de Wodardo reddit ei 50 *s. et servicium unius militis,* and in divers other places. And in Domesday mention is often made of *drenches* or *drenges* which is as much to say as *tenentes per servicium militare.*

[193]

Many others of this kind might be cited to prove that prudent antiquity ever provided by reservation of tenure (amongst other things) for the defence of the realm against the invasion of enemies.

Glanvil. l. 7. c. 9. 10. *Ockham in diversis locis.* Mirror cap. 165. Bracton lib. 2. fo. 36. a. 85. Britton fo. 162. 28. 95. Fleta l. 1. ca. 8.

All our ancient authors treat hereof. See the first part of the Institutes, sect. 103. and see the Grand Custumer of Normandy, cap. 33. &c. fo. 49.

You have heard before *de regali servicio*, before the conquest, but that *regale servicium* (which was knight service) drew unto it relief, but neither wardship of the body or of the land, as hath been said. It is true that the Conqueror in respect of that royall service as a badge of the conquest took the wardship of the land and the marriage of the heirs within age of such tenants, but this extended not to the tenures of the subjects by knights service, as it appeareth by Bracton: *Dicitur regale servicium, quia spectat ad dominum regem, et non alium, et secundum quod in conquestu fuit adinventum; et hujusmodi servicia persolvuntur ratione tenementorum, et non personarum, quia ex tenementis proveniunt, ut si dicatur faciendo inde forinsecum servicium, vel regale servicium, sive servicium domini regis, &c.* So as the Conqueror provided for himself, but other lords at the first by speciall reservation since the conquest provided upon gift of lands for themselves: *Regis ad exemplum totus componitur orbis,* wherein that which we had from the Conqueror we freely confesse, and that which the Normans had from us, we have truly related in other places.

Bract. l. 2. fo. 36. Ubi supra. The tenure (as before it appeareth) was not then invented, but the fruits of the tenure of the king, viz. wardship and mariage, which was Bractons meaning.

The good king H. 1. son of the Conquerour finding that the wardship of the body and lands of his tenants by knight service exacted

exacted by his father was both grievous and unjust, by his great charter *anno primo regni suo*, reciting *Quod regnum suum oppressum erat injustis exactionibus*, &c. (and particularly *tempore patris sui)* did grant (amongst other things) *Quod si uxor cum liberis remanserit, dotem suam et maritagium habebit dum corpus suum legitime servabit, et eam non dabit nisi secundum velle suum, et terræ et liberorum custos erit sive uxor, sive alius propinquior*, &c. To be short by that golden charter, *omnes malas consuetudines, quibus regnum Angliæ injustè opprimebatur, inde abstulit, et lagam regis Edovardi reddidit.* These were called king Edwards laws, not that king Edward made them, *sed quia ex tribus legibus, sc. Anglorum, Danorum, et Merciorum unam legem communem edidit. Vide Ranulph' Cestriens.* Lib. 1. cap. 50.

And where some have objected that wardship is a badge of servitude, for that in the writ of *nativo habendo*, one of the explees (amongst others) is *capiendo redemptionem ab eo pro filiis et filiabus maritandis et aliis villanis serviciis.* That is, taking ransome of him for the marriage of his sons and daughters, and other villain services. To this it is answered, that the king for mariage of his wards taketh no ransomes, but such moderate sums of money, as in respect of the quality and state of the ward, he, or she, all circumstances considered, is able to pay, and in regard thereof, he hath the protection of the court of wards during minority: but if ransomes should be taken, it should not only be against the right institution of wardships before remembred, but also a badge of servitude: and therefore by the statute of Magna Carta, of H. 3. cap. 4, 5, 6. (seeing the crown had a long possession of the wardship of the body and lands of the kings tenant by knights service) it was provided, first, that the king or his grantee or committee should not take of the lands of the heir * but reasonable issues, reasonable customes and reasonable services, without destruction, &c. (and all unreasonable and excessive things are against the common law, *excessivum omne in jure reprobatur.)* Secondly, shall keep up the houses and other inheritance of the heir, and deliver to the heir all his lands stored with ploughs and all other things (woods and all) at least as he received them: whereby it appeareth, that the value of the marriage should be so reasonable, as the heir should not at his full age be enforced for payment thereof to sell either lands or goods. Thirdly, that if the heir be maried, that he be advanced thereby, and not disparaged.

* Note, *reasonable* thrice repeated, that it might be observed.

John earl of Oxford being the kings ward maried without the kings licence, for the which, both for the contempt, and for the duty to the king for so marying, he was fined at three thousand pounds, which was not the value of his lands by one year: and yet he petitioned in parliament to be pardoned of part thereof, which was thought reasonable. And certainly the reasonable rating of wardships of the body and lands is both according to the laws of the realm, and a mean of increase of the kings revenue.

Rot parl. 15 H. 6. nu. 19.

[194]

As to the third: there were of ancient and latter times masters or keepers of the kings wards for the kings best advantage, and the profits and revenue thereof were answered in the kings court of exchequer: as taking one example or two in stead of many for both the points.

* *Rex commisit Randulpho de Nova villa episcopo Cicestr. et Stephano de Segrave custodiam omnium eschaetorum suorum qui accidunt per totum regnum*

* Rot. finium. 14 H. 3. m. 9. Hereof see Mat. Par. anno domini 1232. 16 H. 3. Of Hubert de Burgo, & Stephen Segrave. See also Int. rot. finium, anno 3 E. 1. m. 4. rot. pat. 3 E. 1 m. 33. rot. finium, 13. E. 1. m. 24.

regnum Angliæ, tam in wardis, quam in omnibus aliis eſchaetis quæ regi accidere poſſint, et reſpondend' inde ad ſcaccarium.

a Rot. pat. 25 H. 6. parte 2. m. 24.

[a] See the ſtatute of 51 H. 3. *ſtatut' de ſcaccario.* Sherifs ſhall be keepers of the kings wards, and anſwerable for the iſſues thereof in the exchequer.

b See the firſt part of the Inſtitutes, li. 2. *per totum.*

[b] What care there was of ancient time to preſerve the tree of pious, honourable, and profitable tenures of the king, and for profit eſpecially tenures in *capite* and by knights ſervice, and that the king ſhould be truly anſwered of wardſhips, and other fruits and profits due unto him by reaſon thereof, it notably appeareth by the articles inquirable by the juſtices in eire, and by our ancient books.

* Capit. Itineris in Vet. Mag. Cart. 157, 158. Bract. lib. 3. 116. b. Britton fo. 28. Fleta l. 1. ca. 20.

* *De eſchaetoribus et ſubeſchaetoribus in ſeiſina domini regis facientibus vaſtum, vel deſtructionem in parcis, boſcis, vivariis, vel warrennis infra cuſtodias ſibi commiſſus per dominum regem, quantum et de quibus, et a quo tempore. Item de eiſdem qui occaſione hujuſmodi ceperint bona defunctorum, vel hæredum in manu domini regis injuſte, donec redimerentur ab eis, et quid, et quantum pro hujuſmodi redemptione, et quid ad opus ſuum inde retinuerint, et à quo tempore. Item de eiſdem qui minus ſufficienter terras alicujus in favorem ejuſdem, vel alterius cujuſcunque cui cuſtodia terrarum illarum dari, vendi vel concedi debuerit, in deceptionem domini regis, et ubi, et quando, et quid inde ceperint, et à quo tempore. Item de eiſdem qui prece, precio, vel auxilio, vel favore conſenſerint, vel conſuluerint quod cuſtodiæ domini regis venderentur pro minore precio, quam vendi deberent ſecundum verum valorem, vel maritagia ad dominum regem ſpectantia. Et ſi aliquo modo concelaverint cuſtodias domini regis, vel maritagia hæredum, vel tenentium de rege in capite, vel maritagia dominarum, viduarum maritatarum ſine licentia regis, et ſi quid propter hoc ceperint et quantum, et à quo tempore. Item de hiis qui reſervaverint ad opus proprium cuſtodiam, vel maritagium per leve precium, ſive per concelamentum factum verſus dominum regem, et cujuſmodi damnum rex inde habuerit, et à quo tempore. Item cujuſmodi ſeiſierint terras, et per quantum tempus eas in manu domini regis tenuerint. Item de terris captis in manu domini regis, quæ capi non deberent, et poſtea reſtitutis per præceptum domini regis cum perceptis, utrum percepta reſtituerint ad mandata domini regis, vel non. Et de omnibus prædictis factis et commiſſis infra viginti et quinque annos proxime prædictos prædicti juſticiarii ſe intromittant. Et omnes illi qui ſentiunt ſe ſuper hiis gravatos, et inde conqueri voluerint, audiantur, et fiat eis ſuper hoc juſticia, et ipſe juſticiarii pro hiis quæ dominum regem contingunt diligenter inquirant, &c.*

Vet. Mag. Carta 160, 161. Inter. capit. Eſcaetriæ.

Primo et principaliter inquiratur de feodis militum, et advocationibus eccleſiarum ad dominum regem pertinentibus, viz. *quot ſunt, et quæ ſunt tenementa, et quantitas tenuræ, et per quæ ſervicia.*

[195]

Item, ſi feoda illa integra ſint vel demembrata, non habendo reſpectum ad tempus. Item ſi demembrata, per quem, quando, cui, qualiter, quomodo, et quantum valent per annum. Item ſi tradantur alicui ad terminum vitæ, vel annorum, ſine licentia regis, tunc cui, quando, qualiter, et quomodo, et quantum valent per annum. Et ſi teneantur per medium, per quem medium.

Item de tenementis quæ tenentur de rege in capite, vel teneri debent; ſi aliquis faciat ſe medium inter dominum regem, et verum tenentem ſuum, tunc quæratur ubi, quando, qualiter, et quomodo, et ad quod damnum regis, vel ſi modo tenuram mutaverint.

Item de aliis qui tenent de corona per magnam ſerjantiam, vel parvam, antiquum dominicum domini regis, ſocagium, feodi firmam, vel per aliquod ſervicium, ſi iidem tenentes aliquod alienaverint, vel demembraverint,

verint, cui, quando, quantum, qualiter et quomodo, ſive ſint de aliquo honore, ſive de corona, et de valore annuo. Et ſi aliquis, qui de rege tenuerit per antiquum dominicum vel ſocagium, mutaverit tenuram ſuam, et ad damnum regis, cui, ubi, quando, qualiter, et quomodo, et ad quod damnum regis, et quantum hujuſmodi tenementum valet per annum.

Item ſi aliquis concelaverit aliquem redditum, ſive aliquod ſervicium, ſeu aliquas conſuetudines domino regi debitas, tunc quis, quando, qualiter, et quomodo, et quæ ſervicia, et quem redditum, et quas conſuetudines, et quæ tenementa tenent de quibus debentur hujuſmodi ſervicia, et quantum valent per annum, et ad quod damnum regis hujuſmodi concelamenta ſunt.

Item, de hæredibus quorum cuſtodia et maritagium pertinent ad dominum regem, et dominus rex ea habuerit, quando deberet habere. Et ſi aliquis hujuſmodi hæredum ingreſſus fuerit ſine authoritate curiæ, et abſque legitima ætatis ſuæ probatione ſi infra ætatem, et ſi plenæ ætatis, abſque faciendo regi homagium, vel aliud ſervicium quod ei debet. Et tunc quis ſit ille hæres, quo tempore intravit, et poſt mortem cujus, et per quod ſervicium illa hæreditas teneatur et quantum valet per annum.

Item de viduis ſimiliter quarum maritagium pertinet ad regem, ſi ſe maritaverint ſine licentia regis, cui, quando, cujus conſenſu, et ad quod damnum regis, et quantum tenementa valent quæ tenent in dotem de primo marito ſuo.

Item de hæredibus qui deberent eſſe in cuſtodia regis, et quis cuſtodiam uſurpaverit ſuper regem, et à quo tempore, et quantum tenementa quæ tenent valent per annum.

Item ſi aliquis hujuſmodi hæredum cujus anteceſſor de rege tenuit in capite, ſive de aliquo hærede in cuſtodia regis exiſtente, maritatus fuerit ſine licentia regis, tunc cui, quando, et per cujus conſenſum, et quantum terræ illæ valent per annum, et quantum cepit pro maritagio.

Item ſi dominicæ terræ domini regis in iſto wapentagio ſunt in tali ſtatu ſicut eſſe deberent, vel ſi trahuntur ad firmam, ſi dimittantur ſecundum valorem annuum earundem, et ſi cuſtodes, vel firmarii vaſtum vel deſtructionem, venditionem ſeu exilium fecerint in eiſdem, vel in terris exiſtentibus in manu domini regis per cuſtodiam, vel alio modo, quis, ubi, quando, &c.

Yea ſo precious was immediate tenures of the king, as you read in the parliament roll in 18 E. 1. in theſe words.

Gilbertus de Umphrevill petit licentiam quod poſſit feoffare Gilbertum filium ſuum primogenitum, et Margar. uxorem ejus de manerio ſuo de Overton, tenend' de ipſo Gilberto patre durante tota vita ipſius patris, et poſt ejus deceſſum de capitalibus dominis feodi. Reſpons. Rex non vult aliquem medium. Ideo non conceſſit. [196] Rot. par. 18 E. 1. fo. 4. nu. 52. Note the form of this tenure.

By the ſtatute of 14 E. 3. if the heir of the kings tenant in chief, &c. be found within age, and the next friends of the heir, to whom the inheritance cannot deſcend, ſhall come and offer them to take the ſaid lands, yeelding the value to the king till the age of the heir, as far forth as other will yeeld without fraud; by accord between the chancelor and the treaſurer, they ſhall have commiſſion to keep the ſaid lands by good and ſufficient ſurety till the age of the ſaid heir, and to anſwer the king the value. In this act this treaſurer is intended of the treaſurer of the exchequer. See before in the chapter of the court of exchequer. 14 E. 3. ca. 13. ſtat. 1.

Amongſt the petitions of the commons, they pray that the ſaid ſtatute of 14 E. 3. may be obſerved, which the king granted. Rot. par. 1 R. 2. nu. 79. Rot. par. 50 E. 3. nu. 118.

* Ro. par. 22 E. 4. nu. 6. not in print.

* It is provided by act of parliament in *anno* 22 E. 4. that where ſundry of the kings tenants holding of him immediately, as of his duchy of Lanc', by ſundry recoveries, fines and feoffments in uſe, defeated the king of wardſhips of body and lands: it is enacted, that the king and his heirs ſhall have the wardſhip and cuſtody of the body and lands of every ſuch perſon being within age, to whoſe uſe the fee ſimple or fee tail of any hereditaments ſo holden ſhall grow as heirs by the death of any of his aunceſtors, and if they be of full age to have relief notwithſtanding any ſuch conveyance.

Ibidem nu. 17.

An exact proviſion is made for writs to be granted out of the chancery for the embeſiling of any ſuch heir upon purſuit of the atturny of the duchy.

4 H. 7. ca. 17. A generall law. Note the ſeverall pennings of theſe two ſeverall acts.

By the ſtatute of 4 H. 7. it is provided that the lord of *ceſti que uſe*, no will being declared, &c. ſhall have a writ of right of ward for the body and land, and the heir of *ceſti que uſe* being of full age at the death of his aunceſtor ſhall pay relief. And the heir of *ceſti que uſe* ſhall have like action of waſt, as if the aunceſtor had died ſeiſed, &c.

Dier, 1 & 2 El. fo. 174. b.

Keylway 7 H. 8. 176. between Coniſby and Throckmorton for the heir of Ruſſell.

Upon this ſtatute, a caſe that had in Mich. 1 & 2 Eliz. depended undiſcuſſed thirty years, as the lord Dier reports, but not in the court of wards, (for that court had not then had ſo long continuance) but in the chancery and the court of wards it had ſo long continued, though in 7 H. 8. it had been reſolved by all the judges in the exchequer chamber, that *ceſti que uſe* of lands in fee by knights ſervice in *capite*, and of lands holden of another lord in ſocage dying ſeiſed of the uſe of both, his heir within age, and no will by him declared, that the prerogative ſhall hold place: which reſolution if it had been publiſhed in print, the tedious and chargeable ſuit had not ſo long continued.

Lib. 4. fo. 55. &c. Vid. 2 E. 6. cap. 8. Li. 7. fo. 45. Li. 8. 168, 169. See the 2. part of the Inſt. cap. the ſtatute of 2 E. 6. cap. 8. See 50 E. 3. nu. 184. See hereafter 1 H. 8. cap. 12. This proclamation we have.

Now for traverſes, *Monſtrans de droit*, *&c.* to be relieved againſt offices found for the king, you may read at large in our books, and eſpecially in the Sadlers caſe in the fourth book of our reports, which being the birthright of the ſubject for his relief againſt a falſe office found, cannot be denyed upon juſt cauſe ſhewed, but not to be uſed for delay. This was the offence of Sir Richard Empſon and Edmund Dudley privy counſellors to king H. 7. and maſters of his forfeitures (a new and unaccuſtomed office) who cauſing ſecret and falſe offices (as ſhall appear hereafter) to be found, the parties grieved were denyed to have their traverſe, *Monſtrans de droit*, *&c.* which king H. 7. a little before his death being far gone into a conſumption, with great remorſe of conſcience amongſt other things repented, and by proclamation under the great ſeal in print (amongſt other things publiſhed in theſe words.

See the ſtatute of 1 H. 8. ca. 12. in ratifying hereof.

And that none of his ſubjects ne make no doubt nor difficulty in all cauſes leefull to make traverſes, for his higheneſſe will expreſly, and ſtraightly chargeth and commandeth his chancelour and treaſurer that they not only admit ſuch traverſes but alſo grant the ferms, where the caſe ſhal require, according to the true courſe of his laws.

[197]

Hereupon many men were admitted to their traverſes, and many on the other ſide were without remedy: for by the practice of Empſon and Dudley, many were not onely denyed to traverſe, but inforced

inforced upon ſuch falſe offices to ſue out their generall liveries, whereby they were concluded, and could not by law be admitted to their traverſe.

King H. 8. in the firſt yeare of his reigne intending to give remedy againſt ſecret offices, doth by act of parliament provide, * That every eſcheator and commiſſioner ſhall ſit in convenient and open places, according to the ſtatute heretofore made: and that the ſaid eſcheators and commiſſioners ſhall ſuffer every perſon to give evidence openly in their preſence, to ſuch inqueſts as ſhall be taken before any of them, upon paine of xl. li.

1 H. 8. cap. 8.
3 H. 8. cap. 2.
34 E. 3. cap. 13.
36 E. 3. cap. 13.
23 H. 6. 17.
* By the procurement of Empſon and Dudley offices were found in ſecret places, and men were denied to give in evidence for proof of their rights and tenures.

And by the preamble and other parts of this act of 1 H. 8. the ſiniſter and unjuſt dealing of the ſaid Empſon and Dudley, concerning the finding of officers, are pourtrayed out, whereby the kings ſubjects then of late had beene ſore hurt, troubled, [a] and wronged, and ſome diſherited by nine other wayes. 1. In cauſing untrue offices to be found. 2. In returning of offices that never were found. 3. In changing of the offices that were truly found. 4. That eſcheators and commiſſioners were men of no livelihood, but indigent and unworthy perſons, ready to ſerve turnes, and having nothing to loſe, or to make ſatisfaction to the party grieved. 5. That jurors were returned for the finding of offices of no hability, or behaviour. 6. That the eſcheator or commiſſioner, when the jury were agreed of their verdict, would not receive the ſame, but therein uſe delayes. 7. That the clerk of the petit bag, &c. would refuſe to receive, and file ſuch inquiſitions as were found and offered to them. 8. The like of the officer in the exchequer, of offices returnable into the exchequer. 9. The clerke of the petit bag would refuſe to tranſcribe the offices, &c. into the exchequer. For all which, and the other two before named, remedy is provided by this act, as by the ſame appeareth. At the ſame parliament for the redreſſe of parties grieved for ſuing out of liveries, another act is made, intituled, An act concerning untrue inquiſitions procured by Empſon and Dudley, in theſe words.

[a] See before cap. Of the high court of parliament.

1 H. 8. cap. 12.

Shewen to your diſcreet wiſdomes, that where divers and many untrue inquiſitions by the procurement of Richard Empſon knight, and Edmund Dudley, have beene had and taken within this realme, as well before commiſſioners aſſigned by letters patents of the late king, king Henry 7. as before his eſcheators, as well by vertue of writs of the ſaid late king, as by vertue of their office, by the which inquiſitions ſometime parcell of the ſaid lands contained in the ſaid inquiſitions, and ſometime the whole lands there founden holden of the ſaid late king in capite, where in troth the ſaid lands contained in the ſaid inquiſitions, nor no parcell of them was holden of the ſaid late king in capite, ne of any of his progenitors: to the which inquiſitions the parties then grieved by the ſame, could not, nor might not take their traverſe to the ſame according to the law of the land, but were inforced and conſtrained to ſue their * livery of the ſame out of the hands of the ſaid late king, whereby

* This is intended of a generall livery.

Generall livery concludeth.
[a] Mich. 7 Jacobi resolved by the two chiefe justices, and the chief baron, and the court of wards, in Holmes cases.
1. That the suing of a generall livery concludeth the heire, as here it appeareth by this act of parliament, but otherwise it is of a speciall livery, for that, as to the tenure, is but, *ut dicitur.*
2. That this conclusion or estoppel continueth but during the life of the heire that sueth the generall livery; for jurors are sworne *ad veritatem dicend'*, and are not bound by estoppels.
3. That by suing of livery, and the death of the heire, the office is executed, and hath taken his full effect, and therefore the estoppel expireth therewith, and after the office cannot be traversed. Vide 46 E. 3. fol. 12. 44 Ass. p. 35. *Nota dictum Mowbray, ibidem. Si un tient de roy, &c.* 1 H. 4. 6. 33 H. 6. fol. 7. per Laicon. Observe well the remedies provided by this particular act, &c. whereby the common law is affirmed.

whereby they were, and be [a] concluded to say, that the said lands be holden of the king in chiefe, to their great losse and hindrance, where in truth they were not holden of the said late king, ne of any his progenitors. Wherefore be it enacted, ordained and established * by the king our soveraigne lord, the lords spirituall and temporall, and by the commons in this present parliament assembled, and by the authority of the same, that every person and persons having possession of the said lands contained in the said inquisitions, or any part thereof, may be admitted to have their traverse to the said untrue inquisitions, notwithstanding any livery sued in the time of the said late king, king H. 7. And that it be further enacted by the same authority, that any livery sued of the same in the time of the said late king, ne any thing contained in the same livery, be any conclusion after the course of the common law, or in any wise hurtfull or prejudiciall to any person or persons, that shall happen to tend their traverse to the said office, but that they and every of them shall be admitted to their traverse to the said inquisitions, and to have like advantage in the law, as though no livery had beene sued of the same in the time of the said late king, and this at the reverence of God, and in the way of charity, &c. Provided alway, that they, or any of them which shall tend their traverse to any of the said inquisitions in any manner and forme as is aforesaid, shall not be restored to any mean issues or profits of lands and tenements comprised in the said inquisitions.

See the first part of the Institutes, sect. 441. See before cap. of the high court of parliament.

Now touching liveries which in those days were generall, what a world of troubles the subjects suffered for missing of livery in respect of pretended omissions, and the like, what charging the subjects with values not found by any office, nor appearing by any *melius inquirendum* with mean rates where none were, or for longer time, then they were due, and the like, and these not recovered by course of law, but sending for the parties by pursevants, and by their awfull countenance mixt with menaces and threats, drew them to compositions: which, and other like oppressions and injustice, filled king H. 7. cofers; for by the close roll in *anno* 3 H. 8. it appeareth, that the king left in his cofers fifty and three hundred thousand pounds, most part in foreine coine, which in those dayes was not of least value. Notwithstanding king H. 8. at his parliament holden in *anno* 5 of his reigne, cap. 7. moved for a subsidie, and was denied it; whereupon an act was made for taking out of generall pardons, as a meane to bring money to the king. But I perswade my selfe the reader will inquire what became of these two wicked men, Empson and Dudley. The answer is, that first they were severally indicted as followeth.

5 H. 8. cap. 7.

Juratores præsentant quod Richardus Empson nuper de London miles, nuper consiliarius excellentissimi principis Henrici nuper regis Angliæ septimi, *mi, 10. die Maii, anno regni dicti nuper regis vicesimo, ac diversis vicibus antea et postea apud London, &c. Deum præ oculis non habens, sed ut filius diabolicus imaginans honorem, dignitatem, et prosperitatem dicti nuper regis, et prosperitatem regni sui Angliæ minime valere, sed ut ipse magis singulares favores dicti nuper regis adhibere* * *unde magnatem fieri potuisset, et totum regnum Angliæ secundum ejus voluntatem gubernare, falso, deceptivè, et proditoriè legem Angliæ subvertens, (inter alia) idem Ricardus dictis die et anno apud London in parochia et ward' præd' &c. diversas falsas inquisitiones, et officia de intrusionibus et alienationibus, de maneriis, terris, et tenementis, diversis ligeis ipsius nuper regis inveniri procuravit et excitavit, quod ipsi maneria, terras et tenementa in inquisitionibus illis specificat' de domino rege in capite vel aliter tenerent, cum ita non fuit, ac postea cum dicti ligei dicti nuper regis ad inquisitiones illas sic fact' traversias in curia ipsius nuper regis secundum legem Angliæ tendere et allegare voluissent, iidem ligei ad traversias illas admitti non potuissent, sed se debitis et legitimis traversiis ad officia prædict' faciend' custodivit et retardavit, quousque ipsi cum dicto Ricardo diversas magnas et importabiles fines et redemptiones, tam pro commodo ipsius nuper regis, quàm pro singulari commodo ipsius Ricardi fecer', in magnam depauperationem eorundem ligeorum. Et quod prædictus Ricardus dict' die et anno in parochia et warda prædict', ac diversis vicibus antea et postea, diversos ligeos dict' nuper regis de dicto domino rege diversa maneria, terras, et tenementa per servic' milit' tenent', et mort' antecessor' suis ipsis infra ætatem existent', et in custodia dict' nuper regis ratione tenuræ suæ, cum ad ætates legitimas pervenerunt, et debitam liberationem maneriorum, terrarum, et tenementorum suorum secundum formam et legem Angliæ, ac secundum cursum cancellariæ ipsius nuper regis prosequi voluissent, ad hoc recipi non potuissent, sed ad hoc faciend' totaliter negat' et exclus' fuerunt, quousque ipsi cum prædict' Ricardo diversas magnas et importabiles fines et redemptiones, tam pro commodo ipsius regis, quam pro commodo ipsius Ricardi fecer', in magnam depauperationem eorundem ligeorum ejusdem nuper regis.* (And the conclusion of the indictment is,) *Per quod plures et diversi populi dicti nuper regis hiis gravaminibus et injustis extortionibus multipliciter torquebantur, in tantum quod populi dicti nuper regis versus ipsum regem multipliciter murmurabant, et malignabant in magnum periculum ipsius nuper regis regni sui Angliæ, ac subversionem legum et consuetudinum ejusdem regni.*

* Ambitio.

Proditoriè legem Angliæ subvertens.

Falsas inquisitiones et officia, &c.

Ad traversias admitti non potuissent.

[199]

Pro singulari commodo ipsius Ricardi.

Ad debitam liberationem admitti non potuissent.

The residue of the indictment concerning other exorbitant oppressions and grievances, are worthy to be read, but concerne not the matter in hand.

True it is, that in this indictment (*proditorie*) was used but for aggravation, and as a preparative to greater offences, for in the same yeare they were both indicted of high treason both by the common law, and act of parliament, and in the 2. yeare of H. 8. they lost both their heads. And albeit in some respects the speciall livery is for the benefit of the heyre, yet the fees and charges are so great, and the bonds and covenants, &c. so many, so intricate, and dangerous, as it were worthy to be redressed, for the ease and quiet of the fatherlesse, and widow, (being no benefit to the king, but to fill the purses of clerkes and officers) by authority of parliament; and the rather, for that speciall liveries were of ancient time, as short as the charges thereof; whereof you may reade a notable president, when wardships and liveries were in their cradles, which followeth in these words.

Quorum vestigiis qui insistunt, eorum exitum perhorrescant.

Richardus Dei gratia rex Angliæ, dux Normanniæ, Aquitaniæ, comes Andegaviæ, archiepiscopis, episcopis, abbatibus, comitibus, baronibus, justiciariis,

Vide in the history of Hoveden, pag. 444. 2 R. 1.

justiciariis, vicecomitibus, et omnibus ballivis, et fidelibus suis, ad quos præsens charta pervenerit, salutem. Sciatis nos [a] *concessisse, et præsenti charta nostra confirmasse dilecto et fideli nostro* [b] *Galfrido filio Petri, et Beatriciæ de Sayeo uxori ejus, tanquam justo et propinquiori hæredi, totam terram comitis* [c] *Willielmi de Mandevile, quæ ei jure hæreditario pertinebat, cum omnibus pertinentiis, et libertatibus, et liberis consuetudinibus suis. Quare volumus, et firmiter præcipimus quod prædicti Galfridus et Beatrix uxor sua, et hæredes eorum habeant et teneant de nobis et hæredibus nostris totam prædictam terram cum pertinentiis suis sicut prædictus comes Willielmus de Mandevile eam melius, et liberius, et honorificentius, et integrius, et quietius habuit unquam et possedit, in bosco, et plano, viis, semitis, pratis, pascuis, pasturis, aquis, vivariis, stagnis, piscariis, molendinis, turbariis, in advocationibus ecclesiarum, in custodiis valectorum, et donationibus puellarum, et in omnibus aliis locis et aliis rebus. Hiis testibus Waltero Rothomagensi archiepiscopo, Johanne Eboracensi episcopo, Rogero de Pratellis dapifero nostro, Richardo de Kanvile, Bertrano de Verduno, Radulpho filio Godfredi camerario nostro. Datum per manum magistri R. mali catuli clerici nostri, anno regni nostri secundo, xxiij. die Januarii apud Messanam.*

[a] Nota, *concessisse* is a sure word in omnem eventum, and will answer to a livery.

[b] This Geffery Fitzpeter was after chiefe justice of England.

[c] This William de Mandevile was earle of Essex.

[200]

Now are we arrived at the said act of parliament in *anno* 32 H. 8. wherein, and in the statute of 33 H. 8. besides the exposition of the severall texts, we will observe what alterations these two acts have made.

Ordaineth, maketh, establisheth, and erecteth a court, &c.] Herein three things are to be observed. 1. That this new court could not be erected without an act of parliament. 2. That when a new court is erected, it is necessary that the jurisdiction and authority of the court be certainly set downe. 3. That the court can have no other jurisdiction, then is expressed in the erection, for this new court cannot prescribe.

Pasch. 6 Ja. the bishop of Salisburies case.

Pasch. 6 Ja. the case betweene the king and the bishop of Salisbury, referred to the two chiefe justices and chiefe baron, by the lords of the honourable order of the garter, was this. King E. 4. by his letters patents in French, bearing date 10 *Octobris*, *anno* 15. of his reigne, reciting, that where there was no office of the chancelor of the garter, that there should be such an office of the chancelor of the garter, and that none should have it but the bishop of Salisbury for the time being: we will and ordaine, that Richard Beauchampe, now bishop of Salisbury, should have it for his life, and after his decease, that his successors should have it for ever. And amongst divers other points it was resolved unanimously, that this grant was void, for that a new office was erected, and it was not defined what jurisdiction or authority the officer should have, and therefore for the incertainty it was void. Which being reported to the lords, they were well satisfied therewith, and thereupon the office was granted to Sir John Herbert the kings secretary.

A court of record.] Where it is to be noted, that albeit the proceeding in this court be in English, yet it is a court of record by expresse words of the act.

And shall have also a seale, &c.] This is also necessary to a court.

That all wards, &c.] This clause extendeth as well to the counties palatines of Lancaster, Chester, and Duresme, as to any other the

the parts of the realm of England, but in feverall manners. For as to the wards within the realm of England (out of the faid counties palatines) the writ for the finding of the office, &c. iffueth out of the chancery of England, returnable in the chancery of England. And as to the wards in the counties palatines of Lancafter and Durefme, the writ likewife iffueth out of the chancery of England, but is returnable into the chancery refpectively of thefe two counties palatine, and the chancelors thereof are to tranfcript them into the court of wards.

[a] But for wards in the county palatine of Chefter, no writ iffueth out of the chancery of England, but it ought to be found by force of a writ or commiffion out of the chancery there in the exchequer, and tranfcripted by the chamberlain of that county palatine into the court of wards. [b] *Nos dum hæredes in cuftodia noftra exiftunt, indemnes et fine exhæredatione confervare tenemur.*

[c] And by this claufe of this act of 32 H. 8. the power that the lord chancelor and treafurer had for letting of wards lands, &c. is taken away.

[d] By the ftatute of 18 El. it is enacted, that all inquifitions and offices to be found before any efcheator or commiffioners, by vertue of any writ or commiffion, or otherwife within the faid county palatines of the faid duchie of Lancafter, Chefter, and Durefme, or any of them, fhall be returned by the faid efcheators or commiffioners within one month next after the taking of any fuch office or inquifition into fuch place or places, and to fuch office and offices, as heretofore they have ufually beene accuftomed to be certified and returned into, upon paine to forfeit for every default xl. li. to the ufe of our faid fovereign lady, her heirs and fucceffors. And that the clerk of the faid duchy of Lanc', the vicechamberlain of the faid earldome of Chefter, and the chancelour of the faid county palatine of the faid bifhoprick of Durefme, or other the faid officers or minifters within the faid counties palatines, or their deputy or deputies, and every of them for the time being having authority to receive any fuch office or inquifition, to whofe hands any fuch office or inquifition fhall come to, fhall certifie, or caufe to be certified under his or their hands in parchment the true tranfcript of every fuch office or inquifition taken before any of the faid efcheators or commiffioners unto the mafter of the faid court of wards and liveries, in fuch like manner, form and fort, as is limited and appointed to the clerks of the petit bag in her highneffe faid court of chancery to tranfcript the fame, upon pain to forfeit for every fuch default 5. li. to the ufe of our faid foveraigne lady, her heirs and fucceffors: which tranfcript fo to be certified fhall there remaine of record in like manner and form to all intents and purpofes, as the tranfcripts of other offices already certified into the faid court by the clerks of the petit bag in her majefties high court of chancery, are ufed: any cuftome, ftatute, act, provifo or provifoes heretofore had, made, or ufed to the contrary in any wife notwithftanding.

The ftatute of 32 H. 8. for erection of the court of wards extended only to wards: but the ftatute of 33 H. 8. annexeth to this court liveries alfo. Now in what cafes the heire fhall be in ward or fue his livery, either by the common law, or by the ftatutes, and fpecially of 32 H. 8. and 34 H. 8. &c. and of all incidents

V. Rot. parl. 9 R. 2. 13. the refolution of all the judges of Engl. what right the duke of Lancafter had to the wardfhip of Ifabel the heire of Tho. of Lathom whom Sir John Stanly had married, for the mannor of Lathom holden of him in chiefe as of his county palatine.
V. 26 H. 8. 9. b.
[a] 14 Eliz. Dier. 303.
[b] Mich. 26 E. 1. coram rege. Buck William de Laudares cafe.
[c] 8 H. 6. cap. 16. 18 H. 6. cap. 6.
[d] 18 Eliz. cap. 13.

[201]

dents to the ſame, you ſhall reade plentifull matter both in the firſt part of the Inſtitutes, cap. Eſcuage, and cap. Service de Chivalier: and alſo in the books of my Reports.

Which the kings highneſſe, &c.] Although ſucceſſors be not here named, (yet kings highneſſe) being ſpoken in his royall and politick capacity, which never dieth, doth extend to his ſucceſſors: otherwiſe this court had been diſſolved by the demiſe of H. 8.

[a] Mich. 7 E. 1. in banco. Rot. 126. Warw. Abbot of Malmſburies caſe.

[b] See 33 H. 8. cap. 22. A proviſo for the duchy of Lancaſter.

[c] 14 Eliz. Dier. 303.

[d] Mich. 14. H. 8. *Tenus per Brudnel, Brook et Fitz.* in Keylways report. And ſo was it holden Trin. 40 Eliz. by Popham, Anderſon, and Peryam, upon a caſe referred to them by the lords of the councell, between the earle of Derby and the heirs generall.

[e] See more hereof in the chapter of the court of the duchy of Lancaſter. And Pl. com. fo. 214. & 215.

[f] Pl. com. fo. 115. 116. in Townſends caſe.

[a] All the juſtices in Ireland certified, *Quod homagium tantum dat ſecundum conſuetudinem terræ Hiberniæ cuſtod' et maritag', licet ſervicium militare non debeatur.*

[b] *Intitled to have.*] That is by office to be found.

With their mannors and lands, &c.] This clauſe extendeth only to the inheritances of the ward, and not to any of his goods or chattels, debts or duties, &c. but hereof more ſhall be ſaid hereafter in his proper place,

In the order, ſurvey and governance of the ſaid court.] [c] The generall words of this act extend not into Ireland, for that is a divided and diſtinct kingdome, and hath a proper ſeale. [d] Nor to the Iſle of Man, becauſe it is no part of the realm of England, and out of the power of the chancery of England, and not to be bound by our parliament of England, but by ſpeciall name.

And that the maſter of the ſaid wards] By this clauſe the maſter only hath power to award proces.

Such proces and precepts with reaſonable pains therein limited, as be now commonly uſed in the court of the duchy chamber of Lancaſter being at Weſtm.] [e] Note, the duchy of Lancaſter was created a county palatine by act of parliament in *anno* 50 E. 3. *Adeo plene et integre ſicut comes Ceſtriæ infra eundem com' Ceſtriæ dignoſcitur obtinere.* And hereupon the court of wards is well warranted to be a court of equity, and accordingly from the erection hereof it hath proceeded.

[f] *For or concerning the title of the kings majeſty.*] This is evident.

And that the maſter of the court of wards for the time being ſhall make and appoint all and ſingular particular receivers, feodaries, and ſurveyors in every ſhire, and alſo fees for the execution of the ſame under the ſeale of the ſame office in ſuch wiſe as the ſame officers may be alwayes removeable at the diſcretion of the ſaid court.]

[202]

* See the firſt part of the Inſt. ſect. 1.

Feodarius or *feudatarius* is derived *à feodo ſeu feudo*, which in one ſenſe ſignifieth a * ſeigniory or tenure; his office conſiſteth principally in three things. 1. And principally to be ſkilfull in the knowledge of the kings tenures within his office out of records and authenticall books. 2. At the finding of offices to doe his uttermoſt indeavour to manifeſt the truth concerning the kings tenures. 3. After the office found to ſurvey the wards lands, and rate it.

See Pl. Com. fo. 295. Carils caſe.

See Mag. Cart. cap. 5. The ſtock of goods ſhall be reſtored to the heire. Glanvil, fo. 54. Fleta, li. 1. ca. 11.

Or other cauſe in any wiſe touching or concerning any thing appointed to the order of the ſaid court, for, and on the behalfe of our ſoveraigne lord the king.] By this clauſe, if the heir within age and in ward have any goods and chattels, debts, duties, or other thing due unto him, an information may be exhibited by his majeſties attorny of his wards for his majeſtie on the behalfe of the heir: for this doth touch or concern the value of the wardſhip of the body, which is appointed by this act to the order and ſurvey of this court, for the value

value of the mariage is hereby advanced. But if the heire at the death of his anceſtor be of full age, ſeeing the primer ſeaſon is certain, no ſuit can be in this court for any goods, chattels, debts, &c. belonging to the heir of full age: * for this doth not in any wiſe concern any thing appointed to the order of this court, viz. neither the wardſhip of the body, or of the lands of the heire. * Prærogativa regis, cap. 3.

Alſo be it enacted that the ſaid attorny, receiver generall, and auditors, &c.] The judges of this court are the maſter, the ſurveyor, the attorny, receiver generall, and the auditors of that court. For the words of the ſtatute of 32 H. 8. are, That the ſaid attorny, receiver generall, and auditors, ſhall diligently from time to time attend upon the ſaid maſter in the ſaid court for the hearing and ordering of matters and cauſes, &c. and the ſtatute of 33 H. 8. hath added the ſurveyour in the ſecond place in that court: and albeit *honoris cauſa*, they are to attend on the maſter, as the chief and principall officer of the ſaid court, for ſo he is ſtiled by both the ſaid ſtatutes: yet ſuch attendance is for the hearing and ordering of matters and cauſes, &c. which maketh them judges. And ſee the oath of the ſurveyour which proveth his office to be judiciall: for by the ſtatute of 33 H. 8. his oath is (*inter alia,*) That he ſhall miniſter equal juſtice to rich and poore, &c. and that he take no gift or reward for any matter depending, &c. in that court. And the like oath in effect taketh the attorny, the receiver generall and auditors, by the ſaid act of 32 H. 8. And ſo it was reſolved in auditor Curles caſe when Robert earle of Saliſbury was maſter of the wards and lord treaſurer of England. Hil. 7. Jac. li. 11. fo. 2. & 3. in auditor Curles caſe.

See the ſtatute of Lincolne 29 E. 1. Stanf. *Prær. regis*, ca. *Reſeiſer*. See a notable caſe upon that ſtatute within three years after the making thereof. Hil. 32 E. 1. *coram rege*. Northampton Jorden Twinewikes caſe.

At the parliament holden 18 *Jacobi regis* it was moved on the kings behalfe, and commended by the king to the parliament for a competent yearly rent to be aſſured to his majeſty, his heirs and ſucceſſors, that the king would aſſent that all wardſhips, primer ſeaſons, reliefs for tenures *in capite*, or by knights ſervice ſhould be diſcharged, &c. Wherein amongſt certain old parliament men theſe thirteen things did fall into conſideration for the effecting thereof.

1. That it muſt be done by act of parliament, and otherwiſe it cannot be done.

2. That all lands, tenements, rents, or hereditaments, holden of the king, to be holden by fealty only, as of ſome honour, and ſuch rent, as is now due.

3. That all lands holden of ſubjects, bodies politick or corporate, by knights ſervice to be holden by fealty, and ſuch rent as is now due; for if lands ſhould be holden of them by knights ſervice, the ſame might come to the king.

4. All ſubjects, bodies politick and corporate to be diſabled to take any lands, tenements, rents, or hereditaments of the king, his heirs, or ſucceſſors by any other tenure, then by fealty only, and yearly rent, or without rent of ſome honour. [203]

5. No ſubject, bodies politick or corporate to create by any licenſe, or any other way or means, any other tenure then by fealty

fealty and rent, or without rent upon any eſtate in fee-ſimple, fee-tayl, or otherwiſe.

6. In reſpect of the ſaid diſcharge and freedome of the ſubjects and their poſterities, and that they ſhall be alſo diſcharged thereby of fines and licenſes of alienations, reſpect of homage and reliefs: * a competent rent to be aſſured to the king, his heirs, and ſucceſſors of greater yearly value then he or any of his predeceſſors had for them all, which rent is to be inſeparably annexed to the crown, payable at the receipt only.

* First ſearch muſt be made what the king hath been anſwered for theſe, &c.

7. A convenient rent to be aſſured to the lords for every knights fee, and ſo ratably.

8. Commiſſions for the finding out of the tenures of the king, and the ſubject to be returned, &c.

9. Ideots and madmen to be in the cuſtody of ſome of their kindred, &c. and not of the king, his heirs or ſucceſſors.

10. The court of wards to be diſſolved with penſions to the preſent officers.

11. Proviſion to be made for regulating of gardien in ſocage, and that the anceſtor may appoint gardiens, &c. and that no gardien ſhall make a grant to the king.

12. Proviſion to be made that biſhops ſhall continue lords of parliament, notwithſtanding their baronies be holden in ſocage.

13. That the act ſhall be favourably interpreted for diſcharge of all wardſhips, &c.

Which motion, though it proceeded not to effect, yet we thought good to remember it, together with theſe conſiderations; * hoping that ſo good a motion tending to the honour and profit of the king and his crown for ever, and the freedom and the quiet of his ſubjects and their poſterities, will ſome time or other (by the grace of God) by authority of parliament one way or other take effect and be eſtabliſhed.

* *Spes eſt vigilantis ſomnium.* Hope is the dreame of a waking man.

And we will conclude this chapter with holy ſcripture: *Deus eſt pater orphanorum, et judex viduarum.* And again, *Deus cuſtodit advenas, pupillum, et viduam ſuſcipiet.* And laſtly, in Deuteronomy 27. 19. *Maledictus eſt qui pervertet judicium advenæ, pupilli, et viduæ.*

Pſal. 46. 9. & 67. 6.

Deut. 27. 19.

CAP. XXXVI.

The Court of the Duchy Chamber of Lancaster at Westm'.

FORASMUCH (as it hath been said) the court of wards hath some reference to this court of the duchy, we thought it fit to treat of this court of the duchy next after the said court of wards, for that it may give some light thereunto. Now for that the county of Lancaster is a county palatine, it shall be necessary to shew the beginning and erection thereof.

King Edward the 3. created John his fourth son earl of Richmond, *anno domini* 1355, he 19 *Maii anno domini* 1359 married Blanche youngest daughter of Henry duke of Lancaster (the second duke that England saw.) Duke Henry died of the plague, *anno* 35 E. 3. At the parliament holden *anno* 36 E. 3. the king in full parliament did gird his son John with a sword, and set on his head a cap of furre, and upon the same a circle of gold and pearls, and named him duke of Lancaster, and thereof gave to him, and to his heirs males of his body, and delivered him a charter.

Rot. pat. anno 29 E. 3.

Rot. par. 36 E. 3. nu. 36, 37.

Rot. pat. anno 36 E. 3.

In full parliament, *anno* 50 E. 3. the king erected the county of Lancaster a county palatine, and honoured the duke of Lancaster therewith for tearm of his life in these words.

Rot. pat. anno 50 E. 3. See the 2. pt. of the Inst. Mag. Cart. c. 31.

Edwardus Dei gratia, &c. Sciatis quod si nos debita consideratione pensantes gestus magnificos cunctorum qui nobis in guerris nostris laudabiliter et strenue servierunt, ipsos desideremus honoribus attollere, & pro viribus juxta merita præmiare, quanto magis filios nostros, quos tam in sapientia, quam in gestu nobili alios præcellere conspicimus, et qui nobis locum tenuerunt, et tenere poterunt potiorem, nos convenit majoribus honoribus et gratiis prærogare? considerantes itaque probitatem strenuam, et sapientiam præcellentem charissimi filii nostri Johannis regis Castellæ et Legionis, ducis Lancastriæ, qui laboribus et expensis semper se nobis obsequiosum exhibuit pro nobis pluries in necessitatibus intrepide se guerrarum discriminibus exponendo, et volentes eo pretextu, ac desiderantes eundem filium nostrum aliquali commodo et honore ad præsens (licet non ad plenum prout digna merita exposcunt) remunerare; ex certa scientia nostra, et læto corde [a] *de assensu prælatorum et procerum in instanti parliamento nostro apud Westm' convocat' existen':* [b] *concessimus pro nobis et hæredibus nostris præfato filio nostro quod ipse ad totam vitam suam habeat infra comitatum Lancastriæ cancellariam suam, ac brevia sua sub sigillo suo pro officio cancellarii, deputando, consignando justiciarios suos tam ad placita coronæ, quam ad quæcunque alia placita communem legem tangentia, tenenda, ac cognitiones eorundem, et quascunque executiones per brevia sua et ministros suos faciendas. Et quæcunque alia libertates et jura regalia ad comitatum palatinum pertinentia, adeo libere et integre sicut comes Cestriæ infra eundem comitatum Cestriæ dignoscitur obtinere, &c.*

32 H. 6. fo. 13. the king may make a county palatine by his letters patents without parliament.

[a] De assensu prælatorum et procerum.

12 E. 4. 16.

[b] 5 things to be observed for erecting a county palatine.

1 Cancellaria.

2 Brevia sub sigillo suo.

3 Justiciarios suos tam ad placita coronæ quam alia placita, &c.

4 Quæcunq; alia jura regalia ad com' palatinum pertinentia.

5 Adeo libere et plene prout comes Cestriæ.

See 19 H. 6. 12. 21 E. 4. 8.

[c] But it appeareth by the book of 26 E. 3. 59. b. that the said Henry duke of Lancaster had the like grant; for there in a *præcipe* the

[c] 26 E. 3. 59. b.

the tenant vouched, and that he might be ſummoned in the county of Lanc', and the vouchee challenged, becauſe in the county of Lancaſter the kings writ did not run, *ſed non allocatur*, but a writ ſent to the duke or to his lieutenant to ſummon the vouchee in the ſame manner as it ſhould be done in Cheſter. Vid. 39 E. 3. Voucher 198.

Divers have counties palatines that are not earls, as ſhall appear hereafter.

It is called *comitatus palatinus*, a county palatine, not *à comite* in reſpect of the dignity of an earl, but *à comitatu*, and *à palatio regis*, becauſe the owner thereof, be he duke or earl, &c. hath in that county *jura regalia*, as fully as the king * had in his palace, from whence all juſtice, honors, dignities, franchiſes and priviledges, as from the fountain, at the firſt flowed. Neither by this charter was the duke of Lancaſter created count palatine, but the county was made a county palatine. The power and authority of thoſe that had counties palatines was king-like, for they might pardon treaſons, murders, felonies, and outlawries thereupon. They might alſo make juſtices of eire, juſtices of aſſiſe, of gaol delivery, and of * the peace. And all originall, and judiciall writs, and all manner of indictments of treaſon and felony, and the proceſſe thereupon were made in the name of the perſons having ſuch county palatine. And in every writ and indictment within any county palatine, it was ſuppoſed to be *contra pacem* of him that had the county palatine. But theſe and ſome others are taken away from them that have ſuch counties palatines, and annexed to the crown, and all writs to be made in the kings name, but the teſte is in the name of him that hath the county palatine: and they ſhall have forfeitures of lands and goods for high treaſon, which forfeiture acreweth by the common law. But for treaſons or forfeits given after the erection of the county palatine by any act of parliament, they ſhall not have them.

* [205]

* 20 H. 7. 6. 8.

27 H. 8. cap. 24.

Paſch. 12 Eliz. Dier, 288, 289.

27 H. 8. cap. 24.

Juſtices of aſſiſe, of gaol delivery, and of the peace are and ever ſince the erection of the county palatine of Lancaſter have been made and aſſigned by commiſſion under the ſeal of the county palatine of Lancaſter.

37 H. 8. ca. 19. 36 H. 6. fo. 33. 9 H. 7. fo. 12.

In the county palatine of Lancaſter fines are levyed with three proclamations, &c. before the juſtices of aſſiſe there, or one of them, and all recoveries to be had of any lands or tenements in the county palatine are to be had in the court of that county palatine, and cannot be had at Weſtminſter.

a 22 H. 6. 48.

a In treſpaſſe in the county palatine of Lancaſter, the defendant pleaded a forain releaſe, the court prefixed a day to the parties in bank, the record muſt be removed by *certiorari* in chancery, and by *mittimus* into the bench, there to be tryed.

b 27 E. 3. 84. 21 H. 7. 33. 39 H. 6. 21, 22. 19 H. 6. 12. 32 H. 6. 25. 19 E. 3. trial 66. 45 E. 3 viſne 50. c 9 E. 3. cap. 4. 8 Aſſ. 27. 10 E. 3. 41. 19 H. 6. 12. 53. 21 E 4. 8.

b If iſſue be joyned in the kings bench, or common bench tryable in the county palatine of Lanc', it ſhall be tryed in the county of Lanc' and remaunded hither.

c Where a releaſe or other ſpeciall deed is pleaded in bar in any court at Weſtminſter, within a franchiſe where the kings writ runneth not, it ſhall be tryed where the writ is brought. See the books quoted in the margent. And in this variety of opinions I hold the law to be, that this ſtatute of 9 E. 3. extends not to

a. & b. 27 E. 3. 84. 46 E. 3. viſne 53. *Per touts les juſtices*. 10 H. 4. 40. 10 H. 6. 15, 16. Per Martyn. 8 H. 6. 3. per Strange. Lib. Int. Raſtall fol.

caſes

cafes when any other iffue is joyned tryable in the county palatine or other franchife: and I ground my opinion upon the refolution of all the judges of England in the exchequer chamber, in *anno* 32 H. 6. 25. See 39 H. 6. 21, 22. 21 H. 7. 33. 21 E. 4. 33, 34, 35, 36.

Vid. lib. Intr. fo. 81, 82. pl. 8. Henry Parayes cafe in debt, in *camera Guildhall civitatis London.*

[d] King H. 4. by his charter by authority of parliament, *anno primo* of his reign, doth fever the poffeffions of the duchy, &c. from the crown: and that which John of Gaunt held for life, is eftablifhed for ever, and [e] fpecially by the ftatutes of 1 E. 4. and 1 H. 7. hereafter mentioned: and this feparation H. 4. made, for that he knew he had the duchy of Lancafter (*par multis regnis*) by fure and indefeafible title: and he could not be both *rex* and *dux*, but fpecially that his title to the crown was not fo affured, for that after the deceafe of R. 2. the right of the crown was in the heir of Lionell duke of Clarence, fecond fon of E. 3. John of Gaunt father of H. 4. being the fourth fon: and therefore he intended not, that by the law of the crown the duchy fhould go with the crown, and that he fhould be feifed thereof in right of the crown, as the king afterwards was of the poffeffions of the duchy of York, earldome of March, and others.

[d] Rot. pat. 1 H. 4. intituled Carta regis H. 4. *De feparatione ducatus Lancaftriæ a corona authoritate parliamenti anno regni fui primo.*

[e] Rot. par. 1 E. 4. Pl. com. 219. b.

Humphrey de Bohun earl of Hereford, Effex and Northampton being the firft and laft earl of that name, and feifed of large poffeffions in England and Wales, had iffue two daughters: * Eleanor the eldeft maried to Thomas duke of Glouc', and Mary maried to the Earl of Hertford.

* Vide Rot. parl. 1 H. 6. Partition recited an. 9 H. 5. between H. 5. and the faid Eleanor.

It is enacted that all the mannors and hereditaments which defcended to H. 5. after the deceafe of the faid Mary his mother, as fon and heir unto her, fhould be diffevered from the crown of England, and annexed to the duchy of Lancafter, and to be of the fame nature, as by the kings letters patents eftablifhed by parliament there appeareth; where you may read of many franchifes and liberties belonging to the duchy.

[206]

Rot. par. anno 2 H. 5. nu. 30. 3 H. 5. nu. 15. confirmed, and that no land fhould paffe of duchy, but under the duchy feal. 2 & 3 Ph. and Mar. cap. 20.

[a] Here it is to be obferved, that albeit thefe poffeffions defcended to king H. 5. as heir to his mother, yet he was thereof feifed *in jure coronæ*, and therefore this act diffevereth them from the crown.

[a] See the 1. part Inft. fect. 8.

[b] The duchy of Lancafter as feparated, &c. is by act of parliament affured to E. 4. and his heirs kings of England. By this act all intails of the duchy, or of any land annexed thereunto are cut off, and by this made fee fimple to E. 4. and his heirs kings of England. In an act of parliament without queftion this limitation of a fee fimple is good. See the whole act.

[b] Rot. par. 1 E. 4. nu. 26. Pl. com. 222. Vid. li. 5. fo. the Princes cafe.

[c] It is enacted that H. 7. fhould have, hold, and enjoy to him and his * heirs for evermore the county palatine of Lancafter, and all honors, &c. By which act alfo all former intails are cut off, and in this ftate doth the duchy ftand at this day. [d] All lands, &c. parcell of this duchy given to the king by the ftatute of monafteries, chanteries are ftill within the furvey of the duchie. Within the county palatine of Lancafter the duke having *jura regalia*, his jurifdiction and priviledges therein were very great.

[c] Rot. par. 1 H. 7.

* Nota his heirs without faying (kings of England) as E. 4. did. 21 E. 4. 60. Vid. Dier 1 El. 168. b.

[d] 32 H. 8. cap. 20. 1 E. 6. ca. 14. 1 El. cap. 31.

The

e Rot. par. 9 R. 2. nu. 13. 28 H. 8. Brook Livery 55. Livery within the county palatine, but not of a tenure without. 26 H. 8. 9.

e The duke of Lanc' complaineth by mouth to the king, biſhops, and lords in full parliament; that where after the death of Thomas of Lathome who held the mannor of Lathome in the county of Lanc' of the ſaid duke in chevage, whereby the mannor was ſeiſed into the hands of the ſaid duke of Lancaſter according to his county palatine of Lancaſter, yet notwithſtanding John Stanley knight as in the right of Iſabell his wife daughter and heir of the ſaid Tho. had entered, and taken the profits of the ſaid mannor without any livery or other ſuit made in the chancery of the ſaid duke, for which he prayed remedy. After which, upon full advice of the juſtices of both benches, and others of the kings learned councell, it was declared in the ſaid parliament, that the entry of the ſaid John into the mannor, as aforeſaid, was unlawfull, and that the ſaid John ought to make ſuit by petition, or otherwiſe in the chancery of the ſaid duke for the livery of the ſaid mannor in ſuch caſe to be ſued for.

Vid. 33 H. 8. c. 39. 22 H. 8. c. 20. 3 E. 6. ca. 1. cuſtos rotulorum.

Of the franchiſes and liberties belonging to the county palatine of Lanc. you may read rot. par. 2 H. 5. *ubi ſupra.*

f 2 & 3 Ph. and Mar. ca. 20.

f Lands to be annexed to this duchy under the great ſeal ſhall be as good, as if it had been annexed by parliament.

See the ſtatute of 5 El. cap. 23. concerning writs of *ſignificavit*, and *excommunicato capiendo.*

21 E. 4. 60. 71. Pl. com. 219.

Lands within the county palatine ſhould paſſe by the dukes charter without livery of ſeiſon or attornment, but of lands parcell of a mannor annexed to the duchy without the county palatine, there ought to be livery of ſeiſon, and attornment of tenants, and in the ſame degree is it in the kings caſe. The reaſon hereof is, for that the county of Lanc' was a county palatine, and the duke then had *jura regalia.*

Vid. 33 H. 8. cap. 39. which ſee before in the chapter of the court of wards. See 27 H. 8. ca. 11. there alſo is a chancelor of the county palatine.

The proceeding in this court of the duchy chamber at Weſtm' is as in a court of chancery for lands, &c. within the ſurvey of that court by Engliſh bill, &c. and decree; but this chancery court is not a mixt court as the chancery of England is, partly of the common law, and partly of equity, as hath been ſaid. See before in the chapter of the Court of Chancery.

The proceſſe is by privy ſeal, attachment, &c. as in the chancery.

The officers of this court be the chancelor, the atturny, the receiver generall, clerk of the court, the auditors, ſurveyors, the meſſenger. There is an atturney of the duchy in the chancery, and another in the exchequer. There be four learned in the law aſſiſtants, and of councell with the court.

Hil. 1 E. 6. Brook Travers. 53.

‡ [207]

* *In hoc erratum eſt*, as it appeareth in Pl. com. ubi ſupra.

† It is found for the king, for he is not duke.

Hulmes caſe, Mich. 7 Jac. in curia ward. Travers de office eſtoppel per ſuer de livery.

Where by office a tenure is found of the king *ut de ducatu Lancaſtriæ*, and in truth ‡ it is not ſo, there needeth no traverſe, for the king hath the duchy * as duke and not as king, and a man ſhall not traverſe, but where it is found † for the king: *ſed aliter utitur in diebus noſtris*, as it appeareth in the caſe following.

Le roy (in droit de ſon duchie de Lanc') ſegnior, Rich. Hulme ſeiſie del mannor de Male in le countie de Lanc' tenus del roy come de ſon dit duchie per ſervice de chivalry meſne, et Robert Male (ſeiſie des terres in Male tenus del meſne come de ſon dit mannor per ſervice de chivalry) ten'. Rich. Hulme moriſt; apres que mort, anno 31 *H.* 8. *fuit trove que il moriſt ſeiſie del dit meſnaltie, et que ceo diſcend al Edmonde ſon fitz deins age, et trove le tenure avantdit, &c. et durant le temps que il fuit in ard*

gard Robert Male ten' morist: apres que mort anno 35 *H.* 8. *fuit trove per office que Robert Male morist seisie del dit tenancy peravaile, et que ceo discend alson fitz et heire deins age, et que le dit tenancie fuit tenus del roy come del dit duchy per service de chivalrie (ou in veritie ceo fuit tenus del Edmonde Hulme adonques in gard in le roy come del dit mesnaltie,) per que le roy seisist le gard del heire le ten', et puis* 4 *Jac. regis nunc apres le mort de Rich. Male que fuit lineal heire del dit Robert Male, per un auter office trove fuit que le dit Rich. morist seisie del dit tenancy, et ceo teignoit del roy come de son duchy per service de chivalry son heire deins age, sur ceo Rich. Hulme cousin et heire del dit Rich. Hulme, ad preferre un bill destre admit a son travers de cest darrein office trove in anno* 4 *Jac. Le question fuit, le quel loffice trove in* 35 H. 8. *soit ascun estoppel al dit Hulme a traverser le darrein office, ou si le dit Hulme serra chase primerment a traverser loffice de* 35 H. 8. *Et fuit object que il doit primerment travers loffice in* 35 H. 8. *come in le case de* 26 Ed. 3. fol. 65. *que si* 2. *fynes sont levy de terre in ancient demesne, le* 26 E. 3. fol. 65.
segnior de que la terre est tenus, doit aver briefe de discent a reverser le primier fine, et in ceo le 2 *fine ne serra barre. Et que le primier office estoppera cy longe come ceo remaine in force. A que fuit responde et resolve per les* 2 *chief justices, et chief baron, et le court de gards, que le trover dun office nest pas ascun estoppel, car ceo nest que enquest doffice, et le party greve avera travers a ceo come ad estre confesse, et pur ceo sans question ceo nest pas estoppel; mes quant office est trove fauxement que terre est tenus del roy per service de chivalrie in capite, ou in verity la terre est tenus del auter segnior, ou del roy mesme in socage, si le heire sua generall livery, est tenus in* 46 E. 3. 12. *per Mowbray et Persey que il navera* 46 E. 3. 12.
sute apres d'averre que la terre nest pas tenus del roy, &c. mes ceo nest forsque estoppel al heire mesme que sua la livery et ne concludera son heire: car issint dit Mowbray mesme, expresment in autiel case in 44 Ass. pl. 35. 44 Ass. pl. 35.
que estoppel per suer de livery estoppera solement mesme le heire durant son vie: et in 1 H. 4. fo. 6. b. *la le case est myse de expresse confession et* 1 H. 6. b.
suer de livery per lissue in tail sur faux office, et la est tenus que les jurors sur novel diem clausit extremum *apres le mort de tiel heire sont alarge selonque lour conscience a trover que la terre nest pas tenus, &c. car ilz sont jure* ad veritatem dicendam, *et lour trover est appel* veredictum, quasi dictum veritatis: *quel reason auxi serve quant le heire in fee simple suist livery sur faux office que les jurors apres son mort doient trover selonque le verity, issint est dit in* 33 H. 6. fo. 7. *per Laicon que si* 2 *soers sont* 33 H. 6. fol. 7. per Laicon.
trove heires, dont lun est bastard, si'z joine in sute de livery, cesti que joine ove le bastard in livery ne alledgera bastardy in l'aut', mes nul livre [208]
dit que lestoppel indurer' pluis longement que durant son vie. Et quant livery est sue per un heire, le force et effect del record de cest livery est execute et determine per son mort et pur ceo le estoppel expirer' ove le mort le heire; mes ceo est destre intend dun generall livery, car speciall livery ne concludera omnino, come appear apres. Les parols de generall livery, quant le heire est trove de pleine age, sont. Rex escaetori, &c. Scias quod cepimus homagium I. filii et hæredis B. defuncti de omnibus terris et tenementis quæ idem B. pater suus tenuit de nobis in capite die quo obiit, et ei terras et tenementa reddidimus. Et ideo tibi præcipimus, &c. eidem I. de omnibus terris et tenementis prædict', &c. plenam seisinam habere fac', &c. *Et quant le heire fuit in gard a son plein age, le briefe de livery dirra.* Rex, &c. Quia I. filius et hæres B. defuncti, qui de nobis tenuit in capite, ætatem suam coram te sufficient' probavit, &c. cepimus homagium ipsius I. de omnibus terris et tenementis quæ idem B. pater suus tenuit de nobis in capite die

die quo obiit, et ei terras et tenementa reddidimus : et ideo tibi præcipimus, ut supra. *Quel breif est le sute del heire et pur ceo coment que toutes les parols del breif sont les parols le roy (come tout les breifs le roy sont) et coment que le breif de livery est generall*, de omnibus terris et tenementis de quibus B. pater I. tenuit de nobis in capite die quo obiit, *sans direct affirmac' que ascun mannor in particuler est tenus* in capite, *et nient obstant que ceo nest forsque prosecution dun breif le roy, et nul judgment sur ceo; uncore intant que generall livery est foundue sur loffice, et per loffice fuit trove que divers terres et tenements fuer' tenus del roy* in capite, *a cest cause le suer de cest breif concluder' le heire solement que suist le livery, et apres son mort les jurors in novel breif de* diem clausit extremum *sont alarge, come est avandit, et si cesti jury trove fauxment tenure del roy, auxi le segnior de que la terre est tenus poet travers cest office, ou si terre soit tenus del roy, &c. in socage, le heire poet travers cest darrein office, car per ceo il est greve solement, et ne travers le primer office, et quant le pier suist livery et mort, le conclusion est execute et past, come est dit adevant.* Et nota *la est un speciall livery, mes ceo proceéde de grace le roy, et nest pas sute le heire, et le roy poet grante ceo ou al plein age devant* ætate probanda, &c. *ou al heire deins age, come appiert in* 21 E. 3. 40. *et ceo est generall, et ne affirm directment ascun tenure come le generall livery fist, mes ove un*, ut dicitur, *et pur ceo nest ascun estoppel sans question, et al common ley speciall livery poet over estre grant devant ascun office trove, mes ore per lestatut de* 33 H. 8. ca. 22. *est purvien*, That no person or persons having lands or tenements above the yearly value of 5 l. shall have or sue any livery before inquisition or office found before the escheator or other commissioner, *mes per un expresse clause in mesme lacte*, livery may be made of the lands and tenements comprised or not comprised in such offices. *Issint si office soit trove dascun parcell, &c. ceo suffist, et si le terre trove in loffice nexceade* 20 *l. donques le heire poet suer generall livery apres office ent trove, come est avandit; mes si la terre nexceade* 5 *l. per annum, donques generall livery poet estre sue sans office ent trove per garrant del master de gards, &c.* Vid. Dier 23 El. 377. *que le roigne*, ex debito justitiæ, *nest lye a cest jour puis le dit act de* 33 H. 8. *a graunter speciall livery, mes est a son election a graunt' speciall livery, ou a chaser le heir a un generall livery.*

21 E. 3. 40. 46 E. 3. 33. 46 Ass. p. 47 E. 3. 21. 29 Ass. p. 8. 33 H. 6. 50. 21 H. 6. 28. 37 H. 8. B. estoppell 218. 7 E. 6. ibid. 222. See 4. part. Inst. cap. Pardon. Mich. 39 & 40 El. fol. 397.

[209]

Fuit auxi resolve in cest case que loffice de 35 H. 8. *ne fuit pas traversable, car son travers demesne provera que le roy aver' cause daver gard per cause de gard, et quant le roy vient al possession per faux office ou aut' meane sur pretence dun droit, ou in veritie il nad tiel droit, uncore si appiert que le roy ad ascun auter droit ou interest a aver et tener la terre, la nul traversera cest office ou title le roy, pur ceo que le judgement in le travers est*, Ideo consideratum est quod manus domini regis à possessione amoveantur, &c. *Que ne doit estre quant appiert al court que le roy ad droit ou interest daver la terre, et ove ceo accord.* 7 H. 4. fol. 33. *in le countee de Kents case; et que apres generall livery sue per le heir de Robert Male le office ne poet estre traverse per son heir: Et issint auxi fuit resolve per lassistants del court de gards in Scurfields case in curia wardorum.* Tr. 8 Jacobi.

Which case we have rehearsed in the same language wherein we reported it when it was fresh in memory, and never hitherto was published.

What leases may be made of lands, &c. within the survey of the duchy of Lancaster; see the ordinances of the court of duchy concerning leases to be made, &c. *anno* 20 H. 6.

Mich. 6 & 7 Eliz. Dier 232. 27 H. 8. ca. 11.

See also Dier Mich. 6 & 7 Eliz. the resolution of all the judges concerning leases made by the chancelor of the duchy chamber. And

And if the leaſe either in poſſeſſion or reverſion be made under the duchy ſeal, *Quod dominus rex de adviſamento et aſſenſu concilii ducatus Lancaſtriæ dimiſit, &c.* the leaſe is good, although in truth the chancelor made it, and put to the ſeale of the duchy. For ſuch leaſes under the duchy ſeal, or under the ſeal of the county palatine of lands within the ſame, are of as great force as lands of the crown under the great ſeale.

2 Proviſoes. 2 & 3 Ph. and M. cap. 20. 37 H. 8. cap. 16.

Albeit by ſpeciall proviſion and conſtruction, to a grant of lands and tenements parcell of the duchy of Lancaſter that lye out of the county palatine, there muſt be livery of ſeiſin and attornament, as the caſe requireth, yet the grant under the ſeal of the duchy is matter of record in reſpect of the dignity of the perſon of the king, and needeth no delivery to make it a deed (as deeds between ſubjects ought to have) and if the ſame be denied, *non eſt factum* cannot be pleaded, but *nul tiel record.*

21 E. 4. fo. 60. Rot. par. 1 H. 4. nu. 81. *Vide Cartam* H. 4. *de ſeperatione ducat. Lanc. à corona authoritate parl. anno regni ſui* 1.

And if the king by his letters patents under the ſeal of the duchy doth grant a reverſion expectant upon an eſtate for life or years of lands parcell of the ſaid duchy lying out of the county palatine, the reverſion doth paſſe maintenant to the patentee by force of the letters patents: but he ſhall not have an action of waſte, or diſtraine before attornament. * For this caſe is like to the caſe of a fine between ſubjects, which is matter of record: and ſo the kings letters patents under the duchy ſeal are as high a matter of record (if not higher then a fine.) And this tendeth both to the honour of the king and the ſafety of ſuch as purchaſe ſuch reverſions of the king, that the ſtate of the reverſion ſhould paſſe by thoſe letters patents: otherwiſe if the patentee dye before attornament, the letters patents ſhould be void, and the validity of the kings grant ſhould depend upon the pleaſure of the leſſee, and many inconveniencies ſhould thereupon follow. And all this appeareth by that great and grave reſolution of the caſe of the duchy of Lancaſter reported by Mr. Plowden, that no ſtatute now in force doth ſeparate the duchy from the perſon of the king, nor to have the perſon of the king ſeparate from the duchy, nor to make the king duke of Lancaſter having regard to the poſſeſſions of the duchy, nor to alter the quality of the perſon of king H. 7. but only that the king ſhould have to him and to his heirs the ſaid duchy ſeparate from the other poſſeſſions; in which caſe the duchy at the leaſt is joyned to the perſon of H. 7. and to his heirs, and the perſon of the king remain as it did before, for nothing is ſaid to the quality of the perſon of the king, nor to the alteration of his name. And the perſon of the king ſhall not be infeebled becauſe the duchy is given to the king and his heirs, but remain alwayes of full age, as well to gifts and grants by him made, as to adminiſtration of juſtice: whereupon it was reſolved, that leaſes made by E. 6. being within age of lands, either within the county of Lancaſter or without parcell of the duchy (the royall and politick capacity of the king being not altered) were not voidable by his nonage: a juſt reſolution, and tending to the ſafety and quiet of purchaſers and farmors, and proveth directly that the royall and politick capacity of the king being not altered (as to theſe poſſeſſions) the letters patents of the king of theſe poſſeſſions under the duchy ſeale are of record: and we finde no opinion in our books, or any thing in any record, that we remember, againſt this. So as the law concerning this point is, that for grants of

Rot. parl. 3 H. 5. nu. 15. Rot. parl. 1 E. 4. nu. 26. Rot. parl. 1 H. 7. nu. 2. ſeſſ. 1. 2 & 3 Ph. and Mar. cap. 20. P. 10 H. 4. fo. 7. non omittas, &c. per prerogat. Rot. parl. 2 H. 5. nu. 30. 23 H. 6. nu. 17. 12 E. 4. nu. 7, 8. Dier Mic. 6 & 7 Eliz. ubi ſupra. * Lit. ſect. 580. 1 part of the Inſt. fo. 320. Plowd. Com. 221. b. Vide Rot. parl. 1 H. 4. nu. 81. accord.

[210]

of reversions by letters patents under the kings seal of the duchy of Lancaster, there must be attornament for lands out of the county palatine to make a privity, as in case of a fine for the action of waste or distresse: but of lands within the county palatine, the reversions passe by letters patents under the seal of the county palatine, both for the estate and for the privity of the action and of the distresse: and yet the seal is as high a matter of record in the one case as in the other. And herewith agreeth the continual practise in the court of the duchy of Lancaster. For if a reversion be granted under the duchy seal in fee or in tayl, &c. of the lands of this duchy expectant upon a lease for years, life, &c. a writ in English is usually granted in the kings name under the duchy seal reciting the grant, and commanding the particular tenant to attorn: or if it be of a mannor in possession, a writ likewise in English is usually granted commanding the tenants generally to attorn.

Vide 27 H. 8. cap. 11. for the severall seales. 23 H. 8. cap. 3. Com. of sewers under the seal of the duchy, and they be commissioners of record.

The seal of the duchy of Lancaster remains with the chancelor at Westm. And the seal of the county palatine remains always in a chest in the county palatine under the safe custody of the keeper thereof. All grants and leases of lands, tenements, offices, &c. in the county palatine of Lancaster shall passe under that seal and no other: and all grants and leases of lands, tenements, offices, &c. out of the county palatine and within the survey of the duchy, shall passe under the seal of the duchy, and no other: otherwise such grants and leases shall be void by the apparent intention of the act.

27 H. 8. cap. 16.

Dier ubi supra.

See also pl. com. 222. notable matter concerning leases made of lands within the survey of this court, the king being within age, &c. resolved and decreed to be good.

Pl. com. 222.

This county palatine was the youngest brother, and yet best beloved of all other, for it had more honors, mannors, and lands annexed unto it, then any of the rest, by the house of Lancaster, and by H. 8. and queen Mary, albeit they were descended also of the house of York, viz. from Eliz. the eldest daughter of E. 4.

* For the great roialties, franchises, liberties, priviledges, immunities, quietances, and freedomes, which the duke of Lancaster had for him and his men and tenants, see rot. parl. *die Lunæ post octab. Sancti Martini an.* 2 H. 5. all which are established, ratified and confirmed by authority of parliament, necessary to be known by such as have any of these possessions.

* Roialties, franchises, liberties, &c. Rot. parl. 2 H. 5. nu. 30. not in print, and established and confirmed Rot. parliam. anno 3 H. 5. nu. 15.

CAP.

CAP. XXXVII.

Of the County Palatine of Chester.

SEEING the erection of the county palatine of Lancaster hath reference to the county palatine of Chester, we have thought good to entreat of it in this place, for that one giveth light to the other.

13 E. 3. Vouch. 18. 49 E. 3. 9. 19 H. 6. 12. 36 H. 6. 33, 34. 12 E. 4. 16.

[a] We have spoken of the county of Lancaster raised to a county palatine by act of parliament. We shall now speak of a county palatine created by prescription.

[a] A man may have a county palatine by prescription. 2 E. 4. 17, 18. 22. 12 E. 4. 16. 21 R. 2. ca. 9. Regist. 17. a.

[b] We find that Hugh Lupus sonne of the viscount of Averenches in Normandy by his wife William the Conquerours sister was the first hereditary earle of England created by his uncle the Conquerour earl of Chester, and in the stile of a conquerour, *Totumq; hunc comitatum tenendum sibi et* * *heredibus ita libere ad gladium, sicut ipse rex tenebat Angliam ad coronam, dedit.* † To this earldome is annexed the county of Flint in Wales.

[b] This Lupus did bear azur a head of a woolf erased, argent.

* In Feesimple.

† 21 R. 2. cap. 9.

This is the most ancient and most honourable county palatine remaining in England at this day, * with which dignity the kings eldest sonne hath been of long time honoured.

* 21 R. 2. cap. 9. 17 E. 4. ca. 1.

By this general grant this Hugh earl of Chester had *jura regalia* within the county, and consequently had *comitatum palatinum* without any expresse words thereof, and by force thereof he created eight Cheshire barons, which was the first visible mark of a county palatine. That is to say, Robert Fitz-Hugh baron of Malpas, Richard de Vernon baron of Scibbroke, William Walbank baron of Nantwich, William the son of Nigil baron of Halton, Hamond de Masly baron of Dunham, Gislebert de Venables baron of Kinderton, Hugh the sonne of Norman baron of Hawardyn, and N. baron of Stockport. By the said generall grant he had not the patronage and tenure of the bishoprick of Chester, for thus I reade in the Book of Domesday made in the time of this Hugh earl of Chester. *Cestreshire. Tenet episcopus ejusdem civitatis de rege, quod ad suum pertinet episcopatum; totam reliquam terram comitatus tenet Hugo comes de rege.*

These barons had within their severall courts conusans *de omnibus placitis et querelis in curia comitis motis, exceptis placitis ad gladium ejus pertinentibus,* which you may see at large, Rot. Inspex. Pat. an. 18 H. 6. parte 2. m. 34.

[c] Britton saith, *Voilons nous que justices errant soient assignes de les chapters oier et terminer en chescun countye, et en chescun franchise de 7 ans en 7 ans, et autiel poer voilons que nous* [d] *chief justices de Ireland et Cestre eyent.*

[c] Brit. f. 1. b. 27 H. 8. cap. 5.

[d] Chief Justice de Chester.

[e] Within this county palatine, and the county of the city of Chester, there is, and anciently hath been a principall officer called the [f] chamberlain of Chester, who hath, and time out of minde hath had the jurisdiction of a chancelour; and that the [g] court of exchequer at Chester is and time out of mind of man hath been the [h] chancery court for the said county palatine, whereof the chamberlain of Chester is judge in equity. He is also judge of matters [i] at the common law within the said county, as in the court of

[e] 27 H. 8. c. 5.

[f] Chamberlain of Chester.

[g] Court of eschequer.

[h] Chancery court.

[i] At the common law.

k A mixt court.

l Vice chamberlain.

m The justice of Chester.

of Chancery at Westm; for this court of chancery is a [k] mixt court.

There is also a [l] vice-chamberlain, which is the deputy of the chamberlain. And there is within the same a justice called [m] the justice of Chester, who hath jurisdiction to hear and determine matters of the crown, and of common pleas. Of fines and recoveries levied and suffered as well within the county palatine of Chester as of the city of Chester. See the statutes of 2 E. 6. ca. 28. & 43 Eliz. cap. 15. But of these and other matters concerning this county palatine we have thought good to set down the resolution of four reverend judges (whom we knew) upon view of records and evidences, and mature deliberation thereupon in writing, in these words.

[212]

Sir James Dier, Weston. Harpur. Carns. 10 Febr. 11 reginæ Elizab.

The opinion of Sir James Dier knight, chiefe justice of the common pleas at Westminster, Richard Weston and Richard Harpur esquires, two other justices of the same common pleas, and of Thomas Carns esquire one of the justices of the pleas to be holden before the queens majesty, declared and presented to her highnesse the 10 day of February *anno dom.* 1568. by vertue of her majesties letters to us directed the second day of the same month concerning the jurisdiction and liberties of the county palatine of Chester, and the authority of the chamberlain, and his office there: and concerning the controversie between the lord president and councell in Wales, and the said chamberlains office lately grown upon Thomas Radfords case exhibited unto us: as ensueth.

a King H. 7. made it a county of it selfe. Camden. 459. a.

* By prescription.

First, by that which we have seen and considered, the county of Chester (wherein [a] the city of Chester is now, and by a good time past hath been a county of it self) of * very ancient time before the reign of king H. 3. hath been, and yet is a county palatine, with other members thereunto belonging: and so from time to time hath been received and allowed in the law. And therefore the lawes, rightfull usages, and customes of the said county palatine are to be preserved and maintained.

The chamberlain of Chester.

It further evidently appeareth, that by the like time of antiquity and continuance, there hath been and yet is in the said county palatine one principall or head officer called the chamberlain of Chester, who hath, and ever had all jurisdictions belonging to the office of a chancelour within the said county palatine.

The justice of Chester.

And that there is also within the said county palatine a justice for matters of the common pleas, and the pleas of the crown, to be heard and determined within the said county palatine, commonly called the justice of Chester.

We also see that all pleas of lands or tenements and all other contracts, causes, and matters rising and growing within the same county palatine are pleadable, and ought to be pleaded, heard, and judicially determined within the said county palatine, and not else where out of the said county palatine. And if any be pleaded, heard, or judged out of the said county palatine, the same is void, and *coram non judice*, except it bee in case of error, foreign plea, or foreign voucher.

Error, forein plea and forein voucher.

We also see that no inhabitant of the same county palatine by the liberties, lawes, and usages of the said county palatine ought to be be called or compelled by any writ or proces to appear or answer any matter or cause out of the same county palatine for any the causes aforesaid, but only in causes of treason and error. And the queens writ doth not come, nor ought to be allowed or used within the said county palatine, but under the seal of the said county palatine, except writs of proclamation by the statute of E. 6. *anno regni sui primo.* Treason and error. Seal of the county palatine.

It doth further appear unto us by good matter of record to us shewed, that the court of the exchequer at Chester is, and by the time of antiquity and continuance aforesaid hath been used as the chancery court for the same county palatine, and that the chamberlaine of Chester is the chief officer and judge of that court, and that he is, and time out of mind hath been a conservator of the peace by vertue of the same office, and hath like power, authority, preheminence, jurisdiction, execution of law, and all other customes, commodities, and advantages pertaining to the jurisdiction of a chancelour within the said county palatine of Chester, as the chancelor of the duchy of Lancaster hath used, had and ought to have used and executed within the said county palatine of Lancaster: which more evidently appeareth also by the understanding of the first grant made by king E. 3. to John his sonne then duke of Lancaster, whereby he made the same county palatine of Lancaster, referring the said duke to have his chancelor, liberties, and regall jurisdiction to a county palatine belonging, *adeò libere et integre, sicut comes Cestriæ infra eundem comitatum Cestriæ dignoscitur obtinere.* Court of the exchequer is the chancery court. Chamberlaine judge of that court. A conservator of the peace. See the grant before.

Also it appeareth unto us that the vicechamberlain did lawfully and orderly commit to prison Thomas Radford named in the case presented unto us, for that he refused to put in sureties of the peace within the said exchequer upon affidavit made in that behalf. And that the proceedings of the counsell of the marches touching the enlargement of the said Radford from the said imprisonment, and also their further order and dealing against the said vicechamberlain was, and is without sufficient authority, and contrary to the jurisdiction of the office of the said chamberlain, and the ancient laws and liberties of the same county palatine. Vice-chamberlaine. [213] Councell' of the marches.

And we doe also affirm that the statute of 34 and 35 H. 8. called the ordinances of Wales, whereby the authority of the lord president and councell within the dominion and principality of Wales and marches of the same is established, and hath the force of a law, for or concerning the determination of causes and matters of the same, comprehendeth not the counties of Chester, and the city of Chester, because the same counties of Chester and the city of Chester be no part nor parcel of the said dominion or principality of Wales, or of the marches of the same. The president and councel of Wales and the marches of the same. The counties of Chester, and the city of Chester no part of the marches of Wales.

Between Sir John Egerton plaintif, and William earl of Derby chamberlain of Chester and others defendants, for the trust of an interest of a tearm in lands in the county of Chester, these points were resolved by the lord chancelour and by the chief justice of England, justice Dodderidge, and justice Winche, whom the lord chancelor called to be his assistants as followeth. Hil. 11 Jac. in the chancery.

First, that the chamberlain of Chester being sole judge in equity, or his deputy, cannot decree any cause wherein he himself is Vid. in the charter of Durham, anno 30 E. 1. Coram rege.

is party, for he cannot be *judex in propria causa*, but in that case he may complain in the chancery of England.

21 H. 3. bre. 881.

Vide 21 H 3. *breve* 881. *in rationabili parte versus comitem Cestriæ de hæreditate D. quondam comit' Cestriæ. Comes dicit quod noluit respondere de terra in com' Cestriæ ubi brevia domini regis non currunt extra libertates suas nisi cur' consider', et consideratum fuit per curiam quod respondeat.*

18 Ass. 382. 13 E. 3. tit. jurisd. 5 E. 3. 30. 38 H. 6. 6. 7 H. 6. 37. 8 E. 4. 8. 11 H. 4. 27. &c.

2. If the defendant dwell out of the county palatine, if any of the county palatine have cause to complain against them for matter of equity for lands or goods within the county palatine, the plaintif may complain in the chancery of England, because he hath no means to bring them to answer, and the court of equity can bind but the person, for otherwise the subject should have just cause of suit, and should not have remedy: and when particular courts fail of justice, the generall courts shall give remedy, *ne curiæ regis deficerent in justitia exhibenda.*

* See this case in the chapter of the Chancery, pa. 87.

3. It was resolved, that the king cannot make any commission to hear and determine any matter of equity, but matters of equity ought to be determined in the court of chancery, whose jurisdiction therein have had continuall allowance, and so was it resolved in * Perots case.

See in the chapt. of the County palatine of Durham.

4. Upon consideration had of the said certificate of the lord Dier, and the said other judges, it was resolved, that for things transitory though in truth they were emergent within the county palatine, yet by the generall rule of law, the plaintif may alledge these to be done in any county where he will, and the defendant cannot plead to the jurisdiction of the court, that they were done, &c. within the county palatine; but if the plaintif suppose the transitory cause of action to be in the county palatine, that may be pleaded to the jurisdiction, otherwise it is of things locall.

An office found by commission in the nature of a mandamus issuing out of the chancery at Westminster before the commissioners in *com' Cestriæ* for lands holden *in capite* in the same county, was holden void *per consilium curiæ wardorum*, for it ought to be by writ or commission out of the exchequer in the county palatine, which is the court of chancery there.

[214]

Regist fo. 17. a. 34 H. 6. 42. 6 H 4. 9. Lib. Intr. Rast. 272. Dier 15 El. 320. 321. Dier 18 El. 345, 346.

* Note these generall words extend as well to the chamberlain as to the justice by the rule of the Regist. ubi sup.

If an erroneous judgment be given before the chamberlain in the exchequer in any matter wherein he proceedeth according to the course of the common law, the writ of error shall be directed *Camerario seu ejus locum tenenti*; but if the judgment be given before the justice of Chester, then the writ is directed *Justiciario Cestriæ sive ejus locum tenenti*. And note that in a writ of error to the * county of Chester, day shall be given by so long time, that three counties may be holden before the return of the same writ in the kings bench, which is four months, by which time the justices or lieutenant within the same county may redresse the error, if they will, and this by the usages of the same county; but in a writ of error upon a fine they have no such power: and the plaintif ought to bring the writ of error to the next county after the *teste*, and there it shall be read, *coram judicatoribus ratione tenurarum suarum ibidem*; and the plaintif shall assign the error without praying processe against the tenant or defendant, but only to pray *judicatores* to examine the error, and if error be found they may advise thereon, or presently

reform

reform it, and award restitution, or by their discretion they may award processe returnable at the next county against the tenant or defendant *ad audiend' errores*, (which is reasonable and necessary to be granted) and so return their own judgment given by them or their predecessor, and then there is an end of the businesse, and the record shall remain there without removing; and by this means they shall save an hundred pound forfeiture to the king. But if they affirm the judgment which is erroneous, their affirmation and the record ought to be removed into the kings bench, if the party plaintif be grieved therewith: and if their affirmation be erroneous, although their first judgment was given by their predecessors, notwithstanding they shall forfeit the hundred pounds. And the party grieved by their affirmation or reversall ought to bring a special writ of error peremptory, which shall not be examined by them, for that all this is to be understood where error in law is assigned: for upon the writ of error first brought, if any error *in fait* be assigned, as death of one of the parties, hanging the plea, or the like, which is tryable by the country, they cannot hold plea thereof, but return the record, with the writ into the kings bench. Neither can they hold plea of a release of errors after the judgment or the like, for they are only to examine the errors of the record or processe, and all this doth notably appear in our books. But if no such usage had been, the record ought to have been removed by the writ of error into the kings bench, as it ought to be in other cases.

Egerton the queens solicitor moved in the chancery to have a *certiorari* to the county palatine of Chester for the removing of a record of assise taken in that county between Cotton and others plaintifs, and Venables and others defendants, wherein the recognitors of assise gave a false verdict, and to the intent, that a writ of attaint might be brought in the kings bench, a *certiorari* was prayed. And it was doubted, whether an attaint did lye in this case, out of the county palatine. And by the opinion of Wray and Anderson chief justices, and Manwood chief baron, upon consideration had of the statute of 23 H. 8. cap. 3. whereby it is enacted in these words, That all attaints hereafter to be taken shall be taken before the king in his bench, or afore the justices of the common place, and in no other courts; they resolved and so certified the lord chancelor that for a false verdict given in the county palatine of Chester, the attaint ought to be brought either in the kings bench or common place, and not in the county palatine of Chester, and thereupon a *certiorari* was granted for the removing of the record.

Hil. 29 Eliz.

Vid. 3 El. Dier 202. b. Bendloes 3 Eliz.

Hil. 29 Eliz. *coram rege*. The case was that queen Elizabeth by her letters patents granted the custody of the castle of Chester to John Paston, and Richard Huddlestone esquires, and the survivor of them; John Paston died, and in a *scire fac'* against Huddleston in the exchequer before the chamberlain, (Glasier then being deputy chamberlain) to repeal the said grant, &c. judgment was given against Huddleston that the patent should be adnulled and cancelled, and hereupon Huddleston brought his writ of error. And it was objected that before any writ of error ought to have been granted, Huddleston ought to have sued to the queen by petition to have a writ of error according to the book in 23 E. 3. fo. 24.

Hil. 29 El. Coram rege, Huddlestons case, in brevi de errore.

23 E. 3. fo. 24. F. N. B. fo.

But it was anſwered, that here in this caſe no inheritance was recovered by the judgment, and if Huddleſton that claimed the office * but for tearm of his life ſhould be driven to his petition, wherein great delay might be uſed, his life might end before he could obtain his writ of error, therefore the writ of error in this caſe was to be granted without any petition: and of that opinion was the whole court of the kings bench, and ſo the writ of error did ſtand.

Paſch. 9 E. 2. Coram rege Rot. 32. *Judices et ſectatores com' Ceſtriæ non conſueverunt apponere ſigilla ſua alicui recordo in præſentia juſticiariorum.*

34 H. 8. ca. 13. Before the ſtatute of 34 H. 8. neither the county palatine of Cheſter ſent knights to the parliament, nor citizens out of the city of Cheſter.

27 H. 8. ca. 5. Before the ſtatute of 27 H. 8. the lord chancellor of England appointed no juſtices of peace, juſtices of quorum or goal delivery within the county of Cheſter.

22 E. 4. Juriſd. 61. Lib. Int. Raſt. fo. Si teneatur immediate or mediate. The mannor of C. in the county of York was holden of the prince, as of the county of Cheſter, and that all pleas reall and perſonall riſing within the county, or within any parcell of land holden of the county ought to be impleaded within the ſaid county palatine: for the king by his letters patents may ordain a court at York, or in any other county which ſhall have juriſdiction through the whole realm, and ſo it was reſolved.

Lit. Pat. 6. Apr. 21 H. 7. The city of Cheſter was made a county of itſelf by king H. 7. by letters patents, dat. 6 *Aprilis* 21 of his reign.

5 El. cap. 23. 18 El. cap. 8. See the ſtatute of 5 El. cap. 23. concerning writs of *ſignificavit* and *excom' capiend'*. See the ſtatute of 18 El. cap. 8. making of more juſtices then one.

8 H. 6. cap. 10. Vide cap. 13. By the ſtatute of 8 H. 6. cap. 10. it is provided, That upon every indictment or appeal by which any perſon dwelling in any other county then there where ſuch indictment or appeal is, or ſhall be taken of treaſon, felony, and treſpaſſe, &c. before any exigent awarded, &c. that after the firſt writ of *capias*, another writ of *capias* ſhall be awarded directed to the ſherif of the county whereof he is or was ſuppoſed to be converſant in the indictment, &c. otherwiſe the outlawry to be void.

19 H. 6. 1, 2. In an appeal in the kings bench in the county of Dorſet where the appellee was demurrant at Cheſter, proceſſe continued untill he was outlawed without any *capias* into Cheſter, and it was objected that the *capias* could not iſſue into Cheſhire, for it is a franchiſe into which the kings writ runneth not. Holden at the common law for certain things a writ ſhall iſſue to the franchiſe of Cheſter as for treaſon, and the ſtatute is made by authority of parliament, and is generall as well within franchiſe as without, and therefore the act being generall ſhall be taken generally to extend into Cheſter, *quod conceditur*, but this is a leading caſe.

Vid. lib. Int. Coke, fo. 230, 231, 232, & 296, 297. See an act of parliament. Rot. par. 9 H. 4. nu. 45. touching adjornment in pleas.

CAP.

CAP. XXXVIII.

Of the County Palatine of Durham

THIS is alſo a county palatine by preſcription parcell of the biſhoprick of Durham, which was firſt raiſed, as it is ſaid, ſoon after the time of William the Conqueror.

Yet I find that this county palatine hath been queſtioned (but with evil ſucceſſe.) For at the parliament holden *anno* 11 H. 6. Thomas biſhop of Durham prayed a commiſſion under the great ſeal to certain there named, who by vertue thereof ſat and inquired at Hartlepole being within his county palatine of the rights of the county palatine with all the dependents. Whereupon Sir William Eure knight the kings atturny made divers objections, that the biſhop ought to have no county palatine, neither liberties royall. On the contrary part the biſhop produceth his proofs, and the matter on both parts ſeriouſly debated. In the end judgment was given in parliament for the biſhop, and that the ſaid inquiſitions returned in the chancery or elſewhere ſhould be void. See the record being very long, and yet worthy the reading.

10 E. 3. 41. 12 E. 3. Vouchee 115. 17 E. 3. 36. 5 R. 2. Triall 54. 13 H. 4. Vouchee 39. 11 H. 4. 40. 18 H. 6. 33, 34. 19 H. 6. 12. 52. 21 E. 4. 8. 1 Mar. ſtat. 2. ca. 2. Rot. par. 11 H. 6. nu. 23. See Rot. parl. Paſch. 21 E. 1. rot. 5. a notable record for the liberties of the biſhop of Duresme.

When the biſhop himſelf, that ought to doe juſtice and right to others, will doe injury and wrong within his county palatine, and that he cannot be a judge in his own cauſe: ſee a notable record intituled thus. *Recordum coram domino rege porrectum per manus Willielmi de Bereford et Rogeri de Heigham juſticiar' domini regis ad querelas infra libertatem epiſcopatus Dunelm' audiend' et terminand' aſſignat' in hæc verba.*

Placita apud Dunelm' coram Willielmo de Bereford et Rogero de Heigham juſticiariis domini regis ad veteres querelas Ricardi prioris Dunelm' et aliorum hominum epiſcopatus ejuſdem domini regis prius porrectas et non determinatas audiend' et terminand' aſſignat'. Paſch. 30 E. 1.

Ricardus de Hoton prior Dunelm' queritur de * *Anthonio epiſcopo Dunelm'*, &c. The record is long, but therein you ſhall obſerve ſeverall plaints of the prior againſt the biſhop, whereupon iſſues are joyned, and verdicts given againſt the biſhop, and judgments given worthy the reading. By which record it appeareth that the biſhop had within the county of Dureſme *regalitatem ſuam.*

Northumb. Dunelm.

* This was Anthony Beak, of that ſtate and greatneſſe as never any biſhop was, Woolſey except.

I find alſo another record in the ſame kings time, viz.

Placita coram domino rege apud Weſtm' de termino Sancti Michaelis anno regno regis E. filii regis Henrici 33. *finiente*, 34 *ro.* 32.

Mich. 34 E. 1. Coram rege Rot. 32.

Dominus rex mandavit breve ſuum epiſcopo Dunelm' in hæc verba. Edwardus dei gratia rex Angliæ, dominus Hiberniæ, et dux Aquitaniæ venerabili in Chriſto patri A. eadem gratia epiſcopo Dunelm' ſalutem. Cum Odeliva filia Ricardi de Hurcheworth, Matild' de Swyneburne, et Ricardus Bouche, et Agnes uxor ejus arraniaverunt quandam aſſiſam mortis anteceſſoris infra libertatem veſtram epiſcopatus prædict' * *coram Lamberto de Tykingham, Guyehardo de Charroun, et Petro de Thoreſby per*

* Juſtices of the biſhop. Per breve veſtrum.

per breve vestrum versus Galfridum fil' Johannis le Maschun de Herterpole de uno mesuagio, sex toftis et una carucata terræ cum pertin' in Hurcheworth Brian. Ac prædictus Galfridus Johannem le Maschun de Herterpole intrinsecum versus prædict' Odelivam, Matildam, Ricardum

[217] *et Agnet' inde vocaverit ad warrant'. Et idem Johannes ten' prædict' eidem Galfrido warrantizans Simon' filium Simon' de Mora intrinsecum versus eosdem Odelivam, Matild', Ricardum et Agnet' ulterius inde vocaverit ad warran'. Ac idem Simon' eadem ten' eidem Johanni warrantizans inde vocaverit ad warran' versus eosdem Odelivam, Matild', Ricardum et Agn' per auxilium cur' nostræ Aymerum de Rocheford et Julianam uxorem ejus, Johannem Swayne, et Aviciam uxorem ejus, et*

Forein voucher. *Thom' de Fishborn juniorem forinsecos, qui terras aut tenementa infra libertatem prædictam aut alibi infra districtionem vestram non habent, per quæ per ballivos vestros libertatis prædict' ad warran' illam faciend' distringi possunt, ut accepimus. Nos attendentes expediens esse et necesse quod nos super recordo et processu assisæ prædictæ plenius certioremur, ut partibus prædictis, quod justum fuerit in hac parte ulterius fieri faciamus. Vobis mandamus quod inspectis recordo et processu prædict' si vobis*

Si vobis constiterit ita esse. *constiterit ita esse, tunc recordum et processum assisæ prædictæ cum omnibus ea tangentibus nobis sub sigillo vestro distincte et aperte mittatis et hoc breve, ita quod ea habeamus à die Sancti Michaelis in* 15 *dies ubicunque, &c. partibus eundem diem præfigentes quod sint ibi statur' et receptur' quod curia nostra consideraverit in hac parte, ut nos finito placito warran' prædict' in curia nostra record' et proces' totius negotii memorati vobis remittamus ad procedend' in eodem secundum legem et consuetudinem libertatis prædict'. T. me ipso apud Wynelingfeld* 13 *die Julii anno regni nostri* 33. *Virtute cujus brevis prædictus episcopus misit recordum et processum in hæc verba. Placita de assisis apud Dunelm' coram Guyehardo de Charroun et Petro de Thoresby justiciar' assignat', associat' sibi L. de Trikingham die Martis proxim' post clausum Pasch. anno regni regis E.* 33. *et promot' domini A. Dunelm' episcopi* 22.

Dunelm. Pater Odelivæ avus Matildæ. *Assis' venit recognitur' si Ricardus de Hurcheworth pater Odelivæ fil' Ricardi de Hurcheworth et avus Matildæ de Swyneshurne, et Agn' uxor' Ricardi Bouche fuit seisitus in dominico suo ut de feodo de uno mesuagio, sex toftis et una carucata terræ cum pertin' in Hurcheworth Brian die quo, &c. Et si, &c. quæ Galfridus fil' Johannis le Maschun de Herterpole. Et sciendum quod tertia pars prædict' tenement' excipit' eo quod prædict' Odeliva alias comparuit in curia, et modo non sequitur pro parte sua, &c. Et Galfridus alias venit et dixit quod ipse tenet prædicta tenementa ad terminum vitæ suæ ex dimissione Johannis de Maschun de Herterpole et in forma prædicta vocavit ipsum Johannem ad warran' Simon' fil' et hæredem Simonis de Mora, qui modo venit per sum' et ei warrantiz'. Et vocat ulterius inde ad warran' per auxilium cur' hic et cur' domini regis Aymerum de Rocheford et Julianam uxorem ejus filiam et unam hæredum Nicholai de Swynburne, Johannem Swayne et Aviciam uxorem ejus filiam et alterum hæredem prædicti Nicholai, et Thomam de Fishburne filium Christianæ cohæred' prædict' Julianæ et Aviciæ sum' in com' Northumb. Et quia curia ista jurisdictionem in prædict' Aymero et aliis warrant', &c. qui exec' datus est dies partibus hic die Martis proxim' post festum Sancti Jacobi apostoli. Et dictum est prædicto Simoni quod sequatur versus warrant' suos per auxilium cur' domini, prout sibi viderit expedire, &c. Postea ad diem illum ven' tam prædict' Matilda, Ricardus et Agn', quam prædict' Simon, et iidem Matild' et alii petentes petunt quod procedat ad*

assisam

assisam capiend' per defaltam prædict' Simonis ex quo quod nondum secutus fuit versus warrantos, &c. Et super hoc idem Simon profert breve domini regis huc de mittendo recordum et processum assisæ prædictæ eidem domino regi à die Sancti Michaelis in quindecem dies ubicunque, &c. quæ quidem recordum et processus, et etiam breve domini regis prædict' quod habuit record' consut' per prædict' Matild', Ricardum et Agnet' domino regi mittitur juxta tenorem brevis sui prædict'. Et idem dies præfixus est partibus coram eodem domino rege ubicunque, &c. Et prædict' Ricardus et Agn' po: lo: suo prædict' Matild' in placito prædict', &c. Ad quem diem coram ipso domino rege venerunt partes, et quia constat per recordum prædict' quod prædict' vocati ad warran' sunt extrinseci, et quod vocati sunt ad warran' per auxilium curiæ domini regis qui est superior dominus totius regni, et qui omnibus et singulis de regno suo justitiam facere tenetur, et maxime in defectu aliorum per quorum defectum idem dominus rex vocatur in auxilium; præceptum est vicecom' Northumb' quod summoneat prædict' Aymerum de Rocheford et Julianam uxorem ejus filiam et unam hæred' Nicholai de Swyneburn Johannem Swayne et Aviciam uxorem ejus fil' et alteram hæred' prædict' Nicholai, et Thom' Fishburn fil' Christianæ cohæredis prædictarum Julianæ et Aviciæ, quod sint coram rege à die Sancti Hilarii in 15. dies ubicunque, &c. ad warran', &c. Idem dies datus est petentibus et similiter prædict' Simoni tenen' per warrant' in banco, &c. Idem Simon po: lo: suo Walterum de Middleton et William de Burgham loquela prædict', &c. Et quia prædictus episcopus non misit breve originale simul cum prædict' record', et necesse est prædict' breve hic mittat'; mandatum est prædicto episcopo vel ejus locum tenenti, quod prædict' breve domino regi mittant, ita quod illud habeant ad præfatum terminum, &c. Ad quem diem præd' Simon tenens per warran' venit; et prædict' Matild' de Swynburn, Ricardus Bouche, et Agnes uxor ejus petentes non venerunt, nec, &c. Ideo prædict' Simon inde sine die. Et prædict' Matilda, Ricardus et Agn. et plegii sui de prosequend. in misericordia, &c. Nota.

In an information against Thomas bishop of Durham for a contempt in not certifying a record, he pleads that he is *comes palatinus, et dominus regalis cujusdam terræ vocat'* the bishoprick of Durham, *et habet omnia jura regalia quæ ad comitem palatinum et dominum regalem pertinent, per se, justic', et ministros suos exercenda.* Pasch. 46 E. 3. Coram rege. Rot. 42.

In this county palatine there is a court of chancery which is a mixt court both of law and equity, as the chancery at Westminster: herein it differeth from the rest, that if an erroneous judgment be given either in the chancery upon a judgment there according to the common law, or before the justices of the bishop, a writ of error shall be brought before the bishop himself, and if he give an erroneous judgment thereupon, a writ of error shall be sued returnable in the kings bench.

But now let us see what we find in our books concerning this county palatine.

In a formedon in Durham the tenant pleaded the warranty of the auncestor of the demandant, with assets in a forain county, whereupon the court awarded that the tenant should goe quit without day. And the demandant upon this judgment sued a writ of error before the bishop, and assigned for error, that the justices awarded that the tenant should goe quit without day, where they ought to have continued the plea by adjornment untill the record had been removed. And for this error the bishop reversed the judgment, and day given to the parties before his justices where the plea was pleaded. Mich. 14 F. 3. tit. error 6. F. N. B. 21. g. 8 El. Dier 250.

pleaded. At which day the tenant was essoined, and a day given over. At that day a writ came to remove the record in the common bank, and a day given to the parties in the common bank, and this proceeding of the bishop was according to the usage there. And after by the advice of the whole court a *venire fac'* issued out of the common bank to try the issue joyned at Durham.

32 E. 3. Vouch. 97. 14 H. 6. fo. 3.

If a man in the county palatine of Durham vouch a foreigner to warranty, the demandant may counterplead that the vouchee hath assets within the county palatine for the delay.

13 E. 3. Voucher 165. 45 E. 3. 17. Vid. 19 E. 3. triall 66. 19 E. 3. jurisd. 29. 33 E. 3. ib. 57. 45 E. 3. Visne 50.

In a writ of trespasse *des biens emportes deins un certeine ville*, the defendant said, that the place where the plaintife supposed the taking away, is within the franchise of the B. of Durham, where the kings writ runneth not, but is a franchise royall, *judgement de breife*. Whereunto the plaintife said, that the defendant came in by distresse, and so the court seised of the plea. Finchden giving the rule of the court said, the court is not in this case seised of the plea, but that should be where consuance or franchise is challenged, which lieth not in this case, but the bishop hath franchise royall into which the kings writ runneth not, and therefore for not denying of the exception the writ abated. Note the towne wherein the transitory trespasse was alledged by the plaintife was within the county palatine.

19 H. 6. 52.

If the tenant vouch two, one within the county palatine of Durham, and the other at the common law, summons shall be awarded to the lord of the county palatine, commanding him to summon the vouchee to be at a certain day before the justices here to try the warranty: in this case if the tenant recover in value, the justices shall write to the lord of the county palatine to render in value, *quod fuit concessum*.

Dier 12 El. 288. which was the case of James Pilkington bishop of Durham.

See Dier 12 El. where he that hath *jura regalia* shall have forfeiture of high treason, whereof *vide* before in the chap. of the County Palatine of Lanc.

* 13 H. 4. Vouch. 39. 36 H. 6. ib. 49.

* If the one be vouched, and the tenant prayeth that he may be summoned in the county of York, and the county palatine of Durham, the voucher shall stand, for if he be summoned in the county of York, it sufficeth.

[a] Prærogativa reg. cap. 1.

[a] *Dominus rex habebit custodiam omnium terrarum eorum qui de ipso tenent in capite per servicium militare, de quibus ipsi tenentes fuer' seisiti in dominico suo ut de feodo die quo obierunt de quecunque tenuerunt per hujusmodi servicium, &c. exceptis feodis episcopi Dunelm' inter Tine et Tese.*

16 E. 3. tit. Livery 29. Glanv. li. 7. c. 20. Bract l. 2. fo. 85. 9 H. 3. prær. 25. 21 H. 3. ib. 26.

1. This exception extendeth not to the body. 2. If the bishop did after this statute purchase any seigniory between Tine and Tese it extendeth not to that. 3. That before this statute, the king ought to have had the wardship of the lands, as appeareth in our books, contrary to Poles opinion in this case.

* Prær. regis ca. 3.

* The third chapter of the said statute of *prærogativa regis* doth give the king primer seison, &c. without any saving of the bishop of Duresme.

Trin. 38. El. in curia wardorum.

Sir Thomas Gray knight was seised in fee of the manner of Chillingham in the county of Northumberland holden of the queen by knights service *in capite*, and of the mannor of Rosse in the

county

county palatine of Durham holden of the bishop of Durham by knights service *in capite*, and died seised of both, his sonne and heir of full age. And although on the behalfe of the bishop some presidents were shewed in like case, yet the two chief justices Popham and Anderson *prima facie* did hold, that the primer seison of and for the mannor of Resse belonged to the king.

The town of Creke in the county of York holden of the bishop of Durham, &c. shall be impleaded within the county palatine of Durham, and in no other place: and so is the manner of Howden in the county of York. 22 E. 4. jurisd. pl. 61.

The king shall have the temporalties of the bishop of Durham, and for a church that becommeth void the king shall have a *quare impedit*. 5 R. 2. triall 94.

See the statute of 5 El. ca. 23. concerning the writs of *significavit* and *excom' capiendo*. 5 El. ca. 23.

It was holden by all the justices, that if a man be surety for another to keep the peace, and after he breaketh the peace, and the surety hath lands in the county * palatine of Durham, the king shall command the bishop of Durham or his chancelor to do execution. And so it is in the other counties palatines. In the same manner it is of a statute staple, &c. Recognizances, &c. 21 E. 3. 49. 1 E. 4. 10. Regist. 153. F. N. B. 152. *[220]

Vide 5 E. 3. fol. 58. 17 E. 3. fol. 56. rot. parl. 7 E. 6. rot. pat. 7 E. 6. part. 8. 1 Mar. cap. 3.

CAP. XXXIX.

Of the Royall Franchise of Ely.

IN divers statutes it is named the county palatine of Ely. King H. 1. in the 10 year of his reign, of the rich monastery of Ely made a cathedrall church, and of the abby made a bishoprick, and for his diocesse assigned unto him the county of Cambridge, which before was within the diocese of Linc': in recompence whereof Robert Bluet bishop of Lincoln, then chancelor of England had to him and his successors three mannors, parcell of the possessions of the abby, viz. Spaldwiche, Bicklesworth, and Bugden. And for the chapter of this new bishop, he instituted that there should be a prior and covent. But in respect of the revenues, for that their principall mannors were granted away, the number of monkes being 70 were brought down to 40. And king H. 1. granted to this new bishop and his successors *jura regalia* within the Isle of Ely. But the said prior and convent were in the reign of H. 8. suppressed, and in stead thereof a dean and prebendaries were raised to be the chapter of the bishop, and a grammar school for a master and 24 scholars. 33 H. 8. cap. 10. 5 El. cap. 23.

This royall jurisdiction the bishop hath by prescription grounded upon the said grant as well in pleas of the crown, as in common pleas before his justices.

The

Trin. 3 E. 1. Rot. 62. Coram Rogero de Scryton et sociis suis justiciariis de banc. Trin. 16 E. 1 in communi banco Rot. 89. Cant.

The liberty of the bishop of Ely hath been anciently allowed by the court of common pleas for lands in Wisbich, within the isle whereof a *præcipe quod reddat* was brought.

Again, *Allocatur libertas episcopo Eliensi pro terris infra insulam de Ely prout alias, scilicet in rotulo Martini de Littlebury et sociis suis annis* 55 & 56 H. 3. *anno* 14 *regis nunc coram Thoma de Wayland et sociis suis. Item Mich.* 16 *regis nunc*, rot. 27.

3 H. 6. triall 2.

In trespasse the defendant pleaded an arbitrament made at A. in the Isle of Ely, and thereupon issue was joyned, the plaintif shewed that Ely is a franchise royall, and they of the isle shall not be impannelled out, and prayed a *venire fac'* to the sherif of Cambridge.

Lib. Int. Rast. fo.

Issue being joyned and the visne to come out of Ely, the entry is, *Super quo prædict' (querens) dicit quod E. prædict' est infra insulam Eliens', quodque episcopus Eliens' talem habet libertatem in insula prædicta, quod nullus justiciar' nec aliquis minister domini regis insulam illam ingredi debet ad aliquod officium ibi exercend', nec liberi tenentes nec residentes in eadem insula illam ingredi debent ad aliquam juratam extra insulam illam faciend', et petit breve domini regis de venire fac' hic* 12. *de vicineto de Soham, quæ est propinquior villa in prædict' com' Cantab' extra insulam prædict' adjacen' prædict' villæ de Ely ad triandum exitum præd'. Et quia videtur justiciariis hic quod petitio illa est rationi consonans, ideo præcept' est vic' Cant' quod venire fac' hic tali die* 12. *de vicineto illo, per quos, &c.*

46 E. 3. 8.

[221]

5 E. 2. conusans 68. 21 E. 4. 35.

Sentence was given in the ecclesiasticall court in Cambridge, and the defendant was summoned at Hadington in the isle and franchise of Ely, as he might be, for where the action is intire, and not severall, whereof part is within the franchise and part without, the franchise shall not be allowed. As if one take a man in a place at the common law, and carry him into a franchise and there imprison him, this court shall hold plea, *quia magis dignum trahit ad se minus dignum, et sic de similibus.*

24 E. 3. conusans 74. 20 E. 3. ibid. 85. 49 E. 3. 24. See 23 E. 3. 22. accord.

In an action of account against one as baylif of lands in H. and A. and H. is within the franchise of the Isle of Ely, and because the plaintif might have charged the defendant as bailif of A. and it is no reason that by joyning of them in one writ to disherit the bishop of his franchise, the writ abated.

CAP.

CAP. XL.

Of the County Palatine of Pembroke.

THIS was an ancient county palatine within Wales, and the earle was *comes palatinus*, and had *jura regalia*, and all things belonging to a county palatine, but the juriſdiction hereof was taken away by the ſtatute of 27 H. 8. cap. 26. the county palatine then being in the kings hands.

Rot. parliamenti Hil. 18 E. 1. fo. 6. *Totus com' Pembroke fuit com' palatinus, et habuit cancel. et ſigillum, &c.*
27 H. 8. cap. 26.

And for further proof that it was a county palatine, ſee the charter of E. 3. to Lawrence de Haſtings in theſe words.

Carta regis E. 3. an. 13 regni ſui. 13 Octob. Ro. pat. 13 E. 3. m. 12.

Rex omnibus ad quos, &c. ſalutem. Sciatis quod circumſpectionis et elegantiæ præſagium quod ex aptis conſanguinei noſtri chariſſimi Laurentii de Haſtings juventutis auſpiciis concepimus, merito nos inducunt, ut ipſum in his que honoris ſui debitam conſervationem reſpiciunt, pronis favoribus proſequamur. Cum itaque hæreditas bonæ memoriæ Audomari de Valentia comitis Pembrochiæ (ut dicitur) jampridem ſine hærede de corpore ſuo procreato decedentis ad ſorores ſuas fuerit devoluta, inter ipſas et earum hæredes proportionabiliter dividenda: quia conſtat nobis quod præfatus Laurentius qui dict' Audomar' in partem hæreditatis ſuccedit eſt ex ipſius Audomari ſorore ſeniori deſcendens, et ſic peritorum aſſertione, quos ſuper hoc conſuluimus, ſibi debeatur prærogativa nominis; et honoris juſtum et debitum reputamus ut idem Laurentius ex ſeniori ſorore cauſam habens, aſſumat et habeat nomen comitis Pembrochiæ, quod dictus Audomarus habuit dum vivebat: quod quidem (quantum in nobis eſt) ſibi confirmamus, ratificamus, et etiam approbamus; volentes, et concedentes ut dictus Laurentius prærogativam et honorem comitis palatini in terris quas tenet de hæreditate dicti Audomari, adeo pleno, et eodem modo habeat et teneat, ſicut idem Audomarus illas habuit et tenuit tempore quo deceſſit. In cujus, &c. Teſte rege apud Montem Martini die Octob. anno regni 13.

Note here, that the eldeſt ſiſter ought to have the honor, upon conſultation with learned men.

Prærogativa et honor comitis palatini.

Sicut Audomarus illas habuit.

CAP.

CAP. XLI.

Of the Franchiſe of Hexam and Hexamſhire.

THIS was ſometime parcell of the poſſeſſions of the archbiſhop of York, and claimed by him to be a county palatine.

2 H. 5. cap. 5.
9 H. 5. cap. 7.
8 E. 4. cap. 2.
33 H. 8. cap. 10.
14 El. ca. 13.

At the parliament holden in 2 H. 5. it is reſolved that Hexamſhire was a franchiſe where the kings writ went not.

And in the ſtatute of 33 H. 8. it is named a county palatine.

But at the parliament holden in *anno* 14 Eliz. it was ſeriouſly examined, and in the end four concluſions were enacted by authority of parliament. 1. That whiles it was in the hands of the archbiſhop it was tearmed and named a county palatine, where in right or proof there was none ſuch. 2. That it is within, and parcell of the county of Northumberland. 3. That al pleas of the crown, and ſuits between party and party ſhall receive like triall, &c. as the reſt of the ſubjects of Northumberland ought to have. 4. That the ſherif and other officers of the county of Northumberland may execute his or their office, &c. within Hexam and Hexamſhire. So as whatſoever it was before 14 Eliz. it is now no county palatine, nor franchiſe royall.

CAP. XLII.

Of the Courts of the Cinque Ports.

Domeſday. Chent. Lib. Int. Raſt. fo.

AT the firſt the priviledged ports were but three. For at the making of the book of Domeſday, which was in the 14 year of the Conqueror, there are but three named in that book, viz. Dover, Sandwich, and Rumney, and that theſe three in the time of Edward the Confeſſor were exonerated of ſuch charges and burthens, as others did bear; after two ports were added to them by the Conqueror, viz. Haſtings and Hithe.

Bract. li. 3. f. 118.

Bracton who wrote in the reign of H. 3. nameth Haſtings, Romuall, Heya, * Dover, and Sandwich to be the five ports. Of this number of five were theſe ports called the Cinque Ports, as it appeareth by a writ which Bracton rehearſed in the ſame place, viz.

* Memorandum quod Pharanus de Bolonia venit ad conqueſtum tempore Willielmi regis baſtardi, et in illo conqueſtu perquiſivit wardam de Doveria in feodo, et habuit, et tenuit toto tempore prædict' regis Willielmi uſque ad tempus regis Henrici, avi regis Henrici filii regis Johannis, et dictus rex Hen. avus dedit dicto Pharano 60. libratas terræ in eſchambio pro Doveria, viz. manerium de Wendovre pro xl. libr. terræ, Kingſhull pro x. libr. terræ, et 7 hidas in Eton pro 10 li. terræ. In lib. de Abbathia Miſſ. fo. 114.

Rex Vic' Norff. et Suff. ſalutem. Sciatis quod ſommoniri fecimus ad talem diem apud Shepwey omnia placita de Quinque Portubus ſicut teneri debent,

debent, et solent coram justiciariis apud Shipwey. Et ideo tibi præcipimus quod hoc sciri facias hominibus de Jernemewe, et balivis de Donewiz, ita quod si aliquis conqueri voluerit de aliquo qui sit de libertate vel infra libertatem Quinque Portuum, tunc sit apud Shepwey coram præfatis justiciariis nostris querelam suam propositurus, et justitiam inde recepturus. Teste, &c.

After two more, viz. Winchelsey and Rye were added: for I find a record *anno 1 regis Johannis, quod Winchelsey et Rye debent esse in auxilium villæ de Hastings ad faciend' regis servicium 20 navium, &c,* In Dorf. cart. anno 1 Re. Jo. parte 2. m. 12.

And these have the same franchises and liberties that the former had; and every one of these send two burgesses by the name of barons of the Cinque Ports to the parliament, as by the records of the return of them remaining in chancery at every parliament doth appear. [223] And albeit two be added, yet they hold their former name of the Cinque Ports. These ports or havens doe lye towards France, and therefore prudent antiquity provided, that they should be vigilantly and securely kept, for performance whereof these ports have a speciall governor or keeper, called by his office lord warden or keeper of the Cinque Ports, and is also admirall, and hath the jurisdiction of the admiralty amongst them, and is exempt from the admiralty of England. This warden in former times was ever a man of great fidelity, wisdome, courage, and experience, for that he had the charge of the principall gates of the realm. 50 E. 3. 5. He is also constable of the castle of Dover, his jurisdiction as constable is limited by the statute of *Artic. super Cartas, anno* 28 E. 1. which you may read, and the exposition thereof in the second part of the Institutes. Artic. superCart. cap. 2. 2. part of the Institutes.

The franchise of the Cinque Ports hath been time out of mind partly by ancient parliaments, partly by ancient charters, &c. and confirmed by expresse name by the statute of Magna Carta, ca. 9. and were made five by William the Conqueror. 2 E. 4. 17. 17 E. 4. 16, 17. 36 H. 6. 34. Fortesc. lib. Int. Rast. fo.

For the better understanding of our books; it is to be known that there is a great diversity between the principality of Wales, the counties palatines, &c. and the Cinque Ports. For Wales was originally no part of England, but county palatines were parcell of the realm of England and divided in jurisdiction, and the Cinque Ports are parcell of the county of Kent, and yet *ubi breve domini regis non currit,* but have not *jura regalia,* and therefore regularly no writ of error did lie of a judgement in Wales, otherwise it is in the counties palatines. A judgment here of lands in Wales or in the county palatine is void, but a judgement given here of lands in the Cinque Ports is good if the priviledge be not pleaded, for they be part of the county, and the franchise may be demanded in another action. 9 H. 7. 12. 36 H. 6. 33, 34.

And it is to be observed that within the Cinque Ports there be divers courts, one before the constable of the castle of Dover, (whereof somewhat hath been said before) there be other courts within the ports themselves, before the maiors and the jurats, and another which is called *curia Quinque Portuum apud Shepwey,* whereof we shall speak hereafter.

If any of the kings courts doe write to have a record in the Cinque ports, or for doing of any thing within the same, the writ shall be directed *Constabulario castri de Dover, et gardiano Quinque Portuum,* for 33 E. 3. jurisd. 60.

he is the immediate officer to the kings courts for execution of the kings writs within the Cinque Ports. For example:

30 H. 6. 6 & 7.

If a man plead a record within the Cinque Ports, and the other plead *nul tiel record*, there ſhall goe a writ to the conſtable of Dover to certifie the record, for the courſe is for the kings courts to write to the conſtable, and he ſhall ſend to the barons, that is to the maior and jurats, to certifie him of the record which is before them, and he ſhal certifie the kings court, and ſo the conſtable is the immediate officer to the kings court.

Regiſt. fo. F. N. B. 80. b. 240. a.

Note, though books ſay that the writs ſhall be directed to the conſtable of Dover, yet the writ is to be directed *Conſtabulario caſtri de Dover, et gardiano Quinque Portuum.*

Regiſt. fo. F. N. B. 80. b. 132. 21 E. 3. 49. See 1 E. 4. 10.

Regiſt. 153.

A man hath a judgment in any of the kings courts, and the defendant hath no land or goods but in the Cinque Ports, the plaintif ſhall have a writ to the conſtable of Dover to make execution. And ſo it is if a man will have ſurety of the peace againſt any perſon within the Cinque Ports, then he ſhall have a writ out of the chancery directed to the conſtable of Dover, for the doing thereof.

* Rot. parl. anno 18 E. 1. fo. 6. nu. 115. Inter Abbatem de Feverſham et Baron' de port de Feverſham.

* *Et quia in quadam carta domini regis nunc continetur, quod omnes querelæ verſus ipſos barones Quinque Portuum apud Shepwey terminari debent coram cuſtode Quinque Portuum, præcept' eſt Stephano de Peneceſtr' nunc cuſtodi quod partibus prædictis coram eo certum diem aſſignet et fac' juſticiæ complementum.*

[224]

[a] 30 H. 6. 6 & 7. Dier 23 El. 376. Brook Cinque Ports 25. Temps H. 8. diverſity des courts.

[a] If an erroneous judgment be given in the Cinque Ports before any of the maiors or jurats, it ſhall be redreſſed before the conſtable of Dover at the court at Shepwey, which court was raiſed of ancient time by letters patents of E. 1.

[b] Hil. 18 E. 1. f. 6. Rot. par. nu. 115. Dorſ. clauſ. anno 30 E. 1. m. 13.

[b] The court of the Cinque Ports holden at Shepwey adjudged the abbot of Feverſham (which abby was within the Cinque Ports) for his offence to be impriſoned, for the which the archbiſhop of Canterbury cauſed the kings miniſters of Dover to be cited into the eccleſiaſticall court, &c. The record ſaith, *Quia ſecundum conſuetudinem regni approbatum, et ratione juris regii, miniſtri regis pro aliquibus quæ fecerunt ratione officii ſui, trahi non debeant. Rex prohibuit archiepiſcopo Cant' ne moleſtari faciat miniſtros ſuos Dovor', de eo quod abbatem de Feverſham pro delicto ſuo incarceraſſent per conſiderationem* [c] *curiæ Quinque Portuum de Shepwey*, &c. The whole record is worthy to be read over; this ſhall ſuffice for the end that I aim at.

[c] *Curia Quinque Portuum de Shepwey.* Nota, this for the ſtile of the court.

See Bract. lib. 3. Ubi ſupra.

Vide Fleta lib. 2. cap. 48. the Huſtings *apud* Shepweye.

[d] 50 E. 3. 5. 33 E. 3. tit. Juriſd. 60.

[d] The juriſdiction of the Cinque Ports is generall, and extends as well to perſonall actions, as to actions reall and mixt, or which touch the freehold, but ſo it is not in ancient demeſne, for regularly that juriſdiction extends not to perſonall actions.

1 E. 3. fo. 2. 49 E. 3. 24. 11 R. 2. bre. 636. 46 E. 3. 8. 33 H. 6. 4. 8 H. 4. 7.

If a *precipe* be brought of land, part within the Cinque Ports, and part without, the whole writ ſhall abate: *et ſic de ſimilibus.*

* 39 E. 3. 17. 30 Aſſ. pt. 1. 38 E. 3. 27.

* And there is a diverſity between a franchiſe to demand conuſans, and a franchiſe, *ubi breve domini regis non currit*: for in the firſt caſe the tenant or defendant ſhall not plead it, but the lord of the franchiſe muſt demand conuſans, but in the other caſe the defendant may plead it to the writ.

[e] 49 E. 3. 24.

[e] The mannor of P. within the Cinque Ports was holden of the king as of the honour of Egle, and eſcheated to the king for want of heir,

heir, the king granteth the mannor of P. to another. And it is adjudged that the seison of the king in this case doth not make it of another nature than it was afore: for the priviledge runneth with the land.

CAP. XLIII.

The Court of the Escheator, and of Commissioners for finding of Offices, &c.

THE gift of the office of escheator belongeth to the office of the lord treasurer, who granteth the same by his deed. He is to continue in his office but one year, or once in three yeares.

14 E. 3. cap. 8. 1 H. 8. cap. 8. 3 H. 8. cap. 2.

For the derivation of his name, his antiquity, and some part of this office, see the first part of the Institutes, sect. 4. where the ancient authors, and many authorities be quoted: he ought to be seised of 40. marks land, except escheators in cities and counties palatine.

All writs originall of *diem clausit extremum, mandamus, devenerunt, melius inquirend', quae plura, &c.* are directed to him to finde an office for the king after the death of his tenant, which held by knights service *in capite*, or otherwise by knights service.

This officer in case of escheats for treason, felony, or in case of wardship, or primer season, may find an office *virtute officii*. But in case of wardship, or primer seison, if he finde an office *virtute officii*, if the land, &c. be of the yearly value of 5. li. (or above) he shall lose every time he shall sit 5. pounds.

3 H. 8. cap. 2.

Offices found before him *virtute officii*, he may returne either into the court of chancery, or into the exchequer, saving at this day for wardships, or primer seison, which he must return into the chancery: for by the statute of 32 H. 8. cap. 46. the court of exchequer is barred to deale with the same. And offices found before him *virtute brevis*, are to be returned by him into the chancery.

Lib. 1. fo. 42. b. Alton woods. 4 4. 24. Stanf. prer. 70 b.

If he sit by force of a writ, he ought to take the inquest within a moneth next after the delivery of the writ, and he ought to returne the same within a moneth after he taketh it either by writ, or *virtute officii*.

3 H. 8. cap. 2. 8 H. 6. 16. 18 H. 6. 7.

See *capit' eschaetriae*, whereof the escheator may inquire: and the statute *de eschaetoribus, anno* 29 E. 1. Vide Dier. 248. 249. [a] He is accountable *pro catallis felonum, fugitivorum, et hujusmodi.* [b] All offices found before him, or commissioners ought to be found by the oathes of twelve men, every juror to have lands, &c. to the yearly value of 40 s. in the same county, [c] and indented, and one part by them sealed, and by him the other part, which is to remain with the foreman of the jury, and to be taken in good townes, and open places. For secret offices are abhorred in law, full of vexation and charge, and never have good successe.

Mag. Cart. 1 part. fo. 160, 161. [a] Keylw. 6 H. 8. 17[illegible] [b] 1 H. 8. cap. 8. 3 H. 8. cap. 2. [c] 34 E. 3. cap. 13. 36 E. 3. cap. 13. otherwise void. 8 H. 6. cap. 16. 18 H. 6. cap. 7.

Neither he nor the commissioners can take any enquest of in-

 quiry

quiry of any other perſons, but ſuch as be impanelled and returned by the ſherife.

1 H. 8. cap. 8. 3 H. 8. cap. 2. If he or the commiſſioners ſhall deny any perſon to give evidence openly in his preſence to ſuch enqueſts as ſhall be taken before him for the finding of an office, he ſhall forfeit 40 li. If he, or the commiſſioners, or any of them ſhall refuſe to take a verdict of the enqueſt offering to preſent the ſame, he ſhall loſe 100 li. to the party grieved.

24 E. 3. 55. An office found before commiſſioners is as forcible in law as if it had been found before the eſcheator.

See the 2. part of the Inſtitutes, W. 2. cap. 26. 23 H. 6. cap. 17. 1 H. 8. cap. 8. *[226] The eſcheator ought to take no fee by the ſtatute of W. 1. but of the king onely, but if he find an office by force of any writ, and according to the ſame for the king, hee ſhall have a fee of 40 s. by the ſtatute of 23 H. 6. but if it be found * before him by writ, or *ex officio*, that the lands are holden of a ſubject, or if he find an office for the king *virtute officii*, there is no fee due to him. But the commiſſioners ought to take no fee at all, though an office be found for the king, becauſe they are not within the ſtatute.

[a] 33 H. 8. cap. 22. [b] 32 H. 8. cap. 46. [c] 5 E. 3. cap. 9. 12 E. 4. cap. 9. F. N. B. 100. c. 9 H. 6. fo. 60. [a] The eſcheator finding an office for the king by force of any writ, not exceeding the value of 5 li. ſhall not take above 15 s. and the commiſſioners can take nothing: [b] but the maſter of the wards may allow commiſſioners, counſellours, and feodaries their coſts. [c] The eſcheator may make deputies, but ſuch able men, for whom he will anſwer, and that have ſufficient lands in the ſame county, &c. and the eſcheator ſhall certifie the name or names of his deputy or deputies, under his letters patents into the exchequer within twenty dayes after deputation made. And no deputy ſhall take upon him to occupy that office, except the eſcheator hath lands to the value of 20. li. [d] And if any ſub-eſcheator be made, not having ſufficient, he may be removed by the kings writ directed to the eſcheator *de ſubeſchaetore amovendo*.

[d] 5 E. 3. cap. 4. Regiſter, 177.

[e] 21 E. 4. 23. F. N. B. 100. c. 1 H. 8. cap. 8. 3 H. 8. cap. 2. 9 H. 6. fo. 60. [f] Regiſt. fo. 301. b. [e] If the eſcheator, ſubeſcheator, or commiſſioner, returne a falſe office, an action upon the caſe doth lye againſt them by the party grieved, although they be offices of record, beſides the penalty of 100 l. by the ſtatutes of 1 H. 8. and 3 H. 8. [f] The oath of the eſcheator expreſſing his duty, appeareth in the Regiſter, fo. 301. b.

[g] 10 H. 7. 7. b. [g] If I be poſſeſſed of the goods of a man outlawed in treſpaſſe, and I deliver them to the eſcheator, I am diſcharged, *quod Brian affirmavit:* for he ſaid that the eſcheator is the kings miniſter, and chargeable for the goods.

CAP. XLIV.

Courts in the Univerſities of Cambridge and Oxford.

Liberall arts and ſciences are *lumina reipublicæ.*

IT is true that each of theſe univerſities hath divers courts, juriſdictions, and powers, by the charters of the kings of this realme, divers of which were not grantable by charter, but by authority of parliament, which being eſpyed, queene Elizabeth, (who could (we ſpeake it of knowledge) not onely ſpeak the languages of French, Italian, and Spaniſh, but was learned in the Latine and Greek learned tongues, and excelled all others of her ſex in knowledge both divine and humane,) for the great love and favour that her majeſtie bare to her highneſſe univerſities, and for the great zeal and care that the lords and commons in parliament had for the maintenance of good and godly literature, and the vertuous education of youth within either of the ſaid univerſities; and to the intent that the ancient privileges, liberties and franchiſes of either of the ſaid univerſities, granted, ratified and confirmed by the queenes highneſſe, and her moſt noble progenitors, might be had in great eſtimation, and be of greater force and ſtrength, for the better increaſe of learning, and the further ſuppreſſing of vice: it was enacted by authority of parliament holden in the 13. yeare of her moſt proſperous reigne: 1. That each of the univerſities ſhould be incorporated by a certaine name (albeit they were ancient corporations before.) 2. That all letters patents of the queens highneſſe, or by any of her progenitors or predeceſſors, made to either of the ſaid corporated bodies ſeverally, or to any of their predeceſſors of either of the ſaid univerſities, by whatſoever name or names, the chancelor, maſters, and ſcholars of either of the ſaid univerſities, in any of the ſaid letters patents had beene named, ſhould be good and effectuall, and available in law, to all intents, conſtructions and purpoſes, &c. as amply, fully, and largely, * as if the ſaid letters patents were recited *verbatim* in that act of parliament, any thing to the contrary notwithſtanding. 3. That the chancelor, maſters and ſcholars of either of the ſaid univerſities, and their ſucceſſors for ever, ſhould ſeverally have, hold, poſſeſſe, and enjoy, and uſe to them and their ſucceſſors for ever, all manner of mannors, &c. and hereditaments, and all manner of liberties, franchiſes, immunities, quietances, and privileges, view of frankpledge, law dayes, and other things whatſoever they be, which either of the ſaid corporated bodies had held, occupied or enjoyed, or of right ought to have had, uſed, occupied, and enjoyed, according to the true intent and meaning of the ſaid letters patents whatſoever, any ſtatute, law, uſage, cuſtome, or other thing or things, made or done to the contrary notwithſtanding. 4. That all letters patents of the queenes highneſſe, or any of her progenitors or predeceſſors, and all manner of liberties, franchiſes, immunities,

* Note theſe generall brief and effectuall words.

* Nota hoc.

immunities, quietances, and privileges, leets, law dayes, * and all other things whatſoever therein expreſſed, given or granted to either of the ſaid univerſities, by what name ſoever, be, and by vertue of this act ſhould be eſtabliſhed and confirmed, any ſtatute, law, uſage, cuſtom, conſtruction, or other thing to the contrary notwithſtanding.

Note theſe generall binding and effectuall words. Actus benedictus.

By this bleſſed act of parliament, all the courts, franchiſes, liberties, priviledges, immunities, &c. mentioned in any letters patents, &c. to either of the ſaid univerſities (which were too long here to be recited) * that they might proſper in their ſtudy with quietneſſe, are eſtabliſhed, made good and effectuall in law, againſt any *quo warranto*, *ſcire facias*, or other ſuits, or any quarrell, concealment or other oppoſition whatſoever. See the letters patents of king H. 8. bearing date *primo Aprilis anno* 14. of his reigne, made to the univerſity of Oxford: and other letters patents bearing date 26 *Aprilis*, *anno* 3 *regni* Eliz. made to the univerſity of Cambridge, both which are by expreſſe name eſtabliſhed and confirmed by the ſaid act of 13 Eliz. In which act there is a ſaving to all, other then to the queenes majeſty, her heires and ſucceſſors. *Et ſic omnia in tuto.*

* Haud facile emergunt quorum virtutibus obſtat res vexata domini.

[228]

Touching the juriſdiction and conuſans of divers things belonging to the univerſity of Cambridge, ſee the parliament roll of 5 R. 2. nu. 45, &c. till nu. 66.

The maior, bailifes, and comminalty of Cambridge were accuſed, for that they in the late tumults and uprores confedered with divers other miſdoers, brake up the treaſury of the univerſity of Cambridge, and thereout took and burned ſundry the charters, &c. of the ſaid univerſity, and alſo compelled the chancelor and ſcholars of the ſaid univerſity, under their common ſeals to releaſe to the ſaid maior and burgeſſes, all manner of liberties, and alſo all actions reall and perſonall, and further to be bound to them in great ſummes of money: whereupon it was agreed in forme following: that one writ ſhould be directed to the maior, bailifes, and comminalty of Cambridge, that then were to appeare in the parliament, and to anſwer (the forme thereof doth there appeare.) And that another writ in forme aforeſaid ſhould be directed to the maior and bailifes that were at the time of the offence, (the forme whereof doth there appeare alſo.) The maior and bailifes that then were appeared in proper perſon, and pleaded not guilty, ne witting thereto; the comminalty by their atturneyes appeared at the day. The maior and bailifes, that before were at the time of the offence, appeared alſo in proper perſon, and the ſaid maior anſwered, That he was not privy to any ſuch act, but only by compulſion of others, if any thing were therein done; the which the kings learned councell then did diſprove, as by the record appeareth. The burgeſſes of Cambridge delivered into the parliament the ſaid two deeds ſealed by the chancelor and ſcholars, the one deed contained a releaſe of all liberties and priviledges with a bond of 3000. li. to releaſe all ſuits againſt the ſaid burgeſſes. The other was a releaſe of all actions reall and perſonall, as there doth appeare. Upon the reading of which two deeds, they both were commanded to be cancelled for the cauſes aforeſaid. After this the chancelor and ſcholars aforeſaid by way of petition, and in form of ſundry articles exhibited, ſhewed the beginning and whole diſcourſe of the ſaid maior and bailifs

Nota (*proh dolor*) the ancient charters, records, &c. of the univerſity of Cambridge burnt by rebels.

effectually

effectually and largely. Upon reading of which bill, it was demanded of the said burgesses what they could say, wherfore their liberties late by the king confirmed should not be seised into the kings hands as forfeited.

They require 3. things, viz. 1. A copy of the bill, 2. Councell, and 3. Respight to answer. To the copy of the bill was answered, that sithence they heard the same, it should suffice, for by law they ought to have no copy. To councell, it was said, that wherein councell was to be had, they should have, wherefore they then were appointed to answer to no crime or offence, but only touching their liberties. After many dilatory shifts and subterfuges, the said burgesses touching their liberties only, having no colour of defence, submitted themselves to the kings mercy and grace, saving their answers to all other matters. The king thereupon by common consent of the parliament, and by authority of the same, seised the same liberties into his hands as forfeited. And after the king granted to the chancelor and scholars aforesaid, within the said town of Cambridge and * suburbs of the same the assise, conusance, and correction, of bread, ale, weights, measures, regrators, and forestallers, with the fines, and amerciaments of the same, yeelding therefore yearly at the exchequer 10 l. And certain liberties the king after granted to the said maior and baillies, and increased their former fee farm.

Nota, by act of parliament. Vid. Rot. parl. 8 R. 2. nu. 11.

Nota, suburbs proveth a city.

Nota, the priority of the grant to the university.

This university of Cambridge hath power to print within the same *omnes et omnimodos libros*, which the university of Oxford hath not. See a notable record in parliament, 13 H. 4. concerning the university of Oxford, by the which it was decreed and adjudged by authority of parliament, that the popes bul should not impeach, or alter the right and custome of any thing concerning that university, and therefore was disallowed, too long to be here inserted.

Rot. par. 13 H. 4. nu. 15, 16, 17.

CAP. XLV. [229]

The Courts of the Stanneries in Cornwall and Devon.

THE stile of the court of stannery is, and alwayes hath been, *Magna curia domini regis ducatus sui Cornubiæ apud Crokerenton in com' Devon' coram A. B. custode stannariæ dicti domini regis in dicto com' Devon.*

The stile of th court.

The officers of this court be the steward, underwarden, &c.

The officers.

It is called *stannaria*, *à stanno*, because the lord warden hath jurisdiction of all the tynne in Cornwall and Devon. Tynne is a Saxon word, and derived *à tinnitu*, and the tynners are called *stannatores.*

The jurisdiction of this court is guided by speciall lawes, by customes, and by prescription time out of mind, which so far as we find it to be allowed by the resolution of the judges, or by act of parliament, we will recite.

The jurisdiction.

See the first pt of the Institute sect.

In cancellaria apud Westm. coram Nicho. Bacon milite custod' magni sigilli Angliæ pro stannatoribus, die Veneris, viz. 14 *die Novembris anno regni Elizabethæ reginæ quarto. Inter Martinum Trewynarde quer' in cur' stannar' com' Cornub', et Johannem Killegrew et Georgium Trewynard defend.*

Mich. 4 Eliz. in cancellar. Trewynards case.

Where the 14 day of October last past, the matter in question touching the allowing or disallowing of writs of error, as well between the parties aforesaid, as also for and concerning all other writs of error touching all causes determinable in the stannary court in Cornwall, was by the order of the lord keeper of the great seal of England committed to the hearing and examination of Sir William Cordel knight master of the rols, and Sir James Dier knight chief justice of the common pleas, and justice Weston; to the intent upon the due consideration of the cause they should make report unto the said lord keeper of their opinions and proceedings therein, as in their judgements should seem most agreeable to justice and equity: who having accordingly travelled diligently for the understanding of the truth of the premises upon the deliberate hearing and examining of the cause in the presence of the councell learned of both sides, and upon the perusing and consideration of the ancient prescriptions, customes, liberties, and charters exhibited by the said parties concerning the premises, have this day made their report unto the said lord keeper as followeth. That is to say: that for as much as the said plaintife could not, nor did not shew forth any record or president, whereby any judgements or executions heretofore passed in any of the said stannery courts have been reversed by writ of error in any of the queens majesties courts of her bench or common pleas: and for that it appeareth unto them that divers and sundry inconveniencies were likely to ensue by allowing of such writs of error, and upon other causes and considerations them especially moving; they in their opinions think it not meet nor convenient that any writs of error should passe or be suffered in such case to reverse any of the said judgements or executions. Upon which report made, it is this day ordered by the said lord keeper of the great seale, that the order heretofore taken the 15 of June last past made against the lord warden of the stanneries aforesaid, his officers and others mentioned in the same, concerning the not allowing or not executing of any writ or writs of error; and all and singular the contempts contained in the same order supposed by them to be committed, concerning the not allowing or not executing of any writ or writs of error as is aforesaid, shall be clearly frustrated and void, and they and every of them clearly released and discharged, any thing in the same order to the contrary notwithstanding. And that the said defendants and every of them shall be at their liberty to take their advantage against the said plaintife for their executions had or to be had in any of the said stannery courts according to the custome of the same courts without let or impeachment of any writ or writs of error, or of false judgement sued or to be sued in any of the said courts of the kings bench or common pleas. And that from henceforth, no writ or writs of error or false judgement be hereafter sued in any of the said courts of the kings bench or common pleas to reverse any judgement or judgements in any of the said courts of stanneries heretofore given, or hereafter to be given, untill upon further consideration of

No writ of error lyeth upon any judgement in the stannery courts. Vide simile. Dier 23 Eliz. fo. 376. But judgements shall be reversed by appeal as in the next page appeareth.

[230]

of the ancient grants and liberties of the ſaid courts of ſtannaries, or upon ſome other ſufficient cauſe or matter, it ſhall be otherwiſe ordered and determined by this court of the chancery.

In camera ſtellata apud Weſtm' coram concilio ibidem die Mercurii, viz. 29 die Novemb. anno regni dnæ. Eliz. Dei gratia reginæ Angliæ, Franciæ, et Hiberniæ, fidei defenſor', &c. ſeptimo 1564. Mich. 7 Eliz. Reginæ in Camera Stellata 29 Nov.

Where a matter in variance hath been heretofore moved, and depending in this honourable court, between Martin Trewynard plaintife, and John Raſkarrock, William Gilbert, John Killegrew the yonger, James Drewe, and other defendants by two ſeverall bils exhibited into this court, whereof the laſt bill containeth no other matters of effect being not mentioned in the firſt bill, other then the taking of certaine cattell of the ſaid complainant and others. And where alſo it appeareth this preſent day, that the taking of the ſaid cattell was by certaine of the ſaid defendants lawfully authoriſed for that purpoſe by the ſteward of the ſtannery court of Penwith and caried into the county of Cornwall for an execution upon a condemnation by judgement had in the ſaid court againſt the ſaid plaintife. Touching which condemnation the ſaid complainant hath complained as well in the court of chancery by bill, and in the kings bench by writ of error, as alſo in this court, as appeareth in the firſt of the ſaid two bils here depending, meaning by ſome of theſe wayes to call in queſtion the validity of the ſaid judgement, and was out of the ſaid ſeverall courts by order diſcharged and diſmiſſed, referring the proceeding upon the ſaid judgement to the order of the ſaid ſtannery court, according to divers ordinances by divers ancient charters, cuſtomes, and liberties belonging to the ſtannery ratified by act of parliament. And where it doth alſo appear that the taking of the ſaid cattell, whereupon the ſaid laſt bill in this court is exhibited was only for the execution of the ſaid recovery. And where alſo it doth further appeare, that by the lawes and ordinances of the ſaid ſtannery (if any ſuch cauſe of complaint be miniſtred) the ſame is to be redreſſed by appellation in ſeverall degrees, viz. firſt to the ſteward of the ſtannery court where the matter lyeth, then to the underwarden of the ſtanneries, and from him to the lord warden of the ſame ſtannaries: and for default of juſtice at his hands, to the princes privy councell, and not examinable either here in this court or in any other court. It is therefore this preſent day ordered, that the ſaid ſeverall bills of complaints, and the ſaid defendants named in the ſame, with all the cauſes therein mentioned, be forthwith diſmiſſed out of this court to be determined according to the ſaid lawes and ordinances in the ſaid ſtannery, and not elſewhere.

Erroneous judgements in the ſtannery are to be reverſed by appellation, and to whom this appellation ſhall be made.

[231]

The reſolution of all the judges (by force of his majeſties letters) concerning the ſtanneries in Devonſhire and Cornwall upon the hearing of the councell learned of both parties at ſeverall dayes, and what could be alledged and ſhewed on either party, and upon view and hearing of the former proceedings in the courts of the ſtanneries both before and ſince a certaine act of parliament made concerning the ſtanneries in * 50 E. 3. Term. Mich. 4 Jac. regis.

Firſt, we are of opinion, that as well blowers as all other labourers and workers (without fraud or covine) in or about the ſtanneries

* See this act of parliament hereafter in this chapter.

ries in Cornwall and Devon, are to have the privilege of the ſtanneries during the time that they do work there.

Secondly, that all matters and things concerning the ſtanneries, or depending upon the ſame, are to be heard and determined in thoſe courts according to the cuſtome of the ſame time out of mind of man uſed.

Thirdly, that all tranſitory actions between tynner and tynner or worker and worker (though the cauſe be collaterall, and not pertaining to the ſtannery) may be heard and determined within the courts of the ſtanneries according to the cuſtome of the ſaid courts, albeit the cauſe of action did riſe in any place out of the ſtanneries, if the defendant be found within the ſtannery; or may be ſued at the common law at the election of the plaintiſe. But if the one party only be a tinner or worker, and the cauſe of action being tranſitory and collaterall to the ſtannery do riſe out of the ſaid ſtanneries, then the defendant may by the cuſtome and uſage of thoſe courts plead to the juriſdiction of the court, that the cauſe of action did riſe out of the ſtanneries, and the juriſdiction of thoſe courts, which by the cuſtome of the court he ought to plead in proper perſon upon oath. And if ſuch plea to the juriſdiction be not allowed, then a prohibition in that caſe is to be granted. And if in that caſe the defendant do come to plead to the juriſdiction of the court upon his oath, he ought not to be arreſted *eundo, redeundo, vel morando*, at the ſuit of any ſubject in any corporation, or other place where the ſaid courts of the ſtannery ſhall be then holden.

Fourthly, if the defendant may pleade to the juriſdiction of the court in the caſe before mentioned, and will not, but plead and admit the juriſdiction of the court, and judgment is given, and the body of the defendant taken in execution, the party cannot by law have any action of falſe impriſonment, but the execution is good by the cuſtome of that court. But if in that caſe it doth appear by the plaintiſes own ſhewing, that the contract or cauſe of action was made or did riſe out of the ſtanneries, and the juriſdiction of thoſe courts, or if it appear by the condition of the bond whereupon the action is grounded, that the condition was to be performed in any place out of the juriſdiction of thoſe courts, then all the proceedings in ſuch caſes upon ſuch matter apparent, are *coram non judice.*

Fiſthly, we are of opinion, that no man ought to demurre in that court for want of form, but only for ſubſtance of matter. As if an action be brought there for words which will bear no action, or an action of debt upon a contract againſt executors or adminiſtrators, or ſuch like: in ſuch caſes a demurrer may be upon the matter. And that the proceedings there muſt be according to the cuſtome of thoſe courts uſed time out of minde of man: for that no writ of error doth lye upon any judgement given there, but the remedy given to the party grieved is by appeal, as hath been time out of minde of man accuſtomed.

Sixthly, that the courts of the ſtannery have not any juriſdiction for any cauſe of action that is locall, riſing out of the ſtanneries.

Seventhly, that the priviledge of the workers in the ſtanneries do not extend to any cauſe of action that is locall riſing out of the ſtanneries (for matters of life, member, and plea of land are by

 expreſſe

expresse words excepted in their charters) and no man can be exempt from justice.

Vide lib. Intr. Coke fo. 467. tit. Prohibition, and fo. 23. 293. b. in error. Vide Fleta lib. 6. cap. 7. § *Servitia vero.*

[232]

Such charters, records, and acts of parliament as we have observed concerning the stannery, we will according as we have done throughout this treatise recite *in serie temporis.*

*Johannes dei gratia rex Angliæ, &c. Sciatis quod intuitu Dei, et pro salute animæ nostræ dedimus et concessimus, ac præsenti carta nostra confirmavimus Deo, et ecclesiæ beati Petri Exon', et venerabili patri * Simoni Exon' episcopo et successoribus suis Exon' episcopis decimam de antiqua firma stanni in com' Devon' et Cornub. habendum sibi et successoribus suis cum omnibus libertatibus et liberis consuetudinibus ad eam pertinentibus per manus illius vel illorum qui stanneriam habuerint in custodia, &c.*

In Registro Episcopi Exon.
* This was Simon de Apulia, first dean of York, and consecrate bishop.
8 Johan.
10 E. 2. Inquis. 2. nu. 29.

*Rex Roberto de Courtney salutem. Mandamus vobis quod sine dilatione et difficultate aliqua habere faciatis * Isabellæ reginæ matri nostræ stanneriam com' Devon' cum cuneo et omnibus pertinent'. Teste com' mareschallo, &c.*

Rot. pat. 1 H. 3. m. 4.
* She was the daughter of Aymer earl of Angolesme.

[a] *Rex concessit Johanni filio Rici stanneriam in Cornubia, reddendo mille marcas. Simile anno 5 H. 3. rot finium.*

[a] Rot. fin. 4 H. 3.

[b] *Rex, &c. Sciatis quod commissimus Ric'o dilecto fratri nostro stanneriam nostram Cornubiæ cum omnibus pertin', &c.*

[b] Rot. pat. 10 H. 3. m. 9.

[c] There be two severall charters of liberties and priviledges both bearing date 10 *Aprilis anno* 33 E. 1. the one made *ad emendationem stannariarum nostrarum in com' Devon,* and the other *ad emendationem stannariarum nostrarum in com' Cornubiæ,* [d] which you may read at large in Pl. Com. [e] These charters were allowed in *anno* 35 E. 1.

[c] Rot. pat. 33 E. 1. The liberties and priviledges of the tynners.
[d] Pl. Com. 327. 328.
[e] 35 E. 1. in the treasury.

[f] The charter of 33 E. 1. was confirmed to the tynners of Devon', *de verbo in verbum,* and the like in 1 E. 3. and 17 E. 3.

[f] Rot. pat. 4 E. 2.

[g] Vide rot. *Almaniæ, anno* 12 E. 3. part. 1. nu. 17. An ordinance of the king by advice of his councell concerning tynne.

[g] 12 E. 3. part. 1. nu. 17.

A lease made to *Tideman de Linberghe de cunagio stanneriæ et de emptione totius stanni in com' Devon' et Cornub' pro fine mille marcarum et 3500. marcarum redditus.* These were things done *de facto,* but let us turn our selves to that, which hath the force of a law, viz. [h] an excellent declaration, limitation and exposition of the said charters of 33 E. 1. that was made in the parliament holden in *an.* 50 E. 3. by authority of the same, but never printed, (which we have set down *in hæc verba,* to the end that no syllable of the same should be omitted) it is enacted as followeth.

Rot. pat. 21 E. 3. Vide Rot. pat. 26 Apr. anno 7 E. 6. Gilbert Brockhouse.
[h] Rot. par. 50 E. 3. holden the Monday after the feast of S. Gregory.

A tresexellent et tresredout seignour le roy, supplie sa poure commune del county de Devonshire que luy plese per l'avys des prelats, countees, barons, et auters sages in cest present parliament ordeiner remedie de ceo que les esteynors, et les ministres del esteynery del dit county ont long temps a la dit commune sibien as seigneurs come as autres fait, et font de jour in autre diverses extortions, oppressions et grievances per colour de les franchises a eux grantes per les chartres nostre seigneur le roy, et de ses progenitors encontre la ley et le purport des ditz chartres, et per lour malveis interpretation dicelles: et que les dits chartres et les franchises comprises en ycelles puissent leuz et declarez d' article en article si q; la commune du dit county puissent estre apris droiturelment d'ycelles, et que cest declaration soit mys en record. Et si nul article y soit en les ditz chartres que touche customes ou usages, que plese a nostre dit seignieur le roy d'ordeiner et mander en breif temps suffisants justices

tices seigniours et autres apris de la ley a celles parties denquirer des dites customes et usages, et quils eyent poyur d'oyer et terminer tous les conspiracies, confederations, alliaunces, champerties, extortions, oppressions, grievances, fauxines et maintenances qu'eux les ditz esteynors et lour ministres ont fait a la dite commune, ou a nul de eux qui plendre se vorra, et ce auxi bien al suit le roy, come de la party entendants que le roy nostre seig-
[233] *nior ent gaigner a molt, et d'autre parte se remede ne lour y soit ore fait ilz serront en breise temps pur la greinder party disherites, et destruitz a toutz jours, que Dieu ne voilla. Le tenour d'ascuns des articles de les dites chartres que lour besoignent de declaration sensuent cy apres premerement, cest assassavoir.*

Sciatis nos ad emendationem stannar' nostr' in com' Devon' ad tranquillitatem et utilitatem stannatorum nostrorum prædictorum earundem concessisse pro nobis et hæredibus nostris, quod omnes stannatores præd' operantes in stannariis illis quæ sunt dominica nostra, dum operantur in eisdem stannariis liberi sint et quieti de placitis nativorum, et de omnibus placitis et querelis curiam nostram et hæredum nostrorum qualitercunque tangentibus, ita quod non respondeant coram aliquibus justiciariis vel ministris nostris seu hæredum nostrorum de aliquo placito seu querela infra prædict' stannarias emergentibus, nisi coram custode nostro stannariarum nostrarum prædictarum qui pro tempore fuerit, (exceptis placitis terræ, vitæ, et membrorum) nec non recedant ab operationibus suis per summonitionem alicujus ministrorum nostrorum seu hæredum nostrorum, nisi per summonitionem dicti custodis nostri. Et quod quieti sint de omnibus tallagiis, theoloniis, stallagiis, auxiliis et aliis custumis quibuscunque in villis, portubus, feriis et mercatis infra com' prædictum de bonis suis propriis, &c.

Sur quoy plese declarer si autres persones que les estainors overants in les estayneries averont et emoyeront la franchise grante per la dite chartre du roy desicome la dite chartre voet, quod omnes stannatores prædicti operantes in stannariis illis sint liberi, &c. Et auters personnes que les overours, cest-ascavoir lours maistres que les lovent et lours servants et autres claymont mesme la franchise. Et auxint plese declarer si les ditz overors y averont les franchises en autre temps que quant ilz overont in mesme l'esteynery, desicome la chartre voet dum operantur in eisdem stannariis liberi sint, &c.

Endroit de les dites paroles. Operantes in stannariis illis, et dum operantur in eisdem stannariis, soient clerement entendus, de operariis laborantibus duntaxat in stannariis illis sine fraude et dolo, et non de aliis, nec alibi laborantibus.

Item soit declare si mesmes les overours averont mesme les franchises tant come ils averont aillors que in les desmesnes que feurent au roy laiell nostre seignior le roy que ore est. La quel roy ayell lour grantast la dite chartre autemps del dit grant des franchises desicome la chartre voet, quod omnes stannatores prædicti operantes in stannariis illis quæ sunt dominica nostra, dum operantur in eisdem stannariis sint liberi, &c. Et ilz clamont d'avoir tout soit il einsi quils overont aillours qu'en les dites desmesnes le roy layel.

Endroit de cest article pur ce que il y a une autre article en mesme le chartre, que lour donne conge et licence de fover, in terris, moris, et vastis ipsius domini regis et aliorum quorumcunque in com' prædicto, et aquas, et cursus aquarum ad operationes stannariarum prædictarum divertere ubi et quotiens opus fuerit, et emere buscum ad functuram stanni, sicut antiquitus fieri consuevit, sine impedimento domini regis, hæredum suorum,
[234] *episcoporum, abbatum, comitum, baronum, seu aliorum quorumcunque, &c. Il semble un besoignable chose en ce case que lour custumes et usages soient diligemment*

diligemment enquiz, et que le gardeine de lesteynerie soit charge que il ne soeffre nul overour del dit esteynerie fover en prees, ne autre boys, neve abate autry boys ou autry measons, ne bestover eaue ou cours de eaue per malice. Et si per case le dit gardein se y vorra excuser que les dits esteynors ny voillent obeire a ses maundements, ne cesser lour malice pur luy que tant tost il se face monstrer al grand conseil le roy, et due et hastive remedy ent serra ordeignes.

Item soit declares in speciall comen les justices qu'ore serront assignes d'aller celles marchers pur ent faire la dite enquerre prendront lissue du pais si ascun y chiete entre parties, et coment ceste article precedont touchant les custumes et usages estoit uses devant la fesaunce de la dit chartre l'aiel, et per queux gents tielle issue serra tries, cestascavoir le quel per foreins solement, ou per estaynors seulment, ou per ambideux, &c.

Endroit de cest article, en soit la vys pris du grant conseil et y soient les records en eyre si nulles y soient, et autres evidences et remembrances deins le treasory le roy et aillours, et auxint les remembrances des seigniors queux y ont estre pur le temps serches et duement examines, et auxint soient les liures et evidences quelles les dits estaynors eut ont envers eux venes et regardes, issint que le y purra le mieltz venir al droit verity.

Item soit declare si le gardein del estaynery puisse tenir plee entre esteynor et forein de querele sourdant aillours que in les lieux ou ilz sont overants desicome la chartre voet, quod custos noster prædictus vel ejus locum tenens teneat omnia placita inter stannatores prædictos emergen' et etiam inter ipsos et alios forinsecos de omnibus transgressionibus, querelis, et contractibus factis in locis in quibus operantur infra stannarias prædictas similiter emergen', &c. Quar' il tient plee de tieux quereles sourdants chascune parte deins la dit counte.

Endroit de cest article. Se ont extende la jurisdiction clerement solon les paroles del dit Chartre, cestassavoir, in locis ubi iidem operarii operantur, et nemi aillours, ne en autre manner.

Item plese declarer de ceo que la dite chartre voet einsi. Et si qui stannatorum prædictorum in aliquo deliquerint per quod incarcerari debeant per custodem prædictum arrestentur, et in prisona nostra de Leidford et non alibi detineantur, quousque secundum legem et consuetudinem regni nostri deliberentur. Et en cest case que esteynor soit prise pur felony et liverez au gardein, il est suffert sovent aller a large de quoy grand perill avient moult de fois et aussi de ceo que la deliverance del dit gaolc nest passe fait une foitz en dis ans. Et que pis est per colour de mesme ceste article le dit gardein prent hors dautre prison les emprisones pur arrerages sur accompts, et les mette a Lydeford ou ilz sont in tant fovores quilz my font force de jamays fair gree a lour seigniors.

Endroit de ceste article en soit enquiz diligemment devant les justices que ore y serront proschemement assignes denquerre per quelle authority ilz y fait einsy de puis que en mesme la chartre sont exceptes per speciall toutz plees de terre et de vie, et de membre, et celle enqueste retourne soit declare en especiall sil busoigne.

And according to this act a commission issued out in these words.

*Edwardus Dei gratia Angliæ et Franciæ rex et dominus Hiberniæ dilectis et fidelibus suis * Guidoni de Brian et Johanni de Montague, Roberto de Belknap, Hugoni de Segrave, Henrico Perchaie, et Waltero de Clopton, salutem. Cum dominus Edwardus quondam rex Angliæ avus noster per cartam suam quam confirmavimus ad emendationem stannariarum suarum in com' Devon' ad tranquillitatem, et utilitatem stannatorum suorum* Rot. pat. 50 E. 3. [235]

* These two former were barons and lords of parliament, and sat in the last parliament of 50 E. 3.

suorum earundem concesserit pro se et hæredibus suis, quod omnes stannatores prædicti operantes in stannariis illis quæ fuerunt dominica sua, dum operentur in eisdem stannariis essent liberi et quieti de omnibus placitis nativorum, et de omnibus placitis et querelis curiam suam et hæredum suorum qualitercunque tangentibus: ita quod non responderent coram aliquibus justiciariis vel ministris ipsius avi nostri vel hæredum suorum de aliquo placito vel querela infra prædictas stannarias emergen' nisi coram custode stannariarium prædictarum qui pro tempore fuerit: (exceptis placitis terræ, vitæ, et membrorum,) nec recederent ab operationibus suis per summonitionem aliquorum ministrorum dicti avi nostri seu hæredum suorum nisi per summonitionem communem dicti custodis, et quod quieti essent de omnibus tallagiis, theoloniis, auxiliis, stallagiis, et aliis custumis quibuscunque in villis, portubus, feriis et mercatis infra com' prædictum de bonis suis propriis. Concesserit etiam eisdem stannatoribus quod fodere possunt stannum et turbas ad stannum fundendum ubique in terris, moris et vastiis suis et aliorum quorumcunque in com' prædicto, et aquas, et cursus aquarum ad operationem stannariarum prædictarum divertere, ubi et quoties opus fuerit, et emere buscam ad functuram stanni sicut antiquitus fieri consuevit, sine impedimento ipsius avi nostri vel hæredum suorum, episcoporum, abbatum, priorum, comitum, baronum, seu aliorum quorumcunque. Et quod custos prædictus vel ejus locum tenens teneat omnia placita inter stannatores prædictos emergentia, et etiam inter ipsos et alios forinsecos de omnibus transgressionibus, querelis et contractibus factis in locis in quibus operentur infra stannarias prædictas similiter emergen', et quod idem custos haberet plenam potestatem ad stannatores prædictos et alios forinsecos in hujusmodi placitis justiciandi et partibus justiciam faciend' prout justum, et prius in stannariis illis fuisset usitatum. Et si qui stannatorum prædictorum in aliquo delinquant per quod incarcerari deberent, per custodem prædictum arrestarentur, et in prisona de Lydeford, et non alibi custodirentur, et deliverentur, quousque secundum legem et consuetudinem regni Angliæ deliberarentur. Et si aliqui stannatorum prædictorum super aliquo facto infra com' prædictum non tangente stannarias prædict' se posuerint in inquisitionem patriæ, una medietas juratorum inquisitionis hujusmodi esset de stannatoribus prædictis, et alia medietas de forinsecis. Et de facto totaliter tangente stannarias prædictas fierent inquisitiones sicut fieri consueverint, sicut per inspectionem rotulorum cancellariæ nostræ nobis constat. Ac etiam ex clamosa insinuatione tam magnatum quam communitat' com' prædict' in presenti parliamento nostro graviter conquerentium ad nostrum pervenerit auditum, quod stannatores prædicti ac officiarii, balivi et ministri dict' stannariæ cartam prædictam pro libito suæ voluntatis interpretantes, et debitum intellectum ejusdem cartæ pervertentes, et etiam excedentes, ac quidam alii in magno numero asserentes se fore stannatores cum non fuerint, habitis inter eos conspirationibus, confœderationibus, et alligantiis, quamplurima extorsiones, oppressiones, falsitates, deceptiones, cambipartias ambidextras, manutenentias, transgressiones, damna, gravamina et excessus diversis subditis nostris dict' com' colore cartæ supradictæ per plures vices fecerunt, et indies facere non desistant in nostri contemptum et ipsorum conquerentium grave præjudicium, dict' com' verisimilem destructionem et eversionem manifestam. Nos affectantes singulos subditos nostros sub quieto et debito regimine gubernare, et nolentes tanta maleficia, si per prædict' stannatores, officiarios, ballivos vel ministros, aut alios quoscunque perpetrata existunt, aliqualiter transire impunita; assignavimus vos, quinque, quatuor, tres et duos vestrum, (quorum vos præfat' Robert' unum esse volumus) justiciarios

Pleas of land, life and member are excepted.

[236]

arios nostros ad inquirendum per sacramentum proborum et legalium hominum de com' prædict' tam infra libertates quam extra, per quos rei veritas melius sciri poterit, et aliis viis et modis quibus melius fore videritis de quibuscunque conspirationibus, confœderationibus, alligantiis, extortionibus, oppressionibus, falsitatibus, deceptionibus, cambipartiis, ambidextris, manutenentiis, transgressionibus, damnis, gravaminibus et excessibus per quoscunque stannatores vel alios in com' prædict' factis, et per quos, vel per quem, quibus personis, ubi et quibus temporibus, qualiter et quomodo, et de aliis articulis et circumstantiis præmissa qualitercunque tangentibus plenius veritatem; et ad præmissa omnia et singula tam ad sectam nostram quam dictorum conquerentium et eorum singulorum et aliorum quorumcunque pro nobis, aut pro seipsis prosequi volentium, audiend' et terminand' secundum legem et consuetudinem regni nostri Angliæ: salvis semper dictis stannatoribus libertatibus et privilegiis eis per cartam prædictam concessis. Et ideo vobis mandamus quod ad certos diem et loca quos vos, quinque, quatuor, tres vel duo vestrum (quorum vos præfat' Robert' unum esse volumus) ad hoc provideritis diligenter super præmissa faciatis inquisitiones; et conspirationes, confœderationes, alligantias, extortiones, oppressiones, falsitates, deceptiones, cambipartias, ambidextras, manutenentias, transgressiones, damna, gravamina, et excessus prædicta audiatis et terminetis in forma prædicta, facturi inde quod ad justitiam pertinet, secundum legem et consuetudinem regni nostri Angliæ. Salvis nobis amerciamentis at aliis ad nos inde spectantibus. Mandavimus enim vic' com' prædict' quod ad certos diem et loca quos vos, quinque, quatuor, tres vel duo vestrum (quorum vos præfat' Robert' unum esse volumus) ei scire fac' venire fac' coram vobis quinque, quatuor, tres vel duobus vestrum tot et tales probos et legales homines de baliva sua tam infra libertates quam extra, per quos rei veritas melius sciri poterit et inquiri. In cujus rei testimonium has literas nostras fieri fecimus patentes. Teste me ipso apud Westm' sexto die Julii, anno regni nostri Angliæ 50. Regni vero nostri Franciæ 37. Per consilium in parliamento.

But what was done upon this commission we have not yet found.

The said charter of 33 E. 1. to the tynners of Cornwall was confirmed. Rot. pat. 8 R. 2.

And the charter of 33 E. 1. to the tynners of Devon' was also confirmed. Rot. pat. anno 1 E. 4.

The like confirmation to the tynners of Devon. Rot. pat. 3 H. 7.

See the statute of 11 H. 7. cap. 4. concerning cunage and weights.

It was resolved by the whole court that *stannum*, tyn, otherwise whitelead, nor black lead, nor any other base metall did belong to the king by his prerogative, as gold and silver doe, albeit there may be tried out of the base metall gold or silver, but that is as [237] the seed or strength of the base metall, which being extracted becomes defective. Mich. 4 Jac. In Camera Stellata.

There be five kindes of base metals, viz. *æs, sive cuprum* (because it was found out, as some hold, *in Cypro*) copper, *stannum* tynne, *ferrum* iron, *plumbum* lead, and *orichalcum* latyn. Polybius 209 years before Christ wrote that this island was abundantly stored with tynne. *Britanni qui juxta * Belerium promontorium incolunt mercatorum usu, qui eo stanni gratia navigant, humaniores reliquis erga hospites habentur, hii ex terra saxosa cujus venas sectati effodiunt stannum igne eductum in quandam insulam ferunt Britannicam juxta, quam Vectam vocant;*

Polybius lib. 3. Plinius lib. ca. 8, 9. Diodorus Siculus lib. 5. ca. 8. fo. 142. floruit sub Augusto.

* Aut Vestæum, i. the cape of Cornwall.

vocant: ex hiis insulis mercatores emptum stannum in Galliam portant inde diebus fere triginta cum equis ad fontem Eridani fluminis perducunt. See M. Camden, pa. 134. in Cornwall.

And for as much as tynne is a staple commodity, let us in the next place treat of the court of the mayor of the staple.

CAP. XLVI.

The Court of the Mayor of the Staple.

[a] 27 E. 3. cap. 22. See the first part of the Institutes. Sect. 3. verb. *in la ley. m.*

THIS court is guided by the law merchant, which is the law of the staple, and is holden at the wool-staple at Westm. And there are also two constables, [a] and a certain number of correctors to do that which pertaineth to their office, as in other staples is accustomed.

27 E. 3. cap. 19.

This court (though it was far more ancient) is strengthened and warranted by act of parliament which can best expresse the jurisdiction thereof, and followeth in these words.

27 E. 3. stat. 2. c. 21.

The jurisdiction.

The law merchant.

Item, because the staples cannot long continue, nor the ordinances thereof made and to be made be kept, if good executors and justices be not stablished to make thereof good and ready execution: we have ordained and established, that in every towne where the staple is ordained, a mayor, good, lawfull, and sufficient shall be made and established, having knowledge of the law merchant, to governe the staple, and to doe right to every man after the law aforesaid, without favour, sparing, or griefe doing to any. And in every place where the staple is, shall be two covenable constables now at his beginning put by us, to do that pertaineth to their office, as in other staples is accustomed; and when they shall be dead or changed, then other shall be chosen by the comminalty of the merchants of the said places. And that no maior hold the office over the year, unlesse he be newly chosen by the comminalty of the merchants, as well of strangers, as of denizens. And that the said mayor and constables have power to keep the peace, and to arrest offenders in the staples for debt, trespasse, or other contract, and them to put in prison, and punish after the law of the staple. And a prison shall be ordained for the safe keeping of them that so shall be imprisoned. And the mayors, sheriffs, and bailiffs of the townes, where the staple is, or joyning to the staple, shall be attending to the mayor and ministers of the staple to do execution of their commandments upon pain of grievous forfeiture: and one lord or other of the most sufficient in the country where the staple is, shall [238] be assigned to be aide to the mayor and ministers of the staple to justifie the rebels, which by the said mayor and ministers cannot

cannot be juſtified, and to maintain and counſell them when need ſhall be to the good governance of the ſtaple, and to redreſſe at every mans complaint that that ſhall be done amiſſe by the ſaid mayor or miniſters, or other, and to do right to the complainants in this behalfe. And that the ſame mayor and conſtables do not, nor ordaine any thing contrary to this ordinance, nor make interpretation nor exception to them otherwiſe then the words do purport, but if there be any thing that is doubted, it ſhall be ſhewed to our councell, and there declared by good advice.

[a] See the ſtatute of 36 E. 3. cap. 7. That merchant ſtrangers may either ſue before the mayor of the ſtaple according to the law merchant, or at the common law.

[b] The bounds of the ſtaple at Weſtm. begin at Temple Bar, and extend to Tuthill. In other cities and towns, within the wals: where no wals be, the bounds of the ſtaple ſhall extend through all the city or town.

[c] See 27 E. 3. how triall ſhall be had *per medietatem linguæ: et vide* 11 E. 1. *Cart' Mercator'*.

[d] See the ſtatute of 27 E. 3. that the mayor of the ſtaple may take recogniſances of debt under the ſeal of the office, but not with the ſeal of the party, and how execution ſhall be done thereupon.

[e] The mayor of the ſtaple at Weſtm. and the recorder of the city of London, in the abſence of the two chief juſtices, out of term have power to take recogniſances of debts according to the form of the ſtatute of 23 H. 8. And this is in nature of a ſtatute ſtaple, but it hath beſides the ſeal of thoſe that take it, the ſeal of the party.

[f] The mayor and the conſtables ſhall be ſworn in the chancery to do lawfully that which pertain unto them.

[g] There are five ſtaple merchandiſes of England, viz. wooll, woolfels, leather, lead, and tynne.

This word ſtaple, anciently written [h] eſtaple, commeth of the French word *eſtape*, which ſignifieth a mart or market. So as the court of the ſtaple is, as much to ſay, as the court in the ſtaple market, and is incident to that market, [i] and it was oftentimes kept at Callice, and ſometimes in Bridges in Flanders, and at Antwerpe, Middleburgh, &c. (and therefore it was neceſſary that this court ſhould be governed by law merchant) and at ſeverall times in many places within England, and now (as hath been ſaid) is kept at Weſtm.

We uſe for this word ſtaple, *ſtapula*, as *major ſtapulæ*, *ſtatutum ſtapulæ*, &c. And we may truly ſay that we have but *umbratilem ſtapulam*, which in times paſt was ſo renowned and beneficiall, [k] as it enriched every place where it was holden, and it was commonly ſaid, that riches followed the ſtaple.

See the ſtatute of 2 E. 3. cap. 9. and a writ thereupon. 7 E. 3. in *ſcaccario*. [l] *Et original de ſcaccario anno* 12 E. 3. Rot. 2. ibid. 13 E. 3. Rot. 12. and Rot. Pat. 15 E. 3. 2 part. See the ſtatute of the ſtaple *anno* 27 E. 3. through all the chapters, 36 E. 3. cap. 7. 28 E. 3. cap. 13, 14. 43 E. 3. ca. 1. 12 R. 2. cap. 16.

[a] 36 E. 3. cap. 7. Rot. par. 6 H. 6. nu. 29.

[b] 28 E. 3. ca. 15. The bounds of the ſtaple.

[c] 27 E. 3. ca. 8. 28 E. 3. ca. 13. Rot. Cart. 31 E. 1. nu. 44.

[d] 27 E. 3. cap. 9. F. N. B. 131. d. Pl. com. 62. b. 15 H. 7. 16. Fleta, lib. 2. ca. 57. See 5 H. 4. ca. 12.

[e] 23 E. 8. cap. 6.

[f] 27 E. 3. cap. 23.

[g] 8 H. 6. cap. 17.

[h] 27 E. 3. cap. 8. Dier 4. Mar. 144.

[i] Vid. *Cart. Mercator, ubi ſup.* Merchants as well ſtrangers as ſubjects and merchandizes.

[k] Able to furniſh the king with money. Rot. Parl. 7 E. 4. nu. 9 12 E. 4. nu. 59. Rot. parl. 9 R. 2. nu. 4.

[l] Original. de Scac. 7 E. 3. rot. 9.

CAP. XLVII.

Of the Legall Courts and their Jurisdictions within the Principality of Wales.

THIS principality consisteth of 12 counties, whereof 6. viz. Anglisea, Carnarvan, Merioneth, Flint, Carmorthen, and Cardigan were erected by the act intituled *statutum Walliæ anno* 12 E. 1. [b] and the rest of the statute of 27 H. 8.

Wallia, Wales, so called by the Saxons *Brytwealas, unde Wallenses*, [c] *Walli, i. exteri seu peregrini:* and the Britons call Englishmen to this day *Saisons;* these are of the posterity of the ancient Britons inhabiting on the west part of Great Britany. This was sometime [d] a realm or kingdome and governed *per suos regulos*, [e] *rex E. dedit regi Griffino totum terram quæ jacebat trans aquā que vocatur* [f] *Sed postquam ipse Griffin forisfecit ei, abstulit ab eo hanc terram, et reddidit episcopo Cestriæ et omnibus suis hominibus, qui ante ipsam tenebant.*

[g] By force of a commission directed to divers discreet and learned men as well English as Welsh, viz. Griffith ap Lluellin, Gitten Owen, John King and others, it was found that Owen ap Meredith ap Theodore which married Katherine daughter of France and dowager of king H. 5. was lineally descended from [h] Cadwallader king of the Britains, and gave the armes of the princes of Wales.

And here we are justly occasioned to discover the error of those that have given to our late soveraigne lady queen Elizabeth, of ever glorious and blessed memory, the sirname of Tydur, and consequently to her grandfather, father, brother, and sister: which whether it were out of ignorance or malice some do question, because if she had any sirname at all it was Theodore and not Tydur, which is a nick or by-name. But we rather take it to grow out of ignorance, for that in truth she had no sirname at all; for this Owen her ancestor had no sirname: and therefore was called (Owen ap Meredith, that is the sonne of Meredith, ap Theodore, the sonne of Theodore) ap Grono, &c. All which were Christian names: so as they should rather have called her Elizabeth Owen, his own name, or Elizabeth Meredith, his fathers name, then Theodore his grandfathers Christian name; but Almighty God would not suffer her to have a sirname, because by his grace and goodnesse she should deserve for her imperial vertues to be called [i] Elizabeth the Great.

[k] But *jure feodali* the kingdome of Wales was holden of the crown of England, and thereby as Bracton saith, was *sub potestate regis*. And so it continued untill the 11 year of the reign of king E. 1. when he subdued the prince of Wales rising against him,

See W. 1. cap. 17. the second part of the Institutes, pa. 195.
Stat. Walliæ anno 12 E. 1. in Vet. Mag. Cart. part 2. fo. 3.
[b] 27 H. 8. ca. 26. 34 H. 8. cap. 26.
[c] Lamb. verb. Wallus. 15 E. 3. record. 38. & tit. Error. 2 H. 5. cap. 6. 19 H. 6. fo. 12.
[d] Realme from the French word *roiaume*, and both *à regno*.
[e] Domesday in com. Cestr. Ep. Cestr.
[f] Domesday in com. Hereford. Rex in Arenfield. Rex Griffin et Ble vastaverunt hanc terram T. E. Quandoque rex Griffin nominatur rex Mariadoc.
[g] Rot. pat. anno 7 H. 7.
[h] Cadwallader king of the Britains Mat. Parker archiep. M. S.
[i] This blessed queen raigned the years of Augustus, and lived the age of David, a king elder then any king or queen since the conquest, and yet had *vegetum corpus et vividum ingenium.*
[k] Lib. 7. fo. 21. b. in Calvins case. Tr. 5 E. 3. 40. alien. Bracton (who wrote *tempore* H. 3.) lib. 5. fo. 395. b. Fleta lib. 1. cap. 16. 10 H. 4. fo. 6. acc. Pl. com. 129 a. b. Dier 3 Mariæ 113.

and

and executed him for treaſon, whereof Fleta who lived in thoſe dayes ſpeaketh thus. *Et unico malefactori plura poterunt infligi tormenta, ſicut contigit de Davide principe Walliæ cum per Edwardum quinque judiciis mortalibus torquebatur, ſuis namq; meritis exigentibus, detractus, ſuſpenſus, diſmembratus fuit et combuſtus, cujus caput principali civitati, quatuorq; quarteria ad quatuor partes regni in odium tradit' deferebantur ſuſpendend'.*

[m] The next year viz. in the 12 year of king E. 1. by authority of parliament it is declared thus, ſpeaking in the perſon of the king (as ancient ſtatutes were wont to do) *Divina providentia, quæ in ſua diſpoſitione non fallitur, inter alia ſuæ diſpenſationis munera, quibus nos et regnum noſtrum Angliæ decorari dignata eſt, terram Walliæ cum incolis ſuis prius nobis * jure feodali ſubjectam jam ſui gratia in proprietatis noſtræ dominium, obſtaculis quibuſcunque ceſſantibus, totaliter et cum integritate convertit et coronæ regni prædicti, tanquam partem corporis ejuſdem annexuit et univit.* Yet this wiſe and warlike nation was long after this not ſatisfied nor contented, and eſpecially, for that they truly and conſtantly took part with their rightfull ſoveraigne and liege lord king Richard the ſecond; in revenge whereof they had many ſevere and invective lawes made againſt them in the reigns of H. 4. H. 5. &c. All which as unjuſt are repealed and abrogated. And to ſay the truth, this nation was never in quiet, untill king H. 7. their own country man obtained the crown. [b] And yet not ſo really reduced in his time, as in the reign of his ſonne king H. 8. in whoſe time by certaine juſt laws made at the humble ſuit of the ſubjects of Wales, the principality and dominion of Wales was incorporated and united to the realm of England: and enacted that every one born in Wales ſhould enjoy the liberties, rights, and laws of this realm, as any ſubjects naturally born within this realm ſhould have and inherit, and that they ſhould have knights of ſhires and burgeſſes of parliament, &c. By the which the juriſdiction of the legall courts are thereby ſo perfectly and plainly eſtabliſhed and declared, and their proceedings to be according to the lawes and cuſtomes of England, as we have thought good to refer the judicious reader to thoſe acts of parliament without recitall of them, where he ſhall find the excellent venerable variety of ſeats and courts of juſtice, with their proper juriſdictions according to the laws of England, the golden metwand, whereby all mens cauſes are juſtly and evenly meaſured. Only we will adde certaine things which have not been publiſhed before.

By the ſaid ſtatute of 34 H. 8. it is enacted that there ſhall be holden and kept ſeſſions twice every year in every of the ſaid [c] twelve ſhires, that is to ſay, Glamorgan, Brecknock, Radnor, Carmarthen, Pembroke, Cardigan, Mountgomery, Denby, Flint, Carnarvan, Merioneth, and Angleſie, which ſeſſions ſhall be called the kings great ſeſſions of Wales.

[d] A fine was levied of lands in the county of Carmarthen, and the writ of covenant was *coram juſticiariis noſtris magnæ aſſiſæ in com' Carmarthen*, and becauſe all the judiciall preſidents were in that forme ever ſince the making of the ſtatute, it was adjudged to be good, for *communis error facit jus.*

Alſo in the ſaid act of 34 H. 8. it was enacted, that the kings moſt royall majeſty ſhould from time to time change, &c. all manner

[m] Statutum Walliæ anno 12 E. 1. Vid. 10 H. 4. fo. 6.

[240]

* Note, divers monarchs hold their kingdome of others *jure feodali.* As the duke of Lumbardy, Cicill, Naples, and Bohemia of the Empire. Granado, Leona of Aragon. Navarre, Portugall, of Caſtile. And ſo others.

Dorſ. clauſ. 15 E. 2. m. 13. *De Wallenſibus ad parl. apud Eborum venire fac'* viz. 24 *de diſcretioribus, legalioribus et validioribus hominibus de partibus Southwalliæ, et* 24 *de partibus Northwalliæ* Rot. clauſ. 20 E. 2. m. 3. accord. 21 Jac. ca. 28.

[b] 27 H. 8. ca. 26. 34 H. 8. ca. 26. 37 H. 8. ca. 26. 18 Eliz. cap. 7.

[c] The twelve counties of Wales.

[d] Trin. 34 Eliz. in the caſe of Morgan of the report of the chiefe juſtice Popham.

ner of things before in that act rehearſed, as to his moſt excellent wiſdome and diſcretion ſhould be thought convenient, and alſo to make laws and ordinances for the common-wealth of his ſaid dominion of Wales at his majeſties pleaſure, &c. And albeit the common opinion was that the ſame power in ſo high a degree of truſt, as the alteration of laws, &c. was perſonall to H. 8. and referred to his wiſdome, diſcretion, and pleaſure, and therefore extended not to his ſucceſſors, yet for that the ſubjects of the country and dominion of Wales had been conſtantly loyall and obedient, and had lived in all dutifull ſubjection to the crown of England, to prevent all queſtions and danger the ſaid branch of the ſaid ſtatute of 34 H. 8. is repealed and made void.

So it was reſolved by divers juſtices in Hil. 5 Jac. regis.

21 Jac. regis c. 10.

Hil. 5 Jac.

It was reſolved by all the juſtices upon a reference made to them by the lords of the privy councell upon conſideration had upon the ſtatutes of 34 H. 8. cap. 26. and 18 Eliz. cap. 8. that the juſtices in Wales are to be conſtituted and made by letters patents, as they had been ever ſince the making of the ſtatutes, and not by commiſſion. And upon report of their opinion to the lord chancelour baron Snigge was conſtituted and made by patent accordingly.

Rot. clauſ. anno 20 E. 2. m. 3.

Rex dilecto et fideli ſuo Rico' Damory juſticiar' ſuo Northwalliæ ſalutem. Mandamus vobis quod habito adviſamento cum illis hominibus de partibus prædictis, cum quibus melius fore videritis faciend' diverſimode ſine dilatione venire faciatis ad præſens parliamentum apud Weſtm. convocatum 24 *homines de partibus illis tam Anglicos quam Wallenſes ad conſentiendum hiis quæ ibid. pro communi commodo et pace et tranquillitate regni noſtri et partium præd. favente domino contigerit ordinari, et habeatis ibi nomina præd.* 24 *hominum, et hoc br'e. Teſte rege apud Kenilworth* 11 *Januarii anno* 20 E. 2. rot. clauſ. m. 3.

[241]

12 were Engliſh. and 12 Welſh. Rot. Clauſ. 15 E. 2. in dorſ. m. 13. Wallenſes vocat. ad parliamentum.

By this and others of like nature it appeareth that Welſhmen were in the reigne of E. 2. E. 3. &c. called to our parliaments.

7 H. 4. cap. 15. 11 H. 4. cap. 1. 1 H. 5. cap. 1. 8 H. 6. cap. 7. 10 H. 6. cap. 2. 23 H. 6. cap. 15. 6 H. 6. cap. 4. 27 H. 8. cap. 26. 34 H. 8. cap. 26. 35 H. 8. cap. 11.

But now ſeeing there be ſheriffs throughout all Wales, the writs are directed to the ſheriffs to cauſe to be elected knights, citizens, and burgeſſes, and retornable into the chancery, where before they were retorned into the parliament.

We have ſeen a charter of the earle of Arundell proving, that by the ancient cuſtome of Wales, females could not inherit.

Marchia Walliæ.

Wallica conſuetudo.

Omnibus Chriſti fidelibus præſens ſcriptum inſpecturis Johannes comes Arundel et dominus de Mautravers, ſalutem in domino. Sciatis nos prædict. comitem ad proſecutionem et ſpecialem ſupplicationem communitatis tenen' noſtrorum tam duarum partium quam tertiæ partis dominii noſtri de Oſewaldeſtrie in marchia Walliæ conceſſiſſe pro nobis et hæredibus noſtris et per præſentes confirmaſſe tenen' noſtris prædict', hæred' et aſſig. ſuis, quod eorum filiæ pro defectu exit' maſculini, ac eorum proximi conſanguinei, tam maſculini quam femellæ de cætero hæreditare valeant imperpetuum terras, tenementa et reddit' anteceſſorum et conſanguineorum ſuorum ubique infra dominium noſtrum præd' eiſd' modo et forma quibus utitur in communi lege Angliæ, Wallica conſuetudine prius ibid. de contrario uſitat' in aliquo non obſtante: ſalvis ſemper nobis et hæred' noſtris heriotis, releviis, ſect' cur' et al' conſuetudinib' quibuſcunq; de dictis terris et tenementis ante hanc noſtram conceſſionem nobis quomodolibet pertinen'. In cujus rei teſtimonium huic præſenti ſcript' noſtro conceſſionis ſigillum noſtrum fecim' apponi: hiis teſtibus, Willielmo Ryman, Thoma Baret, Willielmo Sideney armigeris, Hugone Burgh, ſen' dominii noſtri præd', Rich. Irlond, Hoel ap Ogn' Gouch, et aliis. Dat' in hoſpitio noſtro London

don

don vicefimo quinto die menfis Aprilis an. regni regis Henrici fexti poft conqueftum octavo.

At this day women are inheritable in Wales, according to the common law in England.

* *Ordinatio de confuetudinibus Northwalliæ et Weftwalliæ.*

Thefe Britons were ever lovers of the laws of England, for at the parliament holden [a] in 4 H. 4. they petitioned the king, that in all cafes of the crowne throughout every liberty in Wales, the laws of England might be only ufed. Whereunto the king yeilded, and that his councell fhould take order therein. [b] *Quia epifcopi Wallenfes ex antiqua confuetudine teftamentum aliquod condere non potuerunt, rex licentiam dedit epifcopo Bangor, quod poffit condere teftamentum fuum non obftante quod epifcopi Wallenfes ex antiqua confuetudine teftamentum aliquod condere non poffunt.* See the chapter of the Confiftory Courts of Arch-bifhops and Bifhops, fol.

[c] Where execution fhall be made of lands in the marches by the fheriffe of the county next adjojning, *ficut folebat antiquitus.* See the record at large.

[d] *Affach* is a Brittifh word and fignifieth a cuftome in Wales, which was to excufe one of the death of a man by the oath of 300 men. But this ftrange kind of excufe or acquitall is abrogated by ftatute.

[e] There was alfo a certain triall in Wales called a *raythe*, but that is alfo abrogated.

* 9 E. 2. m. 3.
[a] Rot. par. 4 H. 4. nu. 100.
[b] Rot. pat. 13 E. 1. m. 21.
Vid. Hil. 20 E. 1. coram rege. Ro. 37. 22. Wallia Pafch. 10 E. 2. coram rege. rot. 37. 18 E. 2. rot. 73. Trin. 5 E. 3. rot. 40. Coram rege.
[c] Hil. 18 E. 2. rot. 73. cor. rege. Gloc. 18 E. 2. aff. 382. Rot. parl. 18 E. 1. rot. 3. 13 E. 3. jurifdiction. 33. 28 E. 2. ca. 2. 5 E. 3. fo. 30. 45 E. 3. bre. 588. 21 H. 3. bre. 881. fimile.
[d] 1 H. 5. cap. 6.
[e] 6 H. 6. nu. 33.

CAP. XLVIII.

[242]

The Court of the Prefident and Councell in the Dominion and Principality of Wales, and the Marches of the fame.

LEAVING now the legall courts in the dominion of Wales, to proceed by the right rule, *fecundum legem et confuetudinem Angliæ*, let us fpeak fomewhat of the court of equity before the prefident and councell there.

This court is ftrengthened and warranted by the ftatute of 34 H. 8. ca. 26. with a reference to prefcription before it, in thefe words,

Rot. par. 16 R. 2. nu. 44. there was a prefident of Wales.
34 H. 8. cap. 26.

Item, that there fhall be, and remain a prefident and councell in the faid dominion and principality of Wales, and the marches of the fame, with all officers, clerks, and incidents to the fame in manner and form as heretofore hath been ufed and accuftomed: which prefident and councell fhall have power and authority to hear and determine by their wifdomes and difcretions fuch caufes and matters as be, or hereafter fhall be affigned to them by the kings majefty, as heretofore hath been accuftomed and ufed.

They fit by force of the kings commiffion and inftructions, and proceed as in a court of equity by their wifdomes and difcretions. Herefordfhire, Worcefterfhire, Shropfhire, and Gloucefterfhire are included within this commiffion, pretending that thefe four fhires are within the marches of Wales.

That thefe four fhires are no part of the marches of Wales, but ancient fhires of the realm of England, appeareth by fix manner of proofs.

Firft, by expreffe books, viz. 18 E. 2. Aff. 82. 1 E. 3. 14. in Dower. 7 E. 3. 9 E. 3. in Dower. 6 H. 4. fo. 9. in Scire fac. F. N. B. 168.

Secondly, by acts of parliament, viz. Prærog. regis. 17 E. 2. cap. 1. 28 E. 3. cap. 2. 2 H. 4. cap. 12. and 16, 17. 23 H. 6. cap. 5. 27 H. 6. cap. 4. 31 H. 6. cap. 4. 32 H. 8. cap. 13. 13 El. cap. 13.

Thirdly, by records of parliament. 3 R. 2. nu. 29. and 30.

Fourthly, by reafon. 1. Thefe four fhires were ancient Englifh fhires, and governed by the laws of England, and not by the difcretion of the prefident and councell: and this were to bring their inheritances, goods, &c. *ad aliud examen.* 2. At one and the fame time there were in former times earles of the marches of Wales, and feverall earls of thefe four counties, and therefore they could not be one and the fame.

See before in the chapter of the County Palatine of Chefter, pa. 212.

Fifthly, by the refolution aforefaid of thofe four judges concerning Chefhire and Flyntfhire (which were included alfo within the commiffion) that they were not within the marches of Wales, and therefore out of the jurifdiction of the prefident and councell, and fo remain untill this day: for a commiffion without an act of parliament cannot raife a court of equity, as often hath been faid before.

Mich. 2. Jac. regis the cafe of Edward lord Zouch prefident of Wales.

Laftly, by the commandment of the king, all the juftices of England, and barons of the exchequer were affembled concerning the jurifdiction of the prefident and councell of Wales, and the marches of the fame, who upon hearing of councell learned on divers days, and upon mature deliberation refolved *una voce*, that the faid four counties were not within the jurifdiction of the prefident and councell. 2. That forafmuch as the prefident and councell have a limited authority if they proceed in any matter that is out of their jurifdiction either in refpect of the place or of the authority limited to them, a prohibition may be granted, as to the marfhalfea and the like. Which refolution being made known to his majefty, his majefty was gracioufly pleafed, that the lord prefidents commiffion fhould be reformed: whereupon the lord Zouch gave over his place. And yet the commiffion was not after reformed in all points, as it ought to have been.

[243]

Regift. 4 & 8. F. N. B. 39 b. 45 f. 46 a. 171. 159. 185, 186, 187. 19 H. 6. 54.

This is added for the better underftanding of records and hiftories concerning Wales.

Rodry Maure, or Rodry the Great, king of Wales, fon of Merfyn Fryth had iffue three fons. Mervyn, Anarawd, and Cadelh. In the year wherein he died, viz. *anno dom.* 877. (king Alfred, alias Alured, then reigning in England,) this great Rodry divided his kingdome of Wales into three principalities. The firft he called *Guyneth*, the Englifh North Wales, the Latinift *Venedotia.* The fecond principality was called *Powis land*, in Latin *Powifia*, of fome Weft Wales, bordering upon England. The third he called *Dehevbarth*, the Englifh South Wales, in Latin *Demetia.* The

firft

firft principality, fome fay, he gave to Mervin, after others, to Anarawd. The fecond to Anarawd, fome fay, to Cadelh. The third to Cadelh, fome fay, to Mervyn. The firft was the beft, becaufe it was the quieteft. The fecond was often invaded and troubled by the Englifh. Into the third often incurfions were made by the Englifh, the Norman, and the Fleming The divifion of this kingdome (howfoever it was) wrought in proceffe of time fuch a divifion between thefe princes, as it was never quiet untill it came under one monarch and king again: for the royall dignity of a monarch or king, from whence all other fubordinate dignities, *tanquam lumen de lumine*, are derived without any diminution, will fuffer no divifion. *Regia dignitas eft indivifibilis; et quælibet alia derivativa dignitas eft fimiliter indivifibilis.*

The moft woful event that fell out in this realm, when Gorbodug divided this kingdome between his two fons, Ferrex and Porrex, and what heavy event came to paffe, untill it was reduced again under one monarch, let our hiftories tell you: and letting paffe others, I cannot over-paffe the miferable eftate within this kingdome under the heptarchy, untill all was reunited under one foveraign. And this is the reafon, that in England, Scotland, and Ireland, the royall dignity is defcendible to the eldeft daughter or fifter, &c.

But let us look a little into forain parts. Oedipus king of the Thebanes had iffue two fons, Polynices, and Eteocles: he ordained, that after his deceafe, his two fons fhould *alternatim* by courfe, &c. reign in his kingdome. But what was the event? *Fratres de regni hæreditate diffidentes fingulari certamine congreffi mutuis vulneribus ceciderunt.* But to return again to our Wales. Sta. in Theb.

It is divided from England by a ditch after the name of that king that made it, called King Offa his ditch. Camden in the county of Radnor.

King E. 3. at the parliament holden *anno* 17 of his reign, by charter eftablifhed by authority of parliament, created Edward (called the Black Prince) prince of Wales in thefe words, *De concilio prælatorum, comitum, baronum et communium in generali parliamento noftro apud Weftm' die Lunæ in quindena Pafchæ proxime præterito convocato ipfum Edw. principem Walliæ fecimus et creavimus, et dictum principatum fibi dedimus et conceffimus, et per cartam noftram confirmavimus, ac ipfum de dicto principatu, ut ibidem præficiendo præfideat, et præfidendo dictas partes dirigat et defendat, per* [a] *fertum in capite, et annulum in digito aureum, ac* [b] *virgam argenteam inveftivimus juxta morem: habendum et tenendum de nobis fibi et hæredibus fuis regibus Angliæ imperpetuum, &c.* Out of this charter we obferve, that in this creation there is a great myftery, for leffe then an eftate of inheritance fo great a prince could not have, and an abfolute eftate of inheritance in fo great a principality as Wales, the kings meaning was (this principality being fo dear unto him) he fhould not have: therefore a qualified fee therein he had in this form, *fibi et hæredibus fuis regibus Angliæ*, that by his deceafe, or attaining to the crown this dignity might be extinguifhed in the crowne, to the end that the king for the time being fhould ever have the honour and power to create his heir apparent prince of Wales, as he himfelf had been by his progenitor. But otherwife it is in cafe of the duchy of Cornwall, as in the Princes cafe, *ubi fup.* appeareth.

Carta creationis principis Walliæ authoritate parliamenti, anno 17 E. 3.

[a] A chapelet of gold made in form of a garland.

[b] This virge, rod, or fcepter in latter creations for more honor is changed from filver to a verge or fcepter of gold.

Sibi et hæredibus regibus Angliæ.

[244]

See the Princes cafe. Lib. 5.

Vide cartam E. 3. *dat. apud Pontem fract.* 18 *Martii.* 7 E. 3. and Hil. 33 E. 3. *irrotulat' in scaccario ex parte rememorator' Thesaur'.* Rot. 15. the Black Prince created earl being three years old.

* Hil. an. 20 E. 1. Coram rege rot. 14. Wallia.

† Commissionarii.

Inauditum est.

Irrotulatur istud recordum inter placito de banco term' Pasc. an. 14 E. 1.

[a] Ortelius in Carta antiqua Brittanniæ.

[b] Humph. Lloyd apud Ortelium in the same geography.

[c] Idem in Fragm. Britan' Historiæ.

[d] Tacitus. Vide supra pa. 9.

[e] Nota validissimas gentes.

[f] Rot. pat. 9 E. 2. m. 3.

[g] Lib. Int. Co. fo. 549, 550.

And in the same manner is the dignity of the noble and primary county palatine of Chester at the same time granted to the prince, *sibi et hæredibus suis regibus Angliæ.*

* *Ob quamplurimos excessus more hostili vexillo displicato per Gilbertum de Clare comitem Glouc' et Hertf. et homines suos de Morgannon illatos contra Humfredum de Bohun comitem Heref' et Essex et homines suos de Brekenock, dominus rex assignavit* † *episcopum Eliens' et alios commissionar' ad inquirendum, &c Mandavit etiam dominus rex per literas suas dilectis et fidelibus suis Johanni Hastings, Johanni fil' Reginaldi, Edmundo de Mortuo mari, Rogero de Mortuo mari, Theobaldo de Verdon, Johanni Tregose et Galfrido de Cannil, quod intersint apud Brekenock, &c. Et postea venerunt apud Laundon. Voluit idem dominus rex pro statu et jure suo per ipsos justiciarios quod inde rei veritas inquiretur per sacram' tam magnatam, quam aliorum proborum, et legalium hominum de partibus Walliæ et com' Glouc' et Heref' per quos, &c. cujuscunque conditionis fuissent, ita quod nulli parceretur in hac parte, eo quod res ista dominum regem et coronam et dignitatem suam tangit, &c. Dictum est ex parte domini regis Johanni de Hastings et omnibus aliis magnatibus supra nominatis quod pro statu et jure regni, et pro conservatione dignitatis coronæ et pacis suæ apponant manum ad librum, ad faciend' id quod eis ex parte domini regis injungeretur; qui omnes unanimiter respondent, quod inauditum est quod ipsi vel eorum antecessores hactenus in hujusmodi casu ad præstandum aliquod sacramentum coacti fuer', &c. Ac pluries eisdem magnatibus ex parte ipsius regis conjunctim et separatim, libroque eis porrecto, injunctum est quod faciant sacram'; responderunt demum omnes singulatim quod nihil inde facerent sine consideratione parium suorum. Demum comes Glouc' fecit finem cum domino rege pro decem millibus marcarum, et comes Essex pro mille marcis, et uterque eorum committitur mareschallo. (Recordum per longum est, et continet tres rotulos.) Et ob affinitatem, et consanguinitatem cum rege perdonantur plurima, tamen forisfecerunt libertates suas durante vita ipsorum. Et post decessum eorum, hæredes sui rehabeant.*

But now to take our leave of this principality of Wales, this is that the Romans called by the name of [a] *Britannia secunda*, and sometimes [b] Valentia, and by the Britaines themselves called [c] Cambria. And we will conclude this treatise of Wales, &c. with that which that [d] excellent historian speaking of the wars between the Roman and the ancient Britain, saith, *Nec aliud adversus* [e] *validissimas gentes pro nobis utilius, quàm quod in commune non consulunt, rarus ad propulsandum commune periculum conventus: ita dum singuli pugnant, universi vincuntur.*

[f] See 2 part. pat. 9 E. 2. m. 3. *Ordinat' de consuetud' North-walliæ et West-walliæ.*

[g] Vid. Lib. Int. Co. fo. 549, 550. Three notable matters concerning Wales. 1. Of the government of Wales before 27 H. 8. 2. Of lordship, marchers, and their authorities and liberties. 3. The act of 1 & 2 Ph. and Mar. concerning the same.

CAP.

CAP. XLIX.

The Prefident and Councell in the North.

THIS councell is neither warranted by act of parliament, nor by prefcription, but raifed by king H. 8. by his commiffion upon thefe occafions, and in the manner hereafter expreffed. After the fuppreffion of monafteries of the yearly value of two hundred pound or under, which was by act of parliament 4 Febr. *anno* 27 H. 8. in the beginning of 28 H. 8. there was a great infurrection of the lord Huffey and 20800 perfons in Lincolnfhire pretending it to be for the caufe of religion: againft whom Charles Brandon duke of Suff. went and appeafed them. As foon as they were appeafed, a great rebellion for the fame pretence of 40000 of that county, of whom fir Robert Afke was leader: againft whom the duke of Norf. and others went, and difperfed them. Soon after a great commotion for the fame pretence was raifed in Lancafhire of men in that county, and in Cumberland, Weftmerland, and Northumberland: againft whom the earl of Derby was employed, and quieted them. After this Mufagrave Tilly and others to a great multitude did rife, and affaulted Carlifle caftle, whom the duke of Norf. overthrew. Soon after fir Francis Bigot with a great number of people rofe at Setrington, Pickering, Leigh, and Scarborough in Yorkfhire, whom the duke of Norf. pacified. And after this the lord Darcy, Afk, Conftable, Bulmer, and others began a new rebellion about Hull in Yorkfhire, whom the duke of Norf. appeafed. And all thefe rebellions fell out between the beginning of 28 H. 8. and 30 H. 8.

The king intending the fuppreffion of the great monafteries, which in effect he brought to paffe in *anno* 31 H. 8. for preventing of future dangers and keeping thofe northern counties in quiet, in *anno* 31 of his reign raifed a prefident and councell there, and gave them befides two feverall powers and authorities under one great feal, the one of oier and terminer, *De quibufcunque congregationibus et conventiculis illicitis coadunationibus, confœderationibus, Lollardiis, mifprifionibus, falfis allegantiis, tranfgreffionibus, riotis, routis, retentionibus, contemptibus, falfitatibus, manutenentibus, oppreffionibus, violentiis, extortionibus, et aliis malefactis, offenfis, et injuriis quibufcunque, per quæ pax et tranquillitas fubditorum noftrorum in com' Eborum, Northumberland, Weftmerland, Durham, et com' civitatis Eborum, Kingfton fuper Hull, et Newcaftle fuper Tinam gravetur, &c. fecundum legem et confuetudinem regni noftri Angliæ,* [a] *vel aliter fecundum fanas difcretiones veftras audiend' et terminand'.* The other authority was [b] *Nec non quafcunque actiones reales, feu de libero tenemento, et perfonales caufafque debitorum et demandorum quorumcunque in com' prædictis, quando ambæ partes vel al-*

Anno 31 H. 8. 6. parte Roberto Landavens' epifcopo præfidenti concilii, &c. et aliis fact.

[a] Firft, it was refolved by all the judges of the court of common pleas. Trin. 6 Jac. that this claufe is againft law, as the like had been formerly often refolved. See before cap. of the Court of Requefts. [b] 2. It was then alfo clearly refolved, that this latter claufe was againft law, not only for the caufe aforefaid, but alfo for that actions real and perfonall were not to be heard and determined by commiffion, but according to the laws of the realm. Vid. 2 Eliz. Dier 175.

tera

tera pars fic paupertate gravata fuer', quod commode jus fuum fecundum legem regni noftri aliter profequi non poffit, fimiliter fecundum leges et confuetudines regni noftri Angliæ, vel aliter fecundum fanas difcretiones veftras audiend' et terminand'.

But thefe authorities were granted, to the end that commiffioners by mediation might quiet controverfies when one of the parties or both were poor, who are ever moft clamorous. And all the authority they had was expreffed in the patents or commiffion under the great feal, without any reference to inftructions or any inftructions at all. But afterwards, for that the faid commiffion was againft

[246] law, and to the end, that their authority fhould not be known, they procured the firft inftitution to be *ex diametro* altered, viz. that their commiffion fhould not give them any expreffe authority at all, but wholly did refer their authority to certain inftructions which they kept themfelves in private, and were not enrolled in any court, whereunto the fubject might have refort. *Sed mifera fervitus eft, ubi jus eft vagum, aut incognitum.* And thereupon king James being informed hereof by the judges of the common pleas (who had granted prohibitions to the prefident and councell) gave order that their inftructions fhould be enrolled, to the end that the fubject might take advice of learned councell what courfe he might take to enjoy the benefit of the laws of the realm, his beft birthright.

This is left out of the print in latter time, but it is in the parliament rol, &c.

And it appeareth in the fubfidy in *anno* 32 H. 8. cap. 50. that H. 8. raifed not only this prefident and councell, but a prefident and councell alfo having like authority in the weftern parts, pretending it to be for their eafe to receive juftice at their own doors, but they of Cornwall, Devon' &c. defirous to live under the immediate government of the king, and the common law, oppofed it, *et fic commiffio illa cito evanuit,* which commiffion under the great feal we have feen. See in the ftatute of 13 El. where the prefident and councell of York is mentioned, and no man doubteth, but that there is a prefident and councell *de facto*, but what jurifdiction they have is the queftion.

13 El. cap. 13. See in the chapter of the court of requeft, anfwer made to this objection in like cafe.

Thus much (having taken upon us to write) we have clearly and plainly delivered our opinion, and he that fearcheth the fecret of hearts, knoweth that we have publifhed nothing herein or in any other of our works, *reluctante confcientia.*

And in refpect of fome continuance it hath had, and many decrees made, it were worthy of the wifdome of a parliament for fome eftablifhment to be had therein.

CAP.

CAP. L.

The Courts and their Jurisdictions within the City of London; and first of

The Court of the Hustings.

FOR the antiquity and name of this noble city, you may read in Lambard, *inter leges Edovardi regis*, fo. 136. b. *Sed utere tuo judicio, nihil enim impedio.* * But Ammianus Marcellinus an approved author above 1200 years since, calleth it *vetustum oppidum.* And Cornelius Tacitus, (who maried the daughter of Lucius Agricola the Roman, and was here with him by the space of seven years) affirmeth *Quod Londinum tempore Neronis* (which is above 1500 years past) *fuit copia negotiatorum et commeatu maxime celebre.* To be short, it is *camera regis, reipublicæ cor, et totius regni epitome.*

Lib. 8. fo. 130. in the case of the city of London.
* For the antiquity.
For the antiquity and name.

And in searching among such records as we had observed, of or concerning this noble city, we have observed a charter in the Saxon tongue made by William the Conqueror in these words; ƿilliam Cẏnᵹ ᵹreꞇ ƿilliam Biꞅceop ⁊ Goꝺꝼreᵹeꞅ poꞃꞇᵹereꝼan ⁊ ealle þa Buꞃhƿaꞃen þe on Lunꝺen beon, &c. *i.* William the king greeteth William the bishop and Godfrey the portreve, and all the burgesses that in London be, &c.

This is the highest court and of the greatest celebrity within London. It is holden before the maior and sherifs, of all pleas, reall, mixt, and personall. *Nota*, the rule of the Register is, *Quodlibet breve, quod tangit liberum tenementum in London, dirigitur majori sive custodi et vicecomitibus; et alia brevia tantum vicecomitibus.*

Regist. 2. b.
F. N. B. 6. f.

This word hustings is derived of two Saxon words, viz. *hus* which signifieth a house, or bench, and *things*, that is, causes, or pleas, as much to say, as the bench, or court of pleas, for *bancus* or bench is taken for a court, as the kings bench, the common bench, &c.

Fleta lib. 2. in his chapter *De differentiis curiarum. Habet rex curiam suam, &c. Et in civitatibus et burgis et in hustingis London, Lincoln, Winton et Eborum et alibi in libertatibus, &c. Et cap.* 48. *Habet rex curiam suam in civitatibus, burgis et locis exemptis,* [a] *sicut in hustingis London, Winton, Lincolne, Eborum, et apud Shepey, ubi barones et cives recordum habent, &c.* So as neither the name nor the court is appropriated to London.

Fleta, lib. 2. ca. 2. & 28.
[a] F.N.B. 61. q. juris utrum. 62. b. partition. & 199. ex gravi querela. b.

[b] For writs of error to be brought of any judgment in the hustings; see the Register and F. N. B.

[b] Regist. 130, 131 F. N. B. 23 e.

[c] Concerning forain vouchers, and forain pleas, see F. N. B. fo. 6. E. *et stat. de Glouc'.* cap. 12.

[c] F. N. B. 6. e. Glouc. cap. 12.

Of lands holden, no writ doth lye but in London according to the custome. Dier 15 El. 317. Judgment of the outlawries in the hustings is not given by the maior, who is coroner or his deputy, but by the recorder by the custome of this city.

2 part Institutes. 33 E. 3. jurisd. 60. 36 H. 6. 33.

2, 3. The

2, 3. *The two Courts of the Sherifs.*

Regist. ubi sup. F. N. B. 23. a. [248]

In curia civitatis prædict' coram vicecom' sine brevi nostro secundum consuetudinem ejusdem civitatis. If an erroneous judgment be given before the sherifs the party grieved shall sue a writ of error, and remove this before the maior and sherifs in the hustings.

Stephanides cap. de dispositione urbis.

For the antiquity of the sherifs and their courts, Fitz-Stephen, who wrote of the government of London in the reign of king Stephen, of this city saith;

Nota.

Hæc civitas urbe Roma, secundum chronicorum fidem, satis antiquior est, &c. Unde et adhuc antiquis eisdem utuntur legibus communibus institutis; hæc similiter illi regionibus est distincta, habet annuos pro consulibus vicecomites, habet senatoriam dignitatem, et magistratus minores, &c. ad genera causarum, deliberative, demonstrative, judicialis loca sua fora singula, habet sua diebus statutis comitia, &c.

In Lib. abbat de Ramsey. * Tempore H. 1.

In the booke of the abby of Ramsey to a conveyance or concord * without date made in the court of the hustings of London of a certain house in Walbroc within the city, between *Wilcnothus de Walbroc*, and *Renaldum abbatem de Ramsey*, the witnesses were (amongst others) *Willielmus de Einsford vicecomes de London, et Johannes subvicecomes ejus, et Gervasius clericus ejus.* More might be said hereof, but it is clear, that so long as this city hath been a county of it self, so long there have been sherifs, for it cannot be a county without sherifs. There are within the wals of this city 97 parishes, and out of the wals 16 parishes, standing partly within the liberties of the city, and part without in Midd. and Surry.

4. *The Court of Equity before the Lord Mayor, commonly called, The Court of Conscience.*

1 H. 6. 14. Lib. 8. fo. 126. Lib. Int. Rast. Custome 21 and Ville 1.

The custome of London is, and hath been time out of mind, that when a man is impleaded before the sherifs, the mayor upon the suggestion of the defendant may send for the parties and for the record, and examine the parties upon their pleas, and if it be found upon his examination that the plaintif is satisfied, that he may award that the plaintif shall be barred: and this was holden by the court to be a good custome, but by no custome he can examine after judgment. Note, a court of equity may be had by prescription, but cannot be raised by grant, as hath been said in the chapter of the Chancery, and of the County Palatine of Chester.

5. *The Court of the Mayor and Aldermen.*

See 43 El. c. 12. In fine. Lib. 4. fol. 64, 65. Fulwoods case. The print is 28 E. 3. cap. 10. but it should be 27 E. 3. cap. 10. And so resolved by parliament, in 1 H. 4. cap. 15. Altered in the penalty. 17 R. 2. Rot. par. nu. 26. explained by parliament not to extend to error in judgment.

This is a court of record, and consisteth of the lord mayor, the recorder and 23 aldermen, whereof the two sherifs being aldermen are part.

It is ordained and established that the mayor, sherifs and aldermen, which have the governance of the city, shall redresse and correct the errors, defaults and misprisions which be used in the city of London, for default of good governance of the mayor, sherifs and aldermen, &c. This is declaratory of their former power of governance, and for this cause principally amongst others, this court was instituted.

In this court are many courts, as namely,

6. *The Court of Orphans.*

The mayor and aldermen by custome have the custody of orphans within the city. And if they commit the custody of the orphans to another man, he shall have a ravishment of ward, if the orphan be taken away. F. N. B. 142. g. 32 E. 3. gard. 31. 8 R. 2. ibid. 166. Li. 4. 64, 65.

It is enacted, that the mayor and chamberlain of London for the the time being, shall have the keeping of all the lands and goods of such orphans as happen within the city, saving to the king and other lords their rights of such as hold of them out of the same liberty. Rot. par. 1 R. 2. nu. 130. [249]

A recognizance may be acknowledged in this court before the mayor and aldermen to the chamberlain for orphans. Lib. 4. fol. 64. 65, Fulwoods case.

The chamberlain is a sole corporation to him and his successors for orphans: and a recognizance or bond made to him and his successors concerning orphans shall by custome goe to his successor. Lib. 4. ubi sup.

The government of orphans belong to the mayor and aldermen, and they have jurisdiction of them, and therefore if any orphan sue in the ecclesiasticall court, or elsewhere for a legacy, or duty due to them by the custome, a prohibition doth lye. See the first part of the Institutes, sect. 267. how the goods of a freeman of London shall be divided.

For the liberties of London, see 50 E. 3. fo. 143.

An act was made in 7 H. 4. cap. 9. much prejudiciall to the liberties of this city, which is in print, and it was repealed in 9 H. 4. nu. 30. which is not printed. 7 H. 4. cap 9. Rot. par. 9 H. 4. nu. 30.

It would aske a treatise by it self to handle at large the other authorities and powers of the mayor and aldermen in the court of aldermen, and of the other courts within this city, which we will run over as briefly as we can. And the rather, for that in my books of reports I have published many cases concerning the courts, customes, liberties, franchises, and priviledges of this city, and also in the first part of the Institutes, and in this and other parts thereof. Lib. 2. fol. 57. Lib. 4. fo. 18. 54. 64. 65. & 113. Lib. 5. fo. 63. 64. 73. 83. 107. Lib. 8. fol. 122. 125. 126. 127. 129.

Vide Lib. 11. fol. 53. & 194. James Bagges his case. See the first part of the Institutes fol. 176. b. sect. 267. See the second part of the Institutes, Mag. Cart. cap. 9.

7. *The Court of Common Council.*

This court hath some resemblance of the high court of parliament, for it consisteth of two houses, viz. the one of the mayor and aldermen, and the other of such as be of the common assembly resembling the whole comminalty of London. In this court they may make constitutions and lawes for advancement of trade and traffick; for the better execution of the lawes and statutes of the Lib. 5. fo. 62. 63. the chamberlains case. Lib. 8. fo. 123. 125. Le case del city de Londres.

the realme, or *pro bono publico*, and for the good government of the city. So as these constitutions and laws be not contrary to the lawes and statutes of the realm. And this being made by the mayor, aldermen, and comminalty, do bind within this city and the liberties therof. They of the common assembly do give their assent by holding up their hands.

8. *The Court of the Ward-mote.*

Wardmote is derived from ward and mote, that is, the ward court. In London the parishes are as towns, and the wards are as hundreds, and therefore *riens diens gard* was a good challenge at the common law.

7 H. 6. 36. 38. 7 H. 7. 4.

In this city there are 26 wards divided for the government of them amongst the 24 aldermen of the city. This wardmote inquest, consisting of 12 or more of every ward shall enquire of such persons as have not paved or amended their parts and portions of the streets and lanes within the said city, &c.

32 H. 8. cap. 17.

9. *The Court of Hall-mote.*

This is derived of hall and mote, as much to say as the hall court, i. *Conventus civium in aulam publicam*, every company of London having an hall wherein they keep their courts, and this court anciently called hall-mote or folke-mote.

[250]

10. *The Court of the Chamberlaine for Apprentices.*

This court concerning the making free of apprentices. One may be free of London three manner of wayes, viz. by service, as here in case of apprentices: 2. By birthright, the sonne of a freeman: and 3. By redemption, by order of the court of aldermen.

Lib. 8. fo. 129: the case of the city of London.

Now to treat of the great and notable franchises, liberties, and customes of the city of London, would require a whole volume of it self. But there is a most beneficiall statute made for the strengthening and preservation of the same, which I know no other corporation hath. [a] It is enacted that the citizens of London shall enjoy all their whole liberties whatsoever with this clause, *Licet usi non fuerunt vel abusi fuerunt*, and notwithstanding any * statute to the contrary, &c. *Lege statutum*, for by this act the city may claim liberties by prescription, charter, or parliament, notwithstanding any statute made before 7 R. 2. And this is the statute mentioned in our books.

[a] Rot. par. 7 R. 2. nu. 37. Vid. inf. 252. 253.
* Nota hoc. 8 H. 7. 4. b. Dier 22 Eliz. 373. 7 H. 6. 1. 21 H. 7. 16. 17. Pl. com. 36. b. 38, 47. 59. Lib. 8. fo. 129.

11. *The Court of the Conservation of the Water and River of Thames &c.*

The maior of London for the time being hath the conservation and rule of the water and river of the Thames, and the issues, breaches, and lands overflown, &c. from the bridges of Stanes unto

4 H. 7. cap. 15.

unto the water of Yendall and Medwey, and authority as touching punition for using unlawfull nets, and other unlawfull engines in fishing, and to all correction and punishment there concerning unlawfull nets and engines there. In all commissions touching the water of Ley, the mayor of London shall be one. See hereafter cap. Commission of Sewers the statute of 3 Jac. cap. 14. that sewers that fall into the Thames shall be subject to the commission of sewers.

Rot. parl. 2 H. 5. nu. 15.

Rot. parl. 2 H. 5. nu. 16.

3 Jac. cap. 14.

12. *The Court of the Coroner in London.*

The mayor is coroner within the city of London, and the court of the coroner is holden before him or his deputy. *Vide postea* in the chapter of the Coroner.

13. *The Court of the Escheator in London.*

The lord mayor is also escheator within the city, and this court is holden before him or his deputy. See before in the chapter of Escheator.

14. *The Court of Policies and of Assurances in London.*

This court sitteth by force of the commission under the great seal warranted by act of parliament *an.* 43 Eliz. cap. 12. there being an officer or clerk to register assurances, the jurisdiction of which court you may reade in that act of parliament made to encourage merchants to trade and traffick, the benefit whereof appeareth there, and is too long to be recited, and the rather for that we can adde nothing to that act of parliament.

43 Eliz. cap. 12.

15. *The Court of the Tower of London.* [251]

This court is holden within the virge of London before the steward there by prescription of debt, trespasse, and other actions of any summe greater or lesser, whereof you may reade in 4 E. 4. fo. 36. a. b.

4 E. 4. 36. a. b.

Note, where it is said, that the Tower of London is within the city of London, it is thus to be understood, that the ancient wall of London (the mention whereof yet appeareth) extendeth through the Tower, and all that which is invironed with the said wall, viz. on the west part thereof, is within the city of London, that is to say, in the parish of All-Saints-Barking within the ward of the Tower of London. And the residue of the Tower of London, on the east part of that ancient wall is within the county of Middlesex. And this upon view and examination was found out, Mic. 13 Jac. regis, in the case of Sir Thomas Overbury, who was poysoned in a chamber in the Tower on the west part of that old wall. And therefore Weston the principall murderer was tried before commissioners of oier and terminer in London, and so was Sir Gervase Elvice lieutenant of the Tower, as accessary.

16. Of

16. *Of the Jurisdiction and Authority of the President, Censors, and Comminalty of the Colledge of Physicians scituate in Knight-Riderstreet in the Ward of Castle Barnard within the City of London and 7 Miles Compasse.*

Lib. 8. fo. 107. &c. Dr Bonhams case. See the statutes of 3 H. 8. c. 6. & 11. 14 H. 8. cap. 5. 1 Mar. cap. 9. 32 H. 8. ca. 40. 42. 34 H. 8. cap. 8. * Rot. pat. 32 H. 6. m. 17. by what warrant physick is to be given to the king.

Of this colledge, and of their jurisdiction and authority, sufficient hath been said in the 8 Book of Reports in Doctor Bonhams case, whereunto we refer the studious reader. Hereunto we will adde for the safety of physicians, especially of the kings physitians a record worthy of observation.

* *Rex adversa valetudine laborans de assensu concilii sui assignavit Johannem Arundel, Johannem Saceby, et W. Hatcliffe medicos: Robertum Warren et Johannem Marshall chirurgos ad libere ministrandum et exequendum in et circa personam suam; imprimis, viz. quod licite valeant moderare sibi diætam suam et quod possint ministrare potiones, syrupos, confectiones, laxitivas medicinas, clysteria, suppositoria, caput purgea, gargarismata lealnen, epithimota, fomentationes, embrocationes, capitis rasuram, unctiones, emplastra, cerera ventos. cum scarificatione vel sine, emorodorum provocationes, &c. Dantes singulis in mandatis quod in executione præmissorum sint intendentes, &c.*

Upon this, four things are to be observed. First, that no physick ought to be given to the king without good warrant. 2. That this warrant ought to be made by the advice of his councell. 3. They ought to minister no other physick then that which is set down in writing. 4. That they may use the aide of those chirurgions named in the warrant, but of no apothecary; but to prepare and do all things themselves, &c. And the reason of all this is the precious regard had of the health and safety of the king, which is the head of the common-wealth. * The science of physick containeth the knowledge of chirurgery.

* 32 H. 8. cap. 40.

3 E. 3. coron. 163.

If one that is of the mysterie of a physician take a man in cure and giveth him such physick as within three days he dye thereof, without any felonious intent, and against his will, it is no homicide.

Britton cap. 5. De homicides.

But Britton saith, that if one that is not of the mysterie of a physitian or chirurgion, take upon him the cure of a man and he dieth of the potion or medicine, this is, (saith he) covert felony.

Mirror cap. 4. § De homicide. Verb. [*daut' part*]

[252]

Physitians and chirurgions *soient sages en lour faculties, eyent sanes les consciences, cy que rien ne ent failli a faire cure, silz ne scavoient a bone chese mitter, ou silz a bone chese scavoient et sentre mettent nequidant follement ou negligentment, issint que ilz mittont froide per chaude ou le revers, ou trope peu de cure, ou nemi mitter un due diligence, et nosmement in arsons et absciffions que sont defend' a faire forsq; al peril des mesters si lour patients moreront ou perdent memorie, in tiels cases sont ils homicides ou mayhemers.*

And thus much concerning physitians.

For courts holden in other cities, towns corporate, and burghs, our purpose is not, to treat of them, because they are private and sufficiently known; but let us say somewhat of the liberties, franchises, and immunities of this noble city.

Parl. 17 R. 2. nu. 26.

It is enacted, that the statute of 28 E. 3. cap. 10. shall not extend

tend to any erroneous judgement given or to be given in the city of London.

See after cap. 54. the ancient office of garbling of ſpices, &c.

There is a writ in the Regiſter neceſſary to be put in execution for the wholeſomeneſſe of aire in London, and in all other cities, &c. *De vicis et venellis mundandis.* Regiſt. 267. b.

Lourgulary, or lourglary is an offence when any caſt any corrupt thing appoyſoning the water in or about London, compounded of theſe two words *lour* corruption, and *laron* a thief or felon, as * burglary: and if any dye by reaſon of any ſuch offence within a year after, it is felony, and extendeth to all other cities, burghs, &c.

* See the third part. of the Inſtit. cap. Burglary or Burgulary.

It was petitioned to the king, that no man in cities, towns, or elſewhere, do carry maces of ſilver, but only the kings ſerjeants at armes, but that they carry maces of copper and of no other metall. Whereunto the king anſwered, [The ſame ſhall be ſo, except the ſerjeants of the city of London, who may carry their maces of ſilver within the liberties of London before the mayor in the preſence of the king.]

Omnes homines London ſint quieti et liberi, et omnes res eorum per totam Angliam, et per portus maris de theolonio et paſſagio, et ab omnibus aliis conſuetudinibus. V. Carfam H. 1. De liber. London.

In the charter of H. 3. bearing teſte 18 Febr. *anno regni ſui* 11. the king granted to the city of London *vicecomitatum London et Midd. &c.* And in that charter this ſpeciall franchiſe and priviledge is granted to the ſherifes of London and Middleſex for the time being in theſe words. *Ita ſcilicet quod ſi illi qui pro tempore fuerint vicecomites conſtituti aliquod delictum fecerint, unde miſericordiam pecuniæ debeant incurrere, non judicentur ad plus niſi ad miſericordiam vigint' libr' et hoc ſine damno aliorum civium ſi vicecomit' non ſufficiant' ad miſericordiarum ſuarum ſolutionem. Si verò aliquod delictum fecerint, per quod periculum vitæ vel membrorum incurrere debeant, judicentur ſicut judicari debent per legem civitatis: de hiis autem quæ ad prædictum vicecomitatum pertinent reſpondeant vicecomites ad ſcaccarium noſtrum coram juſticiariis noſtris. Salvis eiſdem vicecomitibus libertatibus quas alii cives London habent.*

11 H. 3. 18 Febr. ſpeciall and rare liberties granted to the city of London.

In the charter of the ſame king bearing date 16 *Martii anno regni ſui undecimo ſupradicto*, the king granted to the city of London *Quòd nullus civis civitat' prædict' faciat duellum, et quod de placitis ad coronam pertinent' ſe poſſint diſrationare ſecundum antiquam conſuetudinem civitatis, et quod infra muros civitatis, neque in portſokne nemo capiat hoſpitium per vim vel per liberationem mareſchal', &c. et ſi quis in aliqua terrarum noſtrarum citra mare, vel ultra, ſive in portubus maris citra mare, vel ultra theolonium vel aliquam aliam conſuetudinem ab hominibus London ceperit poſtquam ipſe à recto defecerit, vic' London namium inde apud London capiant.*

Anno 11 H. 3. 16 Martii duellum.

Hoſpitium. Per liberationem mareſchalli.

In another charter of the ſame king bearing date 18 *Auguſti anno* 11 *ſupradict'* the king did diſafforeſt and diſwarren the foreſt and warren of Stanes in the county of Middleſex. Anno 11 H. 3. 18 Auguſti.

And by another charter of the ſame king bearing date 26 *Martii anno regni ſui* 52, the king granted to the citizens of London in theſe words, *Conceſſimus eiſdem civibus quod de placitis ad coronam pertinent', et hiis maxime, quæ infra civitatem prædictam et ejus ſuburbium fieri contingent, ſe poſſint diſrationare ſecundum antiquam conſuetudinem*

Anno 52 H. 3. 26 Martii. De placitis ad coronam.

Super tumulos.

civitatis prædict', co tamen excepto, quod super tumulos mortuorum de eo quod dictur' essent mortui si viverent non liceat præcise jurare, sc. loco mortuorum qui ante obitum suum electi fuerint ad eos disrationandos qui de rebus ad coronam spectantibus appellati fuerint, vel rectati alii liberi et legales eligantur qui idem sine dilatione faciant quod per defunctos memoratos, si venirent fieri oporteret, et quod tam forinseci quam alii attornatos facere possint in hustingo London tam agendo quam defendendo in curia nostra.

Attornati in hustingo.

The citizens or burgesses of London were before and after the conquest governed by portgraves or portgreves untill the reign of R. 1. by whose charter they were governed by two bailiffs: and yet king Richard in the first year of his reign appointed them a mayor, who continued therein untill the eighth year of king John, and then king John appointed a mayor. And forasmuch as sometimes the mayor appointed by the king was no citizen of London, king John in the tenth year of his reign granted to the citizens liberty and authority to choose *de se ipsis* a mayor, &c. And so it continueth unto this day.

An. 10 Johannis.
Mayor de se ipsis

Aldermen.

The aldermen of London were changed by election every year untill 28 E. 3. Then it was ordered they should not be removed without some speciall cause. But rot. parl. 17 R. 2. nu. 25. it is enacted that the aldermen of London shall not from henceforth be yearly chosen, but remain till they be put out for reasonable cause, notwithstanding the ordinances of E. 2. and E. 3. and so it still continueth.

Rot. parl. 17 R. 2. nu. 25. enacted.

Rot. pat. *anno* 1 E. 3. the king granted that the citizens of London should not be constrained to go out of the city of London to any war: and the liberties of this city shall not for any cause be taken into the kings hands. Rot. parl. 1 E. 3. *Authoritate parliamenti.*

Warre.
Liberties not to be taken into the kings hands.

See hereafter cap. of Forests, pag. Cart' H. 1. for their recreation by hunting, &c.

Albeit by the statute of Magna Carta and other acts of parliament, the liberties, priviledges, and franchises of the city of London be confirmed: yet the most beneficiall of them all is that of * 7 R. 2. before mentioned: whereby it is enacted, that the citizens of London shall enjoy the same, with this clause, *Licet usi non fuerint vel abusi fuerint,* [a] and notwithstanding any statute to the contrary.

Mag. Cart. cap. 9. Rot. pat. 11 H. 3.
Rot. parl. 5 R. 2. nu. 19.
50 E. 3. nu. 14?.
* Rot. par. 7 R. 2. nu. 37.
Vid. sup. pag. 250.
[a] Nota hoc.

These notable, rare, and speciall liberties and priviledges we have attempted to remember: but whether herein we have done that good to the city that we intended, we know not, for we have omitted many more of no small number of great rarity and consequence too long here to be recited.

See before pag. 125. *Breve de listis et barris pro duello fac.* Vid. rot. cart. 18 *Februarii* 11 H. 3. against the exaction of the lieutenant of the Tower of Kidelles, &c. 2 part of the Institutes Mag. Cart. cap. 23.

The Court of the Juſtices aſſigned for the Government of the Jews.

Juſticiarii ad Cuſtodiam Judæorum aſſignati.

OMNES Judæi ubicunq; in regno ſunt, ſub tutela et defenſione regis ligea debent eſſe, nec quilibet eorum alicui diviti ſe poteſt ſubdere ſine regis licentia: Judæi enim et omnia ſua regis ſunt. Quod ſi quiſpiam detinuerit eos, vel pecuniam eorum, perquirat rex, ſi vult, tanquam ſuum proprium. Inter leges Edwardi, Lamb. cap. 29. fo. 133. b.

Theſe juſtices did hold a court concerning the cuſtody and government of the Jewes, as (amongſt many other records) it appeareth rot. pat. an. 41 H. 3. m. 4. nu. 6. And that then Philip Baſſet, Philip Luvell, Henry de Bathon, and Simon Paſſel, &c. were then juſtices *ad cuſtodiam Judæorum aſſignat'*. But when the Jewes were utterly (as hath been ſaid) baniſhed, this court ceaſed, which was in 18 E. 1. *anno domini* 1293. See the ſecond part of the Inſtitutes, ſtat. *de Judaiſmo*, rot. clauſ. 18 E. 1. memb. 6. See Tho. Walſ. *in hypodigmate Neuſtriæ* 18 E. 1. Rot. pat. 41 H. 3. m. 4. nu. 6.

The Courts of Stainclife and Frendles Wapentakes.

BECAUSE I find mention made in acts of parliament of the courts of Stainclife and Frendles Wapentakes, &c. I thought good to refer you to thoſe acts. 3 H. 5. cap. 2. 9 H. 6. cap. 10.

CAP. LI. [255]

Of the City of Weſtminſter.

IT hath his name of the monaſtery, which minſter ſignifieth, and it is called Weſtminſter in reſpect of the Eaſtminſter not far from the Tower of London.

This Weſtminſter Sebert the firſt king of the Eaſt Saxons that was chriſtened, founded; and he founded alſo the univerſity of Cambridge, as works and witneſſes of his Chriſtianity. Sebert began his reign anno Domini 603.

But leaving theſe, and others of like nature, to others not lying properly in my way; let us turn our eye to ſuch particular juriſdiction as within this city is exerciſed. For the better underſtanding whereof it is to be known, that within this city there are twelve ſe-

 verall

verall wards, out of which there are elected one burgeſſe and one aſſiſtant in every ſeverall ward; and out of theſe twelve, two are elected yearly in the Thurſday in the Eaſter week for chief burgeſſes to continue for one whole year following. To theſe burgeſſes authority is given by act of parliament in the 27 year of the reign of queen Eliz. (not printed) to hear, examine, determine, and puniſh according to the laws of the realm and lawfull cuſtomes of the city of London, matters of incontinency, common ſcolds, inmates, and common annoyances, and likewiſe to commit ſuch perſons as ſhall offend againſt the peace, and thereof to give knowledge within 24 hours to ſome juſtice of peace within the county of Midd.

This act was at the firſt but a probationer, but is continued to this day.

One thing concerning this ancient monaſtery is obſervable, that after the high court of parliament was divided into two ſeverall houſes (whereof we have ſaid ſomewhat in the chapter of the High Court of parliament) the accuſtomed place of that thrice worthy aſſembly of the knights, citizens, and burgeſſes of parliament (when the parliament was holden in Weſtminſter) was in the chapter houſe of the abbot of Weſtminſter, there to debate and conſult *De arduis et urgentibus negotiis regni, et ſtatum regni et eccleſiæ Anglicanæ concernentibus, &c.* And this continued untill the ſtatute of 1 E. 6. c. 14. which gave to the king colledges, free chappels, chaunteries, and whereby the king enjoyed the ancient and beautifull free chappell of S. Stephens, founded by king Stephen, which had lands and revenues of the old yearly value, of 1085 l. 10 s. 5 d.) Since which time the chappell thereof hath ſerved for the houſe of commons when parliaments have been holden at Weſtminſter.

See before in the chapter of the High Court of Parliament.

Rot. parl. anno 50 E. 3. nu. 8.

Radulphus de Ingham chief juſtice of England, (a very poor man being fined before him at 13 s. 4 d.) in another tearm, moved with pity cauſed the record to be raſed and made 6 s. 8 d: for which he (for his fine) made the clock (to be heard into Weſtminſter Hall) and the clockhouſe in Weſtminſter, which coſt him 800, marks, and continueth unto this day, which ſum was entred into the roll. And almoſt in the like caſe in the reign of queen Elizabeth, Sir Robert Catlyn chief juſtice of England would have had juſtice Southcote (one of his companions juſtice of the kings bench) to have altered a record, which the juſtice denyed to doe, and ſaid openly in court, that he meant not to build a clockhouſe.

Tempore E. 1. Vid. 2 R. 3. f. 10. a.

This monaſtery in *anno* 30 H. 8. was ſurrendred to the king, who erected thereof a dean and chapter. *Anno* 33 H. 8. it was raiſed to a biſhoprick, and Thomas Thurlby made thereof the firſt and laſt biſhop, &c. Queen Eliz. made it a colledge conſiſting of a dean, twelve prebends, a ſchoolmaſter, an uſher, 40. ſcholars, and 12 almeſmen, and ſo it was named the collegiate church of Weſtminſter.

In *anno* 37 H. 8. the kings mannor of Weſtminſter was made an honor.

37 H. 8. cap. 18.

CAP. LII.

Of the City of Norwich, &c.

WITHIN this city there was in the reign of king Edward the Confessor 1300. citizens, and then this city paid to the king 20 l. and to the earl 10 l. And besides these 20 s. and four prebendaries and six sextaries of hony, a bear, and six dogs to bait him. Now it yeeldeth 70 l. to the king, and a 100 s. to the queen, and a palfrey, and twenty pound of white rent to the earl, &c.

In the book of Domesday made by William the Conqueror.

The foundation of the incorporation of this city is very ancient, for in ancient manuscripts it appeareth that *in tempore Steph. regis de nova fundata et ut villa populata communitas fact'.*

This city is highly commended for many things, for it is truly said of it, *Quod suis opibus, frequentia, ædificiorum elegantia, templorum pulchritudine et numero, (parœcias enim plus minus* 30. *complectitur) civium sedulitate, in principem fide, in* * *exteros humanitate, inter celeberrimas Britanniæ urbes merito connumeranda, &c. Mœnibus validis (in quibus crebræ dispositæ turres, et undecim portæ) undique obsepta, nisi ad ortum qua flumen (cum sinuoso flexu* 4. *pontibus pervium septentrionalem urbis partem interluerit) profundo alveo et precipitibus ripis defendit.* * It is preferred before all the cities in England except London. It hath above 30 parishes, and it is as large within the wals as London. It had within it and the liberties six religious houses and one hospitall.

Camden in Britannia.

* Urbanitas ab urbe.

* Alex. Nevill.

For the better establishing of the ecclesiasticall jurisdiction belonging to the bishop of Norwich (of which jurisdiction in generall we are to treat hereafter) it shall not be impertinent to set down the true state of this bishoprick.

In *anno* 27 H. 8. and before William Rugge doctor of divinity of the university of Cambridge was abbot of the [a] monastery of S. Bennets de Hulmo in the county of Norf. and the bishoprick of Norwich becomming void by the death of Richard Nick commonly called the blind bishop, the king nominated the said abbot to be bishop of Norwich. And afterwards the 4. of Febr. *anno* 27 H. 8.

[a] This monastery was founded by king Kanute and increased by Edw. the Confessor, and the monastery made of that strength as it seemed to be *potius castrum quam claustrum*. It was of the order of S. Benedict of black monks.

[b] It was (*amongst other things*) enacted by authority of parliament, that such person as should be elected and consecrated bishop of the said sea should have and enjoy to him and his successors bishops of the said bishoprick of Norwich united and knit to the said bishoprick the monastery of S. Bennets, and all and singular mannors, lands, tenements, &c. belonging to the said monastery, &c. And that the person which should be named bishop of Norwich and his successors bishops of the same bishoprick from thenceforth [c] should be abbots of the monastery of S. Bennets, and have the dignities of the said abbacy

[b] Statut. de 27 H. 8. concerning the bishoprick of Norwich.

[c] The like is not in England.

bacy united, incorporated, and knit to the sea of the said bishop, &c.

See before in the chapt. of the royall Franchise of Ely, that king H. 1. of the monastery of Ely made a bishopr. but king H. 1. had therein one end, and king H. 8. another.

[257]

But peruse the statute, and you shall find that doctor Rugge had *beneficium viscatum*, for the bishoprick lost much more by that act then it gained. And afterwards this doctor was elected and consecrated bishop of Norwich: and being patron, in the right of his bishoprick, of the hospitall of S. Giles in Norwich, he as patron, and Nich. Shaxton master of the said hospitall by their deed acknowledged and inrolled bearing date 6 *Martii*, *anno* 1 E. 6. did give and grant to king E. 6. his heirs and successors the said hospitall and the possessions and hereditaments belonging to the same, and all other their possessions and hereditaments in the said county of Norf. certain concealors *(templorum helluones)* by pretext and colour of the said generall words passed the possessions and hereditaments of the said monastery of S. Bennets de Hulmo in a book of concealments under certain obscure words (which appear in the act of parliament hereafter mentioned) by letters patents of concealment bearing date the 2 day of August, *anno* 27 Eliz. and William Redmain doctor of divinity, and bishop of Norwich caused one Hamond a friend of his to take an estate to him and his heirs of and from the said concealors of all or the greatest part of the said monastery: which I (being then her majesties atturny generall) understanding, and utterly misliking the proceeding herein, conferred with the said bishop about the same, and in the end he was brought to agree, that an act of parliament should passe for the establishment of the said bishoprick and of the possessions thereof, which act (wherewith I was well acquainted) passed at the parliament holden in *anno* 39 El. and is in print, which you may read at large, wherein you shall observe the fraud and falshood of the concealors.

39 El. cap. 22.

What attempts these concealors (gracelesse and wicked men) made to the subversion of the deanery and chapter of the cathedrall church of Norwich, you may read in the third book of my Reports, fo. 73. *Sed (favente Deo et auspice Christo) isti helluones non prævaluerunt.* Which I have the rather remembred both for the establishment of the said bishoprick, as for the repose and quiet of very many fermors, officers, and other persons claiming interests in the said possessions in my native country.

Lib. 3. fo. 73. the case of the dean and chapter of Norwich.

And if any question shall hereafter be made either concerning any of the possessions of this bishoprick, or any other, or of any dean and chapter, or of the colledges in either of the universities, &c. by any concealor or other; their possessions are established by the act of parliament of 21 Jac. cap. 2. intituled, An act for the generall quiet of the subject against all pretence of concealment whatsoever.

21 Jac. cap. 2.

For the courts of justice within this city (which is our principall aime) we have treated of the like before in the city of London. To this we will adde an act of parliament concerning the jurisdiction of this city (whereof we have not found the like that we remember in any other) which in effect is as followeth.

Par. 2 R. 2. nu. 39. not in print.

It is enacted for the citizens of Norwich, that if their customes and usages heretofore used or hereafter to be used, be difficult

difficult or defective in part or in all, or that the ſame need any due amendment for any matter ariſing, whereof remedy was not aforetime had, that then the * bailifs and 24. citizens of the ſame city, ſo therefore yearly to be choſen, or the greater part of them, ſhall from henceforth have power to ordain and provide from time to time ſuch remedies which are moſt agreeable to faith and reaſon, and for the moſt profit, the good and peaceable government of the ſame town, and of ſtrangers thereto repairing, as to them ſhall ſeem beſt, ſo as ſuch ordinances be profitable for the king and his people.

* It hath now a mayor and 24 aldermen. Vide Rot. Cart. anno 4 H. 4.

It is a county of itſelf, and hath two ſherifs and large liberties without the wals. See the ſtatute of 33 H. 6. cap. 7. how many atturnies ſhould be in this city. See before in the chapter of the high court of parliament concerning new draperies, &c. and worſteads, &c. made in this city. See rot. parl. 18 E. 1. fo. 5. concerning the ancient liberties of this city.

33 H. 6. cap. 7.

* *Burgi et civitates fundat' et ædificat' ſunt ad tuitionem gentium, et populorum regni, et idcirco obſervari debent cum omni libertate, integritate et ratione.*

* Int. leges Wil. Conq. Lam. 125. Int. Leges Ethelſtani et Canuti fo. 62. & 106. Oppida inſtaurantur, &c.

* 14 H. 4. It is enacted, that the merchants and artificers of worſteads in Norf. may ſell their ſingle worſteads to any place or perſons being of the kings amity notwithſtanding any inhibition or liberty to the contrary.

* Par. 14. H. 4. nu. 47. not in print.

He that deſires the tearms, true makings, and quantities of worſteads: let him read the ſtatute of 11 H. 4. rot. parl. nu. 48.

[258]

Rot. par. 11 H. 4. nu. 48.

Trin. 13 E. 1. *in banco*, rot. 76. *Inſpeximus cart.* H. 3. *Civibus Norwic. de libertatibus conceſs'.*

Trin. 13 E. 1. in banco rot. 76.

The beautifull cathedrall or mother church of Norwich was begun to be built by Herbert biſhop of Norwich, *anno* 9 *Willielmi Rufi.*

The biſhops of this ſee had the firſt fruits of eccleſiaſticall livings within their dioceſſe before the ſtatute of 26 H. 8. ca. 3. which no biſhop, or archbiſhop of this realm had.

19 E. 3. juriſd. 22. 26 H. 8. cap. 3.

It hath alſo a famous river abounding with fiſh, eſpecially the pearch.

The ſtrong and noble caſtle of Norwich called Blanchflower invironed about with the city, but no part thereof but of the county of Norf. was not (as ſome ſuppoſe) built by Bigot earl of Norf. which ſome upon view thereof have conjectured, for that the arms of earl Bigot are graven on the wals thereof. For we find a charter of king Stephen in theſe words. *Stephanus rex Anglorum archiepiſcopis, epiſcopis, abbat', juſtic', comitibus, baronibus, vicecomitibus, miniſtris, et omnibus fidelibus ſuis Angliæ, ſalutem. Sciatis me dediſſe in feodo et hæreditate * Willielmo comiti Warren' filio meo caſtellum Norwici cum toto burgo, &c.*

And Rafe de Waet earl of Norwich defended this caſtle of Norwich againſt William the Conqueror, who was driven out of England, and travelled with his wife to Jeruſalem.

But true it is that earl Bigot being after owner thereof, did both repair

* This William married Iſabel daughter and heir of William earl Warren, and in her right was earl Warren. Vid. Mat. Par. pag. 92.

repair and enlarge the same, and set his arms upon the wals thereof. And so much for the antiquity (a great ornament of this city) of this castle, which now for want of reparation is ready to fall.

To conclude, this famous and free city is justly to be commended for profession of true religion, their loialty to their prince in all times of tumult, the good government of themselves, and the exercise of works of charity.

This is the chief city of my native country.

Nescio qua natale solum dulcedine cunctos
Ducit, et immemores non finit esse sui.

[259]

CAP LIII.

The Court of the Tourne.

2. Part of the Inst. Mag. Cart. ca. 35. 12 H. 7. 18. Fineux. Rot. pat. 2 R. 2. nu. 5.

WE have spoken of this court (being a court of record) in the Second part of the Institutes, Mag. Cart. cap. 35. whereunto we will adde a charter of William the Conqueror, which we find inrolled 2 R. 2. nu. 5. *pro decano et capitulo ecclesiæ beatæ Mariæ de Lincoln'.*

*Willielmus gratia Dei rex Anglorum, comitibus, vicecomitibus, et omnibus francigenis et qui in episcopatu * Remigii episcopi terras habent, salutem. Sciatis vos omnes, et cæteri mei fideles qui in Anglia manent, quod episcopales leges quæ non bene, nec secundum sanctorum canonum præcepta usque ad mea tempora in regno Anglorum fuerunt, communi concilio, et concilio archiepiscoporum meorum et cæterorum episcoporum et abbatum et omnium principum regni mei emendendas judicavi. Propterea mando, et regia authoritate præcipio, ut nullus episcopus vel archidiaconus de legibus episcopalibus amplius in * hundretto placita teneant, nec causam quæ ad regimen animarum pertinet ad judicium sæcularium hominum adducant, sed quicunque secundum episcopales leges de quacunque causa vel culpa interpellatus fuerit, ad locum quem ad hoc episcopus elegerit, et nominaverit, veniat, ibique de causa sua respondeat, et non secundum * hundrettum, sed secundum canones et episcopales leges rectum deo et episcopo suo faciat. Si vero aliquis per superbiam elatus ad justitiam episcopalem venire non voluerit, vocetur semel, et secundo, et tertio; quod si nec sic ad emendationem venerit, excommunicetur: et, si opus fuerit, ad hoc vindicand', fortitudo, et justitia regis vel vicecomitis adhibeatur: ille autem qui vocatus ad justitiam episcopi venire noluit, pro unaquaque vocatione legem episcopalem emendabit: hoc etiam defendo, et mea authoritate interdico, ne ullus vicecom' aut præpositus, aut minister regis, nec aliquis laicus homo de legibus quæ ad episcopum pertinent se intromittat: nec aliquis laicus homo alium hominem sine justitia episcopi ad judicium adducat; judicium vero in nullo loco portetur nisi in episcopali sede, aut in illo loco quem ad hoc episcopus constituerit.*

* This Remigius was the first bishop of Lincoln; the sea being removed from Dorchester to Lincoln.

* i. In turno.

* This is not intended of the hundred court but that in those times the sherif did hold his tourn *per hundredum*. See Mag. Cart. cap. 35. and the exposition thereupon.

For the confirmation of this charter, see in the register of the bishop of London. *Willielmus Dei gratia rex Anglorum R. Bainardo, et S. de Magna Villa, P. de Vabines, cæterisque meis fidelibus de Essex et de Hertfordshire, et de Middlesex, salutem. Sciatis vos omnes, &c.*

&c. Tenor istius cartæ est in Anglico de verbo in verbum in eadem carta. Consimilis carta ut ante ex libro cartarum archiepiscopi Cantuar'. Against this charter it is objected. First, the time of the enrolling thereof, viz. in 2 R. 2. being never heard of before. Secondly, out of the red book, *inter leges* H. 1. cap. 8. *de generalibus placitis comitatuum, i.* as well of the tourn, as of the county court.

[a] *Sicut antiqua fuerit institutione firmatum, salutari regis imperio, vera nuper est* [b] *recordatione firmatum, generalia comitatuum placita certis locis et vicibus et definito tempore per singulas Angliæ provincias convenire debere, nec ullis ultra fatigationibus agitari, nisi propria regis necessitas, vel commune regni commodum sæpius adjiciant. Intersint autem episcopi, comites, vicedomini, vicarii, centenarii, aldermanni, præfecti, præpositi, barones, vavassores, tungrevii et cæteri terrarum domini diligenter intendentes ne malorum impunitas, aut gravionum pravitas, vel judicum subversio solita miseros laceratione confiniant. Agantur itaque primo debita veræ* [a] *Christianitatis jura; secundo* [b] *regis placita; postremo* [c] *causæ singulorum dignis satisfactionibus expleantur.* Whereupon they conclude, that ecclesiasticall causes were handled in the tourn in the reign of H. 1. long after the said supposed charter. And certain it is that the bishops consistories were erected, and causes ecclesiasticall removed from the tourn to the consistory after the making of the said red book: *ideo penes lectorem sit judicium.*

In the same chapter of the said Red Book it is further said, *Et quoscunque* [d] *shiresgemote discordantes inveniet, vel amore congreget, vel sequestret judicio: debet enim shiresgemot* [e] *bis, hundreda et wapentachia* [f] *duodecies in anno congregari.*

The tourn is a court of record holden before the sherif: the ancient institution thereof was before Magna Carta [g] to hear and determine all felonies (death of man excepted) and common nusances. [h] See the statute of Magna Carta, cap. 17. and the exposition upon the same in the second part of the Institutes.

The stile of this court is *curia visus franc. domini regis apud B. coram vicecomite in turno suo, &c.* and not *turnum vicecom' tent', &c.* for *tornum est nisi perambulatio.* The articles inquirable in the tourn are known and need not be here rehearsed.

[a] Lib. rubeus in custodia remem. regis compositus tempore H. 1. cap. 8. Read the whole chapter. Vide ib. cap. 12.

[b] Int. leges Edw. Lamb. 135. Vid. stat. de Marlbr. cap. 10.

[260]

[a] Ecclesiasticall causes.

[b] Pleas of the crown in the tourn.

[c] Private causes in the county court.

[d] *Turnum* as it is here taken.

[e] And so is the turn holden to this day. Mag. Cart. 35.

[f] And so is the county court holden at this day. Mag. Cart. 35. 2 E. 6. 25.

[g] 22 E. 4. 22.

[h] 2. Part of the Inst. Mag. Cart. cap. 17.

CAP. LIV.

The Court of the Leet or View of Frankepledge.

[See Mich. 7 E. 1. rot. 9 Northampt. abbas de Burgo. See the 2. part of the Inſt. Mag. Cart. cap. 35.]

THIS is a court of record, and at the firſt derived and taken out of the tourn, and is holden before the ſteward, and he is judge thereof. Of the antiquity and juriſdiction of this court, you ſhall read in the ſecond part of the Inſtitutes, Magna Carta cap. 35. And what the ancient juriſdiction of the leet was, you ſhall alſo read in the ſecond part of the Inſtitutes, Mag. Carta cap. 17.

[Int' leges Edw. cap. 35.]

Leþ, leth, or leet is a Saxon word, and commeth of the verb ȝelaþian or ȝeleþian (ȝ being added *euphoniæ gratia*) i. *convenire*, to aſſemble together, *unde conventus*.

If a common nuſans, &c. done within the juriſdiction of the leet be not preſented in the leet, the ſherif in his tourn cannot enquire of it, for that which is within the precinct of the leet is exempt from the tourn, otherwiſe there might be a double charge; but in that caſe a writ may be directed to the ſherif to enquire thereof, &c. againſt the opinion of Fineux in 12 H. 7. if his opinion be not miſreported. And by the book of 29 E. 3. this writ is not taken away by the ſtatute of 28 E. 3. cap. 9. made the year before, which was then freſh in the judges memory.

[29 E. 3. 21. Wilby. 12 H. 7. 18.]

See the ſecond part of the Inſtitutes, in the expoſition upon the ſtatute of 31 El. cap. 7. concerning cottages and inmates, ſpeciall matter concerning the juriſdiction of the leet. See for the juriſdiction of the leet the ſtatute of 2 E. 6. cap. 10. concerning making of malt.

[Rot. par. 17 E. 3. nu. 38.]

The commons petitioned that exceſſive fines ſet on the kings ſubjects by ſuch as have leets may be redreſſed, whereunto the king anſwered, The king would the ſame.

[Mich. 18 E. 1. in banco rot. 156. Norf.]

See a notable caſe concerning the juriſdiction of the leet and court baron, Mich. 18 E. 1. in banco rot. 156. Norf. *Et ibi tenetur quod clericus ad letam venire non habet neceſſe, niſi ejus præſentia ex certis cauſis et conſiderationibus ſit neceſſaria.*

[Stat. de viſu Franc. 18 E. 2. 9 H. 6. 53. b.]

[a Vid. 11 E. 4. 6. b. per Neal and Brian. 1 R. 3. 1. a. 7 H. 4. 14, 15. Brook tit. Leet. 1.]

[b In the ſtat. at large p. 17. Mag. Carta parte 2. 23, 24.]

[c 14 E. 3. cap. 12.]

This court of the leet may enquire of corrupt victuall as a common nuſance, whereof ſome have doubted, both for that it is omitted in the ſtatute of the leet, and of the weak authority of the book of 9 H. 6. where Martyn ſaith, that it is ordained that none ſhould ſell corrupt victuall. And Cottiſmore held opinion that it is *actio popularis*, whereupon it is collected, that the conuſance thereof belongs to the leet. [a] And Martyn and Neal 11 H. 4. agreeing with him ſaid truly, for by the [b] ſtatute of 51 H. 3. *Stat. pillor' et tumbrel', et aſſiſ' panis et cervis'*, and by the ſtatute made in the reign of E. 1. intituled, *Stat. de piſtoribus et braſiatoribus et aliis vitellariis*, it is ordained that none ſhall ſell corrupt victuals. And by the [c] ſtatute of 14 E. 3. it appeareth that this act was ordained in the time of his grandfather, which was E. 1.

Britton

[d] Britton who wrote after the statute of 51 H. 3. and following the same saith thus; *Puis solt inquise de ceux queux achatent per un manner de measure et vendent per meinder measure faux, et ceux sont punies come vendors des vines, et auxi ceux que serront atteints de faux aunes, et faux poys, et auxi les * macegrieves, et les gents que de usage vendent a trespassants mauvase viands corrumpus et woacrus, et autrement perillous a la saunty de home. Et les forstallers, &c. Et fo.* 33. he doth conclude the like passage with these words, *Enconter le forme de nous statutes.*

[d] Britton, f. 77. a.

* *Macellarius*, a butcher or victualler.

Est etiam atrox injuria quæ perpetuam inducit infamiam cum pœna pillorali et tumbrelli, quæ quandoque fit per pistores, brasiatores, et alios qui falsis ponderibus utuntur et mensuris, quæ etiam fit per cibaria corrupta, et semicocta vendentes, &c. But none of these statutes gave the conusance to survey and correct victuallers for corrupt victuall to our court of the leet, therefore further authority therein is desired. Wherein we will produce that which is *omni exceptione majus*, and that is by a resolution in parliament.

[262]

Fleta, lib. 2. ca. 1. §. Est etiam. Et cap. 11. §. Item si dominus.

By the statute of 12 E. 4. cap. 8. it is rehearsed, That mayors, bailifs, and other like governors of every city, borough, and town of substance within this realm of England for the most part have courts of leets and views of frankpledge holden yearly within the same, and surveying of all victuallers there, and correction and punishment of the offenders, and breakers of the assise of the same, to be presented and amercied if default be found in the said courts, &c. And where divers persons intending their singular avail and profit, and to oppresse the said victuallers, and to enter and break the liberty of divers places in this realm having franchises *(that is, leets aforementioned)* and surveying of all victuallers, and correction of the same, had purchased letters patents of king E. 4. to be surveyors and correctors of all such victuallers within divers cities, boroughs and other places, of ale, [a] beere, wine, and other victuals, &c. in [b] wrongfull derogation of the liberties and franchises of the said cities, boroughs, and other places, &c. *as by the said act is rehearsed.* It is established and ordained, that all letters patents granted by that king, or after to be obtained of any office of searching or surveying of wine, ale, beer, or other victual, shall be utterly void and of none effect. And that no person other then such governors before rehearsed, &c. *(that is, in respect of their before rehearsed leets)* shall use or exercise any such office, &c. And besides the declaration of the same to be void and against law, a penalty of 40 l. is inflicted upon such as shall exercise any such office so obtained or after to be obtained. An excellent act of parliament both for the declaration of the law in the case abovesaid, as also that the king by his letters patents cannot make any new office for the surveying, correction, &c. of any thing which belong to the jurisdiction and conusance of any former court which by consequent hath a large extent, and therefore we have cited the same the more at large.

12 E. 4. ca. 8.

Nota.

[a] These words follow after in the act, and nota by this it appeareth, that beer is not of such late time as some suppose. See also Rot. par. anno 4 H. 4. nu. 53. Beer and ale mentioned to be then in Calice. Beer is a Saxon word *bier*, and beer is within the word *cervisia* in the ancient statutes. For it is but as the putting of a new button to an old coat, viz. hops to malt and water, to make it continue the longer. [b] Hereby it appeareth that those letters patents were against law, and that this is a statute declaratory with addition of a penalty.

Some doe hold that it is within the statute of 18 E. 2. some say as an incident to the assise of bread and ale, and others hold that by that

that act power is given to the lord of the leet to enquire of that assise of bread and ale, that is to say, of the statute intituled, The Assise of Bread and Ale, which is the said act of 51 H. 3. in which act sellers of corrupt victuals are to be punished. And herewith (say they) agreeth the book in 1 R. 3. fo. 1. that of corrupt victuall the leet had jurisdiction by the statute, howsoever that is conceived, it is the leet that hath conusance thereof.

Pasch. 18 E. 2. Coram rege Rot. 76. Southt. And albeit malt, *brasium*, be no victuall of it self, as it is adjudged in *anno* 18 E. 2. *Quod venditio brasii non est venditio victualium, nec debet puniri sicut venditio panis, vini et cervisiæ, et hujusmodi contra formam statut'*. Yet because it is the principall ingredient of beer, and serveth to victuall the kings houshold, &c. (as it is said 17 R. 2. cap. 4. in the statute of 17 R. 2.) and tendeth, if it be corrupt and not wholesome, to the great hinderance of health and increase of diseases, we will examine how the law standeth therein at this day.

[263] Mealt or Malt is a Saxon word. In Latin we call it *brasium* derived of *brasso*, i. *ebullio, ferveo*. In the ancient statutes *brasiator* is taken for a brewer. In Fleta, *ubi supra, brasiatrix:* in Britton, *ubi supra, braceresses*, for brewers. In Latin we use the word *pandoxator* or *potifex:* and *brasiator* at this day is used for a maltmaker or malster.

Malt is made of barley, and cannot be well and perfectly made, unlesse it hath the time of 12 dayes in the making thereof, and both 2 E. 6. cap. 10. in the making thereof in the fat, floor, steeping, and sufficient drying of the said malt 3 weeks at the least, except it be in the moneths of June, July, and August, and in those moneths by the space of 17 dayes at the least.

The maltmaker ought not slackly and deceitfully dry the malt, to the intent to have an inordinate increase thereof by swelling of the same, which being not sufficiently dried, within a short * Gurguliones. time will be musty and full of * wivels.

17 R. 2. cap. 4. No person ought to put to sale any malt which shall not be well and sufficiently troden, rubbed, and well fanned, whereby there may be conveniently fanned out of one quarter thereof half a peck of dust, or more.

2 E. 6. cap. 10. No person shall mingle any malt not being well and sufficiently made, or being made of mow-burnt or spired barly, with other good malt, and after put the same to sale. All these be *mala in se*, and punishable by the common law.

And this statute of 2 E. 6. hath added a penalty, if the suit be brought upon this statute. And if the brewer put to sale any beer, which he hath brewed with unlawfull (as all is unlawfull that have not the qualities foresaid) and unwholesome malt, he may be presented for the same in the leet, &c. as selling of corrupt and un- 2 E. 6. cap. 10. wholesome victuall. And by this statute power is given that the justices of peace in every of their sessions, and also the steward in every leet shall hear and determine, as well by presentment of 12 men, as by accusation or information of two honest witnesses of, for, and upon all and every the offences and forfeitures in that act, &c. So as the justices of peace or stewards in leets, may either proceed at the common law or upon this statute. It is further provided by this act, that the bailifs and constables of every borough, and market town or other town where malt shall be made or put to sell, shall from time to time search and survey the same; and if the same be found to be evill made or mingled with evill malt, they by the advice of one justice of peace shall cause the same to be sold at such reasonable price, and under the common price in the market, as to his discretion shall seem expedient. This act extends not to the making of any malt for a mans own provision for his own house or family. And the offences against this act are to be presented within a year.

This act of 2 E. 6. cap. 10. is continued, and yet standeth in force. 27 Eliz. cap. 4. 1 Jac. cap. 25, &c. 4 Car. cap. 4.

That which hath been said (*de malis in se*) of malt, may also be applyed to hops another ingredient in beer, and punishable by the common law. But against divers and many falsehoods practised in packing of foreign hops, for that the subjects of the realm have been by reason thereof of late years abused and deceived unto the value of 20 thousand pounds yearly at the least (for that in sacks of foreign hops there is not found one third part to be good and clean hops, the rest being drosse and soile,) a good law is made *anno* 1 Jac. and every person offending therein shall forfeit the same hops 1 Jac. cap. 18. so brought into the realm. And it is further enacted by the same act, that if any brewer of beer or ale shall imploy and spend any hops unclean, corrupt, or mixt with any powder, dust, drosse, sand, or any other soile whatsoever, he shall forfeit the value of those hops so imployed, to be recovered, &c. in any of the kings courts of record.

The reason wherefore these courts of the tourn and leet are F. N. B. 82. courts of record, and not the courts of the county, of the hundred, and of the court baron (whereof we shall next in order treat) is, for that the tourn and the leet are instituted for the common-weal, as for conservation of the kings peace, and punishment of common nusances, &c. And for conservation of the peace, the sheriffe in the tourn, and the steward in the leet may take recognisances for keeping of the peace. But the said inferior courts of the county, [264] hundred, and the court baron have jurisdiction of private causes under the value of 40 s. between party and party.

- - - Fuit hæc sapientia quondam
Publica privatis secernere, sacra profanis.

And forasmuch as unclean, corrupted, and mingled spices and drugs be so unwholesome and hurtfull, as they tend to the jeopardy of mans body, we will hereunto adde the exposition of the statute of 1 Jac. cap. 19. the penalty of spices not garbled.

Whereas heretofore great deceits and abuses have been committed in uttering, selling, and putting to sale, sundry sorts of uncleane, corrupt and mingled spices, &c. garbleable: to the jeopardy of his majesties person, &c.

Garbleable.] To garble, signifieth in our legall understanding, to sever and divide the good and sufficient from the bad and insufficient; and extendeth not only to spices and drugs mentioned in our statute, but to other wares and merchandizes. As for example. By the statute of 1 R. 3. it is provided that no bowstaves shall be 1 R. 3. cap. 11. sold ungarbled, &c. that is, untill the good and sufficient be severed and divided from the bad and insufficient: and this garbling of

12 E. 4. cap. 2. the ſtatute appointeth who ſhall garble them.

of bows hath reference to the ſtatute of 12 E. 4. cap. 2. where garbling of bows is well expounded, that is, that the bowſtaves be ſearched and ſurveyed, &c. and that ſuch as be not good and ſufficient be marked, &c. Some think that it is derived from the French verb *garber*, to make fine, neat, clean, &c. Others fetch it from *cribler* and that of *cribrare* to ſift or ſever the good from the bad, *unde cribrum, ſic dictum, quia crebris pertuſum eſt foraminibus ad res purgandas à pulvere et immundis (unde cribrarius*, the garbler) which well agreeth with our act.

A ſive and to ſift do come from the Saxons, viz. ſiꝼ, ſiꝼꞇ. This act conſiſteth of a preamble and a body. In the preamble it is rehearſed, That unclean, corrupt, and mingled ſpices, drugs, wares, and merchandiſes garbleable do tend to the jeopardy of his majeſties perſon, and of his ſubjects uſing the ſame in their meats, drinks, and other needfull occaſions, &c.

The ſelling of ſuch unclean, corrupt, and mingled ſpices and drugs uſed in meats, and drinks, is *malum in ſe*, and (as hath been ſaid) in divers like caſes puniſhable by the common law. But this act tendeth to the prevention of ſuch deceipts and abuſes, by garbling and purifying of the ſame before they be ſold, and by puniſhment if they be ſold before they be garbled and purified.

All that is garbleable muſt be garbled and cleanſed and ſealed by the garbler before ſale, upon pain of forfeiture of the ſame or value thereof, for which an action popular is given.

There be 32 kindes of ſpices and drugs by ſpecial name mentioned in this act, viz. { 1 Pepper, 2 cloves, 3 mace, 4 nutmegs, 5 cinnamon, 6 ginger, 7 long-pepper, 8 worme-ſeeds, 9 comyn-ſeeds, 10 anyſeeds, 11 coliander-ſeeds, 12 bynny-pepper, 13 almonds, 14 dates, 15 gals, 16 ſpiknard, 17 galingall, 18 turmerick, 19 ſetwell, 20 caſſia-fiſtula, 21 ginny-pepper, 22 ſeme, 23 barbaries, 24 rice, 25 erins, 26 ſtaveſacre, 27 calamus, 28 fennyrick, 29 caſſia, 30 lignum, 31 graines, 32 caraway-ſeeds.

And in generall words, 1. Gums of all ſorts and kinds garbleable. 2. All other ſpices, drugs, wares, and merchandizes garbleable.

* Nota, garbles ſignifie the duſt or ſoile or uncleanneſſe that is ſevered.

Be it furthermore enacted, that if any of the ſaid ſpices, drugs, wares, or other merchandizes be mixed with * garbles, matter or thing whatſoever after the ſame be garbled, &c. That then the ſaid ſpices, drugs, &c. or the value thereof ſhall be wholly forfeited.

[265]

It ſhall and may be lawfull for the garbler of ſpices, &c. within the city of London and the liberties of the ſame, &c.

There hath been of ancient time an officer in London and the liberties of the ſame, called the garbler of ſpices, &c. who may make his deputies. And this act giveth him authority at all and every time and times * in the day time to enter into any ſhops, warehouſes, or ſeller, to view and ſearch ſuch drugs, ſpices, &c. and to garble and make clean the ſame.

* This had been implyed if it had not been expreſſed.

There is a proviſo, that if any merchant or other perſon (other then merchants alien, or made or to be made denizen) ſhall bring any ſpice, drugs, or other merchandizes garbleable into this realme,

realme, and shall not offer the same to sale or sell the same within this realme, &c. and shall transport the same *bona fide* within eight moneths (accounting 28 dayes to the moneth) after his first landing, &c. shall not incurre any of the penalties of this act.

And this proviso was added in respect of a generall law made in 16 R. 2. that no manner of spicery, after that it be brought into the realm, shall be carried out of the same by alien or denisen, upon pain of forfeiture of the same. And this proviso extendeth only to the natural born subjects, and not to merchants alien, or made or to be made denisens. 16 R. 2. cap. 1.

And by the act of 16 R. 2. cap. 1. it is enacted, that aliens shall sell wines by whole vessels, and spicery by whole vessels and balls, and in no other manner.

The court of the leet may inquire of these offences following by authority of parliament.

De visu franc. Articles of the leet, to which we will adde — 18 E. 2. De visu franc.
Concerning tracing and killing of hares. — 14 H. 8. cap. 11.
Of hostlers making horsebread under the assise. — 32 H. 8. cap. 14.
Of breeders of horses under stature. — 32 H. 8. cap. 13.
Of artillery, butts, and bows. — 33 H. 8. ca. 8, 9.
Concerning shooting in crossebows and handguns. — 33 H. 8. cap. 6.
Concerning victuallers, artificers, workmen, and labourers. — 2 E. 6. cap. 15.
Against great prices and excesse of wines. — 7 E. 7. cap. 5.
For amendment of high wayes, 2 & 3 Ph. and Mar. cap. 3. 5 Eliz. 13. 18 Eliz. 9.
Concerning musters. — 4 & 5 P. and M. c. 3.
For the preservation of the spawn and fry of fish. — 1 Eliz. 17.
Against taking of pheasants and partridges. — 1 Jac. 25.
Against the erection of cottages and inmates. Hereof see before in this chapter. — 23 Eliz. cap. 10. 31 Eliz. cap. 7.

By these and divers other acts of parliament the jurisdiction of this court of the leet hath been much increased, to the end that the subject might have remedy and justice at his own dores: and therefore it is requisite that the steward of this court be learned in the law, for *ignorantia judicis est calamitas innocentis.* See rot. parl. 51 E. 3. nu. 47. concerning taverners.

The style of this court of the leet is, *curia visus franc' pleg' tent' apud B. coram A. B. seneschallo, &c.*

Francus plegius Saxonice ꝼꞃeboꞃoᵹh *freboroe, Anglice,* freepledge.

The constables or petty constables are chosen by the common law at the leet or torn, and are by the common law conservators of the peace, and may take surety of the peace by obligation, and are as ancient as torns or leets be, and began not about the beginning of E. 3. as some have supposed, vide the chapter of the hundred court for the cheif constable, and 9 E. 4. 36. 5 H. 7. 6. 11 H. 4. 12. 38 E. 3. 3.

3 H. 4. 9. 10[illegible]. 4. 17. 44 E. bar. 202. 32 E. 3. ib. 259. 46 E. 3. ib. 214. Vid. Rot. parl. 6 E. 3. post. nu. 6. Fitz. just. of peace 172. 3 E. 3. cor. 288. 12 H. 7. 18. Fineux.

But, to say once for all: repetition without addition is but losse of time, and altogether unprofitable.

CAP.

CAP. LV.

The Court of the County.

See the ſecond part of the Inſt. Mag. Cart. ca. 35.

THE ſtyle of this court is: *Buck. curia prima comitatus E. C. militis vicecomitis com' prædict' tent' apud B. &c.* And the next court *curia ſecunda E. C. vicecom' com' prædict' &c.* And ſo forth.

See the ſtatute of W. 2. cap. 36. againſt procurement of ſuits in this court.

Lib. 6. fo. 12. Jentlemans caſe. Stat. de Merton cap. 3. 44 E. 3. 10. 2 part of the Inſt. Mag. Cart. ca. 35. F. N. B. 119. g. h. Ib. 85. g. &c. & 138. b. &c.

This court is no court of record, and the ſuitors are the judges thereof. But in a *rediſſeiſon* the ſheriffe is judge by the ſtatute of Merton cap. 3. and a writ of error lyeth of his judgement.

Of the antiquity and juriſdiction of this court, you ſhall reade in the ſtatute of Magna Carta, cap. 35. It holdeth no plea of any debt or damages to the value of 40 s. or above, nor of any treſpaſſe done *vi et armis*, becauſe a fine is due thereby to the king. But of debt, detinue, treſpaſſe, and other actions perſonall above 40 s. the ſheriffe may hold plea by force of a writ of *juſticies* to him directed, for that is in nature of a commiſſion to him, and is *vicountel*, and not retornable. And he may before any county court award a ſummons to his bailie retornable within 2 or 3 dayes at his diſcretion, to ſummon the defendant by his goods, &c. to anſwer; and if the bailie retorne *nihil*, and the plaintif removeth the ſame by a *pone* into the common place, that court ſhall not grant a *capias*, for the nature of the writ doth not warrant a *capias*, and the ſheriffe could not grant the ſame, neither doth the writ of *juſticies* alter the nature of the court of the county, for therein the ſheriffe is not judge, but the ſuitors; and upon a judgement given therein a writ of falſe judgement doth lye, and not a writ of error. And in divers reall actions a writ of *juſticies* doth lye as it appeareth in our books, as in *breve d'admeſurement* of dower or paſture, in cuſtoms and ſervices, *meſne*, *quod permittat*, *rationabilibus diviſis*, *ſect' ad molend'*, *de nuiſans*, *de curia claudenda*, *annuity*, *&c.*

4 Eliz. Dier 222. 15 Eliz. 317. a.

In the county court upon the exigent after 5 exact, the coroners give judgement, *Ideo utlagetur per judicium coronatorum.* But by this judgement no goods are forfeited before the outlary appear of record: and that is the reaſon, that no man can claim the goods of outlaws by preſcription. Neither ſhall ſuch an outlawry diſable the party: but if upon a *certiorari* to the coroners they certifie the outlawry, this ſhall ſerve the king for the forfeiture of his goods, but ſhall not diſable the party till the exigent be retorned.

CAP.

CAP. LVI.

The Court of the Hundred.

THIS is no court of record, and the ſuitors be thereof judges. Of the antiquity and juriſdiction hereof vide Magna Carta, *ubi ſup*. And as the leet was derived out of the tourn for the eaſe of the people, ſo this court of the hundred for the ſame cauſe was derived out of the court of the county, and is a court baron in his nature.

2 Part of the Inſt. Mag. Cart. ca. 35. 12 H. 7. 18.

By the ſtatute of 14 E. 3. hundreds (except ſuch as then were of eſtate in fee) are rejoyned (as to the bailywick of the ſame) to the counties, and all grants made of the bailywick of hundreds ſince that ſtatute are void, and the making of the bailiffs thereof belong to the ſheriffe, for the better execution of juſtice and of his office. And ſo it was reſolved by the lord treaſurer Lea and all the barons of the exchequer, and ſo decreed in the exchequer chamber, between Forteſcue of Buckinghamſhire plaintife, and the ſheriffe of the ſame defendant, term. 2 *Caroli regis*, the plaintife having of late divers hundreds granted to him for life in the county of Buck. reſerving a rent, which the ſheriffe diſallowed and put in bailiffs of his own. And a commandment was given by the court to the attorny generall to avoid the like in other counties, for that they were againſt law, and belonged to the office of the ſheriffe, and were occaſions of delayes and hindrances of juſtice. See the ſtatute of W. 2. cap. 36. againſt procurement of ſuits in this court.

14 E. 3. cap. 9. 4 E. 3. cap. 15.

The ſtyle of this court is, *Curia E. C. militis hundredi ſui de B. in com. Buck. tent', &c. Coram A. B. ſeneſchallo ibidem.*

If there be a bailiffe of a liberty appointed by the lord of the liberty, or the ſheriffs bailiffe of any hundred, wapentake, or tything, which have not lands or tenements ſufficient in that county, there lyeth a writ *de balivo amovendo*, grounded upon the ſtatute of 4 E. 3. cap. 9. There are conſtables of the hundred commonly called, chief conſtables, ſo named, becauſe conſtables of towns are called petit conſtables. Theſe conſtables of hundreds were created by the ſtatute of 13 E. 1. and their authority limited to five things. 1. To make the view of armour. 2. To preſent before juſtices aſſigned ſuch defaults as they do ſee in the country about armour. 3. To preſent defaults of ſuits of tourns. 4. Of highwayes. 5. To preſent all ſuch as lodge ſtrangers in uplandiſh towns, for whom they will not anſwer. Divers and many acts of parliament have given the chief conſtable and pety conſtable more authority and power then originally they had, which hath been well collected by others. For no officer that is conſtituted by act of parliament hath more authority then the act that creates him, or ſome ſubſequent act of parliament doth give him, for he cannot

9 E. 2. Linc'. ſtat. Unicum. 4 E. 3. cap. 9. 5 E. 3. cap. 4. Regiſter 178. F. N. B. 164. b.

Stat. de 13 E. 1. De Winch. ca. 6.

Lambard, &c. See cap. Leet for the pety Conſtable.

prescribe as the officer by the common law may. Nota 10 E. 4. fo. 17. the petit constable was an officer by the common law *per curiam*, Vid. 4 E. 3. cap. 3. 25 E. 3. ca. 2. See in the chapter of Hue and Cry in the third part of the Institutes hue and cry alwayes by the common law made by the constables of towns, &c.

Fleta lib. 1. cap. 2. § *De vic' et constabulariis, &c.*

[268]

CAP. LVII.

The Court Baron.

See the second part of the Inst. Mag. Cart. ca. 25.

THIS is a court incident to every mannor, and is not of record, and the suitors be thereof judges, although the plea be holden by force of a writ of right.

There is also a customary mannor whereof you may read in the first part of the Institutes sect. 73. verb. Court, &c.

And this was first instituted for the ease of the tenants, and for the ending of debts and damages under 40 s. at home, as it were at their own doores.

1 Part of the Inst. sect. 73.

See there for the antiquity and institution of this court, and the articles inquirable therein are usuall and well known.

The stile of the court is: *Curia baronis E. C. militis manerii sui prædicti* (having the mannors name written in the margent) *tent' tali die, &c. Coram A. B. seneschallo ibidem.*

In the reigne of E. 1. we have seen court rols having the mannors name in the margent. *Aula ibidem tent' tali die, &c.* the court of the mannor being so called, because it was holden in the hall of the mannor: as the court of the marshalsea is called *curia aulæ hospitii domini regis*, because of ancient time it was holden in the kings hall.

[269]

CAP. LVIII.

The Court of ancient Demesne.

See the second part of the Inst. W. 2. c. 31. f. 456.

THOSE mannors are called the ancient demesnes of the crowne which were in the hands of St. Edward the Confessor or William the Conquerour, and so expressed in the Book of Domesday made or begun in the 14 year of William the Conqueror; for so we finde it in *libro rubro scaccarii in custodia rememb' regis* fo. 47, *quod liber vocatus Domesday compositus fuit anno 14 Willielmi regis conquestoris.* And Radulphus Niger monk of Cogishall in Essex *in vita Willielmi conquestoris* hath these words, *Annis* 1081, 1082, 1083, 1084, 1085, 1086, *rex Willielmus describi fecit omnes barones et feudatos*

See 21 E. 3. 32.

Herein Fitz. in his N. B. fo. 16. ascribing it to

feudatos milites, et quot carucatas terræ quisque habebat et redditus possessionem. And *anno Domini* 1081, was the 14 year of William the Conqueror; and this great and excellent survey lasted 6 years. And in *Lucubrat' Okham* it is worthily called *Liber Judicatorius*, because it is the only triall of ancient demesne; against which, for the uncontrollable truth and verity thereof, there can be taken no averment. And therefore in that respect like the doome and judgement at doomes-day.

Edw. the Confessor, was deceived. Vid. the Preface to the third book of my Reports.

In Chent' archiepi. Cant': Sandwice in anno quo facta est hæc descriptio. In doomes-day it selfe *lege librum*, for hereby it appeareth that it was made in the time of the Conquerour.

All those that hold of these mannors in socage are tenants in ancient demesne: and they plowed the kings demesnes of his mannors, sowed and harrowed the same, mowed and made his medows, and other such services of husbandry for the sustenance of the king and his honourable houshold, maintenance of his stable and other like necessaries pertaining to the kings husbandry. And to the end these tenants might the better apply themselves to their labours for the profit of the king, they had six privileges. First, that they should not be impleaded for any their lands, &c. out of the said mannor, but have justice administred to them at their own dore by the little writ of right close directed to the bailiffs of the kings mannors, or to the lord of the mannor, if it be in the hands of a subject; and if they were impleaded out of the mannor, they may abate the writ. 2. They cannot be impannelled to appear at Westm. or elsewhere in any other court upon any inquest or triall of any cause, 3. They are free and quiet from all mannor of tols in fairs and markets for all things concerning husbandry and sustenance. 4. And of taxes and tallages by parliaments, unlesse they be specially named. 5. And of contribution to the expences of the knights of the parliament, &c. 6. If they be severally distrained for other services, they all for saving of charges may joyn in a writ of *monstraverunt*, albeit they be severall tenants.

See the second part of the Inst. Artic. sup. Cart. cap. 2.

The priviledge of tenants in ancient demesne.

These priviledges remain still, although the mannor be come to the hands of subjects, and although their service of the plough is for the most part altered and turned into money: *Avera in Domesday Grentbrigsh Rexfordham, sed tamen semper inveniat averam vel* 8 *d. in servicio regis*, that is, a dayes work of a ploughman, or 8 d.

This court is in nature of a court baron, wherein the suiters are judges, and is no court of record, for *brevia clausa recordum non habent.*

Nota, the demandant in a writ of right close cannot remove the plea out of the court of the lord for any cause, the tenant may remove the same for 7. causes, viz. 1. For that he holdeth it *ad communem legem.* As if a fine and recovery be levied or suffered thereof in the court of common pleas, this maketh the land frank [270] fee so long as they stand in force. 2. If the land be not holden of the mannor being ancient demesne. 3. If the land be holden by knights service, for as hath been said, the service of the plow and husbandry is the cause of the priviledge. 4. * If there be no suitors, or but one suitor, for that the suitors are judges, and therefore the demandant must sue at the common law, for that there is a failer of justice within the mannor. 5. If the tenant accept a release of his lord of his seigniory, or the seigniory be otherwise extinguished

* Regist. fo. 17 E. 3. 44. F. N. B. 13. c. 41 E. 3. 22. 49 E. 3. 7. 50 E. 3. 14.

tinguished by reason of the seison of the king or otherwise. 6. Of if the lord disseise his tenant and maketh a feoffment in fee. 7. If the lord grant the services of his tenant, and the tenant attorn.

† *Arabant et herciabant ad curiam domini*, i. they did plough, and harrow at the mannor of the lord.

[a] And this priviledge doth not extend to meer personall actions, as debt upon a lease, trespasse, *quare clausum fregit*, and the like, in which by common intendment the title of the freehold shall not come in debate. But otherwise it is of all reall actions, and also in actions of account, replevin, *ejectione firmæ*, writ of mesne and the like, where by common intendment the realty shall come in question.

[b] Lands in ancient demesne are extendable upon a statute merchant, staple, elegit, and regularly all generall statutes extend to ancient demesne.

[c] But a redisseisin although they concern the realty, doth not lie in ancient demesne, because the proceeding in a redisseisin is appointed by the statutes to be made by the sherif, *assumptis secum coronatoribus comitatus, &c.* and in ancient demesne there are no coroners, [d] but otherwise it is in an action of wast.

And as the tenants in ancient demesne are carefull to preserve their priviledges, so the lord is as carefull to preserve his seigniory, and the tenure of this tenancy in ancient demesne. [e] And therefore if the tenant levy a fine, or suffer a recovery in the court of common pleas, &c. whereby for the time the land is become frankfee, the lord by a writ of deceit may not only restore himselfe to his true seigniory, but utterly avoid the fine, and restore his tenant against the recovery and his own fine to the land again in his former estate: and the reason thereof is, for that the recovery or fine was not suffered or levied before a competent judge in the right court, which ought to have been in the court of ancient demesne, [f] and therefore after the reversall in the writ of disceit, it is now *tanquam coram non judice*, and the parties to the fine or recovery shall be fined and imprisoned *pro deceptione curiæ*.

[g] But if in a writ of right close in ancient demesne, the demandant maketh his protestation to sue in the nature of assise of mord', the tenant plead in abatement of the writ, and the writ by judgement is abated, the demandant brings a writ of false judgement wherein the writ is affirmed to be good, the court of common pleas shall proceed as the inferior court should have done, and although that judgment be given to recover the land in the common place, yet the land is not frankfee, but remains ancient demesne, because the beginning and foundation thereof was in ancient demesne.

[h] They may levy a fine in ancient demesne which by a custome it is said to be a bar of the estate taile; but certainly that will not hold.

[i] If the tenant remove the plea for the cause mentioned in the *recordare*, he may come into the kings court, and assign other cause, and twenty, if he hath, to maintain the jurisdiction of the kings court.

† Domesday *sæpe berciare*, or *berseare* of the French word [*berse.*]
[a] Vid. li. 5. fo. 105. Allens case. 44 E. 3. 38. 46 E. 3. 1. 49 E. 3. 7. 44 E. 3. 22. 21 E. 3. 10. 32. 40 E. 3. 4. 28 E. 3. 95. 34 E. 1. Anc' demesne 98. 21 E. 4. Anc' demesne 6. 22 Ass. 45. F. N. B. 136. k. 30 E. 3. 12.
[b] 2 E. 2. Execut. 118. 15 E. 3. ib. 62. 8 E. 2. ib. 136. 7 H. 4. 19. Lib. 5. fo. 105. 19 H. 6. 64.
[c] 4 E. 2. Redisseisin 9.
[d] 7 H. 6. 35. 8 H. 6. 34. 32 H. 6. 35. F. N. B. 189. g. Lib. 5. fo. 105. Allens case. 22 El. Dier 373. 7 H. 7. 11.
[e] 2 E. 4. 26. 8 E. 4. 6. 7 H. 4. 44. 8 H. 4. 24. 17 E. 3. 31. Tr. 16 E. 3. Coram rege rot. 132. Eborum. Tr. 13 E. 3. Coram rege rot. 108 Glouc' (finis) Tr. 3 H. 5. coram rege rot. 9. Essex. (finis) 21 E. 3. 20. 56. 21 Ass. 4. 26 E. 3. 63.
[f] Vid. Dier 22 El. 373.
[g] 3 E. 3. 9. F. N. B. 19. d.
[h] Dier 22 El. 373. 27 Ass. 5. 44 E. 3. 38.
[i] 21 E. 3. 32.

CAP.

CAP. LIX.

The Court of the Coroner.

THIS coroner *coronator* is ſo called, becauſe he deals principally with pleas of the crown or matters concerning the crown: he is eligible by the freeholders of the county, and ſo continues to this day, as of ancient time the * ſherif and [a] conſervators of the peace were, becauſe the people had a great intereſt and ſafety in the due execution of their offices, and ſo long as they were eligible, they continued, notwithſtanding the demiſe of the king, as the coroner doth to this day. And of ancient time this office was of great eſtimation, for none could have it under the degree of a knight. [b] And it appeareth by the writ *de coronatore eligendo*, that he muſt have two properties, viz. ſufficient knowledge, ability and diligence in execution of his office implied in theſe words, *et talem eligi facias, qui melius ſciat, et poſſit officio illi intendere*. [c] And the ſherif after he be elected, ſhall give unto him his oath duly to execute his office: and the court which he holdeth is a court of record. And commonly there are four in every county of England; but in the twelve ſhires in Wales, and in Cheſhire there are but two.

Regiſt. 177. F. N. B. 164.

* Artic. ſup. Cart. cap. 8. & 13. 12 R. 2. cap. 2. 14 E. 3. cap. 7.

[a] Ro. pat. 5 E. 1. Lambard juſtice of peace. 16. b.

[b] Regiſt. 177. F. N. B. 164. Stanf. 48. e. W. 1. cap. 10.

[c] 14 E. 3. ca. 8. He muſt have ſufficient land in the county whereof he may anſwer all people. F. N. B. 164. 34 H. 8. 35 H. 8. cap. 13.

Now concerning his juriſdiction, what it was before the ſtatute of Magna Carta, and what he hath at this day, and of his antiquity, you may read in the ſecond part of the Inſtitutes, Mag. Cart. cap. 17. and the expoſition upon the ſame. Merton cap. 3. Rediſſeiſin, and W. 1. cap. 10. & 26. & Artic. ſuper Cart. cap. 3. and the expoſition of the ſame.

He is to take nothing for doing his office upon grievous forfeiture, but by 3 H. 7. he is to have upon an indictment found of murder 13 s. 4 d. of the goods of the murderer, and if he hath nothing of the amerciament of the townſhip for the eſcape, &c. See alſo the ancient authors, *Mirror des Juſtices*, cap 1. §. *del office del coroner*. Bracton lib. 3. fo. 121, 122, 123. Britton cap. 1. Fleta, lib. 1. ca. 18. *Statutum de anno* 4 *E.* 1. *de officio coronatoris*, and *Stanf. Pl. Coronæ* fol. 48, 49, 50.

3 H. 7. cap. 1.

Vet. Mag. Cart. 4 E. 1. part. 1. 119. Stanf. 49. e. f.

And as the ſherif in his tourn may enquire of all felonies by the common law, ſaving of death of man, ſo the coroner can enquire of no felony but of the death of man, and that *ſuper viſum corporis*: he ſhall alſo enquire of the * eſcape of the murderer, of treaſure trove, deodands, and wrecks of the ſea. But hereof you ſhall read more in the authorities before cited, and in the third part of the Inſtitutes, in the title of Appeals.

35 H. 6. 23.

* 3 H. 7. ca. 1. 4 E. 1. ubi ſup.

He ought to deliver the inquiſition of death taken by him at the next gaol-delivery, or certifie the ſame into the kings bench. * Upon an inquiſition found before him of murder or manſlaughter he ought to put in writing the effect of the evidence given to the jury before him being materiall, and hath power to binde over witneſſes

3 H. 7. ca. 1.

* 1 & 2 Ph. and M. cap. 13.

witneſſes to the next gaol-delivery in that county. See before in the chapter of the Courts in London.

To conclude, beſides his judiciall place, he hath alſo authority miniſteriall as a ſherif, &c. viz. when there is juſt exception taken to the ſherif, judiciall proceſſe ſhall be awarded to the coroners for the execution of the kings writs, in which caſes he is *locum tenens vicecomitis*, and in ſome ſpeciall caſe the kings originall writ ſhall be immediately directed unto him.

Pl. Com.

In defectu vic' pro brevibus regis exequendis, videtur curiæ hic, quod aliis quam coronatoribus non eſt demandand'. Vide Vet. Mag. Cart. parte 2. fo. 19, 20. 21. Stat. Exoniæ. Fleta lib. 1. cap. 18.

Paſch. 9 E. 3. Coram rege rot. 80. Ebor. Weſtm.

[272]

CAP. LX.

The Court of *Pepoudres*, vulgarly Pipowders, *Curia Pedis pulveriſati*.

Bract. l. 5. f. 334. a.

THIS court is incident to every fair and market, as a court baron to a mannor, and is derived of two Latin words, as is apparent, and ſo called, becauſe that for contracts and injuries done concerning the fair or market, there ſhall be as ſpeedy juſtice done for advancement of trade, and traffick, as the duſt can fall from the foot, the proceeding there being *de hora in horam*. And therefore Bracton ſaith, *Item propterea qui celerem debent habere juſtitiam, ſicut ſunt mercatores quibus exhibetur juſtitia pepoudrous, &c.*

Bract. l. 5. f. 334. a.

This is a court of record to be holden before the ſteward of the court, and the juriſdiction thereof conſiſteth in four concluſions. 1. The contract or cauſe of action muſt be in the ſame time of the ſame fair or market, * and not before or in a former. 2. It muſt be for ſome matter concerning the ſame fair or market, done, complained on, heard and determined. 3. It muſt be within the precinct of that fair or market. 4. The plaintif muſt take an oath according to the ſtatute of 17 E. 4. cap. 2. but that concludeth not the defendant. [a] And all this was reſolved, and adjudged in a writ of error brought by Hall againſt Jones, and the caſe was this: Jones being regiſter of the biſhop of Glouc', brought an action upon the caſe in a court of pipowders belonging to the market in Glouceſter againſt Hall for theſe words; Maſter Jones and his clerks have by colour of his office extorted and gotten 300 l. *per annum*, by unlawfull means for many years together above their ordinary fees, for proving of teſtaments and granting adminiſtrations. And not guilty being pleaded, &c. it was tried and adjudged for the plaintif: and divers errors were aſſigned, but the judgment was reverſed for theſe errors following. 1. That this court of pipowders, being incident to the market, hath no juriſdiction but of ſuch things as concern the market; and theſe ſlanderous words did in no ſort concern the market: but if one ſlander the wares of any in the market, whereby he cannot make ſale of them, an action doth lie in that court. 2. It appeared in the record that

6 H. 4. 3. 6 E. 4. 3. b. 7 E. 4. 23. Li. 6 fo. 12. a. & 20.
* See before cap. Juſtices in Eire. ſimile pag. 185.
[a] Mich. 42 & 43 El. Coram rege, Lib. 10. fo. 61. En le caſe del Marſhalſey Jones caſe.

that the words were spoken the day before the market; [b] and no action lyeth in that court but for an injury within the jurisdiction of the court done, complained on, heard and determined on the same market day, the proceeding being *de hora in horam*, and within the precinct of the market. And herewith agreeth 3 Mar. Dier 132. And it was resolved that this court was incident as well to a market as to a fair.

[c] And there may be a court of pipowders by custome without fair or market, and a market without an owner. Another error was assigned, for that it is provided by the [d] statutes of 17 E. 4. and 1 R. 3. that no plea shall be holden in the court of pipowders, except the plaintif or his atturny will make oath, that the contract or other deed contained in the declaration was done or committed within the time of the fair: but this error was disallowed by the court, for although this ought to be done, if the defendant will stand upon it, notwithstanding it shall not be made part of the record.

Vide Lib. Intrat. Rast. fo. 464. Pipowder 1, 2. fo. 18. Execution 3. fol. 158. Gaoler 1.

[b] 7 H. 6. 18, 19. Kelw. 23 H. 7. 99 Doct. and St. fo. 11. 3 Mar. Dier 132. int' Hall and Pinder. 45 E. 3. 1. 1 H. 4. 6. 13 H. 7. 19. b. 12 H. 7. 16, 17.
[c] 13 E. 4. 8. b. 8 H. 7. 4, 5. 12 E. 4. 9. 19 H. 8. Br. incidents 34. 12 H. 6. 3. b.
[d] 17 E. 4. c. 2. 1 R. 3. cap. 6.

CAP. LXI. [273]

The Court of the Clerk of the Market.

HE is to this day called *clericus mercati hospitii regis*, for of ancient time there was a continuall market kept at the court gate, where the king was better [a] served with viands for his houshold then by purveyors, the subject better used, and the king at far lesse charge in respect of the multitude of purveyors, &c. And the officer of the market of the kings houshold retaineth his name still, although the good end thereof according to the first institution ceaseth.

The [b] clerk of the market shall hold no plea but such as were holden in the reign of E. 1. And at this day there is no great need of him, for the justices of assise, the justices of oier and terminer, justices of peace, and the sherifs in their tourns, and the lords in their leets, may and do inquire of false weights and measures.

[c] He doth keep a court and inquireth of weights and measures whether they be according to the kings standard or no, and for that purpose he maketh processe to sherifs and bailifs to return pannels before him, &c. [d] And he is to deliver the estreats of those things which touch his office into the exchequer.

[e] Of drink (that is to say) of wine, ale, and beer, and of corn and grain there ought to be but one measure: *una mensura vini, cervisiæ et bladi, et virgæ*, and of all other merchandize *per totum regnum. De ponderibus vero sicut de mensuris.*

Britton fo. 75. b. Fleta l. 2. c. 20. Rot. par. 50 E. 3. nu. 87. & 152. 13 R. 2. cap. 4. 32 H. 8. cap. 20. 17 H. 8. ca. 24. Lib. Int. Co. 445.
[a] See the 2 part of the Institutes, 28 E. 1. Artic. sup. Cart ca. 2. and the exposition thereupon.
[b] Rot. parl. 8 H. 4. nu. 82.
[c] 16 R. 2. ca. 3.
[d] Stat. de modo mittendi extract. in Scaccarium. Anno 16 E. 1. & 15 E. 2.
[e] Mag. Cart. c. 25. 27 E. 3. ca. 10. 25 E. 3. cap. 9. 24 E. 3. ca. 12. 13 R. 2. cap. 9. 15 R. 2. 4. 16 R. 2. cap. 3. 9 H. 5. cap. 8. 11 H. 7. cap. 4. 12 H. 7. cap. 5. 1 H. 5. cap. 10.

Weights. Trutina campana. Ordinatio menſurar' 31 E. 3.

But notwithſtanding theſe ſtatutes there be within this realm two kind of weights, the one called troy weight, which is commanded by the ſtatute, and this derived from the grain or corn of barley from the middeſt of the ear and dry. 24 of theſe corns or grains make a penny weight, and 20 of theſe penny weights make an ounce, and 12 ounces make a pound troy. A grain contains 20 minutes, a minute contains 24 droits, a droit contains 24 blanks. 12 grains of fine gold make a caret, 24 carets of fine gold make an ounce, and 12 ounces make a pound of fine gold. By this troy weight are weighed according to law pearls, precious ſtones, gold and ſilver, bread, wheat, and ſuch like.

There is another kinde of weight called *aver de pois*. A pound of this conſiſteth of 16 ounces, every ounce having 20 penny weight, every penny weight 21 grains, and $\frac{9}{10}$ of a grain. It is called *aver de pois*, becauſe thereby they have full meaſure. Hereby are weighed all phyſicall drugs, wax, pitch, tarre, iron, ſteele, lead, hemp, flaxe, fleſh, butter, cheeſe, and divers other commodities, but ſpecially every commodity ſubject to waſt. There was another weight called the auncell or anſell weight, which was when the ſcales were fixed to a beam or ſtaffe, and he that weighed by it, uſed his forefinger or hand in the middeſt, wherein was great deceipt, and therefore is put out by the ſtatute of 25 E. 3. cap. 9. 34 E. 3. cap. 5. 8 H. 6. cap. 5. It is derived *ab anſa*, which is the handle of the ballance, and this weight was guided by the hand.

Of meaſures.

Meaſures of troy be of three kinds, viz. of things that be dry, of liquor and of longitude, latitude and profundity.

[274]

Ordinatio menſur'. 31 E. 1. ubi ſup.

Of dry things, 4 grains make a penny weight, 20 penny weight make an ounce, 12 ounces a pound or pinte (for a pound weight is a pinte in meaſure) two pounds or pintes make a quart, two quarts make a pottle, two pottles make a gallon, two gallons make a peck, four pecks make a buſhell, four buſhels make a combe, two combes make a quarter, ſix quarters make a wey, and ten quarters make a laſt.

Of liquor 12 ounces make a pound, 8 pound make a gallon of wine, 8 gallons of wine make a buſhell of London, which is the 8 part of a quarter.

Of wine ſee the ſtatutes of 1 R. 3. cap. 13. 28 H. 8. cap. 14.

See aſſiſa panis et cerviſiæ. 51 H. 3.

Of ale and beer	the ferkine	8	Gallons.
	the kilderkin	16	
	the barrell	32	
	the hogſhead or quarter	63	*Et ſic de cæteris.*

Vet. Mag. Cart. fo. 31, 32. 2 part. Ibidem 44. b. Compoſitio ulnarum et perticarum Vet. Mag. Cart. 2 parte 45, 46. Anno 31. E. 1. ſtatut' de terris menſur'.

See the ſtatute *compoſitio de ponderibus.*

Statut' de piſtoribus, Vet. Mag. Cart. 2 *parte* 23, 24.

Statut' panis et cerviſiæ.

Of longitude, latitude, and profundity, 3 grains of barley in length make an inch, 12 inches make a foot, 3 foot make a yard, a yard and a quarter make an ell, 5 yards and a half make a perche, 40 perches in length make a furlong, 8 furlongs make a mile.

I may ſpeak of the ſellers by the weight of aver de poys, as Tacitus ſpake of the augures in Rome. *Hoc genus hominum ſemper vitabitur, et ſemper in civitate retinebitur.*

But

But now let us ſee what fees the clerk of the market ought to take. By the ſtatute of W. 1. cap. 26. it is enacted that no ſherif or other miniſter of the king ſhall take any reward for doing his office, &c. And the kings clerk of the market is the kings miniſter, and therefore he is within the purvien of this ſtatute. W. 1. an. 3 E. 1. ca. 26.

I find that in 8 R. 2. in open parliament a groat was allowed to him for marking and ſealing of every buſhel, 2 d. of every half buſhell, 1 d. of every peck, and ſo according to that rate. Rot. par. 8 R. 2. nu. 11.

By the ſtatute of 7 H. 7. the chief officer of every city and borough ſhall take for ſealing of every buſhell a penny, of every other meaſure a half penny, of every hundred weight 1 d. and of every half hundred ob. and of every weight under a farthing, and not above. 7 H. 7. ca. 3. 11 H. 4. cap. 4.

The clerk of the market in the reign of queen Eliz. claimed by cuſtome for the examination and view of every buſhell ſealed before by the clerk of the market, whether it were lawfull or unlawfull 2 d. and in like manner of every leſſer meaſure of wood 1 d. and in like manner of inholders meaſures 4 d. and of the meaſures of victuallers 2 d. and divers other fees for examination and viewing of weights and meaſures whether they were lawfull or unlawfull, as is aforeſaid. And it was reſolved by all the judges of England, that no fee was due to the clerk of the market for view and examination only of weights and meaſures for three cauſes. 1. The ſaid parliament roll of 8 R. 2. alloweth a fee for ſealing, and ſo doth 7 H. 7. and 11 H. 7. but no allowance for view or examination. 2. The weights and meaſures are either true, according as before they were ſealed, or falſe: if true, it ſhould be againſt reaſon to charge the innocent, for that were *diſperdere juſtum cum impio;* if falſe, then by the ſtatute of 13 R. 2. they ought to be burnt, and 13 R. 2. cap. 4. the end of the view and examination is to find out falſhood, to 38 Aſſ. p. 11. the end they might be puniſhed, and fined to the king, as appeareth by the ſtatute of 13 R. 2. but no fee is to be taken therefore. 3. Whereas the clerk of the market affirmed that theſe fees had been of long time taken, the judges ſaid, that *malus uſus abolendus eſt*, and the taking of fees for view and examination only was extortion, and that they could not preſcribe againſt the ſaid ſtatute of W. 1. See in the 2. part of the Inſtitutes, the expoſition of the ſaid ſtatute of W. 1.

By the ſaid ſtatute of 13 R. 2. he ought to take no common fine, for before that ſtatute he did uſe to take a reward (which the act [275] tearmeth a fine) for not inquiry of defaults, whereby the king was prevented of his fine, the delinquent not puniſhed, and the people wronged by extortion, and permiſſion of falſe meaſures: and therefore the act provided that no common fine ſhall be taken, as is aforeſaid (but that every perſon which is found in default touching the ſame office be puniſhed according to his deſert. And the clerk 12 E. 4. fo. 8. b. of the market cannot ſet any price of any thing ſaleable in the mar- 23 E. 3. cap. 6. ket, for that belongs not to weights and meaſures: and by the 13 R. 2. cap. 8. common law *arbitrio domini res æſtimari debet*, which cannot be al- 3 H. 8. cap. 8. tered but by parliament; and again, *nemo cogitur rem ſuam vendere etiam juſto precio;* and things ſaleable in the market of one 6 R. 2. cap. 13. kinde are not of one goodneſſe: but he ought to aſſiſe weights and Rot. par. 37 E. 3. meaſures. nu. 39.

It

It is enacted that good examination and correction be had in towns infranchised touching weights and measures, so as the * statutes thereof made be duly observed.

* Which are before in this chapter.

CAP. LXII.

The Court of the Commissioners of Sewers.

QUANDO [a] *aqua profluit*, that is, when water doth issue, vulgarly, sue: hereupon cometh the word *suera*, for a sewer, passage, channell, or gutter of water.

[b] At the complaint of Henry de Lacye earle of Lincolne, a commission of sewers was granted to Roger de Brabason mayor, and the sheriffs of London.

[c] Their authority is by commission under the great seal *in hæc verba*, at this day grounded and warranted by the act of parliament of 23 H. 8.

[d] Of their jurisdiction you may read in my Reports, and see the statutes of 6 H. 6. cap. 5. 8 H. 6. cap. 8. 23 H. 6. cap. 9. 12 E. 4. ca. 6. 4 H. 7. ca. 1. 6 H. 8. cap. 10. 23 H. 8. cap. 5. & 10. 3 E. 6. cap. 8. 1 Mar. cap. 11. 13 Eliz. cap. 9.

Certain necessary observations upon some of these statutes, and principally wherein the statute of 23 H. 8. cap. 5. hath been explained, declared, or altered by any of the said subsequent statutes.

[e] 1 This commission shall be granted to such substantiall and indifferent persons as shall be named by the lord chancelor, the lord treasurer, and the two chiefe justices, or any three of them, whereof the lord chancelour to be one.

[f] 2 Every commissioner before he take upon him the execution thereof shal take the corporall oath mentioned in that act before the lord chancelour, or such as the lord chancelour shall direct by writ of *ded' potestatem*, or before the justices of peace in their quarter sessions, and [g] ought to have lands or tenements of the clear yearly value of 40 marks of some estate of freehold (except as in the statute is excepted) upon pain of forfeiture of 40 li. and no farmer of lands within the precinct of the commission, unlesse he hath lands of some estate of freehold of the yearly value of 40 li. and yet he not to meddle with the lands he hath in farm.

[h] 3 The avowry or justification for a distresse taken by force of this commission shall be generall, that the said distresse, &c. was taken, &c. by force of the commission of sewers for a lot or tax assessed by the said commission, or for such other act or cause, &c.

4 [i] There must be six commissioners, &c. at the least, which shall sit by force of the said commission.

5 [k] That the said act of 23 H. 8. doth not extend to, nor give authority to the commissioners of sewers to reform the great hurt and

[a] Vid. Pasch. 22 E. 1. in banco rot. 52. Kanc' Ric' de Cras com' de sewers. Vi. Regist. 287. a. Certiorar.
[b] Rot. parl. anno 35 E. 1. at Carlisle.
[c] 23 H. 8. cap. 5.
[d] Lib. 5. f. 99. 100. Rookes case. Lib. 10. fo. 137. *Le case de Molyn de Chester*, and fo. 139. Keighleys case. Ib. 141. *Le case de Isle de Ely*. Vid. Regist. 252. b. De antiqua trenchea obstruenda et nova facienda vel habenda ad quod damnum. Ibid. 254. b. De aquæ ductu, et 255. a. F. N. B. 225. e. Tr. 31 E. 3. fol. 44. b. in libro meo M. S. 19 E. 3. barre 279.
[e] 23 H. 8. cap. 5. 10. To whom and by whom this commission shall be granted.
[f] 23 H 8. cap. 5.
[g] 13 Eliz. cap. 9.
[h] 23 H. 8. cap. 5. Lib. Intr. Coke 292. 293.
[i] How many commissioners must sit.
[k] 1 Mar. cap. 11. To what nusances the commission of sewers extend not.

and nuſance by reaſon of the ſand, riſing out of the ſea, and driven to land by ſtorms and winds. A ſpeciall proviſion is there made for the county of Glamorgan.

It is adjudged by act of parliament *anno* 3 *Jacobi regis* cap. 14. That wals, ditches, banks, gutters, ſewers, gates, cauſeys, bridges, and watercourſes in or about the city of London, * where no paſſage for boats is uſed, nor the water therein doth uſually ebbe or flow: which wals, ditches, banks, gutters, ſewers, and other the premiſes, do fall into the river of Thames, are not under the ſurvey, correction and amendment of the commiſſions of ſewers, nor of the ſtatutes made for ſewers in *anno* 23 H. 8. or of any other ſtatute of ſewers, as it is rehearſed by full conſent of parliament: and therefore proviſion is made that thoſe wals, ditches, banks, gutters, ſewers, and other the premiſes, ſhall be ſubject to the commiſſion of ſewers.

3 Jac. cap. 14.

* Nota, an excellent expoſition of the ſtatute of 23 H. 8. by this parliament of 3 Jac.

6 That a commiſſion of ſewers ſhall continue ten years, unleſſe it be repealed or determined by reaſon of any new commiſſion, or by ſuperſedeas.

13 Eliz. cap. 9. How long the commiſſion ſhall endure.

7 That laws, ordinances and conſtitutions made or to be made by force of any ſuch commiſſion, and written in parchment indented under the ſeals of the ſaid commiſſioners or ſix of them, whereof one part ſhall remain with the clerk, &c. and the other part in ſuch place as ſix of the ſaid commiſſioners ſhall appoint, ſhall without any certificate, and without the royall aſſent ſtand and continue in full force notwithſtanding any determination of any ſuch commiſſion by ſuperſedeas, untill the ſame be altered by the commiſſioners of ſewers after to be aſſigned, &c.

13 Eliz. cap. 9. The laws written in parchment & indented, &c. Without certificat or royall aſſent.

8 And if any ſuch commiſſion be determined by expiration of ten years next enſuing the teſte thereof; then ſuch laws, &c. ſo indented and ſealed, &c. ſhall continue for one whole year. And that the juſtices of peace or ſix of them, whereof one to be of the quorum, ſhall have authority during that year to execute the ſaid lawes, &c.

Determination by expiration.

Juſtices of peace.

9 That by the granting of a new commiſſion within that year, the power of the juſtices of peace to ceaſe.

10 The ſaid commiſſioners ſhall not be compelled to make any certificate or retorn the ſaid commiſſions, or of any of their ordinances, laws, or doings, by authority of the ſaid commiſſions.

Nota, no certificat or retourn of the commiſſions or of any the ordinances, laws, or doings.

11 See alſo an alteration by the ſtatute of 13 Eliz. concerning fees.

12 Laſtly, this is certain, that neither the commiſſioners of ſewers, nor any other, have ſuch an abſolute authority, but that their proceedings are bound by law.

Vide the ancient commiſſion of ſewers by the common law in the Regiſter, and F. N. B.

Regiſt. 126, 127. F. N. B. 113, 114.

A generall commiſſion of ſewers enacted by authority of parliament, not printed.

Rot. parl. 2 H. 6. nu. 57.

A generall commiſſion of ſewers enacted by parliament, and in print. But the commiſſion by the ſtatute of 23 H. 8. ſtandeth now in force. And yet by diligent peruſall of the former, and by adviſed comparing of them with the latter, it will manifeſt wherein the former defects were, and how continually by the latter they were ſupplied and amended, and give a great light for the true underſtanding of that which now ſtandeth.

6 H. 6. cap. 5.

Stat. 25 E. 3. ca. 4. 45 E. 3. cap. 2.

See

Hil. 13 E. 2. Coram rege rot. 55 Norf. Pasc. 44 E. 3. Coram rege rot. 2 Mid. [a] 19 E. 3. tit. bar. 279. [b] 2 E. 3. fo. 26. [c] The court of sewers of Rumney Marsh.

See Hil. 13 E. 3. *coram rege, Leges et consuetudines approbatæ pro reparatione murorum maritimorum et mundatione fossatarum et suerarum in paludibus quæ hic exprimuntur per commissionem regis ad hoc faciendum in Mersbland.*

[a] A particular commission granted to S. Joh. de Sutton, and Sir Rob. de Scrope.

[b] A commission concerning the river of Lee.

[c] Rumney Marsh in the county of Kent containing 24000 acres, is at this day, and long time hath been governed by certain ancient and equall lawes of sewers made by a venerable justice Henry de Bathe, in the reign of H. 3. from which laws not only other parts in Kent, but all England receive light and direction: for example: [277] the said generall act of 23 H. 8. ca. 5. in the clause which giveth power to the commissioners to make statutes, ordinances, and provisions, &c. necessary and behovefull after the laws and customes of Rumney Marsh in the county of Kent, or otherwise by any wayes or means, &c,

Both the towne and marsh of Rumney took their name of one Robert Rumney. This Robert (as it appeareth by the book of Domesday) held this town of Odo bishop of Baieux, wherein he had 13 burgesses, who for their service at the sea were discharged of all actions and customes of charge, except felony, breach of the peace and forestalling.

See before in the chapters of the Courts of London, &c. the jurisdiction that the lord mayor hath in the river of Thames.

C A P. LXIII.

The Court of the Commissioners upon the Statutes of Bankrupts.

* The derivation and signification of bankrupt. Cicero pro Flaminio: *In qua civitate nummus moveri nullus potest sine quinq; prætoribus, 3 prætoribus et quinq; mensariis.*

WE have fetched as well the name as the wickednesse of bankrupts from foreign nations: for *banque* in the French is *mensa*, and a banquer or eschanger is * *mensarius* and *route* is a signe or mark, as we say, a cart rout is the signe or mark where the cart hath gone: metaphorically it is taken for him that hath wasted his estate, and removed his banque, so as there is left but a mention thereof. Some say it should be derived from *banque* and *rumpue*, as he that hath broken his banque or state.

25 E. 3. stat. 3. cap. 23. Parl. 50 E. 3. nu. 160. against Lombards. * 51 E. 3. nu. 51. Vid. 50 E. 3. ca. 6. & 2 R. 2. cap. 3. stat. 2. against frauds generally 34 H. 8. cap. 4.

In former times as the name of a bankrupt, so was the offence it self (as hath been said) a stranger to an Englishman, who of all other nations was freest of bankruptcy. And the first statute that we find against this crime, was indeed made against strangers, viz. against Lombards, who after they had made obligations to their creditors, suddenly escaped out of the realm without any agreement made with their creditors. * It was therefore enacted, that if any merchant of the company knowledge himself bound in that manner, that then the company shall answer the debt: so that another merchant which is not of the company shall not be thereby grieved nor impeached: neither do we find either any complaint in parliament, or act of parliament made against any English bankrupt untill the 34 year of H. 8. when the English merchant had

rioted

rioted in three kinds of coſtlineſſes, viz. coſtly building, coſtly diet, and coſtly apparell, accompanied with neglect of his trade and ſervants, and thereby conſumed his wealth.

He is called in Latin * *decoctor, à decoquendo*, for conſuming of his eſtate in riotous and delicate living. The ſaid act of 34 H. 8. is altered by the ſtatutes of 13 Eliz. cap. 7. 1 Jacobi, cap. 15. & 21 Jacobi, cap. 19.

Cicero in Catilinam: *Exercitum collectum ex ruſticis, mendiculis, et decoctoribus.*

And it is to be obſerved, that all the aforeſaid ſtatutes and laws made againſt bankrupts, and for relief of creditors, ſhall be in all things largely and beneficially conſtrued, &c. for the aid, help and relief of the creditors.

A bankrupt is deſcribed by the ſtatute of 13 Eliz. cap. 7. and 1 Jac. cap. 15. but more effectually by the ſtatute of 21 Jac. cap. 19. So as by all theſe three he is perfectly deſcribed. And the commiſſion doth extend to all and every of the ſaid deſcriptions and articles thereof.

The deſcription of a bankrupt.

[a] The authority of the commiſſioners is by commiſſion under the great ſeal; their juriſdiction and power is by force of the ſaid acts of parliament which ought to be purſued, [b] or elſe they are ſubject to the action of the party grieved, for he hath no other remedy. [c] The lord chancelour or lord keeper upon complaint made unto him in writing hath authority to grant the ſaid commiſſion.

[a] The authority of the commiſſioners and their juriſdiction.
[b] Lib. 8. f. 121. Int' Cutt and Delabar.
[c] 13 Eliz. cap. 7. who may grant the commiſſion.

The law hath provided that theſe commiſſioners ought to have * three qualities, viz. wiſdome, honeſty, and diſcretion; which if it be obſerved, it is the beſt means for the due execution of the ſaid ſtatute, and the life of theſe laws doth conſiſt in the due execution thereof: and for ſuch commiſſioners if any action ſhall be brought againſt them, &c. for doing of any thing by force of the ſaid ſtatutes, they may plead generally, and not to be driven to any ſpeciall pleading.

[278]

*Three qualities of every of theſe commiſſioners.

Generall pleading. 1 Jac. cap. 15. 21 Jac. cap. 19.

They have power to examine the offender upon oath, and after he be declared a bankrupt, to examine his wife upon oath, and to examine witneſſes alſo upon oath. See the ſtatute. And they have power to break any the houſes, chambers, warehouſes, &c. trunks and cheſts of ſuch offenders. See the other parts of this act of 21 *Jacobi*, which are plainly and effectually expreſſed, and need not here to be recited.

For the expoſition of the ſaid ſtatute of 13 Eliz. * ſee in my Reports lib. 2. fo. 25, 26. Cullamers caſe. Lib. 8. fo. 98, in Baſpoles caſe, & ibid. fo. 121. *inter Cutt et Delabar.*

* Lib. 2. fo. 25. 26. Cullamors caſe. Lib. 8. fo. 98. Baſpoles caſe. Ib. fol. 121. Int' Cutt and Delabar.

CAP. LXIV.

Commiſſioners for Examination of Witneſſes.

FORASMUCH as the court of ſtar-chamber, the chancery in caſes of equity, the exchequer chamber in caſes of equity, the court of wards, and the duchy of Lancaſter do proceed upon witneſſes examined before commiſſioners, or in court before the examiners, it ſhall be neceſſary (as a matter of great importance to ſay ſomewhat of the power, authority, and duty of the ſaid commiſſioners and examiners, and incidently of witneſſes.

The

See li. 9. fo. 70. 71. Peacocks caſe, for this and ſome of the caſes following.

The commiſſioners, albeit named by the parties reciprocally, ought to ſtand indifferent, and do their uttermoſt endeavour to find out by due examination the whole truth, and to ſuppreſſe no part thereof; for their authority is to that end meerly and wholly from the king by force of his commiſſion.

Lib. 9. ubi ſup.

Neither commiſſioner nor examiner are ſtrictly bound to the letter of the interrogatory, but ought to explain every other matter or thing which riſeth neceſſarily thereupon, for manifeſtation of the whole truth concerning the matter in queſtion.

Lib. 9. ubi ſup.

Neither commiſſioner nor examiner ought to diſcover to either of the parties or to any other, any of the depoſitions or any part of them, which they have taken before publication be granted.

Lib. 9. ubi ſupra.

Neither commiſſioner nor examiner after the examination begun, ought to confer with either party touching the examination, or take new inſtructions concerning the ſame.

Aug. *Serm. 28. de verbis Apoſtoli. Jurare eſt jus veritatis Deo reddere.* Azo. *Juſjurandum eſt affirmatio vel negatio, religione adhibita.* See the third part of the Inſtitutes cap. Perjury.

For as much as the witneſſe by his oath, which is ſo ſacred, as he calleth Almighty God (who is truth it ſelf and cannot be deceived, and hath knowledge of the ſecrets of the heart) to witneſſe that which he ſhall depoſe; it is the duty both of the commiſſioner and the examiner gravely, temperately, and leiſurely to take the depoſition of the witneſſe, without any menace, diſturbance, or interruption of them in hinderance of the truth, which are grievouſly to be puniſhed. And after the depoſitions taken, the commiſſioners and examiners ought to read the ſame diſtinctly to the witneſſes, and ſuffer them to explain themſelves for the manifeſtation of the whole truth. And it is ſafe for the commiſſioner and examiner that the witneſſes ſubſcribe their names or marks to the paper-booke, but they muſt be certified in parchment.

[279]

And albeit the commiſſioners be not equall in ſtate or degree, yet are they all of equall power and authority: for, as it hath been ſaid of old, that there might be priority, but no ſuperiority amongſt commiſſioners.

* 8 H. 6. 13. 2 E. 2. triall 46, &c. Dier 2 Eliz. 185. 13 Eliz. 306. Of witneſſes. Additions to the 1 part of the Inſtitutes. ſect. 1. fo. 6. And to the third part of the Inſtitutes, cap. Perjury. * 12 Aſſ. 12. 23 Aſſ. n. 21 Aſſ. p. 19. [a] Deut. 6. 13. [b] 16 Januarii 14 Eliz. [c] Prov. 19. [d] Bract. lib. 5. fo. 400. b. 2 H. 7. Kelw. 96. a. b. [e] Bract. lib. 5. 359.

Interrogatories ought to be ſingle and plaine, pertinent to the matter in queſtion, and in no ſort captious, leading, or directory.

In ſome caſes the courts of the common law do judge upon witneſſes, but they muſt ever give their teſtimony *viva voce.* * As in dower if the iſſue be whether the huſband be alive or no, &c.

Witneſſe is derived of the Saxon verb *weten, i. ſcire, quia de quibus ſciunt teſtari debent, et * omne ſacramentum debet eſſe certæ ſcientiæ.* In Latin *teſtis à teſtando: et teſtari eſt teſtimonium perhibere: unde regula juris, plus valet unus oculatus teſtis, quam auriti decem: teſtis de viſu præponderat aliis.*

[a] An oath ought to be accompanied with the fear of God, and ſervice of God for advancement of truth, *Dominum Deum tuum timebis, et illi ſoli ſervies, et per nomen illius jurabis.*

Bracton ſaith that an alien born cannot be a witneſſe: which is to be underſtood of an alien infidell: [b] for the biſhop of Roſſe being a Scot born, was admitted to be a witneſſe, and ſworn *anno* 14 Eliz. in the caſe of the duke of Norfolk by the opinion of the juſtices aſſiſtants. [c] *Teſtis falſus non erit impunitus.*

Nocte dieque ſuum geſtat ſub pectore teſtem:

his conſcience alwayes gnawing and vexing him. [d] *Vox ſimplex nec probationem facit, nec præſumptionem inducit.*

[e] *Teſtium numerus ſi non adjicitur, duo ſufficiunt.*

7 *Jurato*

Jurato, creditur in judicio.

[f] *Testibus deponentibus in pari numero dignioribus est credendum.* f Vid. 2 E. 3. triall 45.

[g] *Testmoignes ne poent testefie le negative, mes lassirmative.* g F. N. B. 106. 107.

[h] *Allegans contraria non est audiendus, verum vero consentiens est falsum nec vero nec falso.* h 16 E. 4. 10. a.

Juramentum est indivisibile, et non est admittendum in parte verum, et in parte falsum. i Trin. 13 E. 1. in com. banco. Rich. de Raynhams case.

[i] *Allegans suam turpitudinem non est audiendus.*

Judex non potest esse testis in propria causa.

Jusjurandum inter alios fact' nec nocere, nec prodesse debet.

Facultas probationum non est angustanda.

De crimine in lupanari commisso, lupanares testes esse possunt.

Qui prodit in scenam mercedis ergo, infamis est. Histriones Mercenarii.

Witnesses ought to come to be deposed untaught, and without instruction, and should wish the victory to the party that right hath, and that justice should be administred: and should say from his heart, *Non sum doctus, nec instructus, nec curo de victoria, modo ministretur justitia.* See Britton 134, 135.

CAP. LXV. [280]

Curia Cursus Aquæ apud Gravesend.

OF this court, and others like, which are in private, we intend not to treat, for that the labour herein were infinite, and serveth nothing for the publick, whereat our principall aim hath been.

CAP. LXVI.

The Kings Swanheard.

WHAT authority the kings swanheard hath, being of ancient time by his office *magister deductus cygnorum*, you may reade *rot. patentium anno* 11 H. 4. part. 1. m. 14. rot. pat. 30 E. 3. part 1. m. 20. and lib. 7. fo. 15, &c. *Le case de Swannes*, but court he hath not: no fowle can be a * stray but a swan. Rot. pat. 16. R. 2. part. 1. m. 39. * Tr. 33 E. 1. Essex coram rege rot. 124. 7 H. 6. acc.

So likewise there is an ancient officer of the kings alneger of the kings gift being before any statute: as taking one example for many. [a] In 14 E. 1. Sir Thomas Darlington was by the kings letters patents alneger of broad cloth, and had a fee of the king for the exercise of his office; for the fee that he had of the subject was (as it ought to be) by act of parliament. 27 E. 3. st. 1. cap. 4. [b] Alneger of *aulne* in French, and that of *ulna*, *ulnator*. See before concerning the alnaging of new draperies, cap. of the High Court of Parliament, pag. 31. The kings alneger. a Rot. pat. 14 E. 1. Tho. Darlington militi. This appeareth also by the statutes themselves. 25 E. 3. cap. 1. stat. 4. 27 E. 3. stat. 1. cap. 4. 3 R. 2. cap.

17 R. 2. cap. 2. & 5. 1 H. 4. cap. 13. 11 H. 4. 6. 13 H. 4. 4. 11 H. 6. 1. 31 H. 6. 5. 4 E. 4. 1. 8 E. 4. 1 R. 3. Rot. clauf. 17 R. 2. m. 14.

b The derivation of alneger.

* CAP. LXVII.

23 H. 8. cap. 16. 31 H. 6. cap. 3. 8 E. 4. cap. 2. 22 E. 4. cap. 8.

The Wardens Courts in the East, West, and Middle Marches adjoyning to Scotland.

4 H. 5. cap. 7. 23 H. 8. cap. 16. THEY proceeded according to the law called the March law, or Borders law, but their jurisdiction was increased by act of parliament. The limits of their jurisdiction was within the
31 H. 6. cap. 3. Marches, which were confined to the counties of Northumberland, Cumberland, Westmerland, and the towne of Newcastle upon Tine in the county of York.

For the word [Marches,] see before cap. President and Councell of Wales.

4 Jac. cap. 1. But since king James was monarch of both kingdomes, the batable grounds on both sides are become quiet, and so peaceable, as all the said courts in the east, west, and middle marches are vanished, and hostile laws on both sides by authority of parliament in either of the kingdoms repealed. See the said statute of 4 *Jacobi*. See the first part of the Institutes, sect. 3.

[282]

CAP. LXVIII.

Of *Callais* or *Callis Caletum*.

Rot. par. 50 E. 3. nu. 211, 212. 6 H. 6. nu. 41. See the statute of 27 H. 8. concerning good lawes and orders for Callis and the marches thereof and 1 H. 7. cap. 3. [b] 21 H. 7. 33. 11 H. 8. Kelw. 202. b. Par. 3 R. 2. nu. 48. [c] Pat. 15 E. 3. 2 part. Parl. 9 R. 2. nu. 4. [d] 42 E. 3. cap. 10. lib. 7. in Calvyns case. [e] Rot. parl. 9 R. 2. nu. 4. 9 H. 5. stat. 2. ca. 5. [f] 1 R. 2. nu. 37. [g] Parl. 50 E. 3. nu. 209.

THIS strong port town, the famous and flourishing mart, staple, and vent of English commodities was holden and kept by the space of 211 years by eleven severall kings, viz. E. 3. R. 2. H. 4. H. 5. H. 6. E. 4. E. 5. R. 3. H. 7. H. 8. E. 6. and holden and lost by king Philip and Mary the first queen regnant of this realm, the lord Wentworth then deputy there.

It was governed by Englishmen and by English laws, some particular customes excepted. [b] And of a judgement given there a writ of error did lye retornable into the kings bench. [c] Before the staple at Callais, it was kept at Bruges in Flanders.

[d] The children born there were inheritable in England and so declared by authority of parliament

[e] And there the king had his mint in such manner as in the tower of London. Certaine it is that riches followed the staple wheresoever it was kept. [f] And it could not be appointed in any place but by act of parliament.

[g] The staple being at Callais, upon all rodes forth of the town by the captain, the mayor of the staple furnished him forth of merchants and their servants to the number of 100 bill-men and 200 archers without any wages. And yet it appeareth in the parliament roll of 2 R. 2. nu. 15. that Callais cost the king yearly twenty thousand pounds.

See the parliament roll of 50 E. 3. nu. 211, 212. for the mayors courts, &c. and liberties, and franchises, &c. there. Many acts of parliament have been made concerning this town, and the staple.

ple therein, which need not here to be recited: only we thought it not good totally to pretermit it, because the kings right remains to it, and it may hereafter be restored (which is so much desired) to the right owner.

CAP. LXIX. [283]

Of the Isle of Man, *Insula Euboniæ, modo Mannæ*, and of the Law and Jurisdiction of the same.

THIS isle hath been an ancient kingdome, as it appeareth in lib. 7. in Calvins case, which need not here to be recited. And yet we find it not granted or conveyed by the name of a kingdome, *sed per nomen insulæ, &c. cum patronatu episcopatus.* He hath the patronage of the bishoprick of Sodor, which is a visible mark of a kingdome; albeit of ancient time the archbishop of Canterbury was patron of the bishoprick of * Rochester, and the earl of Glouc' of the bishoprick of Landaf. *Vide Lib. M. S. in Recept. Scaccarii fo.* 166. *et Lib. Parliam. in Turri London temps. E.* 1. *fo.* 19. 21.

Walf. pa. 387. lib. 7. fo. 21. in Calvins case.

* Rot. Cart. 16 Johan. m. 6.

*William le Scrope emit de domino Willielmo de Monte acuto insulam Euboniæ, (*i. *Mannæ:) est nempe jus ipsius insulæ ut quisquis illius sit dominus rex vocetur, cui etiam fas est corona aurea coronari.*

Anno Dom. 1393. Walf. an. 17 R. 2. Corona aurea.

The lord Scrope forfeited the same to H. 4. for high treason. King H. 4. granted the same to Henry earl of Northumberland in these words. *Rex, &c. De gratia nostra speciali dedimus et concessimus Henrico comiti Northumbriæ insulam, castrum,* * *pelam, et dominium de Man, ac omnia insulas et dominia eidem insulæ pertinen' quæ fuer' Willielmi le Scrope chivalier defuncti, quem in vita sua conquestati fuimus, et ipsum sic conquestatum decrevimus, et quæ ratione conquestus illius tanquam conquestata cepimus in manum nostram. Quæ quidem conquestum et decretum in præsenti parliamento nostro de assensu dominorum temporalium in eodem parliamento existentium quoad personam præfati Willielmi, ac omnia, terras, tenementa, bona, et catalla sua tam infra regnum nostrum quam extra ad supplicationem communitatis regni nostri affirmata existunt, &c. Habenda et tenenda eidem comiti et hæredibus suis, &c. per servic' portandi diebus coronationis nostræ et hæredum nostrorum ad sinistrum humerum nostrum et sinistros humeros hæredum nostrorum per seipsum aut sufficientem et honorificum deputatum suum illum gladium nudum quo cincti eramus quando in parte de Holdernes applicuimus, vocatum* Lancaster Sword, *durante processione et toto tempore solemnizationis coronationis supradictæ.*

Of the quality of him. See Walf. Ubi supra.

Rot. pat. 1 H. 4. Rot. 2. Bundello 2. parte 5. m. 36.

* A pele or pile, a fortresse in a small isle belonging to the Isle of Man.

Nota, the title of the king by conquest is affirmed by parliament.

In this little kingdome there are 2 castles, 17 parishes, 4 market towns, and many villages, and in that isle there is a bishoprick, as hereafter shall be shewed.

Anno 5 H. 4. the said Henry earl of Northumberland was attainted of treason, and by act of parliament 1 *Martii*, 7 H. 4. it is enacted that the king should have the forfeiture of all his lands and tenements. And afterwards in H. 4. the king granted the Isle of Man *unà cum patronatu episcopatus* to Sir John Stanlye for life: and after in

Rot. pat. 7 H. 4. parte 2. m. 18. Cum patronatu episcopatus.

in the same year he granted the same isle *unà cum patronatu episcopatus*, to the said Sir John Stanly and to his heirs; *Tenend' de rege hæredibus et successoribus suis per homagium ligeum: reddendo nobis duos falcones semel tantum, viz. immediate post homagium hujusmodi fact': et reddendo hæredibus nostris regibus Angliæ duos falcones diebus coronationis eorundem hæredum nostrorum pro omnibus aliis servitiis, consuetudinibus et demandis, adeo libere, plene, et integre, sicut Willielmus Scrope chivalier vel aliquis alius, &c.*

This Sir John Stanley had issue Sir John Stanley knight, who had issue Sir Henry Stanley lord chamberlain to king H. 6. who created him lord Stanley, who had issue George, who had issue [284] Thomas, whom king H. 7. created earl of Derby to him and the heirs males of his body, who had issue Thomas, who had issue Edward, who had issue Henry, who had issue Ferdinando and William. Ferdinando had issue Anne, Frances, and Elizabeth, and died without issue male: and between these daughters being heirs generall, and William earl of Derby being heir male, question was moved concerning the title of the Isle of Man: which by queen Elizabeth was referred to the lord keeper Egerton, and to divers lords of the councell, and to Popham chief justice of England, Anderson chief justice of the common pleas, and Peryam chief baron, who Trin. 40 Eliz. upon hearing of the councell of both sides, and mature deliberation, resolved these five points. 1. That the Isle of Man was an ancient kingdome of it selfe, and no part of the kingdome of England. 2. They affirmed a case reported by Keilw. *anno* 14 H. 8. to be law, viz. Mich. 14 H. 8. an office was found that Thomas earl of Derby at the time of his death was seised of the Isle of Man in fee; whereupon the countesse his wife, by her councell, moved to have her dower in the chancery: but it was resolved by Brudnell, Brook, and Fitzh. justices, and all the kings councell that the office was meerly void, because the Isle of Man was no part of the realm of England, nor was governed by the law of this land, but was like to Tourny in Normandy, or Gascoign in France, when they were in the king of Englands hands, which were meerly out of the power of the chancery, which was the place to endow the widow of the king, &c. 2. It was resolved by them that the statute of W. 2. *De donis conditionalibus*, nor of 27 H. 8. of Uses, nor the statutes of 32 or 34 H. 8. of Wils, nor any other generall act of parliament did extend to the Isle of Man for the cause aforesaid, but by speciall name an act of parliament may extend to it. 3. It was resolved that seeing no office could be found to entitle the king to the forfeiture of treason, that the king might grant by a commission under the great seal to seise the same into the kings hands, &c. which being done and returned of record is sufficient to bring it into the kings seisin and possession, and into charge, &c. 4. That the king might grant the same under the great seal, because he cannot grant it in any other manner. And herewith agreeth divers grants under the great seal of this Isle, [b] viz. 4 *Junii*, 18 *E.* 1. *rex E.* 1. *concessit Waltero de Huntercombe, &c. Rex E.* 2. *concessit Petro de Gaveston, &c.* 1 *Maii*, 5 *E.* 2. *Gilberto Magaskill*, and in the same year granted *Henrico de Bello monte insulam prædictam cum omni dominio et justitia regali pro termino vitæ, &c.* 5. It was resolved that a fee simple in this isle passing by the letters patents to Sir John Stanley and his heirs, is descendible to his heirs according

Vide 33 H. 8. c. 6. a proviso for the subjects of the Isle of Man. 14 El. cap. 5.

[a] In Turri Lond' 3 Junii. 6 H. 4. such a commission under the great seal was granted to Sir John Stanley and William Stanley, &c. to seise, &c. in this very case.

[b] In tur' Rot. pat. 18 E. 1. and anno 5 E. 2.

to the course of the common law, for the grant it self by letters patents is warranted by the common law in this case: and therefore if there be no other impediment, the isle in this case shall descend to the heirs generall, and not to the heir male; as the grand seigniories and connots in Wales were impleadable at the common law, but the lands holden of them by the customes of Wales, &c. Which resolutions we have thought good to report, because they are the best directions that we have found, both in these, and for the like cases.

By these letters patents it appeareth, that Simon Montacute had intruded into and occupied the said isle *in nostri exhæredationem*, for which he was attached to answer the same in the kings bench at the suit of the king, but what proceeded thereupon we yet find not. Rot. pat. 2 Apr. 6 E. 2.

But now let us come to their laws, and jurisdiction of this isle, the like whereof ye find not in any place. Their judges they call * *deemsters*, which they choose out of themselves. All controversies they determine without proces, pleading, writing, or any charge or expence at all. If any case be ambiguous and of greater weight, it is referred to 12, which they call *claves insulæ*, the keyes of the island. They have coroners *(quos annuos vocant)* who supply the office of a sherif.

* A *dema* a Saxon word for a judge. *Giraldus. sunt duo judices in insula Mannia (olim Ewania nuncupata) qui de litibus ibidem emergentibus cognoscunt.*

But albeit this be so, yet when this isle was in the kings hands, if any injustice or injuries were done to any of his subjects there, the king might grant a commission for redresse thereof: the like whereof we finde rot. pat. anno 20 E. 1. in these words; *Rex dilectis et fidelibus suis Nicholao de Segrave seniori, Osberto de Spaldington, et Johanni de Suthewell, salutem. Sciatis quod assignavimus vos justiciarios nostros ad querelas omnium et singulorum de Insula de Man se conqueri volentium de quibuscunque transgressionibus, et injuriis eis per quoscunque tam balivos et ministros nostros quam alios in prædicta insula illatis audiend' et terminand', et ad plenam et celerem justitiam partibus inde faciend' secundum legem et consuetudinem partium illarum. Et ideo vobis mandamus quod ad certos dies et loca quos, &c. in insula prædicta querelas, &c. audiatis et terminetis in forma prædicta, facturi, &c. salvis, &c. Mandavimus enim custodi nostro insulæ prædictæ; quod ad certos, &c. in insula prædicta venire fac' coram vobis tot et tales, &c. In cujus, &c. Teste rege apud Berewick, 15 die Julii.*

[285]

In the margent, thus; *De querelis hominum Insulæ de Man audiend' et terminand'.*

Nota, secundum legem et consuetudinem Insulæ de Man.

So as albeit the kings writ runneth not into the Isle of Man, yet the kings commission extendeth thither for redresse of injustice and wrong: but the commissioners must proceed according to law and justice of the isle. They have peculiar laws or customes; for example: if a man steal a horse, or an oxe, it is no felony, for the offender cannot * hide them, but if he steal a capon, or a pigge he shall be hanged, &c. Upon the sale of a horse or any contract for any other thing, they make the stipulation perfect *per traditionem stipulæ*. Nota, the true derivation of stipulation. And as they have peculiar laws, so have they a proper language.

* They have no woods.

12 H. 8. fo. 5. a.

This isle hath a bishop instituted by Gregory the fourth bishop of Rome, and he is under the archbishop of York, but hath neither place nor voice in the parliament of England. *In hac insula judex ecclesiasticus citat, definit, et infra octo dies parent, aut carceri intruduntur.* Epūs Soborensis.

The inhabitants of this isle are religious, industrious, and true people without begging or stealing.

CAP. LXX.

Of the Isles of Jersey *alias* Gearsey, *olim Cæsarea*, and Garnsey, *olim Saruia*, and of the Law, and Jurisdiction of the same.

Jersey hath 12 parishes. Garnsey 10.

BOTH these isles did of ancient time belong to the duchy of Normandy: but when king H. 1. had overthrown his elder brother Robert duke of Normandy, he did unite to the kingdome of England perpetually the duchy of Normandy together with these isles: and albeit king John lost the possession of Normandy, and king H. 3. took money for it, yet the inhabitants of these isles with great constancy remained, and so to this day do remain true and faithfull to the crown of England: and the possessions of these islands being parcell of the duchy of Normany, are a good seisin for the king of England of the whole duchy.

Concerning the judicature and customes of these isles whereat we principally aim, it appeareth by the kings records in the Tower, *Quod rex Johannes constituit 12 coronatores juratos ad placita et jura ad coronam spectantia custodienda, et concessit pro securitate insularum, quod balivus de cætero per visum coronatorum poterat placitare sine brevi de nova disseisina fac' infra annum, de morte antecessorum infra annum, de dote similiter infra annum.* And for the most part they proceed according to the customes of Normandy.

Pasch. 17 E. 2. coram rege rot. 67 Jersey.

Drugo Barentyne dicit quod 40. an' est tempus extra memoriam secundum consuetudinem partium illarum.

2 E. 3. fo. 5. b. The abbot of the Mount of S. Mich. case.

King E. 3. assigned Hen. de Guldeford and others, justices errants in the isles of Garnsey and C. by his commission to inquire if he had right in the mannor of C. &c. and there it appeareth that they demanded advisement of the men of the isles learned in their customes, who informed them of the customes of the isles, which the justices followed, and there it appeared that if the information was against the laws of the isles, they may be holpen by the laws of the same. See the book.

Rot. claus. 9 E. 3. & 25 E. 3.

Quod in custumis et aliis rebus tanquam indigenæ et non alienigenæ tractetur, &c. Quod juratores in insula, &c. non protrahunt judicia sua ultra unius anni spacium.

Mich. 41 E. 3. coram rege rot. 109 Jersey in placito transgr.

An action of trespasse was brought by A. in the kings bench for a trespasse done by B. in the isle of Jersey: whereupon in the record this entry was made. *Et quia negotium prædictum in curia hic terminari non potest, eo quod juratores insulæ præd' coram justiciar' hic venire non possunt, nec de jure debent, nec aliqua negotia de insula prædicta emergentia non debent* [a] *terminari nisi secundum consuetudinem insulæ prædictæ, ideo totum recordum negotii mittatur in cancellariam domini regis, ut inde fiat* [b] *commissio domini regis, cui vel quibus domino regi placuerit ad negotium prædictum in insula prædicta audiend' et terminand' secundum consuetudinem insulæ prædictæ.*

[a] Secundum cons. Insulæ præd.

[b] Mich 6 H. 8. 172. b. Kelw. to the baylif and jurates of Jersey. Lib. 7. fo. 20, 21. in Calvins case.

By this it appeareth, that albeit the kings writ runneth not into these isles, yet his commission under the great seal doth, but the commissioners must judge according to the laws and custome of these isles.

[c] *De attornato generali in insulis de Gernsey, Jersey,* [d] *Serk et Aureney fac' virtute brevis domini regis. Rex omnibus balivis et fidelibus suis in insulis de Gernsey, Jersey, Serk et Aureney ad quos, &c. Sciatis, &c.*

[c] Regist. fo. 22.

[d] These little isles of Serk and Aureney doe lye between and neer the other, and were parcell also of the duchy of Normandy.

*&c. in quibuscunque curiis nostris insularum earundem, &c. post adventum ipsius A. in insul' prædict' si contingat * ipsum A. interim venire ad partes illas. Teste, &c.* They are not bound by our acts of parliament, unlesse they be specially named. Vid. 33 H. 8. c. 6.

The king hath granted to the men of the isles of Gernesey, Serk and Aureny, that they during the space of 8 years shall be free of all manner of tols, exactions and customes within the realm as his liege men and denizens. Rot. par. 14 R. 2. nu. 30.

Insulani petunt, quia sunt in mari constituti, quod non ulterius extra insulas prædictas prosequerentur ad eorum periculum, et non facile possunt sequi curias regis in Anglia.

For the isles of Jersey and Garnsey, see Mich. 5 E. 3. *coram rege* rot. 46. Pasch. 17 E. 2. *coram rege* rot. 67.

Within Garnsey there are ten parishes, one market town being the port or haven called S. Peters port by the castle of Cornet. Jersey hath S. Albans and Hillary two little islands adjacent, it hath twelve parishes, and four castles.

CAP. LXXI.

De Insula Vectis or *Vecta*, of the Isle of Wight.

OF this we shall not need to say any thing, because it is and ever hath been part of Hamshire, and ever governed by the laws of England, as the other shires have been: but seeing we have named it, we will relate some things which we have observed.

First, there hath been an ancient baron, *de insula*, of the Isle, or Lisle, and of latter times there was a viscount of the same, which is to be understood of the Isle of Wight: for in the parliament rols of E. 2. I find him called *de insula Vecta*.

Secondly, Henry de Beauchamp earl of Warwick for the singular favour which king Henry the Sixt bare to him, crowned him king of Wight: but we could never find any letters patents of this creation, because (as some do hold) the king could not by law create him a king within his own kingdome, because there cannot be two kings of the same place in one kingdome: and after the same king named him *primus comes totius Angliæ*. But of this it is truly said: *cum illo novus hic et insolitus titulus omnino evanuit.* Camden.

See the statute of 4 H. 7. cap. 16. against taking of farms within this isle, and the power of judicature given thereby to the captain of this isle, or his lieutenant in a certain case.

CAP. LXXII. [288]

Of the Island called Lindesfarne or Leidisfarne, scituate by the River Lied having on the South Eastward the Island of Farn, and is called the Holy Island.

IT hath one castle, one church, and one parish, and a safe haven defended by a block-house.

It is called the holy island, for that it being a solitary place holy men in times past retired themselves thither for their better, and more devout service of God. It was of ancient time a bishops seat, which was after translated to Duresme, and is governed by the law of England.

Farne Isle.

For that this Isle of Farne hath neither church nor towne, but only a castle, I passe it (and other like isles) over.

[289]

CAP. LXXIII.

Of the Forests, and the Jurisdiction of the Courts of the Forest.

Domesday in co' Glouc' et alibi. 2 Mar. Dier 169. 1 part of the Inst. sect. 378. fo. 233. a. Ockam cap. Quod regis foresta. Bracton fo. 231. & 316. Britton fo. 34. Fleta l. 2. c. 34, 35. * 1. pt. of the Inst. sect. 1. fo. 5. b. In the Saxons time forests were called *walds unde waldegrave*, i. *præpositus forestæ*. Virgill. *Sylva*, as in Domesday *saltus à saltando, quia ibi feræ saltant*. * Like to an evill conscience in the false and furious officer of the forest if any such be.

FOR the word *foresta*, see Domesday in Glouc' *et alibi*.

For the derivation and description thereof, and some other things concerning the same; see the first part of the Institutes.

In Latin it is called *saltus*, or *sylva*. And so in Domesday, *sylva est in defens', scilicet, in foresta regis*.

A forest doth consist of 8 things, viz. of soil, covert, laws, courts, judges, officers, game, and certain bounds.

* *Foresta est nomen collectivum*, and by the grant thereof the soil, game, and a free chase doth passe.

And seeing we are to treat of matters of game and hunting; let us (to the end we may proceed the more cheerfully) recreate our selves with the excellent description of Didoes doe of the forest wounded with a deadly arrow sticken in her, and not impertinent to our purpose.

Uritur infœlix Dido, totaque vagatur
Urbe furens, qualis conjecta cerva sagitta,
Quam procul incautam nemora inter Cressia fixit
Pastor agens telis, liquitque volatile ferrum
Inscius: illa fuga sylvas saltusque peragrat
Dictæos, * *hæret lateri lethalis arundo.*

And in another place using again the word [*sylva*] and describing a forest, saith;

Ibat in antiquam sylvam stabula alta ferarum.

King John the 15 of June in the 18 year of his reign at Kummigsmead, *alias* Kyme meade between Stanes and Windsor, granted the like charter as *carta de foresta* is.

Cart de foresta cap. 16.

And now let us set down the courts of the forest.

Within every forest there are these courts.

The court of attachments.

1. The court of the attachments or the woodmote court, this is to be kept before the werderors every forty days throughout the year, and thereupon is called the forty day court. At this court the foresters bring in the attachments *de viridi et venatione*, and the presentment thereof, and the verderers do receive the same, and inroll them, but this court can only inquire, and not convict; but it is to be observed, that no man ought to be attached by his body for vert or venison, unlesse he be taken with the manner within the forest, otherwise the attachment must be by his goods.

1 E. 3. cap. 8. 7 R. 2. cap. 4. Cart. de forest. cap. 6

The court of the lawing of dogs.

2. The court of regard or survey of dogs is holden every third year for expeditation or lawing of dogs by that court.

3. The

3. The court of * swanimote is to be holden before the verderors as judges by the steward of the swanimote thrice in the year, and the foresters ought to present their attachments at the next swanimote court, and the freeholders within the forest are to appear at the swanimote to make enquests and juries. [a] And this court may inquire *de superoneratione forestariorum et aliorum ministrorum forestæ, et de eorum oppressionibus populo nostro illatis.* And this court may not only inquire, but convict also, but not give judgment.

Cart. de forest. cap. 8. Of Swanimote. 1 E. 3. ca. 8. 50 E. 3. assis' 442.

* Swanimote is derived of *swein*, that is, *saxonice*, *minister*, *et mote*, or *gemote*, which is *curia*, i. *curia ministrorum forestæ*, so called because it is but a preparative for the justice seat.

[a] *Ordinat' forestæ*, 34 E. 1. 34 E. 1. cap. 4.

[290]

For the jurisdiction of this court I find a notable case in 45 E. 3. in a writ of trespasse of false imprisonment brought against I. de W. The defendant said that he is forester in fee of the forest, and that at a certain swanimote it was presented by the * foresters, verderors, regarders, and agisters that the plaintif had chased and taken deer within the forest, whereupon the defendant being forester in fee came to the plaintif and prayed him to finde pledges to answer the same before the justice in eire in this country (that is, at the justice seat) and that to doe the plaintif refused, by force whereof he retained him, untill he had performed the statute in that case provided, and justified the imprisonment. The plaintif replied *de son tort demesne sans tiel cause*, and the issue was received by the court. And it was said that before the justice in eire he should have no averment against the presentment of the foresters.

45 E. 3. fo. 7.

* We will hereafter shew from whence these severall names be derived, and the duty of their severall places.

Out of this case we doe observe 6. conclusions. 1. That the law of the forest is allowed, and bounded by the common laws of this realm, and therefore it is necessary, that the judges should know, and be learned in the same. 2. That though the verderors [a] be judges of the swanimote, and the steward but a minister, yet the presentment in that court is as well by them as verderors as by foresters, or keepers, regarders, and agisters, by the law of the forest. 3. [b] That a forester or keeper may arrest any man that kils or chaseth any deer within the forest when he is taken with the manner within the forest, or if the offender be indicted. But then it is demanded, [c] what if a man be so imprisoned, and after offer sufficient pledges, and they are not taken, what remedy for the party, seeing there are very seldome justice seats for forests holden? The answer is, that in the term time he may have *ex merito justitiæ* a *habeas corpus* out of the kings bench, or if he have privilege, out of the court of common pleas, or of the exchequer, or out of the chancery without any priviledge either in the term time, or out of the term in time of vacation, and upon the return of the writ, he may be bailed to appear at the next eir to be holden for the forest, &c. And may also be bailed by force of a * writ *de homine replegiando* directed *custod' forestæ*, [d] if he be arrested by the officers of the forest for hunting, &c. whereof he stands indicted or presented taken with the manner he finding 12 pledges: but if he be adjudged by the justices in eire, and imprisoned he cannot be bailed by that writ *de homine replegiand'* directed *custodi forestæ*, &c. and [e] if he be unjustly proceeded withall there he hath remedy by law, as hereafter, when we treat of the justice seat, shall be declared. And it is

See Domesday Warw. Si vero per mare contra hostes ibat rex, vel quatuor batsneius, vel quatuor libras denariorum ei mittebant.

[a] Ordinatio forestæ. 34 E. 1.

[b] Regist. 8. b. F. N. B. 67. c.

[c] See the 2. part of the Inst. Magna Carta, cap. 29.

* Rot. par. anno E. 3. nu. Int' petitiones.

[d] See the 2 pt. of the Inst. W. 1. cap. 15. Bracton lib. 3. fo. 154. Fleta, lib. 2. c. 2.

[e] F. N. B. 67. a. Register. 1 E. 3. c. 8.

is to be observed, that there is a diversity between the writ *de homine replegiando* directed to the sherif, for he is restrained by the statute of W. 1. cap. 15. to replevy any man imprisoned for the forest, being taken with the manner or indicted, but this statute extends not to the writ *de homine replegiando* directed *custodi forestæ, &c.*

Regist. 80. b. 43 E. 3. 30. a. & b.

The fourth conclusion is, that the offender may be retained by him untill he hath found pledges to appear before the justice in eire, because (as hath been said) the court of the swanimote hath no power of judicature, but if he offer sufficient sureties, he ought not to be imprisoned.

Consuetud' et assisa de foresta. Vet. Mag. Cart. parte 2. fo. 29.

5. That this justice in eire at his sessions may by the law of the forest proceed upon the presentments or verdicts in the court of the swanimote, though they be taken in another court, as the justices in eire might have done in like cases as before in the chapter of justices in eire appeareth.

6. Lastly, Note the issue joyned upon the plea of the forester, viz. *de injuria sua propria absque tali causa*, and allowed by the court, and the consequent thereupon. And thus much for the case the reporter saith, that it was said that the party should * not traverse the presentment of the foresters, verderers, regarders, and agisters: [f] and herewith agreeth 50 E. 3. and note the presentment was in that case by 36. And herein this diversity is to be observed, that if at the swanimote the presentment of the foresters be found true by the jury concerning vert or venison, the offender standeth thereof convict in law, and cannot traverse the same: but an indictment or presentment before the chief justice of the forest at a court of the justice seat by a jury, and not found in the swanimote, may be traversed. 8 E. 3. Itinere Pickering 147. a. because it is not presented but by one jury.

* Nota, the entry is *Præsentatum, et convictum per viridar'.*
[f] 50 E. 3. ass. 442. Ordinat' forest. 34 E. 1. Presentment by 36.

[291]

21 E. 3. 48.

The justice seat.

4. This case also giveth just occasion to speak of the court of the justice seat holden before the chief justice of the forest, aptly called in the said book justice in eire, for so he is, and hath authority and jurisdiction to hear and determine concerning vert and venison &c. by force of letters patents under the great seal, whereof there be two, one for the forest on this side of Trent, the other beyond. By which letters patents the king doth grant unto him *officium gardiani capitalis justiciarii ac justiciarii sui itinerantis omnium et singularum forestarum, parcorum, chacearum et warrennarum suarum cum suis pertin' quibuscunque * ultra Trentam existen', &c. dantes et concedentes eidem* A. B. *plenam authoritatem et potestatem tenore prædictarum literarum patentium omnia et omnimoda placita, querelas, et causas forestarum, parcorum, chacearum et warrennarum prædict' tam de viridi gram', quam de venatione, ac de aliis causis quibuscunque infra easdem forestas,* [a] *parcos, chaseas et warrennas, evenien' sive emergen' audiend' et determinand' : habend', occupand', gaudend' et exercend' offic' præd' cum pertin' per se vel per sufficien'* [b] *deputatum suum sive deputatos suos suffic' durante vita ipsius* A. B. *&c.*

* The like office *citra Trentam mutatis mutandis.* Note, anciently this great officer was created by writ, as other justices in eire were, but now by the statute of 27 H. 8. ca. 24. he is to be created by Let. pat. See before cap. Justices in Eire.
[a] This is to be understood of parks, chases and warrens within the forests, as hereafter shall appear.
[b] That is by the statute of 32 H. 8. cap. 35.

And this court of the justice seat cannot be kept oftener than every third year, and other justices in eir kept their courts every seventh year. And (as before other justices in eire) it must be summoned forty days at the least before the sitting thereof: and one writ of summons is to be directed to the sherif of the county, which writ you shall find hereafter in this chapter.

There

There is another writ of fummons directed *cuftodi foreftæ domini regis vel ejus locum tenenti in eadem*, and this writ confifteth upon two parts. Firft, to fummon all the officers of the foreft, and that they bring with them all records, &c. Secondly, all perfons, which claim any liberties or franchifes, within the foreft, &c. and to fhew how they claim the fame. [c] And this court or juftice feat hath jurifdiction to inquire, hear, and determine two things. 1. All trefpaffes within the foreft, according to the laws of the forefts. 2. All the claims of franchifes, priviledges, and liberties within the foreft, as to have parks, warrens, vivaries, to be quit of afferts, and purpreftures, to cut down his own woods without view of the forefter, &c. Likewife claims of leets, hundreds, felons goods, waifs, ftrays, fugitives, and to kill hares and other beafts of chafe within the foreft, or to have a wood *infra metas foreftæ et extra regardum foreftæ*, that is, to be out of jurifdiction of the foreft, and other franchifes, priviledges, liberties, immunities, freedomes, &c. within the foreft, whereof you fhall read excellent matter in the eire of Pickering in 8 E. 3. rot. 31, where Guilberd of Acton claimed his woods *extra regardum foreftæ*, &c.

c Cart. de foreft. cap. 16. 21 H. 7. 30.

This chief juftice may by the ftatute of 32 H. 8. make his deputy (yet all the writs of commons ancient and late, are *coram* (the juftice *itinerant*) *aut ejus deputato*.)

32 H. 8. ca. 35.

Before any juftice feat be holden, the * regarders of the foreft muft make their regard by force of the kings writ, and the regard is *obambulare*, to goe through and view the whole foreft and every bayliwike of the fame, *ad videndum, inquirendum, imbreviandum et certificandum* all the trefpaffes in the foreft: his office extendeth through the whole foreft, and every part thereof, to inquire of all offences concerning vert and venifon, and of all concealments of any offences or defaults of the forefters, and all other officers of the kings foreft. He is a minifteriall officer, and is conftituted either by letters patents of the king, or by the chief juftice at the juftice feat, or to be chofen by writ to the fherif. The duty of this officer appeareth by the writ hereafter mentioned.

* A regarder is derived of the French word *regardeire*, that is, to view or fee, becaufe he cannot prefent any thing but upon his own fight and view.

To fpeak once for all, the names of all the officers from the higheft to the loweft, put them in mind of their duty: *Conveniunt rebus nomina fæpe fuis: Nomina funt notæ rerum.*

Before a juftice feat there ought to be preparations for the fame, to the end, * that good fervice may be done there, *et quod itinera non fint umbratilia*, as taking one or two examples inftead of many.

*[292]

Rex vic' Not. falutem. Præcipimus tibi quod venire fac' certis die et loco quos ad hoc duxerimus providend' omnes foreftarios et regardatores de [a] *Sherwood* [1] *ad regard' faciend' in foreft' prædict' ante advent' jufticiariorum noftrorum de foreft',* [2] *et loco regardatorum noftrorum qui mortui funt et infirmi alios eligi fac' ita* [3] *quod* [b] 12 *fint in quolibet regard', et nomina illorum imbrevientur.* [4] *Et foreftar' debent jurare quod* 12 *milites ducent per totam balivam fuam, ad videndum omnes tranfgreffiones quæ exprimuntur in* [5] *fcriptis* [c] *capitulorum quæ tibi mittimus, et hoc non omittent pro aliqua re:* [6] *debent etiam milites jurare quod facient regard', ficut debet fieri et folet.* [7] *Et quod ibunt ficut foreftar' eos ducent ad prædicta videnda.* [8] *Et fi foreftar' noluerint eos ducere, vel aliquid forisfact' concelare voluerint, ipfi milites non omittent pro illis quin forisfact' illud videant et imbreviari faciant: et hoc pro nulla re dimittant. Et* [9] *quod regard' fiat circa feft' beati Petri ad Vincula prox' futur'. Tefte, &c.*

Breve de regardo cum artic'.

a Foreft' de Sherwood. i. Limpida Sylva.

b Cart. de foreft. cap. 7.

c 12 capit. patent. inferius. In this writ 9. things are to be obferved.

1 *Videnda*

The 12. chapters abovementioned are these which the regarders duty is to prepare.

Nota, all these 11. are to be upon his view, *super visum*, and in this respect may be resembled to a coroner, *super visum al'*.

1 *Videnda sunt omnia assarta, &c.* Assarts.
2 *Videndæ sunt omnes purprestur' in boscis, &c.* Purprestures in woods.
3 *Videndæ sunt omnes purprestur' in terris arabil', &c.* In arable.
4 *Videnď sunt omnia vasta boscorum, &c.* Wast of woods.
5 *Videnď sunt omnes bosci domini regis, &c.* The kings woods.
6 *Videnď sunt omnes haiæ domini regis, &c.* The hedges of the king.
7 *Item omnes purpestur' et omnia assarta, et omnia vasta, &c.* Generall words.
8 *Videnď sunt omnes aereæ austursorum, espervorum, falconum, &c.* Ayeries of haulks.
9 *Videnď sunt omnes forgæ et mineriæ, &c.* All forges and mines.
10 *Videnď sunt portus maris, &c.* The havens of the sea.
11 *Videnď est mel, si quid, &c.* Hony.

12 *Item milites debent attente inquirere in itinere suo quis habuerit arcus et sagtit' vel baliscas leporarius, burchetas vel aliquid ingenium ad malefaciend' domino regi de feris suis. Balista*, or *arcubalista*, signifieth a crosbow.

Leporaria, a harepipe. *Burcheta* of the French word *berche*, a kind of gunne.

Ordinatio forestæ. 34 E. 1.

Imprimis ordinavimus pro nobis et hæredibus nostris quod de transgres' in forestis nostris de viridi et de venatione de cætero fact', forestar' infra quorum balivas hujusmodi transgres' fieri contigerint, præsentant easdem ad prox' swanimotum coram forestar', viridar', regardator', agistator', et aliis earundem forestarum ministris. Et super præsentationibus hujusmodi ibidem coram forestar' viridar' et omnibus aliis ministris supradictis per sacram' tam militum quam aliorum proborum et legalium hominum de partibus vicinioribus, ubi transgressiones sic præsentatæ fact' fuer' non suspectorum, per quos rei veritas plenius inquiratur. Et sic inquisita veritate præsentationes illæ per communem concordiam et assensum ministrorum prædictorum roborentur et sigillis suis sigillentur. Et si alio modo fuit indictament' pro null' penitus habeatur.

This ordinance being made by the king only without authority of parliament, albeit it was in affirmance of the law, did not binde, and therefore was not executed: and that it was but an ordinance, or declaration made by king E. 1. it appeareth expresly by the statute of 1 E. 3. and by that act of 1 E. 3. the said declaration is rehearsed as a law, the observation whereof is also an excellent preparation for a justice seat.

1 E. 3. ca. 8. sta. 1. F. N. B. 164.

Viridarius à viridi, vert, or gren-hue, for that his office principally concerneth to look to the vert, or grene, and to see it be maintained.

Viridarius is a judiciall officer of the forest, and chosen in full county by force of the kings writ. His office is to observe and keep the assises or laws of the forest, and to view, receive, and inroll the attachments and presentments of all manner of trespasses of the forest of vert and venison, and to do equall right and justice as well to poor as to rich. All this and much more you may read in the oath which he taketh before the sheriffe. There be most commonly four verderors in every of the kings forests.

[293]

Agistator,

Agistator, so called, because he taketh beasts to agistment, that is, to depasture within the forest, or to feed upon the pawnage, and commeth of the French word, *gyser*, to lye, because the beasts that feed there are there levant and couchant, lying and rising. And his office consisteth in *agistando, recipiendo, imbreviando, et certificando*. Agistatores. Const. & Ass. forest. ubi sup.

And this officer is constituted by the kings letters patents: and of these in such forests where there is any pawnage, there be four in number.

Gruarii, (of whom you shall reade in forest records is derived from the French word *gruyer*, which signifieth generally the principall officers of the forest. *Et ipsi gruarii vocantur ad similitudinem eorum qui aucupio regis in grues olim praeerant.* Gruarii. See the Cust. de Norm.

Forestarius is taken for a woodward not only of the king within his forest, but *ex vi termini* of any subject of his woods wheresoever they lye: which appeareth by a writ in Bracton in these words. *Rex vic' salut. Scias quod propter destructionem quae facta est in bosco et terra quam A. de N. tenet in dotem in tali villa de B. de N. Provisum est in curia nostra coram justiciariis nostris, quod idem apponat forestarium suum ad praedictum boscum custodiend', ita quod praedict' A. non habeat in eodem bosco nisi rationabile estoverium suum ad ardendum et claudendum tantum super eandem terram quam ipse tenet in eodem, &c.* But in legall understanding he is taken for a sworn officer ministeriall of the kings forest, and his duty appeareth by his oath, which consisteth on five parts. 1. That he shall be loyall and true to the master of the forest. 2. That he shall truly walk and keep the office of the forestership, and true watch make both early and late both of vert and venison. 3. Truly attache, and true presentment make of all manner of trespasses done within this forest to his knowledge, and specially within the keeping of his bailiwick. 4. The kings counsell, his fellows, and his own, he shall truly keep. 5. No concealment make for no favour, meed or dread, but well and truly to behave himself therein. Forestarius. Bracton, lib. 4. fo. 316. a. & b. & 231. a.

[a] Officers of the forest shall not be sworn on enquests out of the forest.

[b] *Messarius* is a mower or harvester derived *à metendo.* Fleta lib. 2. cap. 75. *messor.* 30 *ass.*

Thestylis et rapido fessis messoribus aestu
Allia serpyllumque herbas contundit olentes. Virgill.

[a] Ordinat. forest. 34 E. 1. cap. 5. Regist. 183. F. N. B.

[b] Assisa et consuet. forest. 6 E. 1. c. 16.

Surcharge of the forest.] *Superoneratio forestae*, is when a commoner in the forest putteth on more beasts then he ought, and so surchargeth the forest. It is taken from the writ *De secunda superoneratione pasturae* in the same sense when the commoner surchargeth. Where it is said *(tempore coronationis regis Henrici avi*, that is, of H. 2.) It is to be known that he was crowned twice, viz. the 20 of December in the first year; he caused his sonne Henry to be crowned king the 15 of June in the 16 year of his reign; Henry his son died the 11 of June in the 28 year of his reign; after whose death king Henry Fitz Empresse was crowned again. Regist. and F. N. B. 126. a. e. &c. surcharge. Mag. Cart. cap. 5.

Desertum, id quod ab hominibus deseritur, et feris relinquitur. Domesday.

Masura terrae, sunt in eisdem masuris 60 domus plus quam ante fuerunt. Mas de t'ra, that is an exchange of land where there is a house. Sudsex Cicestr. et saepe.

Fugacia

Carta Matildis Imperatricis Miloni de Gloceſt.

Fugacia ſignifieth a chaſe, and is all one with *chaſea.* See the charter of Mawde the empreſſe, ſtiling her ſelf *Anglorum domina,* made to Miles of Gloceſter, creating him thereby earl of Hereford, wherein towards the end follow theſe words. *Præcipio quod hæc omnia ſupradicta teneat de me libere et quiete in boſco et plano, in foreſtis et fugaciis, in pratis et paſturis, &c. Præterea autem concedo ut in propriis ipſius prædiis quiſque tam in agris, quam in ſylvis excitet agitetq; feras; meas autem ne venetur, iis præſertim in locis quos privilegio circumſcripſi meo cum pœna præcipio.*

Int. leges Canuti cap. 77. Lamb.

Johannes Roſſus, et alii poſt eum.

That H. 1. made at Woodſtock a park, which was, ſaith he, the firſt park in England. But it is out of doubt that there were parks in the dayes of the Saxons, which were called *deerfald* of two Saxon word of *deor* for deer, and *fald* for a place incloſed with pale, hedge, or wall. And in the book of Domeſday often mention is made by expreſſe name *de parcis. Parcus beſtiarum. Parcus ſylvaticus beſtiarum.*

[294]

Deorfald. Falda ferina.
Domeſday.
Chent. Certh.
Ib. parcus ſylvatic' beſtiarum.
Devonſcoire.
Winchelere.
Hertfordſcire.
Belinton.
Aſſiſ. foreſt.
6 E. 1. cap. 1.

Haia taken for *parcus* of the French word *heye* for an incloſure *Rot. Inquiſit.* 36 E. 3. *in ſcacc' de foreſt'.*

Haia de Kingeſlie in Hamſhire.

Hulmus, i. *inſula* an iſle. *Bercaria,* vid. 1 part. Inſtit. ſect. 1. *Maſtivus mutulatus* is a maſtiffe expeditated or lawed, and not muſled: for no dog by the law of the foreſt ought to be muſled. *Mutulatus* commeth of the verbe *demutulo,* i. *demembro. Biſſa,* i. *cerva,* of the French word *biche* for a hinde. *Mureleges, à legendo mures,* of getting of mice, a wilde cat. *Teſſones* of the French word *teſſon,* for a gray, brock, or badger. *Beſonus* of *biſon* a French word for a wilde oxe.

Ibid. 8 E. 3. Itinere Picker. Guilbert of Actons caſe.

Ham, Saxonicè domus, home, ſometime *villa,* as *Mileham olim Mildham,* becauſe the aire was milde and temperate.

Ib. Artic. 11. Camia continet ſpacium octo palmarum in longitudine. Dorſ. clauſ. an. 16 R. 2. m. 30.

Hue and *cry, huteſium et clamor,* the one being an expoſition of the other, each of them ſignifying crying and ſhowting; *verba dolentis.* And *hue* is derived of the French word *huier* and *crier.* But hue and cry by the foreſt law is not to be made for treſpaſſe in vert, but in veniſon only. This hue and cry cannot be purſued but only within the bounds of the foreſt; and the offence muſt be committed within the foreſt, and not within the purlieu. And this hue and cry may be made by any of the kings miniſters of the foreſt, for any of them may arreſt the malefactor, and none can make hue and cry but he that may arreſt in that caſe, and cannot. And ſo are the generall words, *ſi quis viderit, &c.* to be underſtood.

Si quis viderit, &c. If any townſhip or village follow not the hue and cry, they ſhall be amerced at the juſtice ſeat.

Taken with the *mayneer, à manu* is in 4 kinds, viz. dog-draw, that is, drawing after a deer which he hath hurt. Stable ſtand, viz. at his ſtanding with any knife, gunne, or bow, or cloſe with greyhounds in his leaſh ready to ſhoot or courſe. * Back-bear, that is, carrying away the deer which he killed. Bloody hand, that is, when he hath ſhot or courſed, and is imbrued with blood.

* Bract. lib. 3. fo. 32.

But what if injuſtice be done at the juſtice ſeat? For example, as if a claim be made of any liberty at a juſtice ſeat, and is there allowed, what remedy hath the party grieved in this caſe? which I do the rather propound, becauſe I find not this doubt reſolved in any of the readings upon this ſtatute of *Carta de Foreſta,* or in any that have written of the foreſt laws. And I find this queſtion reſolved

ſolved by a notable book caſe in 21 E. 3. agreeable with the Regiſter and other books; where the caſe was this. *A.* and *B.* before the juſtices of the foreſt of Pickering claymed to have within the wood of *E.* within the ſame foreſt a woodward proper, and alſo to have the windefals in the ſame wood, which claime was allowed by the ſaid juſtices, where in truth the ſaid claime was falſe, to the diſherison of the commoners there: for that the commoners within the ſaid town of *E.* had the choice of the ſaid woodward, and all the windefals for their reaſonable eſtovers as belonging to their freehold. Therupon on the behalf of the commoners the record before the juſtices of the foreſt was removed by *certiorari,* (which in the foreſt law is called a *venire facias* record) into the kings bench (which court is above all eires) and two of the commiſſioners, viz. Robert de Scarburgh and Robert Wich ſued out a *ſcire fac'* upon the ſaid record againſt the ſaid *A.* and *B.* &c. And they declared upon the ſaid writ that all the commoners had the liberties aforeſaid: exception was taken to the writ, that the grievance is as well ſuppoſed to others, as to thoſe two which were plaintifes in the *ſcire fac.* Whereunto it was anſwered, that although the grievance was to others, yet thoſe two that would complain might maintaine this ſuit. And if the others be of record with *A.* and *B.* yet theſe two may ſue, and theſe two might have joyned in aſſiſe. And there it is holden, that if a profit be granted to a comminalty out of the foreſt, the claime ought to be made by them all, but otherwiſe it is within the foreſt, where every one ſhall have his action by himſelf for that which belongs to him; and in the end the writ was adjudged to be good. But in this caſe ſomewhat is implyed, for by the law of the foreſt when a claim is made of any liberty within the foreſt, although no iſſue be joyned thereupon, yet the entry is, *Et quia videtur juſticiariis quod expediens et neceſſe ad inquirendum ſuper præmiſſis rei veritatem antequam ad allocationem clamei prædicti procedatur, inquiratur inde veritas per miniſtros ejuſdem foreſtæ:* and ſometime *tam per miniſtros foreſtæ quam per alios liberos et legales homines,* at the diſcretion of the juſtices for the advancement of truth: and accordingly the foreſters, verderors, regarders, and agiſters doe enquire thereof. [a] Alſo if a claim be made before the juſtices of the foreſt, whereupon there groweth difficulty, or if a demurrer in law be thereupon joyned, the juſtices may adjourn the ſame into the kings bench to be there adjudged, and then the entry is, *Ideo quoad clameum prædict' pro eo quod juſticiarii prædict' nondum adviſantur de judicio inde reddendo, datus eſt dies eidem H. coram domino rege (in tali retorn') ubicunq; &c. de audiendo inde judicium, &c. Et dictum eidem H. quod interim ſequatur bre. de venire fac' inde recordum, &c. Poſtea dominus rex mandavit præfat' juſtic' bre. ſuum in hæc verba.* * *Edw. Dei gratia rex Angliæ, &c. Dilecto et fideli ſuo Rico. de Willowbye ſalutem. Cum vos et ſocii veſtri juſticiarii noſtri ad placita foreſtæ, &c. tenend' aſſignat' quoddam clameum de diverſis libertatibus per dilectum et fidelem noſtrum H. de Percye coram vobis et ſociis veſtris prædictis in eadem foreſt' fact' propter quaſdam difficultates in eodem clameo content' coram nobis adjornaveritis, ut accepimus, vobis mandamus quod ſi ita eſt, tunc omnia clamea prædicta nec non recorda et proceſſ. inde coram vobis habita coram nobis ubicunque fuerimus in Anglia ſub ſigillo veſtro ſine dilatione mittatis juxta adjornamentum*

21 E. 3. 48. a. In ſcire fac. Vid. 25 E. 3. fo. 43. Nichol. Gowers caſe. Vid. Regiſt. 263. b. Breve de inquirendo de libertatibus allocatis.

[295]

[a] 8 E. 3. Itinere Picker. Henry de Percyes caſe which depended in adviſement for difficulty four years before R. de Willowby, and other juſtices of the foreſt.

Venire fac. Record. Certiorari.

* A certiorari before judgement out of the chancery returned into the kings bench directed to R. de Willowbie (being the ancient primary judge) only, becauſe he only hath the keeping of the records.

namentum prædictum hoc bre. nobis remittentes. Teste, &c. anno 12 E. 3.

Virtute cujus brevis clameum prædict', nec non recordum et process. prædict' mittuntur coram rege ad diem prædict' una cum brevi prædicto.

Postea dominus rex mandavit præfato R. de W. quoddam aliud bre. claus. in hæc verba. Edw. &c. dilecto et fideli R. de W. salutem. Cum vos et socii vestri justiciarii nostri ad placita forest' in forest' H. com' Lanc' de Pick' in com' Eborum tenend' assign' quædam clam' de diversis libertatibus per dilectum et fidelem nostrum H. de Percye coram vobis et sociis vestris prædict' in eadem forest' habend' fact' propter quasdam difficultat' in eisdem clameis interveniend' coram nobis adjornaveritis, et quædam alia clamea sua similiter ibidem de quibusdam aliis libertatibus fact' allocaveritis, prout accepimus; nos volentes tam super dictas libertates sic adjornat' quam super al' allocat' certis de causis certiorari, vobis mandamus quod si ita est, tunc omnia clamea præd' nec non record' et process. inde coram vobis, et sociis vestris prædict' habit' coram nobis ubicunque fuerimus in Anglia sub sigillo vestro sine dilatione mittatis, et hoc breve, ut hiis inspectis ulterius fieri faciemus, quod de jure fore viderimus faciend'. T. E. duce Cornub. com' Cestriæ filio nostro charissimo custod' Angl' apud Berkhamsteed primo die Februarii anno regni nostri 13. *Virtute cujus brevis clam' præd' tam adjornat' quam allocat' mittuntur coram rege una cum bri. prædict', &c.*

By all which cases the former question is resolved, which case and consequents thereupon is worthy of serious consideration.

25 E. 3. 43. Nicholas Gower was indicted for that he killed the kings game in the kings forest, when he was the kings steward of the same, and also had taken ransome for indictments, which indictments were removed *coram rege*, and the steward was put to answer thereunto.

[296] 27 E. 1. coram rege rot. 13. Wigorn'. Note the writ of the justice of the forest retorn' into the kings bench. *Breve justiciarii forestæ. Versus Godfridum Episc. Wigorn'.* Ad finem faciend' pro transgress. venationis in foresta de Windesor.

Hugo le Despencer justic' forest' citra Trentam mandavit quoddam breve suum vic' Wigorn' retorn' coram domino rege in crastino Sancti Johannis Baptistæ prox' præterito, &c. in hæc verba. Hugo le Despencer justic' forest' citra Trentam vic' Wigorn' salutem. Mandamus vobis quod distring' Godfridum episcopum Wigorn' per omnes terras et catalla sua in balliva vestra, ita quod nec ipse, nec aliquis per eum ad ea manum apponat, donec aliud a domino rege seu à nobis inde habueritis in mandatis. Et quod de exitibus coram domino rege respondeatis et quod habeatis corpus ejus coram domino rege in festo Sancti Johannis Baptistæ ubicunque tunc fuerit in Anglia, ad finem faciend' pro transgressione venationis per ipsum facta in foresta de Windesore sicut per legalem inquisitionem secundum assisam forestæ coram nobis apud Windesor captam plenius nobis constat. Et unde eidem episcopo per literas nostras ex parte domini regis aliàs mandavimus, quod pro fine suo inde faciendo veniret coram nobis apud London, ita quod esset ibi in crastino Sanctæ Trinitatis prox' præterito, vel sufficientem attornatum suum ibidem mitteret suam plenam potestatem in hac parte habentem: qui ad diem illum coram nobis non venit, nec attornatum in hac parte misit sicut ei ex parte domini regis mandatum fuit; et habeatis ibi hoc breve. Dat' apud Lugtheburghe die Jovis in octab' Ascensionis Domini anno regni regis Edwardi vicesimo sexto. Ad quem diem vic' nihil inde fecit, sed mandavit quod præceperat ballivis libertatis ejusdem episcopi de Oswoldestowe qui nihil inde fecerunt. Per quod præceptum fuit eidem vic' quod non omitteret propter prædictam libertatem, quin distring' prædictum episcopum per omnes te as, &c. Et quod de exitibus, &c. Et quod haberet

haberet corpus ejus coram rege in octabis Sancti Michaelis, ubicunque, &c. ad finem faciend', &c. cum domino rege pro transgress. prædict', &c. Et similiter quia procedi non potuit ad finem capiend' de præd' episcopo, &c. sine record' prædicti Hugonis justic' &c. de transgress. præd. &c. Mandatum fuit eidem Hugoni justic' &c. quod recordum inde coram eo habitum regi mitteret ad præfatum terminum cum omnibus recordum illud tangentibus. Et vic' nullum breve retornavit coram rege ad præfat' terminum Sancti Michaelis: nec prædictus Hugo justic', &c. aliquod recordum misit, &c. propter quod, sicut prius præcept' fuit vic' quod non omitteret propter prædictam libertatem, quin distring' prædictum episcopum per omnes terras, &c. Et quod de exitibus, &c. Et quod haberet corpus ejus coram rege in octabis Sancti Hilarii ubicunque, &c. ad finem faciend' in forma prædict', &c. Et vic' retorn' breve, sed prædictus Hugo justic' nullum recordum misit. Et super hoc venit quidam Aluredus de Northgrave pro prædicto episcopo, et dicit quod præfatus Hugo justic', &c. distringit præd' episcopum per diversa brevia sua in com' Wigorn' et Glouc' ad finem faciend' coram ipso de eadem transgr. et nihilominus paratus est satisfacere domino regi pro prædicto episcopo de prædict' transgress. secundum recordum prædicti Hugonis, et secundum quod cur' regis consideraverit, &c. Et quia dictus Hugo justic' nullum recordum misit per quod procedi potest ad finem capiend' de prædicto episcopo, &c. Ideo quoad prædictum episcopum cessat distr' usque à die Paschæ in unum mensem ubicunque, &c. Et dictum est prædicto Aluredo quod tunc sit ibi ad finem faciend' pro prædicto episcopo, vel quod habeat warrantum de prædicto Hugone justic' quod finem fecit vel finem facere debeat coram prædicto Hugone justic', &c. de transgressione prædict', &c. Et nihilominus mandatum est præfato Hugoni justic', &c. quod venire fac' recordum prædictum, ut prædictum est, coram rege prefatum terminum, &c.

Procedi non potuit ad finem, cap. fine recordo, &c. A certiorari to the justice of the forest for the record.

Episcopus paratus est satisfacere.

Observe well the parts of this record, and a ready way to help the king to his fines after the eire of the forest is ended. [297]

On the other side it is demanded what if a man make a just and lawfull claim to certain liberties at the justice seat, and cannot obtain the same to be allowed by the justices of the forest, what remedy for him that maketh such claim? * Whereunto the answer is, that he shall have a writ *De libertatibus allocandis*, directed to the justices of the forest, which writ doth appear in the Register.

[a] And any person that is to make any claim may the first day of the eire either make it in person or by atturny, F. N. B. 26. g. And he that appears upon a presentment or indictment taken before the justices in eire, and traverseth the indictment, may after appear by atturny. See before cap. Justices in Eire the writ in the Regist. 19. a. W. 2. cap. 10.

[b] And the entry is *A. B. po: lo: suo T. B. vel L. N. de omnibus placitis seu querelis motis seu movendis et ad omnes libertates calumniand', prosequend', et defendend' durante itinere isto:* whereby it appeareth in what generality an atturny may be made.

[c] And this agreeth with the Register, fo. 19. b. by 5 kind of writs which are worthy of observation, viz. [1] *Breve de clameo admittend' in itinere per attornatum primo die itineris, &c.* [2] *De libertatibus exigendis in itinere:* [3] *De attornat' in omnibus placitis et querelis in itinere, et ad libertates calumniandas:* [4] *Aliter in omnibus placitis et querelis in itinere juxta formam stat' de Merton cap. 10. Glouc' cap. 8. et W. 2. cap. 10.* [5] *Aliter de attornatis, &c.*

And these writs are to be granted *ex merito justitiæ*, without any

* Regist. 162. and F. N. B. 229. b. & 230. a. & Int' communia de Scaccar. de anno 14 E. 1. de libertatibus allocandis et vide L. Ockham f. 47, 48.

[a] 8 E. 3. Itinere Hick. 148. a.

[b] 8 E. 3 Itinere Pick. the case of the prioresse of Rocela. Reg. 19. b.

[c] Regist. 19. b.

any denyall as well to the justices in eire of the forest, as other justices in eire for the admitting of atturnies. Vid. 2. part of the Institutes W. 2. cap. 10.

And upon search made I find the like writ beginning, *Omnibus balivis et fidelibus suis, &c.* in the eire of Pickering, 19 b. for the prior of St. Johns of Jerusalem to make an atturny before the justices of the forest.

2 E. 3. fo. 29. Lib. 9. fo. 28. b. Labbot de Strata Marcellas case.

But what if the justice in eire give an erroneous judgment, &c. what remedy hath the party grieved? He may have a writ of error out of the chancery returnable into the kings bench, and there justice shall be done.

d 8 E. 3. Itin' Pick. fo. 165. the case of William of Persay and Petronilla de Kinthorp.

[d] If a man make his claim by grant or prescription, and he or his councell mistaketh his right title in some materiall point, so as the claim is found against him, it is good for him that his true title be found by the same verdict specially, for then may the party by petition make a fine and pray licence to make a new claim, and thereunto he ought to be admitted.

8 E. 3. Itin' Pick. fo. 22. Itin' Lanc' fo. 4.

And concerning claims it is specially to be observed, that by the forest law a grant made of a priviledge within the forest to all the inhabitants being freeholders within the forest or such other comminalties not incorporated, is good.

e 8 E. 3. Itin' Pick. fo. 15. Lanç. f. 64.

[e] If a man make a false claim by claiming more then he ought, he shall be fined for his false claim, but that which he ought to have shall not be seised: as the prior of York claimed by charter to have tithe of all venison, *tam in carne quam in corio*, where he ought not to have it *in corio*, for which he was fined and enjoyed it *in carne*.

Pickerings case.

In the eire of Pickering holden before Richard de Willowby, Robert de Hungerford and John de Hambury justices in eire for the forest of Pickering, *anno* 8 E. 3. a claim was made by Thomas de Pickering and Margaret his wife, viz. *Habere in dominico bosco suo de Locton woodwardum ad custodiendum boscum suum, et quod nullus in eo amputet aut prostrare faciat arborem aliquam sine voluntate sua, et quod ipsi in bosco suo possunt prostrare et dare pro voluntate sua arbores virides et siccas, et dare et vendere arbores suas pro voluntate sua sine visu forestariorum, &c.* and prescribed in the same in the right of the said Margaret, where this prescription was inquired of and allowed to be good in law, but it was found, as to the taking of the trees without the view of the forester, to be untrue.

* *In cur' Scaccar' coram Edw. Sanders capital' bar. et aliis baronibus tempore R. Eliz.* of the report of Popham chief justice.

* The like prescription made by Sellinger to take and cut down timber trees within his own woods within the forest of Haye in the county of † Hereford without the view of the forester, and upon argument and long advisement it was adjudged, that the prescription was good notwithstanding the ordinance of 34 E. 1. and the statute of 1 E. 3. cap. 2. And the reason was, because that statute was but in affirmance of the common law of the forest, and against such a statute a man may prescribe. And that 34 E. 1. was but an ordinance and no statute, see F. N. B. 167. a. Register, which judgment was agreeable to Pickerings case abovesaid, and is of great consequence: for the statute of Carta de Foresta, and most of the statutes concerning forests are likewise *declarativa antiqui juris;* and therefore, as against the common law, so against them a man may prescribe upon a just and reasonable cause; but if they were

†[298] Constit. & Ass. Forest' ubi sup. A man may claim to have dogs inexpeditate and hounds within the forest.

introductiva

introductiva novi juris, then no prescription can be made against them, unlesse he hath another statute to preserve the liberties.

And if a man hath a wood in a forest, and hath no such prescription, the law doth appoint him a means to sell both wood and timber, so it be no prejudice to the game, but sufficient is left besides, and that is, by a writ of *ad quod damnum*, upon return whereof the king doth licence him, &c.

Regist. 257. a. F. N. B. 226. f. 2 E. 2. trns. 9. Ad quod damnum.

By the kings commandment under his signature and signet, all the judges were assembled about certain questions concerning his forests of Leicester in the county of Leicester, and of Bowland in the county of Warwick, to be moved to them by the atturny of the duchy. And the first question which was moved, was, whether the said forests were forests in name only, or in law: which being *questio facti*, the judges could give no answer: but by way of direction they resolved, that if they were forests in law, it must appear of record, for there be certain incidents inseparable to every forest, viz. courts of record, and officers of record, courts of record, as courts of attachments, swanimote, and justice seats. Officers of record, as foresters, verderers, regarders, agisters, &c. who are made (as it appeareth before) by matter of record, &c. but appellation or naming of them forests in offices, pleadings, grants, or other conveyances, are no proofs, that they be forests in law.

Pasch. 5 Jac. Reg.

Vid. Reg. 258. a. Bowland is called libera chasea de Bowland.

2. It was resolved by them, that if they be but free chases and no forests in law, that then the owners of woods within such chases may cut down timber or wood growing therein without view of any officer, or licence of any; but if they cut down so much as they leave not sufficient covert, and bruise wood for the game, they shall be punished at the kings suit. And so it is if a common person hath liberty of chase in other mens woods, the owners of the wood cannot cut down all the woods, but leave sufficient for covert, and bruise, as hath been accustomed, no more then the owners of woods in which others have common of estovers, can destroy the whole woods, but leave sufficient for the estovers.

Temps E. 1. trespasse 249. the case is to be understood of a forest where forester (there named) be, for every forest is a free chase, but not *è converso*. 43 E. 3. 8.

3. And being demanded whether in the kings free chases a man might have common and feeding for sheep, and warren by prescription or grant? It was resolved cleerly they might, but they must not surcharge to the prejudice of the kings game, but the owner of the soil within such a free chase cannot erect a warren without a charter from the king. And it seemeth to me that by prescription a man may have common for his sheep within the kings forest: for, first, I find no authority in our books (that I remember) against it; and that generally a man may common in a forest, it appeareth by *carta de foresta*, cap. 1. 33 E. 1. stat. 5. 34 E. 1. cap. 6. And if for common in generall, especially for common appendant so much favoured in law, and particularly for sheep, as wel as for horses and mares. 12 H. 3. common 25. F. N. B. 230. a. And to conclude this point the prioresse of Wicham prescribed to have common in the forest of Pickering, *pro omnibus averiis suis, except' caprellis*, before the justices in eire in 8 E. 3. rot. 31. which being found to be true was allowed to her, &c. and such a prescription may have a lawfull beginning by the kings grant.

Vid. Dier 6 E. 6. fo. 70.

4. That he that hath a warren within a free chase may build upon his own inheritance within his warren a convenient lodge for preservation of his game. And Popham chief justice before all the rest of the judges cited the said case of Selenger adjudged in the exchequer.

[299] Some question being moved between the earl of Nott. justice in eire in all the kings forests, and the earl of Dorset treasurer of England, concerning the disposing of the kings woods in his forests; for resolving whereof by the kings commandment all the judges of England were assembled, who upon conference and mature deliberation resolved these seven points following.

1. That the justices in eire, and the kings officers within his forest have charge of venison, and of vert or green hue for the maintenance or preservation of the kings game, and therein of all manner of trees for covert, bruise and pawnage. But when need is to sell seasonable woods within his forest, or timber for his majesties use, the same must be sold or taken by force of the great seal, or eschequer seal by the view of the forester to the intent that the woods or the timber shall not be taken in places inconvenient for the game. But the justice in eire, or any of the kings officers within the forest cannot sell or dispose of any wood within the forest without commission: and so the exchequer and the foresters have *divisum imperium*, the one for the profit of the king, and the other for his pleasure.

2. That regularly neither the court of the exchequer, nor any of the kings officers can dispose of the kings timber or woods, but it ought to be done by commission, &c. as is aforesaid, for the kings best profit.

In baga de forestis in custodia rem. regis. 12 E. 2. Com' to sell the underwood in the park of Clarendon. 17 E. 2. Com' to sell windfalls in the park of Northampt. 28 Com' to sell wood in Clarendon. Nota, *minuti blaterones quercuum curli et curbi in foresta de Grovele vend' virtute brevis domini regis. Simile ibidem* 10, 11, 13, *et* 14 E. 4. *Simile* 17 H. 6. *virtute literarum pat.* H. 6.

1 E. 3. stat. 2. c. 2. Constit. & Assi. Forest. ubi sup.

3. That every man in his own woods within the forest may take housebote and heybote by the view of the foresters. The kings fermers that have clauses in their leases to take timber, &c. by view, &c. may take the same accordingly: and so may freeholders by prescription, and coppyholders, which by custome have used to take housebote, &c. take the same by view of the foresters, &c. or otherwise according to the custome.

Vid. Itin' Pick. 8 E. 3. rot. 30. the case of William de Persey and Petronilla his wife.

4. It was resolved, that no officer of the forest could claim windefals or dotard trees for their fees by prescription, because they were once parcell of the kings inheritance, but they ought to be sold by commission, as before it appeareth for the kings best benefit.

5. That he that hath the herbage, or pawnage of a parke by the grant or demise of the king or any other, cannot take any herbage or pawnage but of surplusage over and above the competent and sufficient pasture, and feeding of the game: and if the owner of the game suffer the game so to increase, as there is no surplusage, then he that hath the herbage and pawnage cannot put any beasts in the park.

6. That the owner of the park may divide any competent parcell of the park with rail, pale or hedge for the feed of the game in winter, and he that hath the herbage cannot put any beasts therein.

Lastly,

Rot. par. 18 E. 1. fo. 26. the king may grant estovers in his forest without view of the forester.

Lastly, if the pasture and pawnage of the park be but sufficient to feed the game in winter and summer, the owner thereof may drive out the beasts of him that hath the herbage and pawnage. And thereupon by like assent of all the judges the court of the exchequer took this order following with some reasonable additions.

The order of the exchequer upon the resolution of the judges.

Whereas heretofore some question hath been moved between the lord treasurer of England, and the warden and chief justice, and justice itinerant of all the kings majesties forests, chases, parks and warrens on this side the water of Trent, what appertaineth to each of their offices and places concerning the dealing with and disposing of woods, trees, and coppices within his highnesse parks, forests and chases, which being by his majesty referred to the consideration and determination of his judges, and barons, they have resolved touching the same by one uniform assent, as hereafter followeth, viz. that as the lord treasurer of England for the time being, and court of exchequer have the only ordinary power under the king to deal therein so far forth as the same concerns the inheritance and profit of the crown, as in the sale of woods, trees, coppices and such like: so in like manner it concerns the warden and chief justice and justice itinerant of all the kings majesties forests, chases, parks, and warrens, and their ministers to deale therein so far as it may concern the preservation and maintenance of the game, in respect of the shades, coverts, pawnage, and such like for the deer. And therefore it is resolved by all their opinions, that the lord treasurer of England and court of exchequer may not sell any woods or coppices within any the kings parks, forests, or chases, (except windefals, rootfals, and meer dead and sear trees) without the privity and allowance of the said warden, and chief justice, and justice itinerant, within whose jurisdiction it is: nor may cut down the dead and sear trees, nor carry them or windefals or rootfals away, but at fit times, and by the view of such as have charge of the game, whereby it may be seen unto, that the same may be done at fit and convenient times: and that no trees, other then those that be dead and sear, and meerly windfals and rootfals, may be thrown down or taken away without the privity and allowance of the warden, and chief justice, and justice itinerant of his majesties parks, forests, or chases. [300]

And as for the warden, and chief justice, and justice itinerant, and the keepers and other ministers of parks, forests, and chases appertaining to the king, they may not cut down any trees for new paling or railing, or for repair of lodges, without the warrant and allowance of the lord treasurer of England for the time being: but timber needfull for mending of small defects in old pales or rails that are broken, so as the same do not exceed two or three timber trees in any one forest, park, or chase, in any one year, they may be permitted to take of trees in places fit, without making waste thereof, or any spoile or prejudice to the kings inheritance, making the kings surveyor of the woods speedily acquainted, who is to see that the same hath been accordingly well employed: and needfull browse also in places fit, and times seasonable the keepers may take for the deer, not cutting down the limmes or great boughs of the trees. And therefore it is ordered by this court, that from henceforth where it shall be thought requisite to sell any of the kings woods or coppices within any his parks, forests, or chases, that a writ or commission in nature of an *ad quod damnum* shall be directed unto the warden and chief justice, and justice itinerant within the forests, within whose government the same is to be done, to enquire and certifie what number of trees and what coppices may be sold, and in what places, with least prejudice to the kings game; and that upon the return thereof the sale shall be made of such trees and coppices, as upon such certificat shall be thought fit to be sold. And in like manner it is ordered, that for the new paling, and new railing, and new building of lodges in any place within or about any his majesties parks, forests, or chases, and the great repairs of old pales, rails, or lodges in or about the same; that it is to be done upon certificate from the warden and chief justice, and justice itinerant, and the surveyor of his majesties woods within whose jurisdiction it is, by warrant from the lord treasurer of England for the time being.

42 E. 3. cap. 1. [a] Confirm. Cart. 25 E. 1. [b] Cart. de foresta. cap. 1. & 2. [c] This is an act of restitution, for if the king might have made a forest in other mens woods, then could not the owner have felled down his own woods without view or licence, *et sic ad damnum illius, &c.* [d] Nota, all manner of commons are saved.

It is very observable, that if any act of parliament hath been made against any of the articles of the statute of *carta de foresta*, by the act of parliament of 42 E. 3. the same is made void, and by the statutes of [a] *confirmationes cart'* all judgements given against any of the points of *carta de foresta*, shall be holden for void. And where H. 2. Fitz Empresse claimed that he might make forests not only within his own woods and grounds, but in the woods and grounds of his subjects, and thereupon made divers such forests within his own and other mens woods and grounds: whereupon some readers and others that have followed them are of opinion that H. 2. might *de jure* do that which he did. But this act of *carta de foresta*, which is but a declaratory law restoring the subject to his former right, is directly against that conceipt in these words. [b] *Inprimis omnes forestæ, quas Henricus avus noster afforestavit, videantur per bonos et legales homines; et si* [c] *boscum aliquem alium quam suum dominicum afforestaverit ad damnum illius cujus boscus ille fuerit, statim deafforestetur; et si boscum suum proprium afforestaverit, remaneat foresta, salva* [d] *communia de herbagio et aliis in eadem foresta illis qui prius eam habere consueverunt.* To the same effect is the third chapter. Neither could H. 2. or any other king have made or raised a free chase, park, or warren for himself in any of the grounds of the

[301]

Pl. com' Seignior Berkleys case. fo. 236.

subjects; for it is truly said in Pl. Com'. that the common law hath so admeasured the kings prerogatives, that they should not take away, nor prejudice the inheritance of any. But we agree, that all the lands of the subject are originally derived from the crown. And therefore when the ancient kings had the most part in their own hands, or at least great desarts, waste and woody grounds for want of habitation, they might make what forests it pleased them therein, which may be a reason and cause of a lawfull beginning, and therefore a forest may be by prescription good in law over other mens grounds. But the king in his own grounds may make a forest at this day, which is also proved by these two chapters, for such forests are thereby saved and enacted to stand.

31 H. 8. cap. 5.

King H. 8. intending to make a forest about his house at Hampton Court assigned and limited a certain territory of grounds for nourishing and generation of beasts of venery, and fowls of warren, extending over the lands and grounds of divers and many freeholders, and coppiholders, within the mannors, townships, and villages of Eastmulsey, Westmulsey, Walton, Esher, Weybridge, and part of Cobham: and finding that he could not erect either forest or chase over other mens grounds without their consents, did agree with the freeholders and customary tenants, as by his indenture bearing date the first day of October in the 29 year of his reign, between him on the one part, and Sir Richard Page knight, Thomas Henage esquire, and other the freeholders and customary tenants in the towns and villages aforesaid of the other part, wherein the king doth name it (*ad faciendum populum* for the easier passage) Hampton Court chase. But afterwards (in close words in severall places) that it should have all such and like liberties, jurisdictions, and preheminences, laws, statutes, officers, &c. * as any chase or forest within this realm had, &c. And all offences done within the same, should be punished as if the same had been done within any chase or forest within this realm. And the king did thereby covenant and grant, that the freeholders and coppyholders aforesaid might fell and take their woods, groves, and coppices, at their will and pleasure without any view, &c. and to make their hedges and fences about their corn, &c. to keep out the deer, &c. And (for recompence to both freeholders and coppyholders, &c.) that the third part of the free rent of every freehold should be deducted, and the moiety of the fine of the heir of every coppiholder should be also deducted, &c. which indenture and all the covenants therein being recited, it is enacted by authority of parliament accordingly. By which act and divers generall clauses referring to forests, the king intended to have it a forest. But hereby it plainly appeareth both by the kings said indenture, and by the judgement of the whole parliament, that the king could neither erect any chase or forest over any mans grounds without their consent and agreement. And yet king H. 8. did stand as much upon his prerogative as any king of England ever did.

* Nota.

But to join this new with some that is ancient. In rot. par. *anno* 18 E. 1. there is a notable record in these words:

Rogerus episcopus Coventr' et Lichf. queritur contra Rogerum Extraneum et socios suos justic' domini regis de foresta in com' Staff. Eo quod seis. in manus domini regis boscos ipsius episcopi de maneriis suis de Cannock et Ruggeleghe, &c. Rogerus et alii justiciar' ven' et dicunt, quod in itinere suo praesentatum fuit per viridar', forestar' et alios fideles domini regis, quod praedicti bosci super dominum regem et ejus progenitor' per ipsum episcopum et praedecessores suos purprestabantur. Et eo quod licet eis justiciariis in itineribus suis purpresturas factas infra metas forestae domini regis in manus domini regis seisire, ideo seisire fecerunt, &c. Et episcopus bene concedit quod sunt infra metas forestae: sed dicit quod rex Ric' per cartam suam dat' 4 die Decembris anno regni sui primo dedit Hugoni tunc episcopo Coventr' et Lich. praedecessori suo et successoribus suis dicta duo maneria cum ecclesiis, hundred', et omnibus aliis libertatibus. Et per aliam cartam dat' 30 Nov. anno regni sui primo concessit dicto Hugoni quod omnia maneria sua, terrae et omnes homines sui et feod' ecclesiae de Covent' et Lichf. de Cestr' et Salop, et de Gnowshall et omnium ecclesiarum suarum, libera essent et quieta de foresta, et de placitis forestae, de vastis et assartis et regardis forestae, cum multis aliis libertatibus in eisdem cartis recitatis, &c. Virtute quarum cartarum, ipse et omnes praedecessores sui à tempore confectionis earundem cartarum solebant fugare in dictis boscis, et voluntatem suam inde facere, &c. Et petit quod dominus rex, &c. Et praedict' justic' dicunt quod dominus H. rex pater domini regis nunc fuit in seisina dictorum maneriorum et boscorum. Et scrutatis rotulis, et brevibus scaccarii invenitur primum breve regis H. anno regni sui 14 vic' Staff. direct',

Petitio episcopi Covent. et Lich. contra justiciarios forestae.

Purprestur'.

[302]

Gnowshall.

Nota, in boscis deafforestatis per cartam licet fugare, et voluntatem inde facere; á fortiori, in boscis deafforest' virtute actus parl. de carta de foresta.

direct', et quod sciat, quod reddidit A. tunc episcopo Covent' et Lichf. dicta maneria, &c. Item 2 alia brevia baronibus de scaccario direct' quod computent vic' Staff. 30 s. 6 d. *pro med' pro anno* 14. *Item comp. &c.* 61 s. *pro anno* 10. *pro dictis maneriis, &c. Et præd' justic'*
38 H. 6. fo. 10. ac'. *dicunt, quod patet per easdem cartas quod carta per quam episc. clam' esse quietus de foresta, &c. data fuit et facta ante cartam per quam dictus rex R. dedit episcopo manerium et boscos prædictos, per quod dicunt quod prædictus episcopus non potest clamare dictos boscos esse quietos, &c. per formam dictæ cartæ factæ ante donationem dictorum boscorum: ob quod datus est dies dicto episcopo, &c. in unum mensem ad parliament.*
Adjourned into parliament. *&c. Postea ad parliamentum nunc, &c. venit prediet' episc. in propria persona sua, et reddidit regi dictos boscos ut jus ipsius regis. Et idem do-*
Deafforestatio per. Chart. nota. *minus rex ex gratia sua concessit et dedit eosdem boscos prædicto episcopo per easdem metas, bundas et divisiones per quas ipse et prædecessores sui à tempore confectionis cartæ prædictæ Richardi regis boscos illos tenuer', &c.*
* Nota, infra metas forestæ, et tamen extra forestam. *Et quod habeant et teneant liberos ab omnimodis placitis forestæ, &c.* * *Et quod nec justiciar' forestæ seu forestar' viridar' et regardatores, seu alii ministri quicunq. se intromittant infra metas supradictas licet sint infra*
Foresta de Cannock. *metas forestæ antiquas de Cannok. Et pro hac, &c. idem episcopus cognovit se teneri domino regi in mille libris sterling.*

See hereafter pag. 307. Observe well this record, and the parts of the same. And it is to be known, that where divers perambulations were made in the reign of H. 3. E. 1. and E. 2. that all these perambulations and others that should be made (albeit there be no charters thereof now
1 E. 3. ca. 1. stat. 2. Rot. parl. 1 R. 2. nu. 61. 5 R. 2. 84. extant) are established and made good, both by the statute of 1 E. 3. cap. 1. stat. 2. in print; and by an act of parliament in 1 R. 2. nu. 61. in the roll of parliament and not in print; and by another act of parliament 5 R. 2 nu. 84. not in print. For albeit it be to be presumed that charters have been made according to the perambulations; yet forasmuch as time wears out many things, if charters should now be required, many places should become forest againe, which now are in peace and deafforested.

The form of the perambulation of a forest is, *Perambulatio facta in com' Eborum de foresta de G. die anno regis, &c. apud* E. *coram* A B. C D. *justiciariis domini regis ad dictam perambulationem faciend' assignatis per sacramentum* F G. M P. N S. &c. *Qui dicunt super sacramentum suum, &c.* And so set down the metes and bounds of the forest, shewing what is within the forest, and what to be *extra forestam secundum tenorem Magnæ Cartæ de foresta, eo quod afforestata fuerit post coronationem domini Henrici regis 2, &c. In cujus rei testimonium, &c.*

[303] Nota, the charters be generall and short to this effect. *Rex omnibus ad quos præsentes literæ pervenerint, salutem. Sciatis quod volumus et concedimus pro nobis et hæredibus nostris, quod perambulationes factæ coram* A B. C D. *ad hoc assignat' per præceptum nostrum de forestis nostris in com. Eborum de cætero teneantur et observentur per metas et bundas contentas in eisdem perambulationibus, quarum tenor de verbo in verbum sequitur in hunc modum.* And rehearse the whole perambulation.

Rot. parl. 22 E. 3. nu. 26. A long complaint in parliament against foresters, for afforesting of mens purlieus, for undue triall, and for their extortions, too long here to be rehearsed, but worthy to be read, with a prayer that the great charter may be kept, and that all men may enjoy their purlieus according to the perambulations made in the reign of king E. 1. whereunto the king answered, [The king would the great charter

charter to be kept: and that such as will complaine in the right of their purlieus, may have writs out of the chancery.] See rot. parl. 50 E. 3. nu. 80. and 1 R. 2. nu. 60.

Purlieu containeth such grounds which H. 2. R. 1. or king John added to their ancient forests over other mens grounds, and which were disafforested by force of the statute of *carta de foresta*, cap. 1. and cap. 3. and the perambulations and grants thereupon. And is derived from a French adjective and a French noun, viz. *pur* which signifieth clear, entire, and exempt, and *lieu*, that is, a place entire, clear, or exempt from the forest. And both of these derived from the Latin adjective and noun, viz. *purus locus;* and in this sense the civilians called that *purum locum qui sepulchrorum religioni non est obstrictus*. And the perambulation whereby the purlieu is deafforested is called in French *pourallee*, i. *perambulatio*, so as the purlieu and *pourallee* are two distinct things, and * purlieu is the right name of the place deafforested. Purlieu what it is, and whereof derived. 33 E. 1. stat. 5.

By this it appeareth that chases that never were any forests cannot have any purlieu, and consequently the case in 16 Eliz. Dier 326, 327. is mistaken, for the chase of Whaddon never was any forest. Whereby it may be observed, how necessary the true derivation of words is, according to the example of Littleton, as in divers parts of the first part of the Institutes appears.

By this deafforestation the owners of the grounds within the purlieu may at their will and pleasure fell, cut down, eradicate, and stub up all the timber, woods, and underwoods, convert their pastures, meadows and other grounds to arable, inclose them in with any kind of inclosure, build and erect new edifices upon the same or any part thereof, and to dispose and use the same after the disafforestation, as they never had been afforested.

And where some have conceived, that *quoad* to the owners of the soyle the purlieu is disafforested, but not as to others, but as to them it should remaine a forest, by reason of these words in the first chapter, *ad damnum illius cujus boscus ille fuerit*, those words were added to shew the unlawfulnesse of the afforestation, because it was *ad damnum, &c.* as hath been proved before. And then these men must make a diversity between a deafforestation by force of the first chapter of afforestations in the reign of H. 2. and deafforestations made by force of the third chapter of afforestations, in the reigns of R. 1. and king John, for there the clause of *ad damnum* is omitted, and therefore those afforestations are utterly made void against all men.

The statute of *carta de foresta* hath been above 30 times, and lastly in 4 H. 5. confirmed and enacted and commanded to be put in execution, and we finde no authority in law that we remember against our opinion herein: therefore we proceed and do hold, that in any purlieu a man may as lawfully hunt to all intents and purposes within the purlieu within his own grounds, as any other owner may do in his grounds that never were afforested at all.

Some have endeavoured to limit the purlieu man to hunt by custome or prescription, but all the said statutes were made within time of memory against which they cannot prescribe. Some endeavour to maintain it to be by forest law, but it is questioned whether there be any such forest law, in that point, for *quod non legitur non creditur:* but to conclude this point, no forest law can stand against laws enacted by authority of parliament. Others think, that See the first part of the Institutes sect. 170. [304]

that the said statute of 33 E. 1. stat. 5. or some other statute in the reign of E. 1. E. 2. or E. 3. doe in some sort restrain their hunting, which is utterly denyed, that they are restrained by any such in any of the said kings times; but if any such statutes were, they are, being contrary to the statute of *carta de foresta*, repealed by the statute of 42 E. 3. cap. 1. And all the statutes or assises, either that of Woodstock in the reign of H. 2. or any other in his time, or in the reigns of R. 1. or king John are all abrogated by the statute of *carta de foresta* made in 9 H. 3. cap. 1. and 3. as to the deafforestations, &c. And the statute or assise of Woodstock doth extend to deafforestations before, and not after, the words thereof being, *Nullus faciat aliquam installationem inter foresta' et boscos, &c. p. ipsum vel progenitores suos deafforestatos.* And for the same reason the purlieu man may keep his dogs within the purlieu unexpeditated, and seeing the wilde beasts doe belong to the purlieu man *ratione soli*, so long as they remain in his grounds, he may kill them, for the property *ratione soli* is in him; so as hereby concerning purlieus, and by the resolution of the judges concerning chases, it appeareth, that the makers of the statute of 22 E. 4. mistook the law in both of them, viz. concerning chases and purlieus, but the statute being in the affirmative worketh no prejudice to any. And if he chase them with greyhounds, and the beasts of the forest do flee towards the forest for their safety, if the owner pursue them to the bounds of the forest, and then call back his dogs, and do his endeavour to call them again from the pursuit, although the dogs follow the chase in the forest, and kill the kings deer there, this is no offence, so as the owner enter not into the forest, nor meddle with the deer so killed. But if the dogs fasten upon the deer, before he recover the forest, and the deer drag the dogs into the forest, there the purlieu man may follow his dogs and take the deer.

Rot. par. 51 E. 3. nu. 39.

22 E. 4. cap. 7.

43 E. 3. 8. the earl of Arundels case.

38 E. 3. f. 10. b. simile. 12 H. 8. fo. 10. a.

In some letters patents of the perambulations or purallies of forests made by king E. 3. to any county where lands are disaforested, which we have seen, there is reserved to the king forty days for his wild beasts within the purlieus to return again, and for his raungers within that time to rechase them into the forest, which is taken to be a convenient time for that purpose. And albeit these purlieus be absolutely disaforested, and have no liberty of forest there, yet for conveniency it hath been permitted that the rangers of the forest should as often as the wild beasts of the forest range into the purlieu, with his hound rechase the same: and these rangers have used to present unlawfull hunting and hunters of the kings deer within the purlieu, as in the night, or at unseasonable deer, or killing of the kings deer in purlieus by no purlieu men, but unlawfull hunters or the like: such as should not take advantage of their own wrong both to the king and the purlieu men, and that they are known to be deer belonging to the kings forest, because there are no other within the purlieu; wherein the best rule we can (for avoiding of tediousnesse) give the reader, is to follow the judiciall records and presidents of the eires holden before grave and learned justices in eire, as those of Pickering, Lancaster, and the like, concerning presentment of matters done within the purlieus of the rangers whereunto we do rather incline, when we consider the oath which the rangers have anciently taken and continually in these words. You shall truly execute the office of a ranger in the purlieu

20 E. 3. Rot. pat. 1 pars pro deafforest' forestæ de Kemsam.

Vide Rot. parl. 32 E. 3. nu. 26, 27. a complaint of the purlieu men, and the kings answer.

The oath of the ranger.

purlieu of P. upon the border of the kings foreſt of P. You ſhal rechaſe with your hound and drive the wild beaſts of the foreſt, as often as they ſhall range out of the ſame foreſt into the purlieus: you ſhall truly preſent all unlawfull hunting and hunters of wild beaſts of venery and chaſe * as well within the purlieus, as the foreſt, and thoſe and all other offences you ſhall preſent at the kings next court of attachments, or ſwanimote which ſhall firſt happen: So help you God. And it is to be noted, that in ſuch foreſts, as have no purlieus, there is no ranger.

* This proveth that the purlieus are no part of the foreſt; but diſtinct things.

Rot. par. 51 E. 3. nu. 39. 50 E. 3. nu. 80. 1 R. 2. nu. 60.

It was petitioned in parliament, that no man be impeached for hunting within the purlieu or without the bound of the foreſt, and that there be levied no aſſart rents.

[305]

This petition conſiſting on two parts. 1. Concerning hunting in the purlieu, or out of the bounds of the foreſt, the ſecond concerning aſſart rents.

To the firſt: the king anſwereth, That the charter of the foreſt ſhall be kept, which is a yeelding to the petition for that part, for by that charter the bounds of the foreſts are eſtabliſhed, and no purlieus excepted.

As to the ſecond: he anſwered, That the demand was unreaſonable.

The commons made petition that men might enjoy their purlieus freely, and that perambulations might be made as was in the time of king H. 2.

2 R. 2. nu. 48.

Whereunto the king anſwered, The king thinketh the perambulations are duly made, and who will may complain, and ſhall be heard.

The abbot of Whitby had a foreſt called Whitby foreſt (by the grant of H. 2. and king John with all officers incident thereunto) adjoyning to the foreſt of the earl of Lancaſter called Pickering foreſt, and the game of the foreſt of Pickering ranged into the foreſt of Whitby, *Idem abbas habens exploratores ſuos ſtatim ponere fecit retia, et alia ingenia ſua juxta Hakeneſſe et alibi diſtan' à foreſta iſta per tractum unius arcus et aliquando plus, et poſtea cum canibus excitare fecit feras, ita quod p' excitationem illam plures ferarum illarum in redeundo et fugiendo verſus foreſtam de Pickering decidunt in retibus et ingeniis prædictis et capiuntur, et annuatim capere facit in deſtructionem ferarum foreſtæ prædictæ de Pickering ad dannum domini, et neſcitur quo warranto; per quod præceptum fuit vicecomiti, quod venire faciat prædictum abbatem.* Whereupon the abbot came and pleaded his title to the foreſt, *ut ſupra. Et quod omnes abbates loci prædict' virtute conceſs', &c. prædictos cervos et cervas in locis prædictis ubi retia et ingenia prædicta poſita fuerunt, et quæ fuerunt infra limites foreſtæ ſuæ de Whitby, et quoad quod idem habens exploratores ſuper feras domini, &c. retia et ingenia poni fecit prope foreſtam de Pickering, &c. per quod in redeundo plures feræ capt' fuerunt, quod omnino eſt contra aſſis' foreſtæ, idem abbas dicit, quod ad hoc reſpondere non debet, &c. Et quia manifeſte liquet curiæ, &c. quod feræ de foreſta ad foreſtam aliter conferri non poſſunt, niſi ipſius in cujus foreſta inveniuntur, eo quod ſigno aliquo non conſiſtunt ſignatæ nec diviſas aliquas cognoſcunt. Ideo conſideratum eſt, quod idem abbas eat ſine die.*

In itin' Pick. 8 E. 3. rot. 42.

Nota, for harts, hyndes.

The kings deer are not branded or ſigned with any mark, that they may be known whoſe they are out of the foreſt.

By which record and many others it doth appear, that when the kings game of the foreſt doe range out of the foreſt (and purlieu, if any

7 H. 6. fo. 36.

any be) they belong not to the king, but are at their naturall liberty, *et occupanti conceduntur.*

And this is the reason that some have said, that where the king was seised of the forest of M. in fee, and that a custome was pleaded time out of mind, that if any beast of the forest should range into the free chase of the abbot *de Dien* adjoyning to the said forest, that the foresters of the said forest, &c. might enter into the said chase, and with little dogs rechase the kings beasts of his forest into the forest again, that this custome is against law, for that (besides the reason yeelded in the abbot of Whitbies case) immediately when they are out of the bounds of the forest, the property is out of the king, for the being within the forest maketh the property in that case. But the book of 7 H. 6. is left at large whether the prescription be good or no, and yet aid was thereupon granted: and Dier 16 Eliz. 326, 327. agreeth therewith. But in the abbot of Whitbies case there is no prescription for the king but against him.

Lib. 5. fo. 104. b. Rolstons case.

16 Eliz. Dier 326, 327.

Vide itin' Pick. 8 E. 3. The prior of Ellortons case. Rot. 35. Et ibid. the prior of Maltons case. Rot.

It is to be observed, that by the law of the forest when any claim is made by any ancient charter of any franchise, liberty, or immunity, or discharge within the forest by ancient and obscure tearms and words, the entry is (for example) *Et quia non liquet curiæ manifeste cujusmodi libertates prædict' vocabulorum idem prior habere intendit, dictum est priori quod prædict' vocabula declaret, &c.* And after he that maketh the claim, declareth, that is, explaineth the same, and pleadeth further, *Quod ipse et prædecessores sui semper à confectione cartæ prædictæ sine interruptione usi sunt et gavisi sunt libertatibus prædictis* (according to his declaration) *et hoc paratus est verificare per ministros istius foiestæ, &c. Ideo inquiratur rei veritas per eosdem, &c.* Or the entry is after the declaration made, *Et quia videtur justiciariis quod expediens est et necesse, quod curia certioretur super possessionem ipsius prioris in hac parte, inquiratur inde veritas per ministros ejusdem forestæ,* and thereupon the foresters, verderers, and regarders are sworn, and so much as they find have been continually used, is allowed, and so much as hath not been used is disallowed; so as use and continuall possessions are the best expositors of ancient and obscure words.

[306]

Regula. Hil. 6 E. 3. rot. 179. Coram rege diuturnitas et longæva possessio virtute generalium verborum in antiquis cartis sufficiunt.

For example: *Quietum esse de misericordia forestæ,* is to be quit of all amerciaments in the which he in any sort might fall within the forest. And here *misericordia* is taken as well for a fine, as for an amerciament.

Quietum esse de vasto, if he did wast in his woods within the forest he should not be amercied, nor for any other wast.

Quietum esse de rewardo, that is, to be quit of amerciament wheresoever in any marish within the forest, if the usage hath been accordingly.

8 E. 3. itin' Pick. Lambstons case putura. Geldum in Domesday sæpe pro Scot Anglice. 23 H. 3. gard. 148.

Quiet' de omnibus geldis, i. *quiet' esse de omni putura forestar', et de omni præstatione, ad collectionem garbarum, agnorum et lanæ ad opus forestar' ejusdem forestæ.*

De woodgeldis, i. *quiet' esse de omni collectione in foresta præd' ad opus quorumcunque ministrorum forest' præd' ratione boscorum.*

De horngeldis, quietum esse de omni collect' in foresta de bestiis cornutis asses'.

De fotegeldis, i. *quiet' esse de finibus et amerciamentis pro canibus infra forestam inexpeditatis,* if the usage hath been accordingly, other-

wise

wise not: for ancient charters by the law of the forest must be adjudged according to the continued usage, and not *ex vi termini.*

De bucstall, i. *ubi homines convenire tenentur, ibidem convenire ad stableiam faciend' circa feras, et ad easdem congregand', quietum esse de hoc servicio, quando dominus chaseaverit.*

De tristris, anciently written *traistis*, and is derived of *traist*, i. trust, and signifieth, *ubi alii homines manentes in eadem foresta tempore quo dominus chaceaverit in eadem venire debent, et confisi sunt, Anglicè* are trusted, *ad tenend' leporarios certis locis assignatis pro feris ibidem expectand' et capiend', quietum esse de hoc servicio.*

De fledwite, of *fled*, a Saxon word, a fugitive, one that fleeth, an outlaw, and *wite* a Saxon word also, a freedome.

*De careio, cum aliquæ carræ, seu carectæ cartatæ transeuntes per forestam, et similiter * summagia, seu somagia equorum consuet' sunt solvere secundum magis vel minus ministris ibidem pro chemino ibidem habend'. Quietum esse de hujusmodi solutionibus.* *Summagium* or *sommagium* commeth of the French word *sommier* or *summier*, which signifieth a horse carrying any load. *Chimagium*, a toll for way-faring men through a forest, derived from the French word *chemin* for a way. * Carta de foresta, cap. 14.

De scoto, seu sloto, quando homines faciunt collectum inter se ad aliquod obtinendum seu evitandum. Quietum esse de tali collect'. De talagio, idem ut de scoto.

Extra regardum forestæ. If any man within a forest doe hold his woods or lands by grant or prescription to be *extra regardum forestæ*, the woods or lands are deafforested. 8 E. 3. itin' Pick. fo. 149.

Exilium, i. *cum homines utlegantur in itinere istius forestæ pro transgressione viridis seu venationis.*

De escapio, secundum assisam forestæ si averia alicujus in landis vetitis, vel tempore vetito in eadem inveniantur, prima vice pro quolibet pede averiorum prædict' ipsi quorum fuerint amercientur ad unum denarium; et si secundo ibidem inveniantur, similiter pro qualibet pede unum denarium; et si tertio ibidem inveniantur, averia illa remaneant domino forisfacta, de quibus amerciamentis et forisfacturis per hujusmodi vocabulum, de escapio, extiter' quieti.

De pannagio, that is, to be quit to pay any thing for pawnage. F. N. B. 230.

Assertum, assert, is so called of the effect (as some hold) and is derived (say they) of *ad* and *fero*, *assero*, because of wood grounds, marishes, or wast grounds they are converted to be sown with corn, and therefore in the Register, and F. N. B. it is written *assertare*, with an E, and so it is in Carta de Foresta cap. 4. Bracton hereof saith, *Illud quod fuit aliquando boscus, et locus vastæ solitudinis et communia et jam inde efficitur assartum, vel redactum est in culturam.* And herewith agreeth Fleta, *Illud olim fuit foresta et boscus, &c. et jam efficitur assartum, et reductum est in culturam, et idem dici poterit de mariscis et aliis vastitatibus in culturam redactis.* [307] Regist. 157. Fleta, li. 2. c. 35. F. N. B. 226. f. Cart de forest. cap. 4. Bract. li. 4. fo. 226. Fleta li. 4. ca. 22. Lib. 2. cap. 25. Vide Lucubr. Ockam 20. b.

Others fetch it otherwise, but we hold, that it is derived of the French word *essarter*, to grub up, or cleer a ground of wood, &c. and this appeareth by Domesday. *Herefordsh. Mercheley in eodem manerio sunt 58 acræ terræ pro vect' de sylva*, written over the same *essars, de essart' sylvæ exeunt 17 s. et 4 d.* E being turned into A. Rot. par. 51 E. 3. nu. 39.

Radulphus episcopus Karleol petit versus priorem ecclesiæ Karleol decimas duarum placearum terræ de nova assartarum in foresta de Inglewood, quarum una vocat' Lynthwayt et alia Kirthwayte, quæ sunt infra limites parochiæ suæ de Aspaterick. Et super hoc similiter venit Mr. Hen. de Rot. plac. parl. de anno 18 E. 1. rot. 8. Inter episcopum Karleol' et priorem ejusdem de decimis assa torum.

Burton perſona eccleſiæ de Thoriſby, et eaſdem decimas clamat ut pertinen' ad eccleſiam ſuam. Et prior venit et dicit quod Henr. rex vetus conceſſit dicto Deo et eccleſiæ ſuæ beatæ Mariæ Karleol' omnes decimas de omnibus terris quas in culturam redigerent infra foreſtam, et inde eos feoffavit per quoddam cornu eburheum quod dedit eccleſiæ ſuæ prædict', &c. Et Willielmus Inge qui ſequitur pro rege dicit quod decimæ prædict' pertin' ad regem et non ad alium, quia ſunt infra bundas foreſtæ de Inglewood. Et quod rex in foreſta ſua prædict' poteſt villas ædificare, eccleſias conſtruere, terras aſſartare, et eccleſias illas cum decimis terrarum illarum pro voluntate ſua cuicunque voluerit conferre, &c. Et quia dominus rex ſuper præmiſs' vult certiorari, ut unicuique tribuatur quod ſuum eſt, aſſignetur, &c. et certificent regem ad proxim' parliamentum, &c.

[a] Glanvil. li. 9. cap. 11, 12. Fleta, lib. 2. cap. 35. 18 E. 2. de viſu franc' pleg. Dier 7 El. 240.
[b] Cart. de foreſt. cap. 12.
[c] 8 E. 3. Itin' Pick. fo. 17.
[d] Cart. de foreſt. cap. 7. Fleta. li. 2. cap. 35. cap. Itin' W. 1. cap. 4. de paſtur' pauperum.
[e] Potura. Vid. 45 E. 3. 15. & F. N. B. 209. b. *De potura pauperum*, a drinking or ſuſtenance for the poor. 12 H. 4. 24. Hil. 5 E. 3. Coram rege ro. 30. Eborum. 8 E. 3. Itin' Pick. fo. 150. b. *Putura*
[f] 8 E. 3. Itin' Pick. prior de Ellortons caſe. *Quiet' de geldis* is to be quit *de putura*.
[g] 25 E. 3. cap. 7. ſtat. cap. Itineris *fillenale*, of the Saxon word *fillen*, or *fullen*, and *ale*, i. an ale feaſt, whereat they were filled with ale. Bracton, lib. 3. fo. 117. in reciting of Capitula Itineris, calleth it *filckale*, i. *fildale*, an extortion *colore compotationis*. Vide Fleta, lib. 1. ca. 20. Carta de foreſta, cap. 7.

[a] *Purpreſture.* For this and the derivation, ſee in the ſecond part of the Inſtitutes, Statutum de Bigamis, cap. 4. and the expoſition upon the ſame, and Carta de Foreſta, cap. 4.

[b] *Coopartura* is a thicket or covert of wood.

[c] *Macremium* is derived of the old Normandy word *mariſme* for timber.

[d] *Scotales*, *ſcotalæ*, derived of two Engliſh words *ſcot* and *ale*, as much to ſay as a tribute or contribution of drinking for the miniſters of the foreſt when they came to the houſe of any, whereunto others are contributary within the perambulation of the foreſt, which then was called [e] *potura*, a drinking. And after they claimed the ſame for all victuals for themſelves their ſervants, horſes, and dogs, which was called *putura*; and this doth notably appear by a record in 5 E. 3. in theſe words.

[f] *Putura in chacea de Bowland*, i. *conſuetudo clamata per foreſtarios, et aliquando per balivos hundredorum, recipere victualia, tam pro ſeipſis, hominibus, equis et canibus de tenentibus et inhabitantibus infra perambulationem foreſtæ ſeu hundredi quando eo pervenerint, nihil inde ſolvend'.* Where the ſtatute of Carta de Foreſta ſpeaketh. *Nullus foreſtarius ſeu balivus de cætero faciat ſcotalas, &c.* [g] by the ſtatute of 25 E. 3. it is enacted, that no foreſter or keeper of foreſt or chaſe, nor any other miniſter ſhall make or gather ſuſtenance, nor other gathering of victuals, nor other thing by colour of their office againſt any mans will within their bailiwick or without, but that which is due of old right, that is, thoſe fees, which time out of mind they ought to have within that foreſt, and as ſhall appear to be due by the oath of 12 regarders.

[308]

8 E. 3. Itin' Pick. Sir John de Melſaes caſe.

Chablicia, or *cablicia*, browſe wood, derived of the French word *chablis*, as *boys chablis*, either rent down from trees by the wind, or branches of trees cut for the browſe of deer.

Parkebote, to be quit of encloſing of a park or any part thereof, derived of two Engliſh words, *parke*, and *bote*.

Fleta, li. 1. c. 47.

Brigbote, or *bruckbote*, to be quit of making of bridges.

Pannagium, or *panagium*, is derived from the French word *panage*, i. *paſtura pecorum in nemoribus de glandibus et aliis fructibus arborum.*

Trin. 2 E. 3. coram rege rot. 12.

Expaaltare canes, i. *expeditare canes. Expeditatio* is derived of *ex et pede*, becaufe the dog is lamed in the foot, *inexpeditatus* is unlamed.

Canis in this act is taken for *maſtivus* by thefe words, *talis expeditatio fact' p' aſſiſam communiter uſitatam*, which hath reference to the affife of the foreft, *tempore* H. 2. art. 6. which fpeaketh only *de expeditatione maſtivorum, et aſſis' et conſuetud' foreſtæ*, 6 E. 1. cap. 9. fpeaketh only *de maſtivo*. Carta de foreſta. cap. 6.

Ortelles, this word is taken from the French word *orteiles*, in Englifh, claws.

Pellota, of the French word *pelote*, and they from *pila*: in this act it is taken for the ball of the foot, *ſine pelota*, without the ball of the foot. And therefore by the expreffe words of this act the ball of the foot of the maftiffe is not to be cut off, but the three claws of the forefoot to the fkin. This extendeth only to maftiffs, and to no other dogs, for *ubi non eſt lex, ibi non eſt tranſgreſſio;* and neceffary it is, that fuch as dwell in forefts where there are coverts, that they fhould keep other dogs unexpeditated, and the maftiff expeditated for the defence of their houfe, or for giving of warning of theeves and robbers, &c. *Moloſſus* (the old Britifh word) is a mafe-theef, becaufe he doth mafe or amafe a theef, &c. Carta de foreſta ubi fupra.

Managium et meſagium, is commonly in ancient records taken for *meſuagium*. M. S. Priorat. Covent' fo. 14. b.

The words of this act are *De expeditatione canum exiſtentium in foreſta*, and therefore in purlieus or places deafforefted, a man may keep a maftiff without being expeditated. And that I may fay it once for all, my intention is chiefly to explain the obfcure words of this ftatute of Carta de Forefta, and other acts, and leave the reader to the text itfelf being plain: for, *ſatius eſt petere fontes, quam ſectari rivulos*.

Who may keep greyhounds or other dogs to hunt, or ingens, &c. either in a foreft, or out of the foreft, appeareth by certain ftatutes. 13 R. 2. cap. 13. 19 H. 7. cap. 11. 1 Jac. cap. 27. 3 Jac. cap. 13. Aſſiſa foreſt'.

But if greyhounds be founds running *ad nocumentum*, the forefter ought to retain them, and prefent them in the prefence of the verderers, and fend them to the king, or to the chief juftice of the foreft.

We find not that any chapter or article of Carta de Forefta, doth extend to chafes or parks, but only the 11 chapter. *Quicunque archiepiſcopus, epiſcopus, comes vel baro ad mandatum noſtrum tranſierit per foreſtam noſtram, &c.* which chapter doth not only extend to the forefts of the king, but to his chafes and parks alfo, for fo was the law before the making of this act, which is but in affirmance of the common law of the foreft before this act.

1. In refpect of the perfons, for every lord of parliament, be he fpirituall or temporall, had this priviledge befides thofe that be named in this chapter, as fuch abbots and priors, as were lords of parliament, and fo of dukes, marqueffes, and vifcounts, which were erected and created, afterwards being lords of parliament have the fame priviledge alfo.

2. By reafon of the kind of commandment *ad mandatum noſtrum*, faith the ftatute, which words have reference to the writ of parliament directed to every lord of parliament. *Ideo vobis mandamus, &c.* and is a legall commandment by writ directed feverally to each and every lord of parliament to appear at the kings court of parliament, 8 E. 3. Itin' Pick. fo. 134. A forefter or any other officer of the foreft cannot give a nobleman a courfe in the foreft but it is prefentable.

ment, &c. to treat *de arduis et urgentibus negotiis regni, statum et defensionem regni et ecclesiæ Anglicanæ concernentibus*, and to recreate themselves *veniendo*, and after *redeundo*, they may passing by any of
[309] the kings forests, chases, or parks, hunt and kill one or two of the kings deer. The lords of parliament may doe it at other times *ex gratia*, but by law *eundo et redeundo* to and from the parliament.

3. Here is implied that the lord of parliament may in the absence of the forester or keeper after the blowing of the horn, kill one or two of the kings deer *propriis suis canibus, aut arcu suo proprio*.

Linwood de Venatore Clerico, &c. Cart. de Foresta cap. 11. Assisa forestæ. 6 E. 1. 13 R. 2. cap. 13. 19 H. 7. cap. 11. 1 Jac. ca. 27. *Muta canum* is derived from the French word *muit de cheines*. See 25 H. 8. cap. 19. &c.

4. Here is a secret conclusion of law, that albeit spirituall persons are prohibited by the cannon law to hunt, yet by the common law of the land they may for their recreation, to make them fitter for the performance of their duty and office, use the recreation of hunting, as here it directly appeareth: and in *assisa forestæ* 6 E. 6. it appeareth that the abbot of Peterborow had a right of hunting in the forest of Rockingham. And this appeareth in other statutes, viz. 13 R. 2. 19 H. 7. 1 Jac. And at this day, and time out of mind, the king hath had after the decease of every archbishop and bishop (*inter alia*) *mutam suam canum, &c.* his kennell of hounds, or a composition for the same, which and other things are in the exchequer called *multa*.

5. The last conclusion is, that all cannons against the laws or customes of the realm are void and of none effect.

Of the Drifts of the Forests, *Agitatio Animalium in Foresta*.

The drifts of the forests are said to be when all the cattle as well of commoners as of strangers are driven by the officers of the forest to some certain pound or place inclosed, and the end hereof is threefold, viz. First, to see whether those that ought to common doe common with such kind of cattle as by prescription or grant they ought. Secondly, if they common with such cattle as they ought, whether they doe surcharge or no. Thirdly if the cattle of any stranger be there, which ought not to common at all.

32 H. 8. cap. 13.

By the statute of 32 H. 8. it is enacted, That all forests, chases, commons, moors, heaths, and waste grounds within the realm of England and Wales, and the marches of the same, and every of them shall be driven at the feast of St. Michael the Archangell next comming or within 15. days then next after, and so yeerly to be driven by the lords, owners, and possessors of the said forests or chases, or by the officers of the same, and by the constables, headboroughs, bailifs, bursholders, and tithing men, within whose offices, precincts, and limits the commons, moors, marishes, heaths, and wast grounds being out of the forests and chases be or lie upon pain of xl. s. to be forfeited to our said soveraign lord the king by every of the said officers, bailiffs, constables, headboroughs, bursholders and tithing men, as often, and at every time as the said drift

shall

ſhall be omitted, or left undone, or not effectually done within 15. days after the ſaid feaſt of St. Michael the Archangel, as is aforeſaid. And it ſhall be alſo lawfull to the lords, owners and poſſeſſioners of the ſaid foreſts and chaſes by their officers of the ſame, and by the conſtables, bailifs, headboroughs, burſholders and tithing-men, and every of them within the limits of their offices to make like drift of the ſaid foreſts, chaſes, commons, moors, mariſhes, heaths, and waſt grounds at any other ſeaſon and time of the yeare whenſoever, and as often as they ſhall think meet and convenient.

Out of this act of parliament, as to the drift of the foreſt or chaſe, theſe five concluſions are to be obſerved. 1. By what perſons this drift is to be made, and therein if the foreſt be in the kings hands it muſt be made by all the kings officers of attendance [310] in the foreſt, and by four men and the reve of every town within the foreſt, who to that purpoſe are included under the name of officers. And if they be in a ſubjects hands, then either by the owners or poſſeſſors of the ſaid foreſts, or chaſes, or by ſuch officers, as is before ſaid. 2. At what certain time ſuch drift in foreſts or chaſes is to be made? It appeareth by this act that it ought to be effectually done yeerly within 15. days after the feaſt of St. Michael the Archangel. 3. The ſaid drift may be made at other ſeaſon or time of the year whenſoever, and as often as they ſhall think meet and convenient. 4. That ſtoned horſes under 15 handfull high are prohibited to common in any foreſt. See the ſtatute. 5. For commons, &c. out of any foreſt or chaſe. In theſe words are included purlieus and other grounds wherein men have common, and theſe are to be driven by the owners and poſſeſſioners of the ſame, and by the conſtables, headboroughs, bailifs, burſholders, and tithingmen, within whoſe offices, precincts, and limits the ſaid commons, &c. being out of any foreſt, or chaſe doe lie at ſuch times as are aforeſaid.

Ayeries of hawks 8 E. 3. Itin. Pick. Sir John de Melſaes caſe.

The ſtatute ſpeaketh *de aeriis accipitrum, eſpervorum, falconum, aquilarum, et hieronum*, which is but in affirmance of the common law, for it extendeth to ayeries of other hawks then be ſpecially named, as to ayeries *merleonorum in boſcis ſuis de Leveſham.*

29 H. 8. tit. officers, br. 47.

A foreſter by patent for his life is made juſtice in eire of the ſame foreſt *hac vice*, the foreſterſhip is become void, for theſe offices be incompatible, becauſe the foreſter is under the correction of the juſtice in eire, and he cannot judge himſelf: the ſame law is of a warden of a foreſt and of a juſtice in eir of the ſame foreſt: though the offices of the ſteward and juſtice of the foreſt be both judiciall, yet whether he be ſteward of the ſwanimote, or of the eire he is under the correction of the juſtice in eire, and therefore incompatible.

We have been requeſted to ſet down what perſons and what officers either that then were, or which have been ſince the laſt eire, and how many ſorts of officers, and what number doe belong to a foreſt, which we cannot better reſolve and ſatisfie, then by the records of the eires of foreſts, and ſpecially by the writ of ſummons of thoſe eires, which we have thought good to ſet down *verbatim*, not only

only for answer to the said questions, but for divers other observations as we find it in the said eire of Pickering with the exact and particular return of the same.

Vic' Eborum. The persons that ought to appear before the justices in eire of the forest, &c. Forestr Hen. com. Lanc'. * Under these words are included the constable of the castle, the warden, the ranger, the agisters, the steward, the bowbearer. * Four great learned men justices in eire of the forest. * See Cart de forest. cap. 2. Forestar' Viridar'. To what end the officers are summoned. †[311] *Regardatores.*

*Edwardus Dei gratia rex Angliæ, dominus Hiberniæ et dux Aquitaniæ vic' Eborum salutem. Summon' per bonos summonitores archiepiscopos, episcopos, abbates, priores, comites, barones, milites, et omnes liber' tenentes, qui terras seu tenementa habent infra metas forestæ dilecti consanguinei et fidelis nostri Henrici com' Lanc' de Pick' in com' prædict', et de qualibet vil' ejusdem com' infra metas ejusdem forest' existen' quatuor homines et præpositum et forestar' villarum, et * omnes alios, qui coram justiciar' ad placita forestæ venire solent et debent, quod sint apud Pickering die Lunæ prox' post fest' Sancti Michaelis prox' futur' coram dilectis et fidelibus nostris * Ricardo de Willoughby, Jo. de Shardelowe, Roberto de Hungerford, et Johanne de Hambury, tribus vel duobus eorum quos ad requisitionem dicti consanguinei nostri constituimus justic' ad itinerandum hac vice ad placita forestæ ipsius comitis in com' prædict' à tempore quo Edmundus nuper com' Lanc' pater præd' Henrici, cujus hæres ipse est, placita forestæ in eadem foresta virtute * concessionis sibi per dominum E. nuper regem Angliæ avum nostrum inde fact' ultimum tenuit, auditur' et factur' præceptum nostrum de hiis quæ ad placita præd' pertin'. Fac' etiam venire coram justic' prædictis omnes forestar', viridar' et omnes illos qui fuer' forestar' et viridar' forest' prædict' in com' prædict' post ultima placita prædict' cum † omnibus attachiament' suis tam de viridi quam venatione quæ post ult' placita forestæ sunt emersa et nondum terminat'* (viz.) *tam de illis attachiamentis quæ manent infra metas forestæ, quam de illis quæ manent extra forest': fac' etiam venire coram eisdem justiciariis tribus vel duobus eorum regardatores ipsius comitis in balliva sua, ita quod habeant ibi omnia regarda sua sigillis suis signat' et omnes agistatores præfat' com' in eadem balliva sua cum omnibus attachiament'. Et habeas ibi sum' et hoc breve. T. me ipso apud Westm' 17 die Augusti, anno regni nostri* 8.

Note, the punctuall and direct answer to all the points of the writ.

Ad quod breve Petrus de Saltmersh vic' Eborum retornavit quod fecit plenum retornum istius brevis Hugoni de Nevil ballivo libertatis H. comit' Lanc' honor' de Pickering, cui executio istius brevis restat faciend'; qui sibi respond' quod summon' fecit archiepiscopos, episcopos, abbates, priores, comites, barones, milites, et omnes libere tenen' qui terras et tenementa habent infra met' forest', et de qualibet vill' ejusdem com' infra metas ejusdem forest' existen' quatuor homines et præposit' et forestar' villar' et omnes alios qui coram justiciar' ad placita venire solent et debent, quod sint apud Pickering ad diem in brevi prædict' content' coram præfat' justiciar' tribus vel duobus eorum, auditur' et factur' præcept' domini regis de hiis quæ ad prædict' placita pertinent'. Et quod venire fecit forestar', viridar' et omnes illos qui fuer' forestar', et viridar' forest' præd' in balliva sua post ult' placita præd' cum omnibus attachiamentis præd' tam de viridi quam de venatione quæ post ult' placita forestæ sunt emersa et nondum terminat'. Et etiam quod venire fac' coram eisdem justic' tribus vel duobus eorum regardatores ipsius comitis in balliva sua, ita quod haberent ibi omnia regarda sua sigillis suis signat' et omnes agistatores præfat' comitis in eadem balliva sua cum omnibus agistamentis prout patet in schedula retorn' suo prædicto attachiata.

Forestar

Forestar' de feodo in le westward istius foresta de Pickering, viz. { *Willielmus de Percehay miles.* / * *Petronilla de Kynthorpe, et po. lo. suo Edmundum de Hastinges ad omnia faciend' quæ forestar' incumbunt durante itinere isto, et fecit sacramentum.* }

Forestar' custod' forestæ in le eastward, viz. { *Rogerus de Leicester.* / *Hugo de Yeland,* / *Willielmus le Parker.* }

* Nota, a woman that is a forester in fee cannot execute the office her self, but she may make a deputy during the eire, and her deputy shall be sworn, &c. By Carta de foresta cap. 7. Tot. forestarii ponantur ad forestas custodiend' quot ad illas custodiend' rationabiliter viderint sufficere.

* *Viridar' forestæ de Pickering*, viz. { *Robertus Thurnese.* / *Rogerus Browne.* / *Robertus Playce.* / *Jo. de Kilwardbye.* }

* *Viridarii* 4.

Regardatores forestæ de Pickering. { *Willielmus de Everly.* / *Rogerus le Longe.* / *Johannes Boye.* / *Johannes filius Alani.* / *Galfridus de Kinthorp.* / *Thomas Thurnese.* / *Hugo de Nevill.* / *Rogerus de Alveston.* / *Johannes filius Galfridi.* / *Rogerus de Stapleton.* / *Rogerus Strutcocke.* / *Radulphus de Colloughton.* / *Johannes de la Chemnie.* }

Regardator' 13. By the statute *de Carta de foresta* cap. 7. there are to be 12 at the least, and, as here it appeareth, there may be more.

Agistatores in le westward istius forestæ { *Johannes Dringe.* / *Richardus Russell.* }
Agistatores in le eastward istius forestæ { *Willielmus de Roston.* / *Willielmus Russell.* }

[312]

Agistatores 4.

Nomina forestar' nunc istius forestæ, et eorum qui fuerunt forestar' istius forestæ, et eorum qui fuerunt viridar' istius forestæ.

Nomina forest' et viridar' qui fuerunt.

Alanus de Newton / *Johannes de Wardesden.* } *Capital' forestar' Willielmi de Percehay unius forestar' de feodo forestæ de Pick. in le westward ibidem.*

Henry de Ripley / *Thomas de Dalby* } *Capital' forestar' Petronillæ de Kinthorp alterius forestar' de feodo forestæ de Pickering.*

David de Neuton / *Thomas de Rippely* } *Capit' forestar' Hugon' de Yeland for' custodis forestæ in le eastward.*

Nomina subforestariorum forestæ prædict'.

Johannes de Harley.	*Johannes Munmewe.*	*Forestar' Radulphi de Hastings custod' forestæ prædict' nunc.*
Ricardus de Aleintoftes.	*Johannes Scot.*	
Willielmus Gower.	*Willielmus Courtman.*	
Ricardus de Helmesley.		

Subforestarii. 8.

Nomina subforestar' qui fuer' in foresta ista post ultimum iter, &c.

Galfridus de Hawly.	*Johannes Rouceby.*	*Adamus fil' Willielmi.*
Robertus de Wigan.	*Rogerus fil' Nich.*	*Johannes de Nevil.*
Petrus Lilly.	*Alanus fil' Radi.*	*Thomas de Newton.*

Bernardus de Bergh, qui obiit, fuit viridar' in foresta ista, et Alexander de Bergh filius ejus et hæres venit et reddidit rotulos suos tam de

Viridar'.

de viridi quam de venatione tangen' forestam istam de tempore praedicto.

The law of the forest is, that if a verderor die, his heir is to bring in the rols of his auncestors time, which if he doe, then the entry is *ut supra.*

Adam de Bruis qui obiit fuit viridar' in foresta praedict', et nullus est qui venit ad rotul' reddend', ideo vic' seisiri fac' omnia terras et tenementa quae fuer' praed. Adae quousque, &c. Postea venit Willielmus B. filius ejus et haeres, et fecit finem pro rotulis praedictis, et admittitur per 40 s. *prout patet in rotul' de extractis.*

If the verderor alien his lands or die seised, and no man bringeth in the rols, then shall the land by the law of the forest be seised by the sherif, which the verderor had, untill the rols be brought in, and if the rols be lost, then till he make his fine and have his *ouster le main,* and the entry is, as is next above.

Ricardus de Shelton, qui obiit, fuit constabular' castr' praed. et custos istius forest', et nullus est qui venit ad rotul' et munimenta ist' forest' tangen' reddend', ideo veniant ejus terr' et tenementa tenentes ad respondend', &c.

[313] If the warden of the forest dye, and his heyre, or tertenant bring not in the rols, &c. his heyre or tertenant shall answer for the same.

26 Ass. p. 60. And here it is to be observed, that where the forest of Pickering was appendant or belonging to the castle of Pickering, that he that is the constable of the castle is ever by the law of the forest chiefe warden of that forest. And so it is of the forest of Windsor belonging to Windsor castle, of the forest of Rockingham belonging to the castle of Rockingham, and all other forests belonging to castles. And accordingly here you may observe, that the office of constableship and wardenship are in this record conjoyned one with the other.

Trin. 14 E. 1. in banco rot. 7. Staff. *Philippus de Monte Gomeri qui sequitur pro domino rege, petit vers' Radulphum Quintyn ballivam custodiae liberae hayae regis de Alrewas quae pertin' ad serjantiam regis senescall' forestae regis de Canoco, et quae ab eadem serjantia alienata est sine assensu praedecessorum regis regum Angliae. Et Radulphus venit, et per licentiam reddit domino regi inde seisinam suam, &c.*

Custos forestarum. The duty of a woodward doth appeare by his name, and by his oath. *Nomina sunt notae rerum.*

Hil. 13. E. 3. Coram rege rot. 103. Eborum. 8 E. 3. Itin. Pick. acc. Hil. 13 E. 3. it is thus resolved: *Quilibet woodwardus secundum assisam forestae debet portare hatchettum, et non arcum et sagittas pro sinistra suspicione venationis deponend' ad praesentand' tam de viridi quam de venatione. Et videtur justic' hic et concilio regis quod * capreoli Anglice* roes, *sunt bestiae de warrenna et non de foresta, eo quod fugant alias feras*

* Roe-bucks, capreoli.

Bedellus is an officer of the forest, that doth warne all the courts of the forest, and doth execute the proces of the forest, and make all proclamations as well within the courts, as without; and is derived of the Saxon word *bydder*, to call or warne, or of the French word in Normandy *bedeau*, a bailiffe or apparator.

16 E. 4. fo. 1. a. A master of the game of the forest.

Cart de foresta cap. 8. *Mensis vetitus*, fence month, or defence month, so called, because it is the fawning month, when the does have fawnes, for the preservation whereof they ought to be fenced, and defended from hurt and

and disquiet. It containeth a moneth containing 31 dayes, and beginneth in the fifteenth day before midsommer (that is, the nativity of St. John Baptist) in the beginning of which a swanimote is to be holden, and endeth fifteene dayes after. See the statute of *carta de foresta* cap. 8. whereby it is enacted, *quod tertium swanimotum teneatur in initio 15 dierum ante festum Sancti Johannis Baptistæ, quando agistatores nostri conveniunt pro * faonatione seu feonatione bestiarum nostrarum.*

This word *faonatio*, or *feonatio*, is derived of the French word *faonier*, that is to fawne, or for does to bring forth, &c.

[a] See rot. parl. 18 E. 1. fo. 3. nu. 37. the punishment of a forester for doing trespasse in the forest.

[b] If the king or other lord doth pardon a trespasse in a forest, and the offender at a justice seat by his learned councell plead the same; in the proceeding thereupon we doe observe two things. First, that by the law of the forest, before any allowance thereof, the justices charge the ministers of the forest to enquire whether the delinquent hath done any trespasse in vert or venison after the date of the pardon. Secondly, when the pardon is allowed, then the entry is, *quod invenit manucaptores quod amodo non forisfac'*, i. *non delinqueret aut peccaret.* [c] But if an offender be convicted for trespasse in the forest in hunting, &c. and adjudged to be fined or imprisoned, which fine, though it be paid, yet shall he finde sureties for his good abearing, &c. in these words [d] *quod amodo se bene geret, et in foresta prædicta non forisfac.* i. *non delinqueret seu peccaret. Unde forisfactura pro delicto.*

[e] By the absence or *non venue* of the justices in eyre at the day of the adjornment, the justice seat is discontinued, and how and by what means it may be recontinued, and resummoned, it appeareth in 8 E. 3. *itinere Pickering.*

* The printed book is *venatione*, which ought to be amended, and made *faonatione* or *feonatione*, which signifieth the fawning.

[a] Rot. parl. 18 E. 1 fo. 3. nu, 37.

[b] 8 E. 3. Itin' Pick. Sir Raphe Hastings case.

* This is the word of Carta de de foresta cap. 10.

[c] Ibidem Rob. Saltmershes case.

[d] Carta de forest. cap. 10.

[e] 8 E. 3. Itin. Pick. of William de Persay, and William de Kinthorp fo. 165.

[314]

No jury shall be compelled by any officer of the forest, or any other person whatsoever, to give their verdict in any other place, then where their charge is given, against their good will, nor by malice, menace, or other dures, shall be constrained to give their verdict of a trespasse in the forest, otherwise then their conscience will clearly informe them. This law extendeth to forests only. 7 R. 2. cap. 3.

Albeit there be some beasts that be no beasts of forest, as the buck, &c. and some beasts and fowles that be no beasts and fowles of warren, yet if any man hunt or hawke at them within the forest, it is against the assise of the forest, and punishable by the lawes of the forest, for all manner of hunting or hawking there without warrant is unlawfull, because it disquieteth the beasts of the forest.

We reade that king H. 1. by his charter granted, *quod cives Londoniæ habeant fugationes suas ad fugandum sicut melius, et plenius habuerunt * antecessores eorum, scilicet Siltre, et Middlesex et Suer.*

Carta regis H. 1. civibus London'.

* Nota, the citizens of London had this priviledge before this charter.

The king being seised of a forest, did grant the forest to another in fee, the grantee shall have no forest, because he hath no power to make justices and officers of forest to hold courts, &c. but yet though it cannot take effect *ex vi termini*, as a forest, yet together with the game the same shall passe as a free chase for the savages and conies: for as hath been said every forest is a free chase, *et quiddam amplius.*

42 E. 3. 2. a. in Trans.

Regist. 8. b. *Chasea est ad communem legem*, and is not to be guided by the forest laws, and so are parks.

See the first part of the Institutes, sect. 1. verb. T'res ou ten'ts. But if the king doth grant a forest to a subject, and granteth further that upon request made in the chancery, he and his heires shall have justices of the forest, then the subject hath a forest in law, as the duke of Lancaster had the forests of Pickering and Lancaster, and the abbot of Whitbye had the forest of Whitbye in the county of York, which being not understood, hath been the cause that readers and others have erred. Vide 12 H. 7. Kelw. 13. and 14. &c. 4 E. 3. 55. Malins case. 2 H. 6. 15. Forest de Exmore. 27 H. 8. cap. 7. 1 E. 3. cap. 2. 22 E. 4. cap. 7. 32 H. 8. cap. 13.

Mich. 18 E. 1. in banco rot. 155. Eborum. *Ricardus de Cornubia et 9. alii attach. fuerunt ad respondend' Johanni de Sallaye quare ipsum ceperunt, et in prisona detinuerunt per decem septimanas apud castrum de Knaresburgh, &c. Ricardus et alii dicunt quod castrum et honor de Knaresburgh cum foresta de Bestayne fuit aliquando in seisina domini H. regis, patris domini regis nunc, et eo tempore fuit talis consuetudo in foresta prædicta, quod si quis indictatus fuerit per forestarios coram seneschallo ejusdem honoris de transgressione de venatione facta in eadem foresta, idem seneschallus tales transgressores ubicunque fuerint inventi infra eandem libertatem prædicti honoris, licite potest arrestare et imprisonare, et eos in prisona detinere quousque satisfecerint de transgressione, &c.* By the grant of a forest a chase passeth. *Qui rex Hen. dedit prædict' honorem cum foresta, &c. Ricardo fratri suo com' Cornub' patri Edmundi com' Cornub' qui toto tempore suo usus est tali libertate arrestandi, &c. Johannes è contra dicit, nullam talem fuisse consuetudinem arrestandi malefactores, nisi quando capti fuerunt cum manuopere, et hoc ab antiquiore tempore,* Nota, capti cum manuopere. *quia idem comes non habet ibidem forestam, sed chaceam tantum. Et quod tempore Willielmi de Stotevill domini dictæ chaceæ qui dedit regi J. dictam chaceam, et tempore dicti regis J. et tempore regis H. patris, dum dicta chacea fuit in manu sua, nunquam arrestaverunt aliquos de transgressione in chacea illa, nisi illos qui capti fuerunt cum manuopere, et hoc offert verificare per patriam, &c. Ricardus dicit quod non possunt prædictam verificationem sine prædicto com' verificare. Ideo præc' est vic' quod sum' prædict' com', &c. Consimile placitum et consimilis responsio in eodem rotulo. Item al' in rot.* 163.

[315] Rot. parl. 14 R. 2. nu. 13. King R. 2. granted to Thomas duke of Glocester in speciall taile, the castle of Saint Brionel, and the forest of Deane, (whereby nothing passed, as hath been said, but a frank chase) now by authority of parliament it is enacted, that the said duke should hold the said forest as a forest, and to constitute such justices and officers, &c. as belong to a forest.

But what was the title of the courts of eyre of forests in the hands of subjects? we answer, taking one example of the forest of Pickering in the hands of Henry earle of Lancaster; *placita forestæ Henrici comitis Lanc' de Pickering tent' apud Pickering coram Ricardo de Willowby, Jo. de Shardelowe, Roberto de Hungerford, et Johanne de Hanbury, justiciariis ad itinerand' hac vice, ad placita forestæ prædictæ in com' Eborum assignat' die Lunæ prox' post festum Sancti Michaelis, anno regni regis E. 3. post conquestum* 8.

12 E. 3. coron. 119. felonia. If any felony be committed within the forest, it shall be enquired of before the judges of the common law, and doth not belong to the conusance of the chiefe justice of the forest.

Transgressio. Mich. 9 E. 1. *coram rege* rot. 6. Huntingdon. *Transgressio in foresta regis pro venatione regis non est hic terminanda.*

Nota,

Nota, before Scroope and other justices in eire, according to the course of the common law, a man claimed to be quit of pawnage in the kings forest, and also he claimed in the same forest pawnage of his tenant *pur agistes;* and for that this belonged to the justices of the forest, they would not meddle with it. And the reason of that is, the words of the statute of *carta de foresta,* cap. 16. *Praesententur capitalibus justiciariis nostris de foresta, cum in partes illas venerint, et coram eis terminentur.* So as the termination and ending thereof belongeth to the chiefe justices of the forest, by the expresse words of the statute. And where the statute saith, *coram capitalibus justiciariis nostris, &c.* it is to be knowne, that there is but one chiefe justice of the forests on this side Trent, and he is named *justiciarius itinerans forestarum, &c. citra Trentam.* And there is another *capitalis justiciarius,* and he is *justiciarius itinerans omnium forestarum, &c. ultra Trentam;* who commonly is a man of greater dignity then knowledge in the laws of the forest. And therefore when justice seats are to be holden, there be associated to him such as the king shall appoint, who together with him shall determine *omnia placita, &c. forestae,* with a patent of *si non omnes,* and a writ *de admittendo, &c.* And the chiefe justice of the forest, and these associates, are *capitales justiciarii forestae,* and named *capitales* in respect of the verderors and others, that to some purposes (as hath been said) have inferior judiciall places.

V. Cartam de foresta cap. 16. Temps E. 3. Kelw. 150. b. V. 21 H. 7. 22. & 30.

For these associations and other writs, see a notable president 8 E. 3. Itin. Pickering in the case of William of Persay, &c. fol. 165.

And seeing, as it hath before appeared, the forest laws differ in many cases from the common laws of England, it is good reason they should be determined before men learned in the laws of the forest, as in other cases. As if a trespasse be done either in vert or venison in any forest in the hands of a subject, in the life of the ancestor, lord of the forest, it shall be punished in the life of the heire. But so it is not in the chases or parkes of a subject, for by the common law *actio personalis moritur cum persona.*

If a man committed a trespasse in a forest, and dye, by the forest law the trespasse is dispunishable, agreeable to the rule of the common law.

8 E. 3. Itin. Pick. Hugh Latimers case.

But by the statute of 19 H. 7. he that shall stalk with any bush or beast in any park, chase, or forest, without licence, &c. shall forfeit for every time he so stalketh x. li. to any person that will sue for the same by action of debt, wherein no wager of law, protection, or essoine shall be allowed, and two justices of peace may examine the same, &c. See the statute of 1 H. 7. cap. 7. See the third part of the Institutes, cap. Felony.

19 H. 7. cap. 11. In this act see the great penalty for keeping of nets called deer-hayes and buck-stals by any that hath not any forest, park, or chase.

* If a forestership or a bailiwick of a forest be granted in fee, if it be found out at an eire for the forest, that the grantee hath misdone in his bailiwicke, the bailiwick is forfeited. Nota, the justices in eire have power to enquire thereof. In these offices of foresterships or bailiwicks in fee within a forest, albeit they have an absolute fee simple therein, yet are they of such trust that they cannot be granted over without the kings license, and before such license be granted, there goeth out a writ of *ad quod damnum* to the king, if such license shall be, &c.

* 26 Ass. p. 60.

[316]

Register fo. 257. F. N. B. 226.

There be many beasts of the forest by the laws of the forests of England. The hart in summer, the hinde in winter, and all that proceed as of them: the buck in summer, the doe in winter, and the proceed of them: the hare male and female, and their proceed: the

For the beasts of chase and warren, and fowls of warren being not proper to this treatise.

See the first part of the Inst. sect. 378. Rot. parl. 18 E. 1. nu. 20.

the wild boar male and female, and their proceed: and the wolf male and female and their proceed: the fox male and female, and their proceed: the martin male and female: *capreolus* the roe, as it appeareth before, is no beast of the forest, but it is a beast of chase.

* Lutra animal amphibium.

But I find that in 18 E. 1. John de Claret was amerced in 100 li. *pro uno cervo et duobus * lutris captis in foresta de Pek*, and he petitioned to the king in parliament to be discharged thereof and was denied. Yet I take an otter is no beast of the forest: but all hunting in the forest, as hath bin said, is unlawfull.

The proceads of the hart and hinde. The male the first year a calf, the second a broket, the third a spayad, the fourth a staggard, the fifth a stag, the sixth a hart, and so after. The female, the first year a calf, the second year, a brockets sister, the third year a hinde.

The proceads of the buck and doe. The first year a fawn, the second year a pricket, the third a sorell, the forth a sore, the fifth a buck of the first head, the sixth a great buck.

The proceads of the hare, the first year a leveret, the second a hare, the third a great hare. Of a wilde boar: a pig, a hogge, a hog-stear, a boar, and after a sanglier.

The seasons by the law of the forest for the beasts of the forest are these. Of the hart and the buck, beginneth at the feast of S. John Baptist, and endeth at Holy Rood day. Of the hinde and doe, beginneth at Holy Rood and continueth till Candlemasse. Of the fox at Christmasse, and continueth till the 25 of March. Of the hare, at Michaelmas, and lasteth till Midsummer. Of the bore, from Christmasse till Candlemasse.

Cart. de foresta, ca. 8. 10. 16. &c. And so it is taken 1 Reg. ca. 4. ver. 21. *Venatio cervorum*, the venison of harts. ª Ordinatio forestæ ca. 1. 5.

In the statute of Carta de Foresta in divers places *venatio* signifieth venison in French *venaison*, and so in effect in Duch and other languages. It is called venison or *venaison*, of the mean whereby the beasts are taken, *quoniam ex venatione capiuntur*, and being hunted are most wholesome. ª They are called beast of venary (not venery as some term it) because they are gotten by hunting. No beast of the forest that is *solivagum et nocivum* is venison, as the fox, the wolf, the martin, because they be no meat, but *caro eorum est nociva: a fortiori*, the bear is no venison not only because he is *animal solivagum et nocivum*, but because he is no beast of the forest, and whatsoever is venison must be a beast of the forest, *sed non è converso*. On the other side, *animalia gregalia non sunt nociva*, as the * wilde boar: for naturally the first three years he is *animal gregale*, and after trusting to his own strength, and for the pleasure of man becometh *solivagum*. He is then called sanglier, because he is *singularis*, but he is venison and to be eaten. The hare is venison also, which the poet preferreth before all others,

Aristotle.

Aristotle.

* Sanglier, quia singularis.

Martial.

Inter quadrupedes gloria prima lepus.

Deer à θηρ Græce i. fera bellua κατ' ἐξοχήν, and their flesh is called caro ferina.

So as the red-deer, the fallow-deer, the wilde boar, and the hare, are venison. Whereupon these two conclusions in the law of the forest do follow. First whatsoever beast of the forest is for the food of man is venison, and therewith agreeth Virgil, describing a feast,

Implentur

Implentur veteris bacchi pinguisq; ferinæ.

They had their belly full of old wine and fat venison. So venison was the principall dish of the feast.

2. Whatsoever beast of the forest is not for food of man is no venison. Therefore *capreolus* being no beast of the forest, as hath been said, is not by the law of the forest venison, for though it be food and taken by hunting, it is no venison. Nature hath endued the beasts of the forest which are venison with two qualities, swiftnesse, and feare, and their feare increaseth their swiftnesse.

Pedibus timor addidit alas: but yet the deer are the most fearefull.

[317]

Dente tuetur aper, defendunt cornua taurum,
Imbelles damæ quid nisi præda sumus? Martial.

Having spoken somewhat *de venatione*, it followeth that we should say somewhat *de viridi*, because the statute saith, *Tam de viridi quam de venatione*, and other statutes speak of vert and venison. De viridi, virium verectum, &c. Cart. de forest. cap. 8. 16. 1 E. 1. ca. 8.

* *Viridis*, green hue, *à viriditate*, the French calleth it verd, and we vert, whatsoever beareth green leaf, but specially of great and thick coverts. And vert is of divers kinds, some that beareth fruit that may serve as well for food of [a] men as of beasts, as pear trees, chesnut trees, apple trees, service trees, nut trees, crab trees, &c. and for the shelter and defence of the game: some called [b] *haut-boys*, serving for food and browse of and for the game, and for the defence of them, as oaks, beeches, &c. Some *haut-boys*, for browse and shelter and defence only, as ashes, poples, &c. Of *sub-boys* some for browse and food of the game, and for shelter and defence, as maples, &c. some for browse, and defence, as birch, sallow, willow, &c. some for shelter and defence only, as alder, elder, &c. Of bushes and other vegetables, some for food and shelter, as the hawthorn, blackthorn, &c. some for hiding and shelter, as brakes, gorsse, heath, &c. To sum up all, *Plantarum tria sunt genera: arbores, arborescentes, et herbæ. Arbores*, as *haut-boys, et sub-boys. Arborescentes*, as bushes, brakes, &c. *Herbæ* as herbs and weeds, which albeit they be green, yet our legall *viridis* extendeth not to them.

* Consuet. et assisa de forest. 6 E. 1. cap. 1. 20, 21. Hil. 13 E. 3. Coram rege rot. 103. Virgil. Itur in antiquam sylvam stabula alta ferarum.

[a] Deut. 20. v. 19.

[b] Consuet. et assisa forest. 6 E. 1. c. 2. & 20.

A viridi commeth, as hath been said, *viridarii*, because their office is to see to the preservation of vert, which in troth is the preservation of venison. The poet speaking to the trees, saith,

Quercus es in sylvis pulcherrima, pinus in hortis,
Populus in fluviis, abies in montibus altis.

See for the punishment of trespasse done *de viridi*, either in the kings woods, or in the woods of the subject, *Consuet' et assis' forest', ubi supra.*

The philosophicall poet in describing the most delightfull pleasures of woods, &c. and green hue, saith,

Devenere locos lætos, et amæna vireta
Fortunatorum nemorum, sedesque beatas. Virgil.

And because it should be hard and difficult that any man should hunt and kill the kings deer in his forest and passe away without discovery, unlesse there were procurers, plotters, assisters, and receivers: by the law of the forest, whosoever receiveth within the forest,

Of principall and accessary. 8 E. 3. Itin. Pick. fo. 3. & 5.

forest any such malefactor either in hunting or killing, knowing him to be such a malefactor, or any flesh of the kings venison knowing it to be the kings: in this case he is a principall trespasser, wherein the law of the forest differeth from the common law, for by the common law he that receiveth a trespasse and agreeth to a trespasse after it be done, is no trespasser, unlesse the trespasse was done to his use, or for his benefit, and then his agreement subsequent amounteth to a commandment, for in that case, *Omnis ratihabitio retrotrahitur et mandato æquiparatur*, but by the law of the forest, such a receiver is a principall trespasser, though the trespasse was not done to his use, as well as the procurers and plotters; but by the common law in case of felony such a receiver is but an accessary. But in the case abovesaid, if the receipt be out of the forest, he cannot be punished by the law of the forest, because it is out of the jurisdiction of the forest, which jurisdiction is locall. And seeing the jurisdiction of the forest is locall, the law of the forest hath provided, that the forest should be inclosed by metes and bounds, which indeed are the inclosure of the forest: for as parks are inclosed with wall, pale, or hedges, so forest and chases are inclosed by metes and bounds, and as a parke cannot be a parke without such an inclosure in deed, as is aforesaid, so it can be neither forest nor chase without an inclosure in law, that is, by metes, and bounds. *Metæ sunt clausuræ forestarum et chacearum:* and *Foresta est locus in quo feræ includuntur, venandi ergò, solis metis*. And where by the statute of 6 E. 1. cap. 18. it is provided, *quod omnes metæ forestæ sint integræ domino regi*, that is so to be understood, *quoad jurisdictionem et imperium, et non quoad dominium:* for if rivers or high-ways be bounds, as most commonly they be, yet the king hath no more interest in the soil, way, river, or fishing, then of right he ought, but only for his jurisdiction of his forest which extendeth over the whole way, river, &c. And where mils and other houses, trees, &c. of other men, and such like, be metes and bounds of the forests, yet thereby the king hath no interest in such mils, houses, or trees, &c. And therefore old woodmen have divided metes, *quoad jurisdictionem et imperium*, into metes inclusive, as ways, rivers, &c. and into metes exclusive, as churches, church-yards, chappels, mils, houses, trees, &c. which bound the forest, but are excluded from any jurisdiction; and that the said law of 6 E. 1. is intended only of metes inclusive, if any man kill or hunt any of the kings deer in any part of the river, high-way, &c. being an inclusive boundary of the forest, he is as great an offender, as if he had killed or hunted within the main continent of the forest, albeit the state and interest of the soil of the high-way or river be in other men; but neither of these kinds of metes and bounds are removeable, because they are the inclosure of the kings forest, and if either of them be removed, it is punishable by the laws of the forest. This word *meta* is only used in this statute: in ancient perambulations and records you shall read *secundum metas, mæras, bundas, et* * *marchias forestæ*. *Mæra* is fetched from the Saxon word *mere*, and that of μείρω Grecè, which signifieth to divide or bound. *Bunda* a bound, is derived from the Saxon word *bunna*, signifying a higher thing, as hils, houses, trees, &c. *Marchia* is derived from the Saxon word *march*, now a mark. *Sed meta accipitur pro quocunque termino, limite, seu fine.*

12 E. 4. 9. 15 E. 4. 15. b. 14 H. 6. 26, 27. 37 Ass. 8. 38 Ass. 6. 38 E. 3. 18. 13 H. 7. 12. 13. Nota, that in the highest and lowest offences, viz. high treason and trespasse there are no accessaries, but in felony which is between both, there be accessaries both before and after. See the 3. part of the Instit. cap. Principall and Accessary.

[318]

* 8 E. 3. Itin' Pick. fo. 6. Mæra. Bundæ. Marchiæ. Meta.

His

His ego nec metas rerum, nec tempora pono. Virgil.

And it is to be observed, that a man may have a free chase as belonging to his mannor in his own woods, at well as a warren or park in his own grounds; for the chase, warren and park are collaterall inheritances, and not issuing out of the soil, as the common doth, and therefore if a man hath a chase in other mens grounds, and after purchase the grounds, the chase remaineth.

Regist. Judic. 35, 36. Dier 16 El. 326, 327.

After Easter following the parliament holden in February, *anno* 9 H. 3. according to the statute of Carta de Foresta, Hugh de Nevill, and Brian de Lisle were appointed commissioners to take inquisitions of the ancient metes and bounds of such forests, as either H. 2. or any king after had inlarged. And in the reign of H. 3. divers perambulations, and deafforestations were made, and many other in the reigns of H. 3. E. 1. E. 2. and E. 3. &c. All which were returned into the chancery, and remain of record in the Tower.

Perambulations of forests according to the ancient metes and bounds. Vid. sup. pa. 302.

The commons of Herefordshire pray remedy against the evill customes of the forest of Ewyasone; namely, for taking their cattell comming thereunto as forfeit. Whereunto the royall answer of the king in parliament was in these words, The old good laws and customes of the forest to be observed, and the contrary forbidden by a writ under the privy seal. *Regalis sanè et digna Plantagenestorum genere sententia*, wherewith we will conclude, that new opinions of new authors, or single opinions of readers not grounded upon the authorities of our books or judiciall presidents, are not to be allowed, but the laws both good and old, and specially the statute of Carta de Foresta, and other statutes, and the resolution of the judges thereupon are to be duly observed. See also the old and just articles of the charge in Fleta lib. 2. cap. 35. and reject all new inventions without warrant of law.

Rot. par. anno 9 H. 4. nu. 40.

The good old laws of the forest to be observed.

Nota, the charge and articles inquirable by the good old law of the forest, which is worthy to be advisedly read and followed. Vid. Lib. 2. fo. 80. Lib. 137, 138. Lib. 9. 49, 50.

* Two of the principall and ancient articles, the one concerning venison, and the other concerning vert, be, First, that the chief forester at the justice seat ought to answer for all manner of venison delivered by warrant, or otherwise, in this manner: the twelve jurors ought to present before the justices in eire the number of deer that have been killed since the last eire, and then the chief forester is to answer by what warrant the same were killed, and such warrants as are lawfull ought to be allowed, and such as be unlawfull are to be disallowed. Secondly, the twelve jurors shall present what okes, trees, and other woods have been felled and delivered out of the forest by the officers of the same, and they to answer and shew by what warrants the same were done; whereupon it will appear whether the warrants be sufficient or no, the truth whereof shall be inquired by the foresters, verderers, and regarders. But these or any other minister of the forest are not to be returned of any jury out of the forest.

*[319]

8 E. 3. Itin' Pick. fo. 112, 113.

Vide Register. F. N. B. 167. a. 34 E. 1.

The laws of the forests of England are certain and established by authority of parliament, and not, as in other countries, changeable and floting in uncertainty, *ad principis placitum*.

The commendation of the forest laws of England.

For the antiquity of such forests within England as we have treated of, the best and surest argument thereof, is, that the forests in England (being in number 69.) except the new forest in Hamshire erected by William the Conqueror, as a conqueror, and Hampton Court forest by H. 8. by authority of parliament, are so

The antiquity of forests. The number of the forests is 69. with the forest of Hampton Court.

ancient as no record or history doth make any mention of any of their erections or beginnings.

* Holt Saxonice, sylva Latinè. Levit. 17. 13. 4 Reg. cap. 2. Psal. 50. 10. Psal. 80. 14. 104. 29. 4 Esdr. 5. 15. Jer. 5 6. Ezech. 31. 6.

Our ancestors the Saxons called a forest * **buckholt**, i. *sylva ferina* or *cervina* : we dare not fetch our kind of forest, as some do, from the holy history of scripture, for therein we find no such forests as we have. And it is worthy of observation that in the Custumary of Normandy cap. 10. fo. 17. b. *Le seneschal au prince visiteit les forests et hayes du prince et ronoquoit les forfeits, &c.* So as we fetch not our chief justice of the forest from Normandy, where the kings steward was the chief judge of the forest.

And as forests are of great antiquity, so the care and charge of them was in England always committed to great and honourable personages, and the like was also in forain nations.

Virgil.

Si canimus sylvas, sylvæ sunt consule dignæ.

Suetonius in Cæsare. Vid. Fleta, lib. 2. cap. 35. De veteribus capit' forestæ. Voluptates commendat rarior usus.

For of ancient time the consuls of Rome had the government of the forests, &c. But take Suetonius as he is, *Ab optimatibus datam scribit operam ut provinciæ futuris consulibus minimi negotii, i. sylvæ collesque decernerentur* ; for to say the truth, recreations should not be used as professions, and trades, but to be used as medicines, to make men more able and fit for higher and greater affairs, and therefore they are called recreations, because they newly create spirits, *tanquam instaurationes spirituum* ; but yet these pleasures are accounted *inter res minimi negotii. Nonnulli principes immoderato venatus studio ita correpti, et corrupti sunt, ut ei omnia posthabeant magno dedecore, et ingenti aliorum damno.*

Hæc bis bina, canes et aves, servi atque caballi,
Dicantur dominos sæpe vorare suos.

And to say the truth, the hunter sitteth on a beast, he is compassed about with beasts, and hunteth and chaseth beasts, and therefore not to be used daily as a trade. And it was justly provided by the tenth chapter of this charter of the forest, *Quod nullus de cætero amittat vitam pro venatione nostra, &c.* Hereof John Salisbury speaking of hunting and hunters saith, *In tantum hujus vanitatis instinctu erupere, ut hostes naturæ fierent conditionis suæ immemores, divini judicii contemptores, dum in vindictam ferarum imaginem dei exquisitis judiciis subjugarent, nec veriti sunt hominem pro bestiola perdere quem unigenitus Dei redemit sanguine suo.*

Johannes Sarum lib. 1. de nugis curialium, c. 4. Vid. 31 H. 8. c. 12. *Quod cito evanuit*, repealed 1 E. 6. cap. 12. 1 Mar. cap. 1.

[320]

Duo clarissima mundi lumina, authoritas et ratio.

Thus have we wandred in the wildernesse of the laws of the forest : wherein we have dissented from others, we have produced our authorities, and shewed our reasons, the two maine lights and guides, which herein we have followed. We have faithfully published divers resolutions of the judges concerning forests and forest lawes, wherewith we were well acquainted, which are the safest grounds to build upon. Many things which are evident by the text of Carta de Foresta, and other statutes concerning forests, we have not so much as touched, but left the same to the judicious reader, whom we advise to beware to give credit to our new authors, either vouching of acts of parliament, booke cases or judgements in eire, &c. for we have found many of them mistaken, vouched without warrant, or not understood, which the judicious reader will soone finde : nor to Carta de Foresta of king Canutus granted (as it is published in print) at a parliament holden at Winchester, *anno domini* 1016. We confesse that in that yeare, which was the first

Manwood fo. 1.

yeare

yeare of his reigne, he held a parliament at Winchester, and made divers lawes as well for the honour and worship of Almighty God, as for the good government of his people, which he published in the Saxon tongue, (neither doe we reade that he ever published any law for England in the Danish tongue, as they affirme he did this). In all these laws he never maketh mention of this Carta de Foresta, or of any of these supposed laws of the forest therein contained, which he had just occasion to doe; for amongst his other lawes at the same parliament, he maketh this law the 77. chapter in the Saxon tongue, which is thus translated into Latine: *Praeterea autem concedo ut in propriis ipsius praediis quisque tam in agris quam in sylvis excitet agitetque, feras autem meas ne venetur cum pœna praecipio.* Now in the supposed Carta de Foresta of king Canutus, in the 30. chapter, it is thus contained: *Volo ut omnis liber homo pro libito suo habeat venerem seu viridem in planis suis, sine chasea tamen: et devitent omnes meam ubicunque eam habere voluero.* Which we hold greatly to differ from the true law before rehearsed in two respects. First, that the true law extendeth to woods as well as to plains, and this to plaines only. Secondly, by that they might hunt, &c. by this they cannot; therefore we leave that Carta de Foresta of king Canutus as justly suspected, till we receive better proofe of them: whatsoever it be, it is of little use, for so many of the chapters therein as be contrary to, or differing either from our Magna Carta de Foresta, or any other act of parliament, are certainly of no force.

Thus have we as briefly as we could, treated of the courts of the forest, and incidently of such forest lawes as now stand in force; wherein (as the studious reader may well perceive) we have respected matter more than method. See Carta de Foresta *anno* 9 H. 3. & Cart. 17. *regis Johannis.* Matth. Par. pag. 264.

C A P. LXXIV. [321]

Of Ecclesiasticall Courts, anciently called Halimots, (i. Holy Courts) Circgemots, or Chircgemots.

WHERE some may doubt, how we that professe the common law should write of ecclesiasticall courts, which proceed not by the rules of the common lawes. To this we answer by good authority in our bookes, that the kings lawes of this realme do bound the jurisdiction of ecclesiasticall courts, and that the king is well apprised of all [a] his judges which he hath within his realme, as well spirituall as temporall, as archbishops, bishops, and their officers, deanes, and other ministers, which have [b] spirituall jurisdiction. And that the popes collector or minister (so say our ancient books) had no jurisdiction within the realme.

2 H. 4. 9. Rot. clauf. 4 H. 4. m. 11. optime. Rot. clauf. 11 E. 2. dorf.

[a] Nota, the kings judges.

[b] Spirituall jurisdiction.

And it is declared by the king, the lords spirituall and temporall, and

c 25 H. 8. cap. 21.

* If so, then much more at this day. See before pag. 43.

d The spirituall jurisdiction.

The temporall jurisdiction.

and the commons in ful parliament, [c] That the spiritualty (now being usually called the English church) alwayes hath been reputed, and also found of that sort, that both for * knowledge, integrity and sufficiency of number it hath been always thought, and is also at this houre sufficient and meet of it selfe, without the intermedling of any exterior person or persons, to declare and determine of such doubts, and to administer all such offices and duties as to their rooms [d] spiritual doth appertain: for the due administration whereof, and to keep them from corruption and sinister affection, the kings most noble progenitors, and the antecessors of the nobles of this realme have sufficiently endowed the said church both with honour and possessions. And the lawes temporall for triall of property of lands and goods, and for the conservation of the people of this realme in unity and peace, without rapine or spoile, was and yet is administred, adjudged, and executed by sundry judges and ministers of the other part of the said body politique, called the temporaity: and both their authorities and jurisdictions do conjoyne together in the due administration of justice, the one to help the other.

Of what things they have jurisdiction.

Articuli cleri per totum, lib. 5. fo. 1. Cawdries case.

See before cap. of the Chancery, the articles against cardinall Wolsey art. 1. 13. 14. 17. 18. 19. 22. 24. 25. 29. 30. Bract. lib. 5. cap. 2. &c. Britton fo. 10. b. Rot. parl. 15 E. 3. nu. 22.

e See Dier. Mich. 6 & 7 Eliz.

8 Eliz. cap. 1.

[322]

Parker in libro de Antiquitate Britanniæ Ecclesiæ, sub titulo *Matthæus*. Imprinted 1572.

13 Eliz.

Of what things the clergy hath spirituall jurisdiction, is evident in our books, and particularly in Cawdries case, whereof there is no question. And certain it is, that this kingdome hath been best governed, and peace and quiet preserved, when both parties, that is, when the justices of the temporall courts, and the ecclesiasticall judges have kept themselves within their proper jurisdiction, without incroaching or usurping one upon another; and where such incroachments or usurpations have been made, they have been the seeds of great trouble and inconvenience; for preventing and avoiding whereof, we have composed this treatise of the ecclesiasticall courts of the realm.

The adversary hath made divers objections against our archbishops and bishops made about the beginning of the reign of queene Elizabeth, and by consequent against the bishops ever since. [e] First, that they were never consecrated according to the law, because they had not three bishops at the least at their consecration, nay never a bishop at all, as was pretended; because they being bishops in the reigne of E. 6. were deprived in the reigne of queen Mary, and were not (as was pretended) restored before their presence at the consecration. These pretences being (in troth) but meer cavills, tending to the scandall of the clergy (being one of the greatest states of the realm, as it is said in the statute of 8 Eliz. cap. 1.) are fully answered by the said statute, and provision made by authority of that parliament for the establishing of the archbishops and bishops both in *præsenti* and in *futuro*, in their bishopricks. Of this statute archbishop Parker in his book *De Antiquitate Britannicæ Ecclesiæ* speaking of himself saith, *anno Domini* 1559. *Cantuar' episcopus electus est à decano et capitulo ecclesiæ metropoliticæ Cantuar': posteaq; eodem anno* 17 *Decembris adhibitis quatuor episcopis, &c. lege quadam de hac re lata, requisitus consecratus est.* Another objection was made against our archbishops and bishops, for that the commission (being never inrolled whereby the bishops made in queen Maries time were deprived before the fourth year of the reign of queen Elizabeth: or the record of the approbation of them cannot be found; and therefore it was pretended that the archbishops and

and bishops made by queen Elizabeth, living the former should be no lawfull bishops. But by the statute of 39 Eliz. cap. 8. the archbishops and bishops are adjudged lawfull, as by the said act appeareth. And by these two statutes, these and all other objections against our bishops are answered, which we have thought good to remember, seeing we are to treat of their jurisdiction, *ut obstruatur os iniqua loquentium.*

39 Eliz. cap. 8.

Of the Court of Convocation.

It is called the convocation of the clergy. In England there being two provinces, the one of Canterbury, and the other of York, the bishops and suffragans belonging to York, are the bishops of Duresme, Carlisle, Chester, and the Isle of Man, and all the rest of the bishops are within the province of Canterbury.

In *domo convocationis* the whole clergy of either province are either present in person, or by representation: * but these provinces and they only sit in the parliament time, and this consisteth of two parts, viz. the upper house, where the archbishops and bishops sit, and the lower house where the rest do sit.

The name. F. N. B. 269. B. Regist. fo. See the first part of the Institutes sect. 133. 23 H. 8. cap. 1. 32 H. 8. cap. 23. & 33 H. 8. ca. 31. Anciently called churchgemote. Int. leges Hen. 1. cap. 8. Quosque churchgemot discordantes inveniet, vel amore congreget, vel sequestret judicio. * 21 E. 4. 45. 46.

Anno Domini 686 Augustine assembled in councell the Britain bishops, and held a great synod.

Beda. The antiquity. Newburgh lib. 2 cap. 13. Bract. lib. 3. fo. 123, 124. 6 H. 3. Hol. 203. Rot. parl. 18 E. 3. nu. 1. Rot. parl. 2 H. 4. nu. 29. F. N. B. 269. 8 H. 6. cap. 1.

The clergie was never assembled or called together at a convocation but by the kings * writ, *adjutoria regis,* as Beda saith *ubi supra.* Vid. parl. 18 E. 3. nu. 1. *Int' leges Inæ anno Domini* 727, a convocation of the clergy called *magna servorum Dei frequentia.*

By what authority assembled. * 13 E. 3. Rot. parl. 16. 24. Dors. claus. 17 E. 2. m. 30. 31. 25 H. 8. cap. 19.

Their jurisdiction was to deal with heresies, schismes, and other meer spirituall and ecclesiasticall causes, and therein they did proceed *juxta legem divinam et canones sanctæ ecclesiæ.* [a] And as they could never assemble together of themselves, but were always called together * by the kings writ, so were they oftentimes commanded by the kings writ to deal with nothing that concerned the kings lawes of the land, his crown and dignity, his person, or his state, or the state of his councell or kingdome: as to illustrate this matter to remember one or two examples.

What their jurisdiction was. Merton cap. 9. 21 E. 4. 45. 1. per Vavasor. and b. per Starkey, Brown and Vavasor. 20 H. 6. 13. 34 H. 6. 39. 28 H. 6. 11. Regist. fol. F. N. B. 269. [a] *De procurat. Cler.* See in the chapter of the High Court of Parliament, Regist. 261. and F. N. B. 229. a. and Parl. 6 E. 3. nu. 6. 8 H. 6. cap. 1. * 2 Chron. 29. 15. Ezechias. Num. ca. 10. v. 1, 2. vid. sup. pa. 43.

Mandatum est omnib' episcopis qui conventuri sunt apud Gloucestriam die Sabbathi in crastino Sanctæ Katherinæ firmiter inhibendo quod sicut baronias suas (quas de rege tenent) diligunt, nullo modo præsumant consilium tenere de aliquibus quæ ad coronam regis pertinent, vel quæ personam regis

Rot. pat. 18 H. 3. 2 part. m. 17. De prohibitione fact. Episcopis.

regis vel statum suum, vel statum concilii sui contingunt. Scituri pro certo quod si fecerint, rex inde se capiet ad baronias suas. Teste rege, &c.

[323] See the statute of Carlisle *anno* 35 E. 1.

Stat. de Carlisle 35 E. 1. Rot. pat. 15 E. 2. 1 part. m. 8 pro rege de inhibitione facienda.

Rex, &c Venerabilibus in Christo patribus eadem gratia W. archiepiscopo Cantuariensi, totius Angliæ primati, ac cæteris episcopis et prælatis Cant' provinciæ ad concilium provinciale apud London in proximo conventuris. Mandamus vobis in fide et dilectione quibus nobis tenemini firmiter inhibentes ne in dicto concilio quicquid in nostri, aut status coronæ nostræ vel regni nostri præjudicium statuatis, faciatis, seu quoquo modo libet ordinetis. Teste rege, &c.

De isto negotio scribitur præfatis prælatis per literas de credentia, ut in rotulo clausarum sub eodem datu continetur.

6 E. 3. dors. claus. part 2. m. 15. &c.

Prohibitio fact' archiepiscopo Cant' et clero conventur' post festum Sancti Barth. quod nihil attemptent in præjudicium coronæ.

Vide cap. of the High Court of Parliament, pag. 4. & 5. a. for *procuratores cleri*, & 21 R. 2. cap. 2.

51 E. 3. nu. 42. 46 E. 3. prem. 8. 21 E. 4. 45. ubi sup. Rot. parl. 1 R. 2. nu. 114. * 25 H. 8. cap. 19. 19 E. 3. Quare non admisit acc' 10 H. 7. 6. per Brian. & 2 Ph. & Mar. cap. 8. the prerogatives, and lawes of the crown saved. *Versus finem.*

And further the king did often appoint commissioners by writ to sit with them at the convocation, and to have conusans of such things as they meant to establish, that nothing should be done in prejudice, *ut supra.* * And therefore the statute of 25 H. 8. ca. 19. (whereby it is provided, that no canons, constitution, or ordinance should be made or put in execution within this realm by authority of the convocation of the clergy, which were contrariant or repugnant to the kings prerogative royall, or the customes, laws, and statutes of this realm) is but declaratory of the old common law.

What their jurisdiction now is.

But by the said act of 25 H. 8. their jurisdiction and power is much limited and straitened concerning their making of new canons: for they must have both license to make them, and after they be made, the kings royall assent to allow them, before they be put in execution. But in the end of that act there is an expresse proviso, that such canons as were made before that act, which be not contrariant nor repugnant to the kings prerogative, the laws, statutes or customes of the realm, should be still used and executed as they were before the making of that act. But before that act a disme granted by the clergy at the convocation, did not binde the clergy before the kings royall assent.

2 R. 3. 4. 21 E. 4. 42. 47. 20 H. 6. 13.

26 H. 8. cap. 1.

King H. 8. was acknowledged supream head in divers convocations.

24 H. 8. ca. 12. 1 Eliz. cap. 1.

And if any cause shall depend in contention in any ecclesiasticall court which may or shall touch the king, his heirs, or successors, the party grieved shall or may appeale to the upper house of covocation within 15 dayes after sentence given.

As there be two houses of convocation, so are there two prolocutors, one of the bishops of the higher house, chosen by that house, another of the lower house, and presented to the bishops for their prolocutor.

It is called convocation *à convocando*, because they are called together by the kings writ.

8 H. 6. cap. 1.

The clerks of the convocation called by the kings writ, and their

their servants and familiars shall have such priviledge in comming, tarrying, and going, as the great men, and comminalty of this realm, called to the kings parliament.

Of Subscription.

Subscription required by the clergy is twofold: one by force both of an act of parliament confirming and establishing the 39 articles of religion agreed upon at a convocation of the church of England, and ratified by queen Elizabeth under the great seal of England. Another by canons made at a convocation of the church of England, and ratified by king James, as is aforesaid.

13 Eliz. ca. 12. At a convocation holden at London anno Dom. 1562. and 5to Eliz.

By the act of 13 Eliz. cap. 12. referring to canons made by the clergy of England at a convocation holden at London in *anno Domini* 1562. containing 39 articles of religion, and ratified as is aforesaid.

[324]

The other is by canons of the church of England made and ratified by king James, as is aforesaid.

At a convocation begun at London, anno dom. 1603. 1 Jac. regis § 36.

The subscription hereby required is to three articles.

The first is, that the kings majesty under God is the only supream governor of the realm, and of all other his highnesse dominions and countries, &c.

This book is ratified and confirmed by act of parliament, viz. 2 E. 6. cap. 1. 5 E. 6. c. 1. 1 El. cap. 2. 8 El. cap. 1. 23 El. ca. 1.

2. That the Book of Common Prayer, and of ordering of bishops, priests, and deacons, containeth nothing in it contrary to the word of God, &c.

3. That he allowed of the said 39. articles of religion, and acknowledged them to be agreeable to the word of God.

And in this section, *ubi supra*, 1 Jac. the form of the subscription is set down, which was not expressed in the act of 13 Eliz.

By the statute of 13 Eliz. the delinquent is disabled and deprived *ipso facto*, but the delinquent against the canon of king James is to be proceeded withall by the censures of the church. This statute of 13 is well expounded in Dier 23 El. 377. & lib. 6. fo. 69. in Grenes case.

Dier 23 El. 377. Lib. 6. fo. 69. Grenes case. * Smiths case.

And I heard Wray chief justice in the kings bench, * Pasch. 23 El. report, that where one Smith subscribed to the said 39 articles of religion, with this addition (so far forth as the same were agreeable to the word of God) that it was resolved by him, and all the judges of England, that this subscription was not according to the statute of 13 Eliz. because the statute required an absolute subscription, and this subscription made it conditionall; and that this act was made for avoiding a diversity of opinions, &c. And by this addition the party might by his own private opinion take some of them to be against the word of God; and by this means diversity of opinions should not be avoided, which was the scope of the statute, and the very act it self made touching subscription hereby of none effect.

He must also bring a testimoniall from men known to the bishop, to be of sound religion, a testimoniall both of his honest life, and profession of the doctrine expressed in the said articles; and he ought to be able to answer, and render to the ordinary an account of his faith in Latin, &c.

Besides this subscription, when any clerk is admitted and instituted

tuted to any benefice, he is sworn to canonicall obedience to his diocesan.

Of the High Commission in Causes Ecclesiasticall.

Pasch. 9 Jac. the resolution of the court of common pleas upon mature deliberation, set down in writing by the commandment of king James.

Two questions have been made concerning the jurisdiction of these commissioners.

First, what causes doe belong to the high commissioners by force of the act of 1 El. cap. 1. and of the letters patents thereupon grounded.

Secondly, in what cases the high commissioners by the said act of 1 Eliz. cap. 1. and of the letters patents to them granted, may impose fine and imprisonment, and in what not.

It is said, by force of the statute of 1 El. For that before this act it is agreed, that all ordinaries and ecclesiasticall judges whatsoever, ought in all ecclesiasticall causes to have proceeded according to the censures of the church, and could not in any case have punished any delinquent by fine or imprisonment, unlesse they had authority so to doe by act of parliament. And the papall authority (as hath been confessed) did never fine or imprison in any case, but ever proceeded only by ecclesiasticall censures. Seeing then the state of the question concerning fine and imprisonment dependeth wholly upon the statute of 1 Eliz. and is of greatest consequence, and openeth the way to the other question, for it is confessed that by letters patents only (without an act of parliament) such power to fine and imprison in ecclesiasticall causes cannot be granted; the point of fine and imprisonment shall be first handled. And for that every act of parliament doth consist
[325] of the letter, and of the meaning of the makers of the act: the act of 1 Eliz. doth neither by meaning nor letter give any power to the high commissioners to fine and imprison any, but in certain particular causes, as shall manifestly out of the act it self appear hereafter. And seeing every act of parliament upon consideration had of all the parts thereof together, is the best expositor of it self, the parts of this act of 1 Eliz. doe necessarily fall into consideration.

The title of the act.

First, the title of the act is, *An act restoring to the crown the ancient jurisdiction, &c.* By this the nature of the act doth appear to be an act of restitution.

And this is also manifest by the preamble of the act, where it is said:

The preamble of the act.

Whereas divers good laws were made in the time of the late king Henry the eighth, for the extinguishment of all forain power, and for the restoring unto the crown of this realm the ancient rights and jurisdictions of the same.

1 Ratio.

From whence this reason is drawn, that seeing the expresse letter and meaning is to restore to the crown the ancient jurisdiction ecclesiasticall, and no commissioner by force of that ancient ecclesiasticall jurisdiction could impose fine and imprisonment, that these commissioners having their force from this act of restitution, cannot punish

punish any party by fine or imprisonment, otherwise then shall be hereafter expressed.

The first clause of the body of the act (to let in the restitution of the ancient right and jurisdiction ecclesiasticall within the realm) doth abolish all forain jurisdiction out of the realm.

Then followeth the principall clause of restitution and uniting of the ancient jurisdiction ecclesiasticall, being the main purpose of the act, in these words.

Be it enacted, that such jurisdiction, &c. spirituall or ecclesiasticall, as by any spirituall or ecclesiasticall power or authority hath heretofore been, or lawfully may be exercised or used for the visitation of the ecclesiasticall state and persons, and for reformation, order, and correction of the same, and of all manner of errors, heresies, schismes, abuses, offences, contempts, and enormities, shall for ever by authority of this parliament be united and annexed to the imperiall crown of this realm.

And upon this clause being the finall intention of this act expressed in the title and preamble, doe the subsequent clauses depend; therefore this clause is especially to be considered, and therein these things are to be observed.

First, that by this clause queen Elizabeth was not declared supream head, &c. but by a former clause in this act, viz. that the statute of 1 & 2 Ph. and Mar. cap. 8. (whereby amongst others, the act of 26 H. 8. cap. 1. and 35 H. 8. cap. 3. were repealed) was by this act made utterly void, and consequently the act of repeal being repealed, the acts of 26 H. 8. cap. 1. and 35 H. 8. cap. 3. were amongst others implicite revived, by which acts of 26 H. 8. and 35 H. 8. it is declared and enacted, that the king, his heirs and successors should be taken and accepted the only supream head in earth of the church of England, and should have and enjoy annexed to the imperiall crown of this realm, as well the title and stile thereof, as all honours, dignities, preheminences, jurisdictions, &c. to the said dignity of supream head belonging, &c. By which stile, title, and dignity of supream head of the church of England, king H. 8. his heirs and successors had and have all ecclesiasticall jurisdiction whatsoever. So as the first clause reviving the act of 26 H. 8. &c. thereby queen Elizabeth, her heirs and successors were supream head of the church of England. And there this act extending to raise a commission for the necessity of the time, intended only to restore and annex to the crown such jurisdiction in some particular points as by the intent of the statute, the commissioners should execute, and not to declare by this clause that her majesty should be [326]
supream head of the church, for that was provided for before.

Secondly, that no jurisdiction is by this act restored and united 2 Ratio.
to the crown, but such as before the act had been, or lawfully might be exercised or used for the reformation, &c. correction, &c. Whereupon it is concluded, that seeing that no man could be fined or imprisoned by force of any jurisdiction ecclesiasticall, which had been used, or lawfully might be used before this act, that therefore by this act no power of fining and imprisoning in ecclesiasticall causes is given by this act.

The third observation is, that this clause divideth itself into two branches: the first concerning the visitation of the ecclesiasticall state and persons. This branch was enacted out of necessity, for that all the bishops, and most of the clergy of England, being then popish, it was necessary to raise a commission to deprive them, that would not deprive themselves, and in case of restitution of religion to have a more summary proceeding then by the ordinary and prolix course of law is required. This branch concerns only ecclesiasticall persons: so as, as necessity did cause this commission, so it should be exercised but upon necessity, for it was never intended that it should be a continuall standing commission, for that should prejudice all the bishops of England in their ecclesiasticall jurisdiction, and be grievous to the subject to be drawn up from all the remote parts of the realm, where before their own diocesan they might receive justice at their own doors.

The first commission upon these statutes, whereby about 20 bishops were deprived, and many others of the popish clergy, is said to be lost, and inrolled it is not, as it ought to have been. And it is affirmed by some that have seen it, that it passed not above twenty sheets of paper copy wise; but now the high commission contains above three hundred sheets of paper. And it is likewise affirmed, that never any high commission was inrolled (as they all ought to have been) untill my lord chancelor Egertons time, so as no man before that time could know what their jurisdiction was till that time.

The second branch is, And for reformation, order, and correction of the same *(that is, of ecclesiasticall persons)* and of all manner of errors, heresies, schismes, abuses, offences, contempts, and enormities. So as these two branches extend not to the universality of the supremacy, but only to those points whereunto the commission to be raised by this act should extend, for which purpose nothing is restored or united by this act, but only the visitation of the ecclesiasticall state and persons, and the reformation of the same, and of all errors, heresies, schismes, abuses, offences, contempts, and enormities which be criminall.

The jurisdiction being restored to queen Eliz. her heirs and successors, next and immediately doth the act, &c. give her power to assign and authorise commissioners to execute this jurisdiction restored and united to her, for which purpose it is further enacted.

The clause of assignation of the jurisdiction restored by this act.

That your highnesse, your heirs and successors shall have power and authority by vertue of this act by letters patents, &c. to assigne, name, and authorize, &c. such persons being naturall born subjects, &c. as your majesty, your heirs and successors shall think meet to exercise, use, occupy, and execute under your highnesse, your heirs and successors, all manner of jurisdiction, &c. in any wise touching or concerning any spirituall or ecclesiasticall jurisdiction, &c. and to visit, reforme, &c. all errours, heresies, schismes, abuses, offences, contempts and enormities, which by any manner spirituall or ecclesiasticall power, authority, or jurisdiction, can or may lawfully be reformed, corrected, restrained, or amended.

Out

Out of this clause of assignation it is to be observed, that the substance of the commission of assignation or deputation is described and purtrayed out both for manner and matter by this clause.

1. That it ought to be under the great seal. [327]

2. The commissioners to be assigned ought to be naturall born subjects of queen Eliz. her heirs or successors.

3. Their authority, viz. to exercise, use, occupy, and execute under your highnesse, your heirs and successors, all manner of jurisdiction, &c. and to visit and reform all such errors, heresies, schismes, abuses, offences, &c. which by any manner of ecclesiasticall or spirituall power can, or lawfully may be reformed, corrected, &c.

4. The locall limits and bounds of their commission, viz. within the realm of England, &c.

So as by this clause there is no question, but the commissioners for such causes as are committed to them by force of this act, may, if the commissioners be competent, proceed to deprivation of the popish clergy, which was the main object of the act, or to punish them by ecclesiasticall censures, and by no words, or meaning hitherto can punish by fine or imprisonment, for that no ecclesiasticall power could reform and correct (as the statute speaketh) in that manner. And without question, if the commissioners be competent, that is, if they be spirituall men, they may proceed to sentence of excommunication, which may right well be certified as wel as excommunication before commissioners delegates; both of these authorities being under the great seal, and each of them having authority by force of severall acts of parliament. And excommunication certified by commissioners delegates hath been allowed, as it appeareth in 23 Eliz. Dier 371. And in many cases acts of parliament have adjudged men excommunicate *ipso facto*. But if they be meer lay men, the fault is not in the statute or in the law, but in the nomination: and upon certificate made of the excommunication according to law, a *significavit* or *cap. excom.* shall be awarded out of the chancery, for the taking and imprisoning of the bodies of such excommunicate persons.

3 Ratio.

The high commissioners may excommunicate if they be competent.
Dier 23 El. 371.

Now after the letters patents of the commission are described, and limited, followeth a clause of direction for the commissioners to keep themselves within their commission in these words.

And that such persons so to be named, &c. after the said letters patents to them delivered shall have power and authority by vertue of this act and the said letters patents under your highnesse, your heirs and successors to exercise, use, and execute all the premisses according to the tenor and effect of the said letters patents, any matter or cause to the contrary in any wise notwithstanding.

The clause of execution.

This is a clause of reference meerly to the former parts of the act, and yet by colour of this clause the high commissioners doe pretend to fine and imprison.

That this clause referreth wholly to the former parts of the act, it is apparent by the very words thereof, for first, the words be to exercise, use, and execute all the premisses, which word (premisses) referreth to all the former branches of the act, viz. 1. To the ancient jurisdiction ecclesiasticall restored by this act, by which ancient

cient jurisdiction no person could be corrected by fine or imprisonment. 2. To such jurisdiction spirituall or ecclesiasticall, as by any spirituall or ecclesiasticall power hath heretofore been, or lawfully might be exercised, or used; for these be the expresse words of the main clause of restoring and uniting of the ancient jurisdiction to the crown. But it is agreed, that before this act no man could be punished by fine or imprisonment by any ecclesiasticall power, unlesse it were by force of some act of parliament; therefore by these words in this clause (to execute the premisses) the commissioners cannot fine or imprison. This word (premisses) hath relation to these words in the clause of assignation next going before this clause, viz. to visit, reform, redresse, order, correct, and amend all such errors, heresies, schismes, &c. which by any manner, power, authority, or jurisdiction ecclesiasticall or spirituall can, or may lawfully be reformed, &c. corrected, &c. but no correction before this act could be by fine or imprisonment, but in certain speciall cases.

[328] Then this clause followeth, (according to the tenor and effect of the said letters patents) which words also do wholly refer to the former parts of the act. For if these words (to execute all the * premises) be words of reference, then the addition of these (according to the tenor and effect of the * said letters patents, any matter or cause to the contrary in any wise notwithstanding) must of necessity be referred also to the former parts of the act, by none of which power is given to fine or imprisonment.

* Premises.

* Said.

Also this word (execute) cannot but be referred to the former authority. And it is not said according to the tenor and effect of any letters patents, and yet if the words had been so, the same being coupled to the word (premises) had not restrained them, for they could in that case but only have executed the premises, but the words be according to the tenor and effect of the letters patents before limited by the said act, that is, first that the letters patents be under the great seal. 2. That they be made to naturall born subjects. 3. Their authority is declared with a limitation. 4. The locall limits and bounds of the commission is set down: and this is the true and genuine sense of these words, viz. to execute the premises according to the tenor and effect of the said letters patents. And therefore we marvell how in a case of so great consequence, and so visible to every eye that looks into the act of 1 Eliz. the very words thereof are (for the advantage of the high commissioners) in the very binding clause altered, and changed. For there it is alleaged, that the statute of 1 Eliz. saith, that the high commissioners shall execute the premises by virtue of this act according to their commission indefinitely without reference or restraint, whereas the words of the act be, according to the said letters patents, the effect whereof was limited and expressed before. And by the authority that is claimed by the commissioners, who seeth not, but that confiscation of lands, forfeiture of goods and chattels, &c. as well may be imposed, as fine and imprisonment? But were it not a violent interpretation directly against the letter and meaning of the act, and full of great inconvenience to make of these latter words this construction, viz. that the high commissioners should correct and punish all the errors, heresies, schismes, offences, abuses, contempts, and enormities, &c. under such pains, forfeiture, and penalty, as queen Elizabeth, her heirs, and successors, by any letters patents should impose or appoint; and that consequently

Nota.

quently by force of the generality of this construction, she did impose and appoint fine and imprisonment. Which construction should be first directly against the words and meaning of the act for the causes aforesaid. Secondly, that by the same reason by the generality of such a construction queen Elizabeth might have imposed forfeiture of lands, confiscation of goods, nay corporall punishment, losse of member, and of life also, for incontinency, solicitation of chastity, working on a holiday, or any inferiour offence punishable by the ecclesiasticall law, and yet the sentence of the commissioners in such cases should be both fatall and finall, and uncontroulable by any ordinary means, either by appeal, error, *moderata misericordia*, or otherwise. Thirdly, that this violent construction, under mysticall and cloudy words, should extend to fine and imprisonment, &c. all persons, as well laymen of what estate, degree, or sex soever, in cases ecclesiasticall (where they were not to be fined and imprisoned before) as to ecclesiasticall persons, who were the proper objects of this act. And then by the construction that hath been made of the other side in cases where an executor detaineth a legacy, or a parishioner payeth not his tythes, or the like concerning *meum* and *tuum*, the queen, &c. might have inflicted (as hath been said) what punishment she would, and the high commissioners fine and imprisonment (as it standeth at this day) without limitation of time, be it never so great, or time of imprisonment, be it never so long, and without controlment by any ordinary remedy, be the sentence never so unjust or erroneous; then which nothing could be more absurd and inconvenient. *Talis interpretatio in ambiguis semper fienda est, ut evitetur inconveniens et absurdum.* But this construction should not be *in ambiguis*, but directly against the words and meaning of this act. And seeing it hath been granted that the papall authority or any other having ecclesiasticall jurisdiction could not fine and imprison before this act of 1 Eliz. [329] and that it is expresly said in the preamble of this act, that where in the reign of king Hen. 8. divers good laws were made as well for the extinguishment of forein authority, as for restoring to the crown the ancient jurisdictions, &c. by reason whereof the subjects were kept in order, and disburdened of great and intolerable charges and exactions (which good laws being repealed by queen Mary the said act doth revive and restore) it followeth *à concessis*, and by the letter of this act, that it was never the meaning of the makers thereof to extend the said clause to fine and imprison the subject for ecclesiasticall causes, and to make him subject to greater confiscations, forfeitures, and punishments, where his body before this act was not subject to imprisonment but upon the kings writ *de excom' capiendo*, nor his body, lands, and goods, to fines, or other penalties, or punishments, by them to be imposed, &c. for this were not by this act of restitution to ease them of former intolerable charges (as the statute speaketh) but by this act to make them subject to greater and more heavy pains, punishments, and charges then ever they were before. And the statute of 27 H. 8. cap. 15. saith, that the canons, &c. were overmuch onerous to his highnesse subjects, but they were never so onerous as this act should be. But *uno absurdo dato infinita sequuntur.* We must therefore retire ourselves to the text of the act of 1 Eliz. the only ground of this question, and thereupon the conclusion is, that no letters patents can by vertue of this act of 1 Eliz. give any power to the commissioners to imprison, except it be in certain particular cases, which now fall into consideration. For example. The statute of 1 H. 7. cap. 4. doth give power to bishops, &c. to commit priests convicted of any incontinency to prison, and that no bishop, &c. shall be chargeable therefore in an action of false imprisonment. Now seeing that such jurisdiction ecclesiasticall (that is, to hear, determine, and punish, &c.) as by any spirituall or ecclesiasticall power or authority before the said act of 1 Eliz. had been, or might lawfully have been exercised or used for the visitation of the ecclesiasticall state and persons, and for reformation and correction of the same, and of all manner of errors, heresies, schisms, &c. and that every bishop, &c. might punish such offenders by imprisonment according to the said act, that such power (and the like in any other case by act of parliament if any be) is united to the crown and may be committed over to the high commissioners as before the said act by any spirituall or ecclesiasticall power had been or lawfully might be used, which be the words of the act itself.

1 H. 7. cap. 4.

Vid. stat. of 2 H. 4. ca. 13. & 1 Eliz. ca. 1. and observe them well.

But these generall words, viz. which have been or lawfully might be used, &c. do not extend to any authority or power given by any act of parliament to any ecclesiasticall judge: which act stood repealed and adnulled by a former act of parliament, and had no essence at the time of the making of this act of 1 Eliz. and that for two reasons: first, for that this act of 1 Eliz. doth repeal and revive divers acts of parliament, and therefore shall not be construed to repeal or revive any other by the said generall words. Secondly, for that generall words shall not extend to authorities repealed or adnulled by act of parliament. And so it was adjudged in the lord Darcies case in the kings bench Pasch. 38 Eliz. where the case was, that the lord of the mannor of Thorp Kirby was amongst other franchises and immunities discharged by the letters patents of king E. 4. of purveyance; which charter for the point of discharge of purveyance was adnulled by the statute of 27 H. 8. cap. And after the mannor comming to the hands of king E. 6. he by his letters patents granted the said mannor to the lord Darcie and his heirs: and further granted *Tot, talia, eadem, hujusmodi et consimilia jura, jurisdictiones, franchesias, privilegia, &c. quot, quanta, qualia, et quæ, &c. prout aliquis dominus manerii habuit, tenuit, seu gavisus fuit virtute alicujus cartæ, doni, seu concessionis aut aliquarum literarum patentium per præfatum regem, aut per aliquem progenitorum suorum quorumcunq; fact' concess' seu confirmat', aliquo statuto non obstante.* And it was adjudged as it had been before in the lord Pagets case, Mich. 21 & 22 Eliz. *in scaccario*: that albeit such a generall grant had been enacted and confirmed by act of parliament, yet had not those generall words extended to revive any authority, franchise, priviledge, &c. once granted, and which was after, and before the grant repealed or resumed by act of parliament, unlesse there had been speciall words to revive the same, but should extend to other authorities, franchises, and priviledges which stood not then repealed.

Pasch. 38 Eliz. Coram rege the lord Darcies case.

Mich. 21 & 22 El. in Scaccario, the lord Pagets case.

[330]

1 H. 7. 12, 13.

And there is a far stronger case reported in 1 H. 7. fo. 12. & 13. By authority of parliament all preheminences, prerogatives, franchises, and liberties were given to king H. 7. in taile generally without limitation or saving. And the question was whether the franchises and liberties of lords and other inferior subjects were given: and it was resolved by all the judges that they were not, for that the act was to be intended to do no inferiour subject wrong, but the generall words were to be intended of such as might be intailed without prejudice of the subject: which is a stronger case then this, for besides the prejudice of the inferiour ordinary for his jurisdiction, and for the subject for taking away his appeal, and drawing him from remote parts to his intolerable charge, where he might receive justice at home, the clause preceding of uniting, and latter particular words do limit and expound the generality of the former words.

Now that divers and many other acts of parliament, which are generall in words, have upon consideration of the mischief, and all the parts of the act (for the avoiding of the inconvenience and absurdity that might follow) received a particular interpretation, it appeareth in our books in cases of far lesse inconvenience and absurdity.

Pl. com. in Stowels case, fo. 369. the preamble is to be considered, for it is the key to open the meaning of the makers of the act, and mischiefs which they intend to remedy. The judges of the law have ever in such sort pursued the intents of the meaning of the makers of acts of parliament, as they have expounded acts generall in words to be particular, where the intent hath been particular (which are the words of the book) and therefore upon that rule it is there adjudged, that where the statute of 7 E. 6. is generall; if any receiver or minister accountant, &c. receive of any person any summe of money for payment of any fees, &c. shall forfeit 6 s. 8 d. for every penny; that this do not extend according to the generality of the words to the receiver of common persons, because these words subsequent be added, (otherwise then he lawfuly may by former laws and statutes.) Now the judges restrained the generality to a particular, to the kings receiver only: for that no law or statute was formerly made concerning common persons receivers, &c. But in the case in question, as well the precedent clause of restitution, as the subsequent clause expressing offences in particular, and the words in the same generall sentence viz. under your highnesse, &c. and principally the cause of the making of this act do qualifie the generality of the words. And yet notwithstanding it was resolved by all the court in the said case of Stradling, fo. 203. a. that the receiver of common persons were within the words of the said statute. But there it is said, that if a man consider in what point the mischief was before the statute, and what thing the parliament meant to redresse by this, he shall perceive that the intent of the makers of the act was to punish only the ministers of the king. And a little after the judges say that the stile of that act is. An act for the true answer of the kings revenues. And by this also the intent of the makers of the act is to be collected, and these be the words of the book, which is a far stronger case then the case in question. Pl. Com. fo. 369. Stowels case.

4 E. 4. fo. 4 & 12. Every statute ought to be expounded according to the intent of them that made it, where the words thereof are doubtfull and uncertain, and according to the rehearsall of the statute; and there a generall statute is construed particularly upon consideration had of the cause of making of the act, and of the rehearsall 4 E. 4. 4. & 12.

rehearsall of all the parts of the act. To conclude this point with a generall rule allowed by all laws in construction of statutes. *Quamvis lex generaliter loquitur, restringenda tamen est, ut cessante ratione et ipsa cesset: cum enim ratio sit anima vigorq; ipsius legis non videtur legislator*
[331] *id sensisse, quod ratione careat, etiamsi verborum generalitas prima facie aliter suadeat.* Seeing then so many inconveniences against reason, and the meaning of the makers of the act should follow, it is evident that the generality of the said words in the clause of assignation shall (as they ought) be limited by the clause of restitution, as hath bin said. And it agreeth not well with the stile of the high commission to deal in pety and inferiour causes. And for the recitall of a branch of this act in the statute of 8 Eliz. cap. 1. It referreth to the act of *primo* it self, and is only in the preamble, and therefore doth neither increase nor diminish the same. But albeit they have conusance and jurisdiction of enormous and heinous causes, according to the originall institution, yet cannot they punish the offender in the same by fine or imprisonment, unlesse the same were punishable by fine or imprisonment before the making of the said act of 1 Eliz. by some act of parliament unrepealed at the making of this act.

But it is said (enormous) is uncertain; surely in an act whereof many of the makers are lay and unlearned men, it hath been expounded by law to be equipollent to heinous, horrible and exorbitant. And this appeareth by the statute of 2 E. 3. cap. 2. Commission of oier and terminer, &c. shall not go out, but where the trespasse is horrible. Now if such commission be granted for a small cause, a revocation thereof, which is a flat prohibition, doth lye, as it appeareth in the Register 125, and the words thereof be, *Quia non enormis læsio.* Which word *(enormis)* in that writ doth expresse this word [horrible] in the said act, and there is as great uncertainty in that case upon this word [*enormis*] to prohibit the commissioners of oier and terminer, as in the case now in question concerning the ecclesiasticall commission, and especially in this act of *primo* it ought to be taken to be horrible, exorbitant, *et extra omnem normam;* for that the high commissioners do claim to send for all degrees of men and women, and out of all the parts of England or Wales, be the place never so remote, &c. But the commission of oier and terminer cannot be taken but in the proper county where the fact was done. And yet it is evident by all which hath been said, that his majesty hath, and queen Elizabeth before him had as great and ample supremacy and jurisdiction ecclesiasticall as ever king of England had before them, and that had justly and rightly pertained to them by divers other acts, and by the ancient laws of England, if the said clause of annexation in the said statute of 1 Eliz. had never been inserted.

2 E. 3. cap. 2.

This act of 1 Eliz. provideth against them that should by printing, writing, or words, maintain or defend the jurisdiction spirituall of any forein prince, prelat, &c. within this realm; that every such person being lawfully convicted by the course of the common law, shall for the first offence forfeit and lose all his and their goods and chattels. And if any person so convicted shall not be worth of his proper goods and chattels to the value of 20 li. then such person so convicted shall suffer imprisonment one whole year, &c. Now albeit upon the maintenance or defence of the popes supre-

macy

macy depend so many mischiefs as the principall scope of this and other acts was utterly to abolish and extinguish the same, and that it is high treason in the second degree: yet see how temperately this act doth punish that most dangerous and damnable error. And albeit the proceedings at the common law are reversible by writ of error: yet the statute addeth two cautions, that no persons should be impeached for any of the offences by preaching, teaching, or words, unlesse they be lawfully indicted within the space of one half year. And if any person be imprisoned, and be not indicted within half a year, then the person so imprisoned shall be set at liberty. Now if the party offending in so high and supreme an offence, as the maintaining of the popes supremacy, shall be punished for the first offence so temperately, and with such caution and limitation, it was never the meaning of the statute to charge the subject with fine or imprisonment by the discretion of the commissioners without limitation either of time of imprisonment, or quantity of fine, for lesser crimes and offences, whereunto he was not subject before the making of this act.

But if the meaning of the makers of the act had been to have inflicted newly upon the subject not only fine and imprisonment, but by the same reason confiscation of goods, forfeiture of lands, nay any corporall punishment, &c. they would not under such clowdy and dark words have inflicted those greater punishments for lesser offences without some limitation, as they did for the greatest offences of all, and not to have left lesser offences to the absolute and uncontrollable power of the high commissioners by any ordinary mean. [332]

If the high commissioners might have fined and imprisoned men for offences against the ecclesiasticall laws, to what end were the statutes of 23 Eliz. 28 Eliz. &c. made against men for abstaining and not comming to divine service, &c. and why did those acts inflict a penalty of 20 l. the month, and imprisonment, &c. with a discharge of the penalty, &c. upon submission, if the high commissioners might have fined and imprisoned them absolutely without certainty of any sum, or limitation of any time of imprisonment, and without any ability or power by submission or conformity to ease themselves? and yet absence from divine service is a meer ecclesiasticall cause; and the like may be said of divers other acts of parliament of like nature.

Thus hath this statute been plainly expounded by the parts of the same, according to the naturall and genuine sense, and the originall institution and jurisdiction of the high commission by force of the said act truly expressed.

And concerning the form of commissions and practice by the high commissioners in the reign of the late queen Eliz. by fining and imprisoning for adultery, fornication, simony, usury, defamation, &c. it may be that such fines have been imposed, but, as we be informed, not one of them levied in all the reign of queen Eliz. by any judiciall processe out of the exchequer in the time of Sir Edward Sanders, who was chief baron at the time of the making of the said act, Sir Robert Bell, Sir John Jefferies, Sir Roger Manwood, or Sir William Peryam chief barons of the exchequer: so as in all the late queens time (as we be informed) no fine was levied, or any subject in his body, lands or goods charged therewith,

with, which would not have been by so many worthy men assisted with divers other grave and learned barons pretermitted to be either levied or written for by the court, if by law the same ought to have been levied. And the subjects (for the greatest part) being wrongfully fined, imprisoned, and injured by colour of the high commission, asked no advice to take any ordinary remedy, for that the high commissioners (knowing the weaknesse of their authority) kept the commission secret, and contrary to law and justice suffered not the same to be inrolled in the chancery, so as the subject lived under an unknown commission and authority *(et misera est servitus ubi jus est vagum aut incognitum)* untill of late the lord chancelor (as hath been said) according to law caused the same to be inrolled; and very few upon serious consideration took an exact survey of all the parts of the act of 1 Eliz. And this is the cause why their presidents (if they affirm truly) may be many, especially against the weaker sort: and the judgments and presidents in the kings courts concerning these matters, few, as they give out, charging the judges of the realm with innovation. And yet some being intolerably grieved, sometime to their utter undoing, by the high commissioners, upon complaint made to the highest courts of ordinary justice in this realm, the judges upon consideration had of the statute of 1 Eliz. which is the foundation whereupon the high commission is grounded, have, as often as complaint hath been made, relieved them according to law and justice.

In Atmeres case the whole court of exchequer in the late queens reign, judicially resolved, being the kings proper court, that the high commissioners could not punish any man for working on a holy day, albeit it be a matter of ecclesiasticall conusance, but ought by the true meaning of the statute of 1 Eliz. to be punished by the diocesan, which is to be seen of record.

Taylors case. Mich. 44 & 45 El. rot. 1255. Simile 43 & 44 El. rot. 503.

Also in the reign of queen Eliz. William Taylor clerk, parson of Springfeld in Essex did implead William Massy gent. before the high commissioners for giving unreverent speeches to the minister, &c. for carrying his corn on holy days, * for not suffering the parson and parishioners to come thorough his yard in rogation week in the perambulation, and not giving them a repast as usually he had done, that he whistled and knocked on the parsons barn door, and said he did it to make him musique for his daughters mariage, and many other articles of like nature; and it was ruled upon open motion, and often debating by the whole court of common pleas, that the high commissioners could not deal with such inferiour offences, but are to be left to the proper diocesan, who is to reform the same with lesse charge and travell in the proper diocesse. And thereupon a prohibition was granted by the court of common pleas, whereby it appeareth, that they cannot hold plea of all ecclesiasticall causes.

*[333]

Grayes case, Vid. infra pa. 334. Trin. 44 El. rot. 1233. in com. banco. Simile 40 Eliz. rot. 422 in com. banco. The like in the kings bench. Pasch. 39 Eliz. rot. 100. & Pasch. 41 Eliz. ibidem rot. 235.

The like prohibition was granted out of the common pleas in the said late queens reign, between Robert Pool clerk parson of Winchelsey, and Thomas Gray, to the high commissioners, for that they held plea for assaulting and laying violent hands on the said Robert Pool being a parson, upon open motion and argument by the whole court.

Hil. 3 Jac. regis, in communi banco, between Lyn and Wats for promise of a yeerly sum in marriage.

Trin.

* Trin. 3 Jac. *in communi banco*, between Jeneway parson of T. in Essex, and Porter for defamation, and laying violent hands on a clerk. * Tr. 3. Jac. in com' banco Porters case.

ª And concerning fine and imprisonment, *anno 9 reginæ Eliz.* which was about eight years after the statute of 1 Eliz. Sir James Dier and divers other of the judges were then living, that were present at the making of the said statute, Thomas Lee an atturny of the common pleas, being convented before the high commissioners for hearing of a masse, was by them in their proceedings committed to prison, which matter being returned by *habeas corpus*, he was upon great consideration had, by the lord Dier and the whole court of common pleas discharged of his imprisonment, for that the high commission had no power to imprison him in that case. ª Mich. 9 & 10 El. rot. 1556. Lees case.

The like resolution was in 18 Eliz. by the lord Dier, and the whole court of common pleas, in the case of one Hinde, who being convented before the high commissioners for usury, to answer, &c. was thereupon imprisoned by them, and by *habeas corpus* delivered, for that the imprisonment in that case was unlawfull. 18 El. Dier fo. Hindes case.

By warrant from the high commissioners in the reign of queen Eliz. directed to Richard Butler constable of Aldrington in the county of Northampton, for attaching and arresting of the body of John Simpson of Aldrington aforesaid, and bringing his body before the high commissioners in case of adultery with the wife of Edward Fuste, the constable being assisted with one William Johnson servant of the said Edward Fuste, the said constable with Johnson came to a widows house in Aldrington where the said Simpson was, and the doors being open would have at eight of the clock at night arrested Simpson by the said warrant, which the said constable read unto him, notwithstanding the said Simpson resisted them, and in his own defence (and shewed how) slew the said Johnson that came in aid of the said constable. Now the question before the justices of assise of that county, (Simpson being in the gaol therein) what his offence was? wherein the doubt rested in this, whether the constable might lawfully attach and arrest the body of the said Simpson, (which in law is an imprisonment) for if he had lawfull authority to arrest him, then the offence was wilfull murder in killing one that came in aid of a minister of justice in execution of his office: but if the constable had no lawfull authority to arrest his body by force of the high commissioners warrant, then was it but *se defendendo*, a small offence, which doubt wholly consisted upon construction of the statute of 1 Eliz. for by the letters patents expresse authority is given to the high commissioners to send for the body of any offendor, &c. by pursevant, or by warrant. The matter being weighty, and the said Simpson being by the coroners inquest indicted of wilfull murder, supposing the said warrant to be lawful, the justices of assise thought not good to proceed against him at those assises, but deferred it till the next assises: at what time after this long time of deliberation, and upon conference, [334] it was resolved, that the statute of 1 Eliz. gave no power to the high commissioners to make any warrant to arrest the body of Simpson in that case, but ought to have proceeded by citation: and therefore that Simpson killing the said Johnson had committed no murder: and so the jury upon his arraignment found him not guilty of murder according to the direction of the court, as it appeareth by the record itself. And it was resolved in Grayes case aforesaid, Simpsons case before the judges of assise in Northamptonshire, 42 Eliz. Supra pag. 333. Grayes case.

aforesaid, that for the battery of a minister they could not fine and imprison.

William Thicknes case, in communi banco.

William Thicknes having the priviledge of the court of common pleas, had a *habeas corpus* to the sherif of London for his body, with the cause, he being under their custody, who returned that the high commissioners had committed him to their custody by force of his majesties commission for causes ecclesiasticall, and of the statute in that case provided, for that he was convicted before them of adultery, and other contempts and enormities appertaining to ecclesiasticall conusance. And the case being debated in open court, he was discharged of his imprisonment, for that by the statute of 1 El. they could not imprison him.

25 H. 8. cap. 19.

By the statute of 25 H. 8. cap. 19. it is enacted, that for lack of justice at or within any of the courts of the archbishops of this realm, or in any of the kings dominions, it shall be lawfull to the parties grieved to appeal to the kings court of chancery, and that upon every such appeal commissions shall be directed under the great seal to such persons as shall be named by the kings highnesse, &c. which commissioners so by the kings highnesse, &c. to be named or appointed, shall have full power and authority to hear and finally determine such appeal, and that such judgment and sentence as the said commissioners shall make and decree in and upon such appeal, shall be good, effectual, and definitive. Which words, albeit they be more generall, and with lesse reference to the precedent matter, then the act of 1 El. yet have such commissioners no colour to fine or imprison any: but where the words be [and such judgment and sentence as the said commissioners shall make and decree] these generall words have these words implicite annexed to them [according to the ecclesiasticall laws] shall be good, effectuall, &c. So in the statute of 1 Eliz. such words are implicite to be added to the said clause, viz. that the high commissioners shall execute the premisses according to the said letters patents by the rule of the ecclesiasticall law or authority of parliament. And since the high commission was inrolled and made publique, many prohibitions have been granted according to law and justice upon complaint made by the parties grieved.

And in the reign of the said late queen Eliz. it was resolved, that the high commission should be limited to certain particular enormous and exorbitant causes, which if it were pursued would breed great quiet and repose within the realm.

See Hil. 17 El. rot. 1402. Inter Henr. Evans clericum queren' et Thomam Jefferies clericum defendant.

In the reign of the said late queen a prohibition was granted by Sir James Dier chief justice, and the whole court of common pleas, 10 Febr. *anno* 21 Eliz. to the high commissioners for that they did hold plea *de jure advocationis*.

[a] Hil. 3 Jac.

[b] Mich. 41 & 42 El. rot. 2919. and an attachment thereupon, Mich. 42 & 43 El. rot. 3332.

[a] And in my lord Andersons time in the reign of queen Elizabeth the court of common pleas granted divers prohibitions, as it appeareth before, and two of speciall note [b] between Baker and Broughton, and another between Blackheath and the bishop of Gloucester. And in my lord Gaudies time who succeeded the lord Anderson and enjoyed his place but a short time, yet in that time the court of common pleas granted prohibitions also to the high commissioners.

Many other prohibitions have been granted to the high commissioners out of the court of common pleas of after times.

In the kings bench there are also many prohibitions granted to the

the high commissioners in the times of the lord Wray, lord Popham, lord Fleming, &c. which are to the same effect as those which have been cited be.

And we will conclude with the confession of the lord archbishop Bancroft himself in his 22 article, his own words being: Of latter dayes, whereas certain lewd persons, (two for example sake) one for notorious adultery and other untolerable contempts, and another for abusing of a bishop of this kindome, by threatning speeches and sundry rayling tearmes, no way to be endured, were thereupon fined and imprisoned by the high commissioners till they should enter into bonds to perform further orders of the said court, the one was delivered by *habeas corpus* out of the kings bench, and the other by a like writ out of the common pleas, and sundry other prohibitions have been likewise awarded to his majesties said commissioners upon these suggestions, that they had no authority to fine or imprison any man, &c.

[335]

See the articles and answers in the 2 part of the Institutes, in the exposition of *Articuli Cleri*, &c.

By this article it appeareth, that before the time of the chief justice of the court of common pleas that now is, and before divers of the judges that now be, were called to be judges by the judgment and resolution both of the court of kings bench and common pleas by *habeas corpus*, the parties that were fined and imprisoned by the high commissioners in case of adultery and scandall of a bishop, &c. were by the law discharged, for that the fining and imprisonment of them was unlawfull.

And these were the resolutions of the whole court of common pleas Pasch. 9 *Jacobi regis*, upon often conference and mature deliberation, and accordingly they proceeded.

The Prerogative Court of the Archbishop of Canterbury.

Curia Prerogativa Archiepiscopi Cantuariensis.

This is the court wherein all testaments be proved, and all administrations granted, where the party dying within his province hath *bona notabilia*, in some other diocesse then where he dieth, which regularly is to be to the value of 5 l. but in the diocesse of London it is 10 l. by composition.

The bishops, lords, and commons assented in full parliament, that the king, his heirs and successors might lawfully make their testaments, and that execution shall be done of the same, whereof some doubt was made before. See rot. par. 1 H. 5. nu. 13. the testament of king H. 4. and his executors refused, the archbishop of Canterbury was to grant administration with the testament annexed to the same. See 1 H. 6. nu. 18. the last will and executors of H. 5. 10 H. 6. nu. 27.

Rot. par. 16 R. 2. nu. 10. not in print.

When the king is made an executor of the last will and testament of any other, the king doth appoint certain persons to take the execution of the will upon them (against whom such as have cause of suit may bring their action) and appointeth others to take the account. See rot. par. 15 H. 6. Katherine queen dowager of England, mother of H. 6. made her last will and testament, and thereof constituted king H. 6. her sole executor. And thereupon the king appointed Robert Rolleston, clerk, keeper of the great wardrobe,

Rot. par. 15 H. 6. nu. 32. Obiit 2 Junii 1436. apud Bermondsey.

wardrobe, John Merston and Richard Alreed esquires, to execute the said will by the oversight of the cardinall, the duke of Glouc', and the bishop of Linc', or two of them to whom they should account.

The probate of every bishops testament or granting of administration of his goods, although he hath not goods but within his own jurisdiction, doth belong to the archbishop.

The like court the archbishop of York hath.

From this court the appeal is to the king in chancery. Now touching the jurisdiction of this court, and the consistories of bishops, &c. Such points as have been judicially resolved, are necessary to be remembred, both for the safety of the judge, and the benefit of the party interested.

[336] If a man die intestate having *bona notabilia* in divers diocesses, the judge of this court hath used to assesse a convenient sum to be imployed *in pios usus*, but with these limitations following: 1. It must be after administration granted, and the inventory made and returned, to the end the estate of the intestate may be known. 2. The administrator before any assessement must be called to it, to the intent the judge may be informed of the true state of the intestate, and of his children and kindred, for whose succour and relief there is great piety. The 3. the assessement must be in particular, how much, to whom, and to what use. 4. There must a publique act be made of it before any payment be made. 5. Payment must be made according to the act. Lastly, the judge ought not directly or indirectly to take any thing thereof to his own use, nor for the assessement thereof or entring the publique act, and if he doth, it is extortion.

Mich. 20 Jac. in camera stellata.

And *termino Mich.* 20 *Jacobi regis*, Sir John Bennet judge of this court, for not observing of these rules was sentenced in the star-chamber for extortion, and fined at twenty thousand pounds, imprisoned, and disabled ever after to bear an office, as by the sentence appeareth. And the like orders and rules must be observed in all respects (saving the two former) in commutation of penance, which two former doe not concern this matter. And these rules as well concerning assessements *in pios usus*, upon granting of administrations, as for commutation of penance, may serve for the direction of all the ordinaries and judges in ecclesiasticall courts in England.

21 H. 8. cap. 5. Mich. 6 Jac. reg. rot. 1301. in communi banco.

There was an act made *anno* 21 H. 8. concerning fees for probate of last wils and testaments, and granting of administrations. In the case of James Rowse commissary of the archdeacon of Huntingdon, in an information against him by Edmonde Neale, for extortion upon the said statute of 21 H. 8. whereunto he pleaded not guilty, and was found guilty, the point in question upon the information was, if the probate be not written upon the testament it self, but upon the transcript ingrossed, whether the taking of a fee by the defendant for the ingrossing were within the said statute? And it was upon debate in open court resolved by the chief justice, and the rest of the justices, Walmsly, Warburton, Foster and Daniel, that such a fee taken for the ingrossing was within the statute, for that the act is in the negative. And if the executor request any to ingrosse the testament, he must agree with him,

See the 3 part of the Instit. cap. Extortion.

See the act.

him, that he so request (or * bring one ready ingrossed with him as he did in the case in question, which is a safe and ready way) bu the ordinary or commissary ought not to exact a fee for it of the party as a fee due to him, for divers causes. First, for that the words are expresse for the probation, &c. or for registring, sealing, writing, praising, making of inventories, &c. which word (writing) extends to this case. Secondly, the words be, or any thing concerning the same probate, and when the seal and probate is put to the transcript, this concerns the probate, for the probate is not put to any other writing. Thirdly, if such a construction should be made, that this case is out of the statute, this beneficiall law should be illusory and vain, for if the ordinary or his commissary might take what he would for the ingrossing by his clerks as a fee due to him, the act should be of none effect; and the manner of the precise penning of the act, and the certainty of the fees, and not above, should be all in vain. And the ordinary, if he will, may annex the probate to the testament it self, as seeing he can have no other fee then is in the statute, it may be hereafter he will doe: but for the misreciting of the act of 21 H. 8. in the information, *Curia advisare vult:* and this resolution extending to all courts of ecclesiasticall jurisdiction that have probate of testaments, we thought it necessary to make a memoriall of it.

* Note this.

See the words of the act at large.

The Court of the Arches of the Archbishop of Canterbury.

[337]

This court is called *curia de arcubus*, and hath been anciently holden in Bow church of London. For I read of it in a record of a prohibition *termino Hil. coram rege anno 7 E. 1. rot. 8. in curia Christianitatis coram decano de arcubus London.* Of Bow church in London, where the court hath continually been kept, which and 12 other parishes in London, whereof Bow is the chief, are within the peculiar jurisdiction in spirituall causes of the archbishop of Canterbury, and exempt from the bishop of London.

Hil. 7 E. 1 coram rege. rot. 8. Pasch. 12 E. 1. in banco Essex. Gulielmus de Mortuo mari clericus, &c. See Dier 7 Eliz. 241.

The judge of this court is called the dean of the arches, unto whose officialty in spirituall causes to the archbishop of Canterbury is annexed the peculiar jurisdiction of these 13 parishes. He hath ordinary jurisdiction in spirituall causes of the first instance, and by appeal through the whole province of Canterbury, as it appeareth by the statute of 24 H. 8. cap. 12. His power to call any person for any cause out of any part of his province in the dioces of any other, unlesse it be upon appeal, is restrained by the statute of 21 H. 8. cap. 9. This court in the statute of 25 H. 8. cap. 19. is called the court of the arches, or audience of the archbishop of Canterbury: and from this court of the arches the appeal is to the king in chancery by the said act of 25 H. 8.

24 H. 8. cap. 12. 1 Eliz. cap. 1.

21 H. 8. cap. 9. 25 H. 8. cap. 19.

The Court of Audience. *Curia Audientiæ Cantuariensis.*

This court is kept by the archbishop in his palace, and medleth not with any matter between party and party of contentious jurisdiction, but dealeth with matters *pro forma*, as confirmations of bishops elections, consecrations, and the like, and with matters of voluntary jurisdiction, as the granting of the gardianship of the spiritualties

spiritualties *sede vacante* of bishops, admission and institution to benefices, dispensing with banes of matrimony, and such like.

The Court of the Faculties.

Vi. 28 H. 8. ca. 16. 21 H. 8. cap. 13. 5 Eliz. cap. 16.

This is also a court, although it holdeth no plea of controversie (like the court of audience next before.) It belongeth to the archbishop, and his officer is called *magister ad facultates*. And his power is to grant dispensations, as to marry, to eat flesh on dayes prohibited, (and so may every diocesan) the sonne to succeed his father in his benefice, one to have two or more benefices incompatible, &c. It is called faculties in the statute of 28 H. 8. which in one sense signifieth a dispensation. So as *facultates* (in this sense) *dispensationes et indulta* are *synonyma*.

* Commonly called the master of the faculties. [a] Trin. 44 Eliz. in com. banco. rot. 1525. lib. 4. f. 117. Lib. pl. Co. pa. 512, 513. [b] 2 E. 6. cap. 19. 5 E. 6. cap. 3. See the third part of the Instit. cap. Dier pag. 200. 5 Eliz. ca. 5. 35 Eliz. cap. 7. 27 Eliz. cap. 11. Lib pl. Co. 371. 27 Eliz. ca. 11. 3 Caroli ca. 4. Vid. 35 Eliz. ca. 7.

This authority was raised and given to the archbishop of Canterbury by the statute of 25 H. 8. cap. 21. whereby authority is given to the said archbishop and his successors to grant dispensations, faculties, &c. by himself or his sufficient and substantiall * commissary or deputy for any such matter, whereof heretofore such dispensations, faculties, &c. then had been accustomed to be had at the see of Rome, or by authority thereof. [a] This branch of this act you shall find pleaded lib. plac. Co. pag. 512, 513.

[b] Concerning the power of the archbishop to grant dispensations to any to eat flesh on Fridayes, Saturdayes, embring dayes, vigils, and Lent, the same is limited by the statute of 5 Eliz. cap. 5. And the penalty of 5 Eliz. in that case is diminished and made lesse by 35 Eliz. cap. 7. Note the statute of 5 Eliz. concerning eating of flesh on Wednesdayes is repealed by 27 Eliz. ca. 11. which act of 27 Eliz. is affirmed by the act of 35 Eliz. and by 21 Jac. cap. 28. and expresly by the statute of 3 Caroli cap. 4.

[338]

Curia Peculiarum. The Court of Peculiars.

The archbishop of Canterbury hath a peculiar jurisdiction in divers parishes within the city of London and other diocesses, &c.

The Consistory Courts of the Archbishops and Bishops.

See Lit. sect. 133. 136. 648.

The consistory court of every archbishop and bishop of every dioces in ecclesiasticall causes is holden before his chancelour in his cathedrall church, or before his commissary in places of the dioces far remote and distant from the bishops consistory, so as the chancelor cannot call them to the consistory without great travel and vexation: and he is called *commissarius foraneus*. From these the appeal is to the archbishop of either province respectively: when consistories of archbishops and bishops began within this realm, see before in the chapter of the tourn of the sheriffe.

24 H. 4. cap. 12.

Rot. claus. 30 H. 3. m. 4. mandatum est Thom. de Stanford, &c. Ro. pat. 13 E. 1. m. 21. Rex licent. dedit episcop. Bangor, &c.

It appeareth by many records in the reigns of H. 3. and E. 1. (as taking some one or two examples for many) that by the law and custome of England no bishop could make his will of his goods or chattels comming of his bishoprick, &c. without the kings license. The bishops that they might freely make their wils, yeilded to give to the king after their deceases respectively for ever six things.

1. Their

1. * Their best horse or palfrey with bridle and saddle. 2. A cloak with a cape. 3. One cup with a cover. 4. One bason and ewer. 5. One ring of gold. 6. His kennell of hounds. For these a writ issueth out of the exchequer after the decease of every bishop: For example. *Rex, &c. Vic' Eborum. Praecipimus tibi, quod non omit' propter aliquam libertatem, quin etiam ingred' et distring' omnes executores testamenti et ultimae voluntatis reverendissimi in Christo patris Matthaei nuper archiepiscopi Eborum defuncti, ac administratores et occupatores bonorum et catallorum quae fuer' dicti nuper archiepiscopi, nec non haered' et tenent' terrarum et tenementorum quae nuper sua fuer' per omnes terras et catalla sua in balliva tua. Ita quod nec ipsi nec aliquis per ipsos ad ea man' appon' donec al' inde tibi praeciperimus. Et quod de exitibus earundem terrarum nobis respond', et quod habeas corpora eorum coram baronibus de scaccario nostro apud Westm' à die Paschae in tres septimanas ad respond' nobis de uno optimo equo sive palfrido cum cello et fraeno. Una chlamyde sive cloca cum capella. Uno cipho cum coopertorio. Una pelve cum lavatorio sive aquar'; et uno annulo aureo, nec non * muta canum quae nuper fuer' ejusdem nuper archiepiscopi tempore mortis suae: et quae ad nos ratione praerogativae nostrae spectant et pertinent, et de precio sive valore inde, unde nobis nondum est respons. Et habeas ibi tunc nomina executorum et aliorum praedict' et hoc breve.*

* It is said that this was given by the bishops being secular persons ecclesiasticall for all the secular clergy.

**Muite des cheins*, of *muit* cometh *muta*, signifying a kennell.

The most ancient of this kind that we find and remember (but certainly there were such writs before) is *inter memorand' de scaccario, anno* 2 E. 2. the bishop of Bathe and Wels case. Tr. 36 E. 3. ibid. *Int. com'ia.* the bishop of Chesters case, Hil. 5 E. 4. ibid. adjudge upon demurrer, that the duty being to the king after the decease of every bishop, it extendeth to an archbishop, the archbishop of Yorks cases for every archbishop is a bishop. It is sometimes called *multura* or *mulctura de episcopis*, sometime *monutier, &c.* The king by verdict of twelve recovered ten thousand marks against the bishop of Norwich for that he prosecuted against the abbot of S. Edmonds Bury to appear before him against the kings prohibition, for which it was adjudged that his temporalties should be seised, and his body taken.

Int com' de Hil. 2 E. 2. in scaccar. proces vers. Episc. de Bath et Wels.

Mic. 19 E. 3. coram rege. rot. 157. Norff. Tr. 21 E. 3. rot. 170. coram rege 21 E. 3. fo. 60.

* Upon consideration had of the statutes of 3 R. 2. 7 H. 4. 1 H. 5. & rot. parl. 6 H. 4. nu. 48. & 4 H. 6. nu. 29. If an alien or stranger born be presented to a benefice, the bishop ought not to admit him, but may lawfully refuse him: which we have added, for that the abridgements or late impressions may deceive you.

* 3 R. 2. cap. 3. 7 H. 4. cap. 12. 1 H. 5. cap. 7. Rot. parl. 6 H. 4. nu. 48. 4 H. 6. nu. 29.

The Court of the Arch-Deacon, or his Commissary. [339]

This court is to be holden where and in what places the archdeacon either by prescription or composition hath jurisdiction in spirituall causes within his archdeaconry. And from him the appeal is to the diocesan. He is called *oculus episcopi*.

24 H. 8. cap. 12.

In some acts of parliament and many records and histories you shall read of the bishops pall, *pallium episcopale*. It is a hood of white wooll, to be worn as doctors hoods be upon the shoulders, with four crosses woven into it, &c. the form and colours whereof you may see in the book *De Antiquitate Britannicae Ecclesiae*, page 1. for

20 H. 8. c. 20, &c. Vid. Cassaneus 4 part. Catalogi gloriae mundi fo. 103. a. 26 Consideratio, ubi legas, si placet, multa de pallio.

for a pall is the arms belonging to the see of Canterbury, and therefore expressed there, and commonly in other places.

Vocabular' juris. *Palla est vestis qua altare cooperitur,* viz. *ut lineus pannus consecratus qui super altare ponitur, super quem extenditur corporale.*

Parl. 51 E. 3. nu. 83. The clergy petitioned in parliament, that of every consultation conditionall, the ordinary may of himself take upon him the true understanding thereof, and therein proceed accordingly.

Whereunto the kings answer was, That the king cannot depart with his right, but to yeild to his subjects according to law. *Nota hoc, et stude bene.*

The Court of Delegates and consequently of Appeals.

25 H. 8. ca. 19. It is so vulgarly called, because these delegates do sit by force of the kings commission under the great seal upon an appeal to the king in the court of chancery in three causes. First, when a sentence is given in any ecclesiasticall cause by the archbishop or his officiall. Secondly, when any sentence is given in any ecclesiasticall cause in places exempt. Thirdly, when a sentence is given in the admirall court in suits civill and marine by the order of the civill law. And these commissioners are called delegates, because they are delegated by the kings commission for these purposes.

Now because we have generally spoken of appeals in ecclesiasticall causes, which are grounded upon acts of parliament, it shall be pertinent to our purpose to set down the resolution of the judges, and of the learned in the ecclesiasticall law, which doth summe up in what causes, from what courts, and in what time appeals are to be made, and other necessary incidents concerning the same, as the lord Dier under his own hand hath reported, but are left out of the print, and yet worthy to be known and published, which you shall hear in his own words and language.

Of Appeals.

Appeals. Anno 24 H. 8. ca. 12. First, in cases testamentary, matrimony, and tithes, from the archdeacon or his officiall, if the matter be there commenced, to the bishop of the dioces, and from the bishop diocesan or his commissary in such case, or if the matter be there commenced, within fifteen dayes after sentence given, to the archbishop of the province, and no further.

Item, from the archdeacon or commissary of the archbishop, if the matter be there commenced within fifteen dayes, &c. to the audience or arches of the said archbishop: and from thence within other fifteen days, &c. to the archbishop himself, and no further. And if the cause be commenced before the archbishop, then to be there definitively determined without further appeal.

See infra, this is altered by the statute of 25 H. 8. in the next pag.

[340]

Item, where the matter toucheth the king, the appeal within fifteen days to be made to the higher convocation house of that province, and no further, but finally to be there determined.

25 H. 8. cap. 19. A generall prohibition, that no appeales shall be pursued out of the realme to Rome, or elsewhere.

Item, a generall clause that all manner of appeales, what matter

soever

soever they concern, shall be made in such manner, forme and condition within the realm, as it is above ordered by 24 H. 8. in the three causes aforesaid; and one further degree in appeales for all manner of causes is given, viz. from the archbishops court to the king in his chancery, where a commission shall be awarded for the determination of the said appeale, and from thence no further. Vide supr. pag. praecedent.

Item, that persons exempt shall likewise pursue their appeale in the chancery, *ut supra*, and not to the archbishop.

Note, in case where a sentence is given by commissioners delegates by the prince, as by the late visitors, *anno* 1 Eliz. the party grieved appealing, such appeale is out of the orders prescribed by the said statutes, and the prince in that case may grant a new commission to others to determine that appeale. *Et ceo fuit fait per lopinion del plusors des justices en le case de Goodman deprive del deanery de Wells.*

Nota, Stephen Gardener evesque de Winton fuit deprive al Lambeth per commission del roy E. 6. fait a 10 *persons proceeding sur ceo ex officio mero mixto vel promoto omni appellatione remota summarie de plano, absque omni forma et figura judicii, sola facti veritate inspecta.*

Et vide Mich. 3 & 4 *Eliz. Coveney president del Novel College in Oxon' deprive per le evesque de Winton, visitor del dit colledge, et exempt de tout jurisdiction ordinary, fait appeale al roy in son chancery, et commission illonq; grant a A. Browne et Weston justices, que sur conference ove auters justices et civilians, resolve que le appeale ne gist, ne ascun auter remedie pur le appellant pur ceo que cesti case fuit hors del dit statute de* 24 & 25 *H.* 8. *car cest deprivation est mere temporall, et come p. ley prov'. Ex quo sequitur, que unc assise gist, &c.* This case is in print, Dier fo. 209. a.

Nota, in appellis per doctorem Lewes judic admiral' et al' &c. Forasmuch as an appeale is a naturall defence, it cannot be taken away by any prince or power, and in every case generally when sentence is given, and appeale made to the superior, the judge that did give the sentence is bound to obey the appeale, and proceed no further untill the superiour hath examined and determined the cause of appeale. Neverthelesse where this clause *(appellatione remota)* is in the commission, the judge that gave sentence is not bound to obey the appeale, but may execute his sentence, and proceed further, untill the appeale be received by the superior, and an inhibition be sent unto him: for that clause *(appellatione remota)* hath three notable effects. The first is, that the jurisdiction of the judge that gave sentence, is not by the appeale suspended or stopped, for he may proceed the same notwithstanding. The second, that for proceeding to execution or further proces he is not punishable. The third, that those things that are done by the said judge after such appeale cannot be said void, for they cannot be reversed *per viam nullitatis.*

But if the appeale be just and lawful, the superior judge ought of right and equity to receive and admit the same, as he ought to do justice to the subjects. And so if the cause of the appeale be just and lawfull, he ought to reverse and revoke all meane acts done after the said appeale in prejudice of the appellant. Thus far the report of the lord Dier truly translated.

* At the parliament holden at Clarendon called *assisa de Clarendon anno* 10 H. 2. cap. 8. the formes of appeales in causes ecclesiasticall, are set down within the realm, and none to be made out of the

* Parliam. at Carendon 10 H. 2. cap. 8. Mat. Par. p. 97.

* Rot. clauf. in dorf. anno 8 H. 3. part. 1. m. 29. Rex Dublin archiepifc. &c. Rot. parl. 18 E. 1. rot. 1. William de Valentia. & rot. 3. nu. 39. Wil. de Martingham acc. See Hovenden fol. 284.

‡ [341]

* Hayward doctor of the civill and canon law in the life of William 2.

8 Eliz. cap. 5.

the realm.. *Ne quis appellat ad dominum papam,* * *rex ægrè tulit appell' ad papam in causa bastardiæ, ut contra dignitatem regis de consilio igitur* (the record fpeaking in the perfon of the king) *magnatum et fidelium nobis assistent' vobis mandamus, firmiter injungentes quatenus non obstante appellatione præmissa non differatis pro eo sententiam, &c.* So as the firft article of the ftatute of 25 H. 8. concerning the prohibition ‡ of appeales to Rome is declaratory of the ancient law of the realme.

* And it is to be obferved, that the firft attempt of any appeale to the fee of Rome out of England was by Anfelme bifhop of Canterbury, in the reigne of William Rufus, and yet it took no effect.

See 8 Eliz. cap. 5. an appeale in civill and marine caufes before the lord admirall, &c. a fentence before commiffioners delegates is finall.

See before page 125. upon a fentence given by the conftable and marfhall proceeding by the civill law *in causa armorum,* there lyeth an appeal to the king, but none of the faid ftatutes extend to this kind of appeale.

See rot. cl. *anno* 30 H. 3. part 2. m. 11. *de appellatione pro rege fac' in electione abbatissæ de Shaftesbury.*

The Court of the Commissioners of Review.

Ad Revidendum.

24 H. 8. ubi fupr. 25 H. 8. ubi fupr.

Albeit the faid acts of 24 H. 8. and 25 H. 8. do upon certaine appeales make the fentence definitive as to any appeale, for the words be [fhall be definitive] and that no further appeale fhould be had: yet the king after fuch a definitive fentence, as fupreme head, may grant a commiffion of review, *ad revidendum, &c.* for two caufes. 1. For that it is not reftrained by the ftatute. 2. For that after a definitive fentence the pope as fupreme head by the canon law ufed to grant a commiffion *ad revidend':* and fuch authority as the pope had, claiming as fupreme head, doth of right belong to the crowne, and is annexed thereunto by the ftatutes of 26 H. 8. cap. 1. and 1 Eliz. cap. 1. And fo it was refolved in the kings bench Trin. 39 Eliz. where the cafe was, that fentence being given in an ecclefiafticall caufe in the country, the party grieved appealed according to the faid act of 25 H. 8. to the archbifhop, before whom the firft fentence was affirmed. Whereupon according to the ftatute of 25 H. 8. he appealed to the delegates: before whom both the former fentences were repealed and made void by definitive fentence, and thereupon the queen as fupreme head granted a commiffion of review, *ad revidend'* the fentence of the delegates. And upon this matter a prohibition was prayed in the kings bench, pretending that the commiffion of review was againft law, for that the fentence before the delegates was definitive by the ftatute of 25 H. 8. But upon mature deliberation and debate the prohibition was denyed, for that the commiffion for the caufes abovefaid, was refolved to be lawfully granted. In this cafe I being then the queens attorney was of counfell to maintain the queens power. And prefidents were cited in this court in Michelots cafe, *anno* 29 Eliz. and in Goodmans cafe, and Huets cafe, in 29 Eliz. alfo.

Trin. 39 Eliz. in the kings bench. Hollingworths cafe. Lib. Intr. Raft. fol. 16. Appeale to Rome. Ib. Rome 389.

See

See the ftatute of 8 Eliz. cap. 5. and obferve like words in that ftatute, *ut fupra.*

Upon a fentence given by the high commiffioners, a commiffion of review may be granted to and for the party grieved, as by an expreffe claufe within that commiffion appeareth. And if no fuch claufe had been therein, yet a commiffion of review might have been granted. *Quia ficut fontes communicant aquas fluminibus cumulativè, non privativè; fic rex fubditis fuis jurifdictionem communicat in caufis ecclefiafticis vigore ftatuti in hujufmodi cafu editi et provifi cumulativè, non privativè,* by conftruction upon that act. The high commiffion.

Le Court des Confervators des Priviledges de St. Johns de Jerufalem, &c.

There were two courts holden *coram confervatoribus privilegiorum,* the one *hofpitaliorum,* and another *templariorum.* Of whofe jurifdiction, and of their reftraint to grant any general citations *priufquam exprimatur fuper qua re fieri debeat citatio, et fi viderint hujufmodi confervatores quod petatur citatio de aliqua re cujus cognitio fpectat ad forum regium, hujufmodi confervatores nec citationes faciant nec cognofcant,* as by the ftatute of W. 2. appeareth. [342] W. 2. cap. 43.

See the fecond part of the Inftitutes, the expofition upon that ftatute.

The templers were diffolved in 4 E. 2. and the hofpitlers in 32 H. 8. fo as thefe courts are determined.

Now for a conclufion concerning England, I have referved to fay fomewhat for the honour, and fupream eftate of both the relatives of our foveraign lord the king, and of this his kingdome, which I conceive to be neceffary to that which in this part of the Inftitutes we have taken in hand, for that it graceth and ftrengtheneth all the reft.

By the whole parliament of 24 H. 8. wherein, befides the archbifhops and bifhops of the realm, there were 29 abbots and priors lords of parliament: it was refolved, and fo declared by an act, That by divers and fundry old antique hiftories, and chronicles, it is manifeftly declared and expreffed, that this realme of England is an empire, and fo hath been accepted in the world, &c. 24 H. 8. cap. 12.

But againft the truth hereof, oppofition hath been made. Firft, that this is the only parliament that hath affirmed it. Secondly, that this declaration is unjuft and untrue, and that hiftory or chronicle doth not affirm the fame. Vid. ftat. de 28. cap. 2. in Hibernia.

As to the firft I anfwer: that one act of parliament is *inftar omnium,* being a proof of the unanfwerable and higheft nature, but this is not the only; for fo much in effect (as to this point) is affirmed by all the lords fpirituall and temporall, and the commons by authority of parliament long before the reign of H. 8. that the crown of England hath been fo free at all times, that it hath been in no earthly fubjection, but immediately fubject to God in all things touching the regalty of the fame crown, and to no other. Stat. de 16 R. 2. cap. 5. an. domini 1392.

Publique notaries made by the emperor claimed *de jure* to exercife their offices here in England, but becaufe it was againft the Rot. [illegible] E. 2. [illegible] the dignity of a supream king, they were prohibited by the kings writ.

Bracton who wrote in the reign of H. 3. Lib. 1. ca. 8. nu. 5. anno dom. 1270. Int. leges Edovardi cap. 17. an. dom. 1050.

And long before, these by the ancient law of the crown of England, were due to the king. *Omnis quidem sub rege, et ipse sub nullo, sed tantum sub Deo. (Et ibidem paulo post eodem numero) Ipse autem rex non debet esse sub homine, sed sub Deo, &c.*

And therewith agreeth the law before the conquest. *Rex autem, quia vicarius summi regis est, ad hoc est constitutus, ut regnum terrenum, et populum domini, et super omnia sanctam veneretur ecclesiam ejus et regat, et ab injuriosis defendat, et maleficos ab ea eveliat, et destruat et penitus disperdat.*

Anno dom. 169.

And long before that *anno* 169. *à passione Christi dominus Eleutherius papa Lucio regi Brytanniæ scripsit, ad petitionem regis et procerum regni Brytanniæ. Petistis à nobis leges Romanas et Cæsaris vobis transmitti, quibus in regno Brytanniæ uti voluistis: leges Romanas et Cæsaris semper reprobare possumus, legem Dei nequaquam. Suscepistis enim nuper miseratione divina in regno Brytanniæ legem et fidem Christi, habetis penes vos in regno utranque paginam, ex illis Dei gratia per consilium regni vestri sume legem, et per illam Dei patientia vestrum reges Brytanniæ regnum, vicarius vero Dei estis in regno, &c.* and higher I cannot goe.

22 E. 4. nu. 19.

And by the way it is to be observed in the severall grants by abbots and priors made to king E. 4. they severally stile him by these very words, *supremus dominus noster E. 4. rex.*

25 H. 8. cap. 21.

And by three other acts of parliament, viz. by the statute of 25 H. 8. cap. 21. wherein by authority of parliament it is enacted and declared (directing their declaration to the king) That this your graces realm recognizing no superior under God but only your grace, hath been and is free from subjection to any mans laws, but only to such as have been devised, made and ordained within this realm for the wealth of the same, or to such other, as by sufferance of your grace and your progenitors, the people of this your realm [343] have taken at their free liberty by their own consent to be used amongst them, and have bound themselves by long use and custome to the observance of the same, not as to the observance of the laws of any forain prince, potentate, or prelate, but as to the customed and ancient laws of this realm originally established as laws of the same, by the said sufferance, consents and custome, and none otherwise.

25 H. 8. cap. 21. 1 El. cap. 1. 1 Jac. cap. 1.

And by the statutes of 25 H. 8. cap. 21. 1 El. cap. 1. and 1 Jac. cap. 1. the crown of this kingdome is affirmed to be an imperiall crown.

* Pl. com. 398. b. Doct. & Stud. fo. 164. cap. 55.

As to the second: I might answer * that *le court de parliament est de tresgrand honor et justice, de que nul home doit imaginer chose dishonerable.* And with the Doctor and Student upon the statute of 45 E. 3. cap. that it cannot be thought that a statute that is made by the authority of the whole realm as well of the king, and of the lords spirituall and temporall, as of all the commons, will recite a thing against the truth.

The like charter to the house of Donnington by king Edgar.

But to be short, king Edgar stiled and subscribed himself in his charter, *Basileus, imperator et dominus*, which you may read in the preface to the fourth part of my Reports. Vide rot. pat. 1 E. 4. parte 6. m. 23.

Edward commonly called St. Edward son of king Edgar in a charter

charter which he made to the abby of Ramsey (which I have) stiled himself, *Ego Edwardus totius Albionis Dei moderante gubernatione basileus.*

Another charter of king Edwine to the abby of Crowland intituled, *Carta regis Edwini filii regis Edmundi fratris regis Edgari de terris in Jeckelea.* Wherin he is stiled *Edwinus Anglorum rex et totius Brytannicæ telluris gubernator et rector*, and many others.

To conclude this point with a late and learned writer, whom I will cite for that he agreeth with the former authorities, he saith, that the regall estate and dignity of a king is of two manners. The one is imperiall or supream, such a one is our soveraign lady Elizabeth by the grace of God queen of England, France and Ireland, which soveraign queen holdeth her empire and kingdomes with her people and subjects immediately of the Lord of heaven and earth, without any other mean seigniory or attendancie of corporall or bodily service or allegiance to any other worldly prince or potentate, maugre the head of either her forain enemies or intestine and homeborn traiterous vassals, and also from her sentence (she and we all her faithfull and loyall subjects acknowledging to her estate no superiour) lyeth no appeal.

I. F. of the Inner Temple, in his book intituled, The glory of generosity, p. 140, 141.

There is also a king, and he a homager or feudatory to the estate and majesty of another king as to his superior lord, &c. As that of Navar and Portugall to the king of Castell: the kingdomes of Granado and Leons to Aragon: the kingdomes of Lombardy, Sicill, Naples and Bohemia to the sacred empire: the old kingdome of Burgundy, and now the late erected title of the king of Arles, to the king of the French men, and so forth of the rest.

Nota.

The king which is supream and imperiall is equivalent within his land to the power and authority that Cesar can challenge within his own dominions, and such a king challengeth of right to set upon his head a * crown imperiall with a diademe elevated on high, to signifie the perfection and greatnesse of their estate; but to the other kings homagers a crown not elevated is due. And that we may (as duty is) both with reverence and dutifull fear discern and judge the office and function of our soveraign to be most holy and sacred: let us see with what honours a soveraign king (such a one as is her majesty) is illustrated and made redoubted to his subjects, first, what great majesty, honor, power, and glory is intended by setting a crown upon her head, for in the reverend and majesticall action of coronation, she is first anointed, then blessed, after that consecrated; to signifie unto her and unto us that she is of God, that her power is from Christ, and that she is to rule over Christian people: the crown set on her head is called triumphant, and it is of gold to signifie her excellent majesty; it is called triumphant by reason that the like crown in fashion and form was given the emperours and captains of the Romans in their triumphs over kings and nations. This crown triumphant is most due to her excellent majesty even by the strict course of laws of arms, since that her ancestors have triumphed over many kings and mighty people, as H. 1. over five kings of Ireland, E. 1. triumphed over the Scottish and Welsh nations. E. 3. and H. 5. both of them over France. In the triumphant crown of our soveraign lady there be placed (not only for the ornament of her regall diademe, but also to signifie

* A crown imperiall.

With what majesty crowned.

A crown triumphant.

[344]

the princely virtues of a king) twelve gems or stones of precious esteem.

And for this kingdome of England, the other part of the relative, hear what an ancient poet hath said.

Bartholomæus.

Anglia gens fortis, et fertilis angulus orbis:
Insula prædives quæ toto vix eget orbe,
Et cujus totus indiget orbis ope.
Anglia plena jocis, gens libera et apta jocari,
Libera gens, cui libera mens, et libera lingua;
Sed lingua melior liberiorque manus.

The Answer to certain Objections against the Kings Stile of Defender of the Faith.

This bull you may see in Speeds Chronicle, p. 759. nu. 41. anno domini 1521. 13 H. 8. See Laert. Cherub. Bullar. tom. 1. pag. 619.

And where some doe object that the king our soveraign lord ought not *de jure* to enjoy the title and stile of defender of the faith, *defensor fidei*: for (say they) pope *Leo decimus, anno pontificatus sui*, by his bull granted the same to king H. 8. *et posteris suis.* Well, *veritas à quocunque dicitur, à Deo est.* But they say that by the bull of pope Paul the third, against king H. 8. upon his suppression of the lesser houses of religion in *anno* 27 H. 8. he did not only depose him of this title, but of his crown also, and gave his kingdome to him that could get it: which, say we, was done *de facto, sed non de jure;* and we confesse also that by colour of that bull, pope July the third in his bull to king Philip and queen Mary his direction was *Charissimis in Christo filiis nostris Philippo regi et Mariæ reginæ illustribus*, wherein he omitted the title of defender of the faith: but besides the popes bull, which (as it seemeth) is countermandable at his pleasure, the king hath a surer right thereunto to this stile, for by the full consent of all the lords spirituall and temporall and the commons assembled in parliament, and by authority of the same, in *anno* 35 H. 8. it is enacted, that all his majesties subjects should from thenceforth accept and take his majesties stile as it is declared and set forth in manner and form following, that is to say, in the Latin tongue by these words; *Henricus octavus Dei gratia Angliæ, Franciæ, et Hiberniæ rex fidei defensor et in terra ecclesiæ Anglicanæ et Hiberniæ supremum caput*, and in the English tongue by these words: Henry the eight by the grace of God king of England, France, and Ireland, defender of the faith, and of the church of England, and also of Ireland, in earth supream head: and that the said stile should be from thenceforth by authority aforesaid united and annexed for ever to the imperiall crown of his highnesse realm of England. Hereunto it is objected, that this act of parliament is repealed by the act of 1 Mar. but that is mistaken, for as the treasons made and enacted by subsequent clauses of the said act of 35 H. 8. are repealed by the act of 1 Mar. but the stile and title of the crown without question remaineth of force unrepealed; and accordingly queen Mary in all her severall sessions of parliament before her mariage and after her mariage, she and king Philip used the stile and title of defender of the faith in all their parliaments, letters patents, &c. according to the said act of 35 H. 8. and by the way she used the title also of *supremum caput* in the second session of her parliament in the first year of her reign. And by the resolution of

35 H. 8. cap. 3.

the judges in *anno* 1 Mar. it appeareth that the ſtatutes of 26 H. 8. cap. 1. and 35 H. 8. cap. 3. concerning the ſtile of the king remains in force, for thereupon did the queſtion depend: ſo as albeit pope July in his bull vouchſafed not to give king Ph. and queen Mary their ſtile of defender of the faith, yet both ſhe before, and both of them after their mariage, according to their right took it upon them notwithſtanding the thundring bull of pope Paul the third. Laſtly, all the kings and queens regnant of England have at their coronation time out of minde been ſworn to defend the faith, and therefore were of common right defenders of the faith: by reaſon of which oath they may take upon them the ſtile, and are more firmly bound to perform and do it, then by the popes bull.

1 Mar. Dier 94.

[345]

Having ſpoken of England, and of the pety iſlands and dominions of the ſame, and intending to ſpeak of that noble iſland and kingdome of Ireland, I could not paſſe over that ancient and renowned kingdom of Scotland wholly in ſilence, but as it were to ſalute it by the way, and yet to adde ſomewhat, which none that have written of that kingdom have (to my remembrance) touched.

CAP. LXXV.

OF SCOTLAND.

CONCERNING this kingdome there are many things worthy of obſervation.

1. That theſe two mighty, famous, and ancient kingdoms, viz. England and Scotland (I uſe the words of the act of parliament) were anciently but one.

1 Jac. regis ca. 1.

2. That one religion and ſervice of God is holden and celebrated by both.

Vide 4 Jac. ca. 10. & 7 Jac. cap. 1.

3. That as there is one language in both, ſo there was one kind of government and one law in ancient time that ruled both with many unanimous agreements between them, which evidently appeareth by many proofs. Firſt, that the laws of Scotland are divided as the laws of England be into the common laws, acts of parliament, and cuſtomes. Their common laws are principally contained in two books. The firſt called *Regiam majeſtatem*, becauſe it beginneth (as Juſtinians Inſtitutes do) with theſe words [*regiam majeſtatem.*]

11 Jac. regis ca. 1. & 2. in Ireland.

The ſecond book is called *Quoniam attachiamenta*, becauſe it beginneth with thoſe two words.

The firſt book doth in ſubſtance agree with our * Glanvil, and

* Firſt printed by the perſwaſion and procurement of Sir William Stanford a grave and learned judge of the common pleas anno dom. 1554. 1 & 2 Ph. and Mar. Of whom hear what Hovenden ſaith an. dom. 1180. (et regni H. 2. 26.) Henricus rex Angliæ pater conſtituit Ranulphum de Glanvilla ſummum juſtitiarium totius Angliæ, cujus ſapientia conditæ ſunt leges ſubſcriptæ quas Anglicanas vocamus. This Hovenden lived in the reigne of H. 2. and died in the time of king John. See Pl. Com. 368. b. per Catlyn in Epiſt. to the eight book of reports.

moſt

most commonly *de verbo in verbum*, and many times our Glanvil is cited therein by speciall name.

Secondly, the crown of Scotland is descendible to the daughter or heir female where there is no issue male. If there be many daughters or heirs female, it descends to the eldest. Likewise they have the like descents of lands to subjects as England hath, as none can inherit in the right line ascendant. The eldest daughter hath *initiam partem*. All the daughters of subjects do inherit.

Parliament. Thirdly, they have the high court of parliament, as we in England have, and called by the same name, consisting of the same members, viz. lords spirituall, lords temporall, and the commons. It is summoned and called at the kings pleasure for a certain time. When they meet, the king or his chancelor sheweth the causes of calling them together. But there of later times the lords spirituall do choose eight temporall lords, and the lords temporall choose eight spirituall lords. These sixteen make choice of eight chosen for the counties, and eight of cities and burghs, in all, thirty two. But whatsoever is agreed upon by them, the king doth allow or disallow by moving of his scepter, &c.

Fourthly, they have the same degrees of nobility, as dukes, marquesses, earls, viscounts, barons, &c.

Fifthly, they have the same great officers, as chancelour, that keepeth the great seal, lord treasurer, lord privy seal, secretary, &c.

[346] Sixthly, and the same ministers of justice, as sheriffs, coroners, &c.

Seventhly, the same laws for the most part *quarto modo* appropriated to England, viz. tenant by the curtesie, because they had the same law that England had.

Eighthly, the like writs, *brevia*, as *de recto*, assise of *novel dissin'*, *mordanc'*, *de gard*, *de ideot' inquirend'*, *de divisis fac'*, *replegiar'*, *attachm'*, *&c.*

Ninthly, they agree with *Magna Carta* concerning wardships, &c.

Tenthly, with *Carta de foresta* cap. 11. for it is lawfull for bishops, earls, and barons comming or returning through the kings forests at the kings command to kill one or two beasts in the sight of the forester, or otherwise in his absence to blow his horn, that he appear not to take it thievishly.

11. The lord of whom the land is holden by knights service *per antiquius feoffamentum* shall have the wardship of the body.

12. The sheriffes should cause the acts of parliament to be proclaimed, &c. All which, and many more are the ancient laws of both kingdoms, as it appeareth in the said books of *regiam majestatem*, and *quoniam attachiamenta*, *&c.*

13. The sheriffes there have an inheritance in their office, as sometime in England they had, and yet in Cumberland they have.

14. The same vocables of art are used in the laws of both kingdoms, as *ordelium*, i. the court of water and iron, *filius mulieratus*, *marchetum*, *serplaith* or *serpler*, *judicamenta*, *&c. machameum* or *makemium*, *murdrum* or *murcharum*, *chancemeley*, *mote*, *misericordia*, *messuagium*, *flightwight*, *medletum*, *remanere*, *manerium*, *recognitio per assisam*, *pipoudres*, *pannagium*, *ora*, *nonclayme*, *soc* or *sok*, *serjanteria*, *grand serjanty*, *pety serjeanty*, *sectator* a suiter, sheriffs of inheritance there,

there, the sheriffs court or county court, *toll*, *tunbrellum* or *tumbrellum*, *thainus*, soccage, burgage, *servicium militare*, relief or relieve, *them* and *teme*, theftbote, *in libera eleemosyna*, *terræ dominicales*, *liberum tenementum*, *vidiare duellum*, *warrenna* or *varenna*, *valvasores* or *vavasores*, waif, stray, castleward, *veredictum*, *viridarii*, infangthief, outfangthief, outlawry, outlawed, justice in eire, wreck of the sea, voucher, *vicenetum*, *hamsockne*, *hida terræ*, *bovata terræ*, *heriot* or *heregeld*, *hutesium* or *huesium*, regrateurs, forestallers, a guilde, falsifying of dooms or recovery, *quarentena*, *felonia*, *feodum*, homage, fealty, *estroverium*, *essonium*, *enitia pars*, disparagement, disseisons, disclaimer, *scaccarium*, *collistrigium*, *champertie*, *maeremium*, *averia*, *catalla*, bote, bloodwite, grand assise, assise of novel dissin', barettors, affidavit, adjournment, responsals, attornies, and many others.

There was an heptarchy in Scotland, but now a monarchy. There are there two archbishops, the one of St. Andrew, the other of Glasco: St. Andrew hath eight bishops under him, and Glasco three.

There are there thirty counties or sherifdoms.

The ancient motto of the king of England is, God and my right (*intelligitur*) shall me defend. Of the king of Scotland, In my defence God me defend.

There are also two famous universities, one in St. Andrews, the other in Glasco.

The length of Scotland from Twede to the uttermost coast is 480 miles: it is longer then England, but narrower, and endeth like a wedge.

Of ancient time all the bishops of Scotland were sacred, and confirmed by the archbishop of York.

But by reason of their acts of parliament, which in many points have altered, diminished, and abrogated many of the old, and made new laws and other proceedings: the distinct kingdoms as they now stand have many different lawes.

Item, It is ordained by the king by consent and deliverance of the three estates, that all and singular the kings lieges of the realme live and be governed under the kings laws and statutes of the realm allanerly: and under na particular laws, nor speciall privilege, nor be na laws of uther countries nor realms.

Par. 3 Jac. 1. ca. 48. 11 Martii anno dom. 1425.

Item, It is statute and ordained, that all our soveraigne lordis lieges beand under his obeisance, and in speciall the isles be ruled by our soveraigne lordis awn laws and the common laws of the realm, and be nane uther laws.

[347]

Parl. Jacobi 4. ca. 79. 11 Martii anno dom. 1503.

King James at his parliament holden *anno* 1 of his reigne, endeavoured to have made an union of both kingdomes, and to have erected a new kingdome of Great Britain. And thereupon authority was given to certain commissioners of the higher and lower house of parliament, to treat with certain commissioners of Scotland for and concerning an union of both kingdomes. Amongst these commissioners there grew a question, whether there could be made an union of the kingdomes by raising a new kingdome of Great Britaine before there was an union of the lawes. Which question by the kings commandment was referred to all the judges of England in Trinity terme, *anno* 2 Jac. who unanimously resolved

1 Jac. cap. 2.

ſolved (I being then attorney generall, and preſent) that *Anglia* had laws, and *Scotia* had lawes, but this new erected kingdome of Britannia ſhould have no law. And therefore where all the judiciall proceedings in England are *ſecundum legem et conſuetudinem Angliæ*, it could not be altered *ſecundum legem et conſuetudinem Britanniæ*, untill there was an union of the lawes of both kingdomes, which could not be done but by * authority of parliament in either kingdome.

Vid. ſupra p. 36.

* Ex inſtrumento Lib. Hoſp. Sancti Leonardi in com. Eborum. Egbert rex in parliamento apud Wintoniam mutavit nomen regni de conſenſu populi ſui, et juſſit illud de cætero vocari Angliam. Iſte rex Egbertus obiit anno dom. 673. See a proclamation 15 Septemb. 1603. 2 Ja.

Anno 3 Ja. ca. 3. An act made for things to be done by force of the ſaid act of 1 Ja. cap. 2. in any other ſeſſion of parliament.

Anno 4 Ja. cap. 1. A repeale of hoſtile lawes and of hoſtility between England and Scotland, &c. And it is enacted, that no Engliſhman ſhall be ſent out of England into Scotland for any offence done in Scotland, untill ſuch time as both realmes ſhould be made one in lawes and government. So as the reſolution of the judges was approved by parliament. See a proclamation 20 Octob. 2 Ja. concerning the kings ſtile of king of Great Britaine, wherein all judiciall and legall proceedings, &c. are excepted.

I never read of any union of divided kingdomes, and therefore I conceive it to be without precedent. And in this union many things would fall into conſideration, and thoſe of great weight, other then the union of lawes, though that be a maine one: as for example, the ſeverall crownes are deſcendible to ſeverall heyres of * blood. And queſtion may be made who ſhould be heyre of this new kingdome.

* H. 7.

But the learned poet hath found out an union without danger, directing his verſes to king James.

Cum triplici fulvum conjunge Leone Leonem,
Ut varias atavus junxerat antè roſas.
Majus opus, varios ſine cæde unire leones,
Sanguine quam varias conſociaſſe roſas.

Whoſoever is deſirous to know ſuch miſcellanea as we have obſerved concerning Scotland, let him reade theſe records and authorities following.

The records of parliament from the beginning thereof, for the receivers and tryers of petitions in the lords houſe. Rot. liberat. anno 3 Ed. 1. m. 2. per Johannem Lovetot, rot. paten' anno 20 Ed. 1. Gilberto comiti Glovorniæ et Hereford. Scotia rot. parliament. 21 Ed. 1. inter placita rot. 1. and 2. Hovenden 1194. pag. 7. carta regis R. 1. Mat. Weſtm. anno dom. 1260, pag. 302. H. 3. rot. Scotiæ 21 E. 1. carta f. 1. et l'ræ Alexandri regis Scotiæ, rot. Vaſconiæ 25 E. 1. m. 2. 3. in dorſ. Trin. 25 E. 1. coram rege rot. 6. Norff. Rafe de Tonyes caſe. *Anno* 29 E. 1. *l'ræ quas rex per ſe et quas comites et barones Angliæ per ſe miſerunt domino papæ anno* 29 E. 1. *authoritate parliamenti, quæ irrotulatæ ſunt etiam in ſcaccario.* Vid. Walſingham 48. and 49.

Rot. parl. apud Linc. 29 E. 1. Anno dom. 1300 Literæ omnium nobilium Angliæ, &c. Papæ.

[348]

Rot. pat. 24 E. 1. epiſcopis Scotiæ. Mich. 33 E. 1. coram rege rot. 127. Scotia rot. parl. 35 E. 1. in brevi de parliamento, & auter 1 E. 2. 1 E. 3. fo. 17. Grayes caſe. 6 E. 3. 18. The abbot of Crowlands caſe. 9 E. 3. 6. John Darcyes caſe. rot. pat. 10 E. 3. 2 ps. comes Arundel. rot. parl. 14 E. 3. nu. 15. ſtat. 4. rot. clauſ. 22 E. 3. & 23 E. 3. breve de parliamento magnifico principi, &c.

22 Aſſ.

22 Aff. p. 85. 39 E. 3. fo. 35. rot. parliament. 42 E. 3. nu. 7. 42 E. 3. fo. 25. 8 R. 2. tit. cont. clayme pl. ultimo. 13 H. 4. fo. 5. rot. pat. 2 H. 5. part. 3. m. 1. 8 H. 5. fo. 5. 32 H. 6. 25. 20 E. 4. 6. b. Litt. fect. 100. & 165. 1 part of the Inftitutes. Stat. de 2 & 3 E. 6. cap. 36. Fortefcue cap. 13. Pl. com. 126. Dier manufcript 3 Eliz. 22. b. & 13 Eliz. fo. 68. m. 5. Dier 12 Eliz. fo. 287. in print. Lib. 7. fo. 22, 23, &c. Calvyns cafe. lib. 9. fo. 114. Seignior Zanchers cafe. See before in the chapter of the High Court of Parliament.

Polidor. Virgil. Hollingfh. 1 part. fol. 116, 117. 2 part. 286. Stowe 303. Matth. Weftm. 428, 425, 443, 444, 445. Walfingham 17, 28, 32, 129, &c. Hiftoriæ.

Thus have you all which we have obferved in our reading concerning this matter, and which the benevolent reader may perufe at his pleafure; to whofe cenfure we wholly refer the fame. *Multi multa, nemo omnia novit.*

You have obferved, that thofe of Scotland do agree with us in language, and as hath been faid, differ in lawes. On the other fide, the fubjects of Ireland differ from us in language, and agree with us in lawes, and therefore of them we fhall fpeak fomewhat the more at large.

Amongft variety of authors from whence this noble nation of the Scots originally came, we follow venerable Bede in his hiftory of England, lib. 1. cap. 1. and alfo from whence the * Picts originally came. And there you fhall reade, that the Picts arriving in Britania planted themfelves in the north parts thereof, for the Britains had taken up the fouth part before. And whereas the Picts having having no wives did require the Scots to marry their daughters, the Scots agreed to grant them their boone, under condition, that as often as the matter was in doubt, they fhould choofe their king rather of the next of the houfe of the woman then of the man.

Bede in hiftory of England lib. 1. cap. 1.
* Redfhanks.

Cap. 13.

And that Palladius in the eight yeare of Honorius the emperour, *anno domini* 411. was fent by Celeftinus bifhop of Rome to the Scots that had received the faith of Chrift, to be their firft bifhop.

* That the Scots do nothing differre from the Britains in their converfation.

* Et. lib. 2. cap. 4.

Both thefe famous kingdomes have found by wofull experience, that unwife and incertaine making of leagues, greatly indamageth the commonwealth, and the fatall danger of fuch leagues to the princes themfelves.

Beda in his hiftory of England, lib. 1. cap. 11. Vid. fupr. p. 157.

CAP. LXXVI. [349]

Of the Kingdome of Ireland.

WE fhall not need to undertake another work to write of the courts of juftice there, for that they have the fame which we have in England, and the fame law, faving, where fome that have written of them have in fome maine points miftaken the matter;

1 Jacobi cap. 1. & 11 Jac. &c. cap. 1. & 6. in Ireland Vid. the 1 part of the Inftitutes, fect. 212.

matter; we will convince the ſame by direct matter of record, and we intend to adde ſome things which are neceſſary to be known, which no man that hath written of that country hath vouched, or if they have remembred the ſame, it is with ſo light a touch, as much is omitted out of the record, or caſe reſolved itſelfe, worthy to be known, which we intend to ſupply for the honour of the king, and benefit of his ſubjects there. And the rather, for that I have been informed by many of them that have had judiciall places there, and partly of mine owne knowledge, that there is no nation in the Chriſtian world that are greater lovers of juſtice (whereof we ſhall principally treat) then they are, which vertue muſt of neceſſity be accompanied with many others; and beſides they are deſcended of the ancient Britaines, and therefore the more indeared unto us.

Parliaments in Ireland of ancient time.

First, concerning the parliaments of Ireland, being the higheſt court there, where ſome have ſuppoſed that the ſame beganne in 17 E. 3. we ſhall make it appeare by matter of record, that not only king John, as all men agree, but H. 2. alſo, the father of king John, as * before it hath appeared, and in the next page ſhall be touched, did ordaine and command at the inſtance of the Iriſh, that ſuch lawes as he had in England ſhould be of force and obſerved in Ireland: hereby Ireland being of it ſelfe a diſtinct dominion, and no part of the kingdome of England (as it directly appeareth by many authorities in Calvins caſe) was to have parliaments holden there as England; and thereupon in the reigne of king John himſelfe a parliament was holden there, as by this record enſuing appeareth.

* Pag. 12.

Rot. ann. 18 H. 3. m. 17. nu. 21. See the firſt part of the Inſtitutes, ſect. 212.

ª Nota, Rex de communi omnium conſenſu (ac communi conſilio teneri ſtatuit) is by act of parliament.

ᵇ Nota [omnium] that all received the lawes, &c.

Many things in theſe letters patents are worthy of obſervation.

Rex comitibus, baronibus, militibus, et liberis hominibus, et omnibus aliis de terra Hiberniæ, ſalutem. Quia manifeſtè eſſe dignoſcitur contra coronam, et dignitatem noſtram et conſuetudines, et leges regni noſtri Angliæ, quas bonæ memoriæ dominus Johannes rex, pater noſter, de [a] *communi* [b] *omnium de Hibernia conſenſu teneri ſtatuit in terra illa, quod placita non teneantur in curia chriſtianitatis de advocationibus eccleſiarum et capellarum, vel de laico feodo, vel de catallis quæ non ſunt de teſtamento vel matrimonio. Vobis mandamus, prohibentes quatenus hujuſmodi placita in curia chriſtianitatis nullatenus ſequi præſumatis in manifeſtum dignitatis et coronæ noſtræ præjudicium, ſcituri pro certo, quod ſi feceritis, dedimus in mandato juſticiario noſtro Hiberniæ, ſtatuta curiæ noſtræ in Anglia contra tranſgreſſiones hujus mandati noſtri cum juſtitia procedat, et quod noſtrum eſt exequatur. In cujus, &c. Teſte rege apud Winchcomb* 28. *die Octobris anno regni noſtri decimo octavo. Et mandatum eſt juſticiario Hiberniæ per literas clauſas, quod prædict' literas patentes publicè legi et teneri faciat.* But as true it is that the father of king John, viz. H. 2. when he had conquered Ireland, ſent that treatiſe, intituled, *Modus tenendi parliamentum*, in a faire parchment roll, for their better holding of parliaments there, which you may reade more at large before, cap. The high Court of Parliament, p. 12.

[350]

Rex Henricus 3. *anno regni ſui* 12. *mandavit juſticiario ſuo Hiberniæ, ut convocatis archiepiſcopis, epiſcopis, baronibus et militibus ibidem coram eis legi faciat cartam regis Johannis, quam legi fecit, et jurari à magnatibus Hiberniæ de legibus et conſuetudinibus Angliæ obſervandis, et quod leges illas teneant et obſervent.*

Rot. pat. 30 H. 3.

Quia pro communi utilitate terræ Hiberniæ, et pro unitate terrarum, proviſum

*provisum est, quod omnes leges et consuetudines quæ in regno Angliæ tenentur in Hibernia teneantur, et eadem terra eisdem legibus subjaceat, ac per easdem regatur, sicut Johannes rex cum illic esset * statuit, et firmiter mandavit. Ideo volumus quod omnia brevia de communi jure quæ currunt in Anglia similiter currant in Hibernia sub novo sigillo regis. Teste, &c. Apud Woodstock.*

* Nota.

Major Dublin, qui querebatur vers. thesaurarium scaccarii Dublin, et vers. barones scaccarii de gravaminibus per ipsos illatis, remittitur parliamento, et inde huc: cui per curiam dictum est, quod gravamina sua proponat, qui dicit quod non adhuc est consultus, super quo dies datus est. Ad quem diem nullas proposuit querelas, ideo committitur turri London, et finem fecit domino regi.

Coram rege Mich. 33 E. 1. Rot. 124. Hibernia.

Sometimes the king of England called his nobles of Ireland to come to his parliament of England, &c. And by speciall words the parliament of England may binde the subjects of Ireland, as taking one example for many.

10 Octobris rex affectans pacificum statum terræ Hiberniæ, mandavit Ricardo de Burgo com' Ulton' et aliis nobilibus terræ prædictæ, quod sint ad parliamentum suum quod summoneri fecit apud Westm' in octabis Sancti Hilarii prox' ad tractand' ibid' cum proceribus, &c. regni sui super statu terræ prædictæ.

Rot. parl. 8 E. 2. m. 31.

An excellent president to be followed, whensoever any act of parliament shall be made in England, concerning the state of Ireland, &c.

Anno 35 E. 3. De concilio summonit' pro ter' habentibus in Hibernia.

Rot. parl. 35 E. 3. irrot. fac.

Maria comitissa Norff.	*ad mittendum fide dignos ad colloquium.*
Aelianora comitissa Ormond.	
Jana la Despenser,	
Philippa com. de la Marche,	
Johanna Fitzwater,	
Agnes comitissa Penbroke,	
Margareta de Roos,	
Matildis comitissa Oxoniæ,	
Catherina comitissa Athol.	

[a] *De parliamentis singulis annis in Hibernia tenendis, et de legibus et consuetudinibus ibidem emendandis.*

Hereby it appeareth that there were parliaments holden in Ireland before this time, and order taken at this parliament that they should be holden every yeare, and the like acts were made in England in 4 E. 3. & 36 E. 3. for parliaments to be holden in England.

[a] Rot. parl. anno 10 E. 2. Rot. clauf. 10 E. 2. m. 38. & rot. clauf. 12 E. 2. m. 3. Annales Hiberniæ anno dom. 1309. 2 E. 2. parliam. tent. apud Kilkenniæ per com. Ulton. et Johannem Wagan. Justic. Hiberniæ et Magnates, &c.

[b] *In octabis Sancti Martini apud Nottingham rex de consensu communis consilii sui fecit certas ordinationes pro reformatione status sui Hiberniæ, et ministrorum regis ibidem.*

[b] Rot. parl. 17 E. 2. 1. part. pat. anno prædict. m. 3.

[c] *Volumus et præcipimus quod nostra et terræ nostræ negotia, præsertim majora et ardua, per peritos consiliarios, ac prælatos, et magnates, et quosdam de discretioribus hominibus in parliamentis tractentur, discutiantur et terminentur.*

[351]

[c] Int. Ordinationes pro statu Hiberniæ anno 17 E. 3. in turri, &c.

This ordinance doth regulate the parliaments in Ireland according to the institution and end of the parliaments in England, as in the writ of parliament, which is to confer and treat *de arduis et urgentib' negotiis nos (i. regem) et statum et defensionem regni et ecclesiæ Anglicanæ*

Vid. Lib. Album in ſcaccario. Diverſe acts here made concerning Ireland, and tranſmitted thither to be inrolled in the chancery there.

Anglicanæ concernentibus; the effect whereof is contained in the ordinance of 17 E. 3. but that ordinance doth not erect any parliament there, as ſome have (without any colour) ſuppoſed.

See 20 H. 6. fol. 8. which began Mic. 18 H. 6. rot. 46. coram rege, & 2 R. 3. fo. 12. See before in the Chapter of the High Court of Parliament.

*25 H. 8. cap. 12. F. N. B. 178. a. 12 R. 3. 12. Anno 10 H. 7. Poynings law. * Nota.

And ſeeing good and profitable acts of parliament made in the realm of England ſince the reign of king John extended not into Ireland, unleſſe it were ſpecially named or by generall words included, * as within any of the kings dominions, a right profitable act was made at a parliament holden in Ireland in *anno* 10 H. 7. before Sir Edward Poynings then deputy or prorex in Ireland, and thereupon called Poynings law.

Whereby it is enacted, That * all ſtatutes late made within the realm of England concerning or belonging to the common or public weale of the ſame, from henceforth be deemed good and effectuall in the law, and over that be accepted, uſed, and executed within this land of Ireland, in all points at all times requiſite according to the tenor and effect of the ſame. And over that by the authority aforeſaid, that they and every of them be authoriſed, proved, and confirmed, in this ſame realm of Ireland. And if any ſtatute or ſtatutes have been made within the ſaid land heretofore to the contrary, that they and every of them by the authority aforeſaid be adnulled, revoked, and made void, and of none effect in the law.

And Hil. 10 *Jacobi regis*, it was reſolved by the two chief juſtices and chief baron, that this word [late] in the beginning of this act had the ſenſe of [before] ſo that this act extended to Magna Carta, and to all acts of parliament made in England before this act of 10 H. 7. but it is to be obſerved that ſuch acts of parliament as have been made in England ſince 10 H. 7. wherein Ireland is not particularly named or generally included, extend not thereunto, for that albeit it be governed by the ſame law, yet it is a diſtinct realm or kingdom, and (as hath been ſaid) hath parliaments there.

Books concerning Ireland.

Vide Bracton lib. 5. fo. 395. b. temps E. 1. Voucher 239. 14 H. 3. ſtat de Homage. 13 E. 2. Baſtardy 25. 7 E. 3. 9. 8 aſſ. 17. Britton fo. 1. a. 45 E. 3. 19. Tr. 29 E. 1. coram rege 10 E. 3. 41, 42. 11 H. 4. 7. 8 R. 2. Proces 224. 3 H. 7. 10. 7 E. 4. 27. pl. com. 368. 13 Eliz. Dier 303. 20 Eliz. Dier 360. lib. 7. Calvins caſe. 1 part of the Inſtitutes ſect. 95.

Parliaments in Ireland holden at this day.

How and in what manner a Parliament is to be holden in Ireland, and how Bils ought to paſſe in the ſame.

Hil. 10 Jacobi regis.

The lords of the councell directed their letters to the two chief juſtices and chief baron in theſe words.

After our hearty commendations to your lordſhips. Whereas his majeſty for divers weighty conſiderations hath reſolved to hold a parliament in the realm of Ireland, and that by an act made in the tenth year of H. 7. called Poynings Act, it is provided that all ſuch bils as ſhall be offered to the parliament there ſhall be firſt tranſmitted hither under the great ſeal of that

that kingdom: and having received allowance and approbation here, shall be put under the great seal of this kingdom, and so returned thither to be preferred to the parliament: forasmuch as there are accordingly transmitted hither from thence divers bils as well publick as private, some of which bils were first agreed on here, some others were framed and conceived there, and comming now hither may happily receive amendment or alteration: we have thought meet for avoidance of any question or inconvenience that may arise of the manner and form of proceeding in amending or altering of these bils, hereby to pray and require you, calling to you his majesties attorny and sollicitor to look into Poynings act, and to consider of some such course as shall be fit to be held concerning the same, &c. [352]

Dated *ultimo Januarii* 1612.

Whereupon in this tearm the said chief justices and chief baron, and the attorny and solicitor were assembled two severall dayes at Serjeants Inne, and had consideration not only of the said act of 10 H. 7. cap. 4. but of the act of 3 & 4 Ph. and Mar. cap. 4. intituled, An act declaring how Poynings act shall be expounded and taken. 3 & 4 Ph. and Mar. cap. 4.

For by the said act of 10 H. 7. it is provided that no parliament be hereafter holden in the said land of Ireland, but at such season as the kings lieutenant and councell there first do certifie the king under the great seal of that land, the causes and considerations, and all such acts as them seemeth should passe in the same parliament, and such causes, considerations, and acts affirmed by the king and his councell to be good and expedient for that land, and his license thereupon, as well in affirmation of the said causes and acts, as to summon the said parliament under his great seal of England had and obtained. That done, a parliament to be had and holden after the forme and effect afore rehearsed. And if any parliament be holden in that land contrary to the form and provision aforesaid, it be deemed void, and of none effect in law.

Sur quel act divers doubts et ambiguities fuer' conceive et ascuns de eux fuer' de greinder difficulty que auters.

1. *Et primerment un doubt fuit conceive le quel le dit act de* 10 *H.* 7. *extend al successors le roy H.* 7. *intant que l' act parle solement del roy generalment et ne' de ses successors.* 2 *si le roigne Marie fuit deins cest parol roy. Et coment que ceux ne fuer' matters aascun ambiguity, car cest parol roy que import son politique capacity ne unques mort, et esteant parle indefinite extend in ley a toutes ses successors, uncore ceo est issint expound per le dit act de* 3 *&* 4 *Ph. & Mar. Et que le dit act de* 10 *H.* 7. *extendra* to the king and queens majesty, her heirs and successors.

2. *Ou le act de Poynings dit* (the kings lieutenant and councell there) *scruple fuit conceyve, si le roy appoint un per nosme de le deputie, ou*

lord justice, ou sil constitute 2 lords justices, chief governours or governour, *et le councell, &c. Et quant a ceux est explane per le act de* 3 *& 4 Ph. & Mar. que le dit act de Poynings extend a tout ceux.*

3. *Le greinder et pluis difficult doubt fuit sur ceux parols in lact de Poynings.* And such causes, considerations, and acts affirmed by the king and his councell to be good and expedient for that land, &c. *Le quel le roy poet fair ascun change ou alteration des causes, considerations ou acts que serr' transmitt' icye del lieutenant et councell d' Ireland, car ceo nest pas affirmation mes correction et alteration de eux. Et pur ceo fuit necessary destre explane, que lact de 3 & 4 Ph. & Mar.* [353] *fait in ceux parols.* Either for the passing of the said acts, &c. in such forme and tenor as they should be sent into England, or else for the change and alteration of them, or any part of the same.

4. *Auter question fuit sur les parols del primer act. sc.* That done a parliament to be had and holden, &c. *si a mesme le parliament auters acts que fuer' affirme ou alter icy poent estre enactes per authority del parliament la. Le quel est explaine per le dit darrein act in ceux parols*, for passing and agreeing upon such acts, and no others, as shall be so returned under the great seal of England.

5. *Grand doubt fuit conceive sur les ditz parols* (that done a parliament to be holden) *le quel le lieutenant et councell d' Ireland apres le parliament commence la, et* pendente parliamento *poient sur debate et conference la, transmitt ascun auters considerations, causes, tenors, provisions, et ordinances come sembles a eux bone destre enact' a mesme le parliament deins le realme d' Ireland, le quel est explane per le dit act de* 3 *& 4 Ph. & Mar. in expresse parols, que ils poient, &c.*

Nota lecteur lorder del proceeding et sommons del parliament in Ireland. Primerment le lieutenant et councell la doient certefier de south le grand seale d' Ireland le causes et considerations de toutz tielz acts come semble a eux bone a passer en parliament, issint que le original covient a commencer la. 2 *Ils covient destre affirme ou alter et change et retorne de south le grand seale Dangliterre.* 3 *Licence de south le grand seale a sumoner et tener un parliament.* 4 *A transmitter billes* pendente parliamento *come appiert devant. Et fuit auxi resolve una voce.* 1. *Que les causes, considerations, et billes transmitte icy desouth le grand seale d' Ireland doient destre custodie et preserve icy in le chancery d' Angliterre, et ne remaunde.* 2. *Silz soient affirme, ilz doient destre transcript desouth le grand seale et retorne in Ireland, et tout ceo que passe le grand seale doiet destre invelle icye in le chanceryc.* 3. *Si les acts transmitt icy soient in ascun part alter ou change icy, lacts issint alter et change doient come en un continent destre retourne desouth le grand seale Dangliterre a ceux in Ireland, tout quel doit destre invrolle icy in le chanceryc Dangliterre. Mes le transcript desouth le seale d' Ireland que le remaine in le chanceryc icy, ne serra amend, mes l amendment serra desouth le grand seale Dangliterre come est avandit.* 4. *Les amendments ou alterations icy serr' come est avandit retourne in Ireland sans ascun signification ou certificat dallowance de ceux per ceux de Ireland, car sicome les acts movent originalment de Ireland, issints les amendments ou alterations movent icy in Angliterre.* 5 *Touts les bils que sont transmitt icy de Ireland sont ove le petition del deputye et councell le roy touts ensemble desouth un grand seal d' Ireland.* 6. *Touts les bills que sont affirme ou alter icy soient retourne ensemble desouth un grand seale d' Angliterre.*

And thus much concerning the parliaments of Ireland.

The

The Case of the Earl of Shrewsbury upon the Statute of 28 *H.* 8. *of Absentees.*

Per force de certain letters patents de 28 *Martii* 1612. *del seigniours del privy councell direct al Sir Humfrye Winche, Sir James Lea, Sir Anthony Sentleger, et James Fullerton, ilz certifiont aux seigniors le claim de Guilbert countee de Salop aux dignities del countee de Waterford et barony de Dongarvan in Ireland come ensuist. Le roy* H. 6. *per ses letters patents* anno 24 *de son reign granta à son treschier cosin John countee de Shrewsbury in consideration de ses approved et foyall services in le city et county de Waterford in Ireland,* pro eo quoque quod per eundem consanguineum nostrum prædicta terra nostra Hibernia in partibus illis contra hujusmodi inimicorum et rebellium nostrorum insultus potentius defenderetur, ipsum in comitem Waterford una cum stilo et titulo ac nomine et honore eidem debitis ordinamus, præficimus et creamus habendum, *al dit countee, et a les heires males de son corps. Et oustre per mesme les letters patents granta les castles, seigniories, honors, terres et barony de Dungarvan al dit John countee et a les heires males de son corps, les premisses destre tenus del roy et ses heires per homage et fealty, et le service destre seneschal a son majesty in le realm d'Ireland. Puis al parliament (communement appelle des absentees) tenus al Dublyn in Ireland,* 1 Maii an. 28 H. 8. *fuit enact (per reason del long absence del George countee de Salop hors de mesme le realm) que le roy, ses heirs et assignes avera et enjoyera in droit de son corone d'Angliterre touts honors, mannors, castles, seigniories, franchises, hundreds, liberties, county palatines, jurisdictions, annuities, fees des chivaler, terres, tenements, &c. et touts et singular possessions, hereditaments, et touts auters profits, cibien spirituall come temporall, quecunque queux le dit George countee de Shrewsbury, et Waterford, ou ascun auter person ou persons a son use avoient, &c. Le roy* H. 8. *per ses letters patents,* anno 29 *de son reign recitant le dit statute de absentees,* Nos præmissa considerantes et nolentes statum, honorem, et dignitatem prædicti comitis diminuere, sed amplius augere, ex certa scientia, et mero motu, &c. *granta al dit countee et ses heirs l'abby de Rufford ove les terras a ceo perteynant in le county de Nottingham, et le seigniory de Rotheram in le county de York, les abbeys de Chesterfield Shirebroke et Glossopdale in le county de Derby ove divers auters terres et tenements de grand value destre tenus in capite, et les questions fuer'.* 28 Martii anno Domini 1612.

1. *Le quel per le longe absence del countee de Salop hors de Ireland per que les roys et subjects wanted lour defence et assistance la, enconter le expresse consideration del creation, le title del honor est perdue ou forfeit, le dit countee esteant pier del ambideux realms, et residing icy.*

2. *Le quel per le dit statute des absentees,* anno 28 H. 8. *le title del dignity del countee de Waterford soit prise del dit countee de Shrewsbury cibien come les mannors, terres, tenements et auters hereditaments in mesme lact specifie,*

Et puis per auters letters des seigniours del councell, 27 *Septemb.* 1612. *les deux chief justices et chief baron fuere require a consider del dit case (que fuit enclose deins lour letters) et a certifie lour opinions de ceo.*

Quel case fuit argue per councell erudite del dit county devant les dit chief justices & chief baron, sur que ilz presteront advisement (apres que ilz ont divers foitz lye le preamble et tout le dit act de 28 H. 8.) *jesque a term de* St. Mich. anno decimo Jacobi regis, *et donques fuit unement resolve per eux come ensuist.*

Quant al primer fuit resolve, que intant que nappiert que ascun defence fuit requisite, et que le consideration executory nest trove per office destre infreint, ne judgement done in scire fac', a cest cause que le dit countee de Salop, ceo nient obstant, remain countee de Waterford.

Quant al 2 fuit resolve, que le dit act de 28 *H.* 8. *des absentees nad tolle solement les possessions, que fuer' done a luy al temps de son creation, mes auxi le dignity mesme, car coment que un poet aver dignity sauns ascuns possessions; uncore ceo serroit pleine de inconvenience, et a cest cause le dit act de* 28 *H.* 8. *(come touts auters acts doient estre) serra expound douster tout inconvenience, et pur ceo per les generall parols del act,* (sc. *des honors et hereditaments) le dignity mesme ove les terres dones pur maintenance de ceo sont done al roy, et le dignity extinct in le corone.*

Rot. parl. tent. apud Westm' 16 Jan. anno regis E. 4. 17. Degradatio Geo. ducis Bedford.

Et est digne de observation le cause de degradation de George Nevill duke de Bedford, que fuit fait per force dun act de parliament, 16 *Januarii, anno* 17 *E.* 4. *quel act* reciting the erection and making the said George duke, *expresse le cause de son degradation in ceux parols.*

And for so much as it is openly known, that the said George hath not, nor by inheritance may have any livelyhood to support the said name, estate, and dignity, or any name of estate, as oftentimes it is seen, that when any lord is called to high estate, and have not livelihood convenient to support the same dignity, it induceth great poverty and indigence, and causeth oftentimes great extortion, imbracery, and maintenance to be had, to the great trouble of all such countries where such estate shall happen to be inhabited. Wherefore the king by the advice of his lords spirituall and temporall, and the commons in this present parliament assembled, and by the authority of the same, ordaineth, establisheth and enacteth, that from henceforth the same erection and making of the same duke, and all the names of dignity to the said George or to John Nevil his father be from henceforth void and of none effect, &c.

In quel act 3 *choses fuer' observe,* 1. *Que comment le dit duke navoiet ascun possessions a supporter son dignity, uncore son dignity ne poet estre tolle de luy sans act de parliament.* 2. *Les inconveniences appiert ou grand estate ou dignity nest pas accompany ove livelihood.* 3. *Ceo est bone cause a toller le dignity per parliament, et pur ceo le dit act de* 28 *H.* 8. *serra expound selonque le generalty del letter à toller tiel inconvenience, et coment que le dit countee de Salop soit non solement de grand honor et vertue, mes auxi des grand possessions in Engliterre, uncore ne fuit lentention del act a continuer luy countee in Ireland quant ses possessions in Ireland fuer' tolle de luy, mes que le roy a son pleasure puit conferre cibien le dignity, come les possessions à ascun auter pur le defence de mesme le realm. Et les dits letters patents de anno* 29 *H.* 8. *nad parols a restorer le dignity que lact de parliament ad tolle, auxi ne fuit lentent del roy* diminuere statum, honorem et dignitatem ipsius comitis, sed augere, *ceux sont destre entendes des possessions pur maintenance de son dignity, car tant piert per cest parol* [augere] *car il increase per mesme les letters patents ove exceeding grand bounty le revenues del dit countee de Salop en Angliterre, quel le roy pense fuit un increase de son state, honor et dignity, issint son dignity in Angliterre fuit increase ove large possessions in Angliterre in lieu de tout ceo que fuit tolle de luy per lact de* 28 *H.* 8. *Et ou fuit object que les generall parols* [*des honors et hereditaments*] *sont explain et qualifie*

qualifie per les dits parols relative subsequent (queux le dit George countee de Salop ou ascun auter a sons oeps.) et pur ceo ne serra entende dascun honor ou hereditament mes dont auters poient estoier seisie al use, et ceo nul poet del dit dignity, et pur ceo le dit act extendera a ceo. Mes ceo est destre prise reddendo singula singulis, et les parols queux ledit George countee avoit sont sufficient a passer le dignity, et ove ceo accord le opinion de touts les justices Dengliterre in Nevils case, sur autiels parols in le statute 26 H. 8. in le 7 part de mes reports, fo. 33 et 34.

There is an act made in 3 H. 2. worthy here of remembrance, which never was yet printed. It is enacted, that all manner of persons whatsoever, who have any lands or tenements, offices or other living ecclesiasticall or temporall within Ireland, shall reside or dwell upon the same. And that all such as have there any castles or other forts, shall fortifie the same and furnish it with men able for defence, and thereupon also dwell. And if they at any time depart, then during their absence to appoint some able to supply his room, otherwise the governor to dispose the half of their living to such defence. See the act at large, necessary to be put in execution in these dayes.

Rot. par. 3 R. 2. nu. 42.

Dominus rex vult et præcipit quod de cætero singulis annis semel in anno compotus Hiberniæ, &c. per thesaur' Hiberniæ reddatur ad scaccarium Angliæ, et ibidem audiatur per thesaur' et barones suos. A necessary law, and much for the benefit of the king to be observed.

Rot. par. 21 E. 1. Rot. 3. Hibernia.

A long record touching the custody of the body and lands of heirs within age, wherein these words are contained. *Et cum una et eadem lex esse debeat tam in regno Angliæ quam Hiberniæ.* Like writs of error of judgements given in the kings bench in Ireland, Mich. 32 E. 1. coram rege. Theobald Verdons case, *Breve de errore super bre. de errore rot.* 76. *Pasch.* 30 E. 1. *coram rege rot.* 50. *in breve de errore &c.* William de la Rivers case, et Tr. 33 E. 1. rot. 56. [a] *Concordatum est per omnes de concilio regis, episcopis et aliis in Hibernia unanimiter quod consuetudo usitata in Hibernia de bonis testatorum talis est, quod ubi, &c.*

[b] *Prisage vinorum in Hibernia*, and the manner of the taking of the same.

At a synod holden in Ireland by St. Patrick their apostle, it was unanimously agreed that Irish priests should have wives.

[c] *Tres petitiones porrectæ regi contra Eliam de Ashburnham militem justiciar' domini regis in Hibernia de diversis malefactis, &c. per ipsum perpetratis, qui dicit quod non debet tractari, nisi in Hibernia, et ibidem terminari: et quod oportet ipsum dominum regem informari per indictamentum 12 jur' vel per appellum formatum et attachiament' ad sectam partis secundum legem et consuetudinem regni regis Angliæ hactenus usitat'. Curia vult inde advisari, et interim manucapitur. Postea dominus rex mandavit breve quod caperent manucapt' ad respondendum in Hibernia.*

[d] *Admittitur episcopus Exon' pro fine 200 marc' pro contemptu in non admittendo præsentatum regis ad ecclesiam de Southwell, pro quo contemptu omnia temporalia seisita fuerunt in manus regis, et tunc temporis ante finem fact' vacavit archidiaconat' Cornubiæ ratione quod incumbens electus fuit in* [e] *archiepiscopum Dublin in Hibernia (temporalibus episcopi Exon' ad tunc in manibus regis existen') per quod dominus rex recuperavit vers. episcopum dict' archidiaconat'.*

Trin. 13 E. 1. coram rege rot. 38. in breve de errore Hibernia. Apud Westm'. 22 E. 1. rot. 5. in breve de errore int' Wiliam de Vesey & P. filium Thomæ, & rot. parl. 23 E. 1. 5 E. 2. error 89. 15 E. 3. ibid. 72. 34 Ass. p. 7. reg. F.N.B. fo. 24. c. 11 H. 8. Kelw. 202. 15 E. 3. Record 38. [a] Pasch. 28 E. 1. coram rege rot. 98. Hibernia. [b] Tr. 33 E. 1. coram rege rot. 124. Hibernia. [c] Tr. 18 E. 3. coram rege rot. 148. Hibernia. Sir Elias Ashburnhams case. [d] Pasch. 24 E. 3 rot. 25. coram rege. Cornubia. [e] Bract. li. 5. f. 195. 7 E. 3. 9. 12 E. 3. 41, 47.

In this record two conclusions are to be observed. 1. Though Ireland (as hath been said) be a distinct kingdome of it self, yet it is governed by one and the same law that England is. 2. That when the archdeacon was by the king preferred to a bishoprick, he [357] had the presentation to the archdeaconry in respect of the temporalties of the bishop of Exeter patron of the archdeaconry, and not by any [a] prerogative. And so it is, if an incumbent in Ireland be made a bishop in England.

If a bishop in England be made a [b] cardinall, the bishoprick becomes void, and the king shall name the successor, because the bishopricke is of his patronage.

[c] See 45 E. 3. 9. upon the repeale of a ratification of the incumbent, a *procedendo* out of the chancery here to the justices in Ireland to proceed in the *quare impedit* brought by the king.

I finde an ancient record touching Ireland necessary to be explained in these words.

[d] *Rex thesaurario Hiberniæ, salutem. Cum Edwardus primogenitus noster terram Hiberniæ habeat et teneat de dono nostro cum omnibus pertinentiis suis adeo liberè et quietè sicut eam in manu nostra teneremus, per quod charissima filia nostra Alianora consors dicti filii nostri aurum suum tam de finibus quam sponte oblatis in terra Hiberniæ habere debet, sicut charissima consors nostra Alianora regina Angliæ aurum suum habet de eisdem in regno nostro Angliæ: Vobis mandamus, &c. quatenus præfatæ consorti filii nostri prædicti aurum prædictum de finibus et sponte oblatis, et etiam de quibuscunque aliis finibus prædictis habere facias in forma prædicta. Et hoc, &c. In cujus, &c. Teste rege 29 die Februarii, anno 52 H. 3.*

[a] This is apparent by many authorities. Trin. 32 E. 1. coram rege, rot. 75. John de Bonhams case. 17 E. 3. fo. 40. 21 E. 3. 40. 41 E. 3. 5. 46 E. 3. 32. 6 Eliz. Dier 228. b. pl. 48. resolve.

[b] Rot. pat. 18 H. 6. part 2. m. 24. A bishop made a cardinal.

[c] 45 E. 3. fol. 9.

[d] Rot. pat. anno 52 H. 3. m. 26. Aurum reginæ.

By this record first it appeareth, that, as the law was taken at that day, by gift of king H. 3. his eldest sonne prince Edward was lord of the dominion and lordship of Ireland. Secondly, that albeit the wife of prince Edward was not queen in name, but had the effect of it, therefore she should have a duty called *aurum reginæ*, as well as the queene of England, being but lady in Ireland. [e] For albeit the kings of Ireland were (until the statute of 33 H. 8.) stiled by the name of lord of Ireland, yet was he *supremus*, and *absolutè dominus*, and had royall dominion and authority, and that his consort was *in rei veritate regina*, or else she could not have had *aurum reginæ*.

The like grant was made of the land of Ireland by H. 2. to his son John.

[e] 33 H. 8. cap. 1. And so it appeareth by this act that the king and his progenitors had before this act kingly jurisdiction and royall authority.

[f] Albeit this royall dominion and land of Ireland was of ancient time permitted to be granted *de facto* to the kings sonnes before mentioned, yet by the law the king by his letters patents could not grant so royall a member of his imperiall stile to any, no more then he could doe of the kingdome of England. And that doth well appeare by this, that when king R. 2. by his letters patents created Robert de Vere earle of Lincolne, and marquesse of Dublin to be duke of Ireland, he granted to him for life * *totam terram et dominium Hiberniæ, et insulas eidem terræ adjacentes, ac omnia castra, comitatus, burgos, villas,* * *portus maris, &c. una cum homagiis,* * *obedientiis, vassalis, serviciis, et recognitionibus prælatorum, comitum, baronum, &c.* * *advocationibus et patronatibus ecclesiarum metropoliticarum et cathedralium abbatiarum, &c.* * *constituere cancellar,' thesaurar,' justiciar', &c. cum regaliis, regalitatibus, libertatibus, &c. et omnibus aliis* * *quæ ad regaliam nostram pertinent',* * *cum mero et mixto imperio, adeo plenè, integrè, et perfectè, sicut nos ea tenuimus et habuimus, tenuerunt et habuerunt* progenitorum

[f] See before pag. 12, 14. the grant of king John to the pope declared to be void by the parliament in 40 E. 3.

These thus (*) marked cannot be granted by letters patents.

*progenitorum nostrorum aliqui ullis unquam temporibus retroactis. Tenendum per * homagium ligeum tantum.*

* Per hom. ligeum for tenant for life could not do other homage.

g The said letters patents were authorized by parliament, *assensu prælatorum, ducum, et aliorum procerum, et communitatis nostræ Angliæ in parliamento, &c.* albeit it was *contra legem et consuetudinem parliamenti*, as before it appeareth, pa. 13, 14. to assent to any thing to the disherison of the king and his crown. *Sed novus iste insolitus et umbratilis honor cito evanuit.*

g Rot. pat. 9 R. 2. m. 2. & rot. par. 9 R. 2. nu. 9. & 10 m. 3.

Rot. par 13 R. 2. nu. 21. the king by authority of parliament gave the title of duke of Aquitaine to his uncle John of Gaunt, duke of Lancaster, and it was by consent of parliament, and could not be granted by letters patents, because it was one of the titles and stiles of his royall crowne. And this also did first begin and end in him. [358]

Aurum reginæ.

But now it is necessary to be knowne what this duty of *aurum reginæ* is. Wherein three things are to be considered. First, what authority and warrant in law there is for this duty. Secondly, what it is. Thirdly, what is due thereby. First, in Lib. Rub. in scaccario fo. 46. *de auro reginæ*, where it is said, that it is to be taken *de hiis qui sponte se obligant regi, &c.* This present record of 52 H. 3. Vet. Mag. Carta 2. part. fo. 65. vid. 10 H. 3. stat. de Roteland to the same effect.

A record in the exchequer *termino Hil. anno* 4 E. 1. Another there, Hil. 12 E. 3. rot. 3. *ex parte rem. regis*, and divers other records in the reignes of R. 2. H. 4. &c. untill the reigne of H. 7.

Hil. 4. E. 1. in scac. ex parte rem. reg. Hil. 12 E. 3. ibid. rot. 3.

In acts of parliament, viz. 15 E. 3. cap. 6. 31 E. 3. cap. 13.

Rot. clauf. 12 E. 3. part. 1. m. 21.

2. In divers of these records it appeareth that the queen should have *de sponte oblatis * pro centum marcis argenti unam marcam auri solvend' per ipsum qui sponte se obligat.* And Pasch. 4. *Jacobi regis* the king did require the two chiefe justices and chiefe baron to certifie him what belonged to the queene for this duty at this day. And after many conferences, and hearing of counsell learned on both sides and view of records, at last it was resolved by them all, and so did Popham chiefe justice report to the king, that the duty belonged to the queene with these four limitations. 1. It must be *sponte*, from the subject, and at his pleasure whether he will give it or no, and no right in the crowne. And therefore fines for offences, for alienations, or the like, are no part of this duty. 2. It must be freely, without any consideration of any grant, sale, or lease of any thing wherein the king hath any revenue, estate, or interest. And therefore sales, leases, grants of lands, tenements, wardships, or the like, are out of the same, for there is *quid pro quo*. 3. It must be *sponte super aliqua consideratione, &c.* For example if the subject *sponte* offer to the king for a licence in mortmaine, or to create a tenure of himselfe, or to have a faire, market, or to make a parke, or the like, where the king diminisheth no part of his revenue, state, or interest, there *aurum reginæ* is due to the queene. 4. Of subsidies, fifteens, or any other gratuity of the meere grace or benevolence of the subject, there is nothing due to the queene, and so it was resolved, Hil. 4 E. 1. &c. *ubi supra*. And so much upon this occasion *de auro reginæ*.

Rot. parl. 7 R. 2. nu. 61.

Certaine Irish words necessary to be explained.

a A Tainist was successor apparent under the chiefe lord or captaine of every severall country, and was eligible by the country.

a Thane apud Britannos pro viro nobili, at regis mini

[b] Brehons. Bellagines.

[b] *Brehon.* The Iriſh called their judges *brehons*, and thereupon the Iriſh law is called the brehon law.

[c] Parliament 40 E. 3. at Kilkenny.

[c] At a parliament holden in Ireland by Howel duke of Clarence, lieutenant there, *anno* 40 E. 3. at Kilkenny, and therefore called the ſtatute of Kilkenny, the brehon law is no law, but a lewd cuſtome crept in of latter times, and never was the law of the ancient Britaines from whom they are deſcended.

[d] Cuttings.

[d] *Cuttings.* Under that name they comprehend tallages and impoſitions.

[e] Coſheries.

[e] *Coſheries* are prehendinations, when the chief lord and his retinue, &c. came to his tenants houſe, and fed upon their proviſions till all were ſpent.

Termondland. *Termondlands* are the glebe of the church.

Erick. *Erick* ſignifieth a fine for an offence.

Galloglaſſes. *Galloglaſſes, equites triarii qui ſecuribus utuntur acutiſſimis.*

Kernes. *Kernes ſunt pedites qui jaculis utuntur.*

The *prorex* there in former times hath beene called *cuſtos*, warden, lieutenant, chiefe juſtice, deputy of Ireland.

Theſe expoſitions we have added for the better inſtruction of him who will reade the Iriſh lawes.

[359]

Rot. pat. 9 Johannis regis Johanni mareſcallo, of whom the lord Morly is deſcended.

Rex, &c. Johanni mareſcallo dedimus et conceſſimus pro homagio et ſervicio ſuo mareſcalſiam noſtram totius Hiberniæ cum omnibus pertinentiis, &c. Habendum ſibi et hæredibus ſuis de nobis et hæredibus noſtris.

Regiſt. 294.

See the Regiſter, that if an archbiſhoprick or biſhoprick in Ireland be void, that the chapter ſhall ſue to the king in England to goe to election, and after election made they ought upon certificate thereof made to the king to obtaine his royall aſſent to this election, and thereupon a writ ſhall be directed out of the chancery here, to the chiefe juſtice of Ireland, or his lieutenant rehearſing all this matter, and commanding him to take fealty of the biſhop, and to reſtore him to his temporalties. But now the courſe is in Ireland to make ſuch writs there in the name of the king. But the king names the archbiſhops and biſhops there, as he doth in England; and then the chapter chooſe him whom the king names to them, and thereupon the writs are made of courſe.

F. N. B. 169. 170.

And the reaſon of this change is worthy to be knowne: for the charter of king John for election of biſhops, &c. extended only to the biſhops, &c. of England. [a] But after that the whole dominion of Ireland (as well concerning the church as the commonwealth) was eſtabliſhed to be governed by one law with the kingdome of England, as is aboveſaid, then the courſe of the Regiſter was changed, and the ſame courſe taken there, as it is in England.

[a] Carta Johannis regis 15 Jan. apud novum London ann. 18. Biſhops before were donative by the king. 10 E. 3. 1 b. per Perning. 17 E. 3. 40. per Stone &c.

And whereas heretofore ſome, not without ſcandall, have divided this kingdome into the Engliſh pale, and the wilde Iriſh, [b] let oblivion bury it, or ſilence cover it, for now all are reduced to obedience and civill behaviour. So as a man may juſtly ſay of them as of the old Britaines, *Sunt in bello fortes, et in pace fideles.* And for that ſome have given out that the crowne of England had this country of Ireland of the donation of the pope, we will ingenouſly manifeſt the truth therein by the records and writings themſelves at large.

[b] Auferat oblivio, ſi poteſt, ſi non, utcunque ſilentium tegat.

The charter of king Edgar made ann. Dom. 964. and in the 6. of his reigne.

Altitonantis Dei largiflua clementia, qui eſt rex regum, et dominus dominantium, ego Edgarus Anglorum baſileus, omniúmque rerum inſularum oceani quæ Britanniam circumjacent, cunctarúmque nationum quæ infra

infra eam includuntur imperator et dominus, gratias ago ipsi Deo omnipotenti regi meo, qui meum imperium sic ampliavit et exaltavit super regnum patrum meorum. Qui licet monarchiam totius Angliæ adepti sunt à tempore Athelstani, qui primus regum Anglorum omnes nationes quæ Britanniam incolunt sibi armis subegit, nullus tamen eorum ultra fines imperium suum dilatare aggressus est. Mihi tamen concessit propitia divinitas cum Anglorum imperio omnia regna insularum oceani cum suis ferocissimis regibus usque Norvegiam maximâmque partem Hiberniæ, cum sua nobilissima civitate de Dublina Anglorum regno subjugare, quos etiam omnes meis imperiis colla subdere, Dei favente gratia, coegi. Quapropter et ego Christi gloriam et laudem in regno meo exaltare, et ejus servitium amplificare devotus disposui. Et per meos fideles fautores, Dunstanum, viz. archiepiscopum Ayelyolanum ac Oswaldum archiepiscopos, quos mihi patres spirituales et consiliatores elegi, magna ex parte disposui, &c. Facta sunt hæc anno domini 964. *indictione* 8 *regni vero Edgari Anglorum regis* 6. *in regia urbe quæ ab incolis Ocleayeceastriæ nominatur in natale Domini festivitate sanctorum innocentium feria* 4. *&c.* ✠ *Ego Edgar basileus Anglorum, et imperator regum gentium, cum consensu et principum et archiepiscoporum meorum hanc meam manuficentiam signo meo corroboravi.* ✠ *Ego Alfrye regina consensi et signo crucis confirmavi. Ego Dunstan archiepiscopus Dorobor' ecclesiæ Christi consensi et subscripsi* ✠ *Ego Osticel archiepiscopus Eboracensis ecclesiæ consensi et subscripsi. Ego Alferic dux. Ego Buthnod dux. Ego Aridgari dux* ✠

King Athelstane reduced England to a monarchy.

King Edgar conquered the greatest part of Ireland, with the most noble city of Dublin. Note the piety of this king.

Int. leges Edw. regis & confessoris fo. 137. b. Lamb.

Arthurus qui quondam fuit inclytissimus rex Britannorum, &c. subjugavit sibi strenue (inter alia) Hiberniam, &c.

[360]

And what ecclesiasticall jurisdiction the archbishop of Canterbury had in Ireland of ancient time before it was subject to the crown of England, you may read in Cambdens Britannia, pag. 735. & 765. as namely in the consecration and confirmation of their bishops, by reason of his primacy in Ireland.

A justice in Ireland constituted by letters patents under the great seale of England, cannot be removed from his office but by the king only.

Mich. 5 E. 3. coram rege rot. 43. Hibernia.

Of the Pentarchy of Ireland.

South. The kingdom of Mononia had 7 counties, viz.
- Kerry.
- Desmond.
- Corke.
- Waterford.
- Limricke.
- Tipperay,
- with the county of S[t] Crosses Tipperay.

East. Lagenia 7. viz.
- Kilkenny.
- Caterlough.
- Queenes County
- Kings County.
- Kildare.
- Washford.
- Dublyn.

The middest. Media 3.
- East Meth.
- West Meth.
- Longford.

West. Conacha had 6. counties, viz.
- Towmond.
- Galloway.
- Mino.
- Slego.
- Le Trim.
- Rostaman.

North. Ultonia had 10, viz.
- Louth.
- Cad
- Monaghaia.
- Domagh.
- Doun.
- Antrim.
- Colran.
- Tiroen.
- Tirconel, or Doneal.

Ireland

Ireland hath 33 counties, besides cities, that are counties of themselves.

King H. 2. at a parliament holden at Oxford, *anno regni sui* 23. created his sonne John king of Ireland. But the succeeding kings wrote themselves *domini Hiberniæ*, untill the 33 year of H. 8. in which yeare he took upon him the name of king of Ireland.

Rot. parl. 3 R. 2. nu. 43. in England.
Mines of gold and silver.
Bract. li. 2. fo. 222.
Fleta lib. 4. fo. 119. Pl. Com. in the case of mines.
Coynage at Dublin.
* Rot. pat. 5 H. 6. 1. part.

It was enacted by authority of parliament, that every man during six years might dig in his own proper soyle in Ireland gold or silver, &c. yeelding to the king the ninth part thereof, and that they make plate or coyne thereof at the kings coynage in Dublin, paying the fees: and that none carry thereout any of the said gold, silver, or bullion, but into England, without the kings licence, on paine to lose the same.

* A grant of all mines of gold and silver within England, &c. to the duke of Bedford, regent of France, &c. rendring to the church the tenth part: to the king the fifteenth part; to the owner of the soyle the twentieth part.

[361]

Camden in Hibernia.

To conclude with somewhat which tends to the honour of that noble nation. Certain it is, that whiles the liberall sciences in Europe lay in a manner buried in darknesse, then did their lustre shine forth most clearly here in Ireland; thither did our English Saxons repayre, as to a fayre or market of good letters: whence of the holy men of those times we often reade in ancient writers, *Amandatus est ad disciplinam in Hiberniam:* he was sent into Ireland to study there.

He that is desirous to read more records concerning this kingdome of Ireland, he may read these coram rege in the kings bench. Trin. 13 E. 1. rot. 36. 38. Hibernia. Mich. 17 E. 1. rot. 31. 38. Hibernia. Hil. 19 E. 1. rot. 68. Hibernia. Pasch. 19 E. 1. rot. 69. Hibernia. Trin. 20 E. 1. rot. 40. Pasch. 34 E. 1. rot. 104. Mich. 5 E. 3. rot. 40. & 46. Mich. 6 E. 3. rot. 55. Hibernia.

Of the Precedency of the Great Officers, Nobility, and others of this Realme.

For of the precedency of the king himself and of other kings, and supreme princes, I take not upon me to write, but referre you to learned Camden, *Lib. Annal. anno Domini* 1600. 42 Eliz. pag.

Præcedere est præeundo incedere. Qui præcellit, præcedere debet.
Most ancient is most honourable.
Aristot. 1 Metaph. cap. 3.
31 H. 8. cap. 10. in the preamble.
ed to R. Earl of

At the common law, the king by his prerogative royall might give such honour reputation, and placing to his counsellors and other his subjects, as should be seeming to his wisdome, which prerogative was so declared by act of parliament.

[a] By this prerogative, *Henrico Beauchamp concessit rex Henricus sextus, ut primus et præcipuus esset Angliæ comes, et hoc titulo uteretur; Henricus præcomes totius Angliæ et comes Warwici, Vectæ insulæ regulum dixit; posteaque ducem Warwici creavit, et concessit, ut haberet*

[a] Rot. pat. 23 H. 6. Vid. Rot. pat. 28 H. 6. 2 parte m. 23. Precedency granted to R. Earl of Warwick.

sedem

ſedem in parliamentis, et alibi proximam duci Norf. et ante ducem Buckinghamiæ.

The ſame king created Edmond of Hadham to be earl of Richmond, and granted him precedency before all other earls. He alſo created Jaſper of Hatfield earl of Pembroke, and gave him precedency before all other earls next to his brother the ſaid Edmond earl of Richmond. But hereof theſe examples ſhall ſuffice.

King H. 8. though ſtanding as much upon his prerogative as any of his progenitors, yet finding how vexatious it was to himſelf, and how diſtaſtfull to his ancient nobility to have new raiſed degrees to have precedency of them, and finding that this kind of controverſy for precedency was of that nature, that it had many partakers, ſpent long time, and hindred the arduous, urgent, and weighty affairs of the parliament, was content to bind and limit his prerogative by act of parliament concerning the precedency of his great officers, and of his nobility. And firſt for the lords ſpirituall (who ſit in parliament on the kings right hand) amongſt themſelves. 31 H. 8. cap. 10.

1. The archbiſhop of Canterbury. 2. The archbiſhop of York on the ſame form. 3. The biſhop of London. 4. The biſhop of Dureſme. 5. The biſhop of Wincheſter, and then all the other biſhops of both provinces ſhall ſit and be placed after their ancienties, as before this act was accuſtomed. But having regard to the lords and noble peers of the realm, both the archbiſhops have place above all the great officers and nobility in parliament, councell and commiſſions, ſaving in the ſtar-chamber, the lord chancelor or lord keeper hath the precedency of them. But the other biſhops have place above all the barons of the realm, becauſe they hold their biſhopricks of the king *per baroniam*, but they give place to viſcounts, earls, marqueſſes and dukes.

Concerning the great officers of the realm. 1. The lord chancelor or lord keeper of the great ſeal. 2. The lord treaſurer. 3. The lord preſident of the kings councell. 4. The lord privy ſeal, being of the degree of barons of parliament, or above, ſhall ſit and be placed in parliament on the higher part of the form above all dukes, except only ſuch as ſhall happen to be the kings ſon, the kings brother, the * kings nephew, or the kings brothers or ſiſter ſons. See an act made in 28 H. 8. cap. 18. making it treaſon for marrying, &c. with any of the blood royall within certain degrees: but it is repealed. 5. The great chamberlain of England. 6. The conſtable. 7. The marſhall. 8. The lord admirall. 9. The lord ſteward of the kings houſe. 10. The kings chamberlain ſhall ſit and be placed after the lord privy ſeal in manner and form following, viz. every of them ſhall ſit and be placed above all other perſonages being of the ſame ſtate and degree: as if he be a baron, above all barons: if a viſcount, above all viſcounts: if an earl above all earls, &c. 11. The kings principall ſecretary being a baron of the parliament ſhall ſit above all barons not having any of the offices aforeſaid. But if he be a viſcount, an earl, or any other higher degree, he ſhall not take the place of any viſcount, earl, or higher degree, as it was reſolved in the caſe of Robert Cecil, earl of Saliſbury. And if the ſecretary be a biſhop, he ſhall take the place of all other biſhops not having any of the offices aforeſaid, but not above the archbiſhops.

[362]

Nota, the Lord Steward of England is not here mentioned, becauſe it was intended that when the uſe of him ſhould be neceſſary, he ſhould not endure longer then *hac vice*.

* *i.* the kings granchilde.

Note the degrees within that act.

The general clause.

All other dukes not before mentioned, marquisses, earls, viscounts and barons, not having any of the offices aforesaid, shall all sit and be placed after their ancientie, as hath been accustomed.

All other dukes, &c. If the king should create a duke to the estate of archduke, yet by force of these words he shall not take place of any duke that was his ancient, *et sic de similibus;* otherwise this statute might be made of no force; and an archduke is some other duke.

If any person being lord chancelor, lord keeper, lord treasurer, lord president, lord privy seal, or chief secretary, shall be under the degree of a baron of parliament, they shall in parliaments sit in the uppermost part of the sacks in the middest of the parliament chamber, &c. But in the starchamber, and all other assemblies and conferences of councell, they shall sit and be placed as is above rehearsed; and in * no other place. Lastly, the lord chancelor, lord keeper, lord treasurer, lord president, lord privy seal, being lords of parliament: the great chamberlain, the constable, the marshall, the lord admirall, the lord steward, the kings chamberlain, and the kings chief secretary shall sit and be placed in such order and fashion as is above rehearsed, and not in any other place, by authority of this parliament. Vid. statut. de 10 R. 2. cap. 1.

* The words negative were added to avoid all scruple that the order for precedency set down in this parliament should not be altered by any *non obstante.*

[a] He that is desirous to understand the true rules of precedency of the nobles of this realm in the high court of parliament, &c. let him reade the great case between John earl Marshall and Richard earl of Warwick, in parliament, and the affirmations, answers, and replications on both parts exceeding long, but full of notable rules, reasons, and presidents concerning precedency, both in respect of the blood-royall, and otherwise: together with the lines and pedegrees, seats, and places of many noblemen very delightfull to be read.

[b] Another between William earl of Arundel, and Thomas earl of Devon: wherein you shall reade notable matter concerning the castle and honour of Arundel, precedently adjudged by the lords in parliament in the reigne of H. 4. between the earl of Arundel and the earl of Kent.

[c] If a bishop of this realm be made a cardinall, he shall not take any place of precedency in parliament as cardinall, but take his place in right of his bishoprick, which he holdeth of the king *per baroniam*, in respect whereof he sitteth in parliament.

[d] If a duke or earl, &c. be made protector of the realm in parliament, he shall have no other place but as a duke or earl, &c. Hereby you may perceive how necessary it was to set down by authority of parliament in certainty the place and precedency that great officers should have in parliament, who sit not there in right of their offices, but of their nobility: and the names of dignities of the nobility are parcell of their names, and so ought to be named in the kings writs: but the offices of chancelor, treasurer, and other offices are not parcell of their names, and therefore in the kings writs need not to be so named.

[a] Rot. parl. anno 3 H. 6. in principio, et nu. 10.

[b] Ro. par. 27 H. 6. nu. 18. Vide rot. parl. 11 H. 6. m. 9. nu. 32, 33, 34, 35. between the earl of Arundell and Mowbrey earl of Norf. Rot. par. 3 H. 6 in principio cited in the earl Marshals case.

[c] Hol. Chron. pa. 620. 10. Hall 143. &c. anno 20 H. 6.

[d] Rot. par. 6 H 6. nu. 22, 23, 24.

[363]

[a] 7 H. 6. fo. 15. Vid. rot. parl. 15 E. 3. nu. 7.

It is also enacted by authority of the said act of 31 H. 8. that in all trials of [b] treasons by the peers of this realm, the said great officers of this land shall sit and be placed according to their offices, above all other the peers, as is aforesaid.

[b] This is put for an example, for it extendeth to all trials by peeres, not only in case of treason, but in case of felony, misprision of treason and felony, and so ever since this statute hath it been put in use.

We have perused the list of the names of the lords of parliament ſitting in parliament both of ancient and later time, wherein we can gather no certainty for precedency.

Thus far for avoiding of contention about precedency in parliaments, ſtar-chamber, and all other aſſemblies and conferences of councell, and upon trials by the peers of the realm was neceſſary.

Now he that deſireth to know the places and precedency of the nobility and ſubjects of the realm, as well men as women, and of their children: we for avoiding of tedioufneſſe will refer them to a record of great authority in the reign of H. 7. (for we will not vouch [c] Barth. Caſſaneus or any other foreign author) [d] intituled *Series ordinum omnium procerum, magnatum, et nobilium, et aliorum quorumcunque infra hoc regnum tam virorum quam fœminarum, poſita et diſtincta per nobiliſſimum Jaſparum ducem Bedford et alios nobiles ap. punctuatione domini regis Henrici ſeptimi*: (but this record dealeth not with the places of any of the great officers) [e] whereunto we will refer you: wherein you ſhall ſee what places both the ſons, * wives, and daughters, of lords of parliament, as dukes, marqueſſes, earls, viſcounts, and barons ſhall have, and of banerets, knights, eſquires, and gentlemen, and of their wives and children ſhall have.

[f] If any queſtion be moved in parliament for priviledge or precedency of any lord of parliament, it is to be decided by the lords of parliament in the houſe of the lords, as all priviledges, and other matter concerning the lords houſe of parliament are, as priviledges and other matters concerning the houſe of commons are by the houſe of commons to be decided.

The determination of the places and precedencies of others doth belong to the court of the conſtable and marſhall, unleſſe any queſtion riſeth upon the ſaid act of parliament of 31 H. 8. for that being part of the law of the realme (as all other ſtatutes be) is to be decided by judges of the common law.

[g] *Nobilis eſt qui generis ſui imagines proferre poteſt.* [h] *Flavia gens obſcura quidem et ſine imaginibus.*

Tota licet veteres exornent [i] *undique ceræ*
Atria, nobilitas ſola eſt atque unica virtus.

Major eſt nobilitas quam virtus: virtus enim ſine nobilitate eſſe poteſt, nobilitas autem ſine virtute eſſe non poteſt.

[k] *Arma ſeu inſignia gentilitia ex antiquo habuerunt loco imaginum.* So as now the beſt diſcuſſing of antiquity of gentry is *per inſignia.*

——*Armáque fixit*
Troia.—— *Virgill.*

And by the lawes of England as all the degrees of nobility and honour were derived from the king as the fountaine of honour: * ſo all the lands in England † were originally derived from the crowne of England, and are holden of the ſame mediately or immediately. See before in the chapter of the High Court of parliament.

As names make knowne ſingular perſons, ſo armes diſtinguiſh ſeverall families.

It is worthy of remembrance, and fit for example, that when Thomas Lord Cromwel by a flattering herald was offered in the time of king H. 8. to fetch his pedigree from the ancient lord Cromwel, that he might beare his coat, he anſwered that he would weare

[c] Bart. Caſſanæus in catalogo gloriæ mundi.

[d] Series ordinum tempore H. 7.

[e] Vid. Camden Eliz. pa. 475.

* Which we have added the rather, for that the contention about precedency between perſons of that ſex is ever fiery, furious, and ſometime fatall. Vid. the parliam. rolls ubi ſupra.

[f] Vid. rot. parl. 31 H. 6. nu. 27. See 3 H 6. nu. 10. betweene Mowbray earl of Norf. and Beauchamp earle of Warwick.

[g] Cicero. Plin. lib. 39. apud majores, &c. optime.

[h] Tranquillus in Veſp.

[i] Juvenal. i Cereæ imagines.

[k] Cotte de armes, a coat armour, that is, a long coat over armour with his armes embroidered upon it.

* See the 1 part of the Inſtitutes, ſect. 1. &c. and in that firſt part in divers places many things concerning nobility and their creations, and of the gaining and loſing thereof, &c. viz. ſect. 9. fo. 17. a.b. ſect. 1. fo. 9. b. ſect. 95. fo. 69. a. b. ſect. 112. f. 83. b. ſect. 241. fo. 165. a. ſect. 14, 15. fo. 20. a. ſect. 137. fo. 97. a. ſect. 201. f. 134. a. ſect. 648 fo. 344. a. &c.

† [364]

weare a coat of his own, lest another mans coat might be taken from him: unto whom the king as advanced by him gave this coat, quarterly indented *per fesse*, or and azure, four lions counterchanged: where the old lord Cromwels coat was argent, a chiefe gules, a bend azure. The said act of 31 H. 8. extendeth not to archbishops and bishops, therefore it is necessary to speak somewhat of them also. In ancient time they had great precedency, even before the brother of the king, as it appeareth by the parliament roll of 18 E. 1. and many others, which continued untill it was altered by ordinance in parliament in the reign of king H. 6. as it appeareth by a roll of parliament of that kings reign, entred in the back of the parliament roll. The precedency in parliament, and other places of councell at this day (whereunto we ayme) is, the two archbishops have the precedency of all the lords temporall; and every other bishop in respect of his barony have place of all the barons of the realm, and under the estate of the viscount and other superior dignities. The bishops between themselves have this precedency. First, the bishop of London, and after him the bishop of Duresme, and then the bishop of Winchester, and after him every bishop as he is in seigniority. But to this day, in all acts, ordinances, and judgments, &c. of parliament it is said, the lords spirituall and temporall.

Rot. pat. 9 Jacobi 8. part. 1. nu. 45. Baronets and others.

The first creation of baronets was in *anno* 9 *Jacobi regis*: what place and precedency these baronets and divers others shall hold, you may reade rot. pat. 10 *Jacobi regis* part 10. m. 8. and rot. pat. *anno* 14 *Jacobi regis* part 2. m. 24.

To conclude this chapter with the code of Theodosius, &c. *Ut dignitatum ordo servetur, si quis indebitum sibi locum usurpaverit, nulla se ignoratione defendat, sitque plane sacrilegii reus.*

The EPILOGUE.

THUS have we by the great goodneſſe of the Almighty brought this painfull Work, conſiſting of ſuch, and ſo many varieties and difficulties, concerning the juriſdiction of ſuch, and ſo many diſtinct courts (above the number of 100) to a concluſion: and in ſome few caſes, where we have differed from others in opinion, we have ſhewed the cauſe and beginning of theſe errors (as we take them:) for it is a ſure rule, *Quòd errores ad ſua principia referre, eſt refellere*, to bring errors to their firſt, is to ſee their laſt. Wherein we have ſtrengthened our opinion with our two great guides, authority and reaſon, and not truſted abridgements, polyanthea's, or taken any thing upon truſt, but have ſearched the fountaines themſelves, alway holding this rule, *Quòd ſatius eſt petere fontes, quàm ſectari rivulos:* and our deſired end is, that all theſe high and honourable tribunals, and other ſubordinate courts and venerable ſeats of juſtice may proſper and flouriſh in diſtribution of juſtice, which aſſuredly they ſhall doe, if they derive all their power and ſtrength from their proper roots.

Whileſt we were in hand with theſe foure parts of the Inſtitutes, we often having occaſion to go into the city, and from thence into the country, did in ſome ſort envy the ſtate of the honeſt plowman, and other mechanics; for the one when he was at his work would merrily ſing, and the plowman whiſtle ſome ſelf-pleaſing tune, and yet their work both proceeded and ſucceeded: but he that takes upon him to write, doth captivate all the faculties and powers both of his minde and body, and muſt be only intentive to that which he collecteth, without any expreſſion of joy or cheerfulneſſe, whileſt he is in his work.

Throughout all this treatiſe we have dealt cleerly and plainly concerning ſome pretended courts, which either are no courts warrantable by law, as we conceive them, or which without warrant have incroached more juriſdiction then they ought. *Qui non liberè veritatem pronuntiat, proditor veritatis eſt.* Wherein if any of our honourable friends ſhall take offence, our apology ſhall be, *Amicus Plato, amicus Socrates, ſed magis amica Veritas.* Having ever in memory that ſaying of the kingly prophet, *Keepe innocency and take* Pſal. 37. 38. *heed to the thing that is right, and that will bring a man peace at the laſt.*

And you honourable and reverend judges and juſtices, that do or ſhall ſit in the high tribunals and courts or ſeats of juſtice, as aforeſaid, fear not to do right to all, and to deliver your opinions juſtly according to the laws: for feare is nothing but a betraying of the ſuccours that reaſon ſhould afford. And if you ſhall ſincerely execute juſtice, be aſſured of three things: firſt, though ſome may maligne

Lib. Sap. cap. 17. 12. Nihil eſt timor niſi proditio cogitationis auxiliorum.

ſigne you, yet God will give you his bleſſing. Secondly, that though thereby you may offend great men and favourites, yet you ſhall have the favourable kindneſſe of the Almighty, and be his favourites. And laſtly, that in ſo doing, againſt all ſcandalous complaints and pragmaticall devices againſt you, God will defend you as with a ſhield: * *For thou Lord wilt give a bleſſing unto the righteous, and with thy favourable kindneſſe wilt thou defend him, as with a ſhield.*

* Pſal. 5. 13.

And for that we have broken the ice, and out of our owne induſtry and obſervation framed this high and honourable building of the juriſdiction of courts, without the help or furtherance of any that hath written of this argument before, I ſhall heartily deſire the wiſe hearted and expert builders (juſtice being *architectonica virtus*) to amend both the method or uniformity, and the ſtructure it ſelfe, wherein they ſhall finde either want of windowes, or ſufficient lights, or other deficiency in the architecture whatſoever. And we will conclude with the aphoriſme of that great lawyer and ſage of the law (which we have heard him often ſay) *Bleſſed be the amending hand.*

Ariſtotle.

Edm. Plowden.

Deo gloria et gratia.

F I N I S.

A TABLE

A
TABLE

TO THE

Fourth Part of the Institutes of the Laws of England, concerning the Jurisdiction of Courts.

Agiſtator.

Alien.

Alienation.

Alnage Alnager.

Amercements.

The Office, Authority and Privilege of Ambaſſadours.

Appeals.

He

Of the County Palatine of Chefter.

Chimagium. 306

The honourable Court of Chivalry before the Conftable and Marfhall.

Of the Court of the Cinque Ports.

Claim.

Clerk of the Market. *See* Market.

Commiffion.

Commissions for Examination of Witnesses.

Committees.

Common.

Common-pleas.

Concealers.

Condition.

Safe Conduct. *See* Leagues.

Confession.

Constable.

The Lord Constable of England. *See* Chivalry.

Consultation.

Conusans.

Conviction.

Copy.

Coroners.

The Council-Board, or Table.

Councel.

County.

The Court of the County.

Countermand. *See* Revocation.

The Counting-house of the Kings Houshold.

Domus Compotus Hospitii Regis.

Court.

The

What

Deer.

Delayes.

Deodand.

Deputy.

Dignity. *See* Nobility.

Disceit.

Discontinuance.

Discretion.

Dispensations.

Distresse.

Dogs.

The Book of Doomesday.

Dower.

Drapery.

Duress.

Ecclesiasticall Persons and Livings.

Ecclesiastical Courts, anciently called Halimots, 1 Holy-courts, Circgemots, or Chircgemots.

Delayes in Ecclesiastical Courts. *See* Delayes.

1. Of the Courts of Convocation.

2. Of the high Commission in Causes Ecclesiastical.

3. The Prerogative Court of the Arch-bishop of Canterbury.

4. The Court of the Arches of the Arch-bishop of Canterbury.

5. The Court of Audience.

6. The

What

Errors in the Stannery Courts. *See* Stannery Courts.

Eſcheat.

The Court of the Eſcheator, and of the Commiſſioners for finding of Offices.

Eſtovers.

Eſtoppel.

Eſtreats.

Evidence.

Examiners.

Exchequer-Chamber.

Exchequer.

Banque

A Fine

Forfeiture.

Franchise.

Frank-Fee.

Free-men. *See* Restitution.

Garbler.

Justices of Goale-Delivery.

Garnsey. *See* Jersey.

General Issue. *See* Pleadings.

Glanvil.

Grants.

The

The Kings Houfhold. *See* Counting-Houfe, &c.

Of the Kings Debtors. *See* Debt.

Kingdom.

Kings-Bench.

Knights Service, Knights Fee, &c.

The Court of the Dutchy Chamber of Lancaster at Westminster.

Law.

Leagues, Treaties and Truces.

The

Leases.

The Court of the Leet or View of Frank Pledge.

Liberate.

The Writ *de libertatibus allocandis.*

Licence.

Limitation of Actions.

Livery of Seisin.

Livery out of the Kings Hands.

London.

The Courts and their Jurisdictions within the City of London.

1. The Court of the Hustings.

2. The two Courts of the Sheriffs.

3. The Court of Equity before the Lord Mayor commonly called the Court of Conscience.

4. The

The

Commissions

One

Prefcription.

Prefentation.

Prefident.

Prefidents.

Printing.

Prifage.

Prifon, Prifoners, &c. *See* Falfe-Imprifonment.

Priviledge.

Privy-Seal.

Probate of Wills.

Prohibition.

Property.

Of Scotland.

Sea.

Seals.

Seisin.

Sentence.

Services.

The Court of Commissions of Sewers.

Sheriff.

Statutes.

ED. 1. Westm. 1.

ED. 2.

ED. 3.

R. 2.

H. 4.

In

High Steward of England.

Steward.

Stipulation.

Stray.

Subscription.

Subsidies.

Suits. *See* Actions.

Supremacy.

Surcharge of the Forest.

Surety.

The Kings Swanheard.

Wardwite,

York.

The Rules, Sentences, and other proper Expreſſions, Alphabetically compoſed.

A.

C.

D.

E.

F.

G.

I.

M.

N.

FINIS.